The Qur'ãnic Foundations and Structure of Muslim Society

The Qur'ãnic Foundations and Structure of Muslim Society

by

Dr. Muhammad Fazl-ur-Rahman Ansari
B. Th., M.A., Ph.D.
President
World Federation of Islamic Missions

Volume I

KITAB BHAVAN
NEW DELHI-110002

Kitab Bhavan
Publishers, Distributors, Exporters & Importers
1784, Kalan Mahal, Darya Ganj
New Delhi-110002 (India)

Phone : (91-11) 3277392/93, 3274686
Web Site: www.kitabbhavan.com
E-mail : nasri@vsnl.com
Fax : (91-11) 3263383

Edition ... 2002

ISBN : 81-7151-319-0 (Set)
ISBN : 81-7151-320-4 (Vol. I)

Laser Typesetting at:
Laser Track
Darya Ganj, New Delhi-2

Published in India by:
Nusrat Ali Nasri for Kitab Bhavan
1784, Kalan Mahal, Darya Ganj
New Delhi-110002 [India]

Printed in India at:
Nice Printing Press
Khureji Khas, Delhi-110051

DEDICATED

Most Respectfully

and

In the Name of Allah

to

THE HOLY PROPHET MUHAMMAD

(*Sallallãho 'alaihi wa Sallam*),

the Refulgent Sun

of

Piety, Truth, Justice, Love, Selflessness, Wisdom and Beauty,

who came as

the Last Prophet and Messenger of Allah

to entire Humanity

for teaching the Way whereby

to combat

all Spiritual, Moral, Intellectual, Economic and Political Evils

and

to achieve

the Most Glorious and Comprehensive Success,

and

who accomplished

what stands upto this day as

the Noblest and the Most Profound Revolution

in human history

through

the Impact of

his Superbly-Dynamic and Humanly-Perfect Personality

and

through

the Holy Qur'ãn,

which was revealed to him by Allah

to function as

the Basic Instrument of his Abiding Mission.

CONTENTS

Volume I

Book I
FUNDAMENTALS

Part I. He to whom the Qur'ãn was Revealed

Part II. The Necessity of Divine Revelation

Part III. The Qur'ãnic Revelation

Part IV. Islam: The Religion—in Terms of the Scope and Nature of Qur'ãnic Guidance

Part V. Concluding Observations

Book II

ETHICO-METAPHYSICAL FOUNDATIONS

Part I. The Critique and Dynamics of Morals

Part II. The Metaphysics of Morals

FOREWORD

Dr. Sir Mohammad Iqbal

On

The Predicament of Modern Humanity and the Wayout

The modern man with his philosophies of criticism and scientific specialism finds himself in a strange predicament. His Naturalism has given him an unprecedented control over the forces of nature, but has robbed him of faith in his own future. It is strange how the same idea affects different cultures differently. The formulation of the theory of evolution in the world of Islam brought into being Rumi's tremendous enthusiasm for the biological future of man. No cultured Muslim can read such passages as the following without a thrill of joy:

Low in the earth
I lived in realms of ore and stone;
And then I smiled in many-tinted flowers;
Then roving with the wild and wandering hours,
O'er earth and air and ocean's zone,
In a new birth,
I dived and flew,
And crept and ran,
And all the secret of my essence drew
Within a form that brought them all to view—
And lo, a Man!
And then my goal,
Beyond the clouds, beyond the sky,
In realms where none may change or die—
In angel form; and then away
Beyond the bounds of night and day,
And Life and Death, unseen or seen,
Where all that is hath ever been,
As One and Whole.

—(*Rumi*: Thadani's Translation).

On the other hand, the formulation of the same view of evolution with far greater precision in Europe has led to the belief that 'there now appears to be no scientific basis for the idea that the present rich complexity of human endowment will ever be materially exceeded. That is how the modern man's secret despair hides itself behind the screen of scientific terminology....

Thus, wholly overshadowed by the results of his intellectual activity, the modern man has ceased to live soulfully, i.e., from within. In the domain of thought he is living in open conflict with himself; and in the domain of economic and political life he is living in open conflict with others. He finds himself unable to control his ruthless egoism and his infinite gold-hunger which is gradually killing all higher striving in him and bringing him nothing but life-weariness. Absorbed in the 'fact', that is to say, the optically present source of sensation, he is entirely cut off from the unplumbed depths of his own being. In the wake of his systematic materialism has at last come that paralysis of energy which Huxley apprehended and deplored....... Modern atheistic socialism, which possesses all the fervour of a new religion has a broader outlook; but having received its philosophical basis from the Hegelians of the left wing, it rises in revolt against the very source which could have given it strength and purpose. Both nationalism and atheistic socialism, at least in the present state of human adjustments, must draw upon the psychological forces of hate, suspicion, and resentment which tend to impoverish the soul of man and close up his hidden sources of spiritual energy. Neither the technique of medieval mysticism nor nationalism nor atheistic socialism can cure the ills of a despairing humanity. Surely the present moment is one of great crisis in the history of modern culture. The modern world stands in need of biological renewal. And religion, which in its higher manifestations, is neither dogma, nor priesthood, nor ritual, can alone ethically prepare the modern man for the burden of the great responsibility which the advancement of modern science necessarily involves, and restore to him that attitude of faith which makes him capable of winning a personality here and retaining it hereafter. It is only by rising to a fresh vision of his origin and future, his whence and whither, that man will eventually triumph over a society motivated by an inhuman competition, and a civilization which has lost its spiritual unity by its inner conflict of religious and political values.

—*Reconstruction of Religious Thought in Islam*, p. 176-178.

PREFACE

The basic purpose and function of this book is to state the Philosophy and the Code of Life as given in the Qur'ãn. That Code has developed, however, with *morality* as the central theme. And that should have been so. Because, the value-system which the Holy Qur'ãn has given establishes spirituality as the root, morality as the trunk, and all other aspects of life: economic, political, etc., as off-shoots of morality;—whereby it ensures the emergence of the integrated and progressive individual and the integrated and progressive social order.

The central importance for morality that has emerged thus should impress upon the Muslims the central importance of moral struggle.

Viewed in that perspective, the present book forms a basic contribution in respect of extricating Muslim society from the Crisis of Character which has overtaken all classes of Muslims, and which is the deadliest poison that has ever paralysed or killed any human community.

The method of exposition adopted is simple and direct. Moreover, personal comments have been kept at the barest minimum, so that the Qur'ãn has stayed in its august position free to explain itself. In the *dynamic orthodoxy* that has thus emerged lies, in the belief of the present writer, the salvation of Muslims and of humanity at large.

• • • • •

The typescript of the original draft of this book was ready on June 30th, 1969, and was even handed over to brother Ghazi Nasir-ud-Din, Managing Director of Trade and Industry Publications Ltd., who had come forward with love and devotion to undertake the work of printing. But subsequently it was considered necessary to expound certain topics in detail; as a consequence of which very considerable additions were made, so that the work is being presented finally as a two-volume publication of more than nine hundred pages.

Certain technical discussions relating to philosophical, psychological, sociological, economic and political themes had to be kept out even during the course of the final effort, out of regard for keeping the book handy, lucid and easy of comprehension by the average-educated person. Separate volume or volumes are proposed to be presented on those problems.

The author is conscious of the fact that, although he has availed the talent of the classical translators of the Holy Qur'ãn, there is scope for improvement in respect of the translation of a number of verses. That task is intended to be taken up in the second edition.

In his study of the Qur'ãn, the author had recourse to the classical Arabic Qur'ãnic commentaries and allied literature. But he has quoted mainly from the English commentaries by Abdul Majid Daryabadi and Abdullah Yusuf Ali, because they have projected the best—in fact, the very essence, of the knowledge enshrined in the Arabic classics. Moreover, these two orthodox scholars' commentaries are accessible to the average English-educated Muslim for further study.

The author leads a life wherein he has to perform duties of multifarious types, especially as the President of the World Federation of Islamic Missions, which has several projects to be looked after. Besides that, he has touring duties as an international worker for Islam. It is, therefore, impossible for him to accomplish literary work leisurely and with the concentration which the research-work of the type that has been undertaken in the present book demands. As such, the present task has been accomplished piece-meal by snatching time forcibly from other duties over a period of time, and in consequence there is a possibility of the occurrence of oversights and shortcomings,—even though utmost care has been exercised. The author, who regards himself only as a humble pursuer of Truth and student of Islam, will, therefore, appreciate all genuine criticism and advice from the world of scholarship. He requests his readers, however, not to introduce implications into his statements beyond what has been categorically and clearly said.

• • • • •

ACKNOWLEDGEMENTS

While presenting this book, I consider it my privilege to express my deep debt of gratitude to my revered teachers: Prof. Dr.S.Z. Hasan, M.A., LL. B., Dr. Phil. (Erl.), D. Phil. (Oxon.), under whose guidance I learnt to understand the problems of Philosophy; Hadrat Maulana Saiyid Sulaiman Ashraf, from whom I acquired, at the level of my higher education, knowledge of the Holy Qur'ãn and of the Islamic theological sciences; and Hadrat Maulana Muhammad 'Abdul 'Aleem al-Siddiqi al-Qaderi, through whom I received the Qaderiyya Spiritual Discipline and the mission of serving the far-flung Muslim communities of the globe. The deepest debt of gratitude I owe, however, to my beloved parents of revered memory: Muhammad Khalil Ansari and Husn Ara Begum, who, through their noble character and fruitful teaching and loving concern for my well-being, built up the foundations of my personality and sponsored and guided my education at all stages, thereby enabling me to prepare myself for undertaking this work. I must also acknowledge my debt of gratitude to my wife, Begum Subhia, who, ever since our marriage, has stood by me with grace and fortitude in all the ordeals through which I had to pass in respect of my humble service to the cause of Islam, and without whose earnest co-operation and sincere encouragement the present laborious task could not have been accomplished.

I am grateful also to Mr. Muhammad Ja'fer Shaikh and Mr. Muhammad Ilyas Khan, Joint and Assistant Secretaries respectively of the World Federation of Islamic Missions, for the invaluable help rendered—especially by the former—in the preparation of the typescript; and to my dear pupils: Waffie Muhammad and Imran Nazar Hosein, both of Trinidad (West Indies), and Siddiq A. Nasir of Guyana (South America): to Waffie for assistance in reading the proofs, handling the problem of the Arabic calligraphy, and supervising the printing during the last stage; to Imran for preparing the list of Contents and checking the references; to Siddiq for compiling the Indexes. May Allah bless them all with His choicest Blessings.

Muhammad Fazl-ur-Rahman Ansari

INTRODUCTORY OBSERVATIONS

Why the Qur'ãn Alone?

The enquiry in the present dissertation has been confined strictly to the Holy Qur'ãn, not because the present writer does not give to the *Hadîth* literature its rightful place, but on the following grounds:

Firstly, it alone enjoys the status of being the Scripture of Islam:

Secondly, every word of its text is absolutely authentic as having been preserved to the very letter in the very words in which it was delivered by the Holy Prophet Muhammad (Peace be on him!).

Thirdly, its authority as the basic source-book of Islam has been universally accepted by all sections of Muslims in all ages.

Fourthly, it is *the* Book which should form the *basis* of struggle for the reform of human society, even as the Holy Prophet (Peace be on him!) has been commanded therein: "...and strive against them (i.e., the opponents of the Islamic Way of Life) therewith (i.e., with the Guidance of the Qur'ãn) with utmost strenuousness." (XXV:52).

Fifthly, it claims about itself that it is: "...an exposition (explicit and implicit) of everything..." (XVI:89). Namely: It imparts complete and eternal guidance concerning all aspects of human life.

Sixthly, it is the *only* Book of Guidance compiled under the instruction of the Holy Prophet (Peace be on him!), authorised by him, and delivered by him to the Muslims as the abiding, the infallible and the unchallengeable document of his Teaching for all time,—with no compeer and no substitute. As such, it is the basic instrument of the unity of thought and action in respect of the Islamic Way of Life,—standing in all its uniqueness as totally immune from contradictions and variations.

This characteristic of the Qur'ãn is of tremendous importance in respect of the Islamic System of Belief, on which rests primarily and basically the consolidation of Religious Unity and Uniformity among Muslims—a fundamental virtue the violation of which has been equated by the Holy Qur'ãn with nothing less than the greatest sin, i.e., *Shirk*.

Viewing the *Hadîth* literature in the above perspective: All students of Islam are aware of the sectarian mischief raked up, purely in the name of Prophetic Traditions (*Hadîth*), by certain groups in Muslim history, through the projection of certain allegedly divinely-inspired and divinely-sanctioned offices like those on an infallible *Imãm*, a *Mujaddid*, a *Mahdî*, a Promised Messiah, or a *Mahdî*-cum-Messiah, without the slightest regard for the infallible principles: (i) that any doctrine which is included in the Belief System is *ipso facto* an inalienable part of the Islamic Creed; (iii) that it is not the function of the *Hadîth* literature—however valuable its role otherwise, but only of the Qur'ãn, to lay down the constitutive factors of the Islamic Creed; and (iii) that making belief in the claimants to such offices a part of the Islamic Creed constitutes nothing less than a cruel attack on the very foundation of *Imãn*, being directed to the destruction of the absoluteness and the indivisibility of a Muslim's allegiance and loyalty to the Holy Prophet Muhammad (Peace be on him!) as Guide, Teacher and Leader.

If the Traditions concerning such a personality as that of the *Mahdî*, for instance, are accepted as authentic, that does not make, and cannot make, the belief in the emergence of a great leader (*Mahdî*) at some period of Muslim history a guiding principle of *Imãn*. It remains only a prophecy about a distinguished follower of the Holy Prophet (Peace be on him!).

Similarly, if the Traditions concerning the Second Advent of Jesus (Peace be on him!) are accepted as correct, they relate only to a prophecy about an event of future history, and have nothing to do with the Islamic Creed,—and, as such, have nothing to do with the *Imãn* of a Muslim: neither in its affirmation nor in its denial. Moreover, to project the concept of a 'Promised Messiah' in the person of some x, y, z and to substitute it for the person of Jesus (Peace be on him!)—although it is his personality that has been projected unambiguously in the prophecy—, and to build a sect on that basis, is to indulge in double violation of the Divine Guidance given in the Qur'ãn.

All in all, accepting the Qur'ãn *alone* as the *fundamental* basis for the knowledge of Islamic Guidance is not only the requirement of reason but also the only road to the salvation of Muslims.

Seventhly, the text of the Qur'ãn is grounded in a System of Meaning, through which it is possible to understand Islam fundamentally as a system of Philosophy and a Code of Practice, keeping the exercise of understanding confined to the Qur'ãn itself; and the present book is a plain demonstration of this fact. Of course, there are certain aspect of the

Qur'ãnic Guidance where the projection is of an implicit nature. And it is there that recourse to the *Hadîth* literature becomes necessary,—but only for further clarification and not for adding further dimensions to the basic structure of Islam. Also, it is necessary to know as to how the Qur'ãnic Guidance was put into practice by the Holy Prophet Muhammad himself (On him be Peace!). In other words, it is necessary to know not only the Qur'ãn as a Book of Guidance but also the 'Qur'ãn in Action', viz., the Holy Prophet's *Sunnah.* For that, evidently the *Hadîth* literature is the most indispensable instrument.

But here two important facts have to be kept in view: (i) The Qur'ãn is the basic instrument for understanding Islam. Hence, for the *value-system* of Islam and its entire *fundamental structure*, it is necessary to concentrate on the Qur'ãn alone. (ii) The knowledge thus obtained forms the fundamental instrument for obtaining further guidance on Islam from the *Hadîth* literature.

It should be so, because: (i) it is the Qur'ãn which forms the Criterion of Judgment in respect of Islam—a status explicitly given to it by itself—and not the *Hadîth* literature; and (ii) the Qur'ãn is *absolutely* authentic, while even the best *Hadîth* literature is only *relatively* authentic —namely, authentic only *in a qualified manner*. And, of course, every student of Islam knows all the mischief in the field of *Hadîth* perpetrated by the forces of counter-revolution in the very early period of Muslim history,—a mischief which emerged in the form of sects and schisms, and which forged the Traditions relating to certain aspects of Islamic life and history to an extent that the confusion created thereby has continued to plague the Muslim society upto the present day.

In fact, it is the function of the Qur'ãn to sit in judgment on the *Hadîth*, and not *vice versa*; and, thus, a basic study of Islam in the perspective of the Qur'ãn emerges as the fundamental necessity.

Role of the Qur'ãn As the Book of Guidance

The Qur'ãn came:

* to obliterate all anthropomorphic notions about God and to establish perfect Monotheism—not merely as a theological concept but as a full-fledged philosophy of life.

* to inculcate the establishment and maintenance of a living and dynamic relation with God in order that human beings may attain the highest spiritual and moral refinement and greatness.

* to teach the truth that human beings are basically theomorphic beings—emphasising the 'ascent of Man to God' as opposed to the 'descent of God in Man'—, and that the goal of every human being is the actualisation of his or her potential vicegerency of God through the imitation of Divine Attributes.

* to give to Woman her rightful place in Society, as basically the equal of man.

* to resolve the dichotomy of Faith and Reason
of Religion and Science
of Love and Law
of Beauty and Simplicity
of Participation in godliness and Participation in worldly life.

* to establish in the domain of the philosophy of Religion, the positive concept of *Fulfilment* in place of the universally-prevalent negative concept of *Salvation.*

* to extricate Religion from superstitions.

* to distinguish Spirituality from Mysticism and Psychicism.

* to give a comprehensive Philosophy of Integration, based on the teaching of Unity-ism, thereby providing sure basis for the integration of the life of the Individual as well as of Society; and, beyond that, of Humanity at large.

* to create on Integralistic Culture and an Integralistic Civilisation.

* to make Morality the basis for Spiritual Development, on the one hand, and for Social Evolution, on the other.

* to inaugurate the era of Scientific Advancement by means of teaching the requisite fundamental principles.

* to highlight the role of Inductive Reasoning as the proper instrument for the pursuit of Knowledge.

* to emphasise the quest for Empirical Knowledge, as well as the resultant Technological Advancement and Conquest of Nature, as Exercise in the Worship of God.
* to bestow on Religion the role of functioning as Social Alchemy for the establishment of a Total Welfare Society.
* to harmonise Truth and Justice with Love and Mercy.
* to make Social Justice the very foundation for healthy collective life.
* to establish the concept of Wealth for Welfare.
* to eradicate Poverty, Disease and human Suffering in general.
* to crown Labour with Dignity.
* to proclaim the principle that value lies in Labour, Productivity and Achievement.
* to provide the Golden Mean between the extremist philosophies of Monopoly Capitalism and Communism.
* to open the avenues and provide Guidance for human progress in all healthy directions in general.
* to close the doors on all those perversions in religious and non-religious Thought which go to make Religion an opiate and the Secularistic Philosophies atheistic and immoral;

  and
* to confer on Humanity many other Blessings, besides.

For that, the Qur'ãn gave:

* a well co-ordinated System of Belief,
* a fully-integrated Philosophy, and
* a comprehensive Code of Practice.

The Holy Prophet's *Sunnah*:

Role, Definition and Certain Facets Thereof

* The Qur'ãn has laid fundamental emphasis on the importance of imitation of the Holy Prophet's *Sunnah* as a vital factor in the

practice of Islam, because it begins in accepting him as the sole human Guide, in the post-Qur'ãnic period, in respect of Divine Guidance, and it develops in imitating him more and more as the Perfect Practical Model thereof. The question, therefore, emerges: What does the *Sunnah* stand for? We may concisely answer this question by saying that the Holy Prophet's *Sunnah* stands for the dynamic manifestations of the ethico-religious dimensions of his personality. Or: Looking at it in the perspective of the Qur'ãn, we many define it by saying that it is the realisation by him of the Qur'ãnic value-system in the different dimensions of his personality.

* If the implications of the *Sunnah* are understood properly by a Muslim, it saves him from indulgence in *bid'ãt*, on the one hand, and inspires him with intense fervour for realising in his personality, to his utmost capacity, the ethico-religious Idealism projected by the Qur'ãn.

* The present is not the occasion to project the Holy Prophet's *Sunnah* in detail, because it relates to a personality that has been the richest, the most profound, and the most perfect in history. We may, however, mention here just a few facets selected off-hand, —only to provide a basic idea. They are: (1) Utmost devotion to God: (2) Spending every moment of life productively, and with planning and grace, and not wasting it in frivolities; —and doing all that without the harshness and rigours of Asceticism, but with positive consciousness of maintaining life in God-boundness; (3) Maintaining highest fortitude, with a cheerful countenance and a never-failing smile, even in the most trying and terrifying circumstances; (4) Gentleness and considerateness in dealing with others; (5) Forgiveness— and love—for the worst enemies; (6) Practice of Mercy in all situations,—the conquest of Makkah demonstrating it at its climax; (7) Utmost generosity; (8) Utmost sacrifice for the welfare of others: feeding others, while himself remaining hungry; clothing others, while himself wearing coarse garments patched time and again; not keeping any wealth with him, in cash or kind, but distributing it to the needy before sunset every day; (9) Extreme humility together with full dignity; (10) Highest rational tolerance; (11) Good-will for all

and ill-will towards none (12) Eating less; sleeping less; talking less; (13) Total abstinence from quarrelsomeness; (14) Immaculate cleanliness in respect of the body, the dress and the environment; (15) Practice of truthfulness, honesty, fidelity and self-control at their highest.

* It is heart-rending to observe that the very notion of the obligatoriness of imitating the real *Sunnah*—which has been fundamentally projected above—has progressively departed from the Muslims; while love for externalistic formalities in the name of the *Sunnah*, and that too with much fuss as to juristic hair-splitting, has increasingly taken its place among the so-called orthodox pursuers of religiosity;—all that resulting in the creation of large numbers of Islamically-unbalanced religious personalities.

The Qur'ãnic View of the Individual and the Society

* The mission of the Qur'ãn in respect of both the Individual and the Society is vehemently Integralistic—the principle of Integralism being grounded in the concept of Unity (*tawhid*), and expressing itself in the balanced and harmonious realisation of the basic values of *Piety, Justice, Wisdom, Love, Beauty* and *Selflessness*.

* The Ideational religious approach to human life may either be: (i) ritualistic, or (ii) mystical. The ritualistic approach leads to barren Formalism, or Externalism, which brings into play juristic hair-splitting and bigotry even in purely devotional matters. Often falling victim to the rule disease of 'piety-complex', the adherents of this approach present the picture of a soldier who has acquired only a uniform but no soldierly training. The mystical approach leads to inertia, or to superstitions, or both. As opposed to both of those approaches, the Qur'ãnic approach is Integralistic, i.e., directed to the build-up of an integrated life, which is fundamentally ethico-religious in character. 'Fundamentally ethico -religious means that the Qur'ãn has emphasised the simultaneous pursuit of both Religion and Morality. Indeed, religiosity without regard for the importance of moral refinement and development emerges in the Qur'ãnic view as nothing less than an opiate, because the very concept of 'godliness' loses all meaning without the active pursuit of the highest Morality.

* The mission of a Muslim is: To build up his own personality, his social environment, and the world in general, as good; and for that purpose, to equip himself to possible heights of perfection in respect of, and to co-operate with others in the pursuit of, all healthy and constructive human activities.

* The external make-up of an Islamic personality is fundamentally grounded in natural grace, because the Qur'ãn has ordained no sophistications.

* Religious persons of a particular type feel that they should attach practically all importance to the Law of Grace, and much less or no importance to the Natural Law. No doubt, both of those Laws are operative, under the Divine Plan, in the universe and in the lives of human beings. But, the Holy Qur'ãn demands that a Muslim should function in life with as much regard for the Natural Law as the wisest Materialist, because God Himself has made the function of the natural Law as fundamental, and that of the Law of Grace as supererogatory.

* The adoption of the atheistic mechanistic view of the universe and Man is advocated by its adherents as the only and the necessary condition for Scientific progress. That is, however, fallacious; because the Qur'ãnic concept of the 'Reign of Law' also ensures it in the same measure, and without damage to the spiritual and moral values.

* The Qur'ãn rules out the exploitation of man by man in all forms, whether in the social sphere in respect of the economic and the political matters, or in the sphere of Religion in respect of certain so-called religious practices whereby superstitions are traded in as a commodity. Similarly, it is firmly opposed to all forms of tyranny.

* Wealthiness has been very often wedded to wickedness, and the Holy Qur'ãn has condemned it in that perspective time and again.

* Hence, while Islam permits private enterprise in business and industry, its permission is not unqualified. Because, it permits only controlled freedom in respect of both earning and spending one's wealth, whereby the emergence of Monopoly Capitalism and its child, the luxurious and aristocratic living, both are ruled out, and the possessors of surplus wealth are stopped from adopting the cult of indulgence in 'wealth, wine, and woman',

while the Islamic society as a whole shoulders the responsibility of the provision of basic needs of life to all with dignity.

* We may sum up the Qur'ãnic standpoint in respect of Muslim society by saying in negative terms that, with all the practice of religious rituals, the Muslim society loses a vital part of its Islamic character if: (i) any form of exploitation and tyranny is practised, and economic and political justice is not comprehensively enforced; (ii) the highest moral Idealism is not made the very life-blood of the social order and the basic pursuit of the individuals; (iii) the mission of the conquest of Nature is forsaken,—a mission that necessitates the pursuit of Empirical Knowledge and Technology at the highest level.

Pursuit and Non-Ascetic Character of Spirituality

* The Qur'ãnic ethico-religious Approach does not lead to mysticism, but to what might be termed as *Dynamic Purism* based on *Sidq* and *Safã*. That is the goal and the pride of the orthodox *Sufi* orders in history. They pursued the Qur'ãnic ethico-religious quest with grace and sincerity,—a quest that is the very essence of Islam.

* The ultimate goal of the Qur'ãnic ethico-religious quest is God-realisation. But, its pursuit is impossible without self-realisation, which, therefore, becomes a Muslim's primary obligation.

* The struggle for self-realisation emerges in the Qur'ãnic perspective as basically three-dimensional: the religious, the ethical, and the intellectual.

* In spite of the fact, however, that it is to be undertaken fundamentally as the first step in the exercise of God-realisation, it leads simultaneously to a knowledge which might be named as the 'knowledge of Spiritual Science'. That knowledge is scientific, because it is based, like physical science, on observation and verification. The para-psychologists of today, working at the psychical level alone, have affirmed the ESP, the astral projection, etc. But, Spiritual Science, in the hands of genuine *Sufi* teachers, has attained immeasurably greater heights. The revelation by men like Rumi and Ibn al-Arabi of certain higher truths discovered only recently by physical science, is a case in point.

* It is the *bid'ãt* (i.e., 'spiritual' practices that violate Islam) and superstitions that should be condemned by every genuine Muslim. But, to condemn the Spiritual Science itself is unwarranted.

* Prayer and Fasting play very definite roles in the Qur'ãnic Spiritual Culture.

* Prayer is an exercise in respect of the Communion of the finite with the Infinite. It extricates the finite individual from servitude to the finite and opens to him the road to infinite progress. Prayer is thus for progress. Fasting is the exercise in self-control, which is the key to spiritual progress.

* The enemies of Islam have propagated the allegation that, because of its permission of polygamy, the Qur'ãn teaches sex-indulgence, which does not harmonise with the pursuit of spiritual refinement and progress. Actually, that allegation is based on the age-old misconception of Ascetic ethics, wherein the very fulfilment of the natural biological demand of sex is considered to be unholy, in contra-distinction to the Qur'ãnic view, which holds it as sacred, because it is in conformity with the Divine Scheme, and which condemns only licentiousness as unholy. Thus, the qualified and restricted Qur'ãnic permission for polygamy has not been prescribed as a licence for sex-indulgence but only as an alternative to promiscuity and prostitution,—which it eliminates successfully, in sharp contrast with the Ascetic as well as the Totally-Monogamic social philosophies. As for the former, one has to read only the history of Christianity in the Age of Faith to witness the most ugly storm of licentiousness that overtook even the pursuers of saintliness, not to speak of the common folk. (Besides other literature on the subject, the "*History of Sacredotal Celibacy in the Christian Church*" written by a very devout Christian scholar named Henry C. Lea, published by the University Books Inc., U.S.A., 1966, is enough to provide a correct estimate of the moral disaster perpetrated by that wrong philosophy). Coming to the latter, the modern Western civilization has established the most heinous record of licentiousness,—a record unsurpassed in the history of human civilizations.

* The enemies of Islam extend their allegation to the person of the Holy Prophet Muhammad (Peace be on him!) also, and that to such an extent as to deny to him, with all his superbly-great qualities of character, even basic spiritual goodness and greatness, simply on the basis of his practice of polygamy. But, what are the facts? *Firstly*, his entire personal life was a life of war against ease, opulence, luxuries, and self-indulgence in general. Indeed, it was through and through a life of Austerity, wherein, even at the height of his material power, he lived in a small thatched mud-hut, passed his days in hunger and toil, and spent his nights for the most part standing in prayer to God. *Secondly*, he adopted polygamy towards the dawn of old age, having led an exemplary monogamous life from the age of twenty-five to the age of fifty in the company of a twice-widowed lady who was fifteen years his senior. *Thirdly*, during the polygamous period, while there was a wife like Lady Ayesha, who was a virgin of seventeen at the time of the consummation of marriage, there were those who were widows or divorcees, and there were even those who, at the time of their marriage with him, were already so old as to have crossed the limit of fitness for married life. All these facts demolish the very basis of the aforesaid insinuation completely, and establish, instead, the truth that the Holy Prophet (Peace be on him!) adopted polygamy in the Medinite period of his life *solely* for the sake of his noble and sacred mission,—and that in the perspective of a twofold achievement. Firstly, in the tribal society of Arabia of those days, wherein one of the fundamental conditions of the success of his mission lay in the unification of the mutually-hostile tribes, one of the most potent instrument of their unification, in accordance with the mentality of the Arabs of those days, consisted in uniting them through a kinship centred in his person,—and his marriages did make a signal contribution in that behalf. Secondly, through those different marriages he was able to build in the persons of his wives the most accomplished lady-teachers and embodiments of Islam for the propagation of Islamic knowledge among the womenfolk.

The Past and the Present

* Muslims rose to greatness through the Qur'ãn, which built them up into a World-Force dedicated to the service of Humanity, and they led Humanity for a long time in every phase of human

activity: spiritual, moral, intellectual, aesthetical, economic and political.

But it is a tragedy of human nature that it is easy for human beings to continue to stick to certain Beliefs but difficult to maintain the tempo of the struggle for executing the Practice.

The same has happened to the Muslims, who have fallen from their pinnacle of glory because of their progressive digression from the Qur'ãnic Way of Life.

* Today :

  The old-fashioned as well as the outwardly-westernised religious-minded Muslims, who form the overwhelming majority, are demonstrating in their lives a view of Islam which confines their obligation to devotional and ceremonial practices alone—leaving out even morality;—while:

  The truly-westernised, secularised, modernised Muslims, who are emerging as the major controlling force in many Muslim communities, are groping in the darkness of utter confusion; and in sheer ignorance they look greedily to fashionable un-Islamic and anti-Islamic ideologies and modes of life for imitation and adoption.

* Taking Humanity as a whole:

  In the ideological war that is raging all over the world between the Ideational and the Sensate cultural points of view—between the forces of the other-worldly religions and this-worldly social philosophies, wherein the Higher Values of Life are becoming progressively submerged in the quagmire of Secularism—nay, of rank Materialism, Atheism, Nihilism and Libertinism, leading to grave imbalance in the lives of the Individuals and the Communities to the heights of a Mighty Crisis, a Philosophy and a Code of Life based on Integralism is needed very urgently—a Philosophy and a Code that may establish a Culture wherein all human yearnings, ranging from the Transcendental to the Physical, may find their fulfilment and whereby Humanity may be enabled to achieve its true Destiny.

* That Philosophy and that Code of Life has been given in the Holy Qur'ãn.

* And the present work, being a systematic and comprehensive exposition of the same, forms the need of the hour and deserves serious study by everyone who possesses a serious attitude towards the problems of life.

The Future Role of Islam

The general view of mankind concerning Religion is that its function is confined to the problem of salvation in the next world.

But present-day Humanity has become increasingly interested in achieving salvation in the present world.

Hence Religion has fallen into disrepute as something incapable of solving human problems relating to the earthly life;—nay, even as a definite impediment to human progress.

Here Islam has a unique role to play, because it is definitely, directly and vehemently committed to the salvation of Humanity in both the worlds: the present one as well as the next.

Nay, Islam's role stands at an even higher level, because it substitutes the positive concept of *fulfilment* for the negative concept of *salvation*. And its concept of *fulfilment* comprehends the healthy and harmonious development of the Individual and the Society in all respects: spiritual, aesthetical, moral, intellectual and physical.

All in all, Islam stands in history as Eternal Guidance: the Guidance for yesterday, today and tomorrow.

The Present may be gloomy because of the wrongs committed by the Muslims themselves during the different epochs of their history, including the present. But:

THE FUTURE BELONGS TO ISLAM
—AND TO ISLAM ALONE!

BOOK I

FUNDAMENTALS

PART I

HE TO WHOM THE QUR'ÃN WAS REVEALED

PART II

THE NECESSITY OF DIVINE REVELATION

PART III

THE QUR'ÃNIC REVELATION

PART IV

ISLAM: THE RELIGION

IN TERMS OF

THE SCOPE AND NATURE OF QUR'ÃNIC GUIDANCE

PART V

CONCLUDING OBSERVATIONS

Part I

HE TO WHOM THE QUR'ÃN WAS REVEALED

Chapter I

THE CHRISTIAN-JEWISH CAMPAIGN OF VILIFICATION

Chapter II

BIOGRAPHICAL SKETCH

Chapter III

THE HOLY PROPHET'S PERSONALITY AND CHARACTER AND SIDELIGHTS ON SOME REFORMS

Chapter I

CHRISTIAN-JEWISH CAMPAIGN OF VILIFICATION

In projecting the discussion about the Holy Qur'ān it is necessary to introduce first the personality and the mission of him who was the recipient of its revelation. To do so with any degree of justice would require volumes because of the extreme richness of the personality as well as the mission. The limitations of the present work, however, permit only the briefest introduction. In that connection, again, it seems advisable to present only certain facts, and those too in the words of such Western scholars who, unlike others who were thoroughly drowned in blinding prejudice, felt hesitant in concealing or perverting certain very obvious truths and exerted, with all their background of inherited prejudice, to adopt fair-mindedness in whatever degree possible. In their words, because no judgement can be regarded as more critical than their judgment, and because "the best testimony is that which comes from the enemy's camp", and the Western scholarship in general,—indeed, Christendom and the international Jewry, has exhibited, and continues to exhibit, such limitless cruelty in terms of a planned campaign of misrepresentation and vilification of Islam and the Holy Prophet that in a very brief assessment only this course seems to be beneficial for all those who fall victim to Western propaganda,—such persons existing in large numbers in all the communities.

The campaign of vilification has, indeed, staggering dimensions. Because, it is not only the Christian priests of the medieval ages and the orientalists of the present day[1], but also scholars totally unconnected with the polemics against Islam, who have continued to participate in this

---

1 "During the first few centuries of Muhammadanism", observes Bosworth Smith, "Christendom could not afford to criticize or explain; it could only tremble and obey. But when the Saracens had received their first check in the heart of France, the nations which had been flying before them faced round as a herd of cows will sometimes do when the single dog that has put them to flight is called off; and though they did not yet venture to fight, they could at least calumniate their retreating foe. Drances-like, they could manufacture calumnies and victories at pleasure". (*Muhammad and Muhammadanism*, p. 63. 3rd ed., London, 1889). After this remark, Bosworth Smith records those calumnies (pp. 63-72). To say merely that they are vulgar, wild and obscene would not do justice to their atrocious nature.

filthiest and the most degrading job. Just to cite a few examples selected at random, we may refer to four of them:

(i) Dr. J.H. Muirhead of the University of Birmingham has written a text-book on ethics named "*The Elements of Ethics*", where, just for the sake of insulting Islam, he has irrelevantly inserted the following false statement: "In the lives of the saints among the Turks, as Locke reminds us in his celebrated chapter entitled 'No Innate Practical Principles', the primary virtue of chastity seems to have had no place." (p. 231). This allegation applies actually to Christian monasticism of the Middle Ages. But instead of referring to it, both Locke and Muirhead have foisted a falsehood on Islam!

(ii) In his book: *The Theory of Good and Evil*, which is throughout a work of academic interest on ethical philosophy and which deals only with the western moral theories, Dr. Hastings Rashdall of New College, Oxford, has, without any relevance, hurled a slur on Islam with a touch of innocence thus: "When the Caliph Omar (if the story be not a myth) ordered the Alexandrian library to be burned[2], it is probable that he knew[3] very imperfectly what the Alexandrian library or any other library really was," (Vol. I, p. 137.)

(iii) Max Weber, who enjoys a very high place among modern sociologists, has shown a vulgar ignorance of Islam, if not devilish

---

The Dutch orientalist Snouck Hurgronje supports Bosworth Smith's verdict when he says: "The pictures which our forefathers in the middle Ages formed of Muhammad's religion, appear to be a malignant caricature". (*Muhammadanism*, p. 4). But neither Hurgronje nor the other orientalists could cleanse themselves of the poison inherited from their medieval forefathers, with the result that the West, even after the debacle of Christianity, remains on the whole an inveterate enemy of Islam and Muslims and continues to spread poison against them through all the available media.

2 It was Dr. Rashdall's duty as scholar, if he was not following Paul's principle of "speaking lies for the glory of God", to be absolutely sure about the veracity of his statement before falsely insulting a people who brought the light of learning to Europe. The truth is that the said library was burnt by the co-religionists of Dr. Rashdall, who did so to promote Christianity. ".....Muslims were friends to learning......It was not Muslims but (Christian) monks who burnt the Greek library at Alexandria". (G.D.H. Cole and M.I. Cole: *The Intelligent Man's Review of Europe Today*, London, 1933, p. 31.)

3 Mark how a second insult has been added to the first!

perversion, in his book: *"The Sociology of Religion* (*E.T.*, Ephraim Fischoff), wherein it was his duty to adopt scientific objectivity and to acquire a thorough knowledge of Islam before speaking about it. His entire statement on Islam, from p. 262 to p. 266, is, to say the least abusive. Just to quote a few sentences, picked up off-hand: "….a national Arabic warrior religion…. a religion with very strong class emphasis…. Even the ultimate elements of its economic ethic were purely feudal…. Muhammad's attitude in opposition to chastity sprang from personal motivations….the ethical concept of salvation was actually alien to Islam…. An essentially political character marked all the chief ordinances of Islam….the original Islamic conception of sin has a similar feudal orientation. The depiction of the prophet of Islam as devoid of sin is a late theological construction, scarcely consistent with the actual nature of Muhammad's strong sensual passions and his explosion of wrath over small provocations... he lacked any sort of tragic sense of sin…. unquestioned acceptance of slavery, serfdom, and polygamy; the disesteem for and subjection of women….."[4]

(iv) Arnold J. Toynbee, whose academic labours in the field of history are gigantic, and who was naturally expected to be objective in his approach to all religions, displays in respect of Islam the Crusader's zeal rather than the spirit of intellectual honesty. Indeed, the distortion of facts in his hands and the perversion of truth by him is fully reminiscent of the dark minds of those Christian priests of the Dark Ages for whom the more flimsy a cock-and-bull story that was invented about Islam the more spiritually enjoyable it was. Just to quote a few stray samples of Toynbian rubbish from *A Study of History*, Vol. 12: "Hatra had been under the protection of the trinity of goddesses who, in Muhammad's day, were the protectresses of Makkah. Their potency was so great that Muhammad almost succumbed to the temptation to stultify his mission by proclaiming them to be daughters of the One True God of the pure religion of Abraham." (p. 466). "In the Arabia of Muhammad's day there was a widespread feeling that it was high time for the Arabs to become 'People of the Book'[5], such as the Jews and the Christians were." (p. 467). "Thus, by the time of Muhammad's *hijrah* to Madinah, the Arabs already possessed all the requisites for becoming world-conquerors except

4 A perusal of the present book will reveal even to a casual reader as to how baseless is Max Weber's indictment.

5 Mark how a historian of world renown is projecting a myth!

one, and that was political unity."(p. 469). "If the Hijazi prophet Muhammad had failed, the Najdi prophet Maslamah might have done the equivalent of Muhammad's work; and, if Maslamah, too, had failed, some other prophet would have arisen, in some other part of Arabia, to step into Maslamah's and Muhammad's shoes."(p. 468).[6]

However, we may proceed now to the findings and judgements of some of those Western scholars who could show some fairness in respect of the different aspects of the Holy Prophet Muhammad's personality and mission, to provide a very brief introduction in that behalf.

---

6 Toynbee's vituperative concoctions are so baseless as hardly to deserve any refutation. They are actually based on the old and extremely irrational and groundless Christian accusation of imposture attributed to the Holy Prophet. Some of the modern Western scholars have, however, felt ashamed of it and have controverted and refuted it in strong terms. We will quote later in that connection Montgomery Watt who, in contrast to Prof. A.J. Toynbee, is an Arabicist and specialist in Islamic history, though he too is not a friend of Islam and Muslims.

Chapter II

BIOGRAPHICAL SKETCH

Condition of the World at Muhammad's Advent:

"In the fifth and sixth centuries the civilized world stood on the verge of a chaos. The old emotional cultures that had made civilization possible, since they had given to men a sense of unity and of reverence for their rulers, had broken down, and nothing had been found adequate to take their place....

"It seemed then the great civilization which it had taken four thousand years to construct was on the verge of disintegration, and that mankind was likely to return to that condition of barbarism where every tribe and sect was against the next, and law and order was unknown... The old tribal sanctions had lost their power... The new sanctions created by Christianity were working division and destruction instead of unity and order. It was a time fraught with tragedy. Civilization, like a gigantic tree whose foliage had overarched the world and whose branches had borne the golden fruits of art and science and literature, stood tottering... rotted to the core. Was there any emotional culture that could be brought in to gather mankind once more into unity and to save civilization?"[1]

And, then, speaking of the Arabs, Denison says:

"It was among these people that the man (Muhammad) was born who was to unite the whole known world of the east and south."[2]

Condition of Arabia and the state of Christianity (the precursor of Islam among Revealed Religions):

"The Arabs believed neither in a future state nor in the creation of the world, but attributed the formation of the universe to nature, and its future destruction to time. Debauchery and robbery everywhere prevailed and since death was regarded as the end, strictly so called, of existence, so was there neither recompense for virtue nor punishment for vice. A like moral and religious corruption was to be found among the Christians and the Jews who, for ages, had established themselves

---

1 J.H. Denison: *Emotion as the Basis of Civilization* London, 1928, pp. 265, 269.

2 *Ibid.*

in the Arabian Peninsula, and had there formed very powerful parties. The Jews had come to seek in that land of liberty an asylum from the persecution of the Romans; the Christians had also fled thither in order to escape the massacres occasioned by the Nestorian Eutychianism and Arian dissensions. It is not easy to conceive of anything more deplorable than the condition of Christianity at this time. The scattered branches of the Christian Church in Asia and Africa were at variance with each other, and had adopted the wildest heresies and superstitions. They were engaged in perpetual controversies and torn to pieces by the disputes of the Arians, Sabellians, Nestorians, and Eutychians, whilst the simony, the incontinence, the general barbarism and ignorance which were to be found amongst the clergy caused great scandal to the Christian religion, and introduced universal profligacy of manners among the people. In Arabia the deserts swarmed with ignorant infatuated Cenobites, or recluses, wasting their lives in vain but fiery speculations, and then rushing, often armed, in mobs into the cities, preaching their fantasies in the churches and enforcing assent to them by the sword. The grossest idolatry had usurped the place of the simple worship instituted by Jesus—that of an all-wise, almighty, and all-beneficent Being, without equal and without similitude; a new Olympus had been imagined, peopled with a crowd of martyrs, saints, and angels, in lieu of the ancient gods of paganism. There were found Christian sects impious enough to invest the wife of Joseph with the honours and the attributes of a goddess. Relics and carved and painted images were objects of the most fervid worship on the part of those whom the word of Christ commanded to address their prayers to the living God alone. Such were the scenes which the Church of Christ presented in Alexandria, in Alleppo, and in Damascus. At the time of Muhammad's advent all had abandoned the principles of their religion to indulge in never-ending wranglings upon dogmas of a secondary importance, and the Arabian people could not but see that they had lost sight of the most essential point of the religious doctrine—the pure and the true worship of God—and that, as regards the most disgraceful and the grossest superstition, they were upon a par with their pagan contemporaries."[3]

3 John Davenport: *An Apology for Muhammad and the Koran,* London 1869. p.4.

"Their lies, their legends, their saints and their miracles, but above all, the abandoned behaviour of their priesthood, had brought the churches in Arabia very low."[4]

"It has been the fashion", observes Dr. Emanuel Deutsch, "to ascribe whatever is good in Muhammadanism to Christianity. We fear this theory is not compatible with the results of honest investigation. For, of Arabian Christianity at the time of Muhammad, the less said perhaps the better... By the side of it... even modern Amharic Christianity, of which we possess such astounding accounts, appears pure and exalted."[5]

Birth of Muhammad:

"Four years after the death of Justinian, 569[6] A.D., was born at Makkah, in Arabia, the man who, of all men, has exercised the greatest influence upon the human race."[7]

Muhammad's Youth:

"Our authorities", says Muir, "all agree in ascribing to the youth of Muhammad a modesty of deportment and purity of manners rare among the people of Makkah... Endowed with a refined mind and delicate taste, reserved and meditative, he lived much within himself, and the ponderings of his heart no doubt supplied occupation for leisure hours spent by others of a lower stamp in rude sports and profligacy. The fair character and honourable bearing of the unobtrusive youth won the approbation of his fellow-citizens; and he received the title, by common consent, of *Al-Ameen*, the Trustworthy."[8]

"... Orphaned at birth, he was always particularly solicitous of the poor and the needy, the widow and the orphan, the slave and the downtrodden. At twenty he was already a successful business man, and soon became director of camel caravans for a wealthy widow. When he reached twenty-five, his employer, recognizing his merit, proposed

4 Bruce: *Travels*, Vol. I, p. 501.

5 *The Quarterly Review*, London, No. 954, p. 315.

6 Rather, 571 A.C.

7 John William Draper: *A History of the Intellectual Development of Europe*, London 1875, Vol. I, pp. 329-330.

8 Sir William Muir : *Life of Muhammad*, London 1903.

marriage. Even though she was fifteen years older, he married her, and as long as she lived remained a devoted husband.

"By forty this man of the desert had secured for himself a most satisfying life: a loving wife, fine children and wealth. Then in a series of dramatic and terrifying events, he began to receive through the Archangel Gabriel a revelation of God's word."[9]

Unfolding of Prophetic Consciousness and the Call:

"Ah no!" says Carlyle, "this deep-hearted Son of the Wilderness with his beaming black eyes and open social deep soul, had other thoughts than ambition. A silent great man; he was one of those who cannot BUT be in earnest: whom Nature herself has appointed to be sincere. While others walk in formulas and hearsays, contented enough to dwell there, this man could not screen himself in formulas; he was alone with his own soul and the reality of things. The great mystery of Existence, as I said, glared in upon him, with its terrors, with its splendours; no hearsays could hide that unspeakable fact. 'Here am I'; such SINCERITY as we name it, has in very truth something of divine. The word of such a man is a Voice direct from Nature's own Heart. Men do and must listen to that as to nothing else; all else is wind in comparison. From of old, a thousand thoughts, in his pilgrimings and wanderings, had been in this man. What am I? What is this unfathomable Thing I live in, which men name Universe? What is Life? What is Death? What am I to believe? What am I to do? The grim rocks of Mount Hira, of Mount Sinai, the stern sandy solitudes, answered not. The great Heaven rolling silent overhead with its blue-glancing stars, answered not. There was no answer. The man's own soul, and what of God's inspiration dwelt there, had to answer."[10]

"Certainly he had two of the most important characteristics of the prophetic order. He saw truth about God, which his fellow-men did not see, and he had an irresistible inward impulse to publish this truth. In respect of this latter qualification, Muhammad may stand in comparison with the most courageous of the heroic prophets of Israel. For the truth's sake he risked his life, he suffered daily persecution for years, and eventually banishment, the loss of property, of the goodwill of his fellow-

9 James A Michener: *Islam : The Misunderstood Religion*, Reader's Digest (American Edition) May 1955, p. 68.

10 Thomas Carlyle: *On Heroes, Hero-Worship and the Heroic in History*, London 1888.

citizens, and of the confidence of his friends; he suffered, in short, as much as any man can suffer short of death, which he only escaped by flight, and yet he unflinchingly proclaimed his message. No bribe, threat or inducement, could silence him. 'Though they array against me the sun of the right hand and the moon on the left, I cannot renounce my purpose'. And it was this persistency, this belief in his call, to proclaim the unity of God, which was the making of Islam.

"Other men have been monotheists in the midst of idolators, but no other man has founded a strong and enduring monotheistic religion. The distinction in his case was his resolution that other men should believe. If we ask what it was that made Muhammad proselytizing where other men had been content to cherish a solitary faith, we must answer that it was nothing else than the depth and force of his own conviction of the truth. To himself the difference between one God and many, between the unseen Creator and those ugly lumps of stone or wood, was simply infinite. The one creed was death and darkness to him, the other life and light... Who can doubt the earnestness of that search after truth and the living God, that drove the affluent merchant from his comfortable home and his fond wife, to make his abode for months at a time in the dismal cave of Mount Hira? If we respect the shrinking of Isaiah or Jeremiah from the heavy task of proclaiming unwelcome truth, we must also respect the keen sensitiveness of Muhammad, who was so burdened by this responsibility..."[11]

"...we feel that the words which he (Muhammad) speaks are not the words of an ordinary man. They have their immediate source in the inner reality of things, since he lives in constant fellowship with this reality."[12]

First Converts:

"It is strongly corroborative of Muhammad's sincerity that the earliest converts to Islam were his bosom friends and the people of his household, who, all intimately acquainted with his private life, could not fail to have detected those discrepancies which more or less invariably exist between the pretensions of the hypocritical deceiver and his actions at home."[13]

---

11 Dr. Marcus Dods: *Muhammad, Buddha and Christ*, pp. 17,18.

12 Tor Andrae: *Muhammad*, London 1936, p. 247.

13 John Davenport: *An Apology for Muhammad and the Koran*, p. 17.

Persecution and Migration from Makkah

"Muhammad's message infuriated those rich Arabs whose faith required many idols, and he and his new followers were driven from Makkah, his home."[14]

At Madinah:

"In little more than a year he was actually the spiritual, nominal and temporal ruler of Madinah, with his hand on the lever that was to shake the world."[15]

"...he became head of the state and the testimony even of his enemies is that he administered wisely. The wisdom he displayed in judging intricate cases became the basis for the religious law that governs Islam today."[16]

"...Forced now to fight in defence of the freedom of conscience which he preached, he became an accomplished military leader. Although he repeatedly went into battle outnumbered and outspeared as much as five to one, he won some spectacular victories."[17]

Conquest of Makkah:

"The day of Muhammad's greatest triumph over his enemies was also the day of his grandest victory over himself. He freely forgave the Koraysh all the years of sorrow and cruel scorn in which they had afflicted him and gave an amnesty to the whole population of Makkah. Four criminals whom justice condemned made up Muhammad's proscription list when he entered as a conqueror to the city of his bitterest enemies. The army followed his example, and entered quietly and peacefully; no house was robbed, no women insulted. One thing alone suffered destruction. Going to the Ka'bah, Muhammad stood before each of the three hundred and sixty idols, and pointed to it with his staff, saying, 'Truth is come and falsehood is fled away!', and at these words his attendants hewed them down, and all the idols and household gods of Makkah and round about were destroyed.

---

14 James A. Michener: *op.cit.*

15 John Austin: *Muhammad the Prophet of Allah,* in "T.P.'s and Cassels' Weekly" for 24th September, 1927.

16 James A. Michener: *op.cit.*

17 *Ibid.*

"It was thus Muhammad entered again his native city. *Through all the annals of conquest there is no triumphant entry comparable to this one.*"[18]

"....in comparison, for example, with the cruelty of the Crusaders, who, in 1099, put seventy thousand Muslims, men, women and helpless children to death when Jerusalem fell into their hands; or with that of the English army, also fighting under the Cross, which in the year of grace 1874 burned an African capital, in its war on the Gold Coast, Muhammad's victory was in very truth one of religion and not of politics; he rejected every token of personal homage, and declined all regal authority; and when the haughty chiefs of the Koreishites appeared before him he asked:

"What can you expect at my hands?

"Mercy, O generous brother!

"Be it so; you are free! He exclaimed."[19]

Farewell Pilgrimage and a Great Sermon on Human Rights:

"A year before his death, at the end of the tenth year of the Hegira, Muhammad made his last pilgrimage from Madinah to Makkah. He made then a great sermon to his people... The reader will note that the first paragraph sweeps away all plunder and blood feuds among the followers of Islam. The last makes the believing Negro the equal of the Caliph...they established in the world a great tradition of dignified fair dealing, they breathe a spirit of generosity, and they are human and workable. They created a society more free from widespread cruelty and social oppression than any society had ever been in the world before."[20]

"...this very human prophet of God... had such a remarkable personal influence over all with whom he was brought into contact that, neither when a poverty-stricken and hunted fugitive, nor at the height of his prosperity, did he ever have to complain of treachery from those who had once embraced his faith. His confidence in himself, and in his inspiration from on high, was ever greater when he was suffering under disappointment and defeat than when he was able to dictate his own terms

---

18 Stanley Lane-Poole: *The Speeches and Table-Talk of the Prophet Muhammad*, London 1882, Introduction, pp. 46, 47. (*Italics are the present writer's*).

19 Arthur Gilman: *The Saracens,* London 1887 pp. 184, 185.

20 H.G. Wells: *The Outline of History*, London 1920, p. 325.

to his conquered enemies. Muhammad died[21] as he had lived, surrounded by his early followers, friends and votaries: his death as devoid of mystery as his life of disguise."[22]

21 At the age of sixty-three.

22 H.M. Hyndman : *The Awakening of Asia*, London 1919, p. 9.

Chapter III

MUHAMMAD'S PERSONALITY AND CHARACTER AND SIDELIGHTS ON SOME REFORMS

Personality and Character:

"Muhammad was of middle height, rather thin but broad of shoulder, wide of chest, strong of bone and muscle. His head was massive, strongly developed. Dark hair, slightly curled, flowed in a dense mass almost to his shoulders; even in advanced age it was sprinkled with only about twenty gray hairs, produced by the agonies of his 'Revelations'. His face was oval-shaped, slightly tawny of colour. Fine long arched eye-brows were divided by a vein, which throbbed visibly in moments of passion. Great black restless eyes shone out from under long heavy eyelashes. His nose was large, slightly acquiline. His teeth, upon which he bestowed great care, were well set, dazzling white. A full beard framed his manly face. His skin was clear and soft, his complexion 'red and white'. His hands were as 'silk and satin', even as those of a woman. His step was quick and elastic, yet firm as that of one who steps 'from a high to a low place'. In turning his face, he would also turn his whole body. His whole gait and presence was dignified and imposing. His countenance was mild and pensive. His laugh was rarely more than a smile.

"In his habits he was extremely simple, although he bestowed great care on his person. His eating and drinking, his dress and his furniture retained, even when he had reached the fullness of power, their almost primitive nature. The ~~only~~ luxuries he indulged in were arms, which he highly prized, and a pair of yellow boots, a present from the Negus of Abyssinia. Perfumes, however, he loved passionately, being most sensitive to smells. Strong drink he abhorred.

"....He was gifted with mighty power of imagination, elevation of mind, delicacy and refinement of feeling. 'He is more modest than a virgin behind her curtain', it was said of him. He was most indulgent to his inferiors, and would never allow his little page to be scolded whatever he did. 'Ten years', said Anas, his servant, 'I was about the Prophet, and he never said as much as 'uff' to me'. He was very affectionate towards his family. One of his boys died on his breast in the smoky house of the nurse, a blacksmith's wife. He was very fond of children; he would stop them in the streets and pat their little heads. He never struck anyone in his life. The worst expression he ever use of in conversation was, 'What has come to him? May his forehead become darkened with mud!' When asked to curse someone he replied, 'I have not been sent to curse, but to be a mercy to mankind'. 'He visited the sick, followed any bier he met, accepted the invitation of a slave to dinner, mended his own clothes, milked the goats, and waited upon himself', relates summarily another tradition. He never first withdrew his hand out of another man's palm, and turned not before the other had turned.

"He was the most faithful protector of those he protected, the sweetest and most agreeable in conversation. Those who saw him were suddenly filled with reverence; those who came near him loved him; they who described him would say, 'I have never seen his like either before or after'. He was of great taciturnity, but when he spoke it was with emphasis and deliberation and no one could forget what he said.

"He lived with his wives in a row of humble cottages separated from one another by palm-branches, cemented together with mud. He would kindle the fire, sweep the floor, and milk the goats himself. The little food he had was always shared with those who dropped in to partake of it. Indeed outside the Prophet's house was a bench or a gallery, on which were always found a number of poor who lived entirely upon his generosity, and were hence called 'the people of the bench'. His ordinary food was dates and water, or barley bread; milk and honey were luxuries of which he was fond, but which he rarely allowed himself. The fare of the desert seemed most congenial to him even when he was sovereign of Arabia.

"There is something so tender and womanly, and withal so heroic, about the man, that one is in peril of finding the judgement unconsciously blinded by the feeling of reverence, and well-nigh love, that such a nature inspires. He who, standing alone, braved for years the hatred of his people, is the same who was never the first to withdraw his hand from another's clasp; the beloved of children, who never passed a group of little ones without a smile from his wonderful eyes and kind word for them, sounding all the kinder in that sweet-toned voice. The frank friendship, the noble generosity, the dauntless courage and hope of the man, all tend to melt criticism into admiration.

"He was an enthusiast in that noblest sense when enthusiasm becomes the salt of the earth, the one thing that keep men from rotting whilst they live. Enthusiasm is often used despitefully, because it is joined to an unworthy cause, or falls upon barren ground and bears no fruit. So was it not with Muhammad. He was an enthusiast when enthusiasm was the one thing needed to set the world aflame, and his enthusiasm was noble for a noble cause. He was one of those happy few who have attained the supreme joy of making one great truth their very life-spring. He was the messenger of the one God, and never to his life's end did he forget who he was he was or the message which was the marrow of his being. He brought his tidings to his people with a grand dignity sprung from the consciousness of his high office together with a most sweet humility….."[1]

"His (i.e., Muhammad's) politeness to the great, his affability to the humble, and his dignified bearing to the presumptuous, procured him respect, admiration and applause. His talents were equally fitted for persuasion or command. Deeply red in the volume of nature, though entirely ignorant of letters, his mind could expand into controversy with the acutest of his enemies or contract itself to the apprehension of the meanest of his disciples. His simple eloquence, rendered impressive by the expression of a countenance wherein awfulness of majesty was tempered by an amiable sweetness, excited emotion of veneration and love; and he was gifted with the authoritative air of genius which alike influences the learned and command the illiterate. As a friend and a parent, he exhibited the softest feeling of nature; but, while in possession of the kind and generous emotions of the heart, and engaged in the discharge of most of the social and domestic duties, he disgraced not his assumed title of an apostle of God. With all that simplicity which is no natural to a great mind, he performed the humblest offices whose homeliness it would be idle to conceal with pompuous diction; even while Lord of Arabia, he mended his own shoes and coarse woollen garments, milked the ewes, swept the hearth, and kindled the fire. Dates and water were his usual fare and milk and honey his luxuries. When he travelled he divided his morsel with his servant. The sincerity of his exhortations to benevolence was justified at his death by the exhausted state of his coffers."[2]

"Muhammad…despised grandeur, and lived on principle an extremely frugal life, though he was no ascetic… He is reputed to have behaved very simply, and there is no reason for not supposing that he did. He performed the most menial tasks with his own hands, and was

1 Stanley Lane-Poole: *The Speeches and Table-Talk of the Prophet Muhammad*, Introduction, pp. 27-30.

2 John Davenport: *An Apology for Muhammad and the Qur'ãn*, pp. 52, 53.

essentially puritan, saying the Divine revelation forbade him to wear either gold or silk."[3]

"His deportment, in general was calm and equable; he...was grave and dignified, though he is said to have possessed a smile of captivating sweetness. His complexion was more ruddy than is usual with Arabs, and in his excited and enthusiastic moments there was a glow and radiance in his countenance, which his disciples magnified into the supernatural light of prophecy.

"His intellectual qualities were undoubtedly of an extraordinary kind. He had a quick apprehension, a retentive memory, a vivid imagination and an inventive genius.

"He was sober and abstemious in his diet, and a rigorous observer of fasts. He indulged in no magnificence of apparel, the ostentation of a petty mind; neither was his simplicity in dress affected but a result of real disregard for distinction from so trivial a source.

"In his private dealings he was just. He treated friends and strangers, the rich and the poor, the powerful and the weak, with equity, and was loved by the common people for the affability with which he received them, and listened to their complaints.

"His military triumphs awakened no pride nor vainglory, as they would have done had they been effected for selfish purposes. In the time of his greatest power he maintained the same simplicity of manners and appearance as in the days of his adversity. So far from affecting a regal state, he was displeased in, on entering a room, any unusual testimonials of respect were shown to him. If he aimed at universal dominion, it was the dominion of the faith; as to the temporal rule which grew up in his hands, as he used it without ostentation, so he took no step to perpetuate it in his family."[4]

"Mahomet himself, after all that can be said about him, was not a sensual man...His household was of the frugalest; his common diet barley-bread and water; sometimes for months there was not a fire once lighted on his hearth. They record with just pride that he would mend his

---

3 A.C. Bouquet: *Comparative Religion,* Penguin Books, Harmondsworth, Middle sex, 1954, pp. 269-270.

4 Washington Irving: *Mahomet and his Successors*, London 1909; pp. 192, 193, 199.

own shoes, patch his own cloak...careless of what vulgar men toil for...something better in him than hunger of any sort, or these wild Arab men, fighting and jostling three-and-twenty years at his hand, in close contact with him always, would not have reverenced him so! They were wild men, bursting ever and anon with quarrel, with all kinds of fierce sincerity; without right worth and manhood, no man could have commanded them...No emperor with his tiaras was obeyed as this man in a cloak of his own clouting. During three-and-twenty years of rough actual trial, I find something of a veritable hero necessary for that myself."[5]

"His (i.e., Muhammad's) memory was capacious and retentive, his wit easy and social, his imagination sublime, his judgment clear, rapid and decisive. He possessed the courage of both thought and action; and.... the first idea which he entertained of his divine mission bears the stamp of an original and superior genius."[6]

"Head of the State as well as of the Church", remarks Bosworth Smith, "he was Caesar and Pope in one; but he was Pope without Pope's pretensions, Caesar without the legions of Caesar. Without a standing army, without a body-guard, without a palace, without a fixed revenue, if ever any man had the right to say that he ruled by the right divine, it was Muhammad, for he had all the power without its instruments and without its supports. He rose superior to the title and ceremonies, the solemn trifling, and the proud humility of court etiquette. To hereditary kings, to princes born in the purple, these things are naturally enough as the breath of life; but those who ought to have known better, even self-made rulers, and those the foremost in the files of time—a Caesar, a Cromwell, a Napoleon, have been unable to resist their tinsel attractions. Muhammad was content with the reality; he cared not for the dressings of power. The simplicity of his private life was in keeping with his public life. 'God', says Al-Bukhari, 'offered him the keys of the treasures of the earth, but he would not accept them'."[7]

"Never has a man set for himself, voluntarily or involuntarily, a more sublime aim, since this aim was superhuman: to subvert superstitions which had been interposed between man and his Creator;

---

5 Thomas Carlyle: *On Heroes, Hero-Worship and the Heroic in History*, p. 61.

6 Edward Gibbon: *The History of the Decline and Fall of the Roman Empire*. London 1838, Vol. V. p. 335.

7 Bosworth Smith : *Muhammad and Muhammadanism,* pp. 92.

to render God unto man and man unto God; to restore the rational and sacred idea of divinity amidst the chaos of the material and disfigured gods of idolatry, then existing. Never has a man undertaken a work so far beyond human power with so feeble means, for he (Muhammad) had in the conception as well as in the execution of such a great design no other instrument than himself, and no other aid, except a handful of men living in a corner of the desert. Finally, never has a man accomplished such a huge and lasting revolution in the world, because in less than two centuries after its appearance, Islam in faith and in arms, reigned over the whole of Arabia, conquered, in God's name, Persia, Khorasan, Transoxania, Western India, Syria, Africa, numerous islands of the Mediterranean, Spain, and a part of Gaul.

"If greatness of purpose, smallness of means, and astounding results are the three criteria of human genius, who could dare to compare any great man in modern history with Muhammad? The most famous men created arms, laws and empires only. They founded, if anything at all, no more than material powers which often crumbled away before their eyes. This man moved not only armies, legislations, empires, peoples and dynasties, but millions of men in one-third of the then inhabited world; and more than that, he moved the altars, the gods, the religions, the ideas, the beliefs and the souls. On the basis of a Book every letter of which has become law, he created a spiritual nationality which blended together peoples of every tongue and of every race. He has left for us as the indelible characteristic of this Muslim nationality the hatred of false gods and the passion for the One and Immaterial God. This avenging patriotism against the profanation of Heaven formed the virtue of the followers of Muhammad; the conquest of one-third of the earth to his dogma was his miracle; or rather it was not the miracle of a man but that of reason. The idea of the Unity of God, proclaimed amidst the exhaustion of fabulous theologies, was in itself such a miracle that upon its utterance from his lips it destroyed all the ancient temples of idols and set on fire one-third of the world. His life, his meditations, his heroic revilings against the superstitions of his country, and his boldness in defying the furies of idolatry, his firmness in enduring them for fifteen years at Makkah, his acceptance of the role of public scorn and almost of being a victim of his fellow countrymen; all these and, finally, his flight, his incessant preaching, his wars against odds, his faith in his success and his superhuman security in misfortune, his forbearance in victory, his ambition, which was entirely devoted to one idea and in no manner striving for an empire; his endless prayers, his mystic conversations with God, his death and his triumph after death: all these attest not to an imposture but to a firm conviction which gave him the power to restore a dogma. This dogma was twofold, the unity of God and the immateriality of God; the former telling what God is, the latter telling what God is not; the one overthrowing false gods with the sword, the other starting an idea with the words.

"Philosopher, orator, apostle, legislator, warrior, conqueror of ideas, restorer of rational dogmas, of a cult without images, the founder of twenty terrestrial empires and of one spiritual empire, that is Muhammad. As regards all standards by which human greatness may be measured, we may well ask, is there any man greater than he?"[8]

"...These Arabs, the man Mahomet and that one century,—is it not as if a spark had fallen, one spark, on a world of what seemed black unnoticeable sand; but lo! the sand proves explosive powder, blazes heaven-high from Delhi to Grenada; I said the Great Man was always as lightning out of heaven; the rest of the men waited for him like fuel, and then they too would aflame."[9]

"It is impossible for anyone who studies the life and character of the great Prophet of Arabia, who knows how he taught and how he lived, to feel anything but reverence for that mighty Prophet, one of the great messengers of the Supreme."[10]

Genuineness of Faith in His Divine Mission:

"The essential sincerity of Muhammad's nature cannot be questioned: and an historical criticism that blinks no fact, yields nothing to credulity, weighs every testimony, has no partisan interest, and seeks only the truth, must acknowledge his claim to belong to that order of prophets who, whatever the nature of their physical experience may have been, in diverse times, in diverse manners, have admonished, taught and uttered austere and sublime thoughts, laid down principles of conduct nobler than those they found, and devoted themselves fearlessly to their high calling, being irresistibly impelled to their ministry by a power within."[11]

---

8 Lamartine: *History de la Turquie,* Paris, 1854, Vol. II, pp. 276-277. (Italics are the present writer's).

9 Thomas Carlyle : *op.cit.*, p. 311.

10 Annie Besant: *The Life and Teachings of Muhammad*, Madras 1932, p. 4.

11 Prof. Nathaniel Schmidt: *The New International Encyclopaedia,* 1916, Vol. XVI, p.72.

"His readiness to undergo persecutions for his beliefs, the high moral character of the men who believed in him and looked up to him as leader, and the greatness of his ultimate achievement—all argue his fundamental integrity. To suppose Muhammad as impostor raises more problems than it solves. Moreover, none of the great figures of history is so poorly appreciated in the West as Muhammad...Thus, not merely must we credit Muhammad with essential honesty and integrity of purpose, if we are to understand him at all; if we are to correct the errors we have inherited from the past, we must in every particular case hold firmly to the belief in his sincerity until the opposite is conclusively proved; and we must not forget that conclusive proof is a much stricter requirement than a show of plausibility, and in a matter such as this only to be attained with difficulty."[12]

A Great Exemplar:

"Serious or trivial, his daily behaviour has instituted a canon which millions observe at this day with conscious memory. No one regarded by any section of the human race as Perfect Man had been imitated so minutely. The conduct of the Founder of Christianity has not so governed the ordinary life of his followers. Moreover, no founder of a religion has been left on so solitary an eminence as the Muslim Apostle."[13]

Permanent Impact of Revolution:

"It is not the propagation but the permanency of his religion that deserves our wonder; the same pure and perfect impression which he engraved at Makkah and Madinah is preserved, after the revolutions of twelve centuries...The intellectual image of the Deity has never been degraded by any visible idol; the honours of the prophet have never transgressed the measure of human virtue; and his living precepts have restrained the gratitude of his disciples within the bounds of reason and religion."[14]

Devotion to God and to Righteousness in Conduct:

"The ignorance displayed by most Christians regarding the Muslim religion is appalling...Muhammad alone, among the nations at

12 W. Montgomery Watt: *Muhammad at Makkah,* Oxford 1953, p. 52.

13 D. G. Hogarth: *A History of Arabia,* Oxford 1922, p. 52.

14 Edward Gibbon and Simon Ockley: *History of the Saracen Empire*, London 1870, p. 54.

that time, believed in one God to the exclusion of all others. He insisted on righteousness as the source of conduct, of filial duty, and on frequent prayers to the Everliving God, and of respect to all other peoples, and of justice and mercy to and moderation in all things, and to hold in great respect learning of every kind...Most of the absurdities which Christians would have us believe to exist in the Qur'ãn were never uttered by Muhammad himself, nor are they to be found in a correct translation of the work."[15]

Charge of Voluptuousness Refuted:

"By the force of his extraordinary personality, Muhammad revolutionized life in Arabic and throughout the East. With his own hands he smashed ancient idols and established a religion dedicated to one God. He lifted women from the bondage in which desert custom held them and preached general social justice.

"Muslims think it particularly ironic when Muhammad is charged by Western writers with having established a voluptuous religion. Among drunkards he abolished alcohol, so that even today all good Muslims are prohibitionists. Among the lazy he ordained individual ritual prayers five times each day. In a nation that revelled in feasting he instituted a most rigorous day-time fast lasting a full month each year.

"Western writers have based their charges of voluptuousness mainly on the question of women. Before Muhammad, however, men were encouraged to take innumerable wives; he limited them to four only, and the Koran is explicit that husbands who are unable to maintain strict equality between two or more wives must confine themselves to one..."[16]

Profoundly Practical and Rational:

"In all things Muhammad was profoundly practical. When his beloved son Ibrahim died, an eclipse occurred, and rumours of God's personal condolence quickly arose. Whereupon Muhammad is said to have announced, 'An eclipse is a phenomenon of nature. It is foolish to attribute such things to the death or birth of a human being'."[17]

---

15 G. Lindsay Johnson, F.R.C.S.: *The Two Worlds,* Manchester, 9th August, 1940.

16 James A. Michener, *op.cit.*

17 *Ibid.*

Broad, Liberal and Universalistic Creed for the whole World:

"His creed...necessarily connotes the existence of a universal empire."[18]

"The nobility and broad tolerance of this creed, which accepts as God-inspired all the real religions of the world, will always be a glorious heritage for mankind. On it could indeed be built a perfect world religion."[19]

"More pure than the system of Zoroaster, more liberal than the law of Moses, the religion of Mahomet might seem less inconsistent with reason that the creed of mystery and superstition which, in the seventh century, disgraced the simplicity of the gospels."[20]

"Islam had the power of peacefully conquering souls by the simplicity of its theology, the clearness of its dogma and principles, and the definite number of the practices which it demands. In contrast to Christianity which has been undergoing continual transformation since its origin, Islam has remained identical with itself."[21]

"As a religion the Islamic religion, it must be confessed, is more suited to Africa than is the Christian religion: indeed, I would even say that *it is more suited to the world as a whole*[22] ...the achievement of the Muslim faith enjoys, I maintain, a definite superiority, in proof of which may be cited Muslim abstinence, sense of fraternity, condemnation of usury, and recognition of prophets other than its own. Its quality may be summed up by saying that it takes a man as he is, and while it does not pretend to make a god out of him, it seeks to regulate his conduct so that at least he shall become a good neighbour.[23]

Wisest, Most Learned and Most Enlightened Jurisprudence:

"The Islamic Law which is binding on all from the crowned head to the meanest subject is a law interwoven with a system of the

---

18 Joseph J. Nunan: *Islam and European Civilization,* Demerara 1912, p. 37.

19 Duncan Greenless: *The Gospel of Islam*, Adyar 1948, p. 27.

20 Edward Gibbon: *The History of the Decline and Fall of the Roman Empire*, Vol. V, p. 487.

21 Jean L'heureux, *Etude sur L'Islamisme*, p. 35.

22 Italics are the present writer's.

23 Lancelor Lawton: *The Sphere,* London, 12th May, 1928.

wisest, the most learned and the most enlightened jurisprudence that ever existed in the world."[24]

No Colour Bar:

" 'Take away that black man! I can have no discussion with him', exclaimed the Christian Archbishop Cyrus when the Arab conquerors had sent a deputation of their ablest men to discuss terms of surrender of the capital of Egypt, headed by Negro Ubadah as the ablest of them all.

"To the sacred archbishop's astonishment, he was told that this man was commissioned by General Amr; that the Muslims held Negroes and white men in equal respect—judging a man by his character and not by his colour.

" 'Well, if the Negro must lead, he must speak gently', ordered the prelate, so as not to frighten his white auditors.

"(Replied Ubadah:) 'There are a thousand blacks, as black as myself, amongst our companions. I and they would be ready to meet and fight a hundred enemies together. We live only to fight for God, and to follow His will. We care naught for wealth, so long as we have the wherewithal to stay our hunger and to clothe our bodies. This world is naught for us, the next world is all'.

"Such a spirit...can any other appeal stand against that of the Muslim who, in approaching the pagan, says to him, however obscure or degraded he may be, 'Embrace the faith, and you are at once an equal and a brother'. Islam knows no 'colour line',"[25]

Restoration of Dignity of Womanhood:

"That his (Muhammad's) reforms enhanced the status of women in general is universally admitted."[26]

"You can find others stating that the religion (Islam) is evil, because it sanctions a limited polygamy. But you do not hear as a rule the criticism which I spoke out one day in a London hall where I knew

---

24 Edmund Burle: in his "*Impeachment of Warren Hastings.*"

25 S.S. Leeder : *Veiled Mysteries of Egypt,* London 1912, pp. 332-335.

26 H.A.R. Gibb: *Muhammadanism*, London 1953, p. 33.

that the audience was entirely uninstructed. I pointed out to them that monogamy with a blended mass of prostitution was a hypocrisy and more degrading than a limited polygamy. Naturally a statement like that gives offence, but it has to be made, because it must be remembered that the law of Islam in relation to women was until lately, when parts of it have been imitated in England, the most just law, as far as women are concerned, to be found in the world. Dealing with property, dealing with rights of succession and so on, dealing with cases of divorce, it was far beyond the law of the West, in the respect that was paid to the rights of women. Those things are forgotten while people are hypnotized by the words monogamy and polygamy and do not look at what lies behind it in the West—the frightful degradation of women who are thrown into the streets when their first protectors, weary of them, no longer give them any assistance…

"I often think that woman is more free in Islam than in Christianity. Woman is more protected by Islam than by the faith which preaches Monogamy. In al-Qur'ãn the law about woman is more just and liberal. It is only in the last twenty years that Christian England has recognized the right of woman to property, while Islam has allowed this right from all times… It is a slander to say that Islam preaches that women have no souls."[27]

War Against the Institution of Slavery:

"According to the Qur'ãn, no person can be made a slave except after the conclusion of a sanguinary battle fought in the conduct of a religious war (*Jihãd*) in the country of infidels who try to suppress the true religion. Indeed, wherever the word slave occurs in Koran it is 'he whom your right hand possess', or a special equivalent for neck—'he whose neck has been spared', thus clearly indicating 'a prisoner of war' made by the action of not one man only, but of many….the Arabian prophet recommended: 'When the war has ended, restore them (the slaves or prisoners) to liberty or give them up for ransom'. (*Sura* XLVII: 57)…….

"And elsewhere: 'Alms (which procure righteousness) and destined…to the redemption of slaves.' (*Sura* IX:60)… Further (*Sura* XXIV:33): 'If any of your slaves asks for his manumission in writing

---

27 Annie Besant : *The Life and Teachings of Muhammad,* Madras 1932, pp. 25-26.

give it to him, if you think him worthy of it, and give him also some of the wealth which God has given you'.... The reconciliation of a separated married couple should be preceded by the ransom of a slave, and, if none can be found, the husband should feed sixty poor, or else fast for two months (*Sura* LVIII:4, 5). Whenever the sense of happiness, including that of conjugal felicity, predisposes the heart to gratitude toward the Creator, or whenever fear of God or a punishment, or the desire of a blessing, affect, as such motives can and *do* affect the daily life of a Muhammadan, the emancipation of a slave, as a most proper act of charity is recommended. In short, the 'Cliff', or narrow path to salvation, is charity: 'What is the cliff? It is to free captive (or slave).' (*Sura* XC:12, 13).

"Descending to the second source of the Islamic Law, the authenticated traditions of *Hadis*, we find Muhammad stating that 'the worst of men is he who sells men'; slaves who displeased their masters were to be forgiven 'seventy times a day'; no believer can be made a slave; and 'in proportion to the number of redeemed slaves will members of the body of the releasing person be rescued from the (eternal) fire'."[28]

Contribution to Science and Civilisation:

"It is to Mussalman science, to Mussalman art, and to Mussalman literature that Europe has been in a great measure indebted for its extrication from the darkness of the Middle Ages."[29]

"Europe was darkness at sunset, Cordova shone with public lamps: Europe was dirty, Cordova built a thousand baths: Europe was covered with vermin, Cordova changed its undergarments daily: Europe lay in mud, Cordova's streets were paved; Europe's palaces had smoke-holes in the ceiling, Cordova's arabesques were exquisite; Europe's nobility could not sign its name, Cordova's children went to school; Europe's monks could not read the baptismal service, Cordova's teachers created a library of Alexandrian dimensions."[30]

---

28 Dr. G.W. Leitner: *Muhammadanism*, pp. 17-18. *Cf.* the observation: 'It is indeed an 'abuse of words' to apply the word 'slavery; in the English sense to any status known to the legislation of Islam". (Syed Amir Ali : *The Spirit of Islam* : p. 262).

29 Marquis of Dufferin and Ava: *Speeches Delivered in India*, London 1890, p. 24.

30 Victor Robinson: *The Story of Medicine*, p. 164.

"Our use of the phrase 'the Dark Ages' to cover the period from 699 to 1,000 marks our undue concentration on Western Europe...From India to Spain, the brilliant civilization of Islam flourished. What was lost to Christendom at this time was not lost to civilization, but quite the contrary... To us it seems that West-European civilization is civilization; but this is a narrow view."[31]

"....From a new angle and with a fresh vigour it (the Arab mind) took up that systematic development of positive knowledge which the Greeks had begun and relinquished...Through the Arabs it was and not by the Latin route that the modern world received that gift of light and power."[32]

Peaceful Proselytisation:

"History makes it clear, however, that the legend of fanatical Muslims sweeping through the world and forcing Islam at the point of the sword upon conquered races is one of the most fantastically absurd myths that historians have ever repeated."[33]

In their wars of conquest, however, the Muslims exhibited a degree of toleration which puts many Christian nations to shame."[34]

The Rise of Islam:

"The rise of Islam is perhaps the most amazing event in human history. Springing from a land and a people alike previously negligible, Islam spread within a century over half the earth, shattering great empires, overthrowing long-established religions, remoulding the souls of races, and building up a whole new world—the world of Islam.

"The closer we examine this development the more extra-ordinary does it appear. The other great religions won their way slowly, by painful struggle, and finally triumphed with the aid of powerful monarchs converted to the new faith. Christianity had its Constantine, Buddhism its Asoka, and Zoroastrianism its Cyrus, each lending to his

---

31 Bertrand Russell: *History of Western Philosophy*, London 1948, p. 419.

32 H.G. Wells: *The Outline of History*, p. 327.

33 De Lacy O'Leary : *Islam at the Crossroads*, London 1923, p. 8.

34 E. Alexander Powell : *The Struggle for Power in Muslim Asia*, New York 1923, p. 48.

chosen cult the mighty force of secular authority. Not so Islam. Arising in a desert land sparsely inhabited by a nomad race previously undistinguished in human annals, Islam sallied forth on its great adventure with the slenderest human backing and against the heaviest material odds. Yet Islam triumphed with seemingly miraculous ease, and a couple of generations saw the Fiery Crescent borne victorious from the Pyrenees to the Himalayas and from the deserts of Central Asia to the deserts of Central Africa...Preaching a simple, austere monotheism, free from priest-craft or elaborate doctrinal trappings, he tapped the well-springs of religious zeal always present in the Semitic heart. Forgetting the chronic rivalries and blood feuds which had consumed their energies in internecine strife, and welded into a glowing unity by the fire of their new-found faith, the Arabs poured forth from their deserts to conquer the earth of Allah, the one true God....

"They (Arabs) were no bloodthirsty savages, bent solely on loot and destruction. On the contrary, they were an innately gifted race, eager to learn and appreciative of the cultural gifts which older civilizations had to bestow. Intermarrying freely and professing a common belief, conquerors and conquered rapidly fused, and from this fusion arose a new civilization—the Saracenic civilization, in which the ancient cultures of Greece, Rome and Persia, were revitalized by the Arab genius and the Islamic spirit. For the first three centuries of its existence (circ. A.D. 650-1000) the realm of Islam was the most civilized and progressive portion of the world. Studded with splendid cities, gracious mosques, and quiet universities where the wisdom of the ancient world was preserved and appreciated, the Muslim world offered a striking contrast to the Christian West, then sunk in the night of the Dark Ages."[35]

35 A.M. Lothrop Stoddard *The New World of Islam,* London 1932, pp.1-3.

Part II

THE NECESSITY OF DIVINE REVELATION

Chapter I

PROBLEMS

Chapter II

SOURCES OF GUIDANCE WHAT?

Chapter I

PROBLEMS

I. Problems of Human Life

Life means activity and all activity brings with it certain problems. Those problems have to be solved successfully in order to make the human life a success.

If we analyse the human problems, we find that they fall under two categories, viz: (1) Immediate Problems; and (2) Ultimate Problems.

The immediate problems are the practical day-to-day problems, such as those which refer to the immediate personal needs of the individuals and such problems as the administration of the state, the production, consumption and distribution of wealth, and the relations between the different nations of the world. There is no human being living on earth who has not to face these problems one way or the other during his life. The manner in which they are faced and the efficiency and practical common sense which is shown in connection with their solutions forms the measure of human success.

As regards the ultimate problems, every human being who takes life seriously finds himself face to face with them as soon as he attains the age of maturity and feels the strains, the burdens and the intricacies of life. The first question which arises in this connection is: "What am I?" Every human being is closer to himself than to anyone else. Hence the first problem which should arise in his mind in connection with the ultimate problems should naturally be about his own self.

The question: "What am I?" is a question about the *nature* of human beings. But this simple question opens a whole field of questions which shoot off in a continuous chain and whose links are forged with the unbreakable bond of necessity. Consideration of this first question, therefore, leads to the next one, namely: "From where have the human beings come?" Then a third question arises: "What is the nature of human life?" And then a fourth question: "What is the purpose and end of human life?"

All the above-mentioned questions are, so to say, *personal*. But, then, no human being lives in a vacuum. He lives in a world which is infinitely and immeasurably vaster than his physically-infinitesimal personality, and this world influences his life and his actions at every step. His fortunes, nay, his very life, is interlinked with and dependent upon the world around him. For instance, if the sun were to stop its function, the entire related physical environment would be shattered to pieces. Or, if the heat of the sun rises above or falls below the average to certain levels, the very existence of the human beings on the earth would become impossible.

This being the case, the questions about one's own self lead to questions about the world. The first question in that connection is: "What is this world?", which in other words means: "What is the *nature* of this world?" But the nature of a thing cannot be properly understood unless we have a clear idea about the origin of that thing and the purpose for which it functions. Therefore, the question about "what" leads to questions about "when", "how", "wherefrom" and "whereto". In other words, the enquiry arises: "When did the world come into being?" "How did the world come into being?"; "From what source did the world acquire its life?"; "What is the end towards which it is moving?"; and "What is its final goal (destiny)"?

Among the questions about world, the question: "How did the world come into being?" brings forth a number of further questions, namely:—"If this world came into being by itself, how is that conceivable, i.e., on what ground?" "If this world was brought into being by some other force, what is that force?" "Is it an impersonal force like electricity, or is it a person?" "If it is believed to be an impersonal force, that would mean that it is a blind force like all impersonal forces; and if it is a blind force, how could intelligence, foresight, plan, purpose and law come out of it?" "If it is a person, what is the nature and constitution of that person?" "Is He a person like us—physical, faltering and subject to the processes of decay and death, or is He eternal?" "If not physical, what else is He?" "Is He finite or infinite?" "Is He one in number or two or three or more?"

The above-mentioned questions concerning man, the world and God, are ultimate questions (or fundamental problems). The questions are so vital that every thinking human being is bound to face them at one time or the other during his life and they have such a close bearing on the immediate questions of life that anyone who has any knowledge of human problems will admit that they cannot be shirked.

II. Importance of Ultimate Questions in Practical Life

Some might doubt that these ultimate questions may not after all be as important as they are said to be. Indeed, the modern secular civilization is, for all practical purposes, based on the notion that these ultimate questions have nothing to do with the immediate practical problems of mankind and that the interest that can at all be reasonably taken in them cannot be anything else than academic. In other words, these questions are meant only for philosophers and no practical person should waste his time and energy on them. But if we go deep into the matter, we are bound to come to the conclusion on the basis of our common sense itself that the ultimate questions are infinitely more important than the immediate questions.

The problem can be attacked from different angels. But here it will suffice to quote just one instance of the importance of ultimate questions in the field of the immediate problems of life. Namely, we shall discuss the practical consequences of belief and disbelief in the existence of God.

Taking up disbelief in the existence of God first: If there is no God and the world came into being by itself, it means that it came into being by *chance*. In other words, it is a world of chance in which everything and every event emerges and dies out by chance.

If we consider the nature of "chance" itself, we find that it always indicates an event which has no pre-conceived cause. In any case, it cannot be said to be a planned event. Again, if there is no plan in an event, there can be no purpose, because all purposive activity is planned, whether the planning is conscious (namely, based on intellectual appreciation) or merely instinctive. Resuming the argument, if the world came into being by chance, it is a blind and lawless world. Indeed, the very word "chance" means the absence of law.

Now, if the world is lawless in its inherent constitution and if everything which is born out of it is also in its nature without law, it means that the formulation of any laws by human beings, whether those laws are scientific or ethical or political or economic, would be a violation of human nature and the nature of the world itself. But human beings cannot exist without law. Therefore, they are bound to give up the atheistic hypothesis of the existence of the world in order to live. If they don't and if they carry the atheistic hypothesis to its logical consequences, the only law which they can establish for themselves would be the law of the jungle in political administration and the rule of expediency in moral life.

Speaking from the other side, namely, affirmation of faith in God's existence, if we believe that God exists and that He has created the world, it means that the world came into being through planned creation, is functioning under a system of law and is moving towards a purpose. In other words, plan, purpose and law are inherent in the very constitution of the world. This, in turn, provides the ground for every branch of human law—ethical, political, economic, and so on.

Chapter II

SOURCE OF GUIDANCE—WHAT?

There are three claimants in the field of guidance and everyone of them claims that it can guide humanity in the ultimate problems of life. These claimants are:— (1) Science; (2) Philosophy; (3) Religion. We might take them up one by one and examine the validity of the claim of each.

I. Science

Modern Science entered the field of human thought as the all-solving branch of knowledge and the rival of religion towards the middle of the 18th century. The reason of this new attitude of Science was not that Science nad found out some such unerring methods or instruments of knowledge that could authorise it to make the claim. Rather, it was purely a sentimental affair.

Science came to the modern West from the world of Islam. It was the Muslims who, after the conquest of certain parts of Europe, specially Spain, established the first universities, scientific observatories, laboratories and libraries on the soul of Europe, and the first Christian scientists who, after centuries of darkness and ignorance, lit the torch of scientific knowledge in England, France, Germany and so on, were pupils of Muslim masters.[1] Christianity, as distinct from the original Message of the Holy Prophet Jesus (Peace be on him!), had been anti-Science and anti-reason from the very start. Indeed, it was Christianity which extinguished whatever light of knowledge was to be found in Greece, Egypt and Syria when it became politically powerful.[2] Besides, as already stated, Science came to the modern West through Muslims whom the Christians regarded as their deadliest enemies. Hence, the Christian Church persecuted the scientists, burnt them at the stake and hanged them on the gallows.[3]

That violent persecution made the Western scientists the enemy not only of the Christian Church but of all Religion, and because religion concerns itself basically with the ultimate problems of human life and demands the loyalty of human beings on that score. the scientists entered the field of ultimate problems and started in the nam of scientific facts to

---

1,2, 3. See at the end of this chapter.

oppose the teachings of Christianity concerning such problems as the origin of man, the origin of the world, the existence of the supernatural world and the existence of God. Thus, for instance, Darwin sought to show that man was not a superior being as taught by religion, that he was not a being created in the 'image' of God, but just an animal among animals—merely a higher variety of apes! Indeed, he tried to trace the origin of human beings to the lowest form of life, namely the amoeba, and said that the species had evolved through the process of transmutation, and that the position of man as the strongest of all animals was just due to chance and not because of any Divine decree. His entire thought was actually anti-religious, and others who came after him added to the list of the mistakes of Christian teaching in the name of scientific facts.

But the question remains: "is Science really capable of answering the ultimate questions on the basis of *sure knowledge*?" The answer to this question lies in the analysis of the Scientific Method.

The scientific method of obtaining knowledge consists in observation and experiment. We shall have to examine the validity of observation in order to find out as to how far it can help us in solving with any certainty the ultimate problems.

Scientifically viewed, every observation is made up of three factors, namely: (1) the Observer; (2) the Object which is observed; (3) Conditions under which the observation is made. Let us examine these factors and find out whether they are variable or stable, in order to understand if we can arise at sure knowledge of ultimate things on the basis of *Observation*.

The first factor is the *observer*. Now, observation is bound to vary from observer to observer, because different human beings do not have similarly sharp and accurate powers of observation either as regards their physical senses of sight, smelling, hearing, taste and touch or as regards the intellect which co-ordinates the reports that the brain gets through the physical senses. For instance, a person may be colour-blind or myopic and as such his observation will always differ from the observation of those who have what is called normal eyesight. Similarly, a person may be hard of hearing, or may have lost the smelling sense or the discrimination of taste or the sense of touch, or he may be an idiot or a lunatic. It is thus a well-established fact that the first factor in every observation is a variable factor, which means that different observations can vary on the basis of this factor.

The second factor is the *object which is observed.* It does not require much deep thought to realise that the more immediate, the more concrete and the more comprehensible an object is, the more is the possibility of the observation being correct; and the more remote, the more subtle and the more ungraspable an object is, the less possibility is there for anything like correct observation—nay, even for observation itself. For instance, if we have to find out the chemical properties of Sodium Chloride or of Calcium Carbonate, it is something easily available in its standard form. Also, it is something which is concrete and it is something which can be examined in a test-tube. But even in immediate objects if we turn to Atomic Physics and try to observe the behaviour of the atom it is bound to be a most difficult task, although the atom concerned may be one of Sodium, or of Calcium; or of Carbon. Going to remote objects and trying to observe them is a different matter altogether. For instance, if we try to observe the interplanetary strata, there are bound to be different opinions, even as they are there already. As a matter of fact, even in the case of an object like the moon which is observed and enjoyed even by the child, scientific observation begs for accuracy. For instance, till sometime back scientists had agreed on a certain calculation of the distance between the earth and the moon. But now they say it was a miscalculation and that the real distance is more than what had been believed in.

Coming now to the third factor, namely, the *conditions under which an observation is made*, we find that it also is a variable factor. For instance, if we take a straight rod and dip a portion of it in water, thereby placing one part of it in the medium of water and keeping the other part in the medium of air, we observe that the straight rod appears tilted at the point where air and water meet, although when we view it only in one medium, which may be air or water, it always appears straight. This normal change in the appearance of the shape of the rod is due only to change of conditions of observation and not due to any change in the structure of the rod. Another common instance is that where the distance of an object varies. For instance, when we view a sandy waste in the sultry heat of the sun from a distance, it appears to us as if it is a huge expanse of water—the common phenomenon in the deserts known as mirage. The false nature of this observation becomes known to us only when we approach that supposed lake of water. This means that if we become contented with the first observation, we would always remain in misunderstanding about the supposed lake of water.

We have seen in the foregoing that all three factors which constitute a scientific observation, are variable. In other words, any and every scientific observation is liable to vary in its accuracy according to any one or two or all of these factors. The margin of this possibility of error in scientific observation becomes wider and wider as the objects observed become more subtle and more distant. This means that physical science can be a good guide and source of knowledge only in our immediate, and mostly physical, problems—although even there it is not immune from error. Indeed, it has been making lot of mistakes, as is well known to every student of the history of science. As regards the ultimate problems, which comprehend within themselves the entire universe and all aspects of existence, it should be very plain, even to a person of ordinary intelligence, that it would be extremely unscientific and even foolish to expect their sure and accurate solutions from *physical science.*

We have said in the foregoing that physical science cannot give us sure knowledge in *all cases* even as regards the immediate physical objects. We might illustrate this fact by instances. The human body is the most immediate physical object of observation for a scientific observer. But, in spite of the fact that physical science is carrying man to the moon, it has not succeeded so far even in mastering thoroughly the mysteries of the human body. For instance, the Allopathic system of Medicine and the Homoeopathic system of Medicine are both virtually equally successful in treating human diseases. But the conceptions of human nature on which they are respectively founded are diametrically opposed. This clearly means that neither of them has yet succeeded in grasping the mysteries of human nature (even in its physical aspect) truly and comprehensively. Also, we must bear in mind that if Medical Science, which is a part of Physical Science, had genuinely succeeded in knowing with certainty, accuracy and thoroughness the physical aspect of human nature and the medicines needed for the cure of the different human diseases, the margin of failure in the cure of diseases would have become zero,—which is not the case at present. As regards the details of the human body, here again the same lack of accuracy and finality exists. For instance, there was a time when the scientists of the Allopathic school of medicine were of the opinion that the appendix and the tonsils were useless things and that they could be cast out of the body even as a precautionary measures. The scientific belief about the appendix was so vehemently stated that it gave rise even to an English proverb, namely: "as useless as an appendix". But medical thought is now directed more and more to keeping these organs intact.

We may also give an instance concerning the ever-changing character of scientific conclusions as regards the ultimate problems. We might leave out here the pre-Newtonian scientific thought, in order to be more charitable, and consider only the era starting with Newtonian Physics, which is considered to be the era of the maturity of Science. But what situation do we find here too? Sir Isaac Newton affirmed and proclaimed to the world that the universe was three-dimensional and that Space and Time were two different and independent entities. The entire scientific progress after him proceeded on this assumption. It was held by scientists to be an infallible truth, which they defended and by which they swore day in and day out. But then came Einstein who proved, again *scientifically*, that Newtonian physics was all wrong in its foundations, that the universe was not three-dimensional but four-dimensional, that Time was the fourth dimension of Space and not an independent entity, that instead of *immutability* (on which Materialism had thrived) there was *indeterminacy* in the universe (which renders the scientific affirmation of the existence of God possible),—and Science has proceeded since then to show that Matter itself is unreal. Who knows that tomorrow another great scientist may come and explode the Physics of Einstein also?

II. Philosophy

All Philosophy may be broadly classified into *four schools*, namely: (1) Formal Rationalism; (2) Empiricism; (3) Criticism; (4) Empirical Rationalism. Of these four, nos. (2) and (3) do not deserve consideration in the background of our present problem and that for very definite reasons. No. (2), namely, Empiricism, holds that the only source of obtaining knowledge is sense-experience. It means that the empirical philosopher cannot even aim at trying to understand the whole of Reality, because in their very nature the human senses are very limited in their scope and also liable to error, as we have already seen in the section on Science. Indeed, the only natural and logical consequence of Empiricism is Scepticism, namely, that we *cannot know* Reality. In other words, the philosophy of the Empiricist school itself asserts the incompetence and the failure of philosophical endeavour to answer the ultimate questions. As regards no. (3), namely Criticism, it says that both Reason and Senses are sources of knowledge but that both are *very limited* sources. Hence, the knowledge of the world which we can get through them can only be very limited in its scope as well as character. In other words, according to this school of Philosophy, philosophical effort can succeed only in knowing a part of Reality. This, in its turn, means that comprehensive and sure knowledge, which is the necessary condition for solving the ultimate questions successfully, cannot be obtained from Philosophy. Thus there remain only two schools of Philosophy, namely, *Formal Rationalism* and *Empirical Rationalism* where the belief is found that Philosophy can discover the Ultimate Truth and which alone, therefore, deserve our consideration in connection with the present discussion. Let us examine the validity of their claim.

Formal Rationalism holds that human Reason, unaided by anything else, in capable of knowing the ultimate facts of life and the world.

Empirical Rationalism holds that Reason and Sense-Experience should combine to enable human beings to find out the Ultimate Truth and that, through this combination of the sources of knowledge, Philosophy *can* solve the ultimate problems and guide humanity in that behalf.

Formal Rationalism depends wholly on Logic. Its method is to choose a hypothesis as the starting point of its investigation and on that hypothesis to build up a whole world of philosophical thought by using the instrument of Logic.

Empirical Rationalism may be better named as "Philosophy of Science". Its method is to collect and arrange the facts discovered by Science and to endeavour, by using the instrument of Reason, to form an integrated picture of the world as a whole and thereby to answer the ultimate questions.

If we evaluate Formal Rationalism, we find that, on the face of it, it is incapable of giving us any sure and accurate knowledge of the ultimate problems. This is so, because its starting point is always a hypothesis, which is nothing more than a supposed idea or at best an observation based on common sense, and it has always been chosen by every philosopher arbitrarily. Now, every hypothesis, especially in the realm of abstract thought, is, in the very nature of the case, unverifiable. In other words, it is uncertain. And if it is uncertain, the thought-structure built upon it and the conclusions arrived at must also be uncertain. That is, the knowledge of ultimate problems given by Formal Rationalism cannot be sure and accurate.

As regards Empirical Rationalism, its starting point consists in the scientific facts, namely, sensorial observation, and its method is to reason out the ultimate problems on their basis. But, as we have already seen in the discussion of the Scientific Method, scientific facts are at best workable hypotheses or working material on the scale of observation or the system of reference with which they are connected. Hence, for ultimate problems, they have neither finality, nor perfect accuracy, nor absolute certainty. This means that if the starting point and the working material of Empirical Rationalism lack accuracy, certainty and finality, the conclusions arrived at will also suffer from the same shortcomings. In other words, a solution of the ultimate problems on the basis of sure knowledge is impossible even for the Empirical Rationalist school of Philosophy.

An eminent scientific thinker of modern times admits this truth in the following words: "Many people wrongly think that logical mechanisms are 'standard' and that logical reasoning, and all the more so mathematical reasoning, are inevitably 'true'. This is not always the case. We must beware of the process of human thought because, in the first place, the starting point is often a sensorial observation (therefore of doubtful value) or an observation based on common sense. Now common sense cannot be trusted. It is common sense that leads us to think that the earth is flat; that two plumb lines are parallel (they are both directed toward the centre of the earth and consequently form an angle); that motion in a straight line exists, which is absolutely false as we have to take into consideration not only the motion of the earth around its axis and around the sun, and that of the entire orbit of the earth, but also the motion of the whole solar system toward the constellation Hercules, etc. As a result, a bullet or an aeroplane, which seems to move in a straight line with respect to the earth, for a certain length of time, in reality follows a trajectory more closely resembling a kind of corkscrew with respect to a vaster system of reference, the nearest stars for instance. Common sense tells us that the edge of a razor blade is a continuous straight line, but if we examine it under a microscope it resembles a wavy line drawn by a child. Common sense tells us that a piece of steel is solid; X-rays show us that it is porous and the modern theories of matter teach us that it is in reality made up of trillions of animated, miniature universes having extraordinarily rapid movements and no contact with each other.

"*If, therefore, the starting point, the premises, of a reasoning is false, the conclusion will necessarily, logically, be false.*

"As we have no other means of knowing and describing nature but those given us by our senses and our reasoning faculties—i.e., by our brain cells—we must be extremely cautious and never forget the *reality* of the picture which we construct—a relativity with respect to the recording instrument, man." (Lecomte du Nouy: *Human Destiny*, pp. 5,6).

The competence of Science and Philosophy in unravelling the mysteries of the ultimate problems can be examined through another argument also. As stated in the foregoing, the ultimate problems refer to three main heads, namely: Man, Universe and God. Let us take here the case of Man himself. Can Science or Philosophy, or both combined, provide us true and accurate knowledge of the ultimate problems which refer to Man? If we consider this question cool-mindedly and dispassionately, we find that neither the origin nor the constitution nor the functioning of man can be reasonably conceived to exist in a vacuum. The individual human being is a part of the human race. The human race, in its turn, is part of a larger whole, namely, the animal world. The animal world, in its turn, is part of a larger whole, namely, the organic world (which includes plant life). The organic world, in its turn, is part cf a larger whole, namely, the Earth, (which includes the organic world and the inorganic world both). The Earth, in its turn, is part of a larger whole, namely, our solar system. Our solar system, in its turn, is *immediately* part of a galaxy of *unknown* number of solar systems and *ultimately* a part of the entire Universe which is *unknown to us as a whole thing* and which, according to Modern Science, should be termed as virtually infinite both in Space and Time, and is, therefore, incapable of being grasped in knowledge by our finite powers of perception and reasoning, both logical and mathematical. Thus, the human individual is ultimately part and parcel of a universe which, in its origin, constitution and purpose, is *unknowable as a whole thing*.

Now, if we wish to obtain true, accurate and comprehensive knowledge of the *fundamental laws* which govern the existence of the human individual, we find that just as the human individual does not exist in a vacuum the laws also which govern his existence do not exist in a vacuum. For, the system of laws which governs the existence of the human individual is part of a larger and higher whole, namely, the system of laws which governs humanity as an entity. This larger and higher system of laws is, in its turn, part of another system which is higher and larger than it; and this series goes on—the levels of laws rise higher and higher, tier after tier, until we reach the level where we are confronted with the laws which govern the entire universe *as an entity and fundamentally*.

We are now heading towards the conclusion. To know the nature and destiny of the part we must know the nature and destiny of the whole. Hence, to know the nature and destiny of the human individual we must know the nature and destiny of the whole of which it is a part. As we have already seen, *immediately*, it is part of the human race. But the human race itself is not the *final whole*. Rather, it is a part of a larger whole, and that larger whole is part of a still larger whole, until, if we were to stop even at physical concepts only, we reach the final *whole* which is known as the Physical Universe. This means that unless we know the nature and destiny of the universe, we cannot know the nature and destiny of anything which forms part of it, including the human individual.

All the above discussions lead us positively to the conclusion that neither Science nor Philosophy can ever be capable of giving accurate answers to our ultimate questions on the basis of sure knowledge. And those answers which they have been giving, or might give in future, have been, and shall always be, at best approximations in the nature of partial truths and, in most instances, what the following verse of the Holy Qur'ãn calls "conjectures".

"But they have no *knowledge* thereof. They follow nothing but *conjecture*; and conjecture avails nothing against Truth." (LIII:28).

The question now is: If Science and Philosophy fail in guiding us on ultimate problems, is that the end of the road, or is there a way out? The answer is: Yes, there is a way—the way of Religion.

III. Divine Revelation

The plausibility of the claim of Religion to answer our ultimate questions consists in the *source* of knowledge. Among the various religions of the world, Islam agrees with us that the human faculties of sense and reasoning are, in their very nature, incapable of arriving at accurate and sure knowledge of the ultimate facts both through logical reasoning and mathematical reasoning. But side by side with that it gives us a message of hope and imparts to us a very plain and convincing guidance in that behalf. That guidance may be stated as follows:

There are two factors in every act of knowledge namely, the Subject and the Object. As regards the *process of knowledge*, it is possible in two ways, namely: (1) the subject may *embrace* the object with the instruments of knowledge which, in the case of man, are senses and reason: (2) the object may *reveal* itself to the subject.

The usual path of knowledge is the first one, and it is this which Science and Philosophy employ. And because the finite cannot embrace the infinite, the attempts of Science and Philosophy at solving the ultimate problems end in failure.

The second path of knowledge is the path of *Revealed Religion.* That this path is a matter of experience in the scientific field also is known to all scientists. For instance, there are planets which are far away from the farthest horizon that the most advanced instruments of astronomy have been able to penetrate. Those planets enter that horizon only for a while after very long periods of time. Thus, instead of the powers of the astronomical instruments going out, so to say, to embrace them, they themselves *reveal* their existence by moving for a while into their embrace from a position where their existence cannot be known and after the *revelation* they again disappear into the Unknown. Those whose gaze is fixed and whose instruments of observation are focussed on that horizon see them and *know* them, while others affirm their existence afterwards only *on the basis of authority,* because verification throught observation does not remain possible after the disappearance of those planets.

This much about the physical world—the world of sense-experience—the world which in quality as well as quantity is only a *part* of the Unknown and Infinite Universe. But it brings home to us an important fact. The farther removed a thing is qualitatively (i.e., as regard its difference from us in its nature and constitution and function) or quantitatively (i.e., in Space or Time), the greater becomes the necessity for the first path of knowledge to give place to the second path, i.e., Revelation.

Islam emphasises this all-important fact of Revelation. It affirms the existence of God and says that He is the Creator and Cherisher of the Universe. Also, that He is All-Powerful, All-Knowing and Omnipresent. He possesses perfect knowledge of the origin, the constitution and the function of everything, and His knowledge comprehends the past, the present and the future. And He not only possesses that knowledge but has also revealed to humanity the correct guidance on the ultimate and intricate problems which defy correct and sure solution by means of senses and reason. His Revelations came, much like the distant planets mentioned in the foregoing scientific argument, through the Spiritual Luminaries who appeared on the horizon of humanity from time to time. Those Spiritual Luminaries included men like Adam, Abraham, Moses, Jesus, the last among them being Muhammad (Divine Peace and Blessings be with him and all other Messengers of God); and the last Revealed Book is the Holy Qur'ãn.

Footnotes 1,2,3, (ref: p.35)

The facts referred to are known to all the scholars of history and have been stated by the most eminent authorities of the West and the East. For instance, the renowned British Orientalist, Marmaduke Pickthall, says:

"The Qur'ãn undoubtedly gave a great impetus to learning, especially in the field of natural science: and, if, as some modern writers have declared, the inductive method, to which all the practical modern discoveries are chiefly owing, can be traced to it, then it may be called the cause of modern scientific and material progress.

"The Muslims set out on their search for learning in the name of God at a time when Christians were destroying all the learning of the ancients in the name of Christ. They had destroyed the Library at Alexandria, they had murdered many philosophers, including the beautiful Hypatia. Learning was for them a devils' snare beloved of the pagans. They had no injunction to 'seek knowledge even though it were in China'. The manuscripts of Greek and Roman learning were publicly burnt by the priests.

"....the revolving terrestrial globe happened to be part of the educational equipment of the Spanish Muslim universities at the time when the learned Bruno was burnt at a slow fire by the Inquisition for upholding the Copernican theory of the Earth, and before the even greater Galileo was forced by persecution to recant and sign a solemn declaration that the Earth was fixed immovably, as the Bible said it was. He is said to have murmured under his breath, as he put his name to the lie: *E pur se Muov* ("And yet it moves"). It was from the teaching of the Spanish Muslim universities that Columbus got his notion that the world was round, though he too was forced by persecution to recent it afterwards. When we remember that the Spanish Muslim universities in the time of the Khalifa Abdur Rahman III and the Eastern Muslim universities in the time of Al Ma'mun—I mention these two monarchs because it is specially recorded of their times—welcomed Christian and Jewish students on equality with Muslims; not only that, but entertained them at the Government expense: and that hundreds of Christian students from the South of Europe and the countries of the East took advantage of the chance to escape from ecclesiastical leading strings; we can easily perceive what debt of gratitude modern European progress owes to Islam, while it owes nothing whatsoever to the Christian Church, which persecuted, tortured, even burnt the learned." (*Islamic Culture*, pp. 64, 67, 68).

The learned author of *Islam in the World* says (pp. 142-149):

"The influence of the powerful movement of Islamic culture in Spain rapidly made itself felt throughout Europe. Petrus Alfonsi (b. 1602) who studied at the Arabian medical schools, came to England from Spain as Physician to King Henri I and, in 1120, collaborated with Walcher, Prior of Malvern, in the production of a translation of Alfonsi's astronomical treaties, based upon Arabian sources. In England their united effort represents the first impact of Arabian learning. Its effect was rapid, for immediately afterwards Adelard of Bath earned the distinction of being the first prominent European man of science, outside Spain, to come to Toledo and make a special study of Arabian learning. The cultural links thus formed between England and Muslim Spain were destined to produce important results. They stimulated in England the desire for the new philosophical and scientific learning and led to the achievements of Michael Scot (c. 1175/1232) and Roger Bacon (1214-1294).

"Scot proceeded to Toledo in order to gain a knowledge of Arabic and of Arabian philosophy. At Oxford, Roger Bacon achieved brilliant success as an exponent of the new Arabian-Aristotelian philosophy. In the library of the Dean and Chapter of Canterbury Cathedral is a late thirteenth century illuminated manuscript, '*Vetus Logica*', the earliest known commentary on Aristotle's Logic produced in England following the Arabian 'renaissance' of Aristotelian philosophy. Amongst those scholars who came to Spain from Britain were Robert of England (flourished 1143), first translator of the Qur'ãn. Dental Morley (flourished 1170), etc. Roger Bacon's work '*Optics*' was based on Alhazen's *Thesaurus Opticae*'. The Alchemical teachings of Jabir ibn Hayyan (Geber) and other Arabian writers, are apparent in the work of Albert Magnus, Vincent of Beauvais, etc.

"In a recent study made by the 'Madrid School of Spanish Arabists', (a school which is concerned with the study of Islamic civilisation in Spain and its influence on Christian civilisation in the Iberian Peninsula as well as in the rest of Europe), Julian Ribera demonstrates that many of the institutions of Christian Spain were nothing but a copy or an imitation of similar institutions of Muslim Spain. He discovered Arabic sources for the doctrines of certain thinkers and certain poetic forms of songs of the Middle Ages, and for the medieval Andalusian music and songs of the troubadours, trouveres and minnesingers. Don Miguel Asin Palacios, in studying the origins of philosophy in Spain, traces the influences of such Arabian thinkers as Avempace, Averroes, Abenarabi, Abenmasarra and others. He also establishes the point that one should seek the key of the Divine Comedy of Dante in the Islamic legends of the nocturnal voyage of Muhammad (S.A.). It is further shown that historiographers, mathematicians and lexicologists, etc., owe much to their Muslim predecessors of Spain.

"Emmanuel Deutsch says: "By the aid of the Qur'ãn the Arabs conquered a world greater than that of Alexander the Great, greater than that of Rome and in as many tens of years as the latter had wanted hundreds to accomplish her conquests; by the aid of which they, alone of all the Semites, came to Europe as kings, whither the Phoenicians had come as tradesmen, and the Jews as fugitives or captives. They came to Europe to hold up the light to Humanity: they alone, while darkness lay around, to raise up wisdom and knowledge of Hellas from the dead, to teach philosophy, medicine, astronomy and the golden art of song to the West as well as to the East, to stand at the cradle of modern science, and to cause us late epigoni for ever to weep over the day when Grenada fell'."

Part III

THE QUR'ÃNIC REVELATION

Chapter I

THE QUR'ÃNIC CLAIM TO BE A REVEALED BOOK

Chapter II

THE PROCESS OF COMPILATION

Chapter III

THE PROCESS OF PRESERVATION AND PROPAGATION

Chapter IV

THE QUR'ÃN AS THE ONLY REVEALED BOOK IN THE WORLD

Chapter V

THE STYLE AND STRUCTURE OF THE QUR'ÃN

Chapter I

THE QUR'ÃN : A REVEALED BOOK

The Claim to Revelation :

The Holy Prophet Muhammad (in whom God's Blessings and Peace abide!) was unlettered not, knowing how to read and write, because he had received no formal education in any degree from anyone. The historical testimony in this respect is complete and thorough, even as the Qur'ãnic Revelation contains the proclamation addressed to him and meant to emphasise to his opponents the Divine source of the profound Wisdom that was flowing from his sacred lips:

"And thou (O Muhammad!) didst not recite any book before this (i.e., knew not how to read), nor wast thou (able) to transcribe one with thy right hand (i.e. knew not the art of writing).Otherwise, indeed, those who talk baseless things (against thine Divine Mission) could have (some excuse for having) doubted (the revealed character of the Qur'ãn)." (XXX:48)

The Holy Prophet's sole teacher was God, and no one else:

"...and Allah has revealed to thee (O Muhammad!) the Book and the Wisdom, and has taught thee what thou knewest not; and Allah's Grace unto thee is immense". (IV:113)

Thus, the Holy Qur'ãn is not the product of the Holy Prophet's speculation and thinking. Rather, every word of that Book is the Word of God which was communicated to him through the process of Revelation:

"(This is) the revelation of the Book (i.e., the Qur'ãn) in which there is no (ground for) doubt,—(a Book) from the Lord of the worlds. Will they say: 'he has forged it"? Nay it is the Truth from thy Lord...." (XXXII : 2-3)

"Blessed is He (i.e., Allah) Who sent down the Criterion (i.e., the Qur'ãn) to His servant (Muhammad), that he may be a Warner to all the creatures." (XXV:1)

"Say (O Muhammad!): The (Qur'ãn) has been sent down by Him Who knows the Mystery (that is) in the heavens and the earth...." (XXV:6)

"But Allah bears witness that what he has revealed to thee (O Muhammad!) He has revealed from His (own) Knowledge; and the angels bear witness (also); but enough is Allah for a witness." (IV:166)[1]

Indeed the Holy Qur'ãn calls itself the "Speech of God" (IX:6) and the "most excellent Discourse" "sent down gradually by Allah" (XXXIX:23), communicated to the Holy Prophet Muhammad (Peace be on him!) not as mere 'inspiration' but as the "Arabic Qur'ãn" (XII:2)—as *Recitation* "in plain Arabic language" (XXVI:195), through the process of Prophetic Revelation (XLII:7; etc.) which was the same as in the case of the previous Divine Messengers from Adam to Jesus (Peace be upon them!) (XLII:3), and which descended upon the "heart" of the Holy Prophet not metaphorically but literally, namely, in the form of language in which it was subsequently transcribed by the Scribes.

Being the revealed Word of God, it imparts knowledge which is immune from all possibilities of doubt (II:2), all types of crookedness (XVIII:1), every form of discrepancy (IV:82), and the faintest taint of evil (XXVI:210). On the positive side, it is the embodiment of Truth and Balanced Thought together with the Balanced Way of Life (XLII:17); it is Blessed (with Holiness) (VI:155); it is the Light that is Manifest (IV:174), whose function is to lead forth humanity from the spiritual and moral darkness into the light of the achievement of human destiny (XIV:1); it is the Healing which cures the very basis of spiritual and moral ailments (X:57); it is Mercy and Glad Tidings to those who follow it faithfully (XVI:89); and it is the Criterion which distinguishes clearly the right from the wrong, the good from the evil, the true from the false (II:185); it is the Guide for all humanity (II:185), which imparts detailed and comprehensive guidance in all matters wherein human reason can possibly fail in any measure and in any manner (VI:114, XVI:89): and, imparting new knowledge as it does (II:151), it emphasises that all unbiased persons dedicated to knowledge are bound to uphold its truth at the time of its revelation (XXXIV:6), and to attest it, in later ages, as the horizons of human knowledge expand further and further. (XLI:53)

---

1 We have quoted here just a few verses off-hand. Actually, the Holy Qur'ãn is replete with statements that proclaim explicitly that it is, in its entirety, the revealed Word of God.

The Phenomenon of Prophetic Revelation:

The Prophetic Revelation has nothing to do with the natural mental processes that relate to the human brain. It does not consist even of intentional flashes like those experienced by certain eminent scientists and thinkers in respect of the discoveries of certain facts of knowledge. It is not just an inspiration of notions and ideas. Namely, it is not merely an 'internal' and subjective fact with no 'external' and objective dimension. Rather, it is a concrete objective phenomenon—though, of course supernatural or metaphysical in character. It is 'God's Speech, communicated at the highest level.

Of course, God's Speech (*kalãm*) is not of the same nature as the human speech. For, God is Transcendent in His Being, and so in the nature of His Attributes (XXX:27). That does not imply, however, the impossibility of communication between Him and His creatures. Rather, to the contrary. Because, it is He Who *alone* is the Fountainhead: not only of *existence* but also of *guidance* for every particle of the cosmos:— as the One Who 'encompasses all things' (XLI:54), and Who is, in the case of Man, 'closer to him than his jugular vein' (L:16).

God's Speech is communicated to different things in Creation in the form suitable to their function, the goal being the guidance of those things (VIII:12; XVI:68; XLI:12; XCIX:5). Human beings, not belonging to the category of the Prophets and Messengers, have also been the beneficiaries of this Divine blessing in the form of a *subjective guidance* in terms of inspiration (V:114; XX:38; XXVIII:7). In their case, however, it was *purely a personal affair.*

It appears as if the higher the calibre and the function of anything in the cosmos, the higher, in the sense of more explicit, is the form of manifestation or expression for God's Speech, and the lower the calibre of anything the less its capability to accommodate that manifestation of the Divine Speech which relates to a higher level. Thus, the Speech of God may express itself to an inorganic object or a plant in the form of 'sensation' appropriate to it, to an animal in the form of inner 'perception', to a human being not falling under the category of a Prophet and a Messenger in the form of 'conception'. But in the case of those human beings who were chosen by God to be His Prophets and Messengers, and whose function consequently was not to obtain stray guidance for themselves, but to be the recipients of a full-fledged philosophy of life and a comprehensive code of practical guidance for establishing the Divine Order in the life of humanity, reason leads us to the truth that the Speech of God should have expressed itself through the highest medium—the medium of language, and not through implicit and vague media of inner 'sensation', 'perception' and 'conception'. Thus, although none of the human languages is the 'language of God', the Speech of God has expressed or manifested itself in all the human languages through the Divinely-inspired Teachers who arose in all the communities of the world, in one era or the other, since the time of the Holy Prophet Adam to the advent of the Holy Prophet Muhammad—who came as the last and the final—(May God's Blessings be on all of them!) (XIV:4). There is nothing, in fact, in literal Revelation to the Divine Messengers that may discount it philosophically or scientifically as impossible or even as improbable, provided we do not reduce that phenomenon to the category of the natural phenomena.

Modes of Communication of God's Speech to human beings:

To understand the implication further of what we have said: The word *wahy* has been employed by the Holy Qur'ãn with reference to inanimate as well as animate objects; and, among animate objects, to animals as well as human beings. Then, among human beings, it has been used for communication with the non-prophets, namely, merely righteous persons, as well as for the Prophets and Messengers of God. And it has also been used in connection with the mutual communication between good as well as evil-minded persons. As such it covers different levels of meaning like: creation of an impression, suggestion of an idea, inspiration, revelation—direct and indirect, expressive of different modes of the basic underlying concept of 'communication'.

However, the concept of 'speech' emerges in the Qur'ãn explicitly in respect of God's communication with the human beings in verse 51 of chapter XLII, which we shall shortly quote.

The same verse also leads us to the meaning of the word *wahy* as direct 'Inspiration' by God. Elsewhere, however, the entire revelation of the Qur'ãn, which took place through the medium of the messenger-angel (XXVI:193; etc.), has been affirmed to have taken place through the process of *wahy* (XII:3; etc.). Then the employment of the word, in XLII:51, in respect of the multi-modal communication of God with the Holy Prophet (Peace be on him!) gives to it a most comprehensive scope of meaning. Hence, as it relates to human beings, God's *wahy* to a merely righteous person—a non-prophet, should be taken to signify 'suggestion or creation of an idea'; while as 'Prophetic Revelation'—which, in its ultimate aim, relates to the guidance of humanity at large in a divinely-initiated struggle—it should be accepted as standing for absolutely clear 'Inspiration' and literal 'Revelation'.

With these preliminary observations, we may turn to the Qur'ãn for the different dynamic modes of Divine communication with the human beings. It says:

"And it is not possible (or, fitting) for a human being (in his earthly constitution) that Allah should speak[2] to him otherwise than by *wahy* (—implying direct communication by Allah, which, in the case of non-prophet righteous person, is in the form of the suggestion or infusion of some idea, and, in the case of a Prophet and a Messenger of Allah, is in terms of absolutely clear Inspiration)[3], or from behind a veil (—implying direct communication by Allah to His Prophet and Messenger, to the exclusion of other categories of human beings: a communication wherein a Voice is heard, as happened in the case of Moses at Sinai), or (that) he sends a messenger (in the person of an angel to act as intermediary and) to reveal by His Command whatsoever He wills. Verily, He is Exalted, Wise". (XLII:51)

Modes of Divine Communication with the Holy Prophet (Peace be on him!)

The above-quoted verse is followed immediately by the following:

"And thus (i.e., in the comprehensive manner covered in the different modes of Divine communication presented in verse 51) have We, by Our Command, sent unto thee (O Muhammad) the Inspiration[4]. Thou knewest not (before the establishment of Divine communication) what the Scripture was, not what the Faith......." (XLII:52)

Accordingly, God's communication with the Holy Prophet (Peace be upon him!) was normally in three ways: (i) direct communication

2 Mark the word "speak"!

3 This implication becomes fully established when we compare the mode of *wahy* mentioned in the verse with the two other modes that follow, and give due weight, without any pre-conceived opinion, to the fact that the forms of communication are three *different* types of processes that exclude one another in respect of their distinct natures.

4 This word should be taken here to cover in its implication all the levels of Divine Revelation.

in the form of what has been termed in verse 51 as *wahy*; (ii) direct communication 'from behind the veil'; (iii) indirect communication through an intermediary messenger-angel.

The third being the sole mode of communication employed in respect of the revelation of the Qur'ãn, as we shall shortly notice, the other two modes must be taken to relate to the domain of general communication. Indeed, the Holy Prophet (Peace be on him!), being firmly and absolutely established as *'abd* in the state of harmony with God (VI:162; etc.) and thus in absolute intimacy with, and under the loving care of, God (LII: 48: etc.), his communication with God and God's communication with him was frequent—the communication from God not confined to the revelation of the Qur'ãn.

The above-mentioned modes of communication relate, however, to the Holy Prophet's life in respect of his earthly constitution, in which he normally stayed except—so far as our knowledge goes—on the occasion of *Me'rãj* (Ascension), which can be understood only in terms of a transcendental transformation of his personality by God. Hence, God's communication with him on that occasion should be classed as belonging to a mode different and distinct from the modes mentioned in XLII:51. The reference in the Holy Qur'ãn stands thus:

"By the Star when it goes down, your Companion (Muhammad) does not err, nor is misled; nor does he speak (aught) of (his own) Desire (or, ratiocination). It is naught but Revelation that is revealed (to him). He has been taught by One Mighty in Power, endued with Wisdom; so he attained completion in knowledge[5], while he was in the highest horizon (during his *Me'rãj* or Ascension). Then he (—existing on that occasion, as deducible, in the transcendental dimension of existence—) approached and came closer to Allah, in the transcendental dimension), and it was a distance (in terms of transcendental dimension) of but two bow-lengths or nearer (—implying idiomatically extreme nearness—). Thus He (i.e., Allah) revealed to His Devotee (Muhammad) what He revealed. The (Prophet's) heart lied not in what he saw (it being the direct Vision of, and communication from, Allah)". (LIII:1-11)[6]

5 *Istawã al rajul* means 'he became full grown and mature in body and intellect, or he attained the completion of his make and intellect'. (Lane's *Lexicon*).

6 The translation of these verses and the explanatory remarks inserted within brackets are based on a critical assessment of *Hadith* literature and of the Qur'ãnic philosophy of Religion as upheld by a vast majority of Islamic scholars in history.

[*Note*:- Some scholars who subscribe to no adequate notion either of the nature of human personality or of the dimension of the personality of a Messenger of God—whose view of religious verities is, for all practical purposes, either 'formalistic' or 'naturalistic'—consider it necessary to explain away or minimise every supernatural, or metaphysical, element in the Holy Prophet's personality. As such, they deny that the Holy Prophet (Peace be on him!) was blessed with the vision of God in his *Me'rãj*, saying that the person whom he saw was the angel Jibreel (Gabriel). As for the Hadîth literature, both the views—viz., 'vision of God' and 'vision of Jibreel'—are deducible. But, as regards the Qur'ãn, it affirms the 'vision of God' in the transcendental dimension of existence, i.e., life in Heaven, even for the true followers of the Messengers of God—not to speak of the Messengers of God themselves. The view reported to have been put forward by Lady Ayesha should be taken to relate basically to the impossibility of seeing God with the physical vision; and, as such, it is an absolutely correct view. The Holy Prophet's *Me'rãj* was, however, an event of unique nature in which it should be accepted that his sacred personality had been transformed by God from the physical to the transcendental dimension of existence[7]—the same dimension in which his true followers who, in their status, are simply non-entities as compared with his status as God's greatest Messenger, will exist in Heaven, and will, therefore, become capable of being blessed with the vision of God (LXXV:22,23)]

Reverting to XLII:52, it was not at all necessary for the Holy Qur'ãn, after explicitly affirming all the three modes of Divine communication mentioned in XLII:51, to pin-point each occasion and each guidance as it came to the Holy Prophet (Peace be on him!) from God through the respective modes. Such information can be relevantly sought in the *Hadîth* literature, although even there we cannot expect absolute accuracy in respect of reporting, nor a detailed specification of occasions and modes, basically because of the personal and secret nature of Divine communication. However, that being the only way

---

7 Qualitative transformations are all the time taking place in Nature. Thus, the view presented here is in accordance with the Natural Law. Also: this view synthesises the partial views in which one school of thought—the minority school—emphasises that *Me'rãj* was just a 'spiritual' experience like other spiritual experiences, in which the Holy Prophet's soul *alone* was the subject of experience, while the other school—representing an overwhelming majority of Muslims in history—gives prominence to the participation of the Holy Prophet's body in that entire event.

open to us, we may obtain from there whatever information is in conformity with the Qur'ãn.

There is a consensus of historical reports that the Holy Prophet Muhammad (Peace be on him!) grew up as superbly-normal in mental, physical and moral health and beauty, but abnormally devoted to truthfulness, thoughtfulness, and sympathy for and service to fellow-beings. He passed the greater part of his youth, right from infancy, in the 'lap of Nature', away from the city-life of Makkah, where he was born. As a grown-up young man, he had the occasion to undertake long journeys in the 'environment of Nature' when he crossed time and again, in connection with commerce, the desolate desert vastnesses of Arabia. He was born in a community of idol-worshippers; but he never had anything to do with any idol even unconsciously. He had the mental grace and the personal beauty of the Holy Prophet Abraham (Peace be on him!), from whom he had descended through the Holy Prophet Ishmael (Peace be on him!). But his family had lost the teaching of Abraham and Ishmael, and had preserved only its history.

His contact with the transcendental Reality started crystallising when he began to see true dreams[8]—dreams in which he appears to have seen future events, which happened as he had seen them, or hidden things of this world, which were exactly what he had seen during his sleep, or hidden realities of the transcendental worlds. As this spiritual state continued, his love for solitude increased until, in the very prime of his youth, in spite of his marriage with his beloved wife Khadija (which took place at the age of twenty-five), he began retiring to the wilderness, where, totally cut off from human, animal and even plant life, he would stay engaged in meditation, in the Cave of Hira, which, even to this day, possesses the majesty of the 'Void'. This retreat to the Cave of Hira continued to repeat itself until, at the age of forty[9], on the 12th of Rabi' al-Awwal[10], the pitch darkness of the night inside the Cave and the death-like stillness of the surrounding wilderness were shattered when the Light from God descended (IV:174) and the arch-angel Jibreel,

8 The phenomenon of 'true dreams' continued all though the Holy Prophet's life. The term used by Lady Ayesha is *Ru'yã Sãliha* which means righteous, sound and healthy dreams The statement which follows to the end of the paragraph is based originally on Bukhari's *Sahih; Bãb: Kaifa kãna bada' al-Wayh*—reported by Lady Ayesha, wife of the Holy Prophet.

9 Bukhari: *Sahîh; Bãb: Sifat al-Nabi.*

10 Ibn Kathir: *Al-Bidãyah wa al-Nihãyah*, Vol. II, p. 260—on the authority of Ibn Abbas.

the holy and trustworthy spirit from God, appeared before him and asked him to read, which request was made thrice, each time the angel pressing him in his embrace to activise more and more the transcendental dimension of his personality, to which each time the same reply came, i.e., "I do not know how to read". Then the angel recited to him the first revelation of the Qur'ãn which reads: "Read! (or recite, or proclaim) in the Name of thy Lord and Cherisher Who created (everyone in the universe)—created man out of a (mere) clot of congealed blood: Read! And thy Lord is Most Bountiful,—He Who taught (the preservation, cultivation and promotion of knowledge) through the Pen,—taught man that which he knew not". (XCVI: 1-5). Thereby the Holy Prophet acquired those verses in his memory and returned home highly excited by that most abnormal experience.

Thus came the first revelation of the Qur'ãn, which was the forerunner for all those others that came down over a period of twenty-three years—the actual period of the Holy Prophet's ministry–and constitute, together with that first one, the Qur'ãn as it was completed and as we have it today.

Thus also commenced the period of the Holy Prophet's life in which not only the communication through the messenger-angel but also other modes of Divine communication blessed him very frequently.

The classical Islamic scholars have listed certain modes of Revelation on the basis of *Hadith* literature, with slight differences among themselves. Thus, Suyuti has mentioned five (*Al-Itqãn*, Vol. I, p. 44,), and Ibn Qayyim has listed seven (*Zãd al-Ma'ãd*, Vol. I, pp. 24,25). However, keeping strictly within the bounds prescribed by the Qur'ãnic testimony, as demanded by the nature of the present book, we will not go beyond the basic implications of the three modes mentioned in the holy book—which actually reduce themselves to two, viz., 'direct communication by God' and 'communication by God through the messenger-angle'.

We need not bring testimony from the *Hadith* literature in respect of the revelations that constitute the Qur'ãn, because the holy book itself has explicitly stated the mode of its revelation as consisting in Divine communication through the messenger-angel, Jibreel:

"Verily this is a Revelation from the Lord of the Worlds: The Trusted Spirit (i.e., Jibreel) has brought it down upon thy heart (O

Muhammad!) that thou mayest be of the warners, in plain Arabic language." (XXVI:192-195)

"So verily I call to witness the Planets that recede, moving swiftly (and) hiding themselves; and the Night as it dissipates (gradually melting away in the Day); and the Dawn as it breathes away the darkness;—verily it is a Word (brought) by a messenger honoured (i.e., Jibreel), endued with Power (so that no devilish force can obstruct the path of this powerful messenger), with rank before the Lord of the Throne (i.e., Allah), with authority there (i.e., in the heavens), faithful to his trust. And (O people!) your Companion (Muhammad) is not one possessed (as the calumniators say). Without doubt he beheld him (i.e., Jibreel) at the Clear Horizon[11]. And he (i.e., Muhammad) is not a with-holder of (the knowledge of) the Unseen (which has been bestowed on him by Allah)." (LXXXI:15-24)

"Say (O Muhammad!): the Holy Spirit[12] (i.e., angel Jibreel) has brought down the revelation (of the Qur'ãn) from thy Lord in Truth…." (XVI:102)

Here two importance facts may be noted: (i) although even the dreams of a Prophet are fully meaningful and explicit and are grounded in absolute truth, all the Qur'ãnic revelation came to the Holy Prophet in the state of waking,—on which fact the authorities are unanimous, according to *Kitãb al-Tibyãn* (p. 21); (ii) the messenger-angel seems to have been employed by God for the Qur'ãnic revelations for ensuring

11 *Cf.* The *hadîth* reported and accepted by Bukhari: "Jabir reported that he heard God's Messenger telling about the cessation of Revelation (for a short period after the first one) as follows: '(Once) while I was walking I heard a voice coming from above, and raising my eyes I beheld angel who had come to me at Hira seated on a throne between heaven and earth. I felt over-awed (by the supernatural majesty of the experience,—it being the early stage of the experience of that type. Then I returned to my family and said: Wrap me up, wrap me up! So they wrapped me up. Then Allah Most High sent down the revelation: 'O thou wrapped up (in a mantle)! Arise and deliver thy warning! And preach thou the greatness of thy Lord (*lit.*, thy Lord do thou magnify)! And thy garments keep free from stain! and all pollution shun!' Thereafter the process of Revelation became intensified and continuous'." (Bukhari: *Sahih, Kitãb al-Tafsri*. Cf. Muslim: *Sahih*).

12 Or, the Holy Ghost, who rendered the same service to other Divine Messengers, including Jesus (God bless him!) He is an angel, created by God, and not the third member of Godhead, as erroneously and blasphemously conceived by Pauline Christianity.

their reception by the Holy Prophet (Peace be on him!) in absolute exactitude of *language*, the Qur'ãn being meant to be a book of guidance for humanity for all time.

In respect of Divine communication through the messenger-angel, however, occasions besides those relating to the revelation of the Messages that constitute the Qur'ãn have also been reported in the *Hadîth* literature, wherein the angel's role emerges as very important. For instance, we know that Jibreel was commissioned by God to rehearse the Holy Qur'ãn with the Holy Prophet every year during the nights of the month of Ramadan (Bukhari: *Sahîh; Bãbs: Kaifa Kãna bada' al Wahy* and *Zikr al-Malã'ikah*), and to communicate to him the method of the five daily obligatory Prayers (Bukhari: *Sahîh; Bãb: Zikr al-Malã'ikah).*

In connection with angel Jibreel, we also come across a *hadîth* which is to the effect that, in answer to an enquiry, the Holy Prophet (Peace be on him!) said.

"At times the angel (Jibreel) assumes the human form for me and speaks to me, and I retain (in my memory) what he says."[13]

What was the exact nature of the appearance of the angel in human form, referred to here, cannot be known to us. However, we find it in the *Hadîth* literature to have occurred on a good number of occasions, and, among them, it also happened a number of times that even the Holy Prophet's Companions saw that angel[14].

Coming to the mode of Divine communication 'from behind a veil': Such a phenomenon has been reported in the following *Hadith*[15]:

"(Lady) Ayesha (wife of the Holy Prophet) reported that Harith ibn Hisham enquired from Allah's Messenger: 'How does the Revelation come to you, O Allah's Messenger?' To that he replied: 'It comes to me at times in the likeness of an echoing sound of a bell[16], and that is (the

13 Imam Malik : *Mu'attã; Bãb: Mã jã'a fi al-Qur'ãn.* Cf. Bukhari and Muslim.

14 In this connection, very definite events, stated in very explicit form, have been reported, among others, by Imam Bukhari (*Sahih: Bãbs : Suwãlu Jibreel, Kalifa nazala al-Wahy, Marja' al-Nabî min al-Ahzãb wa Makhrajahu ilã Bani Quraizah, Zikr al-Malã'ikah, Shuhûd al-Malã'ikah Badran*).

15 Imam Malik : *op.cit.*,

16 It was in fact a sound very different from physical sounds,—a sound which is inexplicable in terms of human language (*Al-Itqan*. Vol. I, p. 44). Hence the description should not be understood in the literal sense.

mode) most severe on me; then it is cut off from me, and I definitely remember thereafter what the (Communicator from behind the 'veil') has spoken[17]."

For a clear understanding of the implication of the above *hadîth*, we have to go to the Qur'ãnic testimony which relates to the affirmation of Divine communication 'from behind a veil' with the Holy Prophet (Peace be on him!) (XLII:51, 52), on the one hand, and which states that phenomenon in actual terms in respect of certain other Divine Messengers, on the other. For instance, in the case of the Holy Prophet Abraham (Peace be on him!): "We called unto him: O Abraham! Thou hast already fulfilled the vision...." (XXXVII:104, 105). Again, in the case of the Holy Prophet Moses (Peace be on him!): "And when Moses came to Our appointed tryst and his Lord had spoken to him, he said: My Lord! Show me (Thyself), that I may gaze upon Thee..." (VII:143)

Besides the modes, we come across another aspect of Divine communication also in the *Hadîth* literature, namely, the external ultra-natural symptoms noticed by the Holy Prophet's Companions and reported by them. In that connection, we may first state what Lady Ayesha (Allah be pleased with her!) is said to have reported:

Further: Suyuti, the author of *Al-Itqan*, puts forward the view that this sound preceded the communication of Revelation for the sake of withdrawing the attention of the Holy Prophet from everything else and concentrating it on the Revelation which was to follow (Vol. I, p.44). Imam Ahmad's *Musnad* corroborates this view.

17 As to the communicator of Revelation referred to here, Imam Ahmad and Imam Muslim have narrated Traditions that imply that it was God Himself speaking from behind the 'veil'. Al-Bazzar's *Musnad* brings forth similar evidence. Imam Bukhari devotes to this fact a separate section entitled *Zikr al-Nabî wa riwãyatihi 'an Rabbihî*, where the narrators are personalities of the calibre of Anas ibn Malik, Abu Hurairah and Abdullah Ibn Abbas. The view that the communicator in question was the angel Jibreel also emerges however.

Looking at the problem rationally; the phenomenon of 'the Bell and the Message' appears to bear similarity in form to the present-day communication through the telephone, wherein a bell rings as a prelude to the communication of some message. But, in the case of Jibreel, we learn from the Qur'ãn that he was *sent in person* by God—e.g., the relevant verses quoted in this chapter. Hence, to say, as some have held, that the communicator was Jibreel, is evidently unreasonable. Moreover, the Qur'ãnic testimony in this respect (XLII:51, 52) is final and decisive. As such, we are compelled to hold to the view that the communicator in the case under reference was God Himself.

"Indeed, I saw him while the Revelation came down on him on a very cold day; then, at the expiry of it (i.e., the state of the communication of Revelation), sweat poured forth from his forehead."[18]

Going to other reports, we find that the Holy Prophet (Peace be on him!) attained such a profound state of submergence of his consciousness in the Divine Revelation that those who saw him in that state felt as if his soul had departed from this world (*Kanz al-'Ummãl*, Vol. IV, p. 30), and Imam Bukhari reports in his *Sahih* that the rosy-white colour of his face would change into intense red and his breathing would become louder (*Bãbs: Ghusl al-Khulûq* and *Nazala al-Qur'ãn bi Lisãn-i-Quraish*). Al-Hakim narrates the report from Abu Hurairah that at the time when the Holy Prophet received the Revelation, it was impossible for anyone to fix his gaze at his holy face (*Al-Mustadrak*, Vol. II, p. 222). This report implies the establishment of a halo of undescribable majesty and supernatural character around his face—in fact, around his entire personality. Imam Ahmad relates in his *Musnad* on the authority of Abdullah ibn 'Amru that : *"Sura al-Mã'idah* was revealed to Allah's Messenger while he was riding on a she-camel, which showed expressly her inability to bear (the weight she experienced in physical terms to an extent that) he had to alight (from its back)." (Vol. II, p. 176). This fact is corroborated in several other reports also. Zaid ibn Thabit relates that: ".....then Allah, the Possessor of Blessedness and the Most High, sent down on His Messenger (Muhammad) a Revelation. At that time (I was sitting so close to him by his side that) his folded leg covered my folded leg, whereby I experienced such a heavy load (as to give me the feeling) that my folded leg would be crushed to pieces". (Bukhari: *Sahîh, Kitãb al-Tafsir*).

As to the manifestation of physical effects on the Holy Prophet's personality, Ibn Khaldun, the founder of Sociology and of Philosophy of History, observes in his world-renowned *Muqaddimah*, in connection with his scholarly philosophical discourse on the nature of Prophetic Revelation, that a transformation of the Holy Prophet's personality from the human plane to the angelic plane took place on all such occasions (pp. 98, 99).

However, the phenomenon of 'severity' become toned down to lighter and lighter as time passed; as we find, for instance, in Imam Ahmad's *Musnad* in connection with the revelation of *sura Al-Kauthar* (Vol. III, p. 102).

---

18 Imam Malik : *op.cit.*,

That the Holy Qur'ãn is based on literal Inspiration in the form of Prophetic Revelation and is not the result of the Holy Prophet's own intellectual or spiritual awakening as a seer is borne out also by the mode of the projection of its teachings, wherein clearly it is God Who addresses humankind, including the Holy Prophet, and not the Holy Prophet himself.

Again, anyone who undertakes a comparative study of the language of the Holy Qur'ãn and the language of the *Hadīth* literature, which consists of the utterances of the Holy Prophet on his own behalf, can easily notice the clear difference in the style of expression in both.

Still again, the challenges, thrown by the Holy Qur'ãn to the disbelievers in its divine status, as in X:38, XI:13, XVII:88 and LII:34, bear out that the holy book emphatically affirms about itself that it is the Word of God and not a product of the Holy Prophet's mental effort.

Going into external factors further: Arabic is probably the richest language in respect of its vocabulary, which means for our present purposes that if the very words of the Holy Qur'ãn had not been regarded as revealed with immutable divine sanction behind them, the verses, as they were revealed from time to time during a long period, would have easily and naturally undergone changes at least through the interplay of synonyms;—while it is a well-attested fact that the addition or elimination of such an unimportant word as 'and', for which there is in Arabic only a single letter, was not permitted and could not take place.

Then, entering into internal evidence again: The Holy Prophet's entire attitude towards the revelations that he received belies any assumption as to those revelations being mere 'inspirations' that were projected by him in his own words. For instance, let us consider the verses wherein he has been commanded by God thus: "Move not thy tongue concerning the (Qur'ãn) to make haste therewith (in fear of not remembering exactly the text that was revealed). Verily upon Us is the collecting thereof (in thy mind) and the reciting thereof (exactly as it is revealed to thee). Wherefore when We recite it follow thou the recital thereof. And thereafter verily upon Us (i.e., under Our guidance) is the expounding thereof." (LXXV: 16-19). Movement of the tongue relates to the anxiety of remembering the *words* that he had *heard* and not *thoughts* that could have been *infused* in his mind through inspiration.

Before closing this discussion, it is very necessary to emphasise most vehemently that the nature of Revelation—in fact, of entire prophetic experience, is such that it is incommunicable to and incomprehensible for a non-prophet. Hence, it would be the greatest mistake to view it in terms of the natural laws that relate to the general or basic human level.

Chapter II

THE PROCESS OF COMPILATION

I. Internal Evidence

Although the Qur'ãn was revealed piece-meal, the fact that its Message was meant to be presented to humanity in the form of a book—that it was to be *al-Kitãb*, or, *the* Book—projected itself in the very first revelation wherein God mentioned explicitly the role of the Pen in human history. Indeed, we find the Qur'ãn characterising itself as a book even in the Makkan period of its revelation. Thus, we come across the verses: "Praise be to Allah, Who has sent down unto His Servant (Muhammad) the Book...." (XVIII:1). (This is) a revelation from (Allah) the Compassionate, the Merciful—a Book whereof the verses are detailed..." (XLI:2, 3). "By (this) luminous Book! verily We have made it an Arabic Qur'ãn that haply ye may reflect." (XLIII:2, 3). "A Messenger (Muhammad) from Allah rehearsing (unto them) Writs (*suhuf*) kept pure (from every type of corruption and falsehood) and holy, wherein are discourses (*kutub*) eternal." (XCVIII : 2, 3).

Then, in the portion revealed at Madinah the emphasis on the Qur'ãn as to its being a Book comes before us again. For instance: "This is the Book wherein there is no (ground for) doubt." (II:2). "....(the Prophet) teaches them the Book and the Wisdom...." (LXII:2). Moreover, we come across the following objection raised by the opponents: "They say: (These are) tales of the ancients which he (i.e., Muhammad) has caused to be written..." (XXV:5). This objection too affirms explicitly that whatever portion of the Qur'ãn had been revealed upto that time existed in written form.

All this means that writing down the revelations according to some arrangement was the law that was followed, which means that the Qur'ãn must have been put into writing from the beginning of its revelation to the end according to some principle,—and that writing and compilation should have been executed not merely on palm-leaves and shoulder-bones and pieces of wood and stone but also, and that basically, on paper, or, at least, on parchment, through which alone the form of a 'book' could have emerged after properly arranging and putting together uniform pieces of paper or parchment. Indeed, the incontrovertible truth is that the Qur'ãn grew up as a book from the beginning—growing in its contents with the progress in revelation, and was used as such by the Muslims even at Makkah. Historical facts confirm this fully, as we shall now see.

II. External Evidence

Soon after the commencement of the Revelation, the Holy Prophet (Peace be upon him!) made definite arrangements for the preservation of the revealed Messages in writing[1]. Among those who were entrusted with this task, and whose numbers increased as the numbers of the adherents of Islam increased,— the first one was Abu Bakr, the Companion *par excellence*, the wise and the truthful (*al-Siddîq*), the first adult man to embrace Islam—and that soon after the coming of the first revelation, and one of the respected elders of Makkah. Besides him we find the names of several other personalities mentioned in the historical records as the Holy Prophet's Scribes, who served as such at Makkah and Madinah. The famous Traditionist, Ibn Sayyid al-Nas, has given a list of thirty-eight in the biography of the Holy Prophet entitled: '*Uyûn al-Athar* (Vol. II, pp. 315, 316). The author of *al-Sîrah al-Halabiyyah* affirms a list of twenty Scribes, whose names he has selected from variant traditions wherein the number has gone as high as forty-two, this number having been recorded by al-Kattani (*al-Tartîb al-Idãriyah*, Vol. I, pp. 116-124; Moroccan edition). A critical examination of all the records places the number at twenty-eight, the list including the names of the first four caliphs, namely, Abu Bakr, Omar, Uthman and Ali, and of Mu'awiyah—the fifth head of the Islamic State after the Holy Prophet's demise, and of Zubair ibn al-Awam, Abdullah ibn Masud, Ubayy ibn Ka'ab, Zaid ibn Thabit, Khalid ibn Walid (the famous General), 'Amru ibn al-'As (later on the governor of Egypt) and Abdullah ibn 'Amru ibn al-'As.

Thus the task of writing down every revelation as it came was instituted by the Holy Prophet in a very organised and systematic form. Uthman, the third righteous caliph of Islam, and one of the earliest converts to the faith, bears testimony to it in these words: "Whenever some revelation came down on him (i.e., the Prophet), he would call

1 It may be emphasised here that quite a number of those who joined the Islamic fraternity at Makkah and Madinah were educated persons who knew the art of reading and writing. Moreover, the Holy Prophet gave such importance to the formal education of his followers that even many Muslim ladies received it (Abu Da'ud: *Sunan*, Vol. II, p. 186; etc.), and men like Zaid ibn Thabit acquired, under the Holy Prophet's orders, languages other than Arabic, e.g., Hebrew and Syriac. (*Al-Isãbah*, p. 561; *Al-Tãrîkh al-Saghîr*, p. 53; *Kitãb al-Musãhef*, p. 3.)

upon some of those who had been appointed to write." (Tirmizi: *Jãme'*, Vol. II, p. 134). This fact is corroborated by Imam Bukhari and others. For instance, Bukhari's *Sahih* reports: "Zaid ibn Thabit said that the Prophet dictated to him (the verse) 'Not equal are those believers who sit (at home) and receive no hurt, and those who strive and fight in the Cause of Allah....' " (Vol. III, p. 761). Or, the more comprehensive information contained in the *hadîth* recorded by Ibn Abi Daud and reported by Sulaiman, the grandson of Zaid ibn Thabit, on the authority of his father Kharija: "....(Zaid said:) I was a neighbour of God's Messenger. So, whenever any revelation came (to him), it was practice to call me, whereat I used to write down the revelation (at his dictation)." (*Kitãb al-Musãhef*, p. 3). Darimi's *Sunan* (p. 68) projects the fact that it was not always one person but, probably as a rule, several persons who wrote the revelations, singly but in a joint session, as the Holy Prophet dictated to them. In this connection, the *hadîth* runs like this: "Abdullah ibn 'Amru said: 'While we (the party of Scribes) were engaged in writing in the presence of God's Messenger....' ."

The Holy Prophet did not only dictate the revelations to the Scribes, but also asked them, after they had inscribed, to recite to him what they had written, for correcting any mistake they might have committed. We read in *Majma' al-Zawã'id* (Vol. I, p. 60) that "Zaid ibn Thabit said: '....whenever I had finished (writing down the revelation dictated to me), he (i.e., God's Messenger) asked me to read it out, and accordingly I would recite to him. Then, if there was a mistake, he corrected it. Then he gave it out to the people (for making copies for their use and for memorisation by them)'." (Cf. *Fath al-Mughîth*, p. 250).

This much about the fact that every revelation was written down as it came, with the ulmost care and by several Scribes at a time. Now comes the problem relating to the organisation of the discrete revelation into chapters (*suras*) as it is to be found in the Qur'ãn since the Holy Prophet's time,—only certain chapters having been revealed complete on single occasions. The verdict of history in this respect is that the Holy Prophet himself used to instruct on each occasion concerning the sequence of insertion in a particular chapter of a particular verse or set of verses revealed on a particular occasion; and in case a new chapter was to begin with a particular revelation, the Scribe or Scribes were instructed by him accordingly. Thus, for instance, it has been stated in Imam Tirmizi's *Jãme'* (Vol. II, p. 134): "He (i.e., God's Messenger) used to instruct (the Scribes) to place such and such verses in the chapter where such and such had been stated." In this way did all the chapters of the Holy Qur'ãn—and they are One Hundred and Fourteen in number—come into existence under the Holy Prophet's instruction and under Divine Guidance as communicated to him continuously. (*Majma' al-Zawã'id*, Vol. VII, p. 157; *Al-Itqãn*, vol. I, p. 62. Also refer: Imam Ahmad's *Musnad*).

Now, the chapters in themselves are parts of the Qur'ãn. By putting them together under a certain principle of arrangement, the Holy Qur'ãn assumed the form of a book. The question is: Who gave the existing arrangement in respect of chapters? Here, again, the verdict of history[2] is that this was done by no one else than the Holy Prophet himself. The recorded evidences in this respect are:

(i) Abu Da'ud has recorded the *hadith* in which Hudhaifah informs us that "he saw the Prophet (serially) reciting in the prayer at night the chapters *al-Baqarah*, *Ãl-i-'Imrãn, al-Nisã', al-Mã'îdah* and *al-An'ãm*." (*Sunan*, Vol. I, p. 128). Now, the order of the chapters stated in this *hadîth* is the same as it has existed in the Qur'ãn all through; which shows that the arrangement of all the chapters must have been fixed by the Holy Prophet (Peace be on him!) himself, it being inconceivable that he arranged only the above-mentioned five and left out the rest.

(ii) In Imam Tirmizi's *Jãme'* (Vol. II, pp. 118, 119) there is a *hadîth* which says: "A man enquired 'O God's Messenger! which action is most liked by God?' He replied: ' (The action) of him who finishes a journey and goes on a journey'." Darimi has added to this *hadîth*, in his *Sunan* (p. 41), the following: "It was asked as to what was the meaning of finishing a journey and undertaking another. (To this) he replied: 'A possessor of the Qur'ãn recites it from its beginning to its end, and when he finishes, he returns to the beginning (to finish it again), (making it his routine that) whenever he finishes the journey (of reading and studying the Qur'ãn from beginning to end), he begins the same journey (afresh)'." Here, the very notions of a beginning and an ending for the reading of the Qur'ãn as a book imply the existence of the arrangement of chapters.

The *hadîth* narrated by Imam Tirmizi (*Jãme'* Vol. II, p. 118), wherein the enquiry submitted by Abdullah ibn Amru to the Holy Prophet (Peace be on him!) in respect of the number of days that

2 See in this connection, among others: Al-Zarakshi: *Kitãb al-Burhãn*; Suyûti: *Al-Itqãn;* Shaikh Abdul Haq Muhaddith: *Ash'at al-Luma'ãt.*

was advisable for him to fix for reading the Qur'ãn from the beginning to the end is similar to the above as regards the logical conclusion to which it leads.

(iii) Imam Ahmad has recorded in his *Musnad* a *hadîth* which has a direct bearing on the problems of the arrangement of chapters. Therein, Aus ibn Abi Aus Hudhaifa al-Thaqafi reports that he was a member of a delegation of the Banu Thaqif tribe that had come to the Holy Prophet at Madinah, and that the Holy Prophet used to visit the delegation every night after the 'Ishã prayer; then, it so happened one night that the Holy Prophet was late in coming to them and, on enquiry as to the cause of the delay, he told them: "I had missed the *hizb* (i.e., a definite portion of the Qur'ãn fixed for recitation) meant for today; and I disliked that I should come out without finishing that (task)". "Then", Aus adds, "we enquired from the Companions of God's Messenger in respect of *ahzãb* (plural of *hizb*) of the Qur'ãn (namely, in what manner did they recite the Qur'ãn divided into a number of parts: *azhãb*). To that they replied that they recited (it according to this division): three chapters (beginning with chapter: *al-Baqarah*[3] (on the first day of the week), (the following) five chapters (on the second day), (the following) seven chapters (on the third day), (the following) nine chapters (on the fourth day), (the following) eleven chapters (on the fifth day), (the following) thirteen chapters (on the sixth day), and from the chapter named *Qãf* (numbering 50 in the Qur'ãn to the end of the Qur'ãn (on the seventh day)." (Vol. IV. p. 343). This detail corroborates the arrangement of chapters in the Qur'ãn as it is today, as Hafiz Ibn Hajar al-Asqalani emphasises in *Fath al-Bãrî*, Vol. IX, p. 39.

(iv) We learn from Bukhari's *Sahîh* (Vol. III, p. 141) that a rehearsal of the entire up-to-date Qur'ãn was done by the Holy Prophet in collaboration with angel Gibreel, every year during the month of Ramadan, it having taken place twice in the Ramadan immediately preceding the Holy Prophet's demise. It is evident that any such thing was impossible to happen if the Qur'ãn had been un-arranged

3 The first chapter, named *Al-Fãtihah*, has not been taken into account, because, it being the most basic Qur'ãnic prayer, no devotional action is complete without it. Hence, its recitation has to be repeated every day in connection with that day's *hizb*—and that in its own right. That seems to be the reason why it has not been mentioned as a part of the first day's *hizb*.

at any stage; which means that even the arrangement of its chapters in their serial order was taking place under the Holy Prophet's guidance from the very beginning according to the Divine Plan.

(v) The greatest proof of the fact that the arrangement of the chapters, even as that of the verses, took place under the instruction of the Holy Prophet, who as a result bequeathed the Qur'ãn to humanity exactly in its present form and contents, consists of the following truths: (a) the Qur'ãn is not only a Book of Guidance but also a book for recital for all Muslims. As such, one of the fondest pursuit of the Holy Prophet's Companions was its recital to their utmost capacity. It was obligatory for every Muslim to recite it in the daily prayers; but every Muslim's devotion to it was of such magnitude that he or she tried to go as far beyond the obligatory recitation as possible. All that would have been impossible, however, if the Qur'ãn had not existed from the very beginning as a book thoroughly arranged and perfectly organised internally, (b) if the Qur'ãn had not been perfected in every aspect before the Holy Prophet's demise, variations at least in respect of the arrangement of its chapters would have unavoidably taken place. But no such thing has happened, (c) Muslim scholars have differed among themselves on different issues, the differences even assuming sometimes what may be termed as 'sectarian dimensions', and the races and peoples who have been joining the fold of Islam during the past fourteen centuries came with different backgrounds. But the Qur'ãn has remained what it always was since its completion in the Holy Prophet's time. It means that all Muslims have accepted from the very beginning, and always, that not only its meaning-structure but also its word-structure, and that not only its contents but also its form—which consists of the arrangement of its verses and chapters is divinely-ordained and exists as perfected and completed under the direct instruction of the Holy Prophet (God's choicest Blessings be with him!).

Says Ibn Hazm, the versatile Islamic scholar of the fifth century of the Hijri era: "He who says that the arrangement of the verses and the chapters (of the Qur'ãn) is not Divine through His Prophet, he is ignorant and a fabricator...Had the people arranged (the verses and the chapters) themselves, they could not have avoided one of the (following) three methods (of arrangement): (i) either according to the order of revelation; (ii) or, they would have given priority to the longer chapters, placing the shorter ones after them; (iii) or, vice versa (i.e., from shorter to longer chapters). But because that is not the case, it (the present arrangement) is certainly through the Prophet's own instruction which could not have clashed with the Divinc Order. (In fact) no alternative remains except this." (*Kitãb al-Fasl*, Vol. IV, p. 221).

Chapter III

THE PROCESS OF PRESERVATION AND PROPAGATION

The arrangements instituted by the Holy Prophet (Peace be on him!) were perfect not only in respect of the communication of Qur'ãnic revelations but also concerning their preservation.

In this connection, it should be noted that although paper and parchment were not available in abundance, all important literary work was preserved through writing on parchment or on paper. The concept of writing on parchment or paper has been clearly projected in the Qur'ãn itself when it says: "If We (i.e., God) had sent unto thee (O Muhammad!) a book (or, a writing) on paper (or parchment), so that they could touch it with their hands...." (VI:7).

Supplies of paper, and even of parchment, being very limited, the initial writing of the revelations was very naturally executed by using other writing materials of those days, e.g., flat bones, chiseled stems of palm-leaves and wooden or stone tablets. But, once this initial work had been executed, the writing of the revelations, in accordance with their arrangement dictated to the Scribes by the Holy Prophet, on proper pieces of paper or parchment, which were seemingly in the form of the leaves of a book, was undertaken without fail. The evidence in this respect is explicit. For instance, al-Hakim has recorded the testimony of no less an authority than Zaid ibn Thabit, under the heading of "Compilation of the Qur'ãn during the time of God's Messenger", thus: "He said: 'We (the Scribes) used to *compile* the Qur'ãn from the (recordes of revelations made on) *ruqã*' (i.e., pieces of paper or of parchment[1])."

---

1 Leaves of paper can be stitched together to form a book. Similarly, uniform pieces of parchment can be used for making a book. Hence, whether the Arabs of those days used parchment made of the tanned thin membraneous layer of animal skin, or paper made of rags or reeds, is immaterial; because, although in their texture paper and parchment are different materials, they are similar in respect of their function.

We know that Papyrus, manufactured from reed, was used in Egypt as early as 2500 B.C., while paper made from rags was used by the Chinese since the 2nd century B.C. The existence of paper in Arabia, together with parchment, which was in use there since the 2nd century B.C., cannot be ruled out, as we

(*Al-Mustadrak*, Vol. II, p. 611).[2]

In this way grew up quite a good number of copies of the Holy Qur'ãn under the direct instruction and supervision of the Holy Prophet (Peace be on him!). Then, the copies compiled[3] by the Scribes were handed over to other Companions, as we have already noted, so that they copied them out in order to possess their own copies for reading as well as memorisation. The copies compiled by the Scribes as well as the others continued to grow in content with the progress in revelation until they were declared to be complete by the Holy Prophet, who proclaimed in clear terms: "I am leaving in your midst a thing which (in terms of its importance) is such that you will never fall into error so long as you hold to it firmly; and it is the Book of God (i.e., the Qur'ãn)". (Abu Da'ud: *Sunan*, Vol. I, p. 264).

When we attend to the problem of the number of copies of the Qur'ãn that existed during the Holy Prophet's time and look into the statements contained in Bukhari's *Sahîh* (Vol. III, p. 143), Muslim's *Sahîh* (Vol. II, p. 252), *Tahdhîb al-Tahdhîb* (Vol. VII, p. 243), *'Istî'ab* (Vol. II, p. 565), *Usud al-Ghãbah* (Vol. II, p. 286), Ibn Sa'ad's *Tabaqãt* (Vol. II, p. 112), etc., we become sure of the existence of at least fifteen copies.[4] Then, when we consider the number of the Scribes appointed by the Holy Prophet, the number of copies goes further up. Again: when we consider the total situation in the Muslim community of the Holy Prophet's time

---

find in the references to writing materials given, among others, in Suyuti's *Al-Itqãn* (Vol. I, pp. 58, 59).

2 Cf. *Kitãb al-Burhãn,* Vol. I, p. 256; Darimi: *Sunan*, p. 68.

3 The following *hadîth* indicates that the compiled material was maintained "between two boards", namely, in the form of some sort of binding in book-shape. "Abd al Aziz ibn Rafi said: I and Shaddad ibn Ma'qil visited Ibn Abbas; then Shaddad questioned him: 'Did the Prophet bequeath anything?' He replied: 'No, except what is contained between the two boards (i.e., the Qur'ãn)'. Then we visited Muhammad ibn al-Hanafiyyah and put the same question to him; then he too replied that he (the Prophet) did not leave behind anything except what is contained between the two boards." (Bukhari: *Sahîh*, Vol. III, p. 143).

4 In respect of possessors of complete copies, all recorded evidence compels us to include the first four righteous Caliph i.e., Abu Bakr, Omar, Uthman and Ali,—besides other eminent Companions like Mu'adh ibn Jabal, Ubayy ibn Ka'ab, Zaid ibn Thabit, Abu Darda', Abu Ayyub Ansari, Abdullah ibn Mas'ud, 'Ubadah ibn al-Samit and Tamim Dari.

with reference to widespread activity of racitation and memorisation, we are compelled to consider the number of copies as still higher.

After the demise of the Holy Prophet (Peace be on him!), the number of copies multiplied by leaps and bounds under the compulsion of the law of demand and supply, so much so that before the commencement of the caliphate of Uthman thousands upon thousands of copies had come into existence. Ibn Hazm bears testimony to it thus: "When the Prophet passed away, Islam had already spread in the whole (Arabian) peninsula from the Red Sea to the (southern) coast of Yemen and from the Persian Gulf to Euphrates. There were innumerable townships and villages inside the peninsula where all the inhabitants had declared allegiance to Islam and had constructed the mosques. There was no town, village, or quarter, where the Qur'ãn was not recited at the mosques during prayers. Children and male and female adults, all learnt it, and it was also copied out in writing. After the Prophet's period, Abu Bakr ruled as Caliph for 2½ years.... the recitation grew more and more. There was no town where the copies of the Qur'ãn were not available. After that, Omar became the Caliph and conquered the length and breadth of Persia and the whole of Syria and Egypt. In those countries also there was no inhabited place where mosques were not built and new copies of the Qur'ãn were not made. The leaders of congregational prayers recited it, and the children all over the east and the west (of the Islamic empire) learnt it. This period lasted for ten years and some months. When Omar died, at least one hundred-thousand copies of the Qur'ãn must have been in existence". (*Kitãb al-Fasl,* Vol. II, p. 78).

Since then up to this day, the number of copies that have gone into circulation is beyond all possibility of counting. But the text of the Holy Qur'ãn has not suffered even the slightest deviation and variation. Truly had it been proclaimed by God at the time of its revelation: "We have, without doubt, sent down the Message (i.e., the Qur'ãn), and We are assuredly the guardian thereof". (XV:9).

It is necessary to observe here that the Qur'ãn was propagated by the Holy Prophet not only in written form but also orally, he being not merely the deliverer of the Divine Message but also its Teacher *par excellence* (LXII:2); and the Muslims were asked by him not only to read the holy book but also to memorise it. In this way a double process of preserving the purity of the text of the Holy Qur'ãn came to exist, and a perfect system of teaching it originated with the Holy Prophet himself.

Thus we find Bukhari reporting about Abdullah ibn Mas'ud that he said: "I learnt directly from the mouth of God's Messenger about 79 chapters." (*Sahîh*, Vol. II, p. 141). The same Companion also reported according to Muslim's *Sahîh* (Vol. I, p. 121), that: "God's Messenger asked me to recite the Qur'ãn before him. Thereupon I enquired: "Should I recite to you while it has been revealed to you?' He replied: 'I like to hear it recite by others'. So I recited the chapter *al-Nisã'*."

Thus were the Companions trained by the Holy Prophet as licensed teachers of the Qur'ãn for the masses and they performed this function, under appointment from him[5], with utmost diligence. Just by way of examples: *Miftãh al-Sa'ãdah* (Vol. I, p. 349) reports: "Abu 'Aliyah said: I recited the Qur'ãn to Omar four times"; and, according to Dhahabi's *Tabaqat al-Qurrã'* (p. 606); "When Abu Darda would finish his morning prayer, he would set his students in batches of ten. Once he counted them, and they were more than sixteen hundred."

The system of teaching that developed had the memorisation of the Qur'ãn as its vital part, and a continuous chain of licensed and authorised teachers grew, and has continued to grow from generation to generation, not only to propagate the text of the Qur'ãn but also to preserve its purity, in which connection a whole science has developed; and the uniform oral as well as written[6] transmission down the centuries through successive generations of Qur'ãnic teachers belonging to divers races and countries, has crowned the Holy Qur'ãn with the merit of *tawãtur*[7] to a degree of glory where even the slightest possibility of doubt in respect of the purity of its text is totally eliminated.

That is the only reason why even those hostile western scholars, for whom the highest virtue is to revile Islam on the flimsiest grounds,

---

5 " 'Ubadah ibn al-Samit reported that if God's Messenger was engaged and someone came (to Madinah) as immigrant, he entrusted him to one of us to teach him the Qur'ãn." (*Kanz al-'Ummãl*, Vol. I, p. 231). According to *Isti'ãb* (Vol. I, p. 369) and Tabari's *Tãrîkh* (Vol. III, p. 156), the Holy Prophet appointed several Companions to teach the Qur'ãn to the tribes living outside Madinah. The appointment of teachers has also been recorded in Bukhari's *Sahih* (Vol. III, p. 141), Muslim's *Sahih* (Vol. II, p. 252), and Tirmizi's *Jãme'* (Vol. II, p. 222).

6 These two process have functioned as guards on one another.

7 Namely, unbroken transmission with absolute uniformity.

had to bow their heads in humility when confronted with the problem of the authenticity of the Qur'ãn and had to grudgingly admit the purity of its text—scholars, such as: palmer (*The Qur'ãn*—English Translation; Introduction, p. LIX); Wherry (*Commentary on the Kuran*, I, p. 349); Snouch Hurgronje (*Muhammadanism*, p. 18); William Muri (*Life of Muhammad*, Introduction, p. XXIII); Philip K. Hitti (*History of the Arabs*, p. 123); and Torrey (*Jewish Foundation of Islam*, p. 2). To quote just the last reference: "The Koran was his (i.e., Muhammad's) own creation; and it lies before us practically unchanged from the form which he himself gave it." Had the blinding fire of antagonism to Islam not burned in the heart of Torry in the manner it did, he could have spoken at least in the tone of Bosworth Smith, who said: "In the Koran we have, beyond all reasonable doubt, the exact words of Muhammad without subtraction and without addition". (*Muhammad and Muhammadanism, p. 22). And it is not only Bosworth Smith* who says so, but many others. For instance, F.F. Arbuthnot has confessed that: "....complete text of the Koran....has remained the same, without any change or alteration by enthusiasts, translators, or interpolators, upto the present time. It is to be regretted that the same cannot be said of all the books of the Old and New Testaments." (*The Construction of the Bible and the Koran*, p. 5).

Chapter IV

THE QUR'ÃN AS THE ONLY AUTHENTIC REVEALED BOOK IN THE WORLD

Absolute authenticity in respect of the purity of its text forms the Holy Qur'ãn's distinctive claim—a claim in which it stands unique among all the sacred books of the world: those based on the concept of Divine Revelation and others that are not. Among the former, the Jewish and Christian scriptures stand out most prominently.

As to the Jewish sacred books, from where Christianity derives its base, the reformed Judaism of today has forsaken completely the age-old claim, which is the very foundation of the Jewish faith, namely, the claim relating to their status as divinely-revealed books, as also their authenticity as records of the teachings of Jewish Prophets. According to the *Jewish Encyclopaedia*, the emphasis on divine origin has given way to the admission of "the human origin of the Holy Scriptures", with all their holiness and infallibility shattered, so much so that "the ancient view of a literal dictation by God must be surrendered". Also, "the prophet and the sacred writer were under the influence of the Divine Spirit while revealing by word or pen...(but) the human element in them was not extinguished, and consequently, in regard to their statements, their knowledge, and the form of their communication, they could only have acted as children of their age". (Vol. VI, pp. 608-609).

This ugly situation has emerged for Judaism basically because the Message of God preached and taught by the Jewish Prophets (God bless them all!) was lost, in respect of its original purity, by the Jewish people long ago under the strains and stresses of historical circumstances. What remained was an adulterated and corrupted form of religious teaching and incorrect history, and on that Judaism has been fed ever since. As a result, we find today Jewish scholarship between the devil and the deep sea in respect of the authenticity of the Jewish religion. While "the ancients regarded the whole mass of the national religious writings as equally holy"[1], the moderns have denied completely God's authorship of any Jewish sacred book. "That the real authority of the Bible is intrinsic rather than prescriptive", says Joseph (*Judaism as Creed and Life*), "becomes clear as soon as we think of the circumstances in

---

1 *Jewish Encyclopaedia*, Vol. III, p. 140.

which the Scriptural canon was formed. The decision by which certain books were included in the Bible and others excluded, was a purely human decision. The great teachers[2] sat in judgement upon the claims of various works, and decided upon those claims by the light of reason[3]—in other words, by the internal merits of the works themselves[4]. Nor was the decision always easy[5]. That fate of some books, like Ecclesiastes, and Centicles, and Esther, was, we learn, trembling in the balance even as late as the third century of the present era....The Bible, being the work of godly men, necessarily contains both a Divine and a human element. But since everything human is imperfect, we must not expect to find an absolutely perfect representation of Divine truth even in God's Book[6]....Some of the Biblical stories are clearly legends....The Pentateuch is the work not of one hand but of many hands[7]....Similar views prevail among scholars with regard to other books of the Bible." (pp. 18, 20, 22, 23, 24). Modern scholarship, which has given birth to reformed Judaism, supports the above views of Joseph unanimously. For instance: with respect to the infallibility of the Jewish scripture and its authenticity as the Word of God, Vellentine's *One Volume Jewish Encyclopaedia* tells us: "Jewish tradition....does not hesitate to admit later elaboration and revision of certain books in the Bible.... As an unimpeachable source of history and chronology the Bible is often disappointing, exhibiting statements and data which seem either vague or contradictory, or else fail to agree with what is known of contemporary oriental history and chronology." (pp. 93, 95).

As to the Christian version: "With the advance in the technique of textual criticism during the course of the last generation, with a more

---

2 And not the Jewish Prophets who had delivered the Message of God! And these 'great teachers' also 'sat' long afterwards!!!

3 And not by the light of Revelation!

4 Merits—in what respect?

5 How could it be when there was no standard of judgement?

6 In what sense is it 'God's Book'?

7 According to the *Jewish Encyclopaedia*, the contents of the Pentateuch have been derived from twenty-eight different sources, where the authorship of Moses vanishes into thin air (p. 590). We are also informed that "the many inconsistencies and seeming contradictions contained in it (i.e., Pentateuch) attracted the attention of the Rabbis, who exercised their ingenuity in reconciling them" (p. 589).

searching analysis of the matter of the text, and with the use of the comparative method in evaluating the tradition embodied in the narrative, it has become even more patently evident that orthodox opinion in regard to the authenticity of the Bible cannot be maintained."[8] One has only to go through the findings of the official representatives of Christianity, as recorded in the *Encyclopaedia Biblica*, to discover the impeachment of the authenticity of the Old and the New Testaments by the Christendom of today. In the words of one of the best Biblical apologists, who wrote for the *Encyclopaedia of Religion and Ethics* (vol. VII, p. 263): "It is now a common-place of Biblical learning that God has been at no pains to prevent errors of history and knowledge and defects in the text and its transmission[9] from finding an entrance into the sacred pages of His Written Word[10]." Rev. Bosworth Smith, who seems to be more frank, is more rational in his confession. Comparing the confirmed claim of the Qur'ãn to absolute authenticity with the baseless orthodox Christian claim concerning the Bible, he says: "The Bible in particular makes no such claim....The Bible is the work of a large number of poets, prophets, statesmen, and lawgivers, extending over a vast period of time, and incorporates with itself other and earlier, and often conflicting, documents". (*Muhammad and Muhammadanism*, p. 19).

It may be observed here in passing that it is not only the so-called 'revealed' religions but also the 'unrevealed' ones that suffer from inauthenticity with regard to their sacred texts. Although our present discussion does not directly relate to unrevealed religions owing to their different basis, we may with advantage refer to one such major religion, namely, Buddhism, to reveal the situation on that side[11]. To quote just one authority: "The truth is that the oldest stratum of the existing scriptures

---

8 Sir Richard Gregory: *Religion in Science and Civilisation,* p. 86.

9 "errors of history and knowledge and defects in the text and its transmission" are there only because the Old Testament as well as the New are the products of human brains, where the truth revealed by God has been perverted and missed up with falsehood by human ignorance as well as wrong motives. The Divine Wisdom is absolute and cannot, even in the understanding of a child, admit of the slightest error or defect.

10 But, what *Written Word* from God did Jesus ever give, so far as the Christian testimony goes?

11 Of course, Hinduism, Jainism, Confucianism, Tao-ism, etc., also suffer from the same defect.

(of Buddhism) can only be reached by uncertain inference and conjecture.... I confess that I do not know what the 'original gospel' of Buddhism was..........Buddhism is a body of traditions in which few names stand out, and in which fewer dates are precisely known. It is indeed most exasperating when we try to apply our current ideas of historical criticism."[12]

To revert to the scripture which claim to be revealed, the following verdict of an English scholar is final: "The truth of the message is intimately connected with the authenticity of the record, and a critical theory which assails the one assails the other".[13]

With this verdict—and the principle on which it is based is incontrovertible—Judaism and Christianity, both are ruled out; while the absolute authenticity of the Qur'ãn proves the genuineness of its Message, and here the judgement emerges in all its grandeur that if Divine Revelation alone is the true and valid basis for Religion, then the Holy Qur'ãn alone gives us the true Religion—the Religion revealed by the Creator and Sovereign of the universe and man.

---

12 Edward Conze: *Buddhism, its Essence and Development*, pp. 27, 29, 30.

13 *The Church Times*, February 10, 1905.

Chapter V

THE STYLE AND STRUCTURE OF THE QUR'ÃN

The problem may be viewed in three dimensions, namely, (i) intonation, (ii) diction, and (iii) thought; and the Qur'ãn is inimitable and unique in each.

Intonation:

No other scripture possesses that exquisite and majestic charm of melody that the Holy Qur'ãn has. An English scholar and orientalist of repute bears testimony to this fact when he says: "....the Glorious Qur'ãn, that inimitable symphony the very sounds of which move men to tears and ecstasy."[1]

Diction:

As regards diction: The Arabic language itself, which is the language of the Qur'ãn, is an extremely rich language—a fact attested unanimously by all the Arabicists of the world, Muslim as well as non-Muslim. Over and above that, there is the style employed in the Qur'ãn, whose depths in the dimension of meaning and heights in respect of grandeur are simply immeasurable by human genius—a fact which has given to the language of the Qur'ãn the status of "the purest Arabic"[2] and, "the standard of the Arabic tongue"[3] —all that in a miraculous form. "Whenever Muhammad was asked a miracle as a proof of the authenticity of his mission", says the French scholar Paul Casanova, "he quoted the composition of the Qur'ãn and its incomparable excellence as proof of its Divine origin. And, in fact, even for those who are non-Muslims nothing is more marvellous than its language which with such a prehensible plenitude and grasping sonority with its simple audition ravished with admiration those primitive[4] peoples so fond of eloquence. The ampleness

1 Marmaduke Pickthall: *Meaning of the Glorious Qur'ãn*, Translator's Foreword, 1st para.

2 F.F. Arbuthnot, *The Construction of the Bible and the Koran*, London, p. 5.

3 George Sale: The Qur'ãn: *The Preliminary Discourse*, London and New York 1891, p. 47.

4 In actual fact, the Arabs of those days were not primitive but highly civilised in respect of language.

of its syllables with a grandiose cadence and with a remarkable rhythm have been of much moment in the conversion of the most hostile and the most sceptical.."[5] And the American scholar, Harry Gaylord Dorman, says: It (Qur'ãn) is an ever-present miracle witnessing to itself and to Muhammad, the Prophet of God. Its miraculous quality resides partly in its style, so perfect and lofty that neither men nor *jinn* could produce a single chapter to compare with its briefest chapter, and partly in its content of teachings, prophecies about the future, and amazingly accurate information such as the illiterate Muhammad could never have gathered of his own accord."[6]

It is correct to say that the miraculous quality of the Qur'ãn resides only partly in its literary aspect. Its emphasis on this aspect was, however, necessitated by the arrogance of the Arabs of those days who were proud of their high attainment in literary skill. Thus the challenge was posed to them on their own terms, when the Holy Qur'ãn proclaimed: "Or do they say: 'he has forged it'? Say: 'Bring ye then ten *suras* forged, like thereunto, and call (to your aid) whomsoever ye can, other than Allah!—if ye speak the truth'." (XI:13). "Say (O Muhammad!): 'If the whole of mankind and jinns were to gather together to produce the like of this Qur'ãn, they could not produce the like thereof, even if they backed up each other with help and support". (XVII:88)[7]

It is difficult to translate any book written in any language. Much more so the Qur'ãn, whose miraculous language simply defies translation. All honest translators are unanimous in this behalf. "The Qur'ãn", says Marmaduke Pickthall, "cannot be translated. That is the belief of old-fashioned Sheykhs and the view of the present writer."[8] "Of all the great works," writes Abdul Majid Daryabadi, "the Holy Qur'ãn is perhaps the least translatable. Arabic is not at all easy to translate into a language so widely and radically diferring from it in structure and genius as English, unless it be with the aid of loose periphrasis and lax paraphrase. Even so

5 "L'Enseignement de l'Arabe au College de France", in *Lecon d'overture* for 26th April, 1909.

6 *Towards Understanding Islam*, New York 1948, p. 3.

7 It should be observed that both of these verses were revealed at Makkah, which proves that the Qur'ãn grew from the very beginning in book-form. Also: we find this challenge repeated on three other occasions, viz., II: 23; X:38; LII:34.

8 *op.cit.*,

the fire of the original is quenched, its vivacious perspicuity is lost, and the so-called literal translation looks rugged and dreary. That the language of the Arabs abounds in nuances and both the noun and the verb are extremely flexible, is a fact well known to every student of that tongue. The difficulty is increased hundredfold when one has to render into English, with any degree of accuracy and precision, a work so rich in meaning, so pithy in expression, so vigorous in style and so subtle in implications as the Holy Qur'ãn. To reproduce even partially its exotic beauty, wonderful grandeur and magical vivacity without sacrificing the requirements of the English idiom and usage, is the despair of the translator and an ideal impossible of attainment. The result is that every fresh attempt at translating the Holy Writ brings home, in varying degrees, the truth of the old saying that nothing is so unlike an original as its copy."[9] According to Eduard Montet, ".....the Coran (Qur'ãn)....its grandeur of form is so sublime that no translation into any European language can allow us to appreciate it."[10] Even a Christian clergyman has confessed: "The Qur'ãn in its original Arabic dress has a seductive beauty and charm of its own. Couched in concise and exalted style, its brief pregnant sentences, often rhymed, possess an expressive force and explosive energy which it is extremely difficult to convey by literal word for word translation."[11]

The Qur'ãnic narration is so unique in its style, and so different from the writings of the world's seers and sages, that those who are accustomed only to read human literary productions based on commonplace logical sequence and on the finitude in which human thought expresses itself—the finitude of human perception and conception having its own finite, and hence more intelligible and more crystallised, sequential emphasis—are likely to discover that their minds do not grasp truly the transcendental logic of the Qur'ãnic narration as it flows majestically, starting at *sura al-Fãtiha* and ending at *sura al-Nãs*.

A non-Muslim translator of the Holy Qur'ãn views this problem in his own light and tenders the following advice to the readers of translations: "In the first place, the Western reader must get rid of the assumption that the Koran is more or less like the Old Testament.

9. *The Holy Qur'ãn: English Translation and Commentary*, Lahore and Karachi 1957, Preface, p. IX

10 *Traduction Francaise du Coran*, Paris 1929, Introduction, p. 53.

11 John Naish, M.A. (Oxon.), D.D.: *The Wisdom of the Qur'ãn,* Oxford 1937, Preface, p. VIII.

The misapprehension is natural enough, when the first casual glance picks out the names of Adam, Abraham, Moses, David, Solomon, Jonah, Joseph, Jacob, Job: the Biblical style[12] of the popular translations does not furnish exactly a corrective. Misled by these early impressions, the reader makes the fatal mistake of trying to take it too much at once; he opens at a likely place, the beginning of a *sura*, and is lulled into suspicion by the familiar layout of chapter and verse; he finishes the first *sura* and goes on to several more; he is bewildered by the rapid and seemingly illogical changes of subject, and he quickly wearies of the frequent repetitions of themes and formulas.... The Koran, like the poetry which it resembles in so many ways, is best sampled a little at a time; and that little deserves and needs meditation.... He (the reader) will become gradually familiar with the Koran's claim to be a confirmation of earlier scriptures. He will observe how the Koran assumes a knowledge of the contents of those scriptures, and only later expands the individual narratives into something like connected stories. He now follows step by step the gradual unfolding of the full prophetic powers; and when he comes to the polemic and the legislation he is readier to receive and understand them....the uninitiated enquirer...is screened from it by the double veil of a printed page and a foreign idiom. Yes, a foreign idiom, for the Koran is God's revelation in Arabic, and the emotive and evocative qualities of the original disappear almost totally in the skilfullest translation. When appreciation rests upon these foundations, the charges of wearisome repetition and jumbled confusion become meaningless. Truth cannot be dimmed by being frequently stated, but only gains in clarity and convincingness at every repetition...."[13]

Thought:

The Qur'ãn says about itself that it was *sent down* during the month of Ramadan (II:185), in the Night of Power (XCVII:1), its primary and eternal existence being in a "Tablet Preserved" (LXXXV:21, 22), "in the Mother of the Book, in Our (i.e., God's) Presence, high (in dignity), full of wisdom" (XLIII:4)

---

12 The text of the Bible, as we have already noted, has been composed by eminent human writers, who have very naturally adopted the popular human style. In the translations that style has become even more human. But all that has happened at the cost of loss of the Divine Truth.

13 A.J. Arberry: *The Holy Koran, an Introduction with Selection*, London 1953, pp. 25-27.

The question is: Does the coming down of the Qur'ãn in the Night of Power imply the commencement of revelation to the Holy Prophet (Peace be on him!), or its revelation to him in its entirety on that single occasion, or its descent from the 'Tablet Preserved' in some other dimension?

As to the first, we have already recorded in the foregoing that the first revelation came to the Holy Prophet on the 12th of Rabi' al-Awwal, that being the fact to which a critical study of all the relevant reports leads us.

Taking up the second alternative: It is denied by the Qur'ãn. We are told therein: "And (this is) a Recitation (*lit.*, Qur'ãn) that We have divided (into parts from time to time), that thou (O Muhammad!) mayest recite it to humankind at intervals, and We have revealed it (to thee) be (successive) revelation." (XVII:106)[14]

Thus we are left only with the third alternative, and here we get to the correct answer. Abdullah ibn Abbas, whose authority in respect of the problems relating to the Qur'ãn has been held in very high esteem all through Islamic history, is reported by different authorities, like Nasai, Baihaqi, al-Hakim, al-Tibrani and al-Bazzar, to have held that the entire Qur'ãn, as we have it today, came down in the Night of Power from the "Divine Presence" "to the nether heaven" (i.e., the heaven nearest to the earth), where in the "House of Power, Honour and Glory (*bait al-'izzat*)", it dwelt, like the stars, by the order of God, and from where its portions came to the Holy Prophet (Peace be on him!) as occasions arose, even "as the stars fall from heaven", under the Decree of God,—whereafter the revelations were arranged, under divine guidance, by the Holy Prophet, through his Scribes, in accordance with the original eternal Qur'ãn and not in their chronological sequence. The Commentator Ibn Kathir has concurred with this view in his *Tafsir* (Vol. IV, p. 529), while the famous Suyuti proclaims, quoting al-Qurtubi, thus: "The consensus of learned verdict is to the effect that the Qur'ãn came down all at one time from the 'Tablet Preserved' to the 'House of Power, Honour and Glory' in the nether heaven." (*Al-Itqãn*, Vol. I, p. 40).

The report of Ibn Abbas, directs our attention to *sura Hã Mim* (XLI), which begins with the claim of the Qur'ãn as a revealed book; then, after reference to those who contested its divine origin and the Divine

---

14 *Cf.* XXV:32, LXXVI:23.

Messengership of the bearer of its Message, speaks of the bounties of God as manifested in the earth and of the *wahy* of God to the seven firmaments in respect of the assignment of their duty and command,—thereafter emphasising: "And We adorned the nether heaven with lights, and rendered it inviolable. Such is the Decree of (Him) the Exalted in Might, Full of Knowledge." (verse 12). Maybe, the reference in the adornment of the nether heaven with lights and the establishment of inviolability, is concerned not only with the physical phenomenon as the human beings know it but also with the spiritual phenomenon so explicitly spoken of by Ibn Abbas.

Anyhow, the main point to be noted is that the Qur'ãn we passesses today existed in 'Divine Presence' eternally as a 'Book'[15] and that, although it was revealed piece-meal as occasions arose[16], the Holy Prophet (Peace be on him!) arranged it in accordance with the eternal arrangement as revealed to him. It may be emphasised that *unless this fact is accepted, the style of the Qur'ãn cannot be properly understood.*

Now, a collection of haphazard statements cannot be genuinely named as a book. There should be a sequence and a system inherent in it, which alone bestows that status properly. Thus, because the Qur'ãn insisted upon designating itself as a Book, much before it acquired the book-form with the ending of the Revelation, there must be present in it some definite type of sequence. And that it does possess.

In fact, there are two types of sequences enshrined in the Holy Qur'ãn: one sequence relating to the chronological order of revelations, the other relating to the order in which the revealed messages were arranged.

The chronological sequence guides us, not only in respect of the commencement and progress of the Holy Prophet's mission, but also about the future technique concerning the reform and development of human communities, and of individuals, on the Islamic pattern. Hence Islamic

---

15 That the Qur'ãn calls itself a Book even in the early revelations forms proof of the fact that it was a 'Book' before its revelation to the Holy Prophet (Peace be on him!).

16 It should be clearly noted that though the revelations came as occasions arose, the message contained therein was not confined to the exigencies of the situation.

scholars took the greatest pains in preserving the knowledge of chronological sequence as best as they could.

What light we receive through the consideration of chronological sequence may be illustrated here very briefly by way of example. The first revelation that came to the Holy Prophet (Peace be on him!) and formed, thus, the starting point of his mission, consisted of the first five verses of the *sura* named *al-'Alaq* (XCVI). Now, the basic problem projected in those verses is that of the conflict of Faith and Reason and the solution thereof. The immense importance of this problem in human history in respect of the establishment of peace and harmony between religion, on the one hand, and philosophy and science, on the other, cannot be over-estimated, especially when we consider that the Holy Prophet stood at the helm of the modern era of scientific advancement—of which he himself was to be the inaugurator, while his basic role was to establish Religion on sound footing as God Himself had revealed it before him from time to time. Hence, placing the human knowledge cultivated through the pen in the embrace of a dynamic Faith in God, as those verses do, it was only logical and natural that they should have been revealed first. Moreover, the importance given there to the cultivation of knowledge lend to those verses pre-eminence in view of the fact that it was the Holy Prophet's mission to "teach new knowledge" (II:151)

Then, the first verses that were revealed after the short suspense in Revelation, i.e., LXXIV: 1-5, reflect in essence the five Pillars of Islam, as we find them mentioned in the *Hadith*[17], the first two verses reflecting the Divine Messengership of Muhammad (Peace be on him!); the third verse reflecting the belief in God; the fourth reflecting the concept of purity, for which prayer, compulsory charity and pilgrimage, have been prescribed as Pillars of Islam[18]; the fifth verse reflecting fasting (among the Pillars) in respect of the elimination of impurities—spiritual, moral and physical.

Thereafter, we come to the following verses which, by general consent of the authorities, are accepted as having been revealed in the

17 For instance: Imam Ahmad: *Musnad*, Vol. I, p. 27.

18 The expression: "Thy raiments purify" covers, in the widest sense, physical, moral and spiritual purity,—these three forms of purity bearing reference to the three pillars of Islam mentioned in that connection. The words 'raiment' and 'garment' have been used in the Holy Qur'ān in wider significance than clothes (II:187; VII:26).

first year of the Call, forming thus a part of the very earliest revelations: "And what will make thee comprehend what the uphill road (of virtue) is: (It is:) the setting free of a slave; or the giving of food in a day of privation to the orphan with claims of relationship, or to the indigent (down) in the dust; and to be of those who believe, and enjoin patience, (constancy and self-restraint), and enjoin deeds of kindness and compassion."... (XC:12-17). The emphasis in these verses on the abolition of slavery, which had been one of the greatest curses of the pre-Islamic civilisations, on service to fellow-beings, and on the cultivation of a serene personality, has an importance in understanding the approach of Islam to human problems and its system of priorities in respect of the role of religion.

As regards the arrangemental sequence, the Holy Qur'ãn contains two levels of understanding like Nature, it being the Book of the Religion of Ideal Human Nature (*al-Din al-Fitrat*) authored by the Author of Nature.

The two levels that relate to the understanding of Nature are: the common-sense level and the probe level. Human common sense feels the existence of a system—an order, and witnesses the beauty and the grandeur of the starry heavens, the luminous moon and the blazing sun, the majestic mountains, the enchanting landscapes, and many many other parts of Nature besides. It is, however, the scientists who, through their probe into the depths of the mysteries of Nature, define the system—though not unerringly in every detail—and discover the facts that exist below the surface, revealing the knowledge progressively as they attain level after level.

The two levels that relate to the understanding of the Holy Qur'ãn are: (i) the level of religious consciousness, which is embraced by unperverted human common sense; (ii) the level of theoretic consciousness, which necessitates probe and research below the surface of the Qur'ãnic text. The logic of religious consciousness is the instrument for acquiring understanding at the first level, while the logic of theoretic consciousness serves the other level.

The logic of religious consciousness witnesses in the Holy Qur'ãn the sequence and the concordance as grounded in the demands of Religion. The logic of theoretic consciousness observes the sequence and inter-relatedness as grounded in the requirements of theoretic Reason.

The Holy Qur'ãn has come to guide all human beings, including the common men and women, and not merely the scholars; and its primary function is: (i) *religious* and not *speculative*; (ii) development of human personality and the social order on the basis of Religion, and not speculation in terms of the deduction and induction of Reason; (iii) exhortation for guidance on the basis of the absolute Knowledge and Wisdom of God and in the form of direct and categorical statements of the Truth, and not the presentation for academic interest of any imperfect findings of the struggling human mind which, if it is to succeed in its labours in any measure, has perforce to proceed within the framework of certain fixed categories and under a certain 'system'.

Thus the primary level of sequence in the Holy Qur'ãn is that of the logic of religious consciousness, and in that respect there exists perfect and multi-dimensional sequence[19] from the beginnign to the end,—a sequence that has been demonstrated by the classical commentators. Indeed, even a cursory glance at the Qur'ãnic text bears out this fact. For instance, the very starting point of the Holy Qur'ãn is: "In the Name of Allah, the Beneficent, the Merciful"—the quest for God being the highest quest, nay, the very basic quest, of religious consciousness.[20] Then it continues to speak of God, together with the emphasis on His relation with the universe and man: "Praise be to Allah, the Cherisher and Sustainer of the Worlds, the Beneficent, the Merciful, Ruler of the Day of Judgment". (I:1-3). Then, because man seeks God primarily in the perspective of his needs, the 4th verse is: "Thee (alone) do we worship; and Thine aid (alone) we seek." Then the dimensions, positive and negative, of the Path that leads to the fulfilment of human destiny, have been crisply projected in verses 5-7: "Show us the Straight Path, the path of those on whom Thou hast bestowed Thy Grace; not (the path) of those whose portion is Wrath nor of those who stray." The first chapter ends here, and the second chapter begins. There, the opening verse forms the response to the prayer contained in the first chapter, with the words: "A.L.M. This is the Book; in it is guidance, with no dubiousness, for the godfearing: who believe in the

19 It should be emphatically noted that a multi-dimensional sequence, which is richer than the single-dimensional sequence that is found in the literary works of the greatest human writers, emerges in the Holy Qur'ãn primarily in the order and arrangement that has been given by God through the Holy Prophet to the verses that constitute its text, as well as to the words of rich connotation employed therein.

20 The Qur'ãnic narrative begins with God, both chronologically and arrangementally, in response to religious consciousness. The Biblical narrative begins with the story of "Creation", in response to what? Mark the contrast.

Unseen, are steadfast in prayer and spend out of what We have provided for them; and who believe in the Revelation sent to thee (O Muhammad!), and before thy time, and (in their hearts) have the assurance of the Hereafter. They are on the right path, guided by their Lord, and they shall prospher." (II:1-5). Here the basic qualifications of the Acceptors of the Truth, or the Pursuers of the Straight Path, mentioned in the first chapter, have been referred to. Immediately after that comes the reference to the Rejectors of the Truth, and then of those who swing between Truth and Falsehood, i.e., the Hypocrites,—and so on the narration proceeds. Similarly, when we look at the last portion of the Holy Qur'ãn, we find that, after its multi-dimensional elaboration of the Straight Path, it enters into certain very important and relevant topics. Picking up the last one dozen chapters for the illustration of sequence, the picture that emerges in respect of one dimension of sequence is that, having taught the Islamic Way of Life in detail, the Holy Qur'ãn renders advice to the Muslims with regard to their status as the promoters of the mission for which Islam came. In this perspective, chapter 103 deals with the principles of the rise and fall of nations,—providing to the Muslims certain positive dimensions of the basic emphasis; chapter 104 and 105 project the fatal consequences attendant upon the evils of love of wealth and lust for power; chapter 106 recalls the principles of devotion to God and trust in His Providence as opposed to indulgence in wordly aggrandisement; chapter 107 emphasises that lack of the spirit of human fellowship constitutes the very denial of religion and Divine Judgement; chapter 108 emphasises that the Holy Prophet, who is the highest embodiment of service to others based on love for God, is the recipient of unlimited Divine favours—thus indirectly inviting the Muslims to a life of service to fellow-beings and devotion to God in conformity with the Ideal that the Holy Prophet's life presents; chapter 109 highlights toleration, with devotion to Islam, as the virtue to be pursued, in combination with the virtues emphasised positively and negatively in the preceding chapters just mentioned, by the Muslims in their world-mission relating to the establishment of all that is good for humanity and the elimination of all that is evil; chapter 110 directs to the assurance of the triumph of Truth and emphasises the spirit of humility and godliness that should be observed in victory; chapter 111 reflects the inevitablility of destruction of the forces of evil; chapter 112 lifts up into the appreciation of God concerning such of His Attributes as are basic for faith in Him,—establishment of a dynamic and living relation with Him being the goal towards which entire Islamic activity is directed; chapters 113 and 114, which are the last two, teach the principle that, with all the positive technique taught by the Holy Qur'ãn for the pursuit of godliness, a Muslim should ever remain vigilant against the impact of even the slightest evil,—thus to ensure his progress on the path of godliness and the attainment of the final goal, namely, complete harmony with God.

Here we must record one of the miracles relating to the holy book, to which our attention has been drawn thus:

"Allah has revealed (from time to time) the most excellent Message in the form of a Book, consistent with itself and conformable in its various parts, repeating (its teaching in various aspects)[21] ...."

(XXXIX:23)

The Holy Qur'ãn was revealed in portions during a long period of well-nigh twenty-three years, wherein the Holy Prophet's life passed through very complicated and varied circumstances, and events of very different types took place. Indeed, the situation remained throughout such as to invite discrepancies in the Holy Prophet's conduct and in the projection of principles by him. Had the Holy Qur'ãn been a product of the Holy Prophet's mind it was bound to have registered numerous inconsistencies[22], and those inconsistencies were bound to have been present in it because its piecemeal revelation was recorded once for all on all the occasions of revelation and was preserved as such. But under the circumstances that we have noted, the presence of consistency in it is a definite and miraculous proof of the truth of its revelation, as well as of its preservation, by God.

Now, besides consistency, the conformability of the Holy Qur'ãn in its various parts, as mentioned in the above verse, brings us to the logic

21 The reference here is to multi-dimensional sequence mentioned in the foregoing.

22 Also: if Muhammad (Peace be on him!) had not been truly a Divine Messenger, living his entire life under the guidance of God, his conduct was bound to have registered numerous discrepancies. But we find his whole conduct and his entire career as absolutely self-consistent. Bosworth Smith confesses this fact in these words: "On the whole the wonder to me is not how much, but how little, under different circumstances, Muhammad differed from himself. In the shepherd of the desert, in the Syrian trader, in the solitary of Mount Hira, in the reformer in the minority of one, in the exile of Madinah, in the acknowledged conqueror, in the equal of the Persian Chosroes and the Greek Heraclitus we can still trace a substantial unity. I doubt whether any other man, whose external conditions changed so much, ever himself changed less to meet them: the accidents are changed, the essence seems to be the same in all" (*Muhammad and Muhammadanism*, London 1874, p. 93).

of theoretic consciousness, which, too, is inherent in the holy book, even as the logic of religious consciousness is enshrined therein. The conformability, however, signifies, in the estimation of the best Qur'ãnic authorities, not only uniformity of teaching but also the principle that all the verses of the holy book are inter-related as parts of an intelligible system—whereby the existence of a system of meaning in the Holy Qur'ãn is positively established, as also the technique of the exposition of the system. *The present work is a humble attempt towards the presentation of that system, and the author hopes that he has accomplished that task,—of course, in accordance with his limitations, and not in accordance with the greatness of the Holy Qur'ãn.*

The fulfilment of the demands of theoretic consciousness is contained so richly and so emphatically in the Qur'ãnic Guidance that even non-Muslim scholars, who are naturally devoid of the eye of faith, could not fail to notice it. As examples of this appreciation, we may quote the judgement of two Western scholars.

Eduard Montet observes:

> "Islam is a religion that is essentially rationalistic in the widest sense of this term, considered etymologically and historically. The definition of rationalism as a system that bases religious beliefs on principles furnished by the reason, applies to it exactly. It is true that Muhammad, who was an enthusiast and possessed also the ardour of faith and the fire of conviction, the precious quality that he transmitted to so many of his disciples, brought forward his reform as a revelation; but this kind of revelation is only one form of exposition, and his religion has all the marks of a collection of doctrines founded on the data of reason ....A creed so precise, so stripped of all theological complexities and consequently so accessible to the ordinary understanding might be expected to possess and does indeed possess a marvellous power of winning its way into the conscience of men."[23]

Dr. A. Bertherand remarks:

> " 'To seek knowledge is a duty for every Muslim man and woman'. 'Seek knowledge even though it be in China'. 'The

23 Eduard Montet: *La propagande Chretienne et es adversaires Musulmans*, Paris 1890, pp. 17-18.

savants are the heirs of the Prophets'. These profound words of the great reformer (Muhammad) are an indisputable contradiction to those who seek and exert themselves in putting the responsibility of the intellectual degradation of Muslims upon the spirit of the Qur'ãn. Let them read and meditate upon this great Book and they will find in it, at every passage, a constant attack upon idolatry and materialism; they will read that the Prophet incessantly called the attention and the meditation of his people to the splendid marvels, to the mysterious phenomenon of creation. The incredulous, sceptical and un-believing may convince themselves that the impotance of this Book and its doctrine was not to throw back, eventually, the intellectual and moral faculties of a whole people. On the contrary, those who have followed its counsels have been, as we have described in the course of this study, the creators of a civilization which is astounding unto this day."[24]

24 Dr. A. Bertherand: *Contribution des Arabes au Progress des Sciences Medicales,* Paris 1883, p. 6.

PART IV

ISLAM: THE RELIGION IN TERMS OF THE SCOPE AND THE NATURE OF QUR'ÃNIC GUIDANCE

CHAPTER I

ISLAM AMONG RELIGIONS

CHAPTER II

STRUCTURAL LOGIC, PRINCIPLE OF INTEGRATION, SCOPE AND IDEAL OF GUIDANCE

CHAPTER III

VIEW OF RELIGION AND ATTITUDE TOWARDS EMPIRICAL KNOWLEDGE

CHAPTER IV

STRUCTURE OF RELIGIOUS CREED AND CONCEPT OF RELIGIOUS LEADERSHIP

CHAPTER V

VIEW OF RELIGIOUS QUEST

CHAPTER VI

THE PHILOSOPHY OF UNITY

CHAPTER VII

INTEGRALISTIC MORAL PHILOSOPHY AND COMPREHENSIVE MORAL CODE

CHAPTER VIII

THE INTEGRATED INDIVIDUAL: BASIC QUALITIES OF A MUSLIM

CHAPTER IX

THE INTEGRALISTIC WELFARE SOCIETY

CHAPTER X

INTEGRALISTIC CULTURE AND INTEGRALISTIC CIVILISATION

CHAPTER XI

GENUINE MORAL IDEALISM

Chapter I

ISLAM AMONG RELIGIONS

The Holy Qur'ãn claims that all the problems of human life that relate directly or indirectly to the fulfilment of human destiny, in the earthly environment as well as in the next world, have been dealt with therein explicitly or implicitly:

"....And We have revealed unto thee (O Muhammad!) the Book (*i.e.,* the Qur'ãn) as an (explicit and implicit) exposition of everything (requisite in respect of perfect Guidance)...." (XVI:89)

That comprehensive guidance has been projected, however, under the name of *al-Islãm* ('submission to God')—termed as 'Islam' in popular usage—and on the basis of *Faith in God* and all that it implies. As such, it is *theocentric*, as distinct from the *anthropocentric* and the *nihilistic*.

The terms '*theocentric*', '*anthropocentric*' and '*nihilistic*' refer to three basic attitudes towards Reality that humanity has entertained in history. Among the better-known and representative systems—or, we may call them 'religions' in the broadest sense of the word, the broad[1] classification emerges, subject to certain inherent reservations, thus: systems like Islam, Judaism, Christianity, and certain schools of thought in Hinduism, stand in the civilised sector, and systems like Shintoism stand in the primitive sector, of the first category; systems like Buddhism, Jainism and Confucianism relate to the second; and systems like Marxist Dialectical Materialism and Atheistic Existentialism fall under the third.

In the *theocentric* view *at its highest*, the Ultimate Reality is supra-cosmic, personal and divine. It is 'Being'. It is God. It is the fountain-head of the highest values and ideals. It reveals itself in the Cosmic order, which is its creation. Man is 'from God and for God'. He is the pilgrim of eternity with his source of existence and capabilities in the Ultimate Reality, whose Grace he should seek. His function is to promote harmony with the Ultimate Reality through worship, in order

1 It should be noted that there is a certain amount of intermixing of concepts and attitudes which damage the logic of structural purity in respect of classification. Therefore, only a broad classification with reservations is possible in a summary appraisal.

to acquire perfection adequate to his nature. His ideal is to reflect the Divine Attributes in the mirror of his personality, thereby fulfilling his destiny. His outlook is positive and optimistic, and is grounded in the concept of 'affirmation of personality'.[2]

In the *anthropocentric* view *at its highest*, the Ultimate Reality is intra-cosmic and impersonal. It is 'Becoming'. It is immanent in the Cosmic Order, which consists of the 'natural' and the 'supra-natural'. Man is the child of the cosmos. The 'supra-natural' element in him is the source of his power. His function is to renounce the 'natural', which is evil. His ideal is to efface his personality for attaining freedom from the bondage of the 'natural'. His outlook is negative, because salvation lies through Renunciation. His worship bears reference to ascetic exercises and magical concepts. His ethics is the ethics of asceticism. His goal is the submergence of his personality in the Impersonal Reality.

In the *nihilistic* view *at its highest*, the Ultimate Reality is Illusion, and the cosmos is mere accident. Man is an ephemeral speck of mechanical activity in a chance-order. His power lies in the cunningness what he may be able to employ for 'making the best of a bad bargain'. His ideal is the acquisition of maximum physical happiness, towards which all human struggle is conceived to be directed. The outlook that emerges logically for him is incapable of accommodating any element of hope, because of the notion of double tragedy in terms of the world being a chance-order as well as hostile. His approach to the domain of moral behaviour is possible only through the shifting sands of expediency. His destiny is the annihilation of his personality in the all-consuming Illusion.[3]

We have distinguished the *theocentric* from the *anthropocentric* and the *nihilistic* attitudes to Reality, including not only the first but also the second and the third under the category of 'religion'. That we hve done on the basis that any system of thought which may *bind* anyone to any specific view of life, together with its emotional and ethical implications, is religion, because the very word 'religion' stands

---

2 This statement of the theocentric view is genuinely and comprehensively correct in respect of Islam alone. Because: For instance, Christianity presents the picture of a mixture of certain elements of the theocentric view with certain elements of the anthropocentric view.

3 Ref: For instance, Bertrand Russell's statement in the forthcoming discussion on 'Life after Death'.

etymologically for the idea of being *bound* or *linked* to something. This is how the concept of religion is viewed in the wider sense. Thus, for instance, Ralph Barton Perry says, referring to Marxism and Buddhism, in his *Realms of Value*[4]: "Whether one says that Communism is atheistic or that it has made a god of Economic Force depends on whether one is thinking in terms of a particular religion or in terms of religion in general. The god which Communism denies is a particular variety of God—such as the Christian God. The god it affirms is another variety of universal God. Both gods answer the description of God as Cosmic Power viewed from the stand-point of what men take to be their paramount good. It is clear that esoteric Buddhism as well as Marxian Communism recognises no god in the Christian sense. But Buddhism teaches that Nirvana is the supreme good and that the constitution of things—the view of Karma and ultimate illusoriness of existence—permits Nirvana to be attained. Buddhims is thus a religion in its conjoining of a hierarchy of values with a cosmology; and it can even be said to have its god, if by 'god' is meant the saving grace of man's total environment." (p. 464).

However, taking up the *theocentric view* alone, vital differences exist between the different theocentric systems. In the first instance, these systems are divisible into those which claim to be revealed and those which do not. Thus, for example, Islam and Christiany and Judaism lay claim to Divine Revelation as the source of their guidance, while the theocentric systems of Hinduism make no such claim. Then, as we have already seen, the Divine Revelation which Islam projects is unadulterated and authentic, while in the case of Judaism and Christianity it is adulterated and unauthentic. Again, as regards the 'unrevealed' systems, they are divisible into vulgar (or, primitive) and civilised. Hence, going from lower to higher levels, we arrive at four categories: (1) Unrevealed—of the vulgar or primitive level; (2) Unrevealed—of the civilised level; (3) Revealed but adulterated and unauthentic; (4) Revealed and existing in unadulterated and authentic form.

Religions falling under the above categories admit of comparative normative evaluation in seven dimensions, namely: (1) Concept of God; (2) Outlook; (3) Standpoint; (4) Ideal; (5) Standard of Behaviour; (6) Mission; (7) Programme. It is necessary to undertake it here in order to establish the *nature* of Qur'ãnic Guidance in the perspective of theocentric religions. The evaluation of each category emerges as follows:

---

4 Harvard University Press, Cambridge, Massachusetts, 1954.

I. Unrevealed: Primitive (Shintoism, etc.):

(1) *Concept of God*:	Fetish-worship and Nature-worship, representing the quest for the metaphysical Reality at a superstitious level.
(2) *Outlook*:	Superstitious, rather than rational.
(3) *Standpoint*:	Magical, rather than ethical.
(4) *Ideal*:	Satisfaction of immediate wants.
(5) *Standard of Behaviour*:	Acquisition of immediate gains.
(6) *Mission*:	None.
(7) *Programme*:	Performance of rituals.

Japanese Scholars' Verdicts:

The eminent Japanese scholar, Dr. Genchi Kate, who taught the Shinto religion for many years at the Imperial University of Tokyo, evaluates Shintoism in the historical perspective thus:

"Considered in the broadest historical sweep there are three main cultural stages in the evolution of Shinto. There is, in the first place, the stage of primitive nature-worship or polydemonism; secondly, the stage of higher nature-worship or sheer polytheism; and thirdly, Shinto as an advanced cultural religion wherein beliefs and practices relating to *Kami*-objects have come under the influence of ethical and intellectual influences of a high order. It is at this last named stage that Shinto shows its most definite political pattern."[5]

As regard *Kami*, the key-term of Shintoism, Motoori, another eminent Japanese scholar, expounds its implications as follows:

"Speaking in general, *Kami* signifies, in the first place, the deities of heaven and earth that appear in the ancient records and also the spirits worshipped in the shrines.

"It seems hardly necessary to add that it also includes human beings. It also includes such objects as birds, beasts, trees, plants,

5 Cited in John Clark Archer's: *The Great Religions of the Modern World*, p. 153.

seas, mountains, and so forth. In ancient usage, anything whatsoever, which was outside the ordinary, which possessed superior power, or which was awe-inspiring, was called *Kami*. Eminence here does not refer to the superiority of nobility, goodness or meritorious deeds. Evil and meritorious things, if they are extraordinary and dreadful, are called *Kami*.

"It is also evident that among human beings who are called *Kami* the successive generations of sacred emperors are all included. The fact that emperors are called 'distinct *Kami*' is because from the point of view of common people they are far separated, majestic and worthy of reverence. In a lesser degree we also find, in the present as well as in ancient times, human being who are *Kami*...Furthermore, among things which are not human, the thunder is always called 'sounding-*Kami*'. Such things as dragons, the echo, and foxes, inasmuch as they attract attention and are wonderful and awe-inspiring, are also *Kami*...."[6]

II. Unrevealed: Civilised (Hinduism):

[Note: In respect of this category, we shall deal with Hinduism under two separate headings, viz., (a) Philosophical Hinduism, and (b) Popular Hinduism. This we shall do because of certain very fundamental difficulties. Hinduism is popularly believed to be a consolidated religion and, as such, the oldest among the important religions of the world. Actually, what passes under the name of Hinduism is a collection of different system of religion, and of different philosophies and mythologies, with a strong colouring of the human element in the historical experiences of Asiatic section of the Aryan race. As such, it is a hybrid melange. At best, it is the record of a rich civilisation of the past—a civilisation that had many elements of merit and many deficiencies and even ugly aspects. An earnest student does find there some profound philosophical discussions, which at times shoot off into the fervour of pure Monotheism—thereby confirming the Qur'ãnic stand as to the advent among the Aryans of Divine Messengers the light of whose Message glimmers today, even as in the case of the Messengers whom Judaism and Christianity mention, only through the mists of later distortions. And he finds certain noble moral concepts and words of wisdom and sciences like the science of Yoga. But, he also finds that, unfortunately, humanity

6 *Ibid.*, pp. 147, 148.

cannot benefit from all that any more than it can benefit from the achievements of the philosophers, the psychologists and the spiritualists of other ancient and modern communities, with all the respective differences in outlooks and statures notwithstanding; because: *firstly,* nothing in Hinduism has any divine sanction, and consequently no seeker of God—quest for God being the very essence of a spiritual religion—can place himself under the control of the subjective findings of the Hindu philosophers and sages (which is the highest that Hinduism can offer); and, *secondly*, all that which may be regarded as worthy of appreciation in any sense is mixed up with an overwhelming and dominating mass of puerile beliefs, ugly practices and inhuman social concepts; and it is impossible for even the most radical among the reformers (who have been appearing since the impact initially of Islam and later on of Modern Thought) to purge Hinduism of all objectionable elements in the name of Hinduism itself without creating a new man-made religion. Moreover, unlike Christianity which has the Bible, and unlike which has the Qur'ãn, Hinduism has no single consolidated scripture.

The renowned Hindu scholar and leader, Pundit Jawahar Lal Nehru says (*The Discovery of India*, p. 37):

> "Hinduism as a faith is vague, amorphous, manysided, all things to all men. It is hardly possible to define it, or indeed to say definitely whether it is religion or not, in the usual sense of the world. In its present form, and even in the past, it embraces many beliefs and practices, from the highest to the lowest, often opposed to or contradicting each other."

John Clark Archer, the western scholar of Comparative Religion, observes (*The Great Religions of the Modern World*, pp. 44-45):

> "Hinduism in its vagueness is first of all an item of the Stone Age. It is so ancient....Hinduism has had no founder to furnish a basic message, no early leader comparable with Zoroaster, Jesus or Muhammad....These at least, each in its turn, inspired a 'book of wisdom', a 'gospel', and a 'writing'. Hindus have had no one even like Confucius to edit fully a long, inherited tradition. Strictly speaking, they have had for themselves no such figures as the Jains have in their Vardhaman Mahavira, as Buddhists have in Gotama Sakyamuni or as the Sikhs have in Nanak. In a sense, the founders of Hinduism are legion, their figures as shadowy as 'cloud messengers' of changeful constitution and fitful errand."

However, taking up Hinduism as *one* religion, as it is understood to be, we shall attempt a scientific classification of the basic concepts that constitute its foundations.]

(a) Philosophical Hinduism:

(1) *Concept of God :*	Pantheism with high philosophical fervour, joined to monotheistic approach, on the one hand, and to philosophised idol-worship, on the other.
(2) *Outlook :* (at its highest).	More speculative than religious.
(3) *Standpoint :*	Mystico-philosophical.
(4) *Ideal :*	Individualistic salvation, through meditation and ascetic exercises, as if human life and the world are essentially evil.
(5) *Standard of Behaviour :*	Ascetic.
(6) *Mission :*	Salvation (*muktî*) of the individual from the evil of the ever-repeating cycles of earthly existence.
(7) *Programme :*	Basically mystico-ascetic exercises.

(b) Popular Hinduism :

(1) *Concept of God :*	Nature-worship and Fetish-worship, representing the approach to the metaphysical Reality and grounded in rank Polytheism.
(2) *Outlook :*	Superstitious-*cum*-mystical-*cum*-racial.
(3) *Standpoint :*	Ritualistic and magical, rather than ethical.
(4) *Ideal :*	*Ethically considered* : Preservation of the Social System based on distinctions of race and caste, together with the sanctity of the metaphysics and the ethics from which the said Social System derives its sanction. *Religiously considered*: Deliverance from the painful and inexorable cycle of rebirths.

(5) *Standard of Behaviour* : Adherence to caste-based ethics, as distinct from the universalistic humanistic ethics.

(6) *Mission* : Supremacy of the Hindu section of the Aryan race.

(7) *Programme* : Performance of religious rituals and pursuit of the earthly requirements of life within a caste-ridden-*cum*-autocratic-*cum*-feudalistic-*cum*-capitalistic ethico-politico-economic framework.

III. Revealed, but Adulterated and Unauthentic :

(a) Christianity :

(1) *Concept of God* : Monotheistic, with the concept of a Compound Deity—the Triune God, consisting of three Persons: the Father, the Son and the Holy Ghost.

(2) *Outlook* : Mystical, earthly life being conceived as incompatible with human yearnings.

(3) *Standpoint* : Mystical.

(4) *Ideal* : Salvation of the individual in life-after-death.

(5) *Standard of Behaviour* : Ascetic. In fact, no standard of behaviour or principle of evaluation is needed, because it would necessitate obedience to Law and thus annul the efficacy of Atonement.

(6) *Mission* : To lead its followers into Divine Grace through the mystery of Vicarious Atonement.

(7) *Programme* : Ritualistic and Ascetic exercise for the attainment of 'saintliness'.

(b) Judaism :

(1) Concept of God : Monotheistic, with the concept of a Single Deity—leaning towards Anthropomorphism and the notion of a Racial Deity.

(2) *Outlook :*	This-worldly, adjusted with the vested interests of the Israelites.
(3) *Standpoint :*	Legalistic and Racialistic.
(4) *Ideal :*	Salvation of the Israelite race alone.
(5) *Standard of Behaviour :*	Pragmatic and bearing reference to the interests of the race.
(6) *Mission :*	Welfare of the narrow group.
(7) *Programme :*	Struggle for making the Israelites the dominant race in respect of their being the 'Chosen People of God'.

IV. Revealed : Unadulterated and Authentic (ISLAM alone)

(1) *Concept of God :*	Monotheistic. The Islamic deity is not merely 'god' (*ilãh*) but '*the* GOD' (*Allah*). He is not merely an object of ritualistic worship, but the Possessor of all the dimensions of Highest Excellence,—indeed, of Absolute Perfection. He is the Fountain-head of all Values and Ideals. He is the Omnipotent, the Omniscient, the Omnipresent, the Infinite, the Absolute, the One and the Indivisible God, Who neither incarnates nor has any Partner or Son or Compeer. He is Transcendent in His Being and Immanent in the cosmos through His Love, Knowledge and Power. He is the Creator, the Sustainer, the Nourisher and the Evolver of everything that constitutes the cosmos, equally. He is the Righteous God Who bestows no special favour on any individual or community on the basis of such distinctions as those of race or colour—nay, even in respect of mere formal labels of 'creed'.
(2) *Outlook :*	Universalistic and Integralistic on the basis of spiritual orientation of human life.
(3) *Standpoint :*	Dynamic and Comprehensive.

(4) *Ideal :* Realisation of the status of Vicegerency of God for entire humanity.

(5) *Standard of Behaviour :* Integralistic and Comprehensive, in terms of the concept of 'Fulfilment' and on the basis of the Model of Comprehensive Human Perfection enshrined in the Personality of the Holy Prophet Muhammad (Peace be on him!).

(6) *Mission :* Establishment of all that is good for human beings and eradication of all that is evil, on the basis of godliness and unity of humankind.

(7) *Programme :* Constant spiritual, moral and intellectual struggle (*Jihãd*) for the fulfilment of the above mission in terms of: (i) conquest of the Lower Self by the Higher Self; (ii) conquest of Evil by Good in respect of Social Order; (iii) conquest of Nature for the realisation of 'Vicegerancy of God'.

The foregoing discussion reveals two important facts. *Firstly*, the Qur'ãnic System of Guidance, or, Islam, is grounded in religious approach. It is basically *religion*—religion *par excellence*, in the broader sense as well as in the narrower, or, strict sense—namely, as implying 'belief' in a higher unseen controlling power, with the emotion and morality connected with it'[7]. Hence, it cannot be viewed merely in terms of a conceptual philosophy or a social doctrine. *Secondly*, it is *unique* as regards its normative as well as structural dimensions. In other words, *Islam is religion, but at the same time it stands as a masculine challenge to the generally-accepted notions of religion.* This very basic characteristic of Islam emerges more and more prominently as we proceed in our study.

---

7 *Chambers's Twentieth Century Dictionary*, section, '*R*'.

Chapter II

STRUCTURAL LOGIC, PRINCIPLE OF INTEGRATION, SCOPE AND IDEAL OF GUIDANCE

(A)

Structural Logic :

As a system of Knowledge, the Qur'ãnic Guidance is thoroughly grounded in the Logic of Knowledge, wherein the different knowledge-domains emerge interrelated in a logical sequence that manifests itself thus. Starting objectively: Metaphysics, with its function of providing the world-view and consequently the system of values, stands at the base. Out of it emerges Moral Philosophy which, in its practical aspects, assumes the form of the Moral Code. Expanding into the dimensions of organised society, Moral Philosophy gives rise to Social Philosophy which, for practical purposes, crystalises into the different Social Sciences like Politics, Economics, and Law. Then, from the side of the subject, Psychology and Aesthetics shoot off to constitute organically related complementaries for the 'tree of knowledge' whose roots are in Metaphysics.

Just by Way of Illustration:

When we consider the relationship of *Metaphysics* to *Moral Philosophy*, we find that different metaphysical views lead to different ethical theories under a logical compulsion. Thus, for instance: Pantheism leads to perfectionism, Philosophical Materialism to simple Hedonism, Bio-ism or Vitalism to Evolutionary Hedonism, and Pragmatism to what might be termed as Opportunism.

Similarly, as regards the relationship of *Philosophy* and *Culture : Rationalism,* which consists in the principle that Reason is the avenue of the knowledge of Reality and that the rational alone is real, affirms reality only in the conceptual, the universal, the eternal, the abstract, the necessary, the absolute and the permanent: and, as such gives rise to *Ideational Culture*. As opposed to it, *Empiricism*, which consists in the principle that Sense-experience is the avenue of the knowledge of Reality and that the empirical alone is real, attributes reality only to the 'existent', the particular, the spatio-temporal, the concrete, the contingent, the relative and the changing; and, as such, leads, through skepticism, to *Sensate Culture*.

A proper understanding of this natural and inherent relationship and the resultant balanced and comprehensive journey into the realm of Knowledge leads to a systematic and unitary view of Reality, wherein the fragmentary and partial view-points are modified in mutual adjustments, and a comprehensive and balanced understanding of the human destiny becomes possible.

Then, the higher the point of thought which the human mind may acquire through its exercise in respect of the struggle for knowledge the larger in scope is the *Unity* grasped, and the larger the Unity the higher is the Principle of Integration acquired, and the higher that principle the nearer towards the Truth moves the human mind.

In this connection, the human difficulty—as it has manifested itself in human thought—seems to reside basically in the fact that, left to itself, the human approach is very naturally 'from below upwards', wherein human reason as well as sense-experience find themselves confronted with *Diversity*, and consequently become captives of fragmentary and reactionary views of Reality, to the detriment of human life in respect of the realisation of human yearnings,—as has happened often with the modern so-called 'scientific' thought.

As opposed to this, the view of Reality in terms of Unity is possible only in Revealed Guidance, which originates 'Above'—in the realm of Unity—and thus projects the Whole in its organic relatedness. That possibility is realised by the Holy Qur'ãn in its Structural Logic, wherein Reality is centred in *The One* (CXII:1), Who is the Living, the Eternal, and from where dimensions shoot off in organic 'wholeness' with the base as also among themselves.

(B)

Principle of Integration

Being theocentric in its approach and comprehensive in its outlook, as we have already noticed, the mission of the Holy Qur'ãn is to transform the life of the world with *all* its dimensions into a life of the 'Worship of God' by channelising it into a 'System of Obedience to God' (=*al-Islãm*). It does not endorse the dualistic philosophy of "Give unto God what is God's and unto Caesar what is Caesar's", because everything belongs to God and nothing—absolutely nothing—belongs to Caesar,—in fact, to any creature. Indeed, it is the height of irrationality to believe in God, and, at the same time, to deny His status as the Sovereign of the Cosmos, the Fountain-head of all Values, and the Source of all Guidance, in Whom alone the loyalty of every particle of the Cosmos is centred in the very nature of the case; and consequently the loyalty of those creatures on whom He has bestowed free-will, i.e., the human beings, should also be centred in Him and Him *alone*. And, then, the division of loyalty into parts breeds conflicts, and conflicts breed perversions, and perversions breed neuroses and split-personalities and unbalanced social life.

There can be no two opinions about the fact that it is the *principle of integration* that ensures power, health and life, while non-integration brings about the very opposite. Also, the higher the integration the higher is the measure of the blessings that are obtained as a result. And the higher the integrating principle in the scale of existence the higher is the integration. Then, the deeper we go into Reality, the higher is the integrating principle that emerges before us.

Islam gives the integrating principle in the One True God, *Allah*. Bentham and Mill and the recent pragmatic philosophies give it in the concept of Utilitarianism, which is based on the principle of pure Expediency,—and Expediency is no principle! Hegel and the Hegelians give it in the State deified. The protagonists of nationalism and racialism give it in the Nation deified and the Race deified. The worshippers of the Earth give it in the Motherland or the Fatherland deified. Karl Marx and the Marxists give it in the Economic Force deified.

Islam's integrating principle is grounded in Total Reality. The other integrating principles are founded on discrete parts of Reality. Islam projects the 'Principle of principles', or, the Eternal Principle, which is related to the integration of Reality at all levels, and forms therefore *the* Comprehensive Principle; others put forward at best a principle which relates to one out of the many dimensions of that infinitesimally small part of Reality which relates to the material aspect of human existence on earth. Islam's vision is focussed in absolute depth; the visions of other monistic philosophies are focussed in a narrow view and on tiny patches of what appears to exist on the surface in the immediate physical experience of the human beings.

It is not, however, only the materialistic philosophies that are defective in respect of the principle of integration, but also the spiritually orientated religions of the world, though the problem exists there in a different dimension. Leaving aside the defects in their conceptions of the Spiritual Value, they do emphasise the value itself as basic to human life. But, then, they do not integrate it with the other values, whereby they land themselves in dualism, leaving all the practical affairs of mankind to human ingenuity. In that compartmentalisation, spiritual considerations recede into the background or stay merely ritualistically, and religion becomes imbecile in respect of the practical affairs of human life. As a consequence, the representatives of religion either become the tools of the secular exploiting forces—as has happened in a very large measure in human history, or have to engage themselves in a never-ending conflict with them.

(C)

Scope

Coming to Qur'ãnic Guidance in respect of its *Scope*: Based, as it is, on the Monistic Principle of Evaluation and the consequent Comprehensive Principle of Integration, it covers, on the individualistic level, the spiritual, the moral, the intellectual, the aesthetical and the physical dimensions of human personality, and on the collective level, the social, the economic, the political—in fact, all the dimensions of society,—creating thus a theocentric individual, a theocentric social order, a theocentric culture and a theocentric civilization.

(D)

Ideal

Thus, in the concept of Religion which the Holy Qur'ãn projects, i.e., the concept of the religion of Islam, the following scheme of life emerges. Man's highest merit—nay, his basic function—is the worship of the One True God, Allah (LI:56). This worship is to be undertaken by him, however, not merely as a creature among creatures but as the Vicegerent of God—as a fully-integrated being committed to a cosmic mission. Namely, he has to realise the principle of integration at its highest, because God's Personality enshrines the Perfect Ideal of Integration, and he is His vicegerent. As such, his *worship* should be *dynamic, consequential* and *comprehensive* in its nature; which means that it should not be confined only to the act of *Prayer* but also to: (1) the development of his personality in all dimensions; (2) the establishment of a godly society in which human beings can live a full and integrated life in love, justice and wisdom; and (3) the unravelling of the mysteries of Nature for establishing his status of Vicegerency and for comprehending the majesty and the glory of God.

It is in this perspective that the Holy Qur'ãn makes the pursuit of physical science,—indeed, of all knowledge, and the active struggle for the spiritual and moral emancipation of humanity, and the establishment of social, economic and political justice, *acts of worship.*

and [illegible] (3) the unravelling of the mysteries of Nature [illegible] [illegible] and for [illegible] [illegible] and the glory of God.

[illegible] [illegible] then the [illegible] [illegible] the [illegible] [illegible] of [illegible] and the [illegible] for the [illegible] [illegible] [illegible] of [illegible] [illegible] [illegible]

Chapter III

VIEW OF RELIGION AND ATTITUDE TOWARDS EMPIRICAL KNOWLEDGE

(A)

View of Religion

(i) Fundamental Nature of Religion:

Religion, according to the Qur'ãn, is the *Law of Ideal Human Nature* (XXX:30), which is to be pursued with due regard to the principle of *Balance* (LV: 7,8), *i.e.,* just proportion, correct measure and thorough harmony.

(ii) Fundamental Form of Religion :

The fundamental form which enshrines the concept of Religion in the Holy Qur'ãn is *Islãm* (III:19), which as a religious term means 'submission to the Divine Will' (II:207; etc.), in the sense of conformity to the Divine Plan as enshrined in Nature (III:191; Etc.) and History (VII:176; etc.), and as expressed in Divine Revelation (XXX:8; etc.),—'submission to the Divine Will' being the universal Law of the Cosmos (III:83)

(iii) Fundamental Norm of Religion :

The religion of Islam is based on the fundamental norm of *tawhîd,* or, Unity. This norm consists of a nucleus at the centre and a number of unicentric orbits around it on which the principle of Unity manifests itself at different levels. Thus we have the 'Unity of God' as the Eternal Principle at the centre; with subsidiary unities, which are the creations of the Eternal Principle, at the orbits—unities like the Unity of the Cosmos, Unity of Mankind, Unity of Human Personality, Unity of Faith and Reason, Unity to the Social order, etc., on which we shall elaborate in chapter VI.

(iv) Fundamental Function of Religion :

Being based on the fundamental norm of *tawhîd*, or, Unity, the fundamental function of Islam, in terms of human life on earth, is *Integration,*—namely: (a) integration of human personality; (b) integration of social order; (c) integration of units of mankind divided on the basis of race, colour, language, etc. In other words, that function consists in: (a) the realisation of the ideal of comprehensive, harmonious and balanced development of the Individual and the Society; and (b) the realisation of the ideal of Unity of Mankind.

(v) Form of Fundamental Achievement Envisaged by Religion :

This problem is originally grounded in the views relating to the nature of the world and the nature of man. Hence those religions which teach that the world is evil and that every human being is born in sin—on the basis of either the dogma of inheritance of the 'original sin' of mankind's parents or the hypotheses of *Karma* and transmigration of souls—conceive the form of fundamental religious achievement in terms of 'deliverance from evil'. They stand, therefore, in the category of *Religions of Salvation.*

As opposed to them, the Holy Qur'ãn teaches that the world is good (XXXII:7) and that every human being is born sinless (VI:164; etc.). Hence it emphasises the form of fundamental religious achievement in terms of 'positive acquisition of the Good', as, besides the entire sweep of its philosophy of life, its emphasis on the terms *falãh*[1] (actualisation of latent forces) and *fauz*[2] (success and achievement) affirms. Islam, is thus, the *Religion of Fulfilment,*—and of fulfilment *par excellence,* because it emphasises the acquisition of the Good both in the earthly existence of a Muslim and in the life after death (II:201)

It should be noted here in passing that there is a world of difference between 'deliverance from evil' and 'acquisition of good'. The former is a negative concept, the latter is positive. The former is wedded to pessimism, the latter to optimism. The former bestows a static and effeminate outlook, the latter a dynamic and virile outlook. The former invities to a life of renunciation and asceticism, the latter invites to a life of *Jihãd,* i.e., perpetual struggle against the heaviest odds for the promotion of good and eradication of evil. (III:110; etc)

(vi) Path of Religion :

The Holy Qur'ãn has emphasised the concept of the '*Straight Path*' (I:5), which, in the very nature of the case, denotes the shortest and the most direct path. Then, this 'path' has been defined as the Pursuit of

1 V:38; etc.

2 XXXIII:71; etc.

the law of Ideal Human Nature (XXX:30), which bears the glory of the impact of what God calls His 'spirit' (*rûh*) (XXXII:9). Divine Guidance, in the form of the Holy Qur'ãn and the scripture that were revealed by God for the benefit of the different communities of the world prior to its revelation, forms the exposition of that Law undertaken by God out of love for humanity. The path of Religion consists, therefore, not in mysterious dogmas and magical rites, but in the fulfilment of human destiny in accordance with the demands of Ideal Human Nature and the status of the Vicegerency of God. That necessitates, in its turn, constant exercise in respect of: (a) acquisition of control by the higher self over the lower (or, the animal) self which always forms the greatest obstacle in connection with the pursuit of all idealistic yearnings: spiritual, moral, intellectual, social and aesthetic,—in order to build up human personality in harmony with the demands of ideal human nature; (b) understanding human personality, Nature and History, for the sake of pursuit of harmony in terms of human society; (c) effort for service to, and reform of, the society for the practical establishment of harmony in the social order; (d) subjugation of Nature through the power of knowledge, in order to bring the natural environment into harmony with ideal human aspirations; (e) submission to God, Who is the Basis of all Existence, the Source of all Excellence, and the Fountainhead of all Values, thereby to establish harmony with Him—which harmony alone bestows fundamentally the capability to achieve the human destiny in the true sense.

(vii) Goal of Religion:

In the above discussion, the Islamic goal of religion has emerged in terms of the fulfilment of human destiny, which every individual is *under obligation* to realise in the measure of his personal capability only, as clearly set down in the Holy Qur'ãn: "Allah puts no burden (of duty) upon any soul beyond what it can bear." (II:286). In concrete terms, it means the actualisation, in accordance with one's capacity, of the potential 'vicegerency of God', which has been bestowed on humanity as a whole by its Creator (II:30)

(B)

Attitude Towards Empirical Knowledge Pursuit Thereof : Act of Worship

Says a Western scholar of the Qur'ãn:

"We must not be surprised to find the Qoran the fountain-head of the sciences. Every subject connected with heaven or earth, human life, commerce and various trades is occasionally touched upon, and this gave rise to the production of numerous monographs forming commentaries on parts of the Holy Book. In this way the Qoran was responsible for great discussions, and to it was indirectly due to the marvellous development of all branches of science in the Muslim world.....This again not only affected the Arabs but also induced Jewish philosophers to treat metaphysical and religious questions after Arab methods. Finally, the way in which Christian scholasticism was fertilised by Arabian theosophy need not be further discussed.

"Spiritual activity once aroused within Islamic bounds was not confined to theological speculations alone. Acquaintance with the philosophical, mathematical, astronomical and medical writings of the Greeks led to the pursuance of these studies. In the descriptive revelations Muhammad repeatedly calls attention to the movement of the heavenly bodies, as parts of the miracles of Allah, forced into the service of man and therefore not to be worshipped. How successfully Muslim people of all races pursued the study of astronomy is shown by the fact that for centuries they were its principal supporters. Even now many Arabic names of stars and technical terms are in use. Medieval astronomers in Europe were pupils of the Arabs....

"In the same manner the Qoran gave an impetus to medical studies and recommended the contemplation and study of Nature in general".[3]

Just to speak in respect of the last statement in the above quotation: the Holy Qur'ãn did not merely recommend "the contemplation and study of Nature in general". It did much more when it projected the guidance in respect of the Inductive Method of enquiry, i.e., the Scientific Method; gave the basic principles on which alone the quest of physical science could be established, relating, as it does, to the discovery of identity in Diversity,—the principles, namely, of: (i) Unity of Nature, (ii) Unity of Mankind, and (iii) Unity of Knowledge; and opened the way to the conquest of Nature through its emphasis on absolute Monotheism, on the one hand, and on the Vicegerency of Man, on the other,—thereby causing

3 Dr. Hartwig Hirschfeld: *New Researches into the Composition and Exegesis of the Qoran*, London 1902, p. 9.

4 Ref. Robert Briffault : *The Making of Humanity*, p. 190: "The debt of our science to that of the Arabs does not consist in startling discoveries of

the Muslims to emerge in history as the founders of Modern Science.[4] And not only that. We find therein some very rich scientific concepts, which are of fundamental importance in relation to scientific knowledge. For instance: (i) the concept of "expanding universe"[5], as opposed to the belief in a "block universe"; (XXXV:1); (ii) the concept of a created but evolving universe (XLI:11-12; etc.); ultimately destined to achieve, through crisis, a new birth (XXIX:19; Etc.); (iii) the concept of biological evolution in general (XXI:30; Etc.), evolution of plant life (XXXVI:33; ec.), and evolution in relation to Man (XV:26; XXIII:12-16); (iv) the principle of parity, as for instance, we know it now in physics (LI:49); (v) the concept of the revolutions of planets in their orbits (XXI:33; XXXVI:40); (vi) the concept of the earth as rotating on its axis (VII:137; ec.); (vii) constant movement of the sun towards a goal (XXXVI:38); (viii) the principle of pairs in terms of male and female among plants (XXXVI:36); (ix) the principle of pairs of opposites in "things" about which it was said in the Qur'ãn for the people of those days that "they have no knowledge" (XXXVI:36),—things discovered in modern times, e.g., the positive and the negative in electricity, the proton-electron combination in the constitution of the atom, the 'particle' and the 'anti-particle', and matter and anti-matter; (x) the concept of space-travel, with its difficulties and possibilities (LV:33); (xi) the emergence of till-then-inconceived patterns of vehicles in the post-Qur'ãnic period (XVI:8); (xii) the existence of animal life on other planets and its expected contact in future with the animal life existing on earth (XLII:29)—so on and so forth.

---

revolutionary theories; science owes a great deal more to Arab culture, it owes its existence. The ancient world was as we saw, pre-scientific. The Astronomy and Mathematics of the Greeks were a foreign importation never thoroughly acclimatized in Greek culture. The Greeks systematized, generalized, and theorized, but the patient ways of investigation, the accumulation of positive knowledge, the minute methods of science, detailed and prolonged observation and experimental inquiry were altogether alien to the Greek temperament... What we call science arose in Europe as a result of a new spirit of inquiry, of new methods of investigation, of the method of experiment, observation, measurement, of the development of Mathematics in a form unknown to the Greeks. That spirit and those methods were introduced into the European world by the Arabs".

5 This concept has emerged only recently in modern science, as expounded, among others, by James Jeans ("The Expanding Universe").

Thus, having come to teach "new knowledge" (II:151), the Holy Qur'ãn chartered a new course for the pursuers of science; and in that its function was to stimulate the scientific outlook and the quest for scientific knowledge, and to promote the cultivation of the physical sciences;—and that to an extent that *the Scientific Quest has been made a part of the Worship of God*, having been affirmed as an inseparable complementary of the Religious Quest (III:189, 190). Also, the confirmation by the scientists of the future of what it had taught was to form, in respect of its acceptance as Divine Knowledge, its permanent miracle for the succeeding ages,—even as the proclamation stands:

> "In the time to come We (God) will show them (i.e., human beings) Our Signs in remote regions[6] (of the universe) and in their (own) selves[7], until it becomes manifest to them that this (i.e., the Qur'ãn) is the Truth....." (XLI:53)

---

6 Here the reference is to future discoveries in the fields of astronomy and astrophysics.

7 Here the reference is to future discoveries relating to the human personality in terms of Physics, Chemistry, Biology, Physiology and Psychology.

Chapter IV

STRUCTURE OF RELIGIOUS CREED AND CONCEPT OF RELIGIOUS LEADERSHIP

(A)

Structure of Religious Creed

It is a basic requirement of religion, whether primitive or civilised, and whether 'revealed' or 'unrevealed, to embody its fundamental beliefs in a 'creed'; and the creeds of different religions are naturally different. Besides the differences relating to terminologies and historical perspectives, they also differ in respect of their basic approach to human personality and its relationship with what each religion regards as the ultimate Reality. Among the spiritually-orientated religions—and we are concerned basically with them here—that approach may be fundamentally mythological, or mystical, or ethico-religious. It is degrading if it is mythological. It is enervating if it is mystical. It is dynamic if it is ethico-religious.

The Islamic creed of genuinely, consistently and purely ethico-religious—covering 'this-worldly' as well as the 'other-worldly' Good. It is built up, in the form of Articles of Faith, on belief in seven Qur'ãnic verities, namely: (1) *Allah* (God); (2) the Angels; (3) the Prophets (or, human Messengers of Divine Guidance); (4) Divine Scriptures; (5) *al-Qadr* (or, the 'Law of Measure'); (6) Resurrection; and (7) the Life 'Hereafter'.

Its rationale is grounded in both of its structural components, i.e., (i) the ethical and (ii) the religious.

I. Viewed in the Basically-Ethical Perspective:

(1) Allah is the Supra-Cosmic Ideal of Supreme Good, as the Possessor of Absolute Harmony in all Dimensions of Perfection.

(2) *The Angels* are the Cosmic Ideal of Supreme Good, as possessors of perfect harmony with the Divine Being.

(3) *The Prophets*—all the Prophets of humanity—are the Human Ideal of Supreme Good, as possessors and demonstrators of

humanly-perfect harmony between the human will and the Divine Will.

(4) *The Scriptures*—all the Books of Guidance which came from God to humanity—represent Divine Guidance in respect of the pursuit of harmony between the human will and the Divine Will for the attainment of Supreme Good by the human beings.

(5) *Al-Qadr* forms the basic Norm for the technique of Pursuing the Supreme Good.

(6) *The Resurrection*—Revival after death with the self-same Identity—enshrines the assurance of the attainment of Supreme Good by the human beings.

(7) *The 'Hereafter'*—its concept enshrines the fulfilment of human destiny in terms of the acquisition of Supreme Good.

II. Viewed in the basically-Religious Perspective:

(1) *Allah* is the Fountain head of Guidance as well as of Power, and His Personality forms the Monistic Principle of Evaluation, in respect of the pursuit by humanity of the fulfilment of its Destiny.

(2) *Angels* (who are neither sub-deities nor 'sons' or 'daughters' of God), are the executors of Divine Will, and as such the carriers of Divine Guidance for the entire Cosmos. Their presence demonstrates the fact that the Cosmos is pervaded with Intelligence and Purpose and that its control by God is perpetual. This view is in contrast to the Newtonian view of the 'Indifferent God', the recent view projected in Christendom of the 'Dead God', and the Nihilistic view of 'Blind Cosmos'.

(3) *Prophets* are the human transmitters to, and exemplifiers of, Divine Guidance for humanity.

Here it should be noted that the unique Qur'ãnic doctrine concerning '*Belief in all the Prophets of Humanity*' is related to the Qur'ãnic teaching that: (1) God being One, and mankind being one, the Guidance from God has come to all the human communities since the time of Adam (Peace be on him!) through the Prophets of God that came to them (XIII:7; etc.),—and it has not been confined to any 'chosen people'; (2) it has been—as it ought to have been in the very nature of the case—fundamentally the same i.e., Islam, or, the Philosophy and the Way of Submission to the One God (III:19); and (3) wherever there are resemblances in the teachings of the different religions, they are the remnants of the original Truth revealed by God.

In these Qur'ãnic doctrines of *Universal Divine Guidance* and the *Unity of Religious Truth* emerges a noble and *unique* dimension in the *religious attitude* of a Muslim, which is of tremendous importance for him as well as for humanity. It is the triune dimension of large-heartedness, goodwill and wisdom. Because (1) These doctrines establish in him a rational attitude towards other religions, whereby he tries to view the original reality beneath the crusts of mythology and human interpolations; and possessing, as he does, the Divine Guidance in its pure and authentic revelation, he can undertake a most rational and meaningful probe and research in the field of Comparative Religion, can reconstruct the original religion for the different communities, and can invite them to the same; (2) Knowing, as he does, through his own religion and through history, the unauthenticity of the records of all the pre-Qur'ãnic religions, he is duty-bound to refrain, on principle and not just for expediency, from insulting those personalities of other religions who are considered to be their founders,—which lays the foundation of international goodwill on the basis of Religion from his side. He can criticise, without ill will and only for upholding and distinguishing the truth, the wrong teachings of different religions and the wrongs committed by different religious communities, but he is not permitted by Islam to indulge in insult and abuse of the supreme heads of other religions.

The final part of 'Belief in all Prophets' is the affirmation of belief in the Holy Prophet Muhammad (Peace be on him!) not only as one of the Prophets but as the *last* Messenger of God, who came to seal the Age of Prophet-hood and Prophetic Revelation in the history of mankind (XXXIII:40) and to be the Guide for entire humanity in its Age of Maturity[1] for all time (XXXIV:28).

It is essential to note here that the Qur'ãn does not speak, even indirectly, of the appointment after the Holy Prophet Muhammad (Peace be on him!) of anyone, from within the ranks of its followers or from without, as Prophet of any calibre and in any sense. Also, it does not even hint at the emergence from among its followers, at any period of history,

---

1 Ref. Discussion on 'era of maturity' under the next article of faith.

of any divinely-appointed *Imam* (Religious Leader), or *Mujaddid* (Religious Reviver), or *Mahdi* (the 'Rightly-Guided' Leader who, according to the *Hadîth* literature, will, *in his own life-time and through his personal achievement*, totally annihilate the Jewish Power in Palestine and establish Islam as the Supreme World-Force after the political decline of the Muslims), or *Mahdi*-cum-*Messiah* (which is a recent innovation)—thus blocking the way to the creation, with its sanction, of sects and sectarian Movements around the personalities of claimants to religious Reformer ship for the Muslim community.

(4) Belief in all the *Scriptures* ever revealed to humanity by God fulfils the same function, in terms of 'code of guidance', as 'Belief in the Prophets'. Namely: All the Divine Guidance communicated by God to the Prophets of the world, for the guidance of human communities, in the form of Scriptures, since the earliest times—as a result of which *Muslims* have existed in all periods of human history—has been directed to the basis of ethico-religious fulfilment during the life lived on earth.

As regards the Holy Qur'ãn, it is the last, the final, and the comprehensive revelation of Divine Guidance. Consequently, it performs three functions: (1) it restates the Divine Guidance that had come before its revelation to the different human communities but had subsequently suffered perversion through the vicissitude of history and human interpolation. Thus, its Guidance is fundamentally the same[2] as that contained *originally* in the previous Scriptures (LXXXVII:18, 19); (2) it corrects[3] all the wrong notions found in the different religions, as

---

2 This is the claim of the Qur'ãn, in harmony with its distinctive doctrine of universal Divine Guidance. But, instead of: (a) appreciating the rationale of certain points of resemblance of the Qur'ãnic teachings with the remnants of the original revealed teachings, or with certain parts of historical facts found in the Bible, and (b) evaluating the resemblance in the perspective of the radical differences the explicitly exist between the Qur'ãn and the existing Bible in respect of the *basic* aspects of their teachings, the orientalists are at pains to name Islam as the 'bastard child' of Judaism and Christianity. (Refer, among others, to Prof. Snouck Hurgronje's *Muhammadanism*).

3 This is a great service which the Holy Qur'ãn has rendered to the cause of Religion. But, instead of examining the Qur'ãnic contribution dispassionately, the Jewish and the Christian controversialists, inspite of the absolute unauthenticity of Judaism and Christianity and the indefensible faults and

they came to exist after the introduction of changes; (3) it projects the Divine Guidance in the dimensions that bear reference to the 'era of maturity' in the history of human civilisation, imparting *comprehensive* guidance as a result.

As to the 'era of maturity': Taking humanity as a whole, the history of civilisation presents a picture of definite stages in respect of its evolution, and this evolution has been in the forms of the progressive actualisation of human potentialities in terms of creativity. In this perspective, the present Scientific Era, which the Holy Qur'ãn initiated, forms definitely the 'era of maturity' of human civilisation because of the emergence of, so to say, limitless possibilities of human thrust into the empirical aspect of Reality, which clearly stands out as the 'maturity'-dimension of human civilisation, providing an ever-widening vision of understanding the Reality,—ever wider than possessed by humanity in any pre-Qur'ãnic period of human history, and, consequently, necessitating Divine Guidance in comprehensive measure and directly grounded in the new situation. The same has been provided in the Qur'ãn in terms of the *comprehensive* projection and correlation of all the dimensions of life (XVI:89).

Then, as the emergence of the new dimension of human quest in terms of the conquest of Nature beyond the earth constitutes the completion of the dimensions of civilisation[4], with variations seemingly possible only in correlation within the structure of the quest, the Qur'ãnic comprehensive guidance has also been made by God as the *last* and the *final* revealed guidance from Him.

It should be clearly noted that the Qur'ãn has explicitly qualified the Muslims as those "who believe in that which has been revealed to thee (Muhammad) and that which was revealed *before* thee" (II:4), and does not even indirectly hint at belief in any future Prophetic Revelation (*wahy al-nubûwah*).

---

errors from which they admittedly suffer name the rational and consistent stand of the Qur'ãn as "corruption".

Readers of the present book can very well assess as to how absurd and malicious are the allegations mentioned in footnotes 1 and 2 above. For further edification, they may refer to the Author's : *Islam and Christianity in the Modern World*, published by the World Federation of Islamic Mission.

4 *Cf.* The 'Programme', according to Islam (p. 111).

(5) The concept of *al-Qadr* implies that: (a) the Cosmos as a whole, as also the tiny universe of human personality, is a 'Reign of Law' and not a 'Reign of Magic' (LIV:49); (b) hence, the religious approach should not be 'magical' but in terms of pursuit of the 'law or measure' (LXV:3) which has been revealed in the *hudûd-Allah*, i.e., the *limits* prescribed by God (IX:112, etc.); (c) as a result, the ethico-religious good—as also other forms of good—consists in conformity to measure, or, maintaining the balance (LV:7, 8),—deviation from the measure towards any extreme being evil, the commission of which is 'sin' in Islamic terminology. Thus emerges in the belief in *al-Qadr* the basic technique of pursuing the ethico-religious struggle.

(6) Belief in *Resurrection* after death: (a) lifts up the human vision beyond earthly existence and thus crushes the attitude of earth-rootedness which is the mother of all moral ills; (b) bestows on human values absoluteness, as opposed to expediency, and renders the moral struggle worth-while, meaningful, and genuinely consequential; (c) hence, provides the enthusiasm for moral struggle, in the face of all obstructions and frustrating situations; (d) supplies the basis for the consummation of the reward of moral struggle; (e) establishes the rational ground for the highest sacrifice in the service of all that is good,—including the sacrifice of life, which for a genuine believer in God and the Resurrection is an aspiration of life.

(7) Belief in the *'Hereafter'* relates to the following basic Qur'ãnic concepts: (a) God is the Moral Sovereign of the Cosmos; (b) the Cosmos is a Moral Order; (c) Man has to function on the earth as a moral being with a spiritual base; (d) he has to submit his credentials to the Moral Sovereign, Who is actually the Over-All Sovereign, in order to pass to higher level of existence; (e) hence, he has to face Final Accountability on the Day of Judgement, which will occur when the 'heaven and the earth' have passed through the ports of 'death' into new dimensions of existence (XIV:48).

Finally, it should be noticed that the Islamic Creed is through and through *universal*, and not *sectarian*, because it demands belief not only in the Holy Prophet Muhammad (Peace be on him!) and the

Holy Qur'ãn but in all the Prophets of God and in all the revealed Scriptures that came before in any part of the world.

Closely related to his universalism is the Islamic theocentric Humanism, which has found its expression, in the sphere of inter-religious fellowship, in the following Qur'ãnic proclamation "Say (O Muhammad!): O People of the Book! come to common terms as between us and you: That we shall worship none but the One True God; that we shall associate no equals with Him; that we shall take not, from among ourselves, lords and patrons other than God....." (III:64). The formula of co-operation and fellowship for the promotion of good and the eradication of evil that is contained in this verse is: Commitment of absolute and undivided loyalty and devotion to God and the acceptance of the principle of total elimination of exploitation of man may by man.

(B)

Concept of Religious Leadership

This problem has a vital bearing on human life; because it is related to the relationship with God, on the one hand, and to the character of society, on the other. A religion which endorses the institution of priesthood[5], establishes what might be termed as 'spiritual feudalism', dividing the society into two distinct classes of religious 'masters' and religious 'serfs', and opening the road to the exploitation of the masses by the 'privileged few'. Besides that, it creates a barrier between the human beings and God through the creation of a class of canonised professionals

5 Giving due weight to the basic characteristics that underlie the varied roles played by the institution of priesthood in human history, among the civilised and the un-civilised communities, the concept of the priest as it emerges in its full stature and form is that he is basically a consecrated person, established in an exalted social status in comparison with the lay adherents of a religion—a status acquired on the basis of canonisation either through some ritual or through descent from some particular clan or cause, possessing an unchallengable authority in religious matters, enjoying in the beliefs of the people such powers or privileged position as to be capable in the beliefs of the people such powers or privileged position as to be capable to obtaining from the deity the fulfilment of what he may put forward on behalf of anyone, and therefore the *unavoidable instrument* of the lay-folk for employment in their dealings with the deity. (For a historical discussion, see: *The Encyclopaedia of Religion and Ethics*, Vol. 10; art.: 'Priest, Priesthood').

who become the sole agents for selling the blessing of God, including forgiveness of sins and salvation in the Hereafter. The history of Religion is replete with all this and the attendant evils, wherein humanity has been exploited spiritually, morally and materially—and, wherever possible, even politically, through the establishment of theocracy in the form of government by the priests[6].

What a tremendous amount of misery the institution of priesthood can cause, even in its administrative aspect, to the prestige of *religion* itself, emerges clearly in the ecclesiastical history of mankind. For instance, just to refer to one brief period of Christian history, Will Durant observes in his *The Age of Faith* (New York 1950; pp. 538-540):

".....In 897 Pope Stephen VI had the corpse of Pope Formosus (891-6) exhumed, dressed it in purple robes, and tried before an Ecclesiastic Council on the charge of violating certain Church Laws; the corpse was condemned, stripped, mutilated, and plunged into the Tiber. In the same year a political revolution in Rome overthrew Stephen, who was strangled in jail. For several years thereafter the papal chair was filled by bribery, murder, or the favour of women of high rank and low morality. For half a century the family of Theophylect, a chief official of the papal palaces, made and unmade popes at will. His daughter Marozia secured the election of her lover as Pope Sergius III (804-11), his wife Theodora procured the election of Pope John X (914-28). John has been accused of being Theodora's paramour, but on inadequate evidence.....Marozia after having enjoyed a succession of lovers married Guido, Duke of Tuscany I; they conspired to unseat John; they had his brother Pater killed before his face; the Pope was thrown into prison and died there a few months later from causes unknown. In 931 Marozia raised to the papacy John XI (931-5) commonly reputed to be her bastard son by Sergius III. In 932

---

6 Speaking of the Jewish institution of priesthood, H. Hirschfeld writes: "According to the Levitical code, the Hebrew priest is born, not made.....In order to safeguard the purity of lineage for future generations, the Biblical laws regulating priestly marriages were not only strictly enforced, but also strengthened in various directions.....These restrictive regulations, added to ancestral pride, gradually converted the priestly class into an exalted theocracy which, from the nature of public affairs, at the same time formed the social aristocracy. The priestly family of the Hasmonaeans acquired royal dignity. Later the high priest was the president of the Sanhedrin. Thus power, both spiritual and temporal, and wealth accumulated in some priestly families". (*The Encyclopaedia of Religion and Ethics*, Vol. 10, pp. 322, 323).

her son Alberic imprisoned John in the Castle of Saint Angelo, but allowed him to exercise from jail the spiritual function of the papacy. For twenty-two years Alberic ruled Rome as the dictatorial head of a 'Roman Republic'. At his death he bequeathed his power to his son Octavian, and made the clergy and people promise to choose Octavian pope when Agapetus II should die. It was done as he ordered; in 955 Marozia's grandson become John XII, and distinguished his pontificate by orgies of debauchery in the Lateran palace.

"Otto I of Germany, crowned Emperor by John XII in 962, learned the degradation of the papacy at first hand. In 963, with the support of the Transalpine clergy, Otto returned to Rome, and summoned John to trial before an ecclesiastical council. Cardinals charged that John had taken bribes for consecrating bishops, had made a boy of ten a bishop, had committed adultery with his father's concubine and incest with his father's widow and her niece and had made the papal palace a very brothel. John refused to attend the council or to answer the charges; instead he went out hunting. The council deposed him and unanimously chose Otto's candidate, a layman, as Pope Leo VII (963-5). After Otto had returned to Germany, John seized and mutilated the leaders of the Imperial party in Rome, and had himself restored by an obedient council to the papacy (964). When John died (964) the Romans elected Benedict V, ignoring Leo. Otto came down from Germany, deposed Benedict, and restored Leo, who thereupon officially recognized the right of Otto and his Imperial successors to veto the election of any future Pope. On Leo's death Otto secured the election of John XIII (965-72). Benedict VI (973-74) was imprisoned and strangled by a Roman noble, Bonifazio Francone, who made himself Pope for a month, then fled to Constantinople with as much papal treasure as he could carry. Nine years later, he returned, killed Pope John XIV (983-4), again appropriated the papal office, and died peaceably in bed (985). The Roman Republic again raised its head, assumed authority, and chose Crescentius as consul. Otto III descended upon Rome with an irresistible army, and a commission from the German prelates to end the chaos by making his Chaplain Pope Gregory V (966-9). The young Emperor put down the Republic, pardoned Crescentius, and went back to Germany. Crescentius at once re-established the Republic, and deposed Gregory (997). Gregory ex-communicated him, but Crescentius laughed, and arranged the election of John XVI as Pope. Otto returned, deposed John, gouged out his eyes, cut off his tongue and nose, and paraded him through the streets of Rome on an ass, with his face to the tail. Crescentius and twelve Republican leaders were beheaded, and their bodies were hung from the battlements of Saint Angelo (998). Gregory resumed the papacy, and died, probably of poison, in 999.....

".....The counts of Tusculum in league with the German Emperors, bought bishops and sold the papacy with hardly an effort at concealment. Their nominee Benedict VIII (1012-24) was a man of vigour and intelligence, but Benedict IX (1032-45), made pope at the age of twelve, led so shameful and riotous a life that the people rose and drove him out of Rome. Through Tusculan aid he was restored: but tiring of the papacy he sold it to Gregory VI (1045-6) for one (or two) thousand pounds of gold. Gregory astonished Rome by being almost a model pope...... The Tusculan house.....made Benedict IX pope again, while a third faction set up Sylvester III. The Italian clergy appealed to the Emperor Henry III to end this disgrace; he came to Sutri, near Rome, and convened an ecclesiastical council; it imprisoned Sylvester, accepted Benedict's resignation, and deposed Gregory for admittedly buying the papacy. Henry persuaded the council that only a foreign pope, protected by the emperor, could terminate the debasement of the Church."

The Holy Qur'ãn sounds the death-knell to the institution of priesthood, establishing what might be aptly termed as 'spiritual democracy'. All human beings possess equal human dignity as their birthright (XVII:70) and enjoy the right of access to God equally, because He is equally the God of all (I:1). And because He is nearer to every human being than his jugular vein (L:16), no one needs any priest or priestess in his dealings with Him. He is Himself the Bestower of all Blessings on whomsoever He considers worthy; He Himself judges and forgives the sins of whomsoever He deems deserving; to Him belongs the Absolute Sovereignty and His contact with everyone is direct and constant;—hence, the very notion of a priest or a priestess is regarded by the Qur'ãn as absurd[7]. God's unambiguous proclamation runs through the holy book: "Call on Me; I will answer your (Prayer)...." (XL:60).

Congregational Prayer does necessitate a leader of the congregation. But this necessity has been fulfilled by Islam, not through

7 Says D.R. Mecdonald: "God, Himself, the One, reveals Himself to man through prophets and otherwise, and man, in prayer, can come directly to God. This is Muhammad's great glory. The individual soul and its God are face to face". (*Religious Attitude and Life in Islam*, p. 38).

the appointment of canonised priests, but on the democratic principle that anyone who is highest in learning and piety among a congregation at the time of congregational prayer should lead the congregation.

Not only is every Muslim man and woman his or her own priest or priestess, the transmission of the light of Divine Message is also the obligation of every Muslim, being the collective obligation of the entire Islamic Community (III:110). Of course, the Holy Qur'ãn has projected the concept of specialised workers who should form the spearhead for the fulfilment of that collective obligation (III:104). But, they too have been conceived basically as 'Inviters to the Good' and not as priests.

The religious leadership that emerges thus in the Islamic Community is that of 'teachers' and 'guides' and not of 'priests'. Every Muslim, without any considerations of colour, race, tribe, family, sex, and worldly status, can aspire—in fact, should aspire—for acquiring that status. The qualification he has to acquire for that purpose consists of sound knowledge of Divine Guidance, sound wisdom and sound spiritual and moral personality, as emphasised in connection with the Holy Prophet's Mission (LXII:2). In short, he should be a ***miniature*** *representative* of the Holy Prophet's Personality, and as such should be a spiritual-morally-and-intellectually-illumined person. Whoever acquires this qualification will earn the respect and love of the fellow-Muslims, and even of the fair-minded human beings in general. Therein lies his leadership, which is obviously attained through the democratic process of hard-earned merit. As such, he becomes not only a teacher (***mu'allim***) but also a guide (*murshid*), capable of helping the people not only intellectually but also spiritually,—assisting them in emerging from spiritual darkness into the Light Divine (XIV:1), himself acting through the Light bestowed on him by God (VI:122).

No other category of religious leadership emerges in the Qur'ãnic Guidance. Those who possess only scholastic information, and are scholars of Islam in that sense, and do not fulfil the above-mentioned qualifications, are not entitled to religious *leadership*. Rather, they have been denounced by the Qur'ãn (LXI:2, 3), even as the Jewish religious leaders of yore have been denounced: "The similitude of those who were charged with the (obligations of the) Mosaic Law, but who subsequently failed in (personally acting according to) those (obligations), is that of a donkey which carries huge tomes (but understands them not)....."

(LXII:5). At best, the scholastics can function only as formal transmitters of the information they possess, and nothing more.[8]

In the end, it is essential to note that no religious leader, not even the Super-Leader, i.e., the Holy Prophet Muhammad (Peace be on him!), can function in any way as the substitute for God or as a sub-deity. Also, no religious leader, however great, can possess any absolute authority over the Muslims, because absolute authority resides, among human beings, only in the person of the Holy Prophet, who alone is the absolute Leader of the Muslims for all time, and no one else; so that there is no room in Islam for the creation of sect around personalities.

It is urgent for the Muslim world to pay due heed to the Qur'ãnic Warning: "And be not among those who join gods with Allah,—those who split up their religion and become (mere) sects,—each party rejoicing in that which is with itself!" (XXX:31; 32)—while the prestige of Islam suffers damage after damage and the *millat* as a whole courts defeat after defeat!!!

---

8 As matters stand in the Muslim world today, it is the decline of religious leadership from the Islamic standard in a serious measure that constitutes a major cause of its inability with regard to its emergence from the abyss into which it has been descending since sometime. The remedy for the situation is obvious!

Chapter V

VIEW OF RELIGIOUS QUEST

(i) Nature of Religious Quest :

The Religious Quest proceeds in terms of '*religious experience*'. The Holy Qur'ãn centralises it in the 'Quest for God' (*Jihãd fi Allah*) and tells us that it establishes in the pursuer's consciousness the experience of 'Divine Presence': "As for those who pursue most earnestly the Quest in (or, for) Us (Allah), We surely guide them in Our Paths. And certainly Allah is with[1] (i.e., in dynamic reciprocal relationship[2] with) those who practise *Ihsãn*." (XXIX:69). That living and dynamic contact with God, the All-Holy (LIX:23; etc.) and the All-Wise (II:32; etc.), brings to the pursuer of the Quest, in proportion to the intensity of striving built up by him, on the one hand, *holiness*[3] adequate to human nature—even as a valley or a territory on which the blessings of the All-Holy descend becomes holy (XX:12; V:23; etc.)—, and on the other, *experience* culminating in *basîrah* (i.e., evidence clear as seeing with one's eyes) spoken of in the Qur'ãn thus: "Say thou (O Muhammad!): This is my Way: I do invite unto Allah,—on evidence clear as the seeing with one's eyes,—I and whosoever follows me (practically). Glory to Allah! and I am not of those who join gods with Allah". (XII:108). The Religious Quest is thus basically different from the quests of Philosophy and Science, which relate to the acquisition of *formal discursive knowledge*.

---

1 The Arabic word *ma'a* used in the text for 'with' possesses the emphasis on 'togetherness' and 'company'. It denotes a distinctive form or relationship between God and the Devotee, as compared with the universal and general with-ness of God in reference to everything in Creation.

2 *Cf.* "Remember Me, I will remember you" (II:152), "Verily, Allah helps one who helps Him" (XXII:40); "Call unto Me, and I shall answer your prayer" (XL:60).

3 'Holiness' attainable by a human being is a factual state of human consciousness, and not a mere Idea—a mere concept of speculative thought; and because consciousness is the basic element in Personality, holiness forms the basic achievement in religious quest. This state emerges when the ego, in soaring higher, gets out of the range of the gravitational pull of instinctive urges and passions (LXXIX:40; etc.) and becomes established in the experience of Divine Presence through total surrender to God (II:112; etc.),—acquiring as a consequence, the status of *waliy-Allah* (Friend, of, in the sense of intimacy with, God) (X:62).

In Islamic terminology, the term that emerges for the Religious Quest is *al-Ihsãn*, as laid down explicitly in Bukhari's *Sahîh*: ".....he (the enquirer) asked: 'What is *al-Ihsãn*?' (To that) he (the Holy Prophet) replied: 'It is to pursue the System of Obedience to Allah as if thou art seeing Him (i.e., with the inner vision of 'Divine Presence'); but if it is not possible for thee to see Him (inside thy consciousness), then (this reality should remain thoroughly established in thy mind that) He is seeing thee'....." (Vol. I, p. 12). In the Holy Qur'ãn we find the command: "Verily, Allah enjoins *al-'Adl* and *al-Ihsãn*...." (XVI:90),—*al-Ihsãn* having been related elsewhere in the holy book not only to acts of well-doing to others but also to attitudes and acts that bear direct reference to the practice of self-negation for the sake of God and the attendant purity of the heart and godliness (III:134; V:13; etc.); and we repeatedly come across the theme that "Allah loves those who are *Muhsin* (i.e., pursuers of *Ihsãn*)" (II:195; etc.). Then, the important fact is to be noted that the root from which *Ihsãn* and *Muhsin* emerge is *HSN*, which enshrines the concept of 'beauty'. Hence *al-Ihsãn*, as Imam Raghib al-Isfahani explains, stands in one of its two connotations for "the creation of beauty in one's conduct, which is achieved through beauty in knowledge and beauty in action" (*Mufradãt al-Qur'ãn*, section *HSN*),—thus denoting, as a religious term, the beautification of *Iman* (Faith) and *Islãm* (Exercise in Submission to God); or, as Lane states it on the basis of the findings of other eminent authorities, it relates to the basic Qur'ãnic virtue of *al-Ikhlãs* (undivided loyalty and purity of devotion to Allah—VII:29; XCVIII:5; etc.). and "watchfulness and good obedience" (*Lexicon,* Section *HSN*). All that involves a perpetual conscientious struggle (*jihãd, mujãhada*) on the path of 'Devotion to God' for the sake of establishing purer and purer and more and more living relation with Him,—in one word, the Religious Quest,—the struggle being grounded in the fundamental norm of '*Love* for God' (*hubb Allah*) (II:165) and pursued with utmost regard (*tadarru*') for God's infinite Greatness and Glory (VII:55; etc.).

It is necessary to emphasise here with all the force at the present writer's command that it is the actualisation and the fulfilment of the Quest for God alone which equips a Muslim, according to the Qur'ãn (XXII:78), for becoming capable of 'bearing witness of the Truth of Islam to humanity'—which is his mission (II:143)—and thus *it is an unavoidably necessary qualification, together with the requisite intellectual achievement, for an Islamic religious leader*.

(ii) Standpoint for Religious Quest:

The Qur'ãnic standpoint is *ethico-religious*, as opposed to magical, mystical, ritualistic and legalistic standpoints given by other systems. *Subjectively*, it relates to spiritual and moral transformation of the individual (XCI:9); *objectively*, it is grounded in love for God manifesting itself in love for fellow-beings (II:177; etc.).

(iii) Source of Guidance for Religious Quest:

Religious Quest is to be pursued on the basis of the Qur'ãn and the *Sunnah* (i.e., the dynamics of the Holy Prophet Muhammad's Personality), together with an ever-deepening understanding of Nature and History as repositories of the Signs of God (III: 189; 190; XIV:5; etc.).

(iv) Instruments Employed for Religious Quest :[4]

The Holy Qur'ãn projects two instruments in that behalf, namely, *Faith* and *Reason* (LVIII:11).

Vision of Faith guided by Reason leads to the deepening of Conviction (XXXV:28; etc.), which, in its turn, leads to confident progress in the Quest.

(v) Standard of Behaviour Relating to Religious Quest:

Faith begets *Love*; *Reason* begets *Law*. *Love* and *Law* have, however, been considered as antithetical in the pre-Qur'ãnic religious thought. But, according to the Holy Qur'ãn, they are complementary and should therefore be reconciled (XCVI:1; etc.) in order that a 'sound heart' is built up, which is the demand of Religion (XXVI:89; etc.).

That is so, because: Love relates to *motivation*; while Law relates to *discipline*, which is vitally necessary for human success. But, *discipline* cannot be consequentially *imposed from without*; rather, it should *grow from within*. Hence *Love* should form the *basis* of following the Law.

Also: the ethico-religious (spiritual *plus* moral) approach to life is grounded in *Love,* while the juristic approach is grounded in Law. Hence, because *Love* forms the basis of following the *Law*, the primary emphasis

4 For further edification, refer to our discussion on "*Ethico-Religious Dynamics*"— (Book II, Part, I, Chapter V).

in an ideal religious life should be on the spiritual and moral aspects of human conduct rather than on juristic formalism. It means that emphasis on *Law* should be subordinate to the emphasis on *Love*,—not that *Law* should be discarded. That will ensure healthy development of human personality: Because the spiritual and the moral dimensions of conduct belong to the realm of 'freedom', which renders initiative possible and ensures the flowering of human personality; while the formal, or the juristic, dimension is grounded in 'compulsion', which gives rise to inertia and stultifies the personality.

Hence it is that a much greater portion of the Holy Qur'ãn is devoted to spiritual and moral guidance than to juristics (*al-fiqh*) and the emphasis through and through is on the primacy of the *spirit*, which alone makes the pursuit of the *Law* fruitful (II:177, 263; XXII:37; etc.); while legalistic hair-splitting, which is born of formalistic and externalistic approach to Religion, has been vehemently denounced (II:67-71; Etc).

(vi) Fundamental Ethical Guide-Lights for Religious Quest:

Besides the practice of the entire Qur'ãn ethico-religious system to the best of opportunity and ability, the pursuer of Religious Quest has to fix up some fundamental *ethical* guide-lights on his spiritual Path. These lights are enshrined in the concepts of: Piety, Love, Truth, Justice, Beauty, Wisdom, and Selflessness.

Piety:

Religious Quest is the quest focussed in the direction of the All-Holy. This fact bestows extraordinary importance on Piety (*taqwã*). But Piety has been conceived in the religious practice of mankind in two ways, viz., as *formal piety* and as *practical piety*. The Holy Qur'ãn rejects the former and prescribes the latter (II:177[5]; etc.).

Practical Piety originates in the consciousness of the tremendous seriousness of human life and brings forth unflagging moral earnestness; and it reflects itself in three dimensions, namely:

---

5 About this verse a hostile critic of Islam, Rev. E.M. Wherry, is compelled to remark thus in his *Commentary on the Qur'ãn*: "This is one of the noblest verses in the Kuran. It clearly distinguishes between formal and practical piety. Faith in God and benevolence towards men is clearly set forth as the essence of religion".

(a) An ever-deepening Awareness of the Perpetual Presence of God (LVII:4), Who, besides His other Attributes, is the 'Lord of the worlds' (I:1) and the Judge to Whom account will have to be rendered on the Day of Judgement (I:3),—an awareness which is cultivated through constant and meaningful remembrance of God (III:190-192; etc.) and which compels the pursuer of Religious Quest to act as if he is under constant judgement of the Divine Judge, Whom he can neither evade nor deceive.

The motto that emerges in this respect is: "Act always as if thou art standing before the Divine Judge and witnessing Him; or, at least, that he is witnessing thee." (*Cf.* Bukhari: *Sahîh*, Vol. I, p. 12—*Kitãb-al-Imãn*).

(b) Unswerving attitute of Goodwill towards all Fellow-beings, because the Holy Will of God is in harmony only with the good will (II:195; III: 76; etc.).

The motto that emerges in this respect is: "Always so act that thine action is guided only by goodwill". In other words, the guiding-light is: "Goodwill towards all and ill will towards none".

(c) Constant vigilance in respect of making and maintaining one's self immune from spiritual and moral evil (LIX:18); because then alone the human 'self' can function as a receptacle for the Blessings coming from the All-Holy. (*Cf.*......and He loves those who practise purity". (II:222).

The motto that emerges in this respect is: "Always act with the consciousness that thine goal is God". (LIII:42; etc). That, it may be emphasised, demands utmost spiritual and moral refinement.

Love:

Love is basically directed to God (II:165), Who is the Absolute Good. On the moral plane, it manifests itself in love for the moral good, which projects itself in two dimensions: (a) love for fellow-beings; (b) love for personal goodness, implying that goodness alone should be permitted to reside in the human self.

Love for the good leads to its appreciation wherever found, even in one's enemy.

Thus the motto emerges here: "Appreciate the good wherever found, without any extraneous consideration." (*Cf.* V. 9).

Love for the good also leads to the consciousness of the ugliness of evil, which is the opposite of good. That, in its turn, brings forth hatred for evil.

There, the motto emerges: "Hate evil to the extent of fighting against it." (XXXV:6)

But, 'hate for evil' viewed in the perspective of 'love for fellow-beings' leads to the outlook: "Hate evil, but not the evil-doer"[6]. In this outlook, the evil-doer becomes the deserver of *sympathy* in terms of the spiritual and moral damage that he does to himself. This aspect of the problem of evil evokes in the pursuer of Religious Quest the inspiration and the effort for the spiritual and moral emancipation of the evil-doer[7], as opposed to the spirit of hatred. This outlook found its highest expression in the life of the Holy Prophet Muhammad (Peace be on him!), to which the Holy Qur'ãn bears witness thus: "Haply thou (O Muhammad!) art going to kill thyself with grief, sorrowing after them, if they believe not in this Message (thereby depriving themselves of its blessings)."

(XVIII:6)

It is active sympathy that assumes the forms of *forgiveness*—even when dealing with an enemy, and of *mercy*, which both ought to be practised as the basic principles of conduct.

(XXIV:22; XLI:34-35; XC:17)

Truth:

Truth[8] implies adherence to *Reality*. As such, it is the very salt of life, being the constitutive quality of guidelines (III:17; etc.). It is the light which runs through the cosmos (VI:73; etc.). It is the most basic merit with which God has crowned the Holy Qur'ãn, the Holy Prophet—in fact, all Divine Messengers—, and the religion of Islam (II:119,176; VII:43; XLVII:28; etc.). It is the Attribute of the Divine Being (XXXI:30; etc.). Hence, Truth should be adhered to and pursued without mixing it

---

6 Hating other persons creates spiritual darkness in the moral agent's consciousness.

7 He alone who, among other qualities, personifies this outlook in himself, is entitled to act as a preacher and missionary of religion, according to the Qur'ãn.

8 The Qur'ãn projects the concept of *Truth* comprehensively; employing the term *al-sidq* (truthfulness, veracity) for the subjective aspect, and the term *al-haqq* (reality) for the objective aspect.

with falsehood in the least (II:42)[9]. From the practical point of view, it should manifest itself in human life in two dimensions, namely: (a) personal truthfulness in thought, word and deed; (b) appreciation of truth wherever found.

The motto that emerges here is: "Maintain always the attitude of such strict devotion to Truth and Reality that nothing, not even the fear of death, may have any chance of success in enticing thee into falsehood and un-reality".

Justice:

Justice may be defined as 'given to everyone his duc on the basis of equity'. The Holy Qur'ãn views it in terms of absoluteness, namely, as an imperative which is unconditionally, universally and absolutely binding—binding on everyone, under all circumstances, and in all situations; binding without considerations of sex, caste, tribe, or race; binding without regard to the distinction of Muslim and non-Muslim, or of the ruler and the ruled, or of the rich and the poor; binding even if it hurts one's personal interest (IV:135; V:9; VI:152; etc.). It is the virtue nearest to the virtue of Piety (V:9), which is basic of Religious Quest.

In its widest sense, the *pursuit of Justice* relates to two levels, viz., individualistic and collective.

The individualistic level has two dimensions, viz., justice to one's self and justice to other individuals. Then, there are two aspects of the pursuit in each case, viz., positive and negative. Thus, at the individualistic level, four basic rules of justice emerge in the Qur'ãnic ethics: (a) establish positive devotion to the harmonious development of your personality; (b) remain constantly on guard against all negative factors in respect of every aspect of your personality; (c) give unstintedly to others what is due to them; (d) refrain absolutely from defrauding other in what belongs to them.

---

9 When this adherence is perfect and Truth captures the subconscious state of mind thoroughly, the adherer begins to see true dreams (*al-Ru'yã al-Sãdiqa*) as a manifestation of *al-Bushrã* (Glad Tidings) promised by God "in the life of the Present and in the Hereafter" (X:64). It would be a grave mistake to believe that such a state can be induced merely through 'spiritual recitations', which are consequential in respect of that purpose only when undertaken in conjunction with moral and spiritual purification and integration of the self.

At the collective level, justice takes the following four forms, which have been projected by the Holy Qur'ãn[10]: (a) justice in social relations; (b) justice in respect of the process and enforcement of Law; (c) economic justice; and (d) political justice. The healthy growth of society, which influences the growth of the individual seriously, demands the enforcement of all these forms of justice.

Accordingly, the Qur'ãnic motto emerges: "Always adhere to justice in respect of yourself as well as in the interest of others with absolute sincerity and all comprehensiveness".

Beauty:

The pursuit of spiritual, moral, or any other, Good is good in itself. It is good intrinsically. But the perfection of form is achieved only when it is grounded in the simultaneous pursuit of Beauty, which stands for *grace, balance* and *refinement* in conduct. Thus, Beauty forms the structural component in the Qur'ãnic term for virtue itself, i.e., *al-hasanah* (the Good)[11], and of course it runs through the entire structure of the Qur'ãnic View of Life.[12]

In the Islamic Religious Quest, the primary emphasis emerges naturally in respect of adherence to Beauty in the spiritual, moral and mental spheres. But, what is most remarkable, the physical dimension of life also gets its due to the full—of course, controlled by spiritual and moral values[13] and with the emphasis on *natural grace* as opposed to unbalanced artificiality and sophistication and vulgar ostentation,—in sharp contrast with the view of contempt for the physical in the ideal of 'saintliness' in other spiritually-orientated religious, on the one hand, and with the 'worship' of the physical dimension of life in the modern Sensate Culture, on the other.

Here, the motto emerges: "Always and in all things adopt Beauty as the garb of your behaviour".

---

10 See Vol. II: "The Structure of Islamic Society" for details and references.

11 Ref: "The Critique and Dynamics of Morals" (Book II, Part I).

12 See Vol. II: "The Structure of Islamic Society".

13 Ref. Vol. I: "Art and Morality", and Vol. II: "Duties as Aesthetical Being".

Wisdom:

A human being cannot move forward one step consequentially without *knowledge*. Hence, acquisition of knowledge to the maximum of one's ability and availability of opportunity, stands forth as the fundamental human obligation, and this is what the Holy Qur'ãn has taught.[14] But, *formal knowledge* is only *information*, and does not assist much beyond the minimum level of human aspirations. Rising higher in terms of Values and Ideals necessitates the struggle of diving deeper and with intellectual honesty and sharpness of vision into the System of Meaning which runs through the Reality. According to the Holy Qur'ãn, this struggle should be undertaken in terms of 'Religion' and 'Science' both; and having been undertaken in that *comprehensive* manner, it transforms 'information' into 'experience', and the stage is set for the pursuit of *Wisdom*, which progressively discovers *unity* in *diversity* and enables the possessor to distinguish between *appearance* and *reality* until he arrives at the *Fundamental Unity* pervading the cosmos, which, in its turn, leads him to the *Experience* of *Ultimate Reality* (III:190-191). This is the height of wisdom, about which it has been proclaimed: ".....whosoever is vouchsafed Wisdom he of a surety receiveth abundant good; and none will (truly) grasp the Truth (contained in the Divine Message) save the possessors of Wisdom". (II:269)

Hence, the motto emerges: "Strive for the acquisition of Wisdom, so that thou art able to comprehend the Truth at a level where all doubt ceases."

Selflessness:

The concept of Selflessness is thoroughly projected in the very term employed by the Holy Qur'ãn for him who accepts its guidance, i.e., '*Muslim*', which means: 'the human being who: (a) accepts the ideal of total surrender to God; and (b) pursues that 'ideal actively'. He remains a *formal Muslim* so long as he does not cross from (a) to (b) (XLIX:14). He starts on the road to be Muslim in the proper sense when he crosses into (b). He becomes a *genuine Muslim* only when he undertakes *comprehensively* the active pursuit of the ideal of total surrender to God, which, though it proceeds gradually, definitely implies the *practical affirmation of Faith* (*Imãn*) through its translation into requisite *Action* (*al-'Amal al-sãlih*), elevating him finally to the rank of

---

14 See Vol. II: "Duties as Rational Being".

the *Mo'min* (i.e., the Faithful, or, the Believer in the true sense) (XLIX: 15; etc.).

It implies that the *commitment* of the 'genuine Muslim' is total, expressed thus in the Qur'ãnic *Covenant of Faith*: "Allah has purchased from the Believers their persons and their wealth...." (IX:111). This Covenant enshrines *total selflessness* for the Believer, which is basically not negative but positive inasmuch as it means, in the final analysis, 'affirmation of the self' in God—in Divine Pleasure.

Selflessness being thus a positive state in Islam, adherence to it even at the basic minimum establishes in the personality of its possessor *humility, sweetness, gentleness, large-heartedness, active sympathy for all fellow-beings, simplicity in life, unstinted devotion to labour, fortitude, sincerity* and many other virtues.

From the point of view of Religious Quest, selflessness is the very starting point, being the very basis of Islamic life, subjectively considered.

Hence, the motto emerges: "Always so behave that not the pleasure of thine self but the 'Pleasure of God' is the motivating force for thine action".

(vii) Ultimate Goal of Religious Quest:

Islam is opposed to the doctrine of the Descent of God in Man. It regards the belief in Incarnation as both irrational and blasphemous,—irrational, because it projects the incarnation of the Infinite into the finite, and blasphemous because it involves an attack on the transcendent Majesty and Uniqueness of God. The theory of Incarnation finds its rationale actually in two related dogmas, namely, the dogma of 'original sin', which degrades humanity to the utmost, and the dogma of the physical reality being evil, which renders the human effort for spiritual evolution in the earthly environment illusory. Both of these dogmas are very damaging to the ideal of the spiritual and the moral progress of humanity. They only create despair and skepticism, except for the unverifiable hope in respect of the next life, and there also only for those who may develop faith in Irrationalism and compel themselves to believe in the mysteries of vicarious atonement, or of salvation through transmigration of souls, etc.

Rejecting the above-mentioned beliefs, the Holy Qur'ãn affirms the sinless birth of the human beings and the essential goodness of the world. Going beyond that, it emphasises the 'vicegerency of God' as the status of humanity, and invites human beings to undertake the pilgrimage of eternity[15] in terms of *dynamic* movement towards God (V:38; etc.). Thus it lays down the doctrine of the 'Ascent of Man to God'.

The 'Ascent of Man to God' consists in a spiritual journey, or, the Religious Quest. We learn the following from the Holy Qur'ãn in respect of its progress and achievement.

The spiritually unregenerate person stays in a state of spiritual inertia (VI:122). When his heart is opened to the understanding and appreciation of the ideal of 'Surrender to God' (XXXIX:22), and he undertakes the Religious Quest, he is revived spiritually (VI:122) and his spiritual nearness to God increases (XCVI:19); and as it increases, the harmony with the Divine Life increases; and as that harmony increases, God's Grace bestows upon him 'a Light with which he walks among human beings' (VI:122). Then he continues his spiritual pilgrimage with the help of that Light, acquiring more and more holiness in terms of harmony between himself and God (LXXXIX:28), maturing more and more in terms of the direct experience of Reality, and acquiring deeper and deeper *Conviction* about God (XV:99). In this, the pursuer of Religious Quest attains the realisation of God, on the one hand, and realises himself in terms of the vicegerency of God, on the other; whereby he attains the fulfilment of the highest and the most ultimate yearning of his soul—which constitutes his essential personality—in the state of Beatitude and Felicity. That is the highest possible achievement for the human personality, because of the realisation in it of the ideals of all forms of human consciousness at their highest.[16]

Certain points of basic distinction between mysticism and Islamic religious quest [popularly called Tasawwuf in Muslim History]

Lexicologically, the word 'mystical' has two shades of meaning, viz. : (1) 'relating to mystery'; 'mysterious'; 'sacredly obscure'; (2) 'involving a sacred or secret meaning hidden from the eyes of the ordinary person, only revealed to a spiritually-enlightened mind'. Similarly, the word 'mysticism' carries two shades of meaning, viz.: (1) 'fogginess and unreality of thought (with suggestion of *mist*)'; (2) 'the habit or tendency

15 *Cf.* The concept of '*journey to God*' in XXXVII:99.

16 Ref: Vol. 1: "The Qur'ãnic Conception of Heaven and Hell".

or religious thought and feelding of those who seek direct communion with God or the divine'.[17]

Refined mysticism, as it has emerged in the civilised religions, conforms to the second shade of meeting. And in this respect some superficial affinity might be discernible between Mysticism and the Islamic Religious Quest. But going deeper we find certain very basic differences which are of immense importance.

These differences exist in terms of: (1) philosophy; (2) technique; (3) function; (4) outlook; and (5) goal.

(1) In terms of *philosophy*: Islam differs with all the systems of Mysticism, either largely or wholly, with regard to the teachings concerning God, the World, and Man; and it is self-evident that those differences cannot but influences the structure of the quest most vitally.

(2) In terms of *technique*: All the schools of Mysticism employ as their instruments meditation, contemplation, recitation and asceticism; while Islam employs spiritual devotions to God, and spiritual contact with the Holy Prophet (Peace be on him!) and with the spiritual world as such—all that involving recitation of spiritual Truths as one of the instruments—, intellectual grasp on the Value-System of the Islamic Code of Guidance, study of Nature and History, practice of social morality, meditation, contemplation, and periodic seclusion or 'withdrawal' (*I'tikãf*). Again, the element of asceticism in Mysticism makes its quest possible for only a select few; while the Islamic principle of the practice of Religion in social life and its scheme of placing the basic elements of Religious Quest in the obligatory religious routine of a Muslim[18] makes it possible for every Muslim to undertake it in accordance with his capacity and the availability of opportunity.

(3) In terms of *function*: The function of Mysticism is the annihilation of the animal self, the development of psychical powers and self-realisation in terms of its specific philosophy. The function of Islamic Religious Quest is spiritual and moral integration and development of the 'self' through self-purification, ultimately for reforming the society.

(4) In terms of *outlook*: In Mysticism, the outlook is pessimistic as regards earthly existence, and hence it is passive in relation to it. In the

17 *Chamber's Twentieth Century Dictionary*, section '*M*'.

18 See: the discussion on "The Integrated Individual" (Vol. I, pp. 179-184).

Islamic Religious Quest, the outlook is optimistic based on faith in the goodness of the Divine Plan under which everything exists and every event occurs; and it is dynamic, because the world and worldly life, handled in accordance with the Divine Guidance, are viewed as means to the attainment of human destiny,—which outlook directs the life of the pursuer of Islamic Religious Quest to multi-dimensional and virile activity for interference in the process of history.

The glorious role of genuine *Sûfis*[19] in Muslim history bears historic testimony to this fact. Of all the sections of Muslim society, *only* they and their disciples have propagated Islam in the world; and it is they who have contributed most in respect of spiritual and moral fervour among Muslims. Also, their heroic struggles in the field of political reform form an every important chapter in the history of Islam.

(5) In terms of *goal*: The goal of the mystic is personal salvation. The goal of the pursuer of Islamic Religious Quest—of the true *Sûfi*—is personal fulfilment at three levels, viz., in his inner being, in human society, and finally in God. Thus, it becomes his vital obligation to undertake ceaseless struggle for transforming human society in terms of godliness.

Before closing this discussion, we may refer to the four terms which have become famous in respect of the 'Way of classical orthodox *Sûfi* Teachers'—namely: *al-Sharî'ah*, *al-Tarîqah*, *al-Mã'rifah* and *al-Haqîqah*; and we may emphasise that all these terms are firmly grounded in the teachings of the Qur'ãn.

To begin with: They do not imply four different philosophies or ways of life, but only four stages in the life and experience of a genuine pursuer of *Islãm*.

Thus:

(a) The stage of *al-Sharã'ah* relates to the acquisition of knowledge of the Islamic system of Beliefs and the code of Conduct relating

19 With the awful degeneration of Muslim society, due to certain historical factors well-known to students of Islamic history, the understanding as well as the practice of *Tasawwuf* also has degenerated in more dimensions than one. Also its name has been misused for certain wrong notions and ideas in certain quarters. In spite of that, however, the denial to the Islamic Religious Quest of its rightful place amounts to the very negation of Islam. Also, interpreting *Tasawwuf* in terms of the forms of Mysticism projected by other religions is a flagrant violation of Truth.

to the Path of Islam; and it emerges in response to the primary question: 'What is Islam?'—or, in other words, 'What does Islam demand of a human being?'

The answer to the above question has emerged in the Qur'ãn in all its fullness; and it forms a major part of the present book.

(b) The stage of *al-Tarîqah* refers to the *method* for pursuing *Islãm*, i.e., for travelling on the 'Path of Islam' *meaningfully* and *purposefully,* rather than *formalistically* and *ritualistically*; and it emerges in response to the very vital question: 'How to be a *Muslim*?'—namely, 'What is the *method* of becoming, living and developing as a *Muslim* in the true sense?'

The Qur'ãn supplies the *method* which is enshrined in the verse: "He attains *falãh* who subjects it (i.e., the soul) to *tazkiyah*." (XCI:9). As such, it consists in the pursuit of *tazkiyah*—i.e., eradication of the positive and the negative evils that obstruct or keep in abeyance the development of human personality in the spiritual dimension, and consequently in the moral dimension,—thereby ensuring healthy spiritual growth under the impact of *Islãm*—which operates on the wheels of *Zikr* ('Remembrance of God') and *Fikr* ('Probe into the mysteries of Creation') (III:190, 191), and which ends in the establishment of *falãh* in one's personality (i.e., spiritual development in terms of the harmonious and comprehensive actualisation of the latent capabilities that relate to the transcendental dimension of the personality) (LXXXVII:14). This method is employed in strict adherence to the 'Straight Path' projected in *al-Sharî'ah*.

(c) The stage of *al-Ma'rifah* (or, 'the Realisation', as opposed to the possession of 'formal knowledge') bears reference to the fruits of the strenuous labour (*Jihãd*) undertaken in respect of *al-Tarîqah*.

That stage consists in the progressive realisation in one's Consciousness, through the 'Light from Allah' (XXXIX:22), of the Glory of God, the nature and status of the cosmos, and the true function and destiny of the human being (III:191),—in short, of the Truth of Islam and all that it stands for. In other words, it consists in achieving *basîrah* spoken of in XII: 108; thereby rising to the most meritorious status, with reference to this world's life, of becoming the '*bearer of witness*' of the Truth of Islam to humanity (II:143).

(d) The stage of *al-Haqîqah* (or, 'the Reality') forms actually the highest level of *al-Ma'rifah*.

That stage is said to be attained when the Light that God establishes in His Devotee (*'abd*) (XXXIX:22) illumines all the dimensions of his Consciousness to an extent that he lives and moves *only* under the impact of the Light (VI:122), and not through his Desire (LXXIX:40). At that level of experience, his ego transcends, in terms of its approach to the reality of Existence, the phenomenological level of 'Diversity' and becomes focussed in the realm of 'Unity'—'Unity' being the *haqîqah* (reality) of Existence.

The above facts may be briefly stated in other words thus: The basic function of Islam is to *transform* the human personality on the basis of *Imãn bi Allãh* (Faith in God). That transformation is, in the very nature of the case, *internal process*. As regards *al-Sharî'ah*, it is the law relating to the 'Straight Path' of Islam. But that Path, like every path as such, is meant for undertaking a journey to a goal—the goal in its case being God (II:156). Now, travelling *voluntarily* towards the goal, which Islam emphasises, necessitates: (a) travelling with vigilance and personal enthusiasm and pleasure, which alone enables a person to face the hazards and hardships of journey with equanimity and steadfastness; and (b) proceeding in the journey *meaningfully* and *consequentially*. It is, however, in the very nature of formal Law, even though it may have divine sanction, that, in respect of transformation of personality, it can, by itself, bring about only *superficial* results, which do not endure under the strains and stresses of human life. Then, being externally imposed, it imparts the impression of being a 'burden' rather than a 'pleasure'. Also, the Instinctive Self—which, unless fixed in subjection to the Higher Self, acts normally as the dominating force in human life—always tries to evade the 'Law' in numerous ways. Hence, it is necessary that *al-Sharî'ah* should be *internalised*. Namely, it should be assimilated in *personal experience* as best as possible in every individual case—rather than remaining an imposition 'from outside'—, any meaningful transformation of personality being impossible in the latter case. *Internalisation,* in its turn, demands the adoption of a method (*al-Tarîqah*) and actual meaningful journey (*sulûk*) in the realm of experience. Then, as the transformation proceeds, the appreciation of the Truths that Islam has taught begins to deepen in terms of personal realisation (*al-Ma'rifah*)—realisation with total Consciousness and not merely rationalistic appreciation through discursive thought, which can never provide unshakable *Imãn* (Faith), and realisation not only in respect of the physical problems of human life but, more so—and that is important—in respect of the metaphysical problems, which are of the most basic importance in the Islamic scheme of Guidance. That realisation brings the earnest *Muslim* progressively closer and closer to the understanding of the Reality (*al-Haqîqah*). That understanding attains in due course a standard level when a *Muslim's* Consciousness becomes *fixed* on *Allah*, the Really-Real.

Finally, it may be emphasised that a religion without Religious Quest is like a body without a soul; and, as a modern psychologist has remarked: "A man with a religion purely of the rational type would be in a worse position than the devils". (Thouless: *Psychology of Religion*, p. 90).

Chapter VI

THE PHILOSOPHY OF UNITY

The Holy Qur'ãn has laid the greatest emphasis on the concept of Unity (*Tawhîd*). It is not found there, however, merely as a concept among concepts but as an all-pervading principle which governs all the fundamental domains of human faith and action. As such, it is vitally necessary to understand it in all its dimensions for the sake of understanding the basic Qur'ãnic approach to the vital human problems.

(i) Unity of God :

The Qur'ãnic view of life is grounded in the purest monotheism—the doctrine of the *Unity* of God. God is One. He is indivisible, and He has no partner in the godhead. He is the Reality. He is all-in-all. Belief in Him demands indivisible loyalty and devotion to Him. This emancipates the human beings from every cosmic and earthly bondage and elevates them to the highest pinnacle of glory.

(ii) Unity of the Universe :

The universe has come into existence through creation and God alone is its Creator. Therefore, it is a *unity*—in existence as well as in purpose. And, as such, it is a cosmos and not a chaos. It is a Reign of Law and not a Chance-order. Moreover, it is a Moral Order and not an amoral conglomeration of wayward particles.

Subjectively pitched on the denial of the existence of God by hook or by crook, the materialistic philosophies assume,—*assume* only, because they have no *proof*—the origin of the world in *chance*—a *ghostly* and *meaningless* term *in that respect*. Postulation of chance shuts the door to the affirmation of any meaning, or of the necessary existence of a Monistic Principle as the starting point. But the affirmation of a Meaningful Monistic Principle is the condition of believing in the universe as a *cosmos*, as opposed to *chaos*; and the affirmation of the universe as a *cosmos* is necessary for regarding the human life as *meaningful*. Then, unless human life is *meaningful*, all talk of philosophy, science, economics, politics, social improvement, justice and truth is, to say the least, beside the point.

The principle of Evolution may be presented by the Materialists as the monistic principle underlying the working of the cosmos. But, how, where, why and by whom was that process originated? Evolution remains devoid of any genuine meaningfulness without satisfactory answers to those questions? Indeed, it remains a blind process, even though we may notice some method in it. The difficulties inherent in the hypothesis of Evolution have been commented upon by an eminent French scientist thus:

"One of the greatest successes of modern science was to link the fundamental Carnot Clausius law (also called the second law of thermodynamics[1]), key-stone of our actual interpretation of the inorganic world, with the calculus of probabilities. Indeed, the great physicist Boltzmann proved that the inorganic, irreversible evolution imposed by this law corresponded to an evolution toward more and more 'probable' states, characterized by an ever increasing symmetry, a levelling of energy. The universe, therefore, tends towards an equilibrium where all the dis-symmetries existing today will be flattened out, where all motion will have stopped and where total obscurity and absolute cold will reign. Such will be the end of the world—theoretically.

"Now, we men at the surface of the earth are witnesses to another kind of evolution: that of living things. We have already seen that the laws of chance, in their actual state cannot account for the birth of life. But now we find that they forbid any evolution other than which leads to less and less dis-symmetrical states, while the history of the evolution of life reveals a systematic increase in dis-symmetries, both structural and functional. Furthermore, this trend can hardly be attributed to a 'rare fluctuation' destined to be ironed out statistically, as it has manifested itself steadily for over one thousand million years (probable age of life on this globe), and as the dis symmetries, gloriously unconcerned about the law set by man, became greater as eons passed by until they culminated in the brain of man.

"Once more we repeat that there is not a single fact or a single hypothesis, today, which gives an explanation of the birth of life or of natural evolution. As far as the origin of life is concerned, we have briefly studied the problem in the first part of this book. Willy-nilly, we are, therefore, obliged either to admit the idea of transcendent intervention, which the scientist may as well call God as anti-chance, or to simply recognize that we know nothing of these questions outside of a small

---

1 This law can be worded as follows: An isolated material system can never pass twice identically through the same state. Every successive state entails a definite decrease in its available energy. Hence its irreversibility.

number of mechanisms. This is not an act of faith, but an undisputed scientific statement."[2]

In the hypothesis of the Dialectical Process also the Materialists fail to see that the emphasis should lie not on the process as such but on the monistic *principle* inherent in it. If the world-process is conceived to have started with the simultaneous emergence, through *chance*, of the thesis and the anti-thesis, leading through their interaction to synthesis, that would explain nothing. If it is said that only a thesis emerged first and the anti-thesis was born out of it, that would give us a monistic principle at the start. But the emergence of the original thesis by *chance* makes the entire process blind and does not provide any sanction for any meaningful philosophy of life. The fact is that if it is inferred on the basis of certain phenomena that the world-process consists in repetition *ad infinitum* of a triad in terms of 'thesis—anti-thesis—synthesis', then we are compelled to accept the monistic principle as the controlling force running through the process, because of the culmination of the interaction of the 'thesis' and the 'anti-thesis' in 'synthesis' everytime that the cycle is conceived to be repeated,—the repetition giving to the world-process the form of a chain wherein every new 'synthesis' assumes the form of two prongs in terms of 'thesis' and 'anti-thesis' that finally merge themselves into a 'synthesis'. In other words, dualism is repeatedly reducing itself into monism. This gives the clue to the existence of a monistic principle as the starting point and of the spirit of 'monism' pervading the dialectic.

The Qur'ãn also speaks explicitly, and not just implicitly, of the presence of the dialectic in the world-process in terms of the perpetual conflict of the 'Reality' and the 'unreality', or of Truth and Falsehood (XXI:18; etc.), and it emphasises its importance for human beings in its ethico-religious dimensions. It affirms its origin and starting point, however, not in chance, nor in a blind monistic principle, but in the Will of the Supreme Being who possesses all the attributes of Perfection.

It may also be observed in passing that while the so-called Scientific Materialism emphasises the transformation of Quantity into Quality as the mode of the world-process, the Qur'ãn emphasises the transformation of Quality into Quantity. The former view was actually built on certain wrong scientific notions of the nineteenth century in respect of Matter, which have now undergone radical change lending ever-growing support to the Qur'ãnic view.

---

2 Lecomte du Nouy: *Human Destiny*, pp. 41, 134.

We might state the Qur'ãnic view thus: Because God is the Absolutely-Transcendental Being, His fundamental Attribute is 'Absolute Quality'. The cosmos has emerged in existence, in terms of evolutionary creation—as opposed to 'spontaneous' creation—through the activity of His Will. Quality is 'intangible'. Quantity relates to tangibility. The world-process is the progressive crystallisation of intangibility into tangibility. The intangible is spaceless and timeless,—we may call it 'Idea' in the fundamental sense. The tangible is spatio-temporal. We know that we proceed progressively towards intangibility as we move from 'appearance' to 'reality' in the physical analysis of Matter, which means that intangibility, or spacelessness and timelessness, or Qualitativeness, is the basis of the existence of Matter.

(iii) Principle of 'Unity' in Respect of the Relation of God with the Cosmos:

According to the Qur'ãn: God is Eternal and Absolute, and the cosmos is Transient and Relative. Now, the Relative is not the Absolute. But it has originated in the Will of the Absolute and is sustained by the Absolute. Thus, the Relative has no independent existence of its own, while the Absolute neither *excludes* nor *includes* the Relative. (*Cf.* The philosophical doctrine of the "Ahles-Sunnah wal Jamã'ah": *Lã 'ain wa lã ghair*).

(iv) Unity of Life :

Taking 'life' in the universe as a whole, or '*life*' as such, all 'life' forms a *unity*. In other words: Because the Holy Qur'ãn projects the universe as an organic whole which has come into existence through the unitary action of the Divine Will, all the projections and manifestations of 'life' exist within a single unitary evolutionary principle—human life being distinguished as unique and over-powering because it functions within the framework of Personality.

With respect to the human being, as such, his life before his birth on the earth, his earthly life, and his life after death—all these three phases form a *unity*. Indeed, life is tied to a continuous evolutionary process.

(v) Unity of the 'Natural' and the 'Supernatural' :

The Basis of Existence for all phenomena and things in the entire universe being *one*, and the Source of all laws pertaining to every aspect and every part of the universe being *one*, the 'natural' and the 'supernatural' are only two levels of the activity pervading the cosmos, involving no contradiction. The distinction is actually grounded only in the human framework of reference.

(vi) Unity of Knowledge :

Because the universe is a *unity*, knowledge should be pursued in terms of '*unity*' in the sense that it should form one 'Whole'. The different branches of knowledge should be viewed in the relationship of interdependence. This leaves no ground in the Qur'ãnic view of knowledge for the time-honoured division in terms of 'religious' and 'secular'.

(vii) Unity of Faith and Reason :

It is not, however, only the different branches of knowledge that are complementary among themselves. The time-ḥonoured dichotomy of Faith and Reason, which has played havoc in the history of Christian West, is also a false notion. Cognition (knowing) and conation (feeling) are not antithetic, both being the dimensions of the same human Consciousness. Faith and Reason have also, therefore, to go together: to function in *unity*. Faith without Reason lands human beings in superstition. Reason without Faith deprives humanity of the highest values. Taking up this problem in the very first Revelation, the Holy Qur'ãn has emphasised the *unity* of Faith and Reason and has projected the ideal of Rationally-orientated Faith.

(viii) Unity of Truth :

God has stated the basic Truth in His Revealed Guidance, and has invited His vicegerents, the human beings, to experience the Truth through their observation. Truth does not have different facets; it is one-sided. But its observation through the finitude of human senses and reason gives only partial views which relate to infinitesimally small portions of the whole and are, in the very nature of the case, discrete. However, even the minute and partial views, if interpreted in the scientific spirit, i.e., objectively and without the distortion of the image through the intrusion of subjectivity, are bound to corroborate the Revealed Truth. In other words, true Religion and true Scientific Approach to Truth stand in the relation of *unity*.

(ix) Unity of Religion :

The Holy Qur'ãn teaches that, God being One and humanity being one, Divine Guidance in terms of Religion has not been confined to any particular chosen race. Rather, entire humanity has been blessed with it during the course of human history (XIII:7; etc.). Not could it be different for different communities. This gives the principle of *unity* in respect of Divine Revelation. Also, this teaching provides the venue of appeal to the religions of the world for casting off the shells of later accretions, perversions and distortions brought into existence by human ignorance, ingenuity, or vested interests, and returning to the original Message in the light of reason and with the assistance of the Qur'ãnic Revelation,—finally bringing about the *unification* of religions in the Divine Truth and paving the way to the unity of mankind.

(x) Unity of 'Love' and 'Law' :

'Love' functions as the 'soul' and 'Law' functions as the 'body' of the human code of Conduct; and, in the Qur'ãnic view, genuine flowering of the human personality is possible only when 'Love' and 'Law' function in organic *unity* in the life of a person.

(xi) Unity of Mankind :

Coming to human beings: God, the One, has created them all; and He originated the existence of the human species on the earth through one original pair of man and woman. This gives us the Qur'ãnic principle of the *Unity* of Mankind, in which all prejudices or race, colour, caste and sex are obliterated and the only principle of distinction in respect of status in *achievement* in terms of spiritual and moral character and knowledge. As regards respect for human dignity, it is, in the Qur'ãnic view, the birthright of every human being.

(xii) Principle of Unity in Respect of the Sexes :

Although man and woman are different in respect of some of their functions, and consequently in some of their organs, they have emerged, according to the Holy Qur'ãn, from a single primeval Self. In their basic human nature and status, therefore, they are *united in the bond of humanity*:—they are one and the same, and even in their functions they stand out as complementaries and not as the negation of one another. Consequently both possess equal human dignity.

(xiii) Unity of Human Personality :

With reference to the human personality, the Holy Qur'ãn emphasises its organic wholeness. The human being is a *unitary being*, with the soul, the mind and the body and their different dimensions, of existence and behaviour, forming an integrated organic Whole—a *Unity*. This Qur'ãnic view gives rise to the Qur'ãnic ideal of integration, wherein all the dimensions of human personality: the physical, the moral, the rational, the aesthetical and the spiritual, have to be developed comprehensively and harmoniously in order to achieve the Divine Purpose with regard to human destiny.

It may be emphasised here that similar to what we have noticed in the case of the cosmos, the human being also emerges, in the Qur'ãnic view, as a being who is 'spaceless' and 'timeless' in his origin and constitution. Namely, he originated in a dimension of existence which transcends 'space' and 'time', or, in other words, in the transcendental dimension—a dimension akin to the fifth dimension of the five-dimensional continuum in which we find an electron during its jump from one orbit to the other. And his *essential* constitution is in terms of what is called 'soul' in popular language. As for the birth and the death of the human being on the earth, the Qur'ãnic view may be stated in scientific terms thus. In respect of birth: The soul projects itself, under the Will of God, in the 'dimension of time', bringing about the existence of the *mind*, which is temporal. Then, beyond that, it projects itself into the 'dimension of space', bringing about the existence of the *body*, which is spatio-temporal. At the time of death, the soul resumes its purely transcendental state of existence,—of course, carrying within itself the effects of its earthly career.

(xiv) Unity in Respect of 'Freedom' and 'Determinism' :

According to the Holy Qur'ãn, man is neither the abject slave of inexorable Fate, as the ancient oriental philosophy would have it, nor completely self-determined —the sole maker of his destiny, as the atheistic existentialism of the modern West teaches. Affirmation of inexorable Fate bars the way to all moral struggle,—in fact, to all struggle for improvement, because every sentiment and every idea and every desire of every human being is conceived to be predestined. On the other hand, the view that man is completely free plunges him in the terror and the agony of being infinitely lonely—and that with all the human weakness—in what is regarded as an alien and hostile world. Both of these views end in the philosophy of Pessimism, which is pure poison in relation to human happiness and progress.

The Holy Qur'ãn steers clear of both the above-mentioned stand-points and gives us a view whereby it harmonises the concepts of Freedom and Determinism. It teaches that when God created man, He *endowed* him with personality as well as freedom—a freedom which, though not absolute, is, nevertheless, adequate to human nature. Then it teaches that God has not abandoned man to himself. Man has been made the vicegerent to function in harmony with God, Who is the real Architect of man's destiny. As such, God is man's constant 'companion', and God and man both participate in the making of man's destiny. This 'Mutual Participation' forms the medium wherein Freedom and Determinism stand out in *unity*.[3]

(xv) Unity in Basic Social Life :

The distinctions of the clergy and the laity, of the wealthy and the poor, of the superior caste and the inferior caste, and of the superior race and the inferior race (based on the inhuman dogmas of the 'chosen people' or of the supremacy of one colour of human skin over an-other), have plagued the life of human communities—and that not only among those who have believed in the plurality of gods, like the Hindus, but also among those who have been the so-called upholders of Monotheism, like the Jews and the Christians. Negatively, through the abolition of the institution of priesthood, and positively through the creation of a classless, casteless and non-racial society, the Holy Qur'ãn has sounded the death-knell to all such evil distinctions. It has envisaged a society dedicated to godliness, and it has laid down a value-system wherein the only criteria of superiority are greater spiritual refinement, moral goodness and knowledge. This value-system reduces all the conflicting material distinctions into *unity*.

(xvi) Unity in Terms of Politics :

The establisment of the state is rooted in organisation, and organisation necessitates the emergence of the super ordinate, on the one hand, and the subordinate, on the other. The super ordinate is the repository of the coercive authority and its function is to command to *rule*. As opposed to it, the function of the subordinate is to obey—to be *ruled*. This gives rise to a situation of conflict if supremacy is vested in the state-authority. The ancient thinkers have believed for long in the Divine Right of Kings. They have conceived the kings as above Law. Among the moderns, Hegel has idolised the State to the extent of its being infallible,

3 *Cf.* The position of *Ahles-Sunnah wal-Jamã'ah* in terms of '*bain al-Jabr wa al-Ikhtiyãr*'.

unquestionable and unaccountable. Again, the Marxist State, through its iron regimentation, reduces the subordinates to mere automatons. There, the politbureau is all-in-all.

The Holy Qur'ãn resolves this ugly and painful situation by *uniting* the super ordinate and the subordinate *in subjection* to the principle of the Supremacy of the Law. No human being has a right to rule over another human being. It is the authority of Law—the Law of God, Who alone is the Sovereign—that should reign supreme.

It was this unifying principle which was proclaimed in his inaugural address by the first Caliph of Islam, Abu Bakr the Illustrious (in whom God's Pleasure abides!). He said: "Obey me so long as I obey Allah and His Messenger (Muhammad). But if I deviate from obedience to Allah and His Messenger, obedience to me remains binding on you no more". (Ref: Dr. M.S. Jung: *The Administration of Justice in Muslim Law*, p. vi).

(xvii) Unity of 'Church' and 'State' :

A state which functions without any idealistic foundations is only an expediency-based crude 'police organisation'; and a state which concerns itself only with the physical needs of its citizens, leaving the spiritual and moral needs to a parallel organisation, calling it the 'Church', damages the cause of its citizens. Because, it either breeds a state of the conflict of ideals or promotes the relegation of the fulfilment of spiritual and moral needs to a position of no importance. Being firmly committed to the principle of *Unity*, the Qur'ãn projects the concept of the state in terms of the organised effort of the people for a comprehensive and integrated fulfilment of all the requirements and needs of healthy, progressive and vibrant collective existence. Hence, the Islamic state functions in terms of the *unification* of the 'Church' and the 'State' and shoulders the responsibility of protecting and promoting not only the physical interests but also the spiritual and the moral interests of its citizens.

(xviii) Unity in Terms of Economics :

All human systems and institutions aim at realising some human value or values. Thus capitalism is grounded in the value of Freedom. It was this value which emerged as the highest, by way of reaction to the authoritarianism of the Christian Church, when Europe was blessed with the Renaissance and the Industrial Revolution. The effort to realise this value brought about revolutionary changes in the fields of general social life, politics and economics. In the general social life emerged the phenomenon of increasing respect for anti-authoritarianism leading to disrespect for all authority, including that of the parents, the teachers and the church. This disrespect has assumed enormous proportions today, leading almost to anarchy. In the political field, autocracy gave way to democracy, which became a tremendous source of strength for those Western communities wherein it had the proper opportunity for flourishing in a healthy manner. In the field of economics, the value of Freedom was realised in terms of 'free enterprise'—the *laissez-faire*, which finally built up the giant of Monopoly Capitalism. This process gave tremendous economic power to the advanced states of Europe and America. At the same time, however, it helped to undermine a very important human value, i.e., the value of Equality. Such a result was inherent in the philosophy of Capitalism and could not be avoided.

However, it is human nature to yearn for the realisation not only of the value of Freedom but also of the value of Equality, and of several other values besides. Hence a severe reaction come, and the child of this reaction was Communism, or, the Scientific Socialism of Karl Marx. But, very unfortunately, this reaction was a blind reaction. It was even a crude reaction. Because, without challenging the sincerity and the academic attainments of Karl Marx, it is evident that his mind could not penetrate the true nature of the evil which he wanted to eradicate, and, in his reactionary mood, he just picked up the value of Equality, as a superficial person would do, and made it the foundation of this social philosophy. But with what result? There are so many states in the world today who have adopted the Marxist-Leninist ideology. Everywhere the effort to realise the value of Equality in terms of Scientific Socialism has invariably resulted in depriving the people of the value of Freedom—and that completely. This tragedy, again, like the tragedy of Capitalism, was inherent in the situation.

The truth of the matter is: If a society adopts Freedom as the fundamental value, there will be no Equality. Similarly, if a society adopts Equality as the fundamental value, the value of Freedom will vanish into thin air.

But the realisation of both the values: Freedom and Equality, is necessary for the proper development of the human communities. The question is: how to bring this about?

The Holy Qur'ãn has supplied the answer in its philosophy of Unity, wherein it teaches the establishment of harmonious *union* between the values of Freedom and Equality through the adoption of the value of Justice as the fundamental value on which the human social order should be founded. It is evident that if this is done, the dichotomy of Freedom and Equality will be resolved, and it will be possible to realise both of these values in *due proportion* and without sacrificing either. As a consequence, a synthesis of the merits of free enterprise and controlled economy will emerge, making it possible to establish a welfare society, which will function on the principles, not of class-war or of exploitation of the working class by the moneyed class, but of love, harmony, human fellowship, moral excellence and justice, will ensure a just distribution of wealth on the basis of just reward for *labour*, *talent* and *achievement*, and will guarantee to every citizen the basic needs of life in terms of food, clothing, shelter, medical assistance and education. Therein, no one, to whatever station in life he may belong, will be wronged in any manner, and slavery of all types between man and man will vanish—freedom and equality in respect of human dignity being accepted as the birthrights of every human being.

This is what the Qur'ãnic philosophy of Unity envisages in respect of the economic structure of society, and this is what it actually achieved during the Righteous Period of Muslim history, when the Qur'ãnic orthodoxy had not yet been tampered with.

(xix) Unity of Classes :

It is in the very nature of every human society to undertake and promote diversified activity. Diversification of activity, in its turn, creates diversified groups who contribute to the life and growth of the community through the pursuit, at different *levels* of execution, of different *type* of tasks. Then, each type enjoys a *status* of its own. Thus different types of tasks become graded as of *superior* or *inferior* status in respect of their superior or inferior role in terms of their utility to the community, conferring *ipso facto* superiority or inferiority on the executors of those tasks. Thus groups of people become diversified and differentiated and emerge in terms of their professional superiority or inferiority.

Then, it is in the very nature of organised activity that there is someone who commands, and there are others who obey. That, in itself, creates superiority and inferiority among the members of a society.

Thus, the emergence of classes with positive differentiations is the very condition of the existence of a human society. And those classes emerge on different bases. *Administratively*, the society becomes divided into the ruling class and the class of people who are ruled. *Activistically*, it gets divided into classes according to professions or *types of work*, on the one hand, and in respect of the *quality of labour*, on the other. Then, the factors, of 'type of work' and 'quality of labour' are related to the talent which certain persons possess while others do not, to the labours put in by certain persons for cultivating those talents, and to the measure of the merits acquired by them through sincere labour. Even if it is said that every member of a society owes all his merits and achievements totally to the society, that the society makes him what he is, and that therefore he should submerge his individuality in the society,—even then, on principle, the society has to pay more regard, and take more care of, him on whom it spends more in order that he may be more useful to it. Thus even making the concept of 'labour' as the only standard of evaluation, the emergence of classes with differences in respect of status in social, political and economic terms is unavoidable. The unskilled manual labourer cannot be put on par with the skilled manual labourer. Then, a manual labourer cannot be put on par with an intellectual labourer. Again: Among intellectual labourers, a creative scholar or scientist cannot be put on par with an office-worker or even with a journalistic writer,—nay, even with a teacher. Still again: The head of the state, elected by the people for his exceptional learning, wisdom and sagacity, cannot be put on par with the citizens of his state.

The above situation emerges whether the society is capitalistic or communistic, and whether it is autocratic or democratic.

The real fault with the feudalistic and the capitalistic societies lies in their materialistic approach to life and the consequent exploitation, injustice and want of human sympathy—all these evils being inherent in the feudalistic and the capitalistic social philosophy. "Every man unto himself, and devil take the hindmost", as they say. Or, as the Darwinian atheism formulates it: "Survival of the Fittest".

Human inequalities and qualitative and quantitative gradations are natural to the social life of humanity. But exploitation and injustice and want of human feeling are not natural. What the Holy Qur'ãn does, therefore, is: (1) it emphasises the *human* basis of social life, as opposed to class-distinctions. It does not believe that different professions should unavoidably divide the human beings into mutually hostile classes. (2) It destroys the spirit of estrangement, to which the engagement of different groups of the people in different professions might give rise, through its fundamental *unifying* institution of Brotherhood. (3) It destroys the very foundations of, and the spirit behind, Feudalism and Monopoly Capitalism. (4) It gives a firm teaching and sound laws to keep away exploitation, injustice and tyranny from the society which practices the Guidance it gives. (5) On the positive side, it establishes a Welfare Society based on Piety, Truth, Justice, Love, Wisdom, Beauty and Selflessness,—thereby eliminating all possibilities of the emergence of any type of class-conflicts and the consequent disturbance of the principle of *human unity*.

(xx) Principle of 'Unity' as the Basis of Culture :

The emphasis on 'other-worldliness' creates ideational culture. The emphasis on 'this-worldliness' leads to sensate culture. The Qur'ãn stands for human fulfilment in 'this' world as well as in the 'other' world, *unifies* the Good of this world with the Good of the other world[4], and gives to both the spiritual and the physical values their full due—synthesising them within its *unitary* ideal of human fulfilment. Thus it projects the *unified* integralistic Culture.

(xxi) Unity in Terms of the 'Ideal of Single Goal' :

All human activity proceeds under the impact of different yearnings: the yearning for holiness, the yearning for moral achievement, the yearning for aesthetic refinement, the yearning for knowledge, the yearning for physical happiness, etc. Thus activity becomes diversified, at the individual as well as the collective level, into spiritual, moral, aesthetical, intellectual, physical, social, economic, political, etc. Now, what happens in actual life is that the superficial and unbalanced mind views each of these activities as if it exists independently of the others and believes that it should be pursued as such. Then, because of a diversification of human temperaments and environmental settings, different human beings acquire *special* interest in different types of activity and finally land themselves in the evil of fixing up the goal relating to one particular activity as the *only* or, at least, the *basic* goal of life. Then they go beyond that and transform their personal inclination into philosophy. The errors thus committed infect the minds of even great thinkers. To give just a few examples, in respect of the function of the State: Hegel says that it is moral, while Marx says that it is economic. As regards Man: Aristotle says that he is a social being. Plato emphasises

4 *Cf.* Along with other references the prayer: "Our Lord! Give us Good in this world and Good in the Hereafter." (II:201).

that he is a rational being. Marx asserts that he is an economic being. Then, coming to Culture: the upholders of the ideational school of sociology maintain the view that the spiritual alone is real and consequently hold to the ideal of an other-wordly culture; while the materialistic sociologists believe that the physical alone is real and, as a result, stand as protagonists of sensate culture. Thus, different individuals, different thinkers and different human groups adopt and emphasise different goals, and the pursuit of those different goals leads to endless disharmony and perpetual conflicts within the personalities of the individuals, and between different classes that go to constitute a community, as also between the different nations and races.

The Qur'ãnic concept of *unity* which, at the level of the psychological, the moral and the social phenomena, assumes the form of the principle of *integration*, provides the guidance which can save mankind from disaster in this behalf. Because God has created all the human beings with a plan and a purpose, and has endowed them with the status of His vicegerency, and has created the world such that the human beings can act in it in accordance with their status, the *only goal* worth the name which every human being should by his very nature pursue is the fulfilment of his destiny as the vicegerent of God,—wherein he attains harmony with God, Who is the Source of all life, light, power, happiness and beatitude. This *only goal* is, in fact, the *comprehensive goal* to which the pursuit of all the *partial goals* should bear reference; and for that purpose all the *immediate* goals of human activity (—and every healthy activity *must be* included in the empire of Human Action—) should be pursued in an integrated and balanced manner, harmonising everyone of them with the rest, and all together with the *comprehensive goal*, or, the *ultimate goal*.

Chapter VII

INTEGRALISTIC MORAL PHILOSOPHY AND COMPREHENSIVE MORAL CODE

We have noticed in the foregoing that the Holy Qur'ãn gives a monistic principle of evaluation in its concept of God. That principle plays a vital role in the Qur'ãnic moral philosophy, so that the Qur'ãnic ethical norms are established in what might be named as Divine Ethics.

The Divine Ethics emerges in the Qur'ãnic concept of God as 'ethical Being' Who behaves towards human beings in the ethical way. As for the human being, he has to imitate the Divine Ethics as the vicegerent of God—as best as he can.

God is the Possessor of the Best[1] Attributes (VII:180; XVII:110; LIX:24), and "all that is in the heavens and the earth is devoted to His *tasbîh* (i.e., proclaims His absolute freedom from every type of evil and attests His glory in respect of His absolute perfection)[2]." (LIX:24).

Elsewhere, the act of *tasbih* has been distinguished from the act of prayer: "Beholdest thou not that it is Allah Whose *tasbih* is the function of all (beings that are) in the heavens and the earth, and the birds (in flight) with wings outspread? Surely each one knows its (own mode of) prayer and its (own mode of) *tasbih*. And Allah is Aware of what they do." (XXIV:41)

Then, among the human beings, those who do not ignore the Signs of God—which form the keys to the understanding of the meaning of human life and the nature of human destiny—and establish such a living faith in God that they become capable of appreciating those Signs, surrender of their whole self and *tasbih* enshrined in the realisation of God's absolute Perfection become the guiding lights of their lives : "Only those (human beings) are (genuine) believers in Our Signs, who, when they obtain admonition therewith, fall down prostrate (in adoration of Allah's Glory) and engage in *tasbîh* celebrating the praise of their Lord; and they are never arrogant (in respect of the acceptance of their total dependence on Allah)." (XXXII:15)

---

1 *al-husnã* : The Best (Lane's *Lexicon*).

2 Meaning of *tasbih* according to Lane's *Lexicon*.

Tasbîh has been made a regular daily routine for the Believers: "O ye who believe! Remember Allah with much remembrance and engage in His *tasbîh* morning and evening." (XXXIII:41, 42)

According to Imam Raghib al-Isfahani, the act of *tasbîh* stands for worship in thought, word and deed[3].

Thus: As it relates to thought and word, *tasbîh* is a process of active realisation in one's consciousness of the infinite glory of the Divine Attributes, and thereby of the infinite purity and perfection of the Personality of God; and, as it relates to deed, it is a process of active assimilation of the ethical value-system of those Attributes in one's personality on the basis of a dynamic understanding of the privileged status that God has conferred on him through the infusion of what He calls 'My spirit' (XV:29)—the goal being the realisation of the human vicegerency of God, which starts actualising only when the human personality begins to project the reflection of the Divine Attributes.

The ethical implications of this Qur'ãnic teaching are :

God Himself is the ethical ideal, and the proper ethical function of the human being is to imitate Him[4]. This teaching forms the fundamental base of the Qur'ãnic moral philosophy, and it has been repeatedly brought into focus in explicit terms in the Qur'ãn. For instance:

(i) The mercy, compassion and loving kindness of God is the ever-recurring theme of the holy book. Its very first verse projects it with full emphasis in terms of *rahmah*. Hence the observance of compassionate kindness (*marhamah*) has been made one of the governing principles of Islamic life (XC:17), along with its different dimensions projected in different contexts at different places,—for instance, love and mercy spoken of in respect of their observance by the husband and the wife. (XXX:21)

(ii) God is *al-Barr* (LII:28). Hence, a human being has to act as *barr* through practising *birr* comprehensively (II:177), with special emphasis on social good (III:92). In fact, *birr* has been made one of the governing principles of human life (V:3), and to be from

---

3 *Mufradãt al-Qur'ãn*, sec: *SBH*.

4 *Cf.* The Qur'ãnic verse: "(We take our) colour from Allah, and who is better than Allah at colouring? It is He whom we worship." (II:138).

among the *abrãr* (pl. of *barr*) has been made the ideal. (III:193)

The words *barr* and *birr*, which emerge from the same root, are untranslatable because of the richness of their meanings. The basic connotation is: kindness, affection, gentleness, justice, righteousness, honesty, veracity, considerateness, extensive beneficence[5].

(iii) God is Forgiving (*Ghafûr*) and Merciful (*Rahîm*) Human beings should also be forgiving and merciful in their behaviour towards one another. (XXIV:22)

(iv) God is the Bestower of Good. A human being should also do good to his fellow-being. (XXVIII:77)

(v) God does not wrong any human being even in the slightest measure (X:44); IV:40). The human beings also should not wrong either others or themselves. (II:279; etc.)

One important aspect of this ideal is that it has not been laid down only theoretically, but has also been projected in practical terms in the moral personalities of all the Prophets of mankind, who came to exemplify the Divine Ethics,—and, finally, in the exemplary moral character of the Holy Prophet Muhammad (Peace be on him!), which enshrines comprehensively the Divine Ethics in terms of human perfection and thus forms the perfect human Model for imitation. (XXXIII:21)[6]

As to the implications of the ideal of "imitation of Divine Ethics" for moral philosophy, they may be stated thus:

(i) This ideal is the highest—the most sublime, the noblest and the most consequential—ideal conceivable for humanity, because of its basis in God's Personality.

(ii) This ideal imparts a dynamic approach to human life, because God's Personality is dynamic.

---

5 Lane's *Lexicon*, Sec: '*BR*'.

6 All the Divine Messengers of the world have been, as mentioned above, the embodiments of the ideal. But, because history has not preserved any authentic records of their lives, while historical records are available for a critical assessment of the Holy Prophet Muhammad's imitation of the Divine Ethics, he alone is to be followed as the Exemplar.

(iii) This ideal makes creativity the fundamental mode of human struggle, because God's Personality is committed to continuous creation.

(iv) This ideal supplies an objective moral standard, because it places the standard totally outside of human subjectivity;—and thus it ensures the absolutely pure moral behaviour.

(v) This ideal provides the highest motivation for morality. Because, on the positive side, the entire human moral behaviour has been conceived therein as based on 'love for God' (II:177; etc.); and, on the negative side, the devotee of God is to remain perpetually in a state of 'fear of God', Who is always present with him (LVII:4), is always watching him as to whether he is fulfilling his role of vicegerency (XLIX:18; etc.), and will recompense him after death, i.e., at the termination of his earthly sojourn, as the Lord of the Day of Judgement (I:3; XCIX: 6-8; etc.).

(vi) This ideal enshrines infinite possibilities for human evolution, because the levels of imitation of the infinite perfection of the Divine Personality are infinite.

(vii) This ideal projects an integrated and comprehensive view of human struggle and destiny, because God's Personality possesses the highest integration and comprehensiveness; and, consequently, the Qur'ãnic moral philosophy runs into all the dimensions of human activity and functions as a philosophy governing total human behaviour.[7]

As such, the Moral Code which the Qur'ãn has given is the most comprehensive code possessed by humanity.[8]

---

7 The Holy Qur'ãn integrates the life of humanity both horizontally and vertically. The integration mentioned here is *horizontal integration;* while, through its teaching concerning the role of the Prophets and their genuine followers, it establishes *vertical integration* in human moral history.

8 The entire volume on the "Structure of Islamic Society" forms the Qur'ãnic moral.

Chapter VIII

THE INTEGRATED INDIVIDUAL: BASIC QUALITIES OF A MUSLIM

Man's status and function has been differently viewed in the different schools of moral thought,—the differences emerging basically in the emphasis laid by each on the different aspects of human nature and activity. Thus: for some, man is only an animal among animals; while, for others, he is something more, and as such should be referred to as a 'being'. Then, his function has been emphasised variously in terms of a 'social animal', a 'rational animal', an 'economic animal', a 'moral being', and a 'spiritual being'.

In the Qur'ãnic view, the essential attribute of the human being is *personality*, which consists in the possession of self-consciousness, self-directed will and creative intellect. As such, he is unique among all the creatures living on earth. Nay, his superiority is acknowledged even by the holy celestial creatures known as angels (II:34; etc.). Moreover, he stands in a special relation with God in terms of the attribute of 'personality', which both possess—; and, in consequence, his status among God's creatures is that of the vicegerent of God (II:30). He carries a responsibility on his shoulders which "the heavens and the earth and the mountains" found themselves unable to bear (XXXIII:72). He has a cosmic mission, because "whatever is in the heavens and the earth has been made subservient" to him (XLV:13). Nay, his mission is even beyond that. It is supra-cosmic. For, he belongs to God and unto Him he is journeying (II:156). Indeed, God is his final destination (LIII:42). As such, he is a theocentric being functioning on earth in a spatiotemporal framework of activity and a physical environment; and his vicegerency of God implies that he should function as an integrated being, namely, comprehensively, harmoniously and creatively, in all the dimensions of his personality: physical, spiritual, moral, intellectual, and aesthetical.

It is with this view of status and function of the individual that the Qur'ãn prescribes a comprehensive moral code for him. That moral code is grounded in a value-system which is comprised of the same norms as the ethical guide-lights for the Religious Quest, mentioned already, namely; Piety, Selflessness, Truth, Justice, Love, Wisdom and Beauty.

The existence of this similarity is due to the fact that the Qur'ãnic integralistic philosophy of life aims at integrating not only the individual but also the society. The integration in the former case is achieved horizontally, while in the latter case it is vertical, wherein the individuals at all the levels of human development in terms of that philosophy—from the beginners to the highly-developed—automatically follow the same value-system and the same dynamics, being thus distinguishable from one another only in quantitative terms and not qualitatively. The 'path' is the same, and the 'goal' is the same. Hence the path is open to all, and the goal is open to all. The role of the more-developed is not to consider themselves as a special privileged class but the inspire and assist the less-developed towards ever-greater effort. *Thus a true co-operative spiritual, social, political and economic democracy comes into existence.*

Here the Qur'ãnic philosophy differs radically with those religions which create a distinct class of 'pursuers of saintliness', on the one hand, and a vast mass of 'religious proletariat', on the other,—with principles and ideals and modes of life different for each class.

However, to return to the *basic norms* that should govern the life of every Qur'ãnic individual, i.e., of every Muslim: The acceptance of each of these norms as a guide-light brings into activity certain very basic moral principles[1] even at the minimum level, which might be named as the level of the *Basic Moral Quest*.

[*Note*: It should be understood that the difference between the *Religious Quest*, which we have already discussed, and the *Basic Moral Quest*, which we shall discuss now, is, strictly speaking, not of kind but of degree. They are focussed in the same direction, but differ as to the respective levels of achievement enshrined in them,—the emphasis in the latter case being on the building up of a sound moral life through ethico-religious exercise grounded in 'Faith in God', and in the former case on the achievement of sound experience of nearness (*taqarrub*) to God, and the consequent 'holiness' in *walãyah*, basically through the exercise of 'Love of God' in its progressive intensification. It will thus be noticed that while the two Quests are distinguishable, the latter forms

1 The full-fledged moral code which governs human life Islamically has been presented in Vol. II: "The Structure of Islamic Society", to which the readers should turn for the Qur'ãnic references relating to the basic moral principles projected here.

actually an inseparable part of the former; or, we might term the latter as the preliminary level of the former.]

To Proceed Briefly:

Piety, in the basic sense, has three fundamental dimensions in the Qur'ãnic philosophy, namely: 'faith in God', 'love for God', and 'fear of God'. Adherence to faith in God in the form of the Islamic formula: "There is none worthy of worship except Allah" establishes *humility* and *moral courage* and *optimism* in one's moral behaviour at the very start. Love for God supplies *positive motivation for the highest ideals*. Its cultivation establishes *unfailing love for doing good to humanity as well as for one's betterment*, and *'fills' the human life* so perfectly as to keep away the psychical ailment of the feeling of 'emptiness' of life for good. Cultivation of fear of God, which is, according to the Qur'ãn, actually fear of Accountability and Divine Judgement, brings about the establishment of *conscientiousness, sense of responsibility* and *moral earnestness*.

Selflessness, which, according to the Qur'ãnic philosophy, consist in 'absence of evils relating to the animal self', imparts genuine *dignity* to the pursuer's personality through the exercise of *self-control*, which is its vital base, and ensures *temperance* and true *chivalry* and the *pursuit of all the social virtues* in the highest measure. (It is the urges of the animal self that form the source of all moral evils. Hence, the Holy Qur'ãn teaches that the impelling force of the animal self should be kept in abeyance through the constant cultivation of the basic Qur'ãnic ideal of 'surrender to God',—that being the very function of a Muslim, as contained in the word '*Muslim*' itself).

Truth: Its pursuit, according to the Qur'ãn, is three-dimensional, namely: in thought, in word, and in deed. Adherence to 'truth in thought' establishes a person in *adherence to reality, or, a realistic approach to life*, and in *sincerity*—as opposed to hypocrisy, and in *single-mindedness*. Adherence to 'truth in word' ensure *veracity* and *integrity*. Adherence to 'truth in deed' establishes *honesty* and *effort for efficiency* in one's life.

Justice functions in respect of others as well as in regard to one's self. (1) Adherence to absolute justice in respect of others, as commanded by the Qur'ãn, ensures the *avoidance of doing any undeserved injury* to anyone, even though one's own interests or the interests of one's relatives and friends are injured thereby. (2) Adherence to justice in respect of one's self ensures utmost effort for promoting a *natural healthy* and *vigorous* life, as demanded by the Qur'ãn: (i) The ideal of promotion of life as *natural* commits a person to *simplicity*—as opposed to luxurious and vain sophistication. (ii) The ideal of promotion of life as *healthy* consists, in accordance with the Qur'ãnic philosophy, in the effort for the establishment of *sound physical health, sound moral health, sound spiritual health, sound economic outlook* and *sound social demeanour*; and the duties that emerge are: (a) in respect of physical health: negatively, *to avoid unhealthy foods and drinks* and *to refrain from gluttony*; and, positively, *to stick to healthy foods and drinks only*—and that in *balanced quantities*, with *recurrent fasting*, besides the obligatory one month's fasting during Ramadan—, and to *physical exercise in the form of sports and otherwise, healthy recreation* and *proper rest*; (b) in respect of moral health: to maintain *purity of conscience* and the effort for achieving *soundness in moral behaviour*; (c) in respect of spiritual health: positively, to cultivate more and more a *living and dynamic relationship with God*[2],—the minimum basic obligatory institutional exercises prescribed by the Qur'ãn in that connection being the five daily obligatory prayers (*salãt*), fasting during Ramadan (*saum*), and the payment annually of a fixed portion of one's surplus wealth for the benefit of others, solely out of love for God (*zakãt*); and, negatively, *to avoid all that which hinders or damages the devotion to God*, including all superstitions; (d) in respect of economic outlook: to undertake utmost *sincere effort for earning one's livelihood by lawful means and with dignity,* and *to avoid all waste* of possibilities for economic production; (e) in respect of social demeanour: to maintain one's *dignity in society* through adherence to moral integrity, for which, in addition to its moral teachings, an exercise in the religious perspective has been provided by the Qur'ãn in the institution of the *Hajj*.[3] (iii) The ideal of *vigorous* life commits a person to: (a) pursuance of *earnestness, purposiveness, hard labour* and *a progressive outlook*; and (b) *avoidance of waste of time and energy* in *idleness* or in *vain pursuits*.

Love projects itself in two dimensions, namely, love for one's self, and love for other creatures of God. The *former* demands: (a) doing

---

2 The combination of (a), (b) and (c) ensures what is called 'mental health'.

3 In respect of the wisdom enshrined in the institutions of *salãt, saum, zakãt* and *hajj*, readers may refer to the Author's: "*Philosophy of Worship in Islam*", published by the World Federation of Islamic Missions.

all that lies in one's power for making one's self *sound physically, spiritually, morally, intellectually and economically*; (b) avoiding to the utmost what harms one's self in any way. The *latter* brings into action such virtues as *sympathy, mercy, compassion, kindness, respect, generosity*—in fact, doing good to others in every way and abstaining from injuring them and their lawful interests in any way.

Wisdom, as an ideal of life, commits a person to growth in knowledge and attainment of more and more insight into the reality of phenomena and things. The Qur'ãn wants this pursuit to proceed through a critical study of Divine Revelation, Nature and History, along with the consequential outlook of promoting good and eradicating evil in one's self and in society,—whereby, through *Jihãd*, i.e., ceaseless and vigorous effort, the individual as well as the society attain *power, peace* and *progress*.

Beauty, as an ideal of Qur'ãnic philosophy, commits the pursuer to gracefulness and beautification in every aspect of life. Thus: *sweetness, gentleness* and *gracefulness* emerge in morals and manners; *cleanliness* becomes the watchword in respect of all actions and things, including the body, the dress and the environment: *natural beautification* in conformity with the ideals of Piety and Wisdom is pursued in respect of one's production and one's environment.[4]

---

4 For Qur'ãnic references relating to the details projected in this chapter, refer to Vol. II, relevant sections.

[illegible]

[illegible] things [illegible] in any way. The [illegible] things [illegible] [illegible]

[illegible] knowledge and attainment of truth and morality: any theory [illegible]

[illegible] is an ideal [illegible] [illegible]

[illegible]

Chapter IX

THE INTEGRALISTIC WELFARE SOCIETY

Basically Grounded in the Pursuit of Piety, Truth, Justice, Love, Wisdom, Beauty and Selflessness

The Qur'ãnic Guidance lays such vehement emphasis on Social Good that its social gospel emerges as the very kernel of the religion of Islam, as the unfriendly Canadian orientalist, Wilfred Cantwell Smith, also admits: "While Christianity in recent years has moved towards a social gospel[1], Islam has been a social gospel from the very start."[2]

This is due to the fact that Islam is opposed to the mystico-ascetic approach to life and regards society as the natural framework of activity for human fulfilment.

Islam's social gospel is, however, based on religion and morality, as opposed to the secular social philosophies which are earth-rooted and materialistic in their approach and built up on Expediency as the groundwork of their value-systems. Hence, as regards its foundations, the Islamic society is *theo-centric* and *ethico-religious,* nourished by the pursuit of *godliness*.

As *Theocentric Society*, its social philosophy is grounded in the highest and the most meaningful value-system, because belief in and devotion to God provides the perfect and the comprehensive principle for the highest values and ideals. Indeed, it alone projects the genuine and meaningful sanction for the pursuit of Truth, Justice, Love, Beauty, Austerity and Selfless Service to Fellow-beings.

As *Ethico-Religious Society*, it is based on the theocentric ethical Idealism; which rests upon: (a) the 'love for God' as manifesting itself in the love for humanity, and (b) the 'fear of God' as manifesting itself in the fear of Divine Judgement; which provides, in its concept of God—wherein the ethical aspect of His Personality has been thoroughly emphasised—and the concept of Survival-after-Death in terms of a

1 Mark the movement of Christianity towards the philosophy of Islam and assess the Christian allegation that Islam has borrowed its humanitarian philosophy from the teachings of Christianity.

2 *Islam in the Modern World*, London 1946, p. 22.

dynamic concept of human destiny, the *only* genuine and absolute sanction for morality; and which enshrines the assurance of the realisation of its Social Ideal in its Exemplar, the Holy Prophet Muhammad (Peace be on him!) and in the society established by him at Madinah.

In terms of *spiritual activity*, it is committed to spiritual illumination. Because, God is the 'Light of the heavens and the earth' (XXIV:35); the Holy Prophet (Peace be on him!) is 'Light' (V:17) and the 'Illuminating Lamp' (XXXIII:46); the Holy Qur'ãn is 'Light Manifest' (IV:174); Faith (*Imãn*) is 'Light' (XXXIX:22); the function of Qur'ãnic Guidance, or, Islam, is to bring humanity out of Darkness into Light (XIV:1); a genuine member of the Islamic society is one who receives a Light from God, which shines forth in dealings with fellow-beings (VI:122); and, in the heavenly life, the Light of the Faithful "will run before them and on their right hands, while they say: Our Lord! Perfect our Light for us...." (LXVI:8). Thus, the Islamic society is a *Spiritual-Illumined Society*.

In respect of its *ethical outlook in terms of human dignity*, it invites its members beyond *goodness* to *nobleness*. Because: (i) God is Most Noble (XCVI:3); the Prophet is noble (LXIX:40); the Qur'ãn is noble (LVI:77); the messenger-angel of the Qur'ãn is noble (LXXXI:19); the human race is noble (XVII:70); the norm governing Islamic conduct is to behave nobly (XVII:23; XXV:72; LXXXIX:17), so that the members of Islamic society are to be regarded as more or less noble, and hence deserving more or less honour, in proportion to the nobility in their character (XLIX:13); genuine pursuers of Islam have been promised 'noble provision' (VIII:4) and 'noble (final) reward' (XXXIII:44); and it is the mission of Islam to lead its followers into the 'noble gate' (IV:31) for the attainment of all the dimensions of human nobility. Hence, the Islamic society is a *Noble Society*.[3]

In its *structural aspect*, it lays emphasis on the family as the unit of society (XXV:54; etc.). In fact, the family plays a very important role in Islam's social ethics (XXVI:214; etc.). Because, providing, as it does, the first and the basic social environment to the individual, it is emphasised by Islam as the original field for social morality wherein a person has to

3 The rood work *Karuma*, employed in all the verses quoted, means 'to be noble', i.e., 'to be noble-hearted, high minded, magnanimous, generous, liberal, munificent'. (Ref: *A Dictionary of Modern Written Arabic*, edited by J. Milton Cowan, p. 821). Make here the Qur'ãnic dimensions of nobility!

engage himself in a constant socio-moral exercise, and it is the moral discipline which he acquires there that plays a vital role in respect of his moral behaviour relating to his community, country and humanity at large. The institution of the family is thus the corner-stone of Islamic society; and Islam has provided, for its proper functioning and stability, a code of familial ethics which is built upon: (a) marital piety, (b) parental piety, and (c) final piety,—namely: uncompromising emphasis on: (a) chastity of the husband and the wife, (b) comprehensive parental benevolence, and (c) unflinching goodwill, devotion and respect of the children for their parents and all elders. It should be noted here that Islam's emphasis on *chastity* is absolute, because without that no healthy family life is conceivable. This fact accounts for: (a) the special rules of *modesty* which Islam has laid down for the womenfolk, with which is connected its prohibition of promiscuous intermingling of sexes; and (b) Islam's conditional permission for polygamy. The former is in acknowledgement of the woman's basic role as mother, wherein "the hand that rocks the cradle rules the world";—indeed, the possibilities of the spiritual and moral survival of a community can exist only so long as the womenfolk remain conscientious custodians to the community's spiritual and moral values. As to (b), the qualified permission for polygamy is for warding off prostitution, besides providing for the orphans, in a society having a surplus of womenfolk.[4] All in all, the Islamic society is a *Family-Based Society*.

Being based on the affirmation of the unity of humankind and ideal of human brotherhood (IV:1), Islam regards racialism, tribalism, caste-ism, class-ism and dynasty-ism as nothing less than infidelity to God and treachery against humanity. All the members of the Islamic society, therefore,—whatever their race, or tribe, or dynasty, or colour, or language, are *equal* members and possess, originally and basically, equal fundamental rights. The Islamic society is thus a *Non-Racial, Non-Tribal, Casteless, Classless Society* (XLIX:13). It may also be termed as an *Egalitarian Society*.

The rights which the members of the Islamic society possess fundamentally in equal measure are, however, subject to modification, on *individual basis*—and not on the basis of race, tribe, etc.—in terms of practical demonstration of respect for the discipline of the society and the contribution to the welfare of the society. This must be so, because, in the

---

4 For Qur'ãnic references relating to the facts mentioned in this discussion, see Vol. II: "The Structure of Islamic Society."

first instance, upgrading the merit and degrading the demerit is the very essence of justice and the only way to avoid the frustration of virtue; and, in the second instance, the emergence of gradation among individuals is the unavoidable condition of the functioning of a society, and the existence of the spirit of competition is the necessary prerequisite for progress. Thus, the Islamic society is an *Open Society*, wherein merit is based on achievement alone and not on considerations of physical distinctions in terms of race, or tribe, or family, or colour, or language, or sex (VI:132).

Coming to the *ideological structure*: it is integralistic, 'religion' being the integrating factor. Thus morality is indissolubly joined to 'religion' (II:25; etc.), while economics (III:92[5]; etc.), politics (II:38; V:9[6]; etc.), and law (IV:135[7]; etc.), are related to 'religion' through morality in an unbreakable bond. Thus, ideologically, the Islamic society is an *Integrated Society*.

Then, besides the principle of integration, its structural aspect is also governed by the principle of 'the Balance (LV:7,8), which implies the realisation of *all* the values of human life in balanced manner,—namely, giving to every value its due,—in contrast with the ideational philosophy which emphasises only the spiritual pursuit, and with the materialistic philosophy which confines the human struggle within the bounds of physical needs. Thus, the Islamic society is a *Balanced Society*.

In its *functional aspect*: Being theocentric, ethico-religious, integrated and balanced, its vision is not confined to the day-to-day issues of human life—to which it gives their due—but extends beyond them to the ultimate problems of human destiny. It, therefore, commits itself to the most comprehensive and the highest human ideals, in contradistinction to the materialistic approach which has actually no room for ideals because of its affirmation of the cosmos as 'blind', the human life as a 'gamble', and the human destiny as an 'illusion'.

---

5 The Qur'ãnic ethico-religious basis of economics is the economic welfare of humankind, as emphasised in the verse referred to.

6 The Qur'ãnic ethico-religious basis of politics is the elimination of 'fear and sorrow' and the establishment of justice, as emphasised in the verse referred to.

7 The Qur'ãnic ethico-religious basis of law is equity, as emphasised in the verse referred to.

Then, being the trustee of the mission of humanity for the realisation of the vicegerency of God, it has to imitate God's Attributes, among which is His Attribute of Creativity (XXIII:14). As such, it has to function progressively in its adoption of means for the improvement of human welfare in all aspects of life, through the pursuit of Wisdom and through the conquest of the terrestrial and the celestial environment. The Islamic society is thus an *Idealistic, Dynamic and Progressive Society.*

We have already noted that, structurally, the Islamic society is an egalitarian society. That being so, it functions democratically. Indeed, the Holy Qur'ãn establishes spiritual democracy, social democracy, political democracy, and economic democracy. It establishes spiritual democracy, as we have already noted, by abolishing priesthood and 'spiritual feudalism' completely and by making the acquisition of knowledge the prerogative and the obligation of everyone, including the womenfolk, tearing into shreds the very notion of privileged families and special classes and castes. It establishes social democracy, as already noticed, by abolishing all criteria of tribal, racial and colour distinctions affirming only the superiority of good character. It establishes political democracy by abolishing theocracy as well as all those secular views of government in which any human being may have the opportunity of tyrannising over and exploiting other human beings,—both of these principles forming basic constituents of the Qur'ãnic social philosophy, as already noticed. It established economic democracy—through, among other principles and laws, the basic principle that 'wealth should not be permitted to circulate among the wealthy only' (LIX:7), which makes it imperative that the economic system should be such as to provide a fair measure of equality of opportunity to all the members of the society for securing decent means of livelihood, and thereby sharing in the national wealth honourably through honest labour and sincere achievement, whereas the disabled secure their basic needs honourably through the social-welfare tax imposed by Islam on the well-to-do members of the society (IX:60; etc.). Thus, the Islamic society is a *Democratic Society.*

The guiding light of the Islamic social ethics is *justice*, which has been enjoined by the Holy Qur'ãn in terms of absoluteness and comprehensiveness (V:9: etc.),—whereby the establishment of all forms of social justice, i.e., moral, legal, economic and political, has been enshrined in the Islamic code of life[8]. Thus, the Islamic society is a *Just Society.*

---

8 For references, see Vol. II: "The Structure of Islamic Society".

The concept of Mercy enjoys a basic importance in the Qur'ãn. Because: God is the 'Most Merciful of the merciful' (VII:151; etc.); Whose Mercy 'comprehends everything'[9] (VII:156; etc.); the Holy Prophet (Peace be on him!) is 'mercy unto the worlds'[10] (XXI:107); the Holy Qur'ãn is 'Mercy to the Doers of Good' (XXXI:3); God will cause the Faithful to enter His Mercy after death (LXXVI:31); and the practice of Mercy in human relations has been explicitly emphasised (XVII:24; XXX:21; XLVIII:29; XC:17). Thus, the Islamic society is a *Merciful Society*.

The very basis of the Qur'ãnic philosophy of life is the negation of all forms of selfishness and the affirmation of love for humanity on the basis of love for God. Moreover, the Holy Qur'ãn has emphasised the principle of 'preferring the good of others to one's own comforts' as a basic characteristic of Islamic life (LIX:9). Hence the Islamic society is an *Altruistic Society*.

The Qur'ãn has made knowledge one of the two most fundamental pillars of the pursuit of greatness by human communities (LVIII:11), and the Holy Prophet (Peace be on him!) has made the pursuit of education for the acquisition of knowledge obligatory for every Muslim, man and woman. Hence, the Islamic society is an *Educated Society*.

The Qur'ãn has laid down the 'Limits prescribed by Allah' and has commanded the members of the Islamic society to adhere to the requirements of those 'limits' (II:187: etc.). It has thus channelised human life, and thereby subjected it to discipline. Again: It has emphasised consequential activity (LIX:18). But a truly consequential activity is not possible without proper planning, which, in its turn, necessitates disciplined undertaking. Moreover, the principle of 'discipline' forms the very soul of Islamic conduct (XXIV:51; etc.). The Islamic society is thus a *Disciplined Society*.

---

9 'Imitation of Divine Attributes' being the function of the Muslims, they are under obligation, on this basis itself, to make the practice of Mercy one of the guiding principle of their lives.

10 Imitation of the Holy Prophet's moral character being the very basis of Islamic life, all Muslims are under obligation to practise Mercy towards all creatures, even as the Holy Prophet (Peace be on him!) has commanded: "It is the merciful people on whom the Merciful (God) bestows Mercy. Be merciful to those who are on the earth. (Then) He Who is Above will bestow Mercy on you." (Tirmizi: Jãme', Vol. II, "*al-Birr wa al-Silah*").

The Qur'ãn stresses the 'Brotherhood of the Believers' along with all its implications (XLIX:10). Hence, the Islamic society is a *Fraternal Society*.

The Qur'ãnic laws relating to international relations between Muslims and non-Muslims and the Qur'ãnic ethics of war are based on absolute justice and regard for humanity[11]. Similarly, the Qur'ãn forbids the Muslims from persecuting the non-Muslims for compelling them to change their religion, allowing them thus the right to freedom of conscience (II:256). Also, the Qur'ãn emphasises that Muslims should not abstain from doing good to the non-Muslims, unless they are in a state of active enmity (LX:8, 9). Thus, the Islamic society is a *Humanitarian Society*.

The Qur'ãn has made *Jihãd*, i.e., relentless effort through hard labours to one's utmost capacity, one of the highest and the most unavoidable virtues of a Muslim (XXII:78; etc.), and has stressed that value lies in labour (LIII:39) and achievement (LIX:18, etc.). The Islamic society is, therefore, and *Industrious Society*.

The Qur'ãn condemns 'love of this world's life' (LXXIX:38; 39; Etc.), invites repeated attention to the emptiness of the pleasures of worldly life (III:185; etc.), forbids all vain spending and waste (VII:31; etc.) which is the basis of luxurious living, castigates the infidels for 'loving wealth' (LXXXIX:20), commands the Muslims not to follow the behests of their animal self (IV:135; etc.), and finally invites them to a life dedicated to the love for values (III:15-17)—the highest value being the love for God (II:165), which should manifest itself in the love for fellow-beings (II:177; etc.). This makes *austerity* the ideal in respect of Islamic life, as exemplified at its highest in the life of the Holy Prophet (Peace be on him!), and practised by all those who have walked in his footsteps. The Islamic society is thus an *Austere Society*.

Finally, the *goal* to be achieved through the realisation of the values that govern the Islamic society has been enshrined by the Holy Qur'ãn in the concept of *falãh*[12], i.e., welfare, which has been related explicitly and directly both to the society[13] and to the individual[14]. Then,

---

11 For references, see Vol. II: "The Structure of Islamic Society".

12 III:104, 130; LIX:9; LXII:10; etc.

13 *Ibid.*

14 LXXXVII:14; etc.

the concept of *collective welfare* has been presented in all dimensions: spiritual, moral, physical, economic, political, etc., in contrast with the emphasis on economic welfare *alone*,—as we find in the Marxist Scientific Socialism. This makes the Islamic society a *Total Welfare Society*.

The above *twenty-one* basic dimensions emerge in respect of the society which it is the mission of the Qur'ãn to establish,—a mission that was not only preached but *realised* unambiguously and concretely by the Holy Prophet Muhammad (in whom God's choicest Blessings abide!) in the Islamic society founded by him.

When this society assumes the form of the state, as it did in the state of Madinah, a theocentric, democratic, welfare state, or, a *theo-democratic welfare state*, comes into being. Defining it a little more elaborately, it is the 'Government of God, through the Rule of Divine Law, by the Trustees of the Mission of Islam, who function on the basis of their election by persons of character and wisdom among Muslims and administer the state, within the limits prescribed by God, as Servants of the People, for the attainment by the People of their Comprehensive Welfare'.

We might briefly clarify certain basic concepts involved here.[15]

'Government of God' implies that sovereignty in the Islamic state belongs to God and not to the people. The concept of the 'sovereignty of God', in its turn, ensures political equality for all—the rulers and the ruled, and provides the basis for immunising the society from political tyranny. The sovereignty of God can be challenged and denied only by the atheists. But even in secular political philosophy, which projects the concept of the 'sovereignty of the people', the term 'people' stands for a Corporation and a conceptual entity as it embraces the past, the present and the future generations of the people of a nation-state, bound all the time by the fundamental principles of Constitution established by the 'founding fathers'[16]. Thus, there too, it is a 'transcendental' entity in which sovereignty is affirmed. However, the antinomy that emerges in affirming that the people are 'sovereign' and 'subject' at the same time creates

15 A separate treatise is intended to be presented by the author on the Islamic state, wherein elaboration and comparative evaluation of Islam's political and economic philosophies shall be undertaken.

16 Refer, among other books on political philosophy, to Walter Lippmann's '*The Public Philosophy*', London 1955.

difficulties, which are avoided most rationally in affirming God as *sovereign* and the people as *subjects*.

'Rule by Divine Law' implies that the fundamental structure of political norms, principles and laws has been given by God, and is therefore eternal and unchangeable. This characteristic of the law governing the Islamic state ensures stability in political life and the consequent stability in the total life of the community, and establishes the principle of 'supremacy of law'[17] on firm grounds wherein nobody, not even the head of the state, stands above the law.

'Government by the Trustees of the Mission of Islam' implies that because the entire Islamic *millat* is under obligation to promote the mission, which consists in the effort directed to the establishment of all that is good and the eradication of all that is evil,—and all that keeping the ideal of service to entire humanity in view (IV:110), those who administer the Islamic state have, in the very nature of the case, to function primarily and positively as the 'trustees of the mission of Islam', and not merely as good administrators of a political machinery.

The condition that the administrative hierachy shall come into power through the 'will of the people' and not through hereditary monarchy is clearly laid down by the Qur'ãn,—as, for instance, when it asks the Faithful to delegate the trust of administration to those worthy of it (IV:58), or when it makes mutual consultation the basic principle in respect of the administration of their affairs (XLII:38)—and in the Holy Prophet's *Sunnah*, wherein we find that, with all his absolute authority and wisdom, he did not nominate anyone from among his descendents[18] to be his successor in office as head of the Islamic state but left that office open, as a consequence of which Abu Bakr was subsequently elected.

The condition that the electors should be 'persons of character and wisdom' is the most rational condition in respect of an ideological state. If the persons who are to wield authority in an Islamic state are necessarily to be those who are the best available embodiments of Islamic

---

17 Islam establishes 'supremacy of law' through the separation of the executive and the judiciary also.

18 In fact, he did not nominate anyone at all. As regards nomination from among his descendents, had he established the institution of hereditary rule in Islam, he would have nominated his elder grandson, the illustrious Imam Hasan, who was the son of his daughter, Lady Fatimah (Allah be pleased with her!).

character and wisdom, very naturally they should be elected by those who are themselves practically dedicated to Islam and can understand properly the comparative merits of the different persons for whom they have to cast their votes. Otherwise, democracy is likely to degenerate into *mobocracy*, as it is progressively becoming nowadays under the spell of adult franchise, and to end in disaster. As Walter Lippmann remarks in *The Public Philosophy* (p. 21): "Where mass opinion dóminates the government there is a morbid derangement of the true functions of power. The derangement brings about the enfeeblement, verging on paralysis, of the capacity to govern. The breakdown in the constitutional order is the cause of the precipitate and catastrophic decline of Western society. It may, if it cannot be arrested and reversed, bring about the fall of the West." It is this realistic approach in Islam that accounts for the fact that, in the election of Abu Bakr, it was only the Muslims of Madinah, and not the Muslims of the outlying areas, that participated. It is well-known that the former were the people who had assimilated and imbibed Islamic character and wisdom, because of the blessing of long and continuous contact with and training under, the Holy Prophet (Peace be on him!), much more than the latter. Notwithstanding that, however, it is desirable, and even necessary, in an Islamic state to evolve a system whereby the entire population becomes finally the participant in the elective machinery,—the only condition for the adoption of universal adult franchise being the universal basic education of the people and their training in Islamic living: both of which have been enjoined by Islam. What is of importance in this connection, however, is the acquisition of the real benefits of democracy, and not the technique of democracy. And for obtaining the benefits of democracy, importance lies, in the final analysis, in the spiritual character, moral integrity and statesmanly wisdom of those who are elected to govern.

In respect of collective welfare, Islam lays emphasis, as we have already noted, on comprehensive approach,—that being the demand of its philosophy of Unity. It means that, side by side with spiritual and moral welfare, the Islamic state is *under obligation* to give to the economic welfare of the people its due; and in that respect the teachings of the Qur'ãn are directed through all the channels of economic activity to one goal, namely: the achievement of not only economic justice but of positive economic welfare for every member of the society, so that everyone is enabled to live with honour and dignity.

Such a goal is actually very difficult to achieve, until and unless all the dimensions of human activity are trimmed and fashioned to assist in that achievement. And this is what Islam has done.

In the first instance, it goes to the root of the problem of human suffering when it lays stress on the spiritual and moral reform of the people side by side with the establishment of a healthy economic order. It is self-evident that the dependents of a wage-earner are bound to starve, however much the level of his income is raised within rational limits, if he is addicted to harmful pleasures or wasteful pursuits. Indeed, his own health will starve and he will be crippled. And not only an ordinary wage-earner. Even a wealthy man is bound to suffer through spiritual and moral evils, and so too his family. Hence, Islam has positively commanded that the life of a Muslim should be a life of spiritual grace, moral earnestness and material simplicity. It means that in the godly, austere and industrious society which Islam creates, all types of luxuries are totally banned,—as historically exemplified in the society established by the Holy Prophet (Peace be on him!). Indeed, 'simple and industrious living and high thinking' is incontrovertible the *only* Way of life found in the Qur'ãn and the *Sunnah*, while luxurious living and wasteful pursuits are the dopes needed in the pagan way of life because of its spiritual bankruptcy and materialistic sensuous demands,—and by no stretch of imagination can they be traced in the Qur'ãn and the *Sunnah*, and by no amount of sophistry can they be combined rationally with the lives of the worshippers of Allah.

The prime motive in the production of commodities may either be mounting monetary profit for the producer with selfish disregard for the interests of fellow-beings, which is the very soul of industrial capitalism; or, it may be the service of fellow-beings through the supply of their basic needs. The former is anti-God and anti-human, and therefore completely ruled out in Islam. The latter is godly and humanitarian, and therefore becomes an obligation in the Islamic ethico-religious economic philosophy.

Indeed, the Islamic state is under obligation, in respect of its ethico-religious philosophy, to ordain regimentation of production and consumption both, so that, with the establishment of maximum beneficial production relating to the necessities of human life and a reational austerity in consumption—as distinct from ascetic austerity, the material resources of the community are deployed and employed for the widest and unhampered flow of economic blessings, and the possibilities of the emergence of moral corruption and economic exploitation are eliminated.

Secondly, in the Qur'ãnic principles of widest possible distribution of wealth and of reward on the basis of labour and achievement, on the one hand, and of co-operation, on the other, the principle of peasant-proprietorship emerges in the domain of agriculture—as opposed to the institutions of feudalism and absentee-landlordship—with the creation of co-operatives in farming.

Thirdly, the Holy Qur'ãn blocks the roads to monopoly capitalism through its anti-monopolistic laws in general and the abolition of all forms and all rates of interest in particular.

However, neither private enterprise nor private ownership of property has been banned. Rather, the latter is protected under the Qur'ãnic law. Indeed, the Qur'ãnic economic philosophy stands in definite opposition to the Marxist Scientific Socialism which establishes 'state capitalism', as much as it is opposed to individualistic monopoly capitalism. But the fundamental Qur'ãnic ideals relating to the maintenance of Islamic society as spiritually-illumined, morally healthy and economically dedicated to the welfare of *all* members, make it imperative for the Islamic state to establish a form of economy wherein private sector does not give birth to business magnates and industrial lords, and the state remains in a position to ensure the provision of basic needs to all.

The provision of basic needs to all has to be in the Islamic state fundamentally on the basis of full employment. However, Islam has provided a social welfare tax through *Zakãt* for ensuring basic needs to the disabled and the unemployed. Then, because all that belongs to a Muslim is held by him as 'trust' from God (IX:111), Islam has also commended generosity in terms of voluntary economic well-doing to those in need, to the utmost of one's capacity and considering one's action as a fulfilment of the *right* of the other person—and not merely as ritualistic religious 'charity to a beggar'.

This last fact deserves repeated and vehement emphasis in view of the colossal ignorance concerning Islam's economic philosophy. For

---

19 It should be clearly noted that un-organised voluntary religious charity does not achieve much; and its adverse effect is the creation of the institution of beggary, which is highly degrading and which Islam has vehemently condemned. The fact is that greed for possession of wealth is rooted in the animal self of the human beings, and not many people are capable of helping their fellow-beings with any amount of grace and large-heartedness.

the achievement of its goal of ensuring economic welfare for all, the Holy Qur'ãn does not confine itself to emphasis merely on voluntary charity[19], as other religions do, but adopts a methodical approach to the problem of the economic sufferings of humanity and its solution. These sufferings emerge, in its view, when wealth becomes concentrated in a few hands, bringing in its wake insatiable lust for luxuries, creating the cult of 'wealth, wine and woman', and giving rise to the need of greater and greater exploitation of the weaker members of society. The lust for exploitation, grounded as it always is in a spiritually-hardened heart, is directed to the enjoyment of vulgar pleasures and to exercise in megalomania. When it continues unchecked in a society, moral, economic and political corruption attains progressively such virulence as to act as a dynamite for blowing up the entire spiritual and moral fabric of the community, finally bringing about its destruction. The pithy warning has gone forth in the Qur'ãn: "And how many a community have We (God) destroyed that became reckless in respect of (its structure of) livelihood!....." (XXVIII:58)

Chapter X

INTEGRALISTIC CULTURE AND INTEGRALISTIC CIVILISATION

(A)

Culture

Because of its comprehensive and integralistic approach—which is the demand of its unique Philosophy of Unity, the Holy Qur'ãn reconciles the elements of value in Rationalism and Empiricism[1], affirms the reality of both rational and the empirical (XXII:62; VI:73; etc.)—of course, in accordance with the status of each, demands belief in the Unseen (II:3) as well as in the Seen (III:190; etc.), i.e., in the supra-sensible as well as in the sensible, and synthesises the Ideational and the Sensate, projecting thereby a perfect and sound *Integralistic* or *Idealistic Culture*.

(B)

Civilisation

As already pointed out, the Holy Qur'ãn came not to add one more to the list of the world's religions, or to merely correct certain notions taught by the different religions in respect of the *religious aspect* of human life; but—and that is extremely important for our notice—it came to impart a correct philosophy of *Culture* and, beyond that, to lay the foundations of a new *Civilisation*. The existence of socio-political dimension in the Holy Prophet Muhammad's spiritual struggle, in contrast to the other-worldly character of the spiritual struggle said to have been waged by Holy Prophet Jesus (Peace be on him!), was in response to the demands to the former's all-comprehending Message and Mission, whose range covered the entire area of human thought and behaviour: from the problems of the individual to the problems of the healthy growth of human civilisation.

And a new civilisation did come into existence—a balanced civilisation conceived in terms of the realisation of Piety, Truth, Justice, Love, Beauty, Wisdom and Service to Humanity, and based on the concept of integralistic or idealistic culture, as distinct from the pre-Qur'ãnic

---

1 Ref. p. 108.

ideational and the modern sensate cultures, of the East and the West respectively—as already noticed.

Just to give an idea of what type of civilisation emerged in history under the impact of Islam, we may give here only its briefest account, and that too qualified by the following considerations:

(i) Because of what we shall emphasise later about the intimate relation between the Islamic and the modern Western civilisation, we shall confine ourselves to that period wherein the Islamic civilisation matured in its different dimensions and we shall lay greater emphasis on its, what might be called, sensate aspects[2]. Of course, their Islamic ethico-religious foundations as well as the concomitant high spiritual and moral tone of the Muslims in general—in spite of the deviations of certain members of the aristocracy—are unchallengable.

(ii) We shall state the facts on the authority of a non-Muslim historian, Will Durant, who is one of the most recent writers on the subject, as also a devout Christian and fanatically anti-Islam,—the latter qualification standing guarantee against any misgiving as to the authenticity of the account in respect of the merits of Islamic civilisation.

(iii) It is impossible to make the account in any degree comprehensive because of the extreme dearth of source-materials, as Will Durant himself admits:

"It is a pity that we know these three centuries (750-1050) of Arabic efflorescence so imperfectly. Thousands of Arabic manuscripts in science, literature, and philosophy, lie hidden in the libraries of the Muslim world; in Constantinople alone there are thirty mosque libraries whose wealth has been merely scratched; in Cairo, Damascus, Mosul, Baghdad, Delhi are great collections not even catalogued; an immense library in the Escorial near Madrid had hardly completed the listing of its Islamic manuscripts in science, literature, jurisprudence, and philosophy. What we know of Muslim thought in those centuries is a fragment of what survives; what survives is a fragment of what was produced; what appears in these pages is a morsel of a fraction of a fragment." (*The Age of Faith*, p. 257).

---

2 Some of the ethical aspects shall be dealt with in the next chapter.

The Islamic Civilisation in its Age of Glory

Will Durant observes (The Age of Faith, pp. 179-343):

"In the Qur'ãn.....are rules not only for manners and hygiene, marriage and divorce, and the treatment of children, slaves, and animals, but also for commerce and politics, interest and debts, contracts and wills, industry and finance, crime and punishment, war and peace. Muhammad did not disdain commerce....He threatened hell to lying or cheating merchants; denounced monopolists and speculators who 'keep back grain to sell at a high rate'; and bade the employer 'give the labourer his wage before his perspiration dries'. He prohibited the taking or giving of interest (ii, 275, iii, 130). No reformer ever more actively taxed the rich to help the poor. Every will was expected to leave something to the poor; if a man died intestate his natural heirs were directed to give a part of their inheritance to charity (iv, 8)....he improved the position of woman....

"Muhammad's ethic transcended the limits of the tribe....Distinction of rank or race, so strong among the tribes, was diminished by similarity of belief, 'If a negro slave is appointed to rule you, hear and obey him, though his head be like a dried grape'. It was a noble conception that made one people of diverse nations scattered over the continents....Muhammad (taught)....'Let there be no violence in religion'. 'If they embrace Islam they are surely directed; but if they turn their backs, verily to theE belongs preaching only'. 'Give a respite to the disbelievers. Deal thou gently with them'.....'Kill not the old man who cannot fight, nor young children, nor women'.....'Fight in the way of Allah against those who fight against you, but begin not hostilities. Allah loveth not aggressors'.

".....the Qur'ãn....gave to simple souls the simplest, least mystical, least ritualistic, of all creeds, free from idolatry and sacerdotalism. Its message raised the moral and cultural level of its followers, promoted social order and unity, inculcated hygiene, lessened superstition and cruelty, bettered the condition of slaves, lifted the lowly to dignity and pride, and produced among Muslims (barring the revels of some caliphs) a degree of sobriety and temperance unequaled elsewhere in the white man's world. It gave men an uncomplaining acceptance of the hardships and limitations of life, and at the same time stimulated them to the most astonishing expansion in history.

"Civilisation is a union of soil and soul—the resources of the earth transformed by the desire and discipline of men....All these were busy in Islam....The orange tree.....the Arabs introduced it to Syria, Asia Minor, Palestine, Egypt, and Spain, from which countries it pervaded southern Europe. The cultivation of sugar-cane and the refining of sugar were likewise spread by the Arabs....and were brought by Crusaders to their European states. Cotton was first cultivated in Europe by the Arabs. These achievements on lands largely arid were made possible by organized irrigation; here the caliphs made an exception to their principle of leaving the economy to free enterprise; the government directed and financed the maintenance of the greater canals.

".....Under Muslim rule western Asia attained a pitch of industrial and commercial prosperity unmatched by western Europe before the sixteenth century.

"The state left industry and commerce free, and aided it with a relatively stable currency. Ibn Hawqal (c. 975) describes a kind of promissory note....from the Arabic work *sakk* for this form of credit is derived our work *check*. Investors shared in financing commercial voyages or caravans.....Monopolies were illegal.....

"....In general the Muslim seems to have excelled the Christian in commercial morality, fidelity to his word, and loyalty to treaties signed....normally the Muslim was the soul of courtesy, humanity, and tolerance....In general Muslim society was one of excellent manners....

"If we may believe the traditions, *Muhammad, unlike most religious reformers, admired and urged the pursuit of knowledge*.....Education began as soon as the child could speak.....At the age of six some slave children, some girls, and nearly all boys except the rich (who had private tutors) entered an elementary school....Tuition was normally free....Elementary education aimed to form character, secondary education to transmit knowledge....Tuition in these colleges was free, and in some cases government or philanthropy paid both the salaries of the professors and the expenses of the students....students would travel from one end of the Muslim world to another to meet the mind of a famous teacher....When a visitor entered a Muslim city he took it for granted that he could hear a scholarly lecture at the principal mosque at almost any hour of the day.

"....The first paper-manufacturing plant in Islam was opened at Baghdad in 794 by al-Fadl, son of Harun's vizier. The crait was brought by the Arabs to Sicily and Spain, and thence passed into Italy and France….The invention facilitated the making of books wherever it went. Yaqubi tells us that in his time (891) Baghdad had over a hundred booksellers.

"Most mosques had libraries, and some cities had public libraries of considerable content and generous accessibility. About 950 Mosul had a library, established by private philanthropy, where students were supplied with paper as well as books. Ten large catalogues were required to list the volumes in the public library at Rayy. Basra's library gave stipends to scholars working in it….When Baghdad was destroyed by the Mongols it had thirty-six public libraries. Private libraries were numberless; it was a fashion among the rich to have an ample collection of books…princes like Sahib ibn Abbas in the tenth century might own as many books as could then be found in all the libraries of Europe combined….in a thousand mosques from Cordova to Samarkand scholars were as numerous as pillars, and made the cloisters tremble with their eloquence; the roads of the realm were disturbed by innumerable geographers, historians, and theologians seeking knowledge and wisdom….the conquerors showed such tolerance that of the poets, scientists, and philosophers who now made Arabic the most learned and literary tongue in the world only a small minority were of Arab blood.

"….Ibn Qutaiba (828-89) was one of many Muslims, who attempted to write a *history of the world*….Muhammad al-Nadim produced in 987 an *Index of the Sciences* (*Fihrist al-'ulum*), a bibliography of all books in Arabic, original or translated, on any branch of knowledge….we may estimate the wealth of Muslim literature in his time by noting that not one in a thousand of the volumes that he named is known to exist today.

"….Abu-l-Hasan Ali al-Masudi, an Arab of Baghdad, travelled…..He gathered his gleanings into a thirty-volume encyclopaedia….Al-Masudi survived omnivorously the geography, biology, history, customs, religion, science, philosophy, and literature of all lands from China to France….he summarized his views on science, history, and philosophy in a *Book of Information*, in which he suggested an evolution 'from mineral to plant, from plant to animal, and from animal to man'.

"Algebra….owes its name to the Arabs, who extensively developed this detective science….Al-Khwarizmi contributed effectively to five sciences: he wrote on the Hindu numerals; compiled astronomical tables which, as revised in Muslim Spain, were for centuries standard among astronomers from Cordova to Chang-an; formulated the oldest trigono metrical tables known; collaborated with sixty-nine other scholars in drawing up for al-Mamun a geographical encyclopaedia; and in his *Calculation of Integration and Equation* gave analytical and geometrical solutions of quadratic equations. *This work,* now lost in its Arabic form, *was translated by Gerard of Cremona in the twelfth century, was used as a principal text in European universities until the sixteenth century, and introduced to the West the word algebra* (*al-Jabr*—'restitution', 'completion'. (Thabit ibn Qurra (826-901)….achieved fame in astronomy and medicine, and became the greatest of Muslim geometers….

"The Caliph al-Mamun engaged a staff of astronomers to make observations and records, to test the findings of Ptolemy, and to *study the spots on the sun.* Taking for granted the sphericity of the earth, they measured a terrestrial degree by simultaneously taking the position of the sun from both Palmyra and the plain Sinjr; their measurement gave 56-2/3 miles—half a mile more than our present calculation; and from their results they *estimated the earth's circumference* to approximate 20,000 miles. *These astronomers proceeded on completely scientific principles: they accepted nothing as true which was not confirmed by experience or experiment.* One of them, Abu'l-Farghani, of Transoxiana, wrote (c. 860) an astronomical text which remained in authority in Europe and Western Asia for 700 years. Even more renowned was al-Battani; his astronomical observations, continued for forty-one years, were remarkable for their range and accuracy; he determined many astronomical coefficients with *remarkable approximation to modern calculations*—the precession of the equinoxes at 54.5" a year, and the inclination of the ecliptic at 23° 55'. Working under the patronage of the early Buwayhid ruler of Baghdad, *Abu'l Wafa*….discovered the third *lunar vartidtion 600 years before Tycho Brahe. Costly instruments were built for Muslim astronomers; not only astrolabes and armillary spheres,* known to the Greeks, but quadrants with a radius of thirty feet, and sextants with a radius of eighty. The astrolabe, much improved by the Muslims, reached Europe in the tenth century, and was *widely used by mariners till the seventeenth.* The Arabs designed and constructed it with aesthetic passion, making it at once an instrument of science and a work of art.

"*Even more important than the charting of the skies was mapping of the earth*….Suleiman al-Tajir—i.e., the merchant—about 840 carried his wares to the Far East; an anonymous author (851) wrote a narrative of

Suleiman's journey; this oldest Arabic account of China antedated Marco Polo's *Travels* by 425 years. In the same century Ibn Khordadhbeh wrote a description of India, Ceylon, the East Indies, and China, apparently from direct observation; and Ibn Hawqal described India and Africa. Ahmad al-Yaqubi, of Armenia and Khurasan, wrote in 891 a *Book of the Countries,* giving a reliable account of Islamic provinces and cities, and of many foreign states. Muhammad al-Muqaddasi visited all the lands of Islam except Spain, suffered countless vicissitudes, and in 985 wrote his *Description of the Muslim Empire*—the greatest work of Arabic geography before al-Biruni's *India.*

"Abu al-Rayhan Muhammad ibn Ahmad al-Biruni (973-1048) shows the Muslim scholar at his best. Philosopher, historian, traveller, geographer, linguist, mathematician, astronomer, poet, and physicist—and doing major and original work in all these fields....His first major work (c. 1000) was a highly technical treatise—*Vestiges of the Past....his attitude was that of the objective scholar, assiduous in research, critical in the scrutiny of traditions and texts* (including the Gospels), *precise and conscientious in statement,* frequently admitting his ignorance, and promising to pursue his inquiries till the truth should emerge. In the preface to the Vestiges he wrote like Francis Bacon: 'We must clear our minds....from all cause that blind people to the truth—old custom, party spirit, personal rivalry of passion, the desire for influence'....In 1030 he published his masterpiece, *History of India*....His interest extended to nearly all the sciences. He gave the best medieval account of the Hindu numerals. He wrote treatise on the astrolable, the planisphere, the armillary sphere; and formulated astronomical tables for Sultan Masud. He took it for granted that the earth is round, noted 'the attraction of all things towards the centre of the earth', and remarked that astronomic data can be explained as well by supposing that the earth turns daily on its axis and annually around the sun, as by the reverse hypothesis. He speculated on the possibility that the *Indus valley had been once the bottom of a sea.* He composed an extensive lapidary, describing a great number of stones and metals from the natural, commercial, and medical points of view. He determined the specific gravity of eighteen precious stones, and laid down the principle that the specific gravity of an object corresponds to the volume of water it displaces. He found a method of calculating, without laborious additions, the result of the repeated doubling of a number....He contributed to geometry the solution of theorems that thereafter bore his name. He composed an encyclopaedia of astronomy, a treatise on geography, and an epitome of astronomy, astrology, and mathematics.

He explained the workings of natural springs and artesian wells by the *hydrostatic principle* of communicating vessels.

"Chemistry as a science was almost created by the Muslims....the Saracens introduced precise observation, controlled experiment, and careful records. They invented and named the alembic (al-anbiq), chemical analyzed innumerable substances, composed lapidaries, distinguished alkalis and acids, investigated their affinities, studies and manufactured hundreds of drugs.... 'The most famous of the alchemists was Jabir Ibn Hayyan (702-65), known to Europe as Gebir....'The hundred or more works attributed to him.....were translated into Latin, and strongly stimulated the development of European chemistry....

"....(Muslims) developed in alchemy that experimental method which is the greatest pride and tool of the modern mind. When Roger Bacon proclaimed that method to Europe, five hundred years after Jabir, he owned his illumination to the Moors of Spain, whose light had come from the Muslim East.

"The remains of Muslim biology in this period are scant. Abu Hanifa al-Dinawari (815-95) wrote a *Book of Plants*....adding many plants to pharmacology. Muhammadan botanists knew how to produce new fruits by grafting....Othman Amr al-Jahiz (d. 869) propounded *a theory of evolution like al-Masudi's : life had climbed 'from mineral to plant, from plant to animal, from animal to man.'* The mystic poet Jalal ud-Din (Rumi) accepted the theory....

".....The Muslims established the first opothecary shops and dispensaries, founded the first medieval school of pharmacy, and wrote great treatises on pharmacology. Muslim physicians were enthusiastic advocates of the bath, especially in fevers and in the form of the steam bath. Their directions for the treatment of smallpox and measles could scarcely be bettered today. Anaesthesia by inhalation was practised in some surgical operations; hashish and other drugs were used to induce deep sleep....Medical instruction was given chiefly at the hospitals. No man could legally practice medicine without passing an examination and receiving a state diploma; druggists, barbers, and orthopaedists were likewise subject to state regulation and inspection. The physician-vizier Ali ibn Isa organized a staff of doctor to go from place to place to tend the sick (931); certain physicians made daily visits to jails; there was an especially human treatment of the insane.

".....Ali ibn Isa, greatest of Muslim oculists, whose Manual for Oculists was used as *a text in Europe till the eighteenth century.*

"The outstanding figure in this human dynasty of healers was Abu Bekr Muhammad al-Razi (844-926), famous in Europe as Rhazes....he....wrote some 131 books, half of them on medicine, most of them lost. His *Kitab al-Hawi* (*Comprehensive Book*) covered in twenty volume every branch of medicine. Translated into Latin as *Liber continens*, it was probably *the most highly respected and frequently used medical textbook in the white world for several centuries;* it was one of the nine books that composed the whole library of the medical faculty at the University of Paris in 1395. His *Treatise on Smallpox and Measles* was a masterpiece of direct observation and clinical analysis; it was the first *accurate study of infectious diseases,* the first effort to distinguish the two ailments. We may judge its influence and repute by the forty English editions printed between 1498 and 1866. The most famous of al-Razi's works was a ten-volume survey of medicine, the *Kitab al-Mansuri*....Gerard of Cremona translated it into Latin; the ninth volume of this translation, the *Nonus Almansoris, was a popular text in Europe till the sixteenth century.*

".....Islam knew its greatest philosopher and most famous physician as Abu Ali al-Husein ibn Sina (980-1037)....he found time....to write a hundred books, covering nearly every field of science and philosophy....He translated Euclid, made astronomical observations, and devised an instrument like our vernier. He *made original studies of motion, force, vacuum, light, heat and specific gravity. His treatise on minerals was a main source of European geology until the thirteenth century. His remark on the formation of mountains is a model of clarity*: 'Mountains may be due to two different causes. Either they result from upheavals of the earth's crust, such as might occur in violent earthquake; or they are the effect of water, which, cutting for itself a new route, has denuded the valleys. The strata are of different kinds, some soft, some hard; the winds and waters disintegrate the first kind, but leave the other intact. It would require a long period of time for all such changes to be accomplished....but that water has been the main cause of these effects is proved by the *existence of fossil remains of acquatic animals on many mountains*'.

"Two gigantic production contain Avicenna's teaching: the *Kitab al-Shifa*....an eighteen-volume encyclopaedia of mathematics, physics, metaphysics, theology, economics, politics, and music; and the *Qanun-fi-l-Tibb*, or *Canon of Medicine*, a gigantic survey of physiology, hygiene, therapy, and pharmacology, with sundry excursions into philosophy....He conceives medicine as the art of removing an impediment to the normal functioning of nature.... The *Qanun*, translated into Latin in the twelfth century, *dethroned al-Razi, and even Galen, as the chief text in European medical schools; it held its place as required reading in the universities of Montpellier and Louvain till the middle of the seventeenth century.*

"....Avicenna....His influence was immence: it reached out to Sapin to mold Averroes and Malmonides, and into Latin Christendom to help the great Scholastics; it is astonishing how much of Albertus Magnus and Thomas Aquinas goes back to Avicenna. Roger Bacon called him 'the chief authority in philosophy after Aristole'; and Aquinas was not merely practising his customary courtesy in speaking of him with as much respect as of Plato.

"....Abu Yusuf Ibn Isaq al-Kindi was born in Kufa about 803.... studying everything, writing 265 treatises about everything—arithmetic, geometry, astronomy, meteorology, geography, physics, politics, music, medicine, philosophy....he struggled to reduce health, medicine, and music to mathematical relations. *He studied the tides, sought the laws that determine the speed of a falling body, and investigated the phenomena of light* in a book on Optics which *influenced Roger Bacon.*

"Thirty-nine works of al-Farabi survive....One work....strikes us with its original force: *Al-Madinah al-Fadila—The Ideal City*....the only right is might. Al-Farabi counters this view with an appeal to his fellow men to build a society not upon envy, power, and strife, but upon reason, devotion, and love.

"....From the Alhambra in Spain to the Taj Mahal in India, Islamic art overrode all limits of place and time, laughed at distinctions of race and blood, developed a unique and yet varied character, and expressed the human spirit with a profuse delicacy never surpassed.

"Muslim architecture, like most architecture in the *Age of Faith*, was almost entirely religious....Nevertheless, though the remains are scant, we hear of bridges, aqueducts, fountains, reservoirs, public baths, fortresses, and turreted walls built by engineer-architects....The Crusaders found excellent military architecture at Aleppo, Baalbek, and elsewhere in the Islamic East, learned there the uses of machicolated walls, and took from their foes many an idea for their own incomparable castles and forts. The Alcazar at Seville and the Alhambra at Granada were fortresses and palaces combined.

"We probably own this splendor of ornament to the Semitic prohibition of human or animal forms in art: as if in compensation, the Muslim artist invented or adopted an overflowing abundance of non-representational forms. He sought an outlet first in geometrical figures—line, angle, square, cube, polygon, cone, spiral, ellipse, circle, sphere; he repeated these in a hundred combinations, and developed them into swirls, guilloches, reticulations, *entralacs*, and stars; passing to floral forms, he designed, in many materials, wreaths, vines, or rosettes of lotus, acanthus, or palm tendrils or leaves; in the tenth century he merged all these in the arabesque; and to them all, as a unique and major ornament, he added the Arabic script.

"The brightest name of Muslim Egyptian science is that of Muhammad ibn al-Haitham, known to medieval Europe as Alhazen.... We know al-Haitham chiefly by his *Kitab al-Manazir*, or *Book of Optics*; of all medieval productions this is probably the most thoroughly scientific in its method and thought. *Al-Haitham studied the refraction of light though transparent mediums like air and water and came so close to discovering the magnifying lens that roger Bacon, Witelo, and other Europeans three centuries later based upon his work their own advances toward the microscope and the telescope.* He rejected the theory of Euclid and Ptolemy that vision results from a ray leaving the eye and reaching the object; rather 'the form of the perceived object passes into the eye, and is transmitted there by the transparent body'—the lens. He remarked the effect of the atmosphere in increasing the apparent size of sun or moon when near the horizon; showed that through atmospheric refraction the light of the sun reaches us even when the sun is as much as nineteen degrees below the horizon; and on this basis he *calculated the height of the atmosphere* at ten (English) miles. He analyzed the correlation between the weight and the density of the atmosphere, and the effect of atmospheric density upon the weight of objects. He studied with complex mathematical formulas the action of light on spherical or parabolic mirrors, and through the burning glass. He observed the half-moon shape of the image, during eclipses, on the wall opposite a small hole made in the window shutters; *this is the first known mention of the camera obscura, or dark chamber, on which all photography depends. We could hardly exaggerate the influence of al-Haitham on European science. Without him Roger Bacon might never have been heard of; Bacon* quotes him or refers to him at almost every step in that part of the *Opusmalius* which deals with optics; and Part VI rests almost entirely on the findings of the Cairene physicist. *As late as Kepler and Leonardo European studies of light were based upon al-Haitham's work.*

" '*Never was Andalusia so mildly, justly, and wisely governed as by her Arab conquerors'*. It is the judgement of a great Christian Orientalist, whose enthusiasm may require some discounting of his praise; but after due deduction his verdict stands....al-Maqqari gives a *hundred examples of the justice, liberality, and refinement of the Umayyad rulers of Spain*....they were certainly an improvement upon the illiberal Visigothic regime that had preceded them. Their *management of public affairs was the most competent* in the Western world of that age. *Laws were rational and humane, and were administered by a well-organized judiciary. For the most part the conquered in their internal affairs, were governed by their own laws and their own officials. Town were well policed; markets, weights and measures were effectively supervised. A regular census recorded population and property. Taxation was reasonable compared with the imposts of Rome or Byzantium. The revenues of the Cordovan caliphate* under Abd-er-Rahman III reached 12,045,000 gold dinars ($57,213,750)—*probably more than the united governmental revenues of Latin Christendom; but these receipts were due not so much to high taxes as to well-governed and progressive agriculture, industry, and trade.*

"....The Arab for the most part left the actual work of agriculture to the conquered; however, they used the latest manuals of agronomy, and under their direction agricultural science developed in Spain far in advance of Christian Europe.

".....Christians and Muslims intermarried freely; now and then they joined in celebrating a Christian or Muslim holiday, or used the same building as church and mosque....Clerics and laymen from Christian Europe came in safety and freedom to Cordova, Toledo, or Seville as students, visitors, or travellers.

".....Cordova....*extraordinary general prosperity*....streets were paved, had raised side walks, and were lighted at night; one could travel for ten miles by the light of streets lamps, and along an uninterrupted series of buildings....was *the focus and summit of Spanish intellectual life, though Toledo, Granada, and Seville shared actively in the mental exhilaration of the time*. Muslim historians picture the Moorish cities as beehives of poets, scholars, jurists, physicians, and scientists; al-Maqqari fills sixty pages with their names. Primary schools were numerous, but charged tuition; Hakam II added twenty-seven schools for the free instruction of the poor. Girls as well as boys went to school; several Moorish ladies became prominent in literature or art. Higher education was provided by independent lecturers in the mosques; their courses constituted the loosely organized University of Cordova, which in the tenth and eleventh centuries was second in renown only to similar institutions in Cairo and Baghdad. Colleges were established also at Granada, Toledo, Seville, Murcia, Almeria, Valencia, Cadiz. The technique of paper-making was brought in from Baghdad, and books increased and multiplied. Muslim Spain had seventy libraries; rich men displayed their Morocco bindings, and bibliophiles collected rare or beautifully illuminated books.....*Scholars were held in awesome repute in* Muslim Spain, and were consulted in simple faith that learning and wisdom are one.

".....Abu Muhammad Ali ibn Hazm (994-1064), besides serving as vizier to the last Umayyads, was a theologian and historian of great erudition. His *Book of Religions and Sects,* discussing Judaism, Zoroastrianism, Christianity, and the principal varieties of Muhammedanism is *one of the world's earliest essays in comparative religion*....Maslama ibn Ahmad (d. 1007), of Madrid and Cordova, adapted the astronomic tables of al-Khwarizmi to Spain.....*Ibrahim al-Zarqali* (c. 1029-87) *of Toledo made an international name by improving astronomical instruments; Copernicus quoted his treatise on the astrolabe;* his astronomical observations were the best of his age, and *enabled him to prove for the first time the motion of the solar apogee with reference to the stars;* his 'Toledan Tables' of planetary movements were used throughout Europe. *Abul Qasim al-Zahrawi* (936-1013), physician to Abd-er-Rahman III, was honoured in Christendom as Abulcasis; he stands at the top of Muslim surgeons; his medical encyclopaedia, *al-Tasrif,* included three books on surgery which, translated into Latin, *became the standard text of surgery for many centuries. Cordova was in this period the favourite resort of Europeans for surgical operations.*

"....*Cairo, Alexandria, Jerusalem, Baalbek, Aleppo, Damascus, Mosul, Emesa, Tus, Nishapur, and many other cities boasted of colleges; Baghdad alone had thirty in* 1064. A year later Nizam ul-Mulk added another: the Nizamiya; in 1234 the Caliph Mustansir founded still another, which in size, architecture, and equipment surpassed all the rest; one traveller called it the most beautiful building in the city. It contained four distinct law schools, in which qualified students received free tuition, food, and medical care, and a monthly gold dinar for other expenses; it contained a hospital, a bath-house, and a library freely open to students and staff. Women probably attended college in some cases, for we hear of a *Shaikha*—a lady professor—whose lectures....drew large audiences (c. 1178)....Muhammad al-Shahrastani, in a *Book of Religions and Sects* (1128) analyzed the leading faiths and philosophies of the world, and summarized their history; *no contemporary Christian could have written so learned and impartial a work.*

"Europe knows Persian Poetry chiefly through Omar Khayyam....*His Algebra,* translated into French in 1857, *made significant advances* both on al-Khwarizmi and on the Greeks; its partial solution of cubic equations has been judged 'perhaps the very highest peak of medieval mathematics'. Another of his works on algebra (a manuscript in the Leiden Library) studied critically the postulates and definitions of Euclid. In 1074 the Sultan Malik Shah commissioned him and others to reform the Persian calendar. The outcome was a calendar that required a day's correction every 3770 years—slightly more accurate than ours....

"Jalal-ud-Din Rumi (1201-73)....wrote several hundred poems. The shorter ones, collected in his *Divan* or *Book of Odes*, are marked by such depth of feeling, sincerity, and richness, yet naturalness, of imagery as place them *at the top of all religious poetry composed since the Psalms.* Jalal's main work, the *Mathnawi-i-Ma'nawi* (Spiritual Couplets), is a....religious epic outweighing in bulk all the legacy of 'Homer'.

"*The Muslims continued, in this period* (1057-1258), *their unchallenged ascendancy in science.* In mathematics the most signal advances were made in Morocco and Azerbaijan; we see here again the range of Islamic civilization. In 1229 Hasan al-Marraqushi (i.e., of Marraqesh) published tables of sines for each degree, and tables of versed sines, arc sines, and arc cotangents. A generation later Nasir ul-Din al-Tusi (i.e., of Tus) issued the first treatise in which trigonometry was considered as an independent science rather than an appendage to astronomy; his *Kitab shakl al-qatta* remained without a rival in its field until the *De Triangulis* of Regiomontanus two centuries later. *Perhaps Chinese trigonometry,* which appears in the second half of the thirteenth century, *was of Arabic origin.*

"The outstanding work of physical science in this age was the *Kitab Mizan al-hikmah*....written about 1122 by....Abu'l Fath al-Khuzini. It gave a history of physics, *formulated the laws of the lever,* compiled tables of specific gravity for many liquids and solids, and *proposed a theory of gravitation as a universal force drawing all things towards the centre of the earth.* Water wheels....were improved by the Muslims; the Crusaders....introduced them into Germany.

"*In 1081 Ibrahim al-Sahdi of Valencia constructed the oldest known celestial globe*, a brass sphere 209 millimeters (81.5 inches) in diameter; upon its surface, in forty-seven constellations, were engraved 1015 stars in their respective magnitudes. *The Giralda of Seville* (1190) *was an observtory as well as a minaret; there Jabir ibn Aflah made the observations* for his *Islah al-Majisti*, or *Correction of the Almagest* (1240). The same reaction against Ptolemaic astronomy marked the works of Abu Ishaq al-Bitruji (Alpetraglus) of Cordova, who *paved the way for Copernicus* by destructively criticizing the theory of epicycles and eccentrics through which Ptolemy had sought to explain the path and motions of the stars.

"The age produced two geographers of universal medieval renown. Abu Abdallah Muhammad al-Idrisi was born at Ceuta (1100), studied at Cordova, and wrote in Palermo, at the behest of King Roger II of Sicily, his *Kitab al-Rujari* (*Roger's Book*). It divided the earth into seven climatic zones, and each zone into ten parts; each of the seventy parts was illustrated by a detailed map; these maps were the *crowning achievement of medieval cartography, unprecedented* in fullness, accuracy, and scope. *Al-Idrisi, like most Muslim scientists, took for granted the sphericity of the earth.* Rivaling him for the honor of being the greatest medieval geographer was Abu Abdallah Yaqut (1179-1229)....he completed his *Mu'jam al-Buldan* (1228)—a *vast geographical encyclopaedia* which summed up nearly all medieval knowledge of the globe. Yaqut included almost everything—astronomy, physics, archaeology, ethnography, history, giving the *co-ordinates of the cities* and the lives and works of their famous men. Seldom has any man so loved the earth.

"Botany, almost forgotten since Theophrastus, revived with the Moslems of this age. Al-Idrisi wrote a herbal, but stressed the botanical rather than merely the medicinal interest of 360 plants. Abu'l Abbas of Seville (1216) earned the surname of al-Nabati, the botanist, by his studies of plant life from the Atlantic to the Red Sea. *Abu Muhammad ibn Baitar of Malago* (1190-1248) *gathered all Islamic botany into a vast work of extraordinary erudition, which remained the standard botanical authority till the sixteenth century*, and marked him as the greatest botanist and pharmacist of the Middle Ages. *Ibn al-Awan of Seville* (1190) *won a like pre-eminence in agronomy;* his *Kitab al-Falaha* (*Book of the Peasant*) analyzed soils and manures, described the cultivation of 585 plants and fifty fruit trees, explained methods of grafting, and discussed the symptoms and cures of plant diseases. This was the *most complete treatment of agricultural science* in the whole medieval period.

"*In this as in the preceding age the Muslims produced the leading physicians of Asia, Africa, and Europe. They excelled especially in opthalmology.... Operations for cataract were numerous.* Khalifah ibn abi-Mahasin of Aleppo (1256) was so confident of his skill that he operated for cataract on a one-eyed man. Ibn Baitar's *Kitab al-jami'* made medicinal-botanical history; it listed 1400 plants, foods, and drugs, 300 of them new; analyzed their chemical constitution and healing power; and added acute observations on their use in therapy. But the greatest name in this acme of Muslim medicine is Abu Marwan ibn Zuhr (1091-1162) of Seville, known to the European medical world as Avenzoar. He was the third in six generations of famous physicians, all of one family line, and each at the top of his profession. His *Kitab al-Tasir*, or *Book of Simplification of Therapeutics and Diet*, was written at the request of his friend Averroes, who (himself the greatest philosopher of the age) considered him the greatest physician since Galen. Ibn Zuhr's forte was clinical description; he left classical analyses of mediastinal tumors, pericarditis, intestinal tuberculois, and pharyngeal paralysis. Translation of the *Tasir* into Hebrew and Latin *deeply influenced European medicine*.

"*Islam led the world also in the equipment and competence of its hospitals*. One founded by Nur-ud-din at Damascus in 1160 gave free treatment and drugs during three centuries: for 267 years, we are told, its fires were never extinguished. Ibn Jubayr, coming to Baghdad in 1184, marvelled at the great *Bimaristan Adadi*, a hospital rising like some royal palace along the bank of the Tigirs; here food and drugs were given to the patients without charge. In Cairo, in 1285, Sultan Qalun began the *Maristan al-Mansur*, the greatest hospital of the Middle Ages. Within a spacious quadrangular enclosure four buildings rose around a courtyard adorned with arcades and cooled with fountains and brooks. There were separate wards for diverse diseases and for convalescents; laboratories, a dispensary, out-patient clinics, diet kitchens, baths, a library, a chapel, a lecture hall, and particularly pleasant accommodation for the insane. Treatment was given gratis to men and women, rich and poor, slave and free; and a sum of money was disbursed to each convalescent on his departure, so that he need not at once return to work. The sleepless were provided with soft music, professional story-tellers, and perhaps books of history. *Asylums for the care of the insane existed in all the major cities of Islam.*

"....Muhammedanism produced its greatest theologian, the Augustine and the *Kant of Islam*. Abu Hamid, *al-Ghazali* was born at Tus in 1058....wrote his most influential book—*Tahafut al-Filasifa* (*The Destruction of Philosophy*). All the arts of reason were turned against reason. By a 'transcendental dialectic' as subtle as Kant's....*seven centuries before Hume, al-Ghazali reduced reason to the principle of causality, and causality to mere sequence*....In his *Ihya Ulum al-Din* (*Revival of the Sciences of Religion*) he expounded and defended his renovated orthodoxy with all the eloquence and fervour of his prime; never in Islam the sceptics and the philosophers encountered to vigorous a foe....

"Abu Bakr (Europe'so Abubacer) ibn Tufail (1107-1185)....found time to write, among more technical works, the most remarkable philosophical romance in medieval literature (*Hayy ibn Yaqzan*). It took its title from ibn Sina, and (through Ockley's English translation in 1708) *may have suggested Robinson Crusoe to Defoe.*

"....known to Islam as *Abu al-Walid Muhammad ibn Rushd* (1126-98), and to medieval Europe as Averroes the most influential figure in Islamic Philosophy.....In 1169 Averroes was appointed chief justice of Seville; in 1172 of Cordova....His work in medicine has been almost forgotten in his fame as a philosopher; he was, however, 'one of the greatest physicians of his time', *the first to explain the function of the retina,* and to recognize that an attack of smallpox confers subsequent immunity. *His encyclopaedia of medicine* (*Kitab al-Kulliyat fil Tibb*), translated into Latin, *was widely used as a text in Christian universites*....he added several works of his own on logic, physics, psychology, metaphysics, theology, law, astronomy and grammar....*Malmonides followed in Averroes' steps* in seeking to reconcile religion and philosophy. In Christendom the Commentaries (of Averroes), translated into Latin from Hebrew, fed the heresies of Siger de Brabant, and the rationalism of the School of Padua, and the threatened the foundations of Christian belief. *St. Thomas Aquinas* wrote his *Summae* to stem this Averroistic tide; but he *followed Averroes* in the method of his Commentaries, in divers interpretations of Aristotle....*Roger Bacon marked Averroes next to Aristotle* and Avicenna, and added....'The philosophy of Averroes today (c. 1270) obtains the unanimous suffrage of wise men'.

"*The influence of Islam on Europe was varied and immense.*" (All italics, present writer's).

Modern Civilisation : A Continuation of Arabic-Islamic Civilisation

The present civilisation is, in respect of its merits, the continuation of the Islamic civilisation, with the difference that theocentricism, integralism and comprehensiveness have dropped off under the stress of certain well-known historical circumstances, culminating in its transformation into a purely sensate civilisation. However, its tragic inadequacy and diseased condition is now being taken notice of by all sane-thinking Westerners, together with the necessity of adopting the Islamic philosophy of civilisation for restoring the balanced accommodation of all the values and thereby reverting to the original Islamic civilisation from which it sprang up. The thick curtain of hatred against Islam, nurtured assiduously for centuries by a scheming priesthood, is the only obstacle. But the goodness of human nature is bound to win the day, and the yearnings of the human soul for Truth and Beauty and Justice are bound to attain realisation. The light of reality has already begun to shine forth, as manifested in the following considered judgement of Prof. H.A.R. Gibb, the famous British orientalist:

"*....in its foundations we have seen that Islam belongs to and is an integral part of the larger Western society. It is the complement and counterbalance to European civilisation, nourished at the same springs, breathing the same air.* In the broadest aspect of history, what is now happening between Europe and Islam is the reintegration of western civilisation, artificially sundered at the Renaissance and now reasserting its unity with overwhelming force. The student of history, though fearfully conscious of the pitfalls of analogy, cannot help recalling two earlier (though even then not the earliest) moments in this secular process of creative interaction between the two halves of the western world. It was the glory and the greatness of the Roman Empire that it united them under its *imperium* and that from that unity were born the spiritual forces which have governed the course of Western history ever since. Halfway between that age and ours occurred the first great intellectual adventure of Islam, when it absorbed the heritage of Hellenism and brought it to a new flowering, the seeds from which contributed to the Renaissance in Europe.

"The process could not end there. It is going on before our very eyes, on a wider and vaster scale, though the contrast offered by the Islamic world as a whole to the amazing technical progress of Europe may still blind us to it; and it may be that the sequel will be the same, that *we must wait upon the Islamic society to restore the balance of Western civilisation upset by the one sided nature of that progress*....At all events Islam stands side by side with Europe in distinction from the true Oriental societies of India and the Far East....*for the fullest development of its cultural life, particularly of its spiritual life, Europe cannot do without the forces and capacities which lie within Islamic society*....

"Within the Western world Islam *still maintains the balance between exaggerated opposites. Opposed equally to the anarchy of European nationalism and the regimentation of Russian communism, it has not yet succumbed to that obsession with the economic side of life which is characteristic of present-day Europe and present-day Russia alike. Its social ethic has been admirably summed up by Professor Massignon: 'Islam has the merit of standing for a very equalitarian conception of the contribution of each citizen by the tithe to the resources of the community; it is hostile to unrestricted exchange, to banking capital, to state loans, to indirect taxes on objects of prime necessity, but it holds to the rights of the father and the husband, to private property, and to commercial capital. Here again it occupies an intermediate position between the doctrines of bourgeois capitalism and Bolshevist communism*'.

"*But Islam has a still further service to render to the cause of humanity.* It stands after all nearer to the real East than Europe does, and it possesses a magnificent tradition of inter-racial understanding and co-operation. No other society has such a record of success in uniting in an equality of status, of opportunity, and of endeavour so many and so various races of mankind....*Islam has still the power to reconcile apparently irreconcilable elements of race and tradition. If ever the opposition of the great societies of East and West is to be replaced by co-operation, the mediation of Islam is an indispensable condition. It its hands lies very largely the solution of the problem with which Europe is faced in its relation with the East. If they unite, the hope of a peaceful issue is immeasurably enhanced. But if Europe, by rejecting the co-operation of Islam, throws it into arms of its rivals, the issue can only be disastrous for both.*"[3]

Besides the above judgement of H.A.R. Gibb, the verdict of Arnold J. Toynbee, the fanatical crusader against Islam and zealous upholder of Christian cause, is also worthy of note. He says (*Civilisation on Trial,* London, 1957; pp. 87, 88, 205-209):

"What value are we to place on Islam ourselves?....Islam's creative gift to mankind is monotheism and we surely dare not throw this gift away....*Islam remains, with a mighty spiritual mission still to carry out*....(Italics, present writer's).

"Two conspicuous source of danger—one psychological and the other material—in the present relations of this cosmopolitan proletariat (—i.e., westernised humanity—) with the dominant element in our modern Western society are race consciousness and alcohol; and in the struggle with each of these evils the Islamic spirit has a service to render which might prove, if it were accepted, to be of high and social value.

"The extinction of race consciousness as between Muslims is one of the outstanding moral achievements of Islam, and in the contemporary world there is, as it happens, a crying need for the propagation of this Islamic virtue.....It is conceivable that the spirit of Islam might be the timely reinforcement which would decide this issue in favour of tolerance and peace.

"As for the evil of alcohol, it is at its worst among primitive populations in tropical regions which have been 'opened up' by Western enterprise....the fact remains that even the most statesmanlike preventive measures imposed by external authority are incapable of liberating a community from a social vice unless a desire for liberation and a will to carry this desire into voluntary action on its own part are awakened in the hearts of the people concerned. Now Western administrators, at any rate those of 'Anglo-Saxon' origin, are spiritually isolated from their 'native'

3 *Whither Islam*?, London 1932, pp. 376-379. (Italics, present writer's).

wards by the physical 'colour bar' which their race-consciousness sets up; the conversion of the natives' souls is a task to which their competence can hardly be expected to extend; and it is at this point that Islam may have a part to play.

"In these recently and rapidly 'opened up' tropical territories, the Western civilisation has produced an economic and political plenum and, in the same breath, a social and spiritual void....

"Here, then, in the foreground of the future, we can remark two valuable influences which Islam may exert upon the cosmopolitan proletariat of a Western society that has cast its net round the world and embraced the whole mankind; while in the more distant future we may speculate on the possible contributions of Islam to some new manifestation of religion."

Appendix

Christian Civilisation in its Age of Faith

Before closing this discussion, it is necessary to attend to the Jewish-Christian allegation, referred to in the present work on different occasions, that, as one Orientalist has worded it, "Islam is the bastard child of Judaism and Christianity", and hence whatever is good in the value-system of the Islamic civilisation is in bondage to the Biblical civilisation. In that connection we may give here a brief review of the civilisation nurtured on an international level by Christianity, under the Biblical civilisational value-system, since its coming to power and until the Renaissance in western Europe brought about by the Islamic civilisation,—whereafter the West adopted a secularistic and free-thought approach. We shall present here its basic characteristic features, leaving out certain vital facts for being dealt with in the next chapter under different headings; and our review, here again for avoiding all possibilities of doubt as to accuracy and authenticity, will be submitted in the words of a devout and eminent Christian historian of that civilisation, i.e., Will Durant. Projecting it as 'Civilisation in the Age of Faith', he says (*The Age of Faith*, pp. 44-843):

"*The foster mother of the new civilisation was the Church*....There is an epic grandeur, sullied with superstition and cruelty, in the struggle of the new religion to capture, tame and inspire the minds....to forge a uniting empire of faith...."

"....In paganism the family had been the social and religious unit; *it was a loss that in medieval Christianity this unit became the individual*.

"....*the status of woman was hurt by the doctrine....that woman was the origin of sin and the instrument of Satan.*

"*The Church did not condemn slavery.* Orthodox and heretic, Roman and barbarian alike assumed the institution to be natural and indestructible....*slavery continued throughout the Middle Ages*[4], *and died without benefit of clergy.*

"Next to determination of faith, the greatest power of the Church lay in the administration of sacraments—ceremonies symbolising the conferment of divine grace....More important was the sacrament of penance....According to the Gospel (Matt. xvi, 19; xviii, 18), Christ had forgiven sins, and held endowed the apostles with a similar power to 'blind and loose'. This power, said the Church, had descended by apostolic succession from the apostles to the early bishops, from Peter to the popes; and in the twelfth century the 'power of the keys' was extended by bishops to the priests....Absolution in confession removed from sin the guilt that would have condemned the sinner to hell...The Church claimed the right to remit such punishments....The Church commissioned certain ecclesiastics, usually friars, as *quaestiarii* to raise funds by offering indulgences in return for gifts, repentance, and prayer. These solicitors....developed a competitive zeal....they exhibited real or false relics to stimulate contributions and they kept for themselves a due or undue part of their receipts.

"The official prayers of the Church were often addressed to God the Father; a few appealed to the Holy Ghost; but the prayer of the people were addressed mostly to Jesus, Mary, and the saints. The Almighty was feared....Jesus was closer, but He too was God, and one hardly ventured to speak to Him face to face....It seemed wiser to lay one's prayer before a saint certified by canonization to be in a heaven, and to beg his or her intercession with Christ....Every nation, city, abbey, church, craft, soul, and crisis of life had its patron saint, as in pagan Rome it had a god....The Church arranged an ecclesiastical calendar in which everyday celebrated a saint; but the year did not find room for the 25,000 saints that had been

4 And it continued in Christendom with greater virulence and unspeakable cruelty thereafter also, as we shall notice in the next chapter.

canonized by the tenth century. The calendar of saints was to familiar to the people that the almanac divided the agricultural year by their names....Many saints received canonization through the insistent worship of their memory by the people or the locality, sometimes against ecclesiastical resistance. Images of the saints were set up in churches and public squares, on buildings and roads, and received a spontaneous worship....With so many saints there had to be many relics—their bones, hair, clothing, and anything that they had used. Every altar was expected to cover one or more such sacred memorials....The churches of Constantinople, before 1204, were especially rich in relics; they had the lance that had pierced Christ and was still red with His blood, the rod that had scourged Him, many pieces of the True Cross enshrined in gold, the 'sop of bread' given to Judas at the Last Supper, some hairs of the Lord's beard, the left arm of John the Baptist....In the sack of Constantinople many of these relics were stolen, some were bought, and they were peddled in the West from church to church to find the highest bidder. All relics were credited with supernatural powers, and a hundred thousand tales were told of their miracles. Men and women eagerly sought even the slightest relic, or relic of a relic, to wear as a magic talisman—a thread from a saint's robe, some dust from a reliquary, a drop of oil from a sanctuary lamp in the shrine. Monasteries vied and disputed with one another in gathering relics and exhibiting them to generous worshipers, for the possession of famous relics made the fortune of an abbey or a church. The 'translation' of the bones of Thomas a Becket to a new chapel in the cathedral of Canterbury (1220) drew from the attending worshipers a collection valued at $300,000 today. So profitable a business enlisted many practitioners; thousands of spurious relics were sold to churches and individuals; and monasteries were tempted to 'discover' new relics when in need of funds. The culmination of abuse was the dismemberment of dead saints to that several places might enjoy their patronage and power....The worship of God as Lord of Hosts and King of Kings inherited Semitic and Roman ways of approach, veneration, and address; the incense burnt before altar or clergy recalled the old burnt offerings; aspersion with holy water was an ancient form of exorcism; processions and lustrations continued immemorial rites; the vestments of the clergy and the papal title of *pontifex maximus* were legacies from pagan Rome. The Church found that rural converts still revered certain springs, wells, trees, and stones; she thought it wiser to bless these to Christian use than to break too sharply the customs of sentiment....So a dolmen at Plouret was consecrated as the chapel of the Seven Saints, and the worship of the oak was sterilized by hanging images of Christian saints upon the trees. Pagan festivals dear to the people, or necessary as cathartic moratoriums on morality, reappeared as Christian feasts, and pagan vegetation rites were transformed into Christian liturgy. The people continued to light midsummer fires on St. John's Eve, and the celebration of Christ's resurrection took the pagan name of Eostre, the old Teutonic goddess of the spring. The Christian calendar of the saints replaced the Roman *fasti*; ancient divinities dear to the people were allowed to revive under the names of Christian saints; the Dea Victoria of the Basses-Alpes became St. Victoire, and Castor and Pollux were reborn as St. Cosmas and Damian....The finest triumph of this tolerant spirit of adaptation was the sublimation of the pagan mother-goddess cults in the worship of Mary. Here too the people took the initiative. In 431 Cyril, Archbishop of Alexandria, in a famous sermon at Ephesus, applied to Mary many of the terms fondly ascribed by the pagans of Ephesus to their 'great goddess' Artemis-Diana; and the Council of Ephesus in the year over the protests of Nestorius, sanctioned for Mary the title 'Mother of God'. Gradually the tenderest features of Astarte, Cybele, Artemis, Diana, and Isis were gathered together in the worship of Mary. In the sixth century the Church established the Feast of the Assumption of the Virgin into heaven, and assigned it to August 13, the date of ancient festivals of Isis and Artemis. Mary became the patron saint of Constantinople and the imperial family; her picture was carried at the head of every great procession, and was (and is) hung in every church and home in Greek Christendom. Probably it was the Crusades that brought from the East to the West a more intimate and colourful worship of the Virgin....Just as the sternness of Yahveh had necessitated Christ, so the justice of Christ needed Mary's mercy to temper it. In effect the Mother—the oldest figure in religious worship—became....the third person of a new Trinity....knights vowed themselves to her service, and cities gave her their keys....The Church....made great festivals of the events in Mary's life—the Annunciation, the Vistation, the Purification (Candlemas), the Assumption.

"....In Christian theory the whole human race had been tainted by the sin of Adam and Eve. Said Gratian's *Decretum* (c. 1150), unofficially accepted by the Church as her teaching, 'Every human being who is conceived by the coition of a man with a woman is born with original sin, subject to impiety and death, and therefore a child of wrath'; and only divine grace, and the atoning death of Christ, could save him from wickedness and damnation....*The preaching of this doctrine....gave many medieval Christians a sense of inborn impurity, depravity, and guilt,* which colored much of their literature before 1200.

"....by the age of sixteen the medieval youth had probably sampled a variety of sexual experiences. Pederasty....reappeared....In 1177 Henry, Abbot of Clairvaux, wrote of France that 'ancient Sodom is springing up from her ashes'....The Penitentials—ecclesiastical manuals prescribing penances for sins—mention the usual enormities, including bestiality; as astonishing variety of beasts received such attentions....Cases of incest were numerous. Premarital and extramarital relations were apparently as widespread as at any time between antiquity and the twentieth century....Rape was common....Knights who served highborn dames or damoiselles for a kiss or a touch of the hand might console themselves with the lady's maids; some ladies could not sleep with a good conscience until they had arranged this courtesy. The Knight of La Tour-Landry... if we were to believe him, some men of his class fornicated in church, nay, 'on the altar'; and he tells of 'two queens which in Lent, on Holy Thursday....took their foul delight and pleasance within the church during divine service'. William of Malmesbury described the Norman nobility as 'given over to gluttony and lechery', and exchanging concubines with one another lest fidelity should dull the edge of husbandry. Illegitimate children littered Christendom, and gave a plot to a thousand tales. The heroes of several medieval sagas were bastards—Cuchulain, Arthur, Gawain, Roland, William the Conqueror, and many a knight in Froissar's Chronicles.

"Prostitution adjusted itself to the times. Some women in pilgrimage, according to Bishop Boniface, earned their passage by selling themselves in the towns on their route. Every army was followed with another army, as dangerous as the enemy. 'The Crusaders', reports Albert of Aix, 'had in their ranks a crowd of women wearing the habit of men; they travelled together without distinction of sex, trusting to the chances of a frightful promisculty'....The university students, particularly at Paris, developed urgent or imitative needs, the *filles* established centres of accommodation....In Rome, according to Bishop Durand II of Mende (1311), there were brothels near the Vatican, and the Pope's marshals permitted them for a consideration. The Church showed a human spirit toward prostitutes....A council at Rouen, in the eighth century, invited women who had secretly borne children to deposit them at the door of the church, which would undertake to provide for them; such orphans were brought up as serfs on ecclesiastical properties. A law of Charlemagne decreed that exposed children should be the slaves of those who rescued and reared them[5] ....Penalties for adultery were severe; Saxon law, for example, condemned the unfaithful wife at least to lose her nose and ears, and empowered her husband to kill her. Adultery was common notwithstanding.

"....Feudal masters seduced female serfs at the cost of a modest fine; he who 'covered' a maid 'without her thanks'—against her will—paid the court three shillings. The eleventh century, said Freeman, 'was a profligate age', and he marvelled at the apparent marital fidelity of William the Conqueror, who could not say as much for his father. '*Medieval society*', said the learned and judicious Thomas Wright, '*was profoundly immoral and licentious*'[6].

"....In the Middle Ages....men, good and bad, lied to their children, mates, congregations, enemies, friends, governments, and God. Medieval man had a special fondness for forging documents. He forged apocryphal gospels....he forged decretals as weapons in ecclesiastical politics; loyal monks forged charters to win royal grants for their monasteries; Archbishop Lanfranc of Canterbury, according to the papal Curia, forged a charter to prove the antiquity of his see; schoolmasters forged charters to endow some colleges at Cambridge with a false antiquity; and 'pious frauds' corrupted texts and invented a thousand edifying miracles. Bribery was general in education, trade, war, religion, government, law. Schoolboys sent pies to their examiners; politicians paid for appointments to public office, and collected the necessary sums from their friends; witnesses could be bribed to swear to anything; litigants gave presents to jurors and judges....perjury was so frequent that trial by combat was sometimes resorted to in the hope that God would identify the greater liar. Despite a thousand guild and municipal statutes and penalties, medieval craftsmen often deceived purchasers with shoddy products, false measures, and crafty substitutes. Some bakers stole small portions of dough under their customers' eyes by means of a trap door in the kneading board; cheap cloths were secretly put in the place of better cloths promised and paid for; inferior leather was 'doctored' to look like the best; stones were concealed in sacks of hay or wool sold by weight; the meat packers of Norwich were accused of buying measly pigs, and making from them sausages and pudding unfit for human bodies. Berthold

---

5 Mark the tone of Christian charity towards the orphans!

6 Is the society in Christendom in any way less immoral and licentious today?

of Regensburg (c. 1220) described the different forms of cheating used in the various trades, and the tricks played upon country folk by merchants at the fairs.

"....*Once at war, Christians were no gentler to the defeated, no more loyal to pledges and treaties than the warriors of other faiths*[7] *and times. Cruelty and brutality were apparently more frequent in the Middle Ages than in any civilisation before our own.*

"....In all classes men and women were hearty and sensual; their festivals were feasts of drinking, gambling, dancing, and sexual relaxation; their jokes were of a candor hardly rivaled today; their speech was freer, their oaths vaster and more numerous. Hardly a man in France, says Joinville, could open his mouth without mentioning the Devil.

"....begging flourished....Mendicancy reached....a scope and pertinacity unequalled today except in the poorest areas of the Far East.

"*Cleanliness*, in the Middle Ages, *was not next to godliness.* Early Christianity had denounced the Roman baths....and its general disapproval of the body had put no premium on hygiene. The modern use of the handkerchief was unknown....One result of the Crusades was the introduction into Europe of public steam baths in the Muslim style.

"....In the thirteenth century the chamber pots of Paris were freely emptied from windows into the street....People eased themselves in courtyards, on stairways and balconies, even in the palace of the Louvre.

"....The commonest meat was pork. Pigs ate the refuse in the streets, and people ate the pigs.

"*Drunkenness was a favourite vice of the Middle Ages, in all classes and sexes.* Taverns were numerous, ale was cheap. Beer was the regular drink of the poor, even at breakfast. Monasteries and hospitals north of the Alps were normally allowed a gallon of ale or beer per person per day....A customal of the abbey of St. Peter in the Black Forest includes some tender clauses: 'When the peasants have unladen the wine, they shall be brought into the monastery, and shall have meat and drink in abundance. A great tub shall be set there and filled with wine....and each shall drink....and if they wax drunken and smite the cellarman or the

---

7 On Will Durant's own admission elsewhere in his book under reference, Islam stands excluded here from 'other faiths'.

cook, they shall pay no fine for this deed; and they shall drink so that two of them cannot beat the third to the wagon'.

"....*Gambling was not always forbidden by law,* Siena provided booths for it in the public square.

"....The French and Germans in particular were fond of the dance....Dancing could become an epidemic: in 1237 a band of German children danced all the way from Erfurt to Arnstadt; many died en route; and some survivors suffered to the end of their lives from St. Vitus' dance, or other nervous disorders.

"....Several persons, of any age or sex, might sleep in the same room. In England and France all classes slept nude.

"*Does the general picture of medieval Europe support the belief that religion makes for morality? Our general impression suggests a wider gap between moral theory and practice in the Middle Ages than in other epochs of civilisation.* Medieval Christendom was apparently as rich as our own irreligious age in sensuality, violence, drunkenness, cruelty, coarseness, profanity, greed, robbery, dishonesty, and fraud. It seems to have outdone our time in the enslavement of individuals....It surpassed us in the subjection of women; it hardly euqalled us in immodesty, fornication, and adultery, or in the immensity and murderousness of war. Compared with the Roman Empire from Nerva to Aurelius, *medieval Christendom was a moral setback.*

"....*The intellectual virtues naturally declined in the Age of Faith;* intellectual conscience (fairness with the facts) and the search for truth were replaced by zeal and admiration for sanctity, and sometimes unscrupulous piety....The c*ivic virtues suffered* from concentration on the afterlife....Perhaps *hypocrisy,* so indispensable to civilisation, *increased in the Middle Ages* as compared with the frank secularism of antiquity, or the unabashed corporate brutality of our time." (All italics, present writer's).

Chapter XI

GENUINE MORAL IDEALISM

A Comparative Study in the Perspective of Christian Allegations and Christian Testimony

Preliminary Observations :

Every religion possesses a certain type of moral Idealism. Of course, there are differences among religions in respect of the form and the content of that idealism. But noble ideas and ideals are nevertheless found, however, defective in individual cases their setting, their projection, or their range. Going, however, beyond theoretical assessment into the practical aspect of those ideals, we may consider their worth in the light of the question: 'How far have those ideas and ideals influenced the respective followers of those religions and brought blessings to humanity in practical terms?'

If we compare Islam and other religions in this perspective of evaluation, it will be possible to assess the nature and worth of the Qur'ãnic moral Idealism. For that purpose, we may place Islam and Christianity in the scale of comparison, especially because the Christian propagandists have been, in the past and in the present, foremost in attacking Islam on that ground—other being only their imitators or camp-followers. And those attacks have continued from their side during the past millennium ceaselessly and violently without regard for either justice or Truth. We have already made certain references to Christian misrepresentations in chapter I of Part I of this volume. We may quote here one more—one, which is more recent and which comes from an eminent Christian religious dignitary who has been acclaimed as "one of the greatest missionary-statesmen of the twentieth century", viz., Rev. Dr. Glover. In chap. IV of his publication: Progress of Worldwide Mission (Harper & Bros., New York, 1960), he makes the following observations:

"He (Muhammad) was an Oriental and a Potentate....He was nurtured in the faith that his hand must be against every man. His Arabian armies were possessed by a wild fanaticism and a thirst for plunder and conquest. The Prophet's injunction to them was to exterminate all heathens....

"The sword of Muhammad and the Qur'ãn are the most stubborn enemies of civilisation, liberty and truth, which the world has yet known."

We have already quoted Max Weber's statement on page 2. His allegations relate to the establishment of feudalism, serfdom, slavery and subjection of women by Islam.

The above and other similar calumnies have been actually repeated *ad nauseam*, because Western orientalists, historians, religious writers, missionaries, journalists, and others have been ceaselessly working under a planned effort to malign Islam and the Holy Prophet Muhammad (Peace be on him!)—seemingly convinced that, through widespread and continuous repetition, even totally false statements can accomplish the alienation of humanity at large from goodwill for Islam and the demoralisation of the rising generations of Muslim intelligentsia. The latter, because of persistent westernisation during the past one and a half century of Western domination of the world of Islam and the impoverishment of the agencies of Islamic knowledge and inspiration, are more under the intellectual and cultural influences of the West than of Islam. Hence, the adversaries of Islam hope that, side by side with political and military intrigues, thrusts and assaults, which, engineered by them, have continued unabated to this day—though changing their forms according to circumstances, their anti-Islamic propaganda might finally succeed in weakening Islam to an extent that it may no more be able to challenge their faults and the evils which they endorse.

In his *Age of Faith*, Will Durant has tried, as a good Christian, to tender a lame apology for all that cruelty and blatant dishonesty, though he himself could not escape it on numerous occasions. But, the very term 'religion' loses all grace if there is no adherence to principles of truth and justice by its upholders. Hence, the entire anti-Islamic Christian-Jewish propaganda is a standing disgrace for the very name of Religion.

In our discussion here, we shall confine ourselves only to the testimony of believing Christian scholars, although their appreciation of Islam can in the very nature of the case be only very meagre, and in certain respects very defective, while in others even non-existent. As for Islam's own stand, the present work has projected it on the basis of Islam's scripture itself in all its basic dimensions.

Confining ourselves to Dr. Glover's and Max Weber's allegations, we shall project the realisation in history of the values of mercy, tolerance, regard for freedom of conscience and respect for human dignity in such of their dimensions as bear reference to the allegations made; and because the said allegations have been projected in the perspective of the supposed superiority and sublimity of Christianity, we shall present a comparative evaluation in terms of Muslim as well as Christian history. (Dr. Glover's allegation that Islam is the enemy of civilisation has been already dealt with in the previous chapter). As for the complete rebuttal, it emerges at relevant places in the present work in connection with the exposition of the Qur'ãnic philosophy and code of life. Hence, the statements that follow should be read in conjunction with it.

I

In Terms of Mercy, Toleration and Regard for Human Conscience

(i)

With Reference to War

In connection with the comparative evaluation of Islamic and Christian moral Idealism in terms of the ethics of war, we may take up the most difficult virtue, namely, magnanimity and forgiveness in respect of the enemy. As such, we may refer to the practical effects of the Christian teaching in that behalf and the parallel Qur'ãnic teaching, as recorded in history. Such a comparison will fix the merit of Islam's moral Idealism in the perspective of history, and will at the same time expose the baselessness of Christian propaganda against Islam.

Who have been more tolerant, more humane, more forgiving, more just and more chivalrous in history the believers in the Bible or the believers in the Qur'ãn? Just one pair of events contrasting Christian and Muslim behaviour will suffice—the one relating to the conquest of Jerusalem by the Crusaders on July 15, 1099 A.C., and later on its conquest by Ghazi Salah al-Din al-Ayyubi (named Saladin in European history) in November 1187 A.C., wherein Christendom and Isamdom demonstrated their ethico-religious Idealsim because both fought a *holy war*—a war in the name of religion; and for the Christians it was a war initiated by them right in their Holy Land where Christ had delivered his message of Mercy.

We will quote here only the reputed Christian authorities whose accounts are based on eye-witness reports and first-hand information.

Charles Mills says about the Crusaders and the Crusade:

"They abandoned themselves to every grossness and libertinism. Neither public treasures nor private possessions were spared. Virgin modesty was no protection, conjugal virtue no safeguard....Among the Crusaders, particularly distinguished for ferocity, were two thousands Normans or French. That they destroyed children at the breast and scattered their quivering limbs in the air....that their crimes were enormous, is the general confession of the Latin writers....The Christians dragged the corpses from the sepulchre and despoiled them of their dress, and ornaments. They severed the heads from the trunks, and 15 hundred of them were exposed on pikes to the weeping Turks; and some were sent to the Caliph of Egypt in proof of victory. The dignity of age, the helplessness of youth and the beauty of weaker sex were disregarded by the Latin savages. Houses were no sanctuaries, and the sight of mosque added new virulence to cruelty....the attendants and followers of the camp pillaged the houses of Antioch as soon as the gates had been thrown open; but the soldiers did not for a while suffer their rapacity to check their thirst for blood; when, however, every species of habitation, from the market place to the meanest hovels, had been covered into a scene of slaughter, when the narrow streets and the spacious squares were all alike disfigured with human gore, and crowded with mangled carcasses, then the assassins turned robbers, and became as mercenary as they had been merciless....They were soon reduced to their old resources of dog's flesh and human carcasses. They broke open the tombs of the Musalmans; ripped up the bellies of the dead for gold, and then dressed and ate fragments of the flesh....Their cruelty could not be appeased by a bloodless conquest; extermination, not clemency, marked their victory....Such was the carnage in the mosque of Omar that the mutilated carcasses were hurried by the torrents of blood into the courts; severed arms and hands floated into the current that carried into contact with bodies to which they had not belonged. Ten thousand people were murdered in this sanctuary. It was not only the lacerated and headless trunks which shocked the sight, but the figures of the victors themselves reckoning with the blood of their slaughtered enemies. No place of refuge remained to the vanquished, so indiscriminately did the insatiable fanaticism of the conquerors disregarded alike supplication and resistance. Some were slain, others were thrown from the tops of the churches and of the citadel....It was resolved that no pity should be shown to the Musalmans....the subjected people were, therefore, dragged into the public places, and slain as victims; women with children at breast, girls and boys, all were slaughtered. The squares, the streets and even the uninhabited places of Jerusalem were strewned with dead bodies of men and women and the mangled limbs of children. No heart melted into compassion or expanded into benevolence."[1]

---

1 Charles Mills: *The History of Crusades* (2 Vols.), London, 1821, Vol. I, pp. 68, 71, 185, 228-229, 254, 260.

Referring to the occasion when the Muslims, fighting under Saladin, recovered Palestine from the Crusaders and re-occupied Jerusalem, the same author observes:

"In solemn procession the clergy, the queen, and her retinue of ladies followed. Saladin advanced to meet them and his heart melted with compassion, when they approached him in this attitude and with the air of suppliants. The softened warriors uttered some words of pity....with courteous clemency he released all the prisoners when the women requested, and loaded them with presents."[2]

In the Same Context, Stanley Lane-Poole Remarks:

"After that he (Saladin) commanded that to the dames and damsels whose lords were dead there should be handsomely distributed from his own treasure, to some more and to others less, according to their state, and he gave them so much that they gave praise to God and published abroad the kindness and honour which Saladin had done to them....Islam in its essence and as professed by such a man as Saladin is a religion of noble simplicity and austere self-sacrifice."[3]

Edward Gibbon has the Same Tale to Tell:

"Indeed of a rigorous exaction of his debt he (Saladin) accepted a sum of thirty thousand byzants for the ransom of 7 thousand poor; two or three thousand more were dismissed by his gratuitous clemency....In his interview with the queen (Sybilla of Jerusalem) and her captive husband his words and even his tears suggested the kindest consolations....Thus did the Saracens show the mercy to the fallen city. One recalls the savage conquest by the first crusaders in 1099, when Godfrey and Tancred rode through streets choked with the dead and dying, when defenseless Muslims were tortured, burnt and shot down in cold blood on the towers and root of the temple, when the blood of wanton massacre defiled the honour of Christendom and stained the scene where once the gospel of love and mercy had been preached. 'Blessed are the merciful, for they shall obtain mercy' was a forgotten beatitude, when the Christians made shambles of the Holy City. Fortunate were the merciless, for they obtained mercy at the hands of the Muslim Sultan. If the taking of Jerusalem were the only fact known about Saladin, it was enough to prove him the most chivalrous and great-hearted conqueror of his own, and perhaps of any age."[4]

---

2 *op.cit.*, pp. 330, 441.

3 Stanley Lane-Poole: *Saladin and the Fall of the Kingdom of Jerusalem*, London, 1906, pp. 232, 233, 373.

4 Edward Gibbon: *Decline and Fall of the Roman Empire*, London 1922 Vol. VI, pp. 116, 233.

Before concluding this discussion, we regard it necessary to make certain observations:

(1) In respect of the history of Islam, we have purposely avoided reference to its early period which, being truly idealistic, is naturally expected to enshrine Islamic moral Idealism at its highest. Instead, we have referred to the period in which Muslims had deviated considerably, in the natural historical process, from the Islamic Idealism as such. This we have done to be just to Christianity.

(2) In respect of Christianity: Most unfortunately, the heart-rending record of cruelty and absolute absence of human feeling that has been presented in the foregoing does not stand in history as a solitary lapse. Rather, the political history of Christianity—and even its religious history—, since the acquisition of political power under Constantine, reveals an amazing record of violation without mercy of the Sermon on the Mount and of all the other noble moral teachings given by the Holy Prophet Jesus (Peace be on him!). The injustice, the cruelty, the wanton barbarism which the Christian nations have practised throughout, and continue to practise without blush till today, in international politics and warfare both, forms—as recorded by Christian historians themselves—an amazing example of revolt against God as well as human goodness.

And, then, they have practised utmost cruelty and injustice not only against their political opponents but also against the other people by imposing the most cruel form of slavery upon, and uprooting, defenceless populations, as they did in respect of the Blacks of Africa, and by staging mass murder of indigenous populations, as they did in the Americas and Australasia;—all this for their material power and glory[5] !

5 Even for filthy lucre!!! For instance, in respect of what has been termed in Christian history as 'trade' and which "at all times was little distinguished from piracy": "the first voyage of 1562 of John Jawkins left him the wealthiest man in Plymouth, his second voyage of 1564 left him the wealthiest man in England, and his third voyage of 1567, led to open naval warfare between England and Spain." (*The New Cambridge Modern History*, 1961, Vol. I, p. 457).

(3) A student of history is, indeed, amazed to find that with all their emphasis on religiosity and on certain basic moral principles none of the existening religions except Islam possesses any record, in its history of international and inter-religious relations, of practising the ideal of 'respect for humanity'. Even the Jews with all their 'worship of the One God', whom their centuries-long persecution by the Christians should have made exceptionally conscious of the evils of international cruelty and injustice, are indulging, after acquiring political power, in the same evil—and that, against their own cousins, the Arabs, and against those who gave them asylum when their present friends persecuted them, i.e., the Muslims.

What, then, is the difference in practical terms between 'religion' and 'irreligion'? –

The basic cause seems to lie in the fact that religions other than Islam have, either not given any ethics of war, or have given a wrong one; while Islam has given it in a full-fledged manner, on the one hand, and based it on sound humanitarianism[6], on the other. Then, that ethics has been properly exemplified for practical guidance by the Holy Prophet Muhammad (Peace be on him!).

Thus: The merit of Saladin is not basically his personal merit, but the merit of the Islamic ethics of war and of the Ideal set by the Holy Prophet of Islam[7]—at its highest in his conquest of Makkah. And, the brutality demonstrated by the Christian nations in Palestine and elsewhere in their history, before and after, is due to the absence of ethics of war in

---

6 Ref. Vol. II: "The Structure of Islamic Society".

7 Lest it be understood that Saladin's is a solitary example, we may refer to another. Says Will Durant (*The Age of Faith*, p. 308): "....Alp Arslan lived up to his name—'the lion-hearted hero'—by conquering Herat, Armenia, Georgia, and Syria....Emperor Romans IV collected 100,000....troops to meet Arslan's 15,000....warriors. The Seljuq leader offered a reasonable peace; Romanus rejected it scornfully, gave battle at Manzikert in Armenia (1071), fought bravely....was defeated and captured, and was led before the Sultan. 'What would have been your behaviour', asked Arslan, 'had fortune smiled upon your arms?' 'I would have inflicted upon thy body many a stripe', answered Romanus. Arslan treated him with all courtesy, released him on the promise of a royal ransom, and dismissed him with rich gifts."

Christianity and of its practical model; whereby the Sermon on the Mount alone could not do the job of saving them from committing crimes against humanity in their holy wars. Indeed, sermons do not achieve much by themselves! Because, the human nature is so constituted that, unless it has been properly disciplined spiritually and morally, the human being is always inclined to follow the behest of his instinctive self and to indulge in unbridled vengeance. And, for that spiritual and moral discipline, the first prerequisite is the possession of a sound moral code and a source of inspiration in the personality of him whom a person loves and respects above all as his guide and benefactor,—though, that in itself is only a prerequisite. For, what is finally needed is the *achievement* of the requisite spiritual and moral discipline. It means that not only the followers of other religions and philosophies but even those who are members of the Muslim community in a formal sense, and are thereby related nominally to a humanitarian ethics of war and the highest source of humanitarian inspiration in the Holy Prophet's personality, but have not achieved the requisite spiritual and moral discipline, are likely to behave merely as 'human animals'.

Anyhow, in the final analysis, in respect of teaching as well as inspiration and its practical realisation in history, even today Islam alone provides humanity with what it needs in this behalf; and, those who insult the Holy Prophet Muhammad (Peace be on him!) for his permission of, and participation in, war, and adore the asceitc-pacifist Ideal, would do well to revise their opinion in the interest of humanity;—as also in their own interest, because by insulting him and depriving themselves of the appreciation of his merit, they only insult themselves.

(ii)

With Reference to Post-Conquest Treatment of the Subjected Communities

(a)

Christian Testimony on Christian Conquests

Arnold J. Toynbee says in his *Study of History* (London, New York, Toronto 1962), Vol. I, pp. 211, 212, 225:

"The race-feeling which is thus aroused *in our Western Society* by the present situation and temper of our settlers overseas also *spring naturally from the religious background....This has been a misfortune for Mankind;* for the

Protestant temper and attitude and conduct in regard to Race, as in many other vital issues, is *inspired largely by the Old Testament.... Under this inspiration, the English-speaking Protestant settlers in the New World exterminated the North American Indian, as well as the bison, from coast to coast of the Continent,* whereas *the Spanish Catholics only exterminated the Indian in the Caribbean islands* and were content, on the Continent, to step into the shoes of the Aztecs and the Incas—sparing the conquered in order to rule them as subject populations, converting their subjects to their own religion, and inter-breeding with their converts....*The sense of religious solidarity and fraternity did not, however, restrain the Spaniards and the Portuguese in South America, a century and a half ago, from cold-bloodedly and brutally destroying*—out of sheer greed for (non-existent) gold and for (to them, unutilizable) land—*the wonderful society which had been conjured into existence,* by the genius of the Jesus missionaries, *among the primitive peoples of Paraguay.*" (Italics, present writer's).

The Spaniards might not have employed bullets for wiping out the conquered 'natives' on the Americal mainland, as Toynbee says. But the decimation of the indigenous population occurred nevertheless as a blessing of the Spanish conquest. The *New Cambridge Modern History*, vol. II, p. 583, (1958), gives the following figures for Central Mexico:

"A recent and well documented study gives the following approximate figures of the indigenous (Indian) population on different dates in Central Mexico (then known as New Spain):

1519	11 Million.
1540	6,427,466.
1565	4,409,180.
1597	2,500,000.

(vide S.F. Cook and L.B. Simpson: *The Population of Central Mexico in the Sixteenth Century*, Berkeley, California, 1948)."

That the intolerance practised by Christendom has always gone to the highest level of barbarism in the form of mass murder of human populations, wherever they could carry it out, is fully borne out by history. For instance, in Sudan, the extensive blood-bath undertaken by the crusading Lord Kitchener against the Muslims reduced the population, estimated by the British authorities in 1880 at ten million souls, to less than two million—actually 1,853,000. (Ref: *Encyclopaedia Brittannica*, X, XI, XII editions; 1902, 1911, 1923).

As to those conquests wherein mass murder did not take place, Toynbee, the ardent lover of Christianity attributes to *expediency* and not to any Christian moral idealism. Citing the example of India, he says:

"Finally, in Continental India, where the English could not think of supplanting the conquered 'Natives' as they had supplanted them in North America, but could only impose their rule on them as the Spaniards had imposed theirs on the 'Natives' of Mexico and Peru, the sequel was not the same as it had been in the Spanish Indies....The Reasons are almost too obvious to need mentioning. In the first place, Europeans could not hope to make themselves at home in the Indian climate, even if they had found, or made, the soil of India free from other human occupants. In the second place, the existing 'Native' population of India was too numerous and too far advanced in civilisation to be exterminated, even if our British Israelities had ever contemplated treating the Canaanite in India as they treated him in America." (*op,cit.*, p. 212).

Indeed, Toynbee, with all his subjective devotion to Christianity, is so deeply convinced of the Bible being responsible for all the most amazing and the most callous barbarism and ferocity demonstrated by Christendom in history that he finds himself forced to advocate the subjection of the Christian *sacred* scripture, which Christendom has adored as the Word of God, to the amputator's knife. He says:

"When the first translation of the Bible into a Teutonic language was made by Ulfilas, the Apostle of the Goths, in the fourth century of our era, the translator wisely omitted the Books of Samuel and Kings, on the ground that war and bloodshed were too much in the minds of the Goths as it was, without their proclivity in this direction being consecrated and confirmed by the authority of the sacred book of their new religion. It is a pity that Luther and the English translators did not follow Ulfilas' example—or, indeed, improve on it by omitting Joshur and Judges as well! King James I.'s English Authorzed Version of the Bible, which presents the Old Testament complete and unexpurgated, was published in A.D. 1611. A book called *The New English Canaan*, by Thomas Morton, was published in 1637!" (*op.cit.*, p. 212).

That sheer barbarism was employed as an instrument for converting the heathen[8] is also borne out by Christian history. And it was

8 In respect of conversion, the law of Islam stands radically opposed to the use of force, because of the Qur'ãn's categorical prohibition (II:256). Hence, Muslim history presents a radical contrast to Christian history in this respect. Christian testimony in this behalf has been provided in Thomas Arnold's *Preaching of Islam* (latest edition: Sh. Muhammad Ashraf; Lahore, Pakistan).

employed from the very beginning of the acquisition of political power by Christianity; as, among others, Will Durant testifies:

"Christians divided on almost every point but one—that the pagan temples should be closed, their property confiscated.... Constantine had discouraged, but not forbidden pagan sacrifices and ceremonies; Constans forbade them on pain of death; Constantius ordered all pagan temples in the Empire closed, and all pagan rituals to cease. Those who disobeyed were to forfeit their property and their lives; and these penalties were extended to provincial governors neglecting to enforce the decree." (*The Age of Faith*, p. 8).

We may also notice is this connection that the unparalleled barbarism which Christendom inflicted on the black races of Africa, to which we shall refer shortly, was also conceived by the Christian proselytisers as the instrument for their Christianisation. A brief remark by an eminent Christian scholar may suffice here:

"The Church also supported the slave trade. The Spaniards saw in it an opportunity of converting the heathen, and the Jesuits, Dominicans and Franciscans were heavily involved in sugar cultivation which meant slave-holding. The story is told of an old elder of the Church in Newport who would invariably, the Sunday following the arrival of a slaver from the coast, thank God that 'another cargo of benighted beings had been brought to a land where they could have the benefit of a gospel dispensation'." (Dr. Eric Williams: *Capitalism and Slavery*, London 1964, p. 42).

(b)

Christian Testimony on Muslim Conquests

Says Will Durant[9] in *The Age of Faith* (pp. 187-190, 218, 219, 227):

"Muhammad had appointed no successor to his power, but he had chosen Abu Bakr (573-624) to conduct the prayers in the Madinah mosque this mark of preference persuaded the Muslim leaders to elect Abu Bakr the first Caliph of Islam....Abu Bakr was....simple and abstemious, kindly but resolute; attending personally to details of administration and judgement, and never resting till justice was done; serving without pay till his people overruled his austerity; and then, in his will, returning to the new state the stipends it had paid him....the Muslim leaders were passionate disciples of Muhammad, prayed even more than they fought....The Arab troops were more rigorously

9 It may be remembered that, as a good Christian, Will Durant is always ready to attack and insult Islam and its promulgator on the flimsiest grounds.

disciplined and more ably led; they were inured to leadership....could fight on empty stomachs....'Be just', ran Abu Bakr's proclamation, 'be valiant; die rather that yield; be merciful; slay neither old men, nor women, nor children. Destroy no fruit trees, grain, or cattle. Keep your word, even to your enemies. Molest not those religious persons who live retired from the world'....Omar (the second Caliph)....Having beaten a Bedouin unjustly, he begged the Bedouin—in vain—to inflict an equal number of strokes upon him. He was a severe puritan, demanding strict virtue of every Muslim. ....Muslim historians tell us that he owned but one shirt and one mantle, patched and repatched; that he lived on barley bread and dates; and drank nothing but water; that he slept on a bed of palm leaves, hardly better than a hair shirt; and that his sole concern was the propagation of the faith by letters and by arms. When a Persian satrap came to pay homage to Omar he found the conqueror of the East asleep among beggars on the steps of the Madinah mosque.... The Patriarch Sophronius agreed to surrender Jerusalem if the Caliph would come in person to ratify the terms of capitulation. Omar consented, and travelled from Madinah in stately simplicity, armed with a sack of corn, a bag of dates; a gourd of water, and a wooden dish....He received Sophronius with kindness and courtesy, imposed an easy tribute on the vanquished, and confirmed the Christians in the peaceful possession of all their shrines....Omar forbade the conquerors to buy or till land....

"The Jews of the Near East had welcomed the Arabs as liberators....they stood on equal terms with Christians, were free once more to live and worship in Jerusalem, and *prospered under Islam* in Asia, Egypt, and Spain as never under Christian rule. Outside of Arabia the *Christians* of western Asia usually *practised their religion unhindered*; Syria remained predominantly Christian until the third Muslim century; in the reign of Mamun (813-33) we hear of 11,000 Christian churches in Islam—as well as hundreds of synagogues and fire temples. Christian festivals were freely and openly celebrated; Christian pilgrims came in safety to visit Christian shrines in Palestine; the Crusaders found large numbers of Christians in the Near East in the twelfth century; and Christian communities have survived there to this day. Christian heretics persecuted by the patriarchs of Constantinople, Jerusalem, Alexandria, or Antioch were now free and safe under a Muslim rule that found their disputes quite unintelligible. In the ninth century the Muslim governor of Antioch appointed a special guard to keep Christian sects from massacring one another at church. Monasteries and nunneries flourished....relations between the two religions were so genial that Christians wearing crosses on their breasts conversed in mosques with Muslim friends. The Muhammadan administrative bureaucracy had hundreds of Christian employees....Sergius, father of St. John of Damascus, was chief finance minister to Abd-al-Malik, and John himself, last of the Greek Fathers of the Church, headed the council that governed Damascus. *The Christians of the East in general regarded Islamic rule as a lesser evil than that of the Byzantine government and Church.*

"Despite or because of this polity of tolerance in early Islam, the new faith won over to itself in time most of the Christians, nearly all the Zoroastrians and pagans, and many of the Jews, of Asia, Egypt, and North Africa....Gradually the non-Muslim population adopted the Arabic language and dress, the laws and faith of the Qur'ãn. Where Hellenism, after a thousand years of mastery, had failed to take root, and Roman arms had left the native gods unconquered, and Byzantine orthodoxy had raised rebellious heresies, Muhammadanism had secured, almost without proselytism, not only belief and worship, but a tenacious fidelity that quite forgot the superseded gods. From China, Indonesia, and India through Persia, Syria, Arabia and Egypt to Morocco and Spain, the Muhammadan faith touched the hearts and fancies of a hundred peoples, governed their morals and molded their lives, gave them consoling hopes and a strengthening pride....

"....We must concede that the early Caliphs, from Abu Bakr to al-Mamun, gave successful organization to human life over a wide area, and may be counted among the ablest rulers in history. *They might have devasted or confiscated everything,* like the Mongols or the Magyars of the raiding Norse; *instead they merely taxed.* When Omar conquered Egypt he rejected the advice of Zobeir to divide the land among his followers, and the Caliph confirmed his judgement: 'Leave it', said Omar, 'in the people's hands to nurse and fructify'. Under the caliphal government lands were measured, records were systematically kept, roads and canals were multiplied or maintained, rivers were banked to prevent floods; Iraq, now half desert, was again a garden of Eden; Palestine, recently so rich in sand and stones, was fertile, wealthy, and populous....the *caliphs gave reasonable protection to life and labour, kept career open to talent, promoted for three to six centuries the prosperity of areas never so prosperous again, and stimulated and supported such a flourishing of education, literature, science, philosophy, and art as made western Asia, for five centuries, the most civilized region in the world.*"

(iii)

With Reference to Treatment of Dissenters within the Fold

In the Age of Islam's glory, religious fanaticism in respect of differences within the fold did exhibit itself occasionally,[10], as was natural

10 This phenomenon should actually be traced to Jewish-Christian influence, which came through the very large number of converts from Judaism and Christianity, including the priests of those faiths, entering the fold in the very early days of Islamic history and forming a part of the Muslim community larger than that of the descendants of the original Muslims. As for Islam, it is committed to *positive* struggle for the triumph of Truth on the basis of sublime spiritual and moral principles and does not countenance the *negative* attitude of persecution.

in the case of a community for whom religion was the be-all and end-all of life. But it exhibited itself basically in the issuance of academic condemnatory-verdicts by the jurists, and went on a few occasions to the height of public burning of what was regarded as unorthodox religious literature. But the dimensions of mass barbarism and indescribable tortures which culminated in burning the dissenters at the stake forms the 'pride' of Christianity alone!

Starting from the beginning of Christian political power, and then proceeding straight to Inquisition, we may project here very brief references just to give an idea of the brutality practised in respect of violation of the values of mercy and toleration in Christian history of the ages of Faith and Orthodoxy.

With all his determined endeavour to minimise or explain away the evils that emerged in Christendom under the impact of the Church, Will Durant has been forced to say as follows (*The Age of Faith*, pp. 8, 46, 610, 735-784):

"....Once triumphant, the Church ceased to preach toleration....

"Constantius took theology more seriously than his father.... ecclesiastics loyal to the Nicene Creed were removed from their churches, sometimes by the violence of mobs; for half a century it seemed that Christianity would be Unitarian, and abandon the divinity of Christ[11] ....when Constantius ordered the replacement of the orthodox patriot Paul by the Arian Macedonius, a crowd of Paul's supporters resisted the soldiery, and three thousand persons lost their lives. Probably more Christians were slaughtered by Christians in these two years (342-3) than by all the persecutions of Christians by pagans in the history of Rome.

"....We hear of many heretics, but most of these admitted the basic tenets of the Christian creed....

"The Old Testament laid down a simple code for dealing with heretics: they were to be carefully examined; and if three reputable witnesses testified to their having 'gone and served other gods', the heretics were to be led out from the city and 'stoned with stones till they die' (Deut. xvii, 25)....According to the Gospel of St. John (xv. 6), Jesus accepted this tradition: 'If anyone abide not in

11 Mark the confession, in support of what the Qur'ãn has proclaimed, that the original monotheistic religion preached by Jesus was replaced with its paganised version by the Christian Church—and that through the force of arms! In respect of paganisation, readers may also refer to pages 201, 202 in the foregoing.

me he shall be cast forth as a branch, and shall wither; and they shall gather him up, and cast him into the fire, and he burneth.'....

"....The Templars....aroused the envy, fear, and wrath of King Philip IV the Fair....A tribunal of prelates and monks loyal to the King examined the prisoners; they denied the royal charges, and were put to the torture to induce them to confess. Some, suspended by the wrists, were repeatedly drawn up and suddenly let down; some had their bare feet held over flames; some had sharp splinters driven under their fingernails; some had a tooth wrenched out day after day; some had heavy weights hung from their genitals; some were slowly starved. In many cases all these devices were used, so that most of the prisoners, when examined again, were weak to the point of death. One showed the bones that had fallen from his roasted feet....Several of them died in Jail; some killed themselves; fifty-nine were burned at the stake (1310), protesting their innocence to the end....

"The most powerful of the heretical sects was variously named Cathari....Bulgari....and Albigenses, from the French town of Albi, where there were especially numerous....innocent....gave him (Arnaud, head of Cistercian monks) extraordinary powers to make Inquisition throughout France, and commissioned him to offer a plenary indulgence to the king and nobles of France for aid....Philip Augustus allowed many barons of his realm to enlist....the same plenary indulgence was promised as to those who took the cross for Palestine....When the crusaders approached Beziers (in their heresy-hunt)....scaled the walls, captured the town, and *slew 20,000 men, women and children in induscriminate massacre; even those who had sought asylum in the church*....when Arnaud, the papal legate, was asked should Catholics be spared, he answered, 'Kill them all, for God knows His Own'....Simon de Montfort....For four years Simon continued his campaigns, devastating nearly all the territory....

"....Compared with the persecution of heresy in Europe from 1227 to 1492, the persecution of Christians by Romans in the first three centuries after Christ was mild and humane procedure. *Making every allowance required of an historian and permitted to a Christian, we must rank the inquisition, along with the wars and persecutions of our time, as among the darkest blots on the record of mankind, revealing a ferocity unknown in any beast*[12]."

---

12 To quote Will Durant: Besides "burning at the stake", which was the mode of killing the condemned persons (*op.cit.*, p. 783), "the worst tragedies of the Inquisition were concealed in the dungeons rather than brought to light at the stake" (*op.cit.*, p. 783). In crushing one dissident movement alone, i.e., the Albigensian 'heresy' one million men, women and children were massacred. (vide *Newsweek*. "massacre of the Pure").

II

In Terms of Respect for Human Dignity

(i)

With Reference to the Status of Woman

We shall confine ourselves here only to brief *confessions* by a Christian scholar, and shall leave out elaborate discussion—both theological and historical. (Elaborate presentation of the Qur'ãnic teaching in this behalf has been given in Vol. II).

(a)

Christian Testimony on the Role of Christianity

Will Durant says (The Age of Faith, pp. 825-826):

"The theories of churchmen were generally hostile to woman; some laws of the Church enhanced her subjection.... *To priests and theologians woman was* still in these centuries what she had seemed to Chrysostom—'a *necessary evil, a natural temptation, a desirable calamity, a domestic peril, a deadly fascination, a painted ill*'. She was still *the ubiquitous reincarnation of the Eve who had lost Eden for mankind, still the favoured instrument of Satan* in leading men to hell. *St. Thomas Aquinas,* usually the soul of kindness.... *placed her in some ways below the slave*: 'The woman is subject to the man on account of the weakness of her nature, both of mind and of body....Man is the beginning of woman and her end, just as God is the beginning and end of every creature....Woman is in subjection according to the law of nature, but a slave is not....Children ought to love their father more than their mother'....Man, but not woman, was made in the image of God; 'it is plain from this', argued the canonist, 'that wives should be subject to their husband, and *should almost be servants*'....

"Civil law was more hostile to her than canon law. *Both codes permitted wife-beatings*.... Civil law ruled that *the word of women could not be admitted in court*....it excluded even the most high-born ladies from representing their own estate in the Parliament of England or the Estates-General of France. *Marriage gave the husband full authority over the use and usufruct of any property that his wife owned at marriage*" (Italics, present writer's).

(b)

Christian Testimony on the Role of Islam

Will Durant states (*The Age of Faith*, pp. 180, 181, 183):

"In like manner *He* (Muhammad) *improved the position of woman*.... He allowed women to come to the mosque, but believed that 'their homes are better for them', yet when they came to his services he treated them kindly even if they brought suckling babes: if, says an amiable tradition, he heard a child cry, he would shorten his sermon lest the mother be inconvenienced. *He put an end to the Arab practice of* (feminine) *infanticide* (xvii, 31). *He placed woman on the same footing with man in legal processes and in financial independence, she might follow any legitimate profession, keep her earnings, inherit property, and dispose of her belongings, at will* (iv, 4, 32). He *abolished the Arab custom of transmitting women as property from father to son. Women were to inherit half as much as the male heirs, and were not to be disposed of against their will*....a tradition quotes the Prophet as saying to women, 'It is permitted to you to go out for your needs'....we find Muslim women moving about freely and unveiled in the Islam of his time, and a century thereafter.

"Morals are in part a function of climate; probably the heat of Arabia intensified sexual passion and precocity, and some allowance should be made for men in perpetual heat. *Muslim laws were designed to reduce temptation outside of marriage, and increase opportunity within. Premarital continence was strictly enjoined* (xxiv, 33), and fasting was recommended as an aid. The *consent of both parties was required for marriage*....Muhammad accepted polygamy to balance a high death rate in both sexes, the length of maternal nursing, and the early waning of reproductive powers in hot climes....he *forbade concubinage* (lxx, 29-31).

"*....the ethic of the Qur'ãn is sternly puritan* as Cromwell's; only the uniformed think of Muhammadanism as a morally easy creed." (Italics, present writer's).

(ii)

With Reference to Serfdom and Slavery

(a)

Christian Testimony[13] Relating to Muslim History

Being the uncompromising upholder of human dignity and liberty, an institution like serfdom had no sanction to emerge under the law of Islam. Will Durant admits it, even as Islam's adversary, when he observes: "The Caliphs gave reasonably protection to life and labour." (op. cit., p. 227). And the irreverent critic, H.G. Wells, confesses that *"Islam established in the world a great tradition of dignified fair-dealing"* and *"created a society more free from widespread cruelty and social*

13 For the Qur'ãnic stand in respect of the abolition of these evils, readers should refer to the relevant sections of the present book, especially in Vol. II.

oppression than any society had been in the world before." (Outline of History, p. 325). (Italics, present writer's).

In respect of the institution of Slavery, Will Durant admits that the Holy Prophet (peace be on him!) "did what he could do to mitigate its burdens and its sting" (p. 180), and observes: "*The Qur'ãn recognised the capture of non-Muslims in war, and the birth of children to slave-parents, as the sole legitimate sources of slavery*; no Muslim (just as in Christendom no Christian) was to be enslaved." (p. 209). As such, it was mostly and basically the unransomed prisoners of war[14], the exaggeration of whose numbers is discounted by Will Durant himself (p. 209), that formed in the Muslim world what has been wrongly termed as slave class. However, with all his want of love and respect of Islam, he finds himself forced to say:

> *"The Muslim.... handled them (slaves) with a genial humanity that made* their lot no worse—*perhaps better, as more secure—than that of a factory worker in nineteenth-century Europe.... The offspring of a female slave by her master, of a free woman by her slave, was free from birth. Slaves were allowed to marry; and their children, if talented, might receive an education. It is astonishing how many sons of slaves rose to high place in the intellectual and political world of Islam, how many, like Mahmud and the early Mamluks, became kings."* (p. 209). (Italics, present writer's).

(b)

Christian Testimony Relating to Christian History

Serfdom:

Will Durant observes *(The Age of Faith, pp. 552-564):*

"The same factors that paved the way of feudalism between the thrid century and the sixth established it between the sixth and the ninth....

"An institution that had lasted throughout known history appeared inevitable and eternal, even to honest moralists....Pope Gregory I....continued to

---

14 If there were 'slaves' of any other category, they must be taken to have come in reprisals against the continuous mischief of the neighbouring non-Muslim communities. For instance, Will Durant says, referring to Christian slave-trade: "Muslims and Greeks were kidnapped by (Christian) slave traders along the shores of the Black Sea, western Asia, or northern Africa for sale as farm hands, domestic servants, eunuchs, concubines or prostitutes....The slave trade flourished in Italy, probably due to the nearness of Muslim countries which could be preyed upon with a good conscience...." (*op.cit.*, p. 554).

use hundreds of slaves on the papal estates, and approved laws forbidding slaves to become clerics or marry free Christians. The Church....permitted the enslavement of Muslims and of Europeans not yet converted to Christianity. Thousands of captured Slaves and Saracens were distributed among monasteries as slaves; and slavery on church lands and papal estates continued till the eleventh century. Canon law sometimes estimated the wealth of church lands in slaves rather than in money; like secular law. It considered the slave as a chattel; it forbade church slaves to make wills, and decreed that any peculium or savings of which they died possessed should belongs to the Church. The archbishop of Narbonne, in his will of 1149, left his Saracen slaves to the bishop of Beziers. St. Thomas interpreted slavery as one consequence of Adam's sin....emancipation sometimes proved more difficult on ecclesiastical than on secular properties.

"The decline of slavery was due not to moral progress but to economic change....Servitude continued....

"Typically the serf tilled a plot of land owned by a lord of baron.... He could be evicted at the owner's will....it is impossible to calculate the total of serf's obligations. For late medieval Germany it has been reckoned at two-third of produce....stories told how Satan excluded serfs from hell because he could not bear their smell....His (i.e., serf's) manners were rough and hearty, perhaps gross....he had to survive by being a good animal....he was greedy because poor, cruel because fearful, violent because repressed, churlish because treated as a churl. He was the mainstay of the Church....

"*....the Church became to largest landholder in Europe, the greatest of feudal suzerains*....her 'feudalities', or feudal rights and obligations, became a scandal....Feudalism feudalized the Church". (Italics, present writer's).

White Slavery:

Speaking of this institution, assiduously cultivated in Christendom through the beneficence of the Church, Dr. Eric Williams makes the following observations in his *Capitalism and Slavery* (pp. 12-18):

"The political and civil disturbances in England between 1640 and 1740 augmented the supply of white servants. *Political and religious nonconformists paid for their unorthodoxy by transportation* most to the sugar islands. ....*Religious intolerance sent more workers to the plantations.* In 1661 Quakers refusing to take the oath for the third time were to be transported; in 1664 transportation....was decreed for the third offence for persons over sixteen assembling in groups of five or more under pretence of religion....*The prisoners were granted in batches to favourite courtiers, who made handsome profits from the traffic in which, it is alleged, even the Queen shared.* A *similar policy* was resorted to after the Jacobite rising of the eighteenth century.

"The status of these servants became progressively worse in the plantation colonies. *Servitude....tended to pass into a property relation* which asserted a control of varying extent over the bodies and liberties of the person during service as if he were a thing. Eddis, writing on the eve of the Revolution, found *the servants groaning 'beneath a worse than Egyptian bondage'*....Defoe bluntly *stated that the white servant was a slave.*" (Italics, present writer's).

Black Slavery:

In his valuable historical document entitled African Glory (Wett & Co., London 1955), Mr. J.C. Degroft Johnson projects the beginnings of the Negro slave trade thus:

"In 1441-42 Antonio Gonsalves and Nuno Tristan passed Cape Blanco on the Saharan coast, and on the return journey called at Rio d'Ouru, or, River of Gold, whence they brought back some gold dust and *the slaves. These slaves having been sent by Prince Henry to Pope Martin V, the latter conferred*[15] *on Portugal the right of possession and sovereignty over all lands that might be discovered between Cape Blanco and India.*

"Prince Henry the Navigator, having now received the support of the Church[16], carried horses on his ships to enable his sailors to hunt down their human prey on the Saharan coast. Great was the rejoicing in Catholic Christian Lisbon as each succeeding batch of African slaves arrived." (p. 127). (Italics, present writer's).

In his highly-scholarly work, *Capitalism and Slavery*, the Christian scholar-statesman of the West Indies, Dr. Eric Williams, projects a historical record which, though it deals mainly with the British slave trade, brings into broad relief the fact that rejoicing in the Negro slave trade was shared by all the Christian powers capable of participating in the Rape of Black Africa. He says (pp. 35-48, 192, 209):

"With free trade and the increasing demands of the sugar plantations, the volume of the British slave trade rose enormously....The importation into Jamaica from 1700 to 1786 was 610,000, and it has been estimated that the total import of slaves into all the British colonies between 1680 and 1786 was over two million.

"Mutinies and suicides were obviously far more common on slave ships than on other vessels, and the brutal treatment and greater restrictions on the movements of the slaves would doubtless have tended to increase their

---

15 What a gift, and what a reward, and what a holiness!

16 Mark the role of the Church in blessing the Rape of Black Africa!

mortality....The sole aim of the slave merchants was to have their decks 'well covered with black ones'. It is not uncommon to read of a vessel of 90 tons carrying 414....The space allotted to each slave on the Atlantic crossing (called the 'Middle Passage') measured five feet in length by sixteen inches in breadth. Packed like 'rows of books on shelves', as Clarkson said, chained two by two, right leg and left leg, right hand and left hand, each slave had less room than a man in a coffin. It was like the transportation of black cattle, and where sufficient Negroes were not available cattle were taken on. The slave trader's aim was profit and not the comfort of his victims....

"Prior to 1783, however, *all classes in English society presented a united front with regard to the slave trade. The monarchy, the government, the church, and public opinion in general, supported the slave trade....*

"The (Christian) Spanish monarchy set the fashion which European royalty followed to the very last. The palace-fortresses of Madrid and Toledo were built out of the payment to the Spanish Crown for licenses to transport Negroes. One meeting of the two sovereigns of Spain and Portugal was held in 1701 to discuss the arithmetical problem posed by a contract for ten thousand 'tons' of Negroes granted the Portuguese. The Spanish queen, Christina, in the middle of the nineteenth century, openly participated in the slave trade to Cuba. The royal court of Portugal, when it moved to Brazil to avoid capture by Napoleon, *did not find the slave atmosphere of its colonial territory uncongenial. Louis XIV fully appreciated the importance of the trade to metropolitan France and France overseas. The plans of the Great Elector for Prussian aggrandizement included the African slave trade.*

"Hawkins' slave trading expedition was launched under the patronage of Queen Elizabeth....slave traders held high offices in England. *Of The Royal Adventurers trading to Africa in 1667, a list headed by royalty included two eldermen, three dukes, eight earls, seven lords, one countess, and twenty-seven knight.*

"The Church also supported slave-trade....Sherlock, later Bishop of London assured the planters that 'Christianity and the embracing of the Gospel does not make the least difference in civil property'. Neither did it impose any barriers to clerical activity; for his labours with regard to the Asiento, which he helped to draw up as a British plenipotentiary at Utrecht, Bishop Robinson of Bristol was promoted to the see of London. The bells of the Bristol churches pealed merrily on the news of the rejection by Parliament of Wilberforce's bill for the abolition of the slave trade. The slave trader, John Newton, gave thanks in the Liverpool churches for the success of his last venture before his conversion and implored God's blessing on his next. He established public worship twice everyday on his slaver, not for the slaves but for the crew. 'I never knew', he confessed, 'sweeter or more frequent hours of divine communion than in the last two voyages to Guinea'. The famous Cardinal Manning of the nineteenth century was the son of a rich West Indian merchant dealing in slave-grown produce. Many missionaries found it profitable to drive out Beelzebub by Beelzebub. According to the most recent English writer on the slave trade, they 'considered that the best way in which to remedy abuse of Negro slaves was to set the plantation owners a good example by keeping slaves and estates themselves, accomplishing in this practical manner the salvation of the planter and the advancement of their foundations'. The Moravian missionaries in the islands held slaves without hesitation; the Baptists, one historian writes with charming delicacy, would not allow their earlier missionaries to deprecate ownership of slaves. To the very and the Bishop of Exeter retained his 655 slaves, for whom he received over £ 12,700 compensation in 1833....Quaker nonconformity did not extend to the slave trade. In 1756 there were eighty-four Quakers listed as members of the Company trading to Africa, among them the Barclay and Baring families. Slave dealing was one of the most lucrative investments of English as of American Quakers, and the name of a slaver, the Willing Quaker, reported from Boston at Sierra Leone in 1793, symbolizes the approval with which the slave trade was regarded in Quaker circles....An inscription to Foster Cunliffe (a Liverpool slave trader) in St. Peter's Church describes him thus: 'a Christian devout and exemplary in the exercise of every private and public duty, friend to mercy, patron to distress, an enemy only to vice and sloth, he lived esteemed by all who knew him....and died lamented by the wise and good'....

"....It was held in 1677 that 'Negroes being usually bought and sold among merchants, so merchandise, and also being infidels, there might be property in them'. In 1729 the Attorney General ruled that baptism did not bestow freedom or make any alteration in the temporal condition of the slaves; in addition the slave did not become free by being brought to England....So eminent an authority as Sir William Blackstone held that 'with respect to any right the master may have lawfully acquired to the perpetual service to John or Thomas, this will remain exactly in the same state of subjection for life', in England or elsewhere.

"The barbarous removal of the Negroes from Africa continued for at least twenty-five years after 1833, to the sugar plantations of Brazil and Cuba.

"....What was characteristic of British capitalism was typical also of capitalism in France. Gaston-Martin writes: 'There was not a single great shipowner at Nantes, who, between 1714 and 1789, did not buy and sell slaves....it is almost as certain that none would have become what he was if he had not sold slaves'." (Italics, present writer's).

We may close this most brutal tale of heinous crimes against humanity with the observations of Professor Emil Torday who, lecturing at Geneva in 1931 under the auspices of the 'Society for the Protection of Children of Africa', said[17]:

---

17 Quoted by J.C. Degroft Johnson, *op.cit.*, pp. 153-165.

"This, too is an age of propaganda. We excel our ancestory only in system and organisation; they lied as fluently and as brazenly. Central Africa was a territory of peace and happy civilisation. Traders travelled hundreds and sometimes thousands of miles from one side of the vast continent to the other without molestation; the stranger was always an honoured guest to the African. The tribal wars from which the European pirates claimed to deliver the people were mere sham-fights; it was a great battle when half a dozen men perished on a battlefield. Some may question the use of the word 'pirates' but it must be admitted that even the mode employed by Sir John Hawkings to procure his first stock of slaves for the new world was worse than that of an accredited pirate.

"Pierre de Vaissiers gives us the incident of a captain who poisoned his human cargo when held up by calms or adverse winds. Another killed some of his slaves to feed the others with the flesh of their slaughtered friends.

"It is little wonder, then, that slaves died not only from physical ill-treatment, but also from grief, rage, and despair. Some undertook hunger strikes: some undid their chains and hurled themselves on the crew in futile attempts at insurrection. *In order to combat the grief and melancholy among the slaves it became the custom to have them on deck once a day and force them to dance, but even in these cases many a slave took the opportunity to* jump overboard, uttering cries of triumph as he cleared the vessel and disappeared *below the surface.* There are indeed limits to the degradation which the human spirit will endure.

"....the slaves were forced into crowded canoes and taken to the ships, where the use of whips and spears compelled them to climb reeling and trembling up the swaying rope-ladders....

".... It is difficult to determine accurately the extent of the de-population of Africa occasioned by the slave trade. *One French historian quoted by Utting says it is not exaggeration to say that 100,000,000* people were lost to Africa as a result of it. *Dr. W.E.B. Du Bois, the eminent Afro-Asian historian, also believes that Africa lost about 100,000,000 souls as a result of the slave trade.*

"Next it must be stressed that many died in the slave wars ... Whitened skeletons littered the slave routes as if to blaze a trail for others to follow. Such was the carnage. Between 1690 and 1820 Jamaica alone received no fewer than 800,000 slaves; yet in 1820 only 340,000 slaves existed in the island. *Think of the numerous West Indies islands, under the domination of so* many European countries, think of the United States of America, of Canada, of Mexico and of the South American Republics, which have large Negro populations even today, and then picture those blacks who perished in Africa before the journey to the new world had really begun; think of those who perished during the Middle Passage; then again consider of those who fell dead as a result of the slave whips; and let us reflect on the lot of those sick, injured, and aged slaves who were cast adrift to die of hunger and starvation. Finally, let us remember that band of brave Negro men and women, particularly the Koromantee Negroes, who found the state of bondage insufferable and who died at the state in the cause of liberty." (Italics, present writer's).

Conclusion

Finally, may we be permitted to emphasise that the role of the Christian civilisation in the ages of faith being what has been recorded in the forgoing, the following judgement of Bertrand Russell, in his well-known book: *Why I am not a Christian*? (London, 1967), stands unchallenged for all time:

"In the so-called ages of faith, when men really did believe the Christian religion in all its completeness, there was the Inquisition, with its tortures, there were millions of unfortunate women burnt as witches, and there was every kind of cruelty, practised upon all sorts of people in the name of religion.

"You find as you look around the world that every single bit of progress in human feeling, every improvement in the criminal law, every step towards the diminution of war, every step towards better treatment of the coloured races, every mitigation of slavery, every moral progress that there has been in the world, has been consistently opposed by the organised Churches of the world. I say quite deliberately that the Christian religion, as organised in its Churches, has been and still is the principal enemy of moral progress in the world." (p. 25).

Appendix

Islam's Role in Africa in the Background of the Role of Christianity

Virulent missionary propaganda has been carried on in respect of Africa in which, in order to hide the crimes of Christendom against Africa's black populations, the name of Islam has been most falsely dragged in respect of Negro slavery. Hence, a brief discussion in respect of Islam's role among the black races of Africa has become absolutely necessary. In this connection we will bring forward the testimony of the Afro-American Christian scholar Dr. Blyden. Combining eminence in scholarship with a first-hand knowledge of Africa, he wrote thus, towards the end of the nineteenth century, in his book: *Christianity, Islam and the Negro Race* (London, 1887):[18]

"After the first conquests of the Muslims in North Africa, their religion advanced southward into the continent not by arms, but by scholars and books and mosques, by trade and inter-marriage. *They could not have brought a force*

18 Italics in all quotations, present writer's.

sufficient to subjugate the people, for they had to deal with large, powerful and energetic tribes. The Nigritian and Soudanic tribes have never been subdued by a foreign foe, but they have over and over again driven back both Arabs and Europeans." (p. 256).

"You can understand why it is then that Islam has such a hold upon the African tribes who have embraced it. They gather under the beams of the Crescent not only for religious but for patriotic reasons, till they are not only swayed with one idea but act as one individual. The faith becomes a part of their nationality, and is entwined with their affections. Arguments from outsiders have no weight with them. There are 'names and phrases which have such effect upon their minds and so thrill them as supersede and transcend all argument....That theory which attributes the success of Islam in Africa to what are frequently denounced as the sensual aspects of the religion is based upon ignorance, not only of the system but of the elementary facts of human nature. No religion could exert so powerful a sway over two hundred millions[19] of people of all races and climes for more than a thousand years which appealed chiefly to the lower passions." (p. 266).

"It is not too much to say that the popular literature of the Christian world since the discovery of America, or at least for the last 200 years, has been anti-Negro. The Muhammadan Negro has felt nothing of the withering power of caste. There is nothing in his colour or race to debar him from the highest privileges, social or political, to which any other Muslim can attain. The slave who becomes a Muhammadan is free." (p. 18).

"With every wish, no doubt, to the contrary, the European seldom or never gets over the feeling or distance, if not of repulsion, which he experiences on first seeing the Negro. While he joyfully admits the Negro to be his brother having the same nature in all its essential attributes, still owing to the diversity in type and colour he naturally concludes that the inferiority which to him appears on the surface must extend deeper than the skin, and affect the soul. Therefore very often in spite of himself he stands off from his African convert even when under his training he has made considerable advance in civilization and the arts....And the (European) missionary looking from a comfortable social distance surveys the Europeanised native, sometimes with pity, sometimes with dismay, seldom with thorough sympathy." (p. 34).

"Muhammadanism and learning to the Negro were coeval. No sooner was he converted than he was taught to read, and the importance of knowledge was impressed upon him. The Christian Negro came in contact with mental and physical proscription and the religion of Christ contemporaneously. If the Muhammadan Negro had at any time to choose between the Qur'ãn and the sword, when he chose the former he was allowed to wield the latter as the equal of any other Muslim; but no amount of allegiance to the Gospel relieved the Christian

---

19 Now seven hundred million.

Negro from the degradation of wearing the chain which he received with it, or rescued him from the political, and in a measure ecclesiastical, proscription which he still undergoes in all the countries of his exile. Everywhere in Christian lands he plays at the present moment the part of the slave, ape, or puppet." (pp. 15, 16).

"The Muhammadan Negro is a much better Muhammadan than the Christian Negro is a Christian, because the Muslim Negro as learner is a disciple, not an imitator....With the disciple progress is from within; the imitator grows by accretion from without. The learning acquired by a disciple gives him capacity; that gained by an imitator terminates in itself. The one becomes a capable man; the other a mere sciolist. This explains the difference between the Muhammadan and the Christian Negro." (p. 44).

"The introduction of Islam into central and west Africa has been the most important, if not the sole preservative, against the desolations of the slave trade." *(p. 78).*

"Mungo Park, in his travel seventy years ago, everywhere remarked the contrast between the pagan and the Muhammadan tribes of interior Africa. One very important improvement noticed by him was abstinence from intoxicating drinks....Thus throughout Central Africa there has been established a vast Total Abstinence Society; and such is the influence of this Society that where there are Muslim inhabitants even in Pagan towns it is a very rare thing to see a person intoxicated. They thus present an almost impenetrable barrier to the desolating flood of ardent spirits with which traders from Europe and America inundate the coast....The abstemiousness of Islam is one of its good qualities which we should like Africans to retain, whatever may be the future fortunes of that faith on this continent. The Negro race in their debilitating climate do not possess the hardihood of the North American Indian or of the New Zealander; and under the influence of that apparently inseparable concomitant of European civilization, they would in a much shorter time than it has taken the last named races reach the deplorable distinction of being 'civilized off the face of the earth'." (pp. 79, 80).

Dr. Blyden's book created a big stir in the British press. Among those who boldly came forward to espouse the cause of truth and to confirm the learned doctor's verdicts on the roles of Islam and Christianity in Africa were Bosworth Smith, who wrote a long article in the *Nineteenth Century* for December 1887, and an eminent Englishman who had travelled widely in Africa, Mr. Joseph Thomson by name, who wrote in high praise of Islam's role in the London *Times* (November 10, 1887). We may quote here the latter's verdict on the allegation of Islam's association with slave trade in Africa. He said:

"It has been argued by some of your correspondents that in Eastern Africa and the Nile basin you see Islam in its true colour in congenial association with the slave trade and all forms of degradation and violence. A more baseless statement could not be conceived. I unhesitatingly affirm—and I speak from a wider experience of Eastern Central Africa than any of your correspondents possess—that if the slave trade thrives, it is because Islam has not been introduced to those regions, and for the strongest of all reasons, that the spread of Muhammadanism would have meant the concomitant suppression of the slave trade."

Part V

CONCLUDING OBSERVATIONS

Chapter I

THE IMMEDIATE ENVIRONMENT FOR THE QUR'ÃNIC REVOLUTION

Chapter II

THE HOLY PROPHET'S DIVINE MISSION

Chapter I

THE IMMEDIATE ENVIRONMENT FOR THE QUR'ÃNIC REVOLUTION

The Holy Qur'ãn emerged in Arabia and, though it claimed to be the message of God for entire humanity, very naturally its immediate encounter was with the Arabs, who possessed a religious philosophy, a system of religious rituals, a social structure, an ethical outlook and a moral code, along with the *Ka'bah* at Makkah—which had been established in hoary antiquity as the house of Worship for the One True God—still enjoying the status of Arabia's central holy place under the control of the descendants of Abraham through Ishmael, though no longer for monotheism but only for idolatry.

In that encounter, Arab paganism, with all its material resources, fought against Islam tooth and nail until, tottering step by step in the process, it finally vanished lock, stock and barrel.

One of the aspects of that bloody conflict was that, even in the worst crisis—and crises were many, Islam did not compromise in the slightest measure,—and in this its reform movement stands in human history as radically different from other known reform movements which crystallised into distinct religions, as they exist today; because the latter built on the existing material, some of which alone was discarded for projecting new dimensions. This is what we find, for instance, in the teachings of Gautama Buddha, who came forward to reform Hinduism—as a result of which Buddhism came into existence; and in the teachings of Christ, who stood up to reform Judaism—as a result of which the Christian religion was born.

Thus, Islam is neither a reaction brought about by the theoretical or the practical dimensions of Arab life, nor is it in any way a product of Arab environment. Hence it cannot be called Arab religion. Nor can it be called Muhammadanism, because unlike Gautama Buddha, for instance, Muhammad has not claimed to be the author of Islam. Rather, he has emphatically renounced all such claim, proclaiming God as its Author.

To come to the *religion, social structure* and *ethics* of the pagan Arabs:

As accepted on all hands, the Arab '*cult of worship*' was a magical cult based on sheer polydaemonism and fetish-worship, possessing not even the faintest semblance of any civilised features. The Qur'ãn confronted it with the purest form of Monotheism and wiped it out completely.

The *outlook in respect of human life* was based on a thorough-going Pessimism. The present world was regarded as the only world that existed, and Time was considered to be the great Destroyer. The existence of human beings was believed to be confined to the span of earthly life commencing with birth and terminating in death. Thus, the worldly relations were ephemeral, life was an empty dream, and struggle for anything idealistic was vanity. This crude materialistic view of the world and human life led to the establishment of Nihilism as the 'religious philosophy'[1]. As of the Qur'ãn, it agreed in respect of the transient character of the worldly joys, which forms an incontrovertible truth. But, then, it gave a philosophy which was the very opposite of the Arab pagan view. It taught: (a) the earthly life possesses reality—as opposed to vanity, and meaningfulness—as opposed to 'emptiness'; (b) only to regard it as the be-all and end-all of human existence is wrong, because; (c) it is actually a *means* to a higher *end*,—the end being evolution of the human personality, and it being only a stage in the stages of that evolution; (d) as *means*, however, it has to be pursued and cared for with all earnestness; and, therefore; (e) *Pessimism* is a false view, and *Optimism* alone deserves to be adopted.

In respect of *social structure*, the most ferocious and inhuman form to tribalism[2] constituted its foundation—a tribalism that had led to prolonged internecine wars and tremendous social mischief. The Holy Qur'ãn challenged it and uprooted it on the basis of its principles of Human Unity and Brotherhood of the Believers, which cuts right across all ties of tribal and racial kinship and establishes the social structure on ethico-religious foundations.

The pessimistic nihilistic outlook had very naturally led the pagan Arabs to full-blooded Hedonism *in the domain of morality*. For them, it

---

1 Ref: The Holy Qur'ãn, VI:29; XXIII: 82, 83; XLV: 23, 24; L: 2, 3; etc. Also: 'Abid b. al-Abras : *Diwãn*; and the Seven *Mu'allaqãt*.

2 Dozy names it as 'a violent and terrible passion' (*Histoire des Musulmans d'Espagne*, I, 7. Leiden, 1932.

was a bad world, and life was a 'bad bargain'. The pursuit of 'wealth, wine and woman' had, therefore, become their greatest passion, to which the praises of voluptuousness in pre-Islamic poetry bear full testimony[3]. Indeed, the pagan Arabs were a godless, thoughtless, reckless people, whom only a miracle could change,—and the miracle came in the person of the Holy Prophet Muhammad (Peace be on him!) who, with his unique personality and his unique message in the form of the Qur'ãn, as his weapons, blew up the sands of pagan morality and built up the edifice of the morals of godliness.

To revert to Arab morality: Along with hedonism as their basic moral philosophy, the pagan Arabs possessed certain moral concepts like loyalty, generosity, courage, patience, veracity and regard for honour. Unfortunately for them, however, they possessed no refined moral sense, nor did they have any idea of ethical norms and principles. Hence, their notions of those virtues were either defective or positively vicious. A brief examination will suffice.

Loyalty:

The pagan virtue of loyalty was grounded purely in materialistic considerations, with absolutely no idea of anything higher. It was rooted in tribalism—in kinship by blood, and as such it could induce the pagan Arabs to demonstrate the highest self-sacrifice and to undergo the worst

---

3 For this purpose, even the reference to the famosu Seven *Mu'allaqãt* alone is enough. In his *Literary History of the Arabs* (p. 136), Prof. R.A. Nicholson has projected the pagan hedonistic conception of life in the words of a pre-Islamic poet thus:

Roast meat and wine, the swinging ride
On a camel sure and tried,
Which her master speeds amain
Over low dales and level plain:
Women marble-white and fair
Trailing gold-fringed raiments rare:
Opulence, luxurious ease,
With lute's soft melodies——
Such delights hath our brief span;
Time is change, Time's fool is man:
Wealth or want, great store or small,
All is one, since death's are all!

sufferings in upholding it, whither the cause was morally right or wrong. In consequence: Based on the outlook: 'My tribe, right or wrong', it was no more than an irrational and immoral passion; as we find plainly expressed, for instance, by Durayd b. al-Simmah, in a verse quoted by Nicholson: "I am of Ghaziyya: if she be in error, then I will err; and if Ghaziyya be guided right, I go with her"[4]. To enter into a solemn covenant with someone outside one's tribe, for safeguarding any of his specific interests, was rare. Such a covenant was, however, honoured with full loyalty. But, the pagan spirit being one of overbearing haughtiness and show of vulgar 'manliness', the practice of loyalty in this respect also was not based on any considerations of humanitarian moral obligation but on crude self-esteem.

As opposed to the above pagan view, the Holy Qur'ãn establishes the virtue of loyalty on *principles*: spiritual and moral. A Muslim should be loyal to God and to the Holy Prophet Muhammad (Peace be on him!)—a bond of loyalty which exists in the form of an explicit and solemn Covenant that comes into being simultaneously with the acceptance of Islam (XLVIII:10). Besides that, he has to practise loyalty in the entire sweep of social relations on the *principle* of upholding all that is good and striving against all that is evil for humanity (III:110),—on the basis of the universalistic Divine Law and not on petty tribalism or racialism.

Generosity:

It was intimately related to the pagan view of 'honour', as Zuhari b. Abi Sulmã projects it in terms of 'a shield of his personal honour'[5]. It was more a demonstration of self-projection than of benevolence. In other words, it was motivated purely by the spirit of ostentation and vainglory, the notion of its role as a moral virtue being consciously absent from the pagan consciousness. This fact becomes evident when we find the pre-Islamic poets boasting of even their excessive drinking of wine as a hall-mark of generosity! Thus Arab paganism stood not for generosity as such, but for thoughtless prodigality.

The Holy Qur'ãn, too, gives a high place to generosity in its moral code. But it denounces vehemently the pagan notions connected with it, namely: lavish wasteful spending (XVII:27), and spending for

---

4 *op.cit*, p. 83.

5 *Mu'allaqah*, V. 51.

ostentation and vainglory (II:264). Indeed, thoughtless extravagance is regarded as no less a vice than niggardliness (IV:36, 37; XVII:27, 29; etc.); and Muslims have been commanded to practise *disciplined* generosity (XXV:67; etc.), and that with the purest of motives, i.e., love of God (II:177; etc.). Hence, generosity is a purely moral act in Islam—well-balanced and consequential for its executor as well as for its recipient.

Courage:

Military prowess was the demand of the vicissitudes attendant on the cult of tribalism, wherein reckless courage constituted the very means of survival; and it was meant to be practised indiscriminately and without any ethical considerations, namely, as a burte passion—as an uncontrolled and irresistible animal impulse, employed for plunder or for destroying the members of a rival tribe. Indeed, the sages of paganism preached openly that the courage of an Arab consisted not merely in striking dauntlessly at the enemy who had committed aggression, but basically in the attitude whereby 'he should rather take the initiative (of murdering people) and perpetrate aggression (even) when no one does him any wrong'[6]. Thus, for Arab paganism bravery was only another name for the practice of brute and barbaric ferocity.

The Holy Qur'ãn, too, commends and commands courage (VIII:45; etc.) and deprecates cowardice (VIII:15; etc.). But therein courage has been projected as a noble and thoroughly disciplined trait of human character; and it has been emphasised in both of its aspects, namely, physical courage and moral courage. As *physical courage*, or, military prowess, it has been firmly grounded in justice (V:9), mercy (XC:17) and peace (VIII:61), on the one hand, and in the highest ideals of fighting in the 'Way of God' (IV:74; etc.) and of attaining the sublime blessing of martyrdom (II:154; etc.), on the other—which makes a Muslim absolutely fearless of death. As *Moral courage*, it has been affirmed as an inseparable part of Islamic character (V:57).

Patience:

The rough and difficult conditions of life, with scarcity, pestilence, famine and fratricidal wars always haunting them, had made extraordinary endurance and patience eminent virtues in the sight of the desert Arabs, for whom it was essentially a vital part of courage to face

6 Zuhair b. Abi Sulmã: *Mu'allaqah*, vv. 38, 39.

hardships dauntlessly on the battlefield and elsewhere. As such, it was not actually a moral virtue with an idealistic content but a bare necessity relating to their physical existence and survival.

As compared with that view, the Holy Qur'ãn has filled the concept of patience (*sabr*) with a rich spirituomoral content (II:153, 155; etc.), elevating it to the status of a high moral principle and an eminent constituent of godliness (II:177), whereby the promotion of the best of man as well as the advancement of the cause of Truth and Goodness in the life of humanity are ensured (II:156; III:146-148).

Veracity:

The qualities of rugged straightforwardness, courage and vigour which the desert life breeds, establish an appreciation of the virtue of veracity, or, truthfulness, as a manly trait of character. Moreover, simple truthfulness is a virtue which has been appreciated throughout human history, among the most primitive as well as the civilized communities, as an admirable mode of human expression. Thus, the pagan Arabs also regarded veracity, or, truthfulness, as an eminent virtue.

As compared with the simple Arab pagan view, the Holy Qur'ãn has projected the concept of 'Truth' comprehensively in terms of, so to say, both of its poles: subjective and objective, namely, as *sidq* and *haqq*, and has presented an elaborate philosophy of Truth with its spiritual, moral, social, cosmic and supra-cosmic dimensions[7]. Similarly, it has given an elaborate exposition of the concept of Falsehood (*Bãtil*).

Regard for Honour:

The pagan Arabs possessed a deep sense of honour. Its entire concept revolved, however, around their philosophy of tribalism. It was embedded in the notion of exultation in ancestral virtues (*hasab*), which formed the criterion of the excellence to which the tribes laid their claim, as also the real source of personal glory for every member of a tribe. The honour of the tribe was thus the honour of every individual, and the greatest virtue of the individual was to cultivate and maintain a violent and blind passion for defending and promoting it, and finally bequeathing it to posterity,—regarding no sacrifice and no suffering as too great in that regard[8].

---

7 We have dealt with it elaborately in our "*Dynamics of Moral Revolution*".

8 Ref: *Mufaddaliyãt* and the Seven *Mu'allaqãt*.

It was this peculiar sense of honour that had created in the pagan Arabs the spirit of violent arrogance (*ibã'*),—a spirit that caused them to regard submission to the authority of man[9], or even of God[10], as highly dishonourable for themselves.

Also, it was this vulgar sense of honour that had given birth to, and nourished for centuries, the spirit of blind and persistent vengeance, which Nicholson calls "a tormenting thirst which nothing could quench except blood, a disease of honour which might be described as madness"[11].

Again, it was this blind sense of honour that was responsible for the practice of female infanticide[12], the womenfolk being regarded as nothing more than chattels in the pagan Arab society.

Still again, it was this irrational sense of honour which was responsible for the existence of a feudalistic aristocratic social order in which honour belonged only to those of noble descent (*nasab*), namely, the aristocracy, and not to the 'base-born', i.e., those who could not trace their lineage to any heroic person: the serfs and the slaves[13].

As compared with all that, the Holy Qur'ãn, based as its teachings are on a genuine notion of moral good and evil and on universalistic ethical ideals, has counteracted, in a radical and revolutionary manner, the pagan concept of 'honour' as well as its different practical ethical implications. In its view, all human beings, irrespective of their tribe or sex, are equally honourable in respect of their humanity (XVII:70); while, in terms of achievement, it is neither *hasab* (ancestral glory) nor *nasab* (pedigree) that can confer greater honour on a human being, but only sound godly moral character (XLIX:13). The only division of humanity which it endorses is that of upholders of Truth and Goodness and the upholders of Falsehood and Evil (LXIV: 2; etc.), and the only conflict which it consequently permits is for the establishment of Truth and Goodness in, and the eradication of Falsehood and Evil from, the life of mankind (III:110; IV:76; etc.). As opposed to pagan arrogance, it preaches

---

9 'Abid b. al-Abras: *Diwãn*: IV, 20; etc.

10 *The Holy Qur'ãn,* II: 206, XCVI: 6,7; XVI: 22; etc:

11 *op.cit*., p. 93.

12 *The Holy Qur'ãn,* LXXXI:8, 9; etc.

13 For references, see Ibn Ishaq: *Sîrat al-Nabî.*

the practice of humility in respect of both human beings (XXV:63; etc.) and God (LVII:16; etc.), and projects the virtue of honour in terms of self-respect (LXIII:8) in the light of that humility; and it teaches self-restraint in anger, forgiveness (III:134), and compassionate kindness (XC:17; etc.), as laws of life. It kills the spirit of vengeance by asking the Muslims to meet evil with good (XLI:34), and to leave the matter of punishment to God, Who is the 'Lord of Vengeance' on behalf of the oppressed (III:4). Even in respect of murder, which was the source of immense and never-ending cruelty in the pagan 'cult of Honour', it teaches the law of equity as based not only on absolute justice but also on mercy (II:178). It elevates the woman to the status of the twin-half of man,—equal to him spiritually, morally and legally (IV:I; XXXIII:35; etc.).

Chapter II

THE HOLY PROPHET'S DIVINE MISSION

The Holy Prophet was born and brought up among the pagan Arabs whose spiritual, moral and social outlooks we have discussed in the previous chapter. But, how different, radically different, from their philosophy of life is the revolutionary Message of the Qur'ãn?

There was a sprinkling of Jewish and Christian groups also present in that country since some centuries, who were as backward in terms of culture as the pagan Arabs. Even so, however, they possessed better religious philosophy and ethical teachings. But how different, radically different, from their philosophies of life is the Qur'ãnic philosophy?

Indeed, the Qur'ãn emerged in history with a philosophy which in its structure, dimensions and outlook differed vitally from all the existing religions and philosophies, adding new dimensions even where it agreed and correcting the wrongs wherever they existed in any religion—not only in respect of Arab paganism but also with reference to other religions of the world. And, no wonder, the Holy Prophet Muhammad (Peace be on him!) claimed the Qur'ãn as the greatest of the miracles bestowed on him by God.

And, then, another important fact, to which we have made a passing reference in the foregoing, deserves full notice— the fact, namely, that the departure of the Qur'ãn from the prevalent thought in religion or ethics or social structure is not of a reactionary character but positive in its nature. In other words, the Qur'ãnic message emerges in a positive, original, constructive, and comprehensive principle which contains within it *potentially* the entire system of its philosophy[1], like the seed of a tree which is said to contain the tree within it potentially,—even as the holy book says: "Seest thou not how Allah sets forth a parable?—A Goodly Word (i.e., the Divine Message) (is) like a goodly tree, whose root (it) firmly fixed and its branches (reach) to the heavens, (and) it brings forth its fruit at all times, by the leave of its Lord..." (XIV:24). Thus, it did not grow out of something pre-existing through re-adjustments and pruning

1 Ref: "The Philosophy of Unity", pp. 157-172 (Vol. I).

but emerged as an exclusive and self-subsisting reality, which supplied the sound model of thought and action in every sphere of life so that any belief or any principle of action which had affinity with it to any extent—even if only in name—became transformed by coming into contact with it, casting off its wrong dimensions and the wrong approach to reality contained in it.

It is this we find in the case of the pre-Qur'ãnic Arab virtues of generosity, courage, loyalty, veracity, patience, etc. In that connection, it may be observed, beyond what we have already noticed, that certain noble moral concepts—noble in terms of their nomenclature—have been possessed by all human communities, including the most primitive. It is, however, not the names of those concepts but their contents that are important. Otherwise, to possess the basic notion of generosity, or courage, or loyalty, etc., is the very demand of human nature. Indeed, it is the very condition of human existence.

In the final analysis, the fact cannot be denied that what could not be achieved up to this day in terms of comprehensive and balanced Wisdom by the greatest thinkers of the world—Aristotle, Plato, Kant, Hegel, Marx, etc.—, and by the greatest religions, was achieved through the Qur'ãn by an illiterate person who had no access to any wisdom of the world and who was born and brought up in a community whose highest intellectual achievement was nihilistic and hedonistic poetry. Yes, he was illiterate and enjoyed not the slightest advantage of any Wisdom in his environment,—unlike Jesus Christ, who was born and brought up in the prophetic lore of the Israelites, unlike Gautama Buddha, who received the highest education as a prince and whose environment was saturated with the accumulated learning of the Hindu sages, and unlike Aristotle, Plato, Hegel, Karl Marx, and others, who had drunk deep at the fountains of knowledge that existed through the labours of previous thinkers. And, then, he gave that Wisdom not through any academic process of research and creation and polishing up of thought from inside academies and libraries, but in an extempore manner—orally and in bits, whose collection under his guidance assumed the form of a Book that contain a thoroughly consistent and comprehensive philosophy and code of life. If, therefore, the Qur'ãn is not the greatest existing miracle of history—what else it is? And how could such a super-human achievement take place without a super-human basis of achievement? Indeed, there is no way but to accept the Qur'ãn as the Word of God. And that it claims to be from the beginning to the end.

Those who believe in the existence of God and in the genuineness of the phenomenon of Divine Revelation, and yet refuse to accept the Holy Prophet Muhammad (Peace be on him!) as the Messenger of God and the Holy Qur'ãn as a divinely-revealed Book, land themselves in the quagmire of absolute irrationality. And the same can be said about the other categories of the Unbelievers also.

This irrationality becomes evident when we examine the attitudes adopted in respect of his claim by his opponents, their judgments emerging in the following terms: (1) it was an act on his part of downright lying, forgery and imposture; (2) it was a case of self-deception under the influence of some serious and peculiar form of madness.

As to the first: Human nature being what it is: He who never spoke a lie in his dealings with human beings,—nay, he who conspicuously shone out as the very personification of Truth and Integrity (*al-Sãdiq* and *al-Amin*) from the very beginning of his life, how could he indulge day in and day out, for twenty-three years, in forging lies in the name of God? Then, who can possibly forge lies deliberately and consciously in the name of God? Only a die-hard atheist with a firm *devilish* mind; because a simple philosophical atheist with any degree of human character would regard any such thing as obnoxious. But, what do we find in his case? Practice of the highest human virtues of truth, justice, mercy, forgiveness, sweetness, sympathy, generosity, selfless service to and suffering for the cause of humanity, etc.[2], on the one hand, and the total submergence of his personality in living and positive devotion to God and the utmost sacrifice in His Way, on the other[3]. Then, had he been an adventurer, employing the name of God as a subterfuge, why should he have insisted on belittling himself by attributing all his merits not to himself but to God, and by confining his status to that of a human being and a Servant

2 Even the tributes paid by the non-Muslim scholars, which we have quoted elsewhere, are enough to give some idea as to what type of character and personality he possessed.

3 Both the Qur'ãn and the *Sunnah* bear irrefutable evidence to the fact that, with all the superhuman labour that he had to undertake for building up the multi-dimensional spiritual, moral, social, economic and political Revolution that he accomplished in history and with all his self-imposed rigours and sufferings of poverty, he would regularly pass a large part of the night, when others would sleep, in standing in prayer before God, until sometimes the skin of his feet would crack and bleed.

of God?—while it was easy for him, with all his dynamic personality and with all the primitive and vulgar superstitiousness of his countrymen, to claim some form of divinity for himself. All of us know that a human being like Jesus has been elevated to the status of the Son of God and has been accepted as such by a large section of mankind in spite of the monotheism projected by the Bible, and Gautama Buddha has been worshipped by his followers very much as a god in spite of the atheistic foundations of Buddhism. Moreover, if his mission would have been based merely on political adventurism, what need was there for him to antagonise his countrymen by confronting them with the challenge of a radically different religion and undertaking, as a consequence, the most poignant sufferings and the greatest risks? Therefore, only a person who has been totally blinded by prejudice can even think of bringing forward the allegation of imposture.

As to the second: The foundations of human behaviour being what they are: What do we really find? The records of his life are in existence. And what do they reveal? Only one thing: that he possessed a most sound physical health and a most sound mind that any human being ever possessed. And the fact that, even under the stress and strain of the greatest adversity, he never lost his equanimity of mind but greeted the worst crisis always with superhuman fortitude and forbearance and an unfailing smile, as also the fact that he combined in his personality utmost mercy with the utmost bravery, speak volumes not only of his spiritual, moral and mental grace and greatness but also of the extraordinary soundness of his nerves. Indeed, only a mentally diseased person can think about him that he could ever be mentally diseased.

In the final analysis: If Truth has any reality and Reason any value, and both of them any meaning: The Holy Prophet Muhammad (in whom God's greatest Blessings abide!) is, by all canons of Truth and Reason, the Messenger of God to humanity.

BOOK II

ETHICO-METAPHYSICAL FOUNDATIONS

PART I

THE CRITIQUE AND DYNAMICS OF MORALS

PART II

THE METAPHYSICS OF MORALS

Part I

THE CRITIQUE AND DYNAMICS OF MORALS

Chapter I

THEORY OF MORAL JUDGMENT

Chapter II

THE MORAL LAW

Chapter III

ENDS TO WHICH THE MORAL LAW IS DIRECTED

Chapter IV

PENAL ETHICS

Chapter V

ETHICO-RELIGIOUS DYNAMICS

FUNDAMENTAL CLASSIFICATION

Laws stated in the Qur'ãnic Moral Code, the presentation of which has been undertaken in the second volume of the present book, are actually ethical judgements. But there are certain principles which form the theoretical core of all moral philosophy, because they deal with the *nature* of Morality. We may call them 'basic ethical principles', and state them under the following fundamental classification:

I. Theory of *Moral Judgement*.

II. Then, if the standard of moral judgement is Law, discussion relating to the *Moral Law* with regard to:

(a) its nature;

(b) the spirit according to which it is to be practised;—and also:

III. (a) The *Immediate End* or *Ends* to which the Moral Law is directed.

(b) The *Ultimate End*, if any, which morality—although it is to be practised within its domain as an absolute value—should serve:

IV. *Penal Ethics*, or, Theory of Punishment.

V. *Moral*, or, in the Qur'ãnic perspective, *Ethico-Religious*, *Dynamics*.

FUNDAMENTAL CLASSIFICATION

[illegible]

Chapter I

THEORY OF MORAL JUDGEMENT

The *Moral Judgement* is the judgement, from the point of view of morality, of approval or condemnation of a mode of conduct. It relates to the following factors:

(I) The Object of Moral Judgement, i.e., that which is approved or disapproved as good or bad. It can be conceived either as the motive of a performed voluntary action or as the consequence thereof.

(II) The Subject of Moral Judgement, i.e., that which sits in judgement over the modes of conduct of the moral agent.

(III) The Predicate of Moral Judgement, i.e., the term of moral approval or condemnation.

(IV) The Standard involved in the Moral judgement, with reference to which the value of a mode of conduct is assessed. It can be conceived either as Law or as End.

Now, as to the Qur'ãnic teaching in that behalf:

I. Object of Moral Judgement:

The *object of moral judgement* is, in the first instance, voluntary action which involves will, as opposed to reflex action which lacks will. Thus it has been affirmed:

"Allah will not call you to account for that which is unintentional in your oaths, but He will take you to task for that which your hearts have garnered...." (II:225)

Again:

"....But if one is forced by necessity, without wilful (i.e., voluntary) disobedience, nor transgressing the limits, then he is guiltless...." (II:173)

The voluntary action comprises within it such elements as:

(a) The *conflict* between two motives, the motive of the performance of Duty (i.e., the *consciousness of an obligatory Law*) and the motive of the fulfilment of Desire (i.e., the *instinctive urge* in defiance of the moral law).

Duty is constituted of:

(i) the consciousness of an obligatory Law;

(ii) the feeling of reverence associated with it;

(iii) the consciousness of want of moral value in the idea of failing in duty.

Desire is constituted of:

(i) the idea of the end;

(ii) the feeling of pleasantness associated with the idea;

(iii) present state of uneasiness from want of something.

(b) Besides the conflict, there is involved *deliberation*, i.e., the weighing and balancing of each of the two conflicting factors in the voluntary action.

(c) Deliberation is followed by choice of either of the two conflicting motives of Duty and Desire, which is a *free choice* and every morally-conscious agent knows that it is free.

(d) Finally, there is *resolution* to fulfil either the Desire or the Duty, thereby passing beyond mere intention.

(e) The resolution is followed by the *execution* or the actual performance of the action.

(f) The performance of the action brings in the *consequences*, or the result of the performance, which is causally determined by numerous factors in control of the agent without *taufiq*.[1]

---

1 This is the verdict of the Qur'ãn (XI:88). The question arises: what is the significance of *taufiq*? *Taufiq* means: 'conformation'. As a Qur'ãnic term it implies the existence of harmony between the effort of the moral agent and the extraneous factors through Divine Grace. The occasion for Divine Grace, in its turn, arises, according to the Holy Qur'ãn, only when the moral agent takes the initiative (XIII:11)—which initiative, again, should be in consonance with the Law that governs the cosmological process and is reflected in history. We have discussed that Law in our "*Dynamics of Moral Revolution.*"

The analysis of voluntary action brings out and the Holy Qur'ãn affirms that man is responsible only to the extent of the *freedom* he possesses:

> "Allah does not hold anyone responsible except to the limit of his capability". (II:286)

Now because, this capability is confined to the freedom of choice in respect of conflicting motives, the real object of moral judgement is the motive[2], as the following verses confirm:

> "....And there is no blame on you in the mistakes that you make unintentionally, but (what counts is) that which your hearts intend purposely...." (XXXIII:5)
>
> "....Save him who is compelled thereto (i.e., unto the declaration of unbelief), while his heart is still contented with Faith...." (XVI:106)

Namely, if his motive is not to defy the truth, the transgression committed by him under duress will not be condemned.

> "....When, the Hypocrites come to thee (O Prophet!), they say, 'We bear witness that thou art indeed the Messenger of Allah". Yea, Allah knows that thou art indeed His Messenger. But Allah bears witness that the Hypocrites are indeed liars (in respect of their motive)". (LXIII.1)

---

2 The Holy Prophet (Peace be on him!) says:

"Verily the value of actions lies in the motives (by which they are prompted)." (Bukhari: *Sahîh*; Vol. I, p. 2).

It should also be noted that motives not translated into action (i.e., *lamam*) do not form the object of moral judgement, as we have been told:

"....those who avoid great sins and abominations, save the slight and unwilled deviations from virtue...." (LIII:32).

This is the Qur'ãnic view of the object of moral judgement. But there is a view opposed to it which regards 'consequence' as the object. That view is, however, unacceptable; because, in the first instance, consequence is determined not by the human will but by causal nexus. Secondly, morality is reduced thereby to expediency. Thirdly, because vice too is an expediency, virtue can hardly be separated from vice.

"It is not their (i.e., the sacrificial animals') meat, not their blood, that reaches Allah: it is your (motive for) piety that reaches Him...." (XXII:37)

Viewing the problem from another angle, it is the conflict between Desire and Duty that gives rise to the moral situation, wherein emerges the question: what is really binding as moral obligation? Now, the Qur'ãnic verse: "O ye who believe! Stand out firmly for justice, as witnesses to Allah, even as against yourselves, or your parents, or your kin, and whether it be (against) rich or poor...." (IV:135), implies that the moral imperative expressed in the words "stand out firmly for justice" is the standard to be adhered to without regard to any other consideration whatsoever, which means that an action is morally approvable only when it is performed in obedience to the imperative, and condemnable if performed in defiance of it. The value resides thus in the *motive* of the performed action, which relates to the performance of Duty[3] in the case of virtue, and to the defiance of Duty and obedience to Desire[4] in the case of vice, and is subjected as such to moral approval and disapproval.

[*Note on Desire*: It should be clearly noted that it is not *desire* as such, nor the higher desires that relate to high and noble ends, but only the desires relating to the *instinctive urges*, called *hawã'* in Qur'ãnic terminology, obedience to which, in defiance to the sense of duty, is what is meant here by 'obedience to Desire', as the verses quoted in footnote 2 signify.

The correctness of this Qur'ãnic view is self-evident even though certain great religions like Buddhism[5], and certain great moral

---

3 Cf. the verses:

"And for such as had entertained the fear of standing before their Lord's (tribunal) and had restrained (their) soul from the lust of the instinctive urges, or evil Desire, (out of respect for Duty), their abode will be the Garden." (LXXIX: 40, 41).

4 *Cf.* The verses:

"Then, for such as had rebelled (against Duty) and chose the life of this world (—the life of following Desire in the sense of slavery to the lust of instinctive urges); lo! Hell will be his home". (LXXIX: 37-39).

5 For a critical appraisal of the Buddhist point of view relating to the present discussion, as also to other philosophical and ethical problems, and its

philosophers like Kant are opposed to it. For instance, maintaining that all desire is bad, Kant says: "The inclinations themselves being sources of want, are so far from having an absolute worth for which they should be desired, that on the contrary it must be the universal wish of every rational being to be wholly free from them". (*Grundlegung*, 2; *E.T.*, Abbot, p. 46). Schopenhauer terms Kant's view as the 'apotheosis of' lovelessness'. (*Ueber die Grundlage der Moral*; *E.T.*, Bullock, 1903, p. 49); because, in Kant's estimation, even the most unselfish acts of benevolence towards, and love for, other human beings lose all their moral worth unless inspired by pure sense of duty and unless emptied of all *desire* to be benevolent towards fellow-beings.

If we take into consideration the facts of human psychology in reference to the proper realisation of the moral ideal, we are bound to hold to the Qur'ãnic view that some desires deserve to be suppressed, some to be moderated, and some to be encouraged and enhanced, ultimately subordinating all to the spiritual yearning of obtaining Divine Pleasure,—keeping the sense of duty always dynamically alive and the action entrenched in the purest motivation.

However, Kant's deification of Duty acquires meaning in the Qur'ãn itself, in the idea of Absolute Duty to God, because the Divine Will is directed absolutely to *all* that is good—including the supreme good of humanity—and to good and good alone, and the negation of all Desire relating to this world at that level, except the inspiration of fellowship with the Absolute Ideal that is also absolutely Real, would be permissible, because it leads *ipso facto* to perfection above all the perceptions that might be aimed at in relation to earthly life.]

II. Subject of Moral Judgement:

The Qur'ãnic view with regard to the *subject of moral judgement* is that it is the Conscience, or, Moral Reason, of the moral agent, because it maintains:

---

comparison with the Islamic point of view, readers should refer to the penetrating and masterly exposition presented by the young Muslim thinker from the West Indies, Imran Nazar Hosein, in his brilliant book: "*Islam and Buddhism in the Modern World*" (published by the World Federation of Islamic Missions, Karachi, Pakistan).

"O but the human being (in his Conscience[6], or, Moral Reason) is endowed with discernment concerning himself".

(LXXV:14)

And this is possible because of the duality of human nature:

"By the Soul, and Him Who gave it proportion and order, and inspired it (with the conscience of) what is wrong for it and (what is) right for it." (XCI:7, 8)

Verse 8 implies that the human self is capable of wickedness (*fujûr*), which is the urge of the lower self, or, the "Impelling Self" (XII:53), and also of virtue (*taqwã*), which is the urge of the higher self, or, the moral Reason named as the "Reproaching Self" (LXXV:2). But the urge of the lower self should be made subordinate to the urge of the higher self in order that it becomes finally powerless in respect of compelling the individual to follow the path of Desire in defiance of the call of Duty,—the human self attaining finally the stage of the Beatified Self (LXXXIX:27)

III. Predicate of Moral Judgement:

In respect of the *predicate of moral judgement*, which is constituted of the terms of moral approval and disapproval, it is necessary to have in view the nature of the Qur'ãnic value-system

---

6 In respect of the *nature* of Conscience, there are two views in modern moral philosophy. One of them holds that it is 'Moral Sense',—that is, it is based on Feeling. The other maintains that it is Reason,—that is, its basis is Knowing. According to the Holy Qur'ãn, it may best be termed as 'Moral Reason'. This view we obtain from the word *basîrah* in the Arabic original of the word.

As regards the *function* of Conscience, again, there are two schools of thought. One, which Sidgwick names as 'unphilosophical Intuitionism', maintains the Conscience is a *dictator*, dictating all the time and in all acts as to the course of moral action. The other school, which is called 'philosophical Intuitionism', holds that Conscience is a *legislator*, legislating in respect of the morality of human actions. According to the Holy Qur'ãn, Conscience is the *judge* (or, the evaluator)—as *basîrah*, whose function is to judge whether a certain action is morally approvable or disapprovable in the light of the standard laid down by the Divine Law, that standard having reference to consequences also, as we shall shortly see.

Thus the Holy Qur'ãn steers clear of the mistakes committed by the modern intuitionist thinkers in respect of the nature and function of Conscience.

wherein morality does not stand in isolation from the other values, especially the spiritual[7]. Consequently, the Holy Qur'ãn has not employed just one set of terms, like 'right' and 'wrong' and 'good' and 'bad', to denote the moral virtues and vices. Rather it has used different sets, and even single words, in different contexts, with the basic notions of moral goodness and evil running through them. Thus we find the following sets of opposites:

(i)	*sãlihãt* and *sayyi'ãt:*	(XLV: 21);
(ii)	*khayr* and *sharr:*	(XCIX:7, 8; etc.);
(iii)	*birr* and *ithm*:	(V:3);
(iv)	*hasanah* and *sayyi'ah*:	(XXVII:89, 90);
(v)	*ma'rûf* and *munkar*	(III:104; etc.);
(vi)	*halãl* and *harãm*	(X:59; etc.);
(vii)	*tayyib* and *khabîth*:	(II:267; etc.).

As for single words, they, along with their connotations (all relating to evil in different gradations and categories), are:

(i)	*fasad* (II:205; etc.):	corruption—a word capable of denoting all types of evil action.
(ii)	*'udwãn* (II:85; etc.):	disobedience.
(iii)	*junãh* (II:158; etc.):	sin.
(iv)	*fãhishah* (IV:22; etc.):	anything abominable beyond measure
(v)	*khatî'ah* (IV:112; etc.):	mistake, fault in small or large measure, and intentional or unintentional.

7 *Cf.* Rashdall: "If, finally, we ask what is the relation of the idea of value to the idea of 'moral' value, I should answer that all that has value has moral value, in the sense that it must be moral, in due proportion to the amount of that value, to promote it; but by moral value we generally mean the particular kind of value which we assign to a good character". (*Theory of Good and Evil*, Vol. I, p. 138).

(vi)	*rijs* (V:93; etc.):	something intensely filthy and unclean.
(vii)	*najas* (IX:28):	something that is unclean according to Reason or Law.
(viii)	*jurm* (XI:35; etc.):	sin—the Qur'ãnic use almost invariably with reference to *kufr*.
(ix)	*lamam* (LIII:32):	slight and unwilled deviation from virtue—possibly in thought alone.
(x)	*ma'siyah* (LVIII:8, 9):	disobedience.
(xi)	*dhanb* (XL:3; etc.):	slip, lapse; trespassing correct boundaries of action intentionally or unintentionally. (Mark that *dhanb* is related to *dhanab* which means tail).

We are, however, really concerned with the seven sets of opposites that we have mentioned.

In that connection, the first fact to be noted is that the terms used in these sets fall into three categories, namely: evaluative, classificatory and descriptive; and among these categories it is only the first that is of value to us in the present discussion. This becomes clear when we examine the semantic structure of each term and fix up its connotation. For this purpose we will take up here the positive terms contained in the sets.

(i) *sãlihãt*: Good deeds. The word *sãlih* means sound, good, righteous, and its semantic constitution contains emphatic reference to belief in God, prayer, and goodwill and love for humanity. However, the practice of *sãlihãt* is repeatedly joined to Faith. Thus this term connotes 'faith expressed in outward conduct'.

It may also be noted that this term has not been used in the Qur'ãn in its singular form, *sãlihah*, which seems to be one of the necessary conditions for choosing a term for our purpose.

(ii) *khayr*: Good. It has been used in the Qur'ãn as a comprehensive term for 'good', covering religious belief, worldly happiness and good in general.

(iii) *birr*: Godliness, righteousness, probity, kindness, charitable gift. The semantic constitution of this term seems to be similar to that of *sãlih*.

(iv) *hasanah*: Good deed, benefaction, charity. Its masculine form, *hasan*, means: beautiful, nice, good, agreeable, exquisite; while the word *husn* means: beauty, excellence, perfection. In its semantic constitution, it covers not only the 'good' in respect of both the worldly and the religious spheres of life, as we find in the case of *khayr*, but also *a powerful emphasis on moral goodness and on beauty, or, grace in conduct.*

(v) *ma'rûf*: It seems to express a very general and comprehensive idea of religious goodness in the sense of compliance with the Divine Law. Literally, it means 'known', 'familiar', and hence 'approved'. Thus in the Qur'ãnic usage, *al-m'arûf* should be taken to mean: 'that which is known to ideal human nature' and hence familiar to and in harmony with it, whereby any act which is *m'arûf* is a good act in the light of what the Qur'ãn teaches as to the goodness of all that is in conformity with ideal human nature (XXX:30). However, it should be noted that the application of this term in the Qur'ãn bears reference more vitally to the legal aspect of human relations than to morality.

(vi) *halãl*: Lawful. It is a legal term. So too is *harãm*, its opposite.

(vii) *tayyib*: Good, pleasant, agreeable, delicious. The Qur'ãn has employed it to denote religious goodness as well as goodness pertaining to worldly things.

Among these seven terms, the first four are evaluative; the next two classificatory; and the last is descriptive. Again, among the evaluative terms, *hasanah* emerges as the term related to the Qur'ãnic predicate of moral judgement, which may be defined as 'moral Good[8] joined to spiritual purity and aesthetic grace'. This selection is confirmed by the Divine Command:

"Verily Allah commands (observance of absolute) Justice and adherence to the *hasanah*...." (XVI:90).

IV. Standard of Moral Judgement:

Coming now to the *standard of moral judgement*, it is Law, as has been clearly set down, among others, in the following verses:

"And those who do not judge on the standard of what Allah has revealed, verily they are transgressors." (V:50).

"And those who do not judge on the standard of what Allah has revealed, verily they are unjust." (V:48).

"And those who do not judge on the standard of what Allah has revealed, verily they are infidels". (V:47).

This means that only actions performed in obedience to 'Law'—the Law grounded in the transcendental value of Divine Pleasure—are morally approvable or virtuous[9], and those performed

---

8 In respect of the predicate of moral judgement Kant has adopted the term 'right' in keeping with his ethical system, while others have chosen the term 'good' whereby moral judgements can be reasonably considered as judgements of value containing at the same time the idea of 'ought' or obligation. Now, it is evident that the term 'good' is more appropriate—more correct—than the term 'right'. In respect of 'good', again, the concept of 'good' is bound to vary in different ethical systems in accordance with the nature or scope of the 'good' conceived. In this respect, the Qur'ãnic concept of the predicate is most perfect.

9 *Cf.* the verses:

"Say: 'Truly, my prayer and my (service of) sacrifice, my life and my death are (all) for Allah, the Cherisher of the Worlds: No partner hath He: This am I taught, and I am the first of those who bow to His Will". (VI:162, 163).

in defiance of 'Law' and obedience to 'Desire' are morally condemnable, or vicious.[10]

10 *Cf.* the verse:

"....and follow not the lusts (of the instinctive urges), for they will mislead thee from, the Path of Allāh...." (XXVIII:26).

Chapter II

THE MORAL LAW

I. Nature of the Moral Law :

The Qur'ãn affirms the following characteristics in respect of the nature of Moral Law:

(i) Besides the regard for the transcendental value of Divine Pleasure—which in itself makes the action most highly disinterested from the practical human point of view—it should not be conditioned by any interest other than morality. We are told:

> "O ye who believe! Stand out firmly for Allah (i.e., act solely out of respect for the Moral Law given by Allah) as witnesses to fair dealing, and let not the hatred of others to you make you swerve to wrong and depart from justice. Be just...." (V:9)

Again:

> "And among mankind is he who would sell his 'Self' to the seeking of Allah's Pleasure (alone) (i.e., seeking no other end but only the intrinsic good contained in the observance of the divinely ordained Moral Law)...." (II:207)

(ii) The Moral Law has been conceived as universally binding, i.e., binding on all rational beings—a principle contained in the following Qur'ãnic affirmation[1] :

"Do they seek for other than the Divine Law?—while all (creatures) in the heavens and on the earth have, willing or unwilling, bowed to His Will (i.e., accepted the Divine Law), and to Him shall they all return." (III:83)

(iii) The Moral Law is to be obeyed as unconditionally and absolutely binding[2] :

---

1 *Cf.* the Holy Prophet's verdict:

"None of you can have (real) belief (in Islam) until he loves for all human beings what he loves for himself." (Ahmad: *Musnad*, Vol. III, p. 272).

2 Because it emanates from the Absolute Good Will and is directed to the establishment of good will among human beings. As to the merit of good

"They (i.e., the human beings) have never any choice (but to obey the Divine Law)". (XXVIII:68)

Again, as regards Muslims:

"The answer of the Believers, when summoned to Allah and His Messenger (Muhammad) in order that he (Muhammad) may judge between them, is no other than this: They say, 'We hear and we obey': It is such as these that will attain felicity". (XXIV:51)

[*Note on Kant's Categorical Imperative*: Before we proceed to the next section, it is necessary to discuss Kant's famous Categorical Imperative.

Among eminent moral thinkers of the modern age, Kant enjoys the distinction of not only being the most eminent but also of presenting an ethical philosophy which is nearer to the Qur'ãnic ethical view than any other, so near in fact that in certain aspects the standpoints of the Holy Qur'ãn and of Kant appear to be identical. This necessitates that while we have stated the Qur'ãnic view concerning the 'standard as Law', we should have a clear understanding of the Kantian Categorical Imperative.

To begin with: Kant names the normative laws as 'imperatives' and says that they are of three kinds, namely: (i) the *hypothetical imperative*, which is not universally applicable and holds only under certain conditions; (ii) the *assertorial imperative*, which can be conceived as universally applicable, but only in respect of the attainment of certain ends; and (iii) the *categorical imperative*, which holds universally as well as unconditionally. He further says that the Moral Law is the *only* law that falls under the category of the categorical imperative; and he lays down the rule: "There is nothing good without qualification except the good will", thus denying all teleology in morals whereby action is conceived to be morally good in respect of its being conducive to certain desirable consequences. (Kant: *Fundamental Principles of the Metaphysics of Morals*, Sec. II, *E.T.*, Abbot, pp. 31-33).

---

will, Kant expresses it beautifully thus: "If with its greatest efforts (the good will) should yet achieve nothing and there should remain only the good will (not to be sure a mere wish but the summoning of all means in our power), then like a jewel, it would still shine by its own light, as a thing which has its whole value in itself". (Kant: *Fundamental Principles of the Metaphysics of Morals*, Sec. I, *E.T.*, Abbot, p. 10).

Trying to understand Kant's view of the Categorical Imperative critically, the very first criticism that emerges is that, as defined by him, it is a 'form without content'; or, it is the 'ideal' divorced from the 'real'. Hence it cannot enjoy as such the status which Kent gives to it in his philosophy. To put it concretely: 'To will always what is good' ought to be accepted as a valid principle, but that does not as such provide any guidance in respect of 'willing the good' in particular situations.

As regards the Holy Qur'ãn, it also prescribes a categorical imperative with regard to the maintenance of the good will. But in the Qur'ãnic view, what is unconditionally and universally binding is strictly the obligation of Obedience to the Moral Law, which derives its authority, not from any utopian transcendental deduction—as in Kant, but from the absolute authority of the Absolute Good Will of the Moral Ruler of the universe, i.e., God. Moreover, it does not stop at the 'form' of the Categorical Imperative but also teaches its practical application in the concrete situations of moral action

Kant lays down three laws in respect of the application of the Categorical Imperative, viz., (i) 'Act only on that maxim which thou canst at the same time will to become universal law'; (ii) 'Treat every rational being including thyself always as an end and never as a mere means' (iii) 'A principle of moral conduct is morally binding on me if, and only if, I can regard it as a law which I impose on myself'.

As to the first law, it stands challenged on different counts. Firstly, numerous situations, in practical human life are conceivable where this law cannot be validly applied; for instance, becoming a teacher of a particular branch of knowledge, which is morally good but cannot be universalised. Secondly, Kant has bestowed on an unreal abstraction of one condition (i.e., obedience to a universal law) the status of being the essential condition for good will. Thirdly, he has confused the merit of performing an action with its goodness. Fourthly, he has erred in holding, as Professor Broad has pointed out (*Five Types of Ethical Theory*, p. 124 f), that a right action—right in respect of the factor of universality—must always be right, no matter what the inclinations of the agent are. For instance, if a man and a woman are married on considerations of Pure Reason, where alone the principle of universality resides, and no consideration is given to their respective inclinations and their unique circumstances, that marriage may prove to be evil for both of them, and not good in any sense of the word. Thus, the mere formal consistency which Kant has emphasised—i.e., that the rule of an action should be willed to be the rule of every person—can never by itself make an action good in terms of morality.

As to the second law, its validity may be said to have been challenged by Kant himself, inasmuch as his ethical philosophy makes every human being, in respect of the realisation of the moral law, a mere means, so that he no more remains 'an end'!

As to the third law, it is correct in the sense that moral law, as distinguished from the political law, is surely a law that our own moral consciousness—our own conscience, and not any other factor, should make us incline to obey. It should form the behest of our higher self. Yet moral law should not be accepted as *merely* self-imposed, because the self can also dispense with it even as it can impose. Consequently it should be combined with the element of *absolute authority*, and such an authority can only be the authority of God.]

II. The Spirit according to which the Moral Law is to be practiced :

The law is meant to be pursued as if it is *self-imposed*, i.e., it should form the behest of the higher self of the moral agent. But here would arise the difficulty: how to regard the Divine Law, which is externally imposed as a 'Law self-imposed'. This difficulty arises, however, in the want of understanding with respect to the expression 'divine origin'. Being of divine origin should not be taken to mean, according to the Qur'ãnic teaching, that the Divine Law is foreign to the nature of man and is merely thrusted from outside on him by God to be obeyed. Rather, it is simultaneously the 'Divine Law' as well as the 'Law of ideal Human Nature', and constitutes, therefore, the very behest of the higher human self.

The identity of the 'Divine Law' and the 'Law of ideal Human Nature' has been explicitly proclaimed thus:

> "So set thy purpose for religion as by nature[3] upright—the nature (framed) of Allah in which He hath created the human beings[4].

3 The *nature* conceived by the Holy Qur'ãn is governed by a universal law which is fundamentally rational.

4 Here the Holy Qur'ãn refers to ideal human nature, i.e., the nature bestowed on humanity by God at the dawn of creation. It is not the same thing as Rousseau and some other moralists speak of in terms of 'primitive' or 'original' nature, because their view does not go beyond the spatio-temporal dimensions,

There is no altering the laws of Allah's creation. That is the right religion, but most men know not."[5] (XXX:30)

Here it should be noted that the 'ideal nature' is the same, and has been always the same, in all human beings, of whatever race or tribe or country. In the Holy Qur'ãn, this is implied in the fact that Divine Law relating to the 'ideal nature' has been revealed to all the communities of the world at one or the other period of human history (XIII:7). In history, it is confirmed by the fact that basic moral concepts have been the same in different civilisations and different ages—their differences consisting basically in the imperfect understanding of those concepts, or in their application to concrete problems of life. Mr. C.S. Lewis has put forward this truth ably thus: "Think of a country where people were *admired* for running away in battle, or where a man felt *proud* of double-crossing all the people who had been kindest to him. You might just as well try to imagine a country where two and two made five. Men have differed as regards what people you ought to be unselfish to—whether it was your own family or your fellow-citizen or everyone. But they have always agreed that you oughtn't to put yourself first. Selfishness has never been admired. Men have differed as to whether you should have one wife or four. But they have always agreed that you mustn't simply have any woman you liked". (*Broadcast Talks*, p. 11). It means that we should affirm the existence of an absolute universal law, based on ideal human nature and underlying the moral judgements of human beings.

---

wherein the modifications of the 'ideal' in respect of its manifestations must be presumed to have commenced at the very early period of human history—as we notice in the Holy Qur'ãn in connection with "the story of the two descendants of Adam" (V:30).

5 *Cf.* Cicero: "True law is right reason in agreement with nature; it is of universal application, unchanging and everlasting; it summons to duty by its demands and averts from wrongdoing by its prohibitions." (*Republic*, iii. 22).

Chapter III

ENDS TO WHICH THE MORAL LAW IS DIRECTED

I. The Immediate Ends :

Morality being an action determined by Law, the difficulty arises: how to accommodate the purposive character of human activity in the scheme of moral life. It is, however, resolved when we find in the Holy Qur'ãn that the Law is directed to a four-dimensional End, those dimensions being:

(i) Moral and Spiritual Well-being of the Moral Agent.

The Holy Qur'ãn says:

"O ye who believe! If you are careful of your duty to Allah (i.e., if you obey the Divine Law), He will grant you a Criterion (to judge between right and wrong), remove from you your (moral and spiritual) ills, and bestow on you forgiveness.....

(VIII:29)

(ii) Moral and Spiritual Well-being of Others.

The Holy Qur'ãn says:

"Ye are the best group, evolved for the service of humanity, enjoining what is right, forbidding what is wrong...."

(III:110)

(iii) Material Well-being of Others.

The Holy Qur'ãn says:

"....and do thou good (to others) as Allah has been good to thee...." (XXVII:77)

(iv) Material Well-being of the Moral Agent:

The Holy Qur'ãn says:

"....and forget not thy portion (of Happiness) in this world...."

(XXVIII:77)

The Law is directed to the above four-dimensional End, without either the Law or the End becoming subservient to each other. Because the very act in obedience to the Law is at the same time the immediate fulfilment of the End. Thus the Holy Qur'ãn harmonises the concepts of the 'Law' and the 'End', and establishes the principle that virtue should be regarded as consequential activity and not merely as 'Duty for the sake of Duty'.

Here it should be properly understood that the End is to be conceived as an organic whole, and its four dimensions are to be realised in harmony, namely, on the principle of *balance* enunciated and emphasised in the Holy Qur'ãn (LV:7-9). Otherwise, they are capable of coming into clash with one another, thereby thwarting the goals of integrated development of the individual and the creation of a social order based on the concept of integralistic culture—both being the Qur'ãnic goals of morality.

It may be observed in passing that this Qur'ãnic view of the four-dimensional End is richer and more sound than Kant's formula wherein two dimensions of the End alone emerge explicitly, viz. (i) the moral perfection of the agent (or, the morally struggling individual), in the sense of the attainment of a perfectly good will, and (ii) the happiness of others. (Kant: *Preface to the Metaphysical Elements of Ethics*, *E.T.*, Abbot, pp. 296-302).

In this connection Prof. Lillie observes:

"....this double standard of morality is surely a strange one for the philosopher who emphasied consistency and denied the relevancy of pleasant consequences to the rightness of actions. If perfection or the good will is the only good or the highest good for ourselves, it surely must also be the highest good for other people and, however little we can do for other people's perfection, to do that little is far more important morally than to seek their happiness. And if happiness be a good for other people, it surely must also be a good for ourselves." (*Introduction to Ethics*, p. 175).

II. The Ultimate End:

While the Holy Qur'ãn is definitely committed to the view that the moral value has to be pursued at its own level as an absolute value, in order that the purity of motive and consequently the purity of moral action is not damaged, it does not subscribe to Kant's barren philosophical stand point which regards morality as the Supreme Good. Rather, it views morality in the perspective of spirituality, or, the transcendental dimension of the human personality, and hence it prescribes a spiritual end as the ultimate end for which a Muslim should always aspire, regarding it as the Supreme Good. That end is the absolute harmonisation of the human will with the Divine Will through the Qur'ãnic technique of the spiritualisation of morality[1]. Says the Holy Qur'ãn:

> "But the most righteous shall be removed far from it (i.e., the Fire),—he who spends his wealth for increase in self-purification, and has in his mind no favour from anyone for which a reward is expected in return, but only the desire to seek the Countenance of his Lord Most High, and soon will he attain (complete) satisfaction.
> (XCII:17-21)

---

1 It may be pointed out here that this is the actual pursuit of *Tasawwuf*, which is a vital dimension of Islamic orthodoxy; and this is also the actual implication of the Sufi doctrine of *fanã'*.

Chapter IV

PENAL ETHICS

As in the case of every organised society, it is the function of the Islamic Social Order to ensure the preservation of the values that it upholds through a Criminal Code which, though built up on spiritual and moral foundations, is to be enforced by the state-authority. Indeed, the Holy Qur'ãn does not confine itself to mere sermonising on morals and does not want the upholders of its message and mission to be mere passive spectators or imbecile critics with respect to evil and evil-doers. Rather, it commissions them to control the incentives to crime and to combat the forces of moral evil and social ill-health actively and with masculine grace.[1]

Among the Western thinkers who, in modern times, have devoted their attention to a philosophical assessment of the problem of punishment, two stand out prominent, i.e., Kant and Bentham. The former, who is famous for his categorical imperative and moral purism, holds to the retributive character of punishment, while the latter, who is famous for his utilitarianism, has projected utility as the basic consideration in respect of punishing criminals. But neither the absolute standard of Kant nor the utilitarian view of Bentham have satisfied the later legal thinkers when they have found themselves confronted with complicated legal situations. As a consequence, different other theories, which are 'dubious mixtures'[2] of the above-mentioned two, have come into existence—of course, with the Benthamian bias, making confusion worse confounded, because crime, which it is the aim of all these theorists to control, has continued to increase in the Western society and in those others that are its camp-followers.

Coming to the Holy Qur'ãn, there the obligation of punishment is, besides being legal, also moral and even spiritual, whereas it is only a

---

1 III: 110; XXII:41.

2 Professor K.O. Shatwell, Dean of the Faculty of Law at the University of Sydney, Australia, names them as "unproven theories" and deplores "that crime like the ever rolling stream with which we are all familiar is today not only in danger of over-flowing its banks but to some extent has already done so". (See, his paper on "Crime and the Punishment of Crime" read at the Third Commonwealth and Empire Law Conference held at Sydney, and reported in the *Pakistan Legal Decisions,* Lahore, 1966, p. 103).

legal obligation in the secular systems. It being so, the Qur'ãnic outlook on the nature of punishment is that the values, which form the life-blood of the social order, should be preserved, if need be, even at the cost of mutilating, or taking the life of the criminal, and no softness should be observed because that would degenerate finally into the adoption of expediency, the condoning of crimes, and the consequent deterioration of the moral standards[3].

The ultimate end is the spiritual purification of the criminal through subjection to an ordeal and of the society through the establishment of the correct moral and spiritual tone by means of creating genuine fear of evil consequences of crimes among the would-be criminals and thus restraining them from deviating from the right path—the path of virtue. The end is contained in the principle of comprehensive spiritual purification, which has been declared by the Holy Qur'ãn to be the mission of the Holy Prophet (Peace be on him!) (LXII:2-3)

As regards the gradation of punishment, the Qur'ãnic principle that emerges is that the higher the value that is violated, the severer the punishment, and the lower in grade the violated value, the lighter—comparatively speaking—the punishment. Thus the Qur'ãnic evaluatory scale of crimes stands, from above downwards in the following order: Fornication, Theft, Murder.

Now: Fornication is a crime against honour, as also against the healthy existence of family life, and thus against the very foundations of human society—because, as the Holy Qur'ãn teaches (IV:1), it is the family and not the individual which forms the basic unit of human society; theft is a crime against property; and murder is a crime against life.

The outlook of the Holy Qur'ãn in respect of the punishment of these crimes is not the same in each case. It is the most severe in the case of fornication, because it has been commanded that Muslims should not show the slightest compassion in inflicting the punishment, or else they will land nothing less than their Faith itself in jeopardy (XXIV:2). As for theft, decoity and treason, once they fall in the punishable category and have been detected, there remains absolutely no possibility of condonement. Coming to murder: although the Holy Qur'ãn prescribes retribution, it also permits payment of ransom if the aggrieved party agrees. This seems to be due to the fact that the inducement to commit murder is

3 This is what is happening in the West today, as we shall shortly see.

mostly rooted in the crimes against honour and property. Hence, once the crimes against honour and property have been dealt with more severely, as the Holy Qur'ãn does, the crime of murder can be dealt with less severely, provided there exists a genuine ground for it, without damaging the social health.

Viewing the Qur'ãnic punishments in the light of ethics, the punishments relating to fornication, adultery and homosexuality are reformative in the sense that they imply the spiritual purification of the offenders; the punishments prescribed for theft, dacoity and treason are of deterrent character; and the punishment in respect of murder is based on retribution which is tempered with mercy (II:178). The guiding light in all cases, however, is the procurement of spiritual good[4] of the individuals concerned and of the society.

As for the principle of severity in respect of punishments, it is grounded in the following facts:

(a) The Qur'ãnic view of the human being is that he is essentially a spiritual being and the Vicegerent of God, and not just an animal among animals. In consequence, the crimes in question acquire extraordinary gravity as forming fundamental violations of the human status.

(b) Like every criminal code which emerges on the basis of an overall philosophy and code of life and is rationally enforceable in that perspective alone, the Qur'ãnic penal code is meant to be enforced in a specific form of society—the Islamic society.

---

4 Not the observation of Rashdall: "....the moment we insist upon the effect produced on the sufferer's soul by his punishment, the retributive theory is deserted by the reformatory or the deterrent....If it be urged that avenging of the Moral Law (in the infliction of physical punishment) is right because it is the expression of the avenger's indignation (—as Kant would have it—) that is an intelligible answer; ....though this can be hardly regarded as an ultimate end but rather a means to further end—the spiritual good of the man himself and of society at large." (*Theory of Good and Evil*, pp. 285-301).

In contrast stands the defective and rigid view of Kant, who is one of the greatest of modern philosophers: "Juridical punishment can never be administered merely as a means for promoting another good, either with regard to the criminal himself or to civil society, but must in all cases be imposed only because the individual on whom it is inflicted *has committed a crime*....The penal law is a Categorical Imperative...." (*Kant's Philosophy of Law, E.T.* by Hastie, 1887, p. 195).

(c) The Islamic society, i. e., the society based positively in both theory and practice on the Qur'ãnic Guidance and constituted of morally struggling and spiritually orientated individuals, is, in its turn, a society which is dedicated to the ever-active realisation of moral, legal, economic and political justice, which functions positively and devotedly for the eradication of the incentives to crime, and whose ultimate goal is through and through spiritual.[5]

Considered in terms of efficiency in respect of the eradication of crime, the success of the Qur'ãnic penal code stands at the highest in human history.

Coming to the modern Western outlook, it is radically opposed to the Qur'ãnic gradation of values. There, the highest in the scale is the crime against life, and after that comes the crime against property. As regards crimes relating to sex, chastity is not considered to be a value worthy of being protected with the arm of law! Rather, it is the sex-crimes that receive legal and, in some quarters, even ecclessiastical protection. How horrifying is the situation in this respect can be seen in the published proceedings of the legislative bodies in certain Western countries and in the facts and reports broadcast in the respectable journals of Europe and America. And, as already stated it is not only the laity but also the clergy (!) of Christian Church who have fallen victim to an absolutely immoral point of view in respect of sex-crimes. In evidence thereof, we may quote from a book entitled "*God Speaks out on New Morality*"[6] (pp. 104, 105). Giving, the heading: "Shocking Homosexuality in the Ministry", the authors of the book have reported:

> "Here is a London newspaper report: 'The Archbishop of Canterbury, Dr. Geoffrey Fisher, spoke in the House of Lords in supports of a change in British Law to make homosexual acts between consenting adults in private no longer a criminal offence. The Archbishop said: the right to decide one's own moral code and obey it, even to a man's hurt, was a 'fundamental right of man given to him by God, and to be strictly respected by society and by a criminal code'. *That from the head Minister of the Church of England*!.....

5 Ref: Discussion on the nature of Islamic society in Chapter IX of Part IV (Vol. I, Book I).

6 Compiled by Faculty Members and published by the Graduate School of Theology, Ambassador College, Pasadena, California, U.S.A. (1964).

"A Congregationalist minister, Pastor Robert W. Wood, wrote a book, *Christ and the Homosexual*. A newspaper review of his book in a Pasadena paper said: 'Mr. Wood seems.....interested in proving that 'homosexuality is the creation of God (since God is the Creator of everything); and as such it is just as good as any other creation of God'. He says further that homosexual love'— *he means lust* can be truly sacramental, or holy, in the eyes of God. He has seriously discussed the desirability of performing marriages between two persons of the same sex.

" 'A homosexual' he says, 'can be a successful clergyman'.... Mr. Wood maintains that the rate of homosexuality in the clergy is higher than in most other professions. The author even suggests that this perversion may one day be useful in solving the problem of over-population.' (It certainly did solve the 'over-population.' (It certainly did solve the 'over population' of Sodom and Gomorrah!!!). 'He says that homosexuality is not a sin, and that under certain conditions in certain ways it may even be morally right'.

"I have much, much more evidence....many more such reports. Theological seminaries—several of them—are know to have, as students being trained to become pastors of churches, a high percentage of homosexuals. I have reports that homosexuals are organised—and that there is a determined campaign to seek out, seduce, and 'covert' to this loathsome perversion *child* 'converts'.....

"Some men who profess to be the ministers of Jesus Christ argue that the Bible nowhere condemns fornication or homosexuality."

If ministers of the Christian Church, like the Archbishop of Canterbury and Pastor Robert W. Wood and many others, regard the *unnatural* crime of homosexuality as 'holy in the eyes of God', very naturally the Western civilisation of today accepts the *natural* crime of fornication much holier, and consequently the Western societies have gone forward to an unimaginable extent in that respect. This fact is so well-known that it hardly requires any documentation.

Viewing the situation in respect of crime in general, it seems as if the Western society[7] finds itself helpless in facing the challenge of crime. And this helplessness has reached a point where what was once regarded with utmost seriousness of conviction as an offence is now being legalised only because that offence is being widely committed, having received licence from a wrong philosophy of punishment for a long period of time.

It should not be too much to emphasise here that the whole fault lies with the West's legal philosophy, which in its turn is based on certain perverted concepts in the realm of moral philosophy.

The following observations of a former Chief Justice of Pakistan, Mr. A.R. Cornelius (a Christian), in respect of the consequences for morality of the legal procedures and punishments awarded under the present-day westernished Criminal Law, are worthy of note by those who object to the severity of punishments prescribed by the Holy Qur'ãn. He says[8]:

> "....As for criminal cases, it is probably correct to say that under the present system every decision has the quality of breeding more cases of the same kind...case in which guilty persons are acquitted probably form the majority. On the other hand, there are a number of cases in which innocent persons are convicted, on the basis of oral evidence, and even suffer death.
>
> "Cases are common enough where 10 or 15 persons have jointly slaughtered 3 or 4 of their enemies, and carried their heads in triumph aloft on spears through the village. One supposes that when they are acquitted, as they often are, the village lives in a state of terror from these persons when they return and the whole balance of life is upset once again, as it was when the murder took place and during the ensuing Police Investigation. By the inscrutable working of the judicial system, a situation has been created, to which under the necessities of life the people have to adapt themselves, and, at the cost of a part of their true character, they do so. Unfortunately, what is damaged in the process is that part of their character which is the distinguishing feature of the strong and noble human being. Belief in truth diminishes. Denial of the strength of evil becomes impossible...."

---

7 And so, too, its camp-followers in Asia and Africa!

8 *Pakistan Legal Decisions*, Lahore 1965, pp. 157-158.

Elsewhere, Mr. Cornelius observes[9]:

"I may appropriately end this paper by stating *my doubts regarding the utility of imprisonment*[10] in all cases as a mode of punishment for a crime. At a time when the common person all over the world is finding it increasingly difficult to provide subsistence for himself, there is something of an absurdity involved in the consideration that he can procure such subsistence and a good many amenities and facilities besides (such as medical care) by simply committing a crime....the ever-increasing burden of maintaining prisons and highly-paid staff to provide accommodation, care, proper food and other amenities for persons of proved anti-social quality is one from which an intelligent citizenry may justifiably seek to be relieved if alternative methods, cheaper and not less effective, can be found to create the desired effects of punishment, retribution and reformation."

9 *Pakistan Legal Decisions*, 1956, p. 149.

10 Italics, present writer's.

Chapter V

ETHICO-RELIGIOUS DYNAMICS

Morality, according to the Holy Qur'ãn, is conscientious action in accordance with the Moral Law. But conscientious action is not possible without the possession of purity of motive by the moral agent, which, in its turn, necessitates a continuous psychological effort, named in Islamic terminology as *tazkiyah*:

> "By the Soul and the proportion and order given to it; and its enlightenment as to its wrong and its right;— truly he succeeds (in his spirituo-moral struggle) who subjects it successfully to *tazkiyah* (or, purifies it), and he fails who corrupts it." (XCI : 7-10)

The word *tazkiyah* means literally the removal of undesirable growths and impurities. As a spirituo-moral term it denotes the self-imposed effort of the moral agent for eradicating those tendencies within the human self which form obstacles in the path of moral development,— the eradication consisting in resolving the conflict between good and evil that rages in the human breast.

This internal conflict is, however, closely influenced by the conflict of good and civil existing in the society.

Thus, the Qur'ãnic view is that, for the realisation of morality, evil must be subdued and good must be made to prevail at both the levels: the individual and the collective. Namely, it is not only the internal conflict which should be resolved but also the external conflict. This is in keeping with the Qur'ãnic integralistic outlook as opposed to the ideational outlook of Christianity, Hinduism, Buddhism, etc. Hence we may discuss briefly[1] the techniques of both.

I. Technique of Resolving the Internal Conflict:

The Holy Qur'ãn affirms, as we shall notice more fully in the "Metaphysics of Morals", the existence of two aspects of human nature, namely, *al-Nafs al-Ammãrah* (the Impelling or Carnal Self)[2], and *al-Nafs*

---

1 Elaborate treatment necessitates a separate monograph, which the present author intends to present later.

2 XII:53.

al-Lawwãmah (the Reproaching or Moral Self)[3], and of the conflict between them. Moreover, it affirms that this situation of conflict has to be resolved through discarding the behests of the Carnal Self at the instance of the Moral Self, thereby enabling the self to be transformed into *al-Nafs al-Mutma'innah* (the Self-at-Peace, or the Beatified Self)[4]. It is through undertaking this process that an individual can avoid neurosis, develop as an integrated personality, and become capable of acting with due respect for the Moral Law.

This leads us the question: What are the conditions that are required to be fulfilled for bringing about this transformation?

Those conditions are: (i) there must be such a comprehensive and sound Moral Code that may ensure to an individual the moral perfection adequate to human nature; (ii) there must be a Model[5], or Exemplar, of moral perfection, who may impart the assurance that moral values can be realised and moral norms can be actualised; (iii) Acquisition of *tazkiyah* should be a historical fact and not a mere theoretical possibility.

The Qur'ãnic Guidance fulfils all these conditions:

Firstly, it imparts a comprehensive Moral Code, as we shall shortly see in Volume II.

Secondly, it gives at a Model of moral perfection in the person of the subject of Qur'ãnic Revelation, viz., the Holy Prophet Muhammad (Peace be on him!).

> "Ye have indeed in the Messenger of Allah an Excellent Model (i.e., Pattern of Conduct) for him who looks to Allah and the Last Day, and remembers Allah much." (XXXIII:21)

---

3 LXXV:2

4 LXXIX:27.

5 Professor Muirhead observes: "As Professor Mackenzie puts it, 'For the communication of the art of conduct example is better than precept, and experience is better than either; so that even if it were the business of ethics to lay down precepts, these precepts would still not suffice for instruction in the art of life'." (*The Elements of Ethich*, p. 28).

According to Prof. William Lillie: "....the example of good men's lives and the training of practical experience are likely to be more effective influence in producing good conduct." (*Introduction to Ethics*, p. 20).

Thirdly, it affirms the transformation of the human personality through *tazkiyah* not merely as a possibility but as an established historical fact:

> "Assuredly Allah hath shown grace to the Believers when He raised up unto them a Messenger from among themselves, who rehearseth unto them His Signs, *purifies them* (*of spiritual and moral evils*), and teaches them the Scripture and the Wisdom (– thereby imparting comprehensive knowledge[6] of, among other things, the oral dynamics and the moral code); although afore they were in flagrant error." (III:164)

Coming to the technique to *tazkiyah* the Qur'ãnic Guidance bestows certain powerful feelings that reside in a true Muslim's soul. They are: intense love for God and fear of the Displeasure of God, on the one hand, and intense love for the Holy Prophet (Peace be on him!) and absolute loyalty to him, on the other. It is these which, in the emotional life of a Muslim, are meant to subdue the force of feeling associated with Desire (or, the feeling that leads to the defiance of the Moral Law) and make *tazkiyah* possible.[7] Thus says the Holy Qur'ãn:

Love for God and Fear of God's Displeasure:

> "....and those who believe are most intense in their love for Allah." (II:165)

> "O ye who believe! fear Allah (in respect of His Displeasure) with fear due to Him, and die not except ye be Muslims (i.e., in a state of submission to Allah). (III:102)

Love and Respect for the Prophet:

> "The Prophet is nearer to the Believers than themselves (i.e., entitled to their utmost love and respect)." (XXXIII:6)

Love for God is Based on:

(i) His Absolute Perfection:

---

6 XVI:89.

7 The view that *tazkiyah* can be brought about through the Consciousness of Law seems to be untenable, because an abstract law or idea can never be so effective in moulding the human personality as the impact of another personality. Thus, the cultivation of love for the Holy Prophet (in whom God's Blessings abide!) assumes supreme importance.

"(He is) Allah, the Possessor of Absolute Perfection." (CXII:2)

and (ii) His concern for us, as detailed in the discussion on "God."[8] Indeed, He is *al-Wadûd*, "the Loving One". (LXXXV:14)

Love for the Prophet (Peace be on him!) is based on:

(i) The grandeur of his spiritual and moral personality:

"And thou (O Muhammad!) art (established) on an exalted standard of character". (LXVIII:4)

"O Prophet! We have sent thee as....Illuminating Lamp (*par excellence*—a lamp that illumines for humanity the path of righteousness leading to God). (XXXIII:46)

and (ii) his concern and function for us:

"Assuredly there hath come unto you a Messenger from among yourselves: aught that harasses you grieves him: full of concern (is he) for you (in respect of your acquisition of the Good): to the Believers he is most kind and merciful". (IX:128)

"....and he (Muhammad) relieves them of the burdens and the shackles and have been upon them." (VII:157)

Love for God should express itself basically in following the Holy Prophet (Peace be on him!) both as Teacher of Godliness and as Model of Human Perfection:

"Say: If ye (O Muslims!) love Allah, follow me (practically, as your ideal of human perfection): Allah will love you and forgive you your sins: For Allah is Oft-Forgiving, Most Merciful". (III:31)

Love for the Holy Prophet (*Peace be on him*!) *should express itself* in unrestricted and unqualified loyalty to him—a loyalty which should be *practice* as distinct from being merely *emotional*:

"But no, by thy Lord, they can have no (real) Faith until they make thee judge in all disputes between them, and find in their souls no resistance against thy decisions, accepting them with the fullest submission." (IV:65)

---

8 See "Metaphysics of Morals" (Vol. I, Part II).

In connection with the function of the Holy Prophet (Peace be on him!) for his followers, we may also note:

(i) it is the spiritual impact of his personality that has been prescribed by God as the most powerful instrument of *tazkiyah* in the life of a Muslim;

(ii) the Holy Prophet's basic function of bringing about *tazkiyah* in his followers—a function for which his other functions (as Teacher) are a means—transcends the limitations of space and time;

(iii) the Holy Prophet's spiritual impact was available not only to the Muslims of the period of his physical existence but has remained available ever since and will remain available up to the Last Day.

These facts are contained in the following Qur'ãnic verses:

"It is He Who has sent amongst the non-possessors of Revealed Truth[9] a messenger from among themselves, to rehearse to them His Signs, to purify them, and to instruct them in the Scripture and the Wisdom,—although they had been, before, in manifest error—as well as (to confer those benefits upon) others of them (i.e., of the Believers) who have not yet joined them (but will do

9 This should be accepted as the correct connotation of the term '*al-Ummiyyun*' employed in the Arabic text. No doubt, the word '*ummi*' stands, amongst its different connotations, for an 'unlettered' person also. But to translate '*al-Ummiyyun*' as 'the un-lettered' creates more difficulties in understanding the Qur'ãn that it solves,—indeed, irresolvable difficulties. However, once we employ the semantic approach and turn to the Qur'ãn itself for guidance, the problem of connotation is solved unambiguously and without difficulty. For instance, this term has been used in III:20 in contradistinction to the category to 'those who have received the Scripture'. Then, in verses 78 and 79 of *sura* II, emerges the emphasis on the 'non-possession of Revealed Truth' in spite of the formal possession of a scripture, because there it bears reference to the Jews who are definitely among 'those who have received the Scripture'. All this means that the term '*al-Ummiyyun*', as employed in their verse under discussion, should be translated as 'the non-possessors of the Revealed Truth'. And, might we also say that, although the primary reference is to the Arabs of those days, the secondary reference covers virtually entire humanity, because even those who claimed to possess a Scripture did not possess the Revealed Truth in its unadulterated form. (The view propounded here is supported by the verdict of Abdullah ibn Abbas.—Refer, among others, to Ibn Jarir al-Tabari's *Tafsir*, Vol. II, p. 258.

so in future up to the Last Day): And He is Exalted in Might, Wise. Such is the Bounty of Allah which He bestows on whom He will (—and He has bestowed it on Muhammad). And Allah is the Lord of Grace Unbounded". (LXII:2, 3, 4,)

What is needed *most* for *tazkiyah*, therefore, is the cultivation of love and reverence for God and the Holy Prophet (Peace be on him!) to a point of intensity where it may become possible for the moral agent to absorb the Divine blessing through the Holy Prophet's spiritual personality, thereby acquiring that spiritual refinement and that moral force which may enable him to overcome all evil propensities and to act according to the highest demands of morality with pleasure and ease.

For this purpose, the Remembrance of God (*Zikr-Allah*) and offering *salãt* and *salãm* (i.e., invocation of God's Blessings and salutation) to the Holy Prophet, the Beloved of God, as often and as much as possible, and with devotion and concentration of thought, form a basic practice, as enjoined by the Holy Qur'ãn. (XXXIII: 41, 56)

Now, development of intimate and living relation with God is fundamental to *tazkiyah.* But intimacy can be cultivated only through love. Love, in its turn, demands obedience to the beloved without demur. Indeed, the richer the exercise in obedience the greater the stabilisation of love in richness and depth.

However, love originates in appreciation, and appreciation is not possible without knowledge. The Muslim begins his quest for God *the Unknown* with *faith*—a faith which, though basically innate, is acquired in its proper dimensions from the Messenger of God, who stands thus as the *axis* around which the entire structure of the Faith moves. Or, we might say, the Messenger of God is the 'door' through which alone the seeker of God can enter upon the Straight Path that leads to God; and this Straight path, again, is nothing else than what is revealed in the personality of the Messenger of God. Thus the Messenger of God is the unavoidable Medium, the *wasîlah* spoken of in V:38; while God is the Goal. (LIII:42)

This being so, the exercise in love for and obedience to God begins with the cultivation of love for and obedience to the Messenger of God—the Holy Prophet Muhammad (in whom abide God's Choicest Blessings!). The Messenger of God being human, no human being can have difficulty in knowing him, which is the prerequisite for loving him and obeying him.

Now, because the Messenger of God is not merely a wise man and a social reformer, and because the transcendental dimension of his personality—his intensely intimate relation with God—is its most vital aspect, approach with respect of *knowing* him must of necessity be two-fold, namely: *intellectual* and *spiritual*.

In respect of the *intellectual approach*, again, the avenues are two, viz., the Qur'ãn and the *Sunnah*. The Qur'ãn enshrines his Prophetic Consciousness and is the Mirror of his Personality, as Lady Ayesha, with her extraordinary wisdom and piety, emphasises[10]. The *Sunnah*, critically assessed, is the human record of his behaviour as the Perfect Man and as the Witness to God and the Vital Proof of God's existence (XXXIII:45)

Both the above sources of knowledge should be constantly studied as a serious exercise, until all the dimensions of the excellence and the greatness of his personality are assimilated in one's consciousness and they entrench themselves in memory as guiding refulgent stars. Such a knowledge will grow in depth as the study continues, and with that will grow the love which it automatically begets,— and, along with love, will grow the inspiration to imitate him and to obey him without hesitation. Then, because obedience to God consists in obedience to the Messenger of God (IV:80), obedience to God will be simultaneously achieved—even though only functionally.

The goal, however, being the establishment of a living, vibrant and dynamic relation with God, Who is transcendent in His being, a powerful exercise in *spiritual approach* to, and realisation of, the Holy Prophet's Personality is also vitally necessary, in order to build up the affinity for the pursuit of that highest goal, as also to obtain the strength, through the blessings of the spiritual impact of the Holy Prophet's Personality, for the pilgrimage to God. It is for this end that God has commanded the Muslims, as mentioned above, to engage in *salãt* and *salãm*, wherein the greater the devotion the richer is the spiritual purification, and the richer the spiritual purification the sublimer is the

10 She says: "The character of the Prophet (in whom Allah's Blessings and His Peace abide!) is (enshrined in) the Qur'ãn." (*Mishkãt al-Masãbih Bãb al-Witr, al Fasl al-Awwal*, p. 111, *Cf.* Muslim: *Sahih*).

purity of motive in moral action—of course, when that exercise is combined with conscientious and whole-hearted practical devotion to the Holy Prophet as Teacher and as Exemplar.

Cultivation of love for and obedience to the Holy Prophet paves the way for the love of God and obedience to Him. Indeed, love and obedience develop simultaneously in both respects, not only because attention focussed on the Messenger of God gets concurrently fixed up on God, but more so because in the spiritual quest of a Muslim the remembrance of God forms the fundamental exercise with which the exercise of *salãt* and *salãm* is combined as complementary.

Remembrance of God, as the fundamental exercise, is directed to seeking the Nearness to God (XCVI:19), and cannot therefore be something formal. As such, *firstly*, it should be undertaken in a state of 'withdrawal' (LXXIII:8), withdrawing attention from everything else and concentrating it solely on God. *Secondly*, it should be undertaken abundantly (III:41; VIII:45; XXXIII:41; LXII:10; etc.)—nay, under all conditions and at all times (III:191). *Thirdly*, it should be joined to contemplation of the Signs of God which pervade the entire universe (III:191 etc.) *Fourthly*, it should be combined with a study of Divine Guidance as contained in the Holy Qur'ãn (XXXVIII:29), and with a serious exercise in moulding one's life in accordance with it to the fullest extent possible (II:206; etc.). *Fifthly*, this entire exercise should proceed most conscientiously as well as most intelligently (VII:205; etc.), in order that the practical results and the tangible fruits of all this labour of lover may be grasped at every step for enabling the pilgrim of eternity to undertake his spiritual flights and moral development at higher and higher levels with the attainment of ever-increasing refinement of the soul, on the one hand, and purity of will for moral action, on the other.

Indeed, this intellectual-cum-spiritual struggle in the domain of *tazkiyah* continues in the life of the conscientious, struggling Muslims, until he becomes capable of establishing a living and abiding Communion with God, thereby attaining finally the realisation of God to an extent that establishes him firmly in submission to the Divine Will (which is the very meaning of the word 'Islam') and bestows upon him purity of motive in moral life, with perfection adequate to human nature,—even as we are told in the Qur'ãn :

"O ye who believe! If ye keep your duty to Allah, He will grant you a Criterion (for judging by its light the rightness and wrongness of motives), will rid you of your evil propensities and deeds, and will bestow on you forgiveness (in respect of your natural shortcomings and past sins); For Allah is the Lord of Grace Unbounded." (VIII:29)

It should be noted here that, because Islam is not just Moralism, moral purification is only the immediate goal, while spiritual purification is the ultimate goal, for which the former forms the organically-necessary basis. Spiritual purification or refinement, again, is not an end-in-itself but only a means to the development of the transcendental dimension of Personality[11]. It is this activisation, which leads through *tazkiyah* to 'holiness,' and 'holiness' is the distinctive quest of religion as opposed to the quests of philosophy and the physical sciences—nay, even of the normative and the social sciences, as we have already noticed in our discussion on the Religious Quest. The acquisition of 'holiness,' in its turn, brings the seeker of God, at different levels of attainment, progressively nearer and nearer to God, the All-Holy, in respect of earning His Pleasure,— which is the highest ideal in Islam:

> "But the greatest (achievement) is the Good Pleasure of Allah. That is the Felicity Supreme". (IX:72)

> "But ah! O thou the Soul at-peace, return to thy Lord well-pleased (thyself) and well-pleasing unto Him! Enter thou, then, among My Devotees! Yea, enter thou My Heaven!" (LXXXIX:27-30)

Thus, the fact cannot be over-emphasised that *Faith in God* is meant in the Holy Qur'ãn to be *lived* and not merely to be *held,* and it is impossible to live it without passing through the rigorous discipline of *tazkiyah.*

And it is not only *Faith in God* but also *Faith in the Messenger of God* which should be *lived*, and lived dynamically; because it is the

---

11 We may recall here what we have already recorded in our discussion relating to the "Unity of Human Personality" in Chapter VI of Part IV. The Qur'ãnic concept of human personality includes three dimensions: the physical, the psychical, and the transcendental. The physical is spatio-temporal; the psychical is temporal; and the transcendental is spaceless and timeless, or, beyond space and time. It is the transcendental dimension which forms the channel of Communion with God, on the one hand, and the substratum of human personality on the other,—substratum for the progressive emergence out of it of the temporal and the spatio-temporal dimensions of personality at the beginning of earthly career, and substratum for he survival of personality with the self-same Identity after the earthly death.

Messenger of God who has been appointed by God as the Divine Instrument of *tazkiyah* for all time. (LXII:2-4; etc.)

There are some for whom, because of superficiality of thought or because of some temperamental prejudice, the reality of all that is nonphysical or metaphysical is, for all practical purposes, nothing more than that of a 'regulative idea' with which human beings are not practically concerned. Such an outlook gives birth to a virtually materialistic view of religion with all the inherent contradiction. In such a view, the religious verities become restricted and confined to a formal *belief* (*'aqîdah*), on which Dialectical Theology thrives 'with all its barrenness, to the detriment of a consequential and dynamic *faith* (*Imãn*).

It is in the above perspective that the question emerges: God is Eternal, Ever-Living and Omnipresent; hence communion with Him is possible. But the Messenger of God was a human being who died long ago. How can communication and establishment of intimate spiritual relation with him be possible?

The Qur'ãnic answer to this misgiving is very clear and unambiguous. *Firstly*, the human personality is not annihilated at death; it is only transferred from one level of existence to another with its Identity intact,—the life after death being a new *life*. *Secondly*, the levels of existence after death are *qualitatively* different in the case of each category of human beings, including the Muslims. Thus, about the martyrs it has been said: "And call not those who are slain in the way of Allah 'dead'. Nay, they are alive; only ye perceive not." (II:154). And again: "Think not of those who are slain in the way of Allah, as dead. Nay, they are living. With their Lord they have provision: Jubilant (are they) because of that which Allah hath bestowed upon them of His bounty, rejoicing for the sake of those who have not joined them but are left behind: that there shall no fear come upon them, neither shall they grieve. They rejoice because of favour from Allah and kindness, and that Allah wasteth not the wage of the Believers." (III: 167-171). Here the qualitative distinction between the life of the ordinary Muslim and the life of the martyr, after death, is very clear. The martyr's life after death is not just life, but it is a full life of enjoyment and activity and of attachment to those Muslims whom he has left behind in their earthly existence.

Now, who are these martyrs that have been spoken of? They are the spiritual children of the Messenger of God,—and, in that respect, not in the highest category but next in rank to those others who acquire the status of *Siddīq*. The status of the life-after-death of the Holy Prophet Muhammad (Peace be on him!), who is not only superior to his followers but, as the Leader of all the Messengers of God (III:81), is supreme in entire Creation, should be in all justice accepted as immeasurable,—not to speak of accepting him as the Living Spiritual Medium for the Blessings of God that relate to the transcendental dimension of human personality.

The fact is that the goal of Islamic life is the establishment of a '*fellowship*' of unique type at the transcendental plane, *right here on earth*, which is possible only if activity at the transcendental level of existence is absolutely real and genuine. The Holy Qur'ãn affirms the acquisition of that fellowship thus:

"Those who submit to Allah and the Messenger (establishing harmony with them), they are (blessed) with (the spiritual fellowship of) the Prophets, the Intensely Truthful and Sincere (Servants of Allah), the Martyrs (who are Witnesses to Allah), and the Possessors of Sound Godliness in general. Ah! What a beautiful Fellowship! Such is the Bounty of Allah, and Allah sufficeth as Knower (and because He affirms it, the factual character of that fellowship should not be questioned by anyone)." (IV:69)

That fellowship is spiritual fellowship—fellowship in the transcendental dimension of existence. It is a living and consequential fellowship, and not a mere idea. It is a dynamic fellowship, like that of the sun, the moon and the earth, wherein the sun is the source of light and life created by God for everything existing on the earth and elsewhere, and the moon is the reflector of sun's light and energy for the earthly creatures and other things. Then, just as water always flows through a channel from the higher to the lower level, spiritual blessings also flow similarly on the invisible transcendental beam. To receive them, however, it is necessary to rise to the spiritual level where fellowship becomes possible with the spiritual luminaries, among whom the greatest and the central luminary is Muhammad, the Beloved of God *par excellence* in whom God's Choicest blessings abide in abounding measure[12]. Indeed, just as iron is transformed into a magnet in its fellowship with the magnet, and just a perfumeless thing becomes perfumed simply through fellowship with the perfume embodied in a rose or a jasmine, so does the pursuer of *tazkiyah* acquire holiness at higher and higher levels in the fellowship of those on whom God has bestowed holiness.

12 The Holy Qur'ãn, CVIII:1.

One further important problem may also be examined here. The question may be raised: If *tazkiyah* involves such a high-level and rigorous discipline, together with an intellectual effort, how is it possible for the common man and woman to acquire the purity of motive demanded by the Qur'ãn?

The answer is: The Islamic society has been conceived to be composed of individuals who are dedicated to the ideal of being spiritually progressive, morally integrated, intellectually awakened and economically and politically emancipated. This ideal is to be pursued by the Islamic community on a collective scale, with fanatical enthusiasm and rigorous discipline. Such a process imparts the impact of the virtues of better-talented individuals to those of lesser calibre through contagion of personality. This is the law of social psychology which has always governed all ideological societies, whether theistic or atheistic, including the early Islamic society and the present-day idealistic Communist society of China.

The fact is that there are natural gradations in respect of calibre and achievement in every society. All human beings are not gifted with every quality in equal measure. Hence what really counts is the spiritual, moral and intellectual achievements of those who can rise above the common level in any measure. The ideal is basically pursued *in all its dimensions* by them alone. And this brings us to the problem of Islamic leadership.

Tazkiyah and Islamic Leadership:

The foundations of Islamic society are basically ehtico-religious. Hence, anyone who honestly comes forward to lead the Muslims to the goal prescribed for them in the Holy Qur'ãn should possess a personality refulgent in its spiritual, moral and intellectual dimensions.[13] This is the verdict of the Qur'ãn, and this is the verdict of Islamic history.

---

13 Let it be noted that these three dimensions are so essential for leadership that they bear reference not only to God-affirming societies but also to Godless societies, such as the Communist, where an effort is made to forge an idealism—even though with materialistic bias. Under that idealism emerges a 'cult of the spirit' and a moral discipline of a certain type suited to the requirements of the ideology.

Again, rigorous discipline for Communist leadership, and even for the rank and file, is a vital element in Communist idealism.

And it is all this, more than anything else, which has bestowed success on Communist revolutions.

But how can such a personality be built up? By mere emotionalism? By mere mysticism? By mere intellectualism? By mere ritualism? By mere formal puritanism? By mere externalism and legalism? By mere ritualistic missionary-ism? By mere political agitationism in the name of Islam? No. A thousand times, No!

The only alchemy which can transform the human personality into 'pure gold' is the alchemy of the rigorous discipline of *tazkiyah*, with its rigours enhanced in the measure of the height of achievement desired. This is what has been taught and demonstrated by the Holy Prophet (in whom abide God's choicest Blessings!), and this is what has been practised throughout Islamic history by those who had truly grasped the dynamics of leadership in Islam and were consequently able to achieve historic success. One such personality was Saiyyid Abd el-Qader al-Jilani of Baghdad, the *Ghaus al-A'zam* (Grand Master) of the Qaderiyyah Spiritual Discipline, who built up, with the spiritual dynamism of his personality and without any political power, the forces that crushed the menace of the Assassins for good, on the one hand, and the might of the Crusaders' barbaric hordes entrenched in Palestine at that time, on the other.

The Holy Prophet was *born* as Messenger of God, having been ordained by God as such at the dawn of Creation (III:81). Hence, he needed no spiritual exercise for earning that office. But we find him withdrawing from the life of the world to the Cave of Hira, in the stark solitude of wilderness, for fifteen years before he proclaimed his divine mission. Then, throughout his ministry, his exercise in the transcendental dimension with its spending of nights in prayers and the days in fasting and prayers both, in the midst of handling the multifarious duties relating to the most glorious and comprehensive revolution of human history; with its majestic austerity enshrining extreme selflessness; with its flowering in the moral domain at the highest level; and with the flood of multi-dimensional blessings for humanity surging from his august pesonality—that exercise is the most conspicuous trait of his character. *In that he established the Sunnah for every future Islamic leder.*

There were in history many of his followers who realised the obligatoriness of this *Sunnah*, in opposition to other leaders whose personal limitations kept them away. One of the glorious products of this *Sunnah* was the great Saiyyid Abd el-Qader al-Jilani, to whom we have referred. It is recorded in history that, in imitation of the Holy Prophet's exercise of retreat to Hira, he was accustomed to retreat to the forest every evening during the course of his formal education, and after the completion of that education he withdrew to the wilderness and stayed there in solitude for many years in total devotion to God, finally acquiring through an extremely rigorous discipline that high level of *tazkiyah* which not only elevated him to great eminence in godliness but enabled him to change the course of history.

The history of Islam is studded with a host of other spiritual luminaries, commonly called *Sufis*, on whom the rigorous discipline of *tazkiyah* bestowed greatness in their achievements for the cause of humanity. Among them was Khwaja Mu'in al-Din of Sanjar (later of Ajmer) who, alone with his spiritual dynamism and without any army or political thrust, pitched the banner of Islam in the heart of an inimical and alien population, changing the course of history in the South-Asian sub-continent permanently. Among them was Sheykh al-Islam Abdullah al-Ansari of Heart who fought with his spiritual armour alone against the corruptions of the tyrants and brought them down to their knees with masculine grace. Among them were the *Sufis* of the Naqshbandia Order who, under the most adverse circumstances when the prestige of the Muslims was at its lowest ebb, conquered, without any material means and purely through the power of their spiritual personalities, the hearts of the haughty enemies of Islam who had destroyed the political power of the Muslims under Halaku Khan—defeating at the same time the Buddhist and the Christian religious forces that were fully entrenched in the field. And, among them were a host of others who, through their *tazkiyah* and in contradistinction to those Muslim religious leaders who were devoid of *tazkiyah*, acquired the glorious distinction of becoming the sole pioneers in respect of the most difficult task of converting vast and widespread human communities to Islam.

Alas, the Islamic leaders of today have turned their backs on *tazkiyah,* with the result that they cannot benefit even the Muslims, not to speak of humanity at large. And the world of Islam presents a scene of unspeakable mass destruction of Islamic values, with the forces of the new-fangled secular 'isms' pouncing upon the Muslim communities like vultures.

The world of Islam will have to revive the pursuit of comprehensive *tazkiyah* in accordance with the norms and principles laid down in the Qur'ãn and the *Sunnah*, in order that genuine Islamic leadership of the Muhammadan Pattern emerges on a high level and in a large measure and acts fruitfully for the fulfilment of the mission of Islam.

As matters stand in respect of the Muslim religious leadership of the present day, neither those who are popularly known as *Sufis* nor those who have become anti-*Tasawwuf*, and neither the political agitators among the '*Ulamã* nor the professional preachers and writers among them, seem to possess any chances of achieving success in defeating the forces of evil that sway the world.

II. Technique of Resolving the External Conflict:[14]

The conflict between good and evil rages not only within the inner world of the human personality but also in the external world of social phenomena. That conflict also has to be resolved if the moral development of the human beings in general has to be ensured. This is so, because man is a social being, and he is born and grows in society, whose good and evil influences have a potent influence on the formation of his character in either direction, i.e., good and evil. The social order has to be, therefore, of necessity transformed into, and maintained as a moral order, if the individual is to attain his true moral stature. That is why the Holy Qur'ãn has commissioned the Muslim Fraternity to strive for transforming the human society into moral order (III:110)

The transformation of the society into moral order, however, presents a challenge to all morally struggling individuals. Hence, every Muslim has been commanded and commissioned to meet this challenge with all his might and to wage a determined struggle without respite all his life to defeat the forces of evil and to enthrone the forces of good. The Holy Qur'ãn calls it *Jihãd*[15] and says:

---

14 For a comprehensive understanding of this problem, readers are referred to the author's: "*Dynamics of Moral Revolution.*"

15 The word *jihãd* means: the act of exerting one's utmost for achieving an end. As a Qur'ãnic term it stands for waging relentless war against evil, whether it exists in the personality of the moral agent—in his inner self—or in his societal environment. Islam evaluated the former as 'Greater Jihãd' and the latter as 'Lesser Jihãd, evidently because the former is the very basis for the latter.

"O ye who believe! Keep your duty to Allah, seek the Medium of Approach (*al-Wasîlah*)[16] unto Him, and strive with might and main (*jãhidû*) in His Way (which comprehends spiritual and moral *tazkiyah* at individual and collective levels): that ye may succeed." (V:38)

Again:

"And strive hard for Allah (which includes eradication of vice and establishment of virtue on earth)—as is due unto Him hard striving (*jihãd*). He has chosen you (for this striving), and has not placed upon you any narrowness in religion." (XXII:78)

In human nature we find that there are only two incentives which bring out the best in man and lift him up in the scale of personality, namely, ambition and danger. *Jihãd* provides both. Now, the greater and the more difficult of achievement the ambition,—and what social ambition can be greater than the transformation of human society into a moral order—, the greater the dangers that are involved. And the greater the dangers involved, the greater the incentive for the maintenance of disciplined struggle and integrity of character; and the greater the said incentive, the greater the *tazkiyah*.

Appendix I

Art and Morality

Vulgar aestheticism, with its base in erotic art, forms a very serious obstacle in the way of moral progress. Coming into conflict with the genuinely moral yearnings, it exerts a profound immoral influence if

---

16 According to the Holy Qur'ãn, God is All-Seeing, All-Knowing, Everywhere-Present, and Above all need of the least dependence in anything on anyone. But just as He has created the angels to act as the Medium for the execution of His Will in the universe, He has created the Holy Prophet Muhammad (Peace be on him!) to act as that Medium for the Muslims through which they can acquire the spiritual capacity for *meaningful* and *consequential* approach to Him—an approach which should assume the level of *contact* in the transcendental dimension, flowering finally into the establishment of genuine and living *intimacy* with God. In both cases, the Medium is there, not because of any deficiency in God's Power, but because of the demands placed in the constitution of the universe and Man by God for the executions of His Plan.

it is permitted to hold sway, even as it is exerting on a progressively more and more damaging scale among the Westernised human societies—especially in the countries of origin, where vulgar pursuit of aestheticism is assuming alarming proportions day-by-day leading the affected communities headlong to ultimate spiritual and moral destruction.

Now, while the Holy Qur'ãns itself affirms the aesthetical value and prescribes aesthetical duties, as we have recorded elsewhere in this book[17], it is with the same vehemence opposed to the immoralisation of the aesthetical pursuit. Indeed, it lends the entire weight of its philosophy of life firmly to the principle that the aesthetical value cannot stay purely unless it is wedded to the highest spiritual and moral considerations. It is convinced that aestheticism based on sensuousness is the mother of all moral ills and spiritual perversions.

Behind this attitude of the Qur'ãn, which has withstood the test of history, there is its scheme of values wherein the gradation is: (I) Religion; (ii) Morality; (iii) Knowledge; (iv) Art[18].

This gradation of values emerges when we consider, in the first instance, the oft-repeated Qur'ãnic expression:

"those who possess Faith and practise the Virtues." (II:25; Etc.—mentioned 49 times).

Here 'religion' forms the highest value, and next to it stands 'morality'.

Then, in the following verse, 'religion' stands first and 'knowledge' stand second:

> "....Allah will exalt those of you who possess Faith and those who are endowed with Knowledge.... (LVIII:11).

---

17 Ref: Volume II, pp. 49-59.

18 Only such cultures as are pessimistic in outlook and stand consequently in need of dopes, can reasonably idolise Art and give it a status higher than that of Morality or Religion or Knowledge in their gradation of values. Indeed, they are in need of employing momentary 'contemplation of the beautiful' as an escape from the sense of misery and the consequent agony to which the pessimistic outlook on life gives rise. This cannot be possible in the case of the Qur'ãnic philosophy of life which upholds vigorously an optimistic outlook and regards pessimism as nothing less than Infidelity: *Kufr* (XII:87).

However, because, according to the Qur'ãnic philosophy of life, Faith is meaningless without the possession of sound Morality, which makes religion and morality twins, as in the previously quoted verse, the gradation finally deducible from the above verses is: Religion, Morality, Knowledge.

As for the pursuit of the Beautiful, the Qur'ãnic standpoint is:

(a) That pursuit can be undertaken both ways: good and evil; and hence it should always be treated in terms of morality. Thus we are told:

"Lo! We have made that which is on the earth an ornament (i.e., source of beauty) thereof (i.e., with reference to the life on it, which is related to sensuous pleasure—both refined and vulgar) that We may try them (i.e., the human beings): which of them is best in conduct (with respect to their aesthetical pursuit wherein the test is whether they indulge in vulgarity and indecency or adopt in that respect the highest moral standards)." (XVIII:7)

(b) All sensuous vulgar pursuit in the aesthetical domain is from the Devil and should therefore, be avoided[19]:

"Lo! he (i.e., the Devil) commandeth indecency and abomination...." (XXIV:21)

And the Holy Book has reminded us that it is the mission of the Devil to play beauty for misleading mankind, inasmuch as he had proclaimed at the dawn of Creation:

"....I verily shall employ Beauty for them (i.e., the human beings) in the earth (i.e., based on the earthly environment, inducing them to the love of sensuous pleasure and to the adoption, for that purpose, of the materialistic and hedonistic approach to Art), and shall mislead them all,—except such as are Thy perfectly devoted servants". (XV: 39, 40)

Thus, the aesthetical pursuit has, in the very nature, of the case, to be subordinated always to the demands of morality, whereby alone the moral tone and social health of the human can be ensured.

---

19 For certain direct commands relating to this problem, refer to XXIV: 31, 60; etc.

Appendix II

The Problem of Despair and the Gospel of Emancipation

In many human beings the consciousness of past sinfulness creates a sense of despair—sometimes involving great severity—as to the possibility of their moral emancipation; and it can actually damage their prospects with respect to moral reformation, unless they are offered some principle that may ensure to them that the evil spiritual consequences of their past sins could be washed away, enabling them to build up a healthy moral life with hope and confidence and serenity, and without any lurking sense of past guilt that may disturb their moral enthusiasm.

The Holy Qur'ãn has supplied that principle in its teaching that sincere repentance (*taubah*[20]) brings immediate forgiveness from God which washes away the spiritual stains of guilt. It says:

> "O ye who believe! Turn to Allah with sincere repentance: Belike your Lord will expiate from you your misdeeds...." (LXVI:8)

The fact is that doubtlessly the commission of sins leads a person farther and farther away from moral purity. But once a person performs *tauḅah*, i.e., repents truly and with all the force of his personality, his latent will for good is revived and activised, reinforcing his moral fibre. This is what we learn from the story of Adam, the father of humanity. The Holy Qur'ãn attributes his entanglement in the Devil's deception not to deficiency in knowledge but to deficiency in will.

It says:

> "And verily We made a covenant of old with Adam, but he forgot: and We found in him no firm resolve[21] (in that affair)".
>
> (XX:115)

---

20 The act of *taubah* is actually three-dimensional, because it consist of (i) sincere acknowledgement in one's heart of the wrong committed; (ii) firm establishment in one's consciousness of a proper estimate of the evil nature of that wrong and the consequent dissociation from it; (iii) firm resolve in respect of avoiding its commission in the future. As such, it might be termed as a 'contract with the future'.

21 "*wa lana najid lahû 'azmã*" in the Arabic text may also mean: "and We did not find in him determination (to disobey)"—implying that Adam's act of eating from the forbidden tree was not voluntary, and, consequently, Adam's sinlessness was not impaired in spite of that act.

The wrong which Adam committed was of an innocent type, consisting, as it did, not in moral turpitude but only in error of judgement. But even so, it did not repeat itself, because his repentance brought about the *tazkiyah*, i.e., purified him of the deficiency in his will, as we read in the Holy Qur'ãn:

> "Then Adam learnt from his Lord words (of penitence), and He relented towards him; for He is Oft-Returning, Most Merciful." (II:37)

The Attribute of God as 'Oft-Returning' (*Tawwãb*) in the above verse is expressive of the Islamic teaching that God's attitude towards the sinners is one of continued mercy and compassion. Persons with weak but a good heart may relapse time and again from their commitment in respect of *taubah*. But they should not lose heart. Rather, they should re-affirm their *taubah* with greater determination, each time they fail, and keep up the exercise for their firm establishment on the path of virtue. For that they will have to return again and again to the seeking of God's mercy; and they will not fail to get it, because God is Oft-returning, Most Merciful.

Besides inviting to Repentance, the Holy Qur'ãn has also stated the law:

> "Lo! good deeds annul ill deeds: Be that the word of remembrance to those who remember (their Lord)." (XI:114)

However, the following proclamation forms the greatest Message of Hope even for the worst sinners, provided they repent truly and start their life in conformity with the Divine Law:

> "Say: 'O My Servants who have transgressed against their souls! Despair not of the Mercy of Allah: for *Allah forgives all sins:* verily, He is Oft-Forgiving, Most Merciful. Turn ye to your Lord (in repentance) and bow to His (Will), before the Penalty comes on you: after that ye shall not be helped." (XXXIX: 53, 54)

Indeed, evils already committed can be blotted out, with regard to the spiritual effects on the human personality, if: (a) an evil-doer repents truly, and (b) wages a determined struggle for pursuing Good in Submission to God.

Part II

THE METAPHYSICS OF MORALS

Chapter I

THE MAN

Chapter II

THE WORLD

Chapter III

THE GOD

RELEVANT METAPHYSICAL PROBLEMS

Moral consciousness seeks not only the Moral Good but also the *realisation of the Moral Ideal*, which consists in the triumph of moral good and the defeat of moral evil.

Both of these problems are ethical in character. But their solutions necessitate a metaphysics. Because they cannot be solved without a proper solution of the relevant problems concerning the nature, function and purpose of man and of the world, and the existence and Attributes of God, and the bearing of those Attributes on the working of the world and the life of man.

Now, in respect of the realisation of the moral ideal, the question emerges: What are the conditions that make it possible?

The answer that presents itself to the human reason is: The foremost condition is that man ought to be *free* to realise that ideal. But even if he is free, he cannot realise such a grand ideal in his short span of earthly life and with the obstacles that he has to face within and around him, He must, therefore, be *immortal*. But even if he is immortal, the realisation of the ideal remains inconceivable unless *the world is so constituted as to admit of success in his moral struggle*. But that it can be only if it has been *created* for that very purpose. The duality in human nature, however, which forms the internal obstacle in the realisation of the moral ideal, and the existence of insurmountable difficulties which seem to be embedded in the life of the world, both give the impression of incompatibility with it. Hence the need from the moral point of view for an All-Perfect Being, Who could, out of sheer Grace, remove this disharmony and incompatibility. That is the realisation of the moral ideal would be possible only if *God* exists.

Thus: Freedom of the Will, Immortality of Man, Creation of the World, its Harmony with the Moral Struggle, and the Existence of God and His Gracious Interference to lean man to success, are the metaphysical implications of the realisation of the moral ideal, and form, therefore, the Metaphysical Basis of the Moral Code,—or, in other words, the Metaphysics of Morals.

In the discussion of these verities, we shall proceed, on the basis of the Holy Qur'ãn, under the basic classification of Man, World and God.

Chapter I

THE MAN

I

BASIC PRINCIPLES

The following observations seem relevant in connection with our present discussion concerning the origin, function, nature, purpose and destiny of man:

1. Man should be a created being. Namely, he should possess no aboriginal nature independent of the Creator's design. In other words, his nature should only be that which has been conferred on him by his Creator in conformity with the purpose of his creation—the realisation of the moral ideal forming a vital part of that purpose.

2. Man should be a purposive being and an evolutionary being, in order that struggle for some serious purpose and capability to rise higher and higher may form the very essence of his personality.

3. Man should be a moral being, in order to be capable of leading moral life and pursuing moral struggle.

4. Man should be supreme in Creation, in order to be able to mould the forces of the world around him for the realisation of the moral ideal.

5. But even if man is supreme in Creation, he is a finite being—an imperfect being—and his powers cannot be unlimited; and as such he must suffer from definite shortcomings and weaknesses. Moreover, he is a created being and, as such, dependent on his Creator. He, therefore, needs help from the Creator, Who, with all His Attributes of Perfection and through His Grace, should be prepared to help him in the realisation of the moral ideal. To obtain this Divine Help and Grace and to save himself from pessimism, despair and frustration, man should by nature be a

worshipping being—namely, faith in God and quest for God should be ingrained in his nature.

6. Morality cannot be realised except in society. Man should, therefore, be a social being.

7. Man's nature should be essentially good in order that his struggle for the realisation of virtue in his life and in the life of mankind should form the natural demand of his nature and be thereby rational (=reasonable) for him.

8. Man's personality should contain within it the conflict between Duty and Desire in order to provide the moral situation.

9. Man should possess Freedom of Will, without which moral struggle would be absolutely inconceivable.

10. Imperfect as the world and the human personality are, Man should survive his earthly existence with the selfsame Identity and should be subject to Resurrection and Final Accountability for his moral actions in this world—it being a necessary condition for the realisation of the moral idea! wherein virtue should be adequately rewarded and vice adequately punished.

11. The consequences of the realisation of the moral ideal should be such as to be capable of forming the highest aspiration of Man in order to provide the highest incentive for moral struggle in the face of hardships, sufferings and trials, which must always form vital concomitants of that struggle and which can sometimes assume the most poignant forms.

II

IN THE LIGHT OF THE QUR'ÃN

I. *Man—A Created Being:*

The Holy Qur'ãn says:

"But does not Man call to mind that We (God) *created* him *before*, when he was naught." (XX:67)

II. *Man–A Purposive being and an Evolutionary Being:*

Purposiveness has been affirmed thus:

"Deem ye that We have created you (O humankind!) in vain (i.e., with no serious purpose) and that unto us ye are not to be returned (for account). So exalted be Allah, the True King...."

(XXIII:115, 116)

As for the evolutionary character of the human personality it has been affirmed, among other verses, in the following:

"Man We did created (at the earthly stage) from a quintessence of clay; then We placed him as (a drop of) sperm in a place of rest, firmly fixed; then We made the sperm into a clot of congealed blood; then of that clot We made a (foetus) lump; then We made out of that lump bones and clothed the bones with flesh; then We developed out of it another creature (—a creature who is not a mere animal but a being endowed with spiritual, moral, aesthetic and intellectual faculties and capable of pursuing ideals). So blessed is Allah, the Best to create! After that, at length ye will die. Again, on the Day of Judgement, will ye be raised up."

(XXIII: 12-16)

"Verily, We created Man from a drop of mingled sperm, in order to try him: So We gave him (the gifts of) Hearing and Sight (i.e., endowed him with responsibility). We showed him the Way (of Right and Wrong): whether he be grateful or ungrateful (rests on his will)." (LXXVI: 2, 3)

"And surely He hath created you by stages (i.e., by various steps or changes from the original form till ye acquired the full stature of human personality)." (LXXI:14)

III. *Man—A Moral Being:*

That Man has been created with the purpose of pursuing moral struggle has been affirmed thus[1]:

"....(Allah) created Death and Life, that He may try you as to who among you is best in conduct." (LXVII: 2)

Elsewhere, the very purpose of creation of the world itself has been stated to be the pursuit of moral struggle by Man:

"He it is Who created the heavens and the earth in six (Cosmic) Days—and His Throne (of Authority) was on the Waters (from where life evolved)—that He might try you (as to) which of you is best in conduct." (XI:7)

IV. *Man—Supreme in Creation:*

(a) Man is a creature honoured and honourable:

"And assuredly We have honoured the Children of Adam (i.e., humankind)." (XVII: 70)

(b) Man has been made the vicegerent of God on earth and, as such, supreme among all the creatures on the earth:

"Behold! thy Lord said to the angels: verily I am going to place a vicegerent on the earth." (II:30)

(c) The angels made obeisance to Adam, thus acknowledging Man's superiority in Creation:

"And recall what time We said unto the angels: prostrate yourselves before Adam, they prostrated themselves...." (II:34)

(d) Everything on the earth has been created for Man:

"He it is Who created for you (i.e., for your service, O humankind!) all that is on the earth." (II:29)

---

1 *Cf.* also the verse LXXVI: 3, quoted above, where the existence of moral consciousness in Man has been clearly affirmed. That Man is a being created for *struggle* has been directly emphasised in the following verse: "Verily We have created Man into toil and struggle." (XC:4).

(*e*) *Everything in the heavens and on the earth has been made subservient to Man:*

"And he has subjected to you (O humankind!), as from Him, all that is in the heavens and on the earth. Behold! in that are Signs indeed for those who reflect." (XLV:13)

V. *Man—A Worshipping Being:*

Man's need for God arises in his weaknesses and shortcomings, which are found in him as definite facts of his life. The Holy Qur'ãn says:

(*a*) *Man is weak and susceptible to error:*

"Allah intends to lighten your (difficulties): For Man has been created weak (i.e., weak in flesh, weak in judgement and weak in respect of overpowering desire)." (IV:28).

In this respect, Man needs Divine Grace.

As regards the initial weaknesses of the human will, the reference to Adam's lapse is significant (XX: 115). The Holy Qur'ãn mentions elsewhere that immediately after that lapse, Adam acquired perfect firmness of resolve (XX: 122) through repentance (VII: 23). There is guidance in this for all human beings that they have to train their will by committing themselves to higher ideals, by cultivating patience and constancy in that respect, and through communion with God. The Holy Qur'ãn says:

"O ye who believe! seek help with patient Perseverance and Prayer (Communion with Allah): verily Allah is with those who patiently persevere." (II; 153).

(*b*) *Man is given to impatience, i.e., desires easy success:*

"Man is a creature of haste[2]." (XXI:37).[3]

(*c*) *Man suffers from sentimentalism:*

"And if We let Man taste mercy from Us, and thereafter withdraw it from him, verily he is despairing, blaspheming.

---

2 The word *'Ajal*, translated as 'haste', signifies "the seeking, and pursuing, or endeavouring after, a thing before its proper time, or season". (Lane's Lexicon)

3 *Cf.* Also XVII: 11.

"And if We let him taste favour after harm has touched him, he says: the ills have departed from me; verily he becomes elated, boastful. Not so do those who practise patience and constancy, and work righteousness; for them is forgiveness (of sins) and a great reward."
(XI: 9, 10, 11)

In respect of (b) and (c) above, the human personality needs tuning to submission to the Divine Will in order to avoid failure, as expressed in verse 11 above.

(*d*) *Man is a contentious creature:*

"....Man is in most things contentious." (XVIII:54)

In respect of this weakness, Man needs a Moral Code based on universal laws and given by the Supreme Authority, i.e., God, in order to provide true arbitration and the consequent harmony and peace in human relations.

We have pointed out above that the situation arising out of human weaknesses and shortcomings can be remedied through Divine Guidance and Grace. The Holy Qur'ãn has affirmed it repeatedly. In fact, it forms the keynote of its teaching. We may quote here just one verse:

"O ye who believe! If you are careful of (your duty to) Allah, He will grant you a Creation (to judge between right and wrong), remove from you (all) evils (that may afflict) you (including your weaknesses and shortcomings), and forgive you: for Allah is the Lord of Grace Unbounded." (VIII:29)

Now Divine Guidance and Grace cannot come to Man without his belief in the existence of God. And this belief should not be a mere logical necessity for him, as Kant would have it, but embedded in his very nature—in what is called his Unconscious. The Holy Qur'ãn mentions this fact in terms of the 'Covenant of Monotheism' which all human beings made in the world of spirits as the time of Creation. It says:

"And when thy Lord brought forth from the children of Adam their posterity from their backs, and (after endowing them with sufficient intelligence and understanding) made them to testify as to themselves (saying): am I not your Lord? They said: Yea! We do testify. (Thus was the belief in God inscribed upon the soul of Man). (That was) lest ye should say on the Day of Resurrection (by way of excuse for atheism, polytheism or idolatry): verily of this we have been unaware."

(VII:172)

We are also told that seeking Divine Help in times of need is ingrained in human nature:

"When harm touches human beings, they cry to their Lord, turning to Him in repentance...." (XXX:33)

"When a wave covers them (i.e., those who are unmindful of Allah otherwise) like the canopy (of clouds) (i.e., a storm overtakes them at sea), they call to Allah, offering Him sincere devotion." (XXXI:32)

"When we are further told that the human beings with healthy minds remember God at all times:

"....Possessors of understanding, namely, those who remember Allah standing, sitting and lying on their sides...." (III: 190, 191)

Then the Holy Qur'ãn proceeds to emphasise that the human heart finds its true peace only through confidence in Divine Help which comes to him by establishing the relation of intimacy with God through Remembrance (*al-Zikr*).

"Lo! in the remembrance of Allah hearts do find rest (i.e., serene tranquillity and steady peace of mind)." (XIII:28)

As for God Himself and His role for Man, the Holy Qur'ãn proclaims that he is Beneficent, Merciful, Forgiving, Loving and Bestower of Grace, and is always ready to help him. We shall deal with this aspect of the problem in the discussion about God.

But, the facts of human nature, and human life being what they are, *the Holy Qur'ãn exhorts Man to cultivate the worshipping aspects of his nature through communion with God and to maintain a constant worshipful attitude towards Him, thereby ensuring optimism and hope and success in his moral struggle.* Some of the verses having a bearing on this read:

"And your Lord has said: call unto Me, and I shall answer your prayer. Verily those who are stiff-necked against My worship, anon they will enter Hell abject." (XL:60)

"And when My devotees ask thee regarding Me, then verily I am Nigh; I answer the call of the caller when he calleth unto Me; so let them answer Me and believe in Me, haply they may be rightly guided." (II:186)

"And remember Allah much that ye may prosper (in the health of the mind and the spirit, and thus attain true success in life, including moral life)." (LXII:10)

"Verily I! I am Allah! no God there is but I; so worship Me, and establish prayer for My remembrance." (XX:14)

VI. Man—A Social Being:

It has been proclaimed:

"Your creation (in the past) and your resurrection (in the future) are only as though of one soul." (XXXI:28)

This statement implies that all the individuals constituting humanity in the past, the present and the future, possess among themselves such an intimate bond of unity that the benefits and the sufferings of one individual should be conceived morally to be the benefits and sufferings of every other individual. In other words, Man is a social creature in his origin, nature, purpose and destiny.

Of similar import is the following verse:

"On humankind! fear your Lord (in your dealings with one another), Who created you from a single primeval Self, created, of like nature, the spouse thereof, and from them twain scattered (like seeds) countless men and women:—fear Allah, through Whom ye demand your mutual (rights), and be careful of your duty to Allah and (in respect of) the wombs (i.e., the ties of family relationship); verily Allah ever watches over you." (IV:1)

We have also been told:

"And He it is Who has made you (His) agents, inheritors of the earth, and has raised some of you over others in degrees, that he may try you in the gifts ye receive. Verily thy Lord is Swift in punishing: yet He is indeed Oft-Forgiving, Most Merciful." (VI:165)

This verse indicates that the very structure of human society, built up as it is on human inequality in respect of talents and functions, has been made by God, in its very nature, of such a type as to form the ground for moral struggle by the individuals, in whatever degree they may have received the different Divine gifts. Morality and social life have been thus affirmed by the Holy Qur'ãn to be interdependent. And because Man is a moral being in his very creation, he has been made a social being also by God.

VII. Essential Goodness of Man's Nature:

The Holy Qur'ãn says:

"Assuredly We have created Man in the best make[4] (having the goodliest nature). (XCV:4)

This verse establishes the essential goodness of human nature in contradistinction to ideational culture where Man has been conceived to have been born either with the stigma of sin or fettered to the chains of re-incarnation; and it proves human competence for pursuing good successfully and fighting evil on individual and collective levels.

The story of Adam may also be mentioned in the present context. That the angels, who are holy and pure, prostrated before him, while *Iblīs*, the embodiment of evil, refused to do so, indicates that, in his very creation, Man has affinity with the angels and thereby with goodness, while evil is set in disharmony with him and, consequently, with his nature.

In short, Man is the goodliest specimen of God's handiwork, born sinless and with essentially good nature.

VIII. Conflict in Human Nature:

However, essentially good though human nature, is, Man has been created to pursue moral struggle and, therefore, while he is capable of scaling the loftiest heights of perfection adequate to his nature, he can also sink to the lowest of the low in Creation, as it has been said:

"Thereafter (i.e., in consequence of wrong use of his opportunities and misuse of his free will by Man) We (as the Author of the Universal Scheme) abase him (to be) the lowest of low (—he himself having destroyed his original purity and goodness),—save those who believe and practise reighteousness. Theirs shall be a reward unfailing." (XCV: 5, 6).

---

4 Note that *taqwîn* means: make, mould, symmetry, form, nature, constitution.

This double capacity—for moral success and for moral failure—is grounded in the conflict with which human nature has been endowed, as the Holy Qur'ãn says:

"By the Sun and his (glorious) splendour, by the Moon as she follows him, by the Day as it shows up (the Sun's) glory, by the Night as it conceals it, by the Firmament and its (wonderful) structure, by the Earth and its (wide) expanse, by the Soul and Him Who gave it proportion and order, and inspired it with the wickedness thereof (which comes through the devil and is developed to a responsible human act by Man's own free will) and the piety thereof (which comes through the angels and is developed to a responsible human act by Man's own free will), truly he succeeds that keeps it pure and he fails that corrupts it." (XCI: 1-10)

The conflict between wickedness and piety in the human soul, mentioned above, is there;—and it must have been so, because the moral situation can arise only in a situation of conflict. That conflict develops in the following way:

On the one side, there is excessive love of instinctive desires in human nature, the reality of which has been emphasised in these words:

"Fair-seeming in the eyes of human beings is the love of things they covet (under the impact of instinctive urges): women and sons, heaped up hoards of gold and silver, horses branded (for blood and excellence), and (wealth of) cattle and well-tilled land. All that is the enjoyment of the life of the world: but in nearness to God is the best of goals." (III:14)

On the other side, there is ingrained in the human soul the pursuit of ideals—the highest among them being the ideal of attaining nearness to God, referred to at the end of the above verse. Leading one's life in the pursuit of noble ideals has been beautifully emphasised in the verses which immediately follow. There, it has been said:

"Say (O Muhammad!): shall I give you glad tidings of things far better than those (i.e., objects of instinctive desires recounted in III:14)? For the righteous are Gardens in nearness to their Lord with rivers flowing beneath; therein is their eternal home; with companions pure (and holy); and the Good Pleasure of Allah. For in Allah's sight are all His servants,—(namely) those who say: 'Our Lord! we have indeed believed, wherefore forgive us our sins and protect us from the agony of the Fire': those who practise *sabr* (i.e., patience, perseverance and self-control), who are truthful, who worship devoutly, who spend (for their fellow-beings), and who pray for forgiveness in the early hours of the morning."

(III: 15-17)

It may be observed that, according to the Holy Qur'ãn, the attraction for the objects of instincts is neither condemnable in itself nor irrelevant to the requirements of the "best make" in which Man has been created. The Qur'ãnic moral guidance aims at the balanced, appropriate and just satisfaction of both of the aspects of human nature—the sentient and the rational[5]—that have been bestowed upon it by its Creator, to which the following verse bears reference through the emphasis on ideal human nature:

"So set thy purpose for religion as one by nature upright—the nature (framed) of Allah, in which He hath created man. There is no altering (the laws of) Allah's creation. That is the right religion (containing the philosophy of human conduct), but most men know not." (XXX:30)

It should be noted, however, that, according to the Holy Qur'ãn, the human self has, as already stated, three stages of, and states in, development:

(i) the *nafs-al-ammãrah.*

(ii) the *nafs-al-lawwãmah,*

(iii) the *nafs-al-mutma'innah,*

Now, what renders the pursuit of the instinctive demands questionable is the *nafs-al-ammãrah*[6], or the Impelling Self, which impels the moral agent to satisfy these demands unchecked, and thus to commit evil, as the Holy Qur'ãn says:

"....Verily the Self impels to evil, unless my Lord do bestow His Mercy, but surely my Lord is Oft-Forgiving, Most Merciful."

(XII:53)

---

5 The conflict between these two aspects of human nature may present a difficult situation only to those—like the Christians, the Buddhists and the Hindus—according to whom not the wrong manner of fulfilling the instinctive wants but the instinctive wants themselves are evil.

6 "*Ammãrah*" signifies: prone, impelling, headstrong, passionate.

Then there is the stage, and the state, of *nafs-al-lawwãmah* or the Reproaching Self, which reproaches when the instinctive demands are fulfilled under the impact of *nafs-al-ammãrah*. The Holy Qur'ãn refers to *nafs-al-lawwãmah* in the following verses:

"And I do call to witness the Reproaching Self." (LXXV:2)

Therefore, the healthy development of the human self lies in counteracting the evil force of the Impelling Self and conquering it. Once it is conquered, the human self outgrows the torture of self-reproach and becomes *nafs-al-mutma'innah* or the Beatified Self[7]. The Holy Qur'ãn refers to the Beatified Self and its reward thus:

"O thou Beatified Soul! return unto thy Lord well-pleased (thyself) and well pleasing (unto Him). Enter thou among My Devotees and enter thou My Garden." (LXXXIX:27-30)

Reverting to the *excessive attraction for the objects of instincts*, it may be said that the instinctive urges have their respective goals which can be achieved through much less instinctive exertion than what is required by the disproportionately excessive demand that afflicts an unbalanced personality. Thus, if personality is integrated through *tazkiyah*, and the *necessary minimum* fulfilment of—instead of excessive indulgence in—the instinctive urges becomes the guiding light of human conduct, the surplus energy available thereby can be utilised in the pursuit of higher values—that being necessary for all cultural development and progress.

IX. Man Possesses Free Will:

Viewing the conflict and the urge for moral betterment in human nature we are led to the conclusion that for realising morality and the moral ideal it is essential that Man should be *free*.

For realising morality, he should be free to choose between the two conflicting motives within his inner self, i.e., the motive of the fulfilment of Desire (command of *nafs-al-ammãrah*) and the motive of the fulfilment of Duty (behest of *nafs-al-lawwãmah*).

For realising the moral ideal, he should be free not only to choose between the above-mentioned conflicting motives within his own self but also to struggle in the social situation for transforming the

---

7 *Lit.* Self-at-Peace: the self in complete satisfaction and free from all pain and sorrow.

world of human relations into a moral order in the face of the conflict that rages there.

We are, therefore, confronted now with the questions:

(i) what is Freedom of Will?

(ii) how is Freedom of Will conceivable?

and (iii) does the Holy Qur'ãn affirm Freedom of Will?

(i) *What is Freedom of Will?*

Freedom of Will consists in the independence of the will of the moral agent from all internal restraint and external constraint in the choice of motive in the situation of moral conflict.

(ii) *How is Freedom of Will Conceivable?*

The question 'how is Freedom conceivable?' can be answered in this way. If, in the act of Creation, "being" (*wajûd*) has been bestowed as an act of Grace on the *shai'*, i.e., the aimed-at Idea, and Personality and Freedom of Will have been conferred upon Man as acts of Grace by the fiat of the Divine Will, the concept of necessity is eliminated with reference to human will and freedom becomes conceivable as a final and ultimate fact.

However, as emphasised earlier, the proper attitude in response to the question: how is human Freedom of Will possible?, is: somehow it is a fact; we may or may not be able to explain 'how' in the manner of exact sciences.[8] Indeed, it is only the speculative consciousness that stumbles; while moral consciousness affirms it as vehemently as the speculative consciousness stumbles.

---

8 The observation of the famous English philosopher, Locke, in respect of intuitive judgements is worthy of note. He says: "But God has not been so sparing to men to make them barely two-legged creatures and left it to Aristotle to make them rational....He has given them a mind that can reason without being instructed in syllogizing." (*Concerning Human Understanding*, Book IV, Ch. 17).

Among the scholars of Moral Philosophy in the present time, Prof. William Lillie judges the same problem thus: "....it is certainly the case that direct or intuitive judgement plays a far larger part in normative sciences, and especially in ethics, than it does in the physical descriptive sciences" (*An Introduction to Ethics*, p. 18).

That Freedom of Will is a fact is known to us intuitively. Indeed, it is deeply ingrained in our consciousness, on account of which we insist on moral responsibility and believe in the validity of moral approval and condemnation.

It may be emphasised that human freedom is restricted to the choice of the motive and does not extend to the consequence, which follows as *necessity*. It should, however, never mean that the consequence is *necessarily* against the yearning of the moral agent.

(iii) *Does the Holy Qur'ãn affirm Freedom of Will?*

It may be observed at the very outset that the Holy Qur'ãn affirms the human Freedom of Will in clear terms. Its basic statement in this connection is:

"We (God) did indeed offer the Trust to the heavens and the earth and the mountains; but they refused to undertake it, being afraid thereof: but Man undertook it[9],—he[10] is indeed very unjust (to himself in not fulfilling his responsibility in respect thereof) and very ignorant (in respect of the evil consequences of not fulfilling his responsibility), —(with the result) that Allah has to punish the Hypocrites, men and women, and the Unbelievers (*lit.*, 'polytheists'), men and women; and Allah turns in Mercy to the Believers, men and women: For Allah is ever Forgiving, Merciful." (XXXIII: 72, 73)

According to the Commentators of the Holy Qur'ãn, "Trust" stands here for "moral responsibility, which is human sense of answerableness for all acts of thought and conduct. Its first and foremost prerequisite is freedom of choice, which is the real function of a human

---

9 Speaking of the acceptance of the Trust by Man, Sir Muhammad Iqbal observes: "In the case of man in whom individuality deepens into personality, opening up possibilities of wrongdoing, the sense of the tragedy of life becomes much more acute. But the acceptance of selfhood as a form of life involves the acceptance of all the imperfections that flow from the finitude of selfhood. The Qur'ãn represents man as having accepted at his peril the trust of personality which the heavens; the earth, and the mountains refused to bear." (*Reconstruction of Religious Thought in Islam*, London 1934, pp. 121, 122).

10 The word "he" actually stands here for those among humankind who are unfaithful to the Trust.

being as a moral agent. The 'trust' referred to is obviously the trust of free choice or accountability". (*English Translation and Commentary of the Holy Qur'ãn* by Maulana Abdul Majid Daryabadi, p. 680, n. 136).

We may now quote other important verses which clearly and directly affirm and proclaim the possession of freedom of will by Man,—namely:

"Do what ye will (i.e., act as you choose in accordance with your free will). Verily He (God) sees (clearly) all that ye do." (XLI:40)

"We have shown him (i.e., Man) the Way (of Right and Wrong); (now it rests on his will) whether to be grateful (by using the gift of free will in the service of Good) or ungrateful (by serving Evil through his free will)". (LXXVI:3)

"Say: The Truth is from your Lord; let him who will, believe, and let him who will, reject it."[11] (XVIII:29)

"That is the Day of Certainty. Whosoever therefore wills, let him betake unto his Lord a resort." (LXXVIII:39)

"....a warning to humankind,—to any of you that chooses (through his will) to go forward (towards Good) or to lag behind." (LXXIV: 36, 37)

Man is, however, a created being. As such he cannot be independent of his Creator in anything. Even free will is not possessed by him of his own right, unlike his Creator Who owns it in His own right. Man's freedom of will has been conferred on him by his Creator as an element of Personality. Hence the human will functions as a 'State within State'.

In other words, Man's *limited* freedom functions within the *absolute* Freedom of the Creator's Will. We will see later in this discussion that the Creator's Will is not, and can never be, capricious, irrational, arbitrary and unjust, and does never interfere in the freedom of human will. How the human free will functions as free will while remaining

11 "Thus", says Iqbal (*op.cit.*, p. 151), "the element of guidance and directive control in the ego's activity clearly shows that the ego is a free, personal causality. He shares in the life and freedom of the Ultimate Ego, who, by permitting the emergence of a finite ego, capable of private initiative, has limited this freedom or His own free will."

within the Will of God?—this question relates to an *ultimate fact* which is beyond the powers of human reason to comprehend fully.[12] But logically it is valid; because, on the one hand, human reason demands that Man must possess free will in order to be a moral being, and moral consciousness affirms vehemently that he does possess free will; and, on the other hand, if there is a Creator of the cosmos—as He is there, His existence being affirmed by reason and Revelation both—everything in the cosmos, including human will and its freedom, must be encompassed by Him[13] and cannot ever be conceivable as independent of Him.

It is this fact, and not the negation of human freedom of will, that has been emphasised in the following verses:

"Nay, verily this (Qur'ãn) is an Admonition: so let him who will (i.e., has the will to do so) heed it. But they shall not heed except as Allah wills (in His infinite Wisdom and in accordance with His Universal Scheme). He is the Lord of Righteousness and the Lord of Forgiveness."[14]
(LXXIV: 54-56)

"This is an Admonition: then whosoever (shall exert his) will, may chose a way unto his Lord. But ye will not except as Allah wills[15] (in His infinite Wisdom and in accordance with His Universal Scheme); for Allah is full of Knowledge[16] and Wisdom[17]. He will admit to His Mercy

---

12 What we can understand from the Holy Qur'ãn is that the human will is *sustained* by the Divine Will and the Divine Will assists the human beings in the light of the motive chosen by the human will, whether the motive is for good or for evil.

13 *Cf.* the Holy Qur'ãn : IV:126.

14 Commenting on this verse, A. Yusuf Ali says: "Righteousness as well as Forgiveness have their source in God's Will. Man's righteousness has no meaning except in relation to the Universal Will." (*The Holy Qur'ãn:* English Translation and Commentary, p. 1647, n. 5808).

15 "Man in himself is weak; he must seek God's Grace, without it he can do nothing; with it he can do all. For God knows all things, and His Wisdom comprehends the good of all." (A. Yusuf Ali, *op.cit.*, p. 1660, n. 5861).

16 i.e., "His supreme knowledge comprehends all conditions and circumstances" —a knowledge which He employs for he benefit of mankind.

17 i.e., "His Wisdom surpasses the insight of all finite beings"—a wisdom used to rectify the evils of the deviations of human will.

whom He will[18] (in accordance with the requirements of His Gracious Nature and of the demands of Absolute and Universal Divine Justice); but the wrongdoers—for them He has prepared a grievous Penalty (in accordance with the misuse of their free will). (LXXVI: 29-31)

"Verily this (i.e., the Qur'ãn) is not less than a Message to (all) the Worlds (i.e., it is universal)—upon whomsoever among you wills to go straight[19]: but ye shall not will except as Allah, the Cherisher of the Worlds, wills[20]." (LXXXI:27-28)

---

18 A. Yusuf Ali says: "That is, according to His Just and Wise Plan. If the will is right, it obtains God's Grace and Mercy. If the will of man rejects God, man must suffer Penalty." (*op.cit.*, p. 1661, n. 5862).

19 "i.e., such alone can profit by it. This repudiates the doctrine of *Karma* and determinism, in all its forms and varieties." (Maulana Abdul Majid Daryabadi, *op.cit.*, p. 938, n. 167).

20 Commenting on this verse, A. Yusuf Ali says: "Cf. LXXIV: 55-56. God is the Cherisher of the Wolds, Lord of Grace and Mercy, and His guidance is open to all who have the will to profit by it. But that will must be exercised in conformity with God's Will (verse 29). Such conformity is Islam. Verse 28 points to human free will and responsibility; verse 29 to its limitations. Both extremes, viz.: cast-iron Determinism and the idea of Chaotic Free will are condemned." (*op.cit.*, p. 1697, n. 5996).

An important point to be noted here is that the expression 'but ye shall not will except as Allah wills' is to be found in the Holy Qur'ãn only in the three verses quoted above. Another important point to be noted is that in all these verses, there is reference only to the acceptance of Spiritual Truth—to Good and not to Evil. This is so, because Good and Good alone has its source in God; and hence the pursuit of Good is not possible except when there is identity between the human will for Good and the Divine Will. Also, these verses mean that the acceptance of the Divine Faith can be possible only for those who possess, as moral beings, the good will. And because the will of Man cannot bear fruit without the assistance of the Divine Will—its freedom being limited to the choice of the motive alone—, no one as a spiritual being will receive the strength from the Divine Will to accept the True Faith unless he possess the good will already as a moral being.

Here we may take notice of a verse wherein Divine Will has been mentioned with reference to the existence of evil. The verse is: "If Allah had willed (i.e., if it had been God's Plan), they would not have taken false gods." (VI:107). But this verse does not say that God assists evil. It only says that, on the one hand, He has the power to eliminate evil, and that, on the other hand, He does not interfere when the wrongdoers adopt evil through their free will. This point has been made clear emphatically in another verse which reads: "And

We said in the foregoing that God's Will is not, and can never be, capricious, irrational, arbitrary and unjust. There are numerous verses in the Holy Qur'ãn which emphasise this fact vehemently. For instance, the following:

"Verily Allah deals not unjustly with Man in aught. It is (actually) Man that wrongs his own soul." (X:44)[21]

This is a general statement which covers the human life. As for the Day of Judgement specially—the Day of final reward and punishment, the Holy Qur'ãn proclaims in unambiguous terms thus:

"Then, on the Day, not a soul will be wronged in the least, and ye shall but be repaid the needs of your past Deeds." (XXXVI:54)[22]

Having negated injustice on the part of God, we may now quote the verse which affirms the law of Absolute Justice in God's dealings with man:

"Never will I (God) suffer to be lost the work of any of you, be he male or female." (III:195)

The Holy Qur'ãn affirms positively that no action of God can ever be irrational and arbitrary. It says:

"Verily, my Lord (Allah) is on the Straight Path."[23] (XI:56).

---

they say: if it had been the Will of (God) Most Gracious, we would not have worshipped these (idols). They have no knowledge thereof, they are only guessing." (XLIII:20).

As for the Divine Plan in permitting the existence of evil, it relates to the provision of those conditions whereby alone can the moral and spiritual struggle be pursued, which, in its turn, forms the foundation on which alone the evolution of human personality to greater and greater heights is possible. More of it on some other occasion. (In this connection see the author's book on the *Dynamics of Moral Revolution*, to be published shortly).

21 Other similar verses are: II:57; III:117; VII:160; IX:70; IX:80; XVI:28; XVI:118; XXIX:40; XXX:9.

22 *Cf.* XXI:47.

23 According to A. Yusuf Ali, "the standard of virtue and righteousness is in the Will of God, the Universal Will that controls all things in goodness and justice." (*op.cit.*, p. 539, n. 1552).

Further, the Holy Qur'ãn negates capriciousness absolutely when it speaks of the Perfect Knowledge and Wisdom of God on page after page. It proclaims:

"Verily Allah is Perfect in Knowledge and Perfect in Wisdom." (LXXVI:30)

Then, besides perfection in knowledge and wisdom, God is *Rabb-ul-Ãlameen*[24] (The Cherisher of everything in the cosmos), *al-Rahmãn*[25] (Most Gracious), *al-Raheem*[26] (Most Merciful), *al-Ra'oof*[27] (Full of Kindness), *al-Wadood*[28] (Loving), *al-Ghaffãr*[29] (Most Forgiving), *Al-Hafeez*[30] (The Protector). And He is even more than all that, because He is *Zul-Fadl-il-'Azeem*[31] (the Lord of Abounding Grace) Who gives to man more than he deserves.

There are, however, certain verses in the Holy Qur'ãn which, if read unintelligently and without full reference to other connected verses, might give the wrong impression to the superficial reader that God guides and leads astray, and rewards and punishes, human beings arbitrarily and that, therefore, the human will enjoys no freedom whatsoever. But if we understand the meanings and implications of all such verses properly, we find that they nowhere negate the freedom of human will in the manner and in the measure that it has been conferred on Man by God. We give herein below some such typical verses, along with their proper connotation and explanation.

God says in the very early part of the Holy Qur'ãn:

"As to those who reject Faith (deliberately), it is all the same to them whether thou warn them or do not warn them, they will not believe (because they have no will to believe). Allah has set[32] a seal on their hearts (by their being inured to disobedience and disbelief), and on their hearing and on their eyes is a veil; and unto them shall be a torment

---

24 I: 2.	25. I:3.	26. I:3	27. III:30.
28. XI:90.	29. XX:82.	30. XI:57.	31. LVII:29.

32 It may be noted that the Holy Qur'ãn refers all actions to God, because, according to it, nothing can occur outside His Knowledge and Power.

It is also important to note that the sealing of the hearts by God is *not the cause* of disbelief *but follows* the deliberate rejection of Faith.

mighty (as a just retribution for the misuse of the free will conferred on them by God[33]). (II:6, 7)

At another place, we have been told:

"If Allah so willed (i.e., if it had been the Divine Plan), He could make you all one People.[34] But He leaves straying[35] whom He pleases, and He guides whom He pleases: and ye shall certainly be called to account for all your actions." (XVI:93)[36]

In understanding this verse, some people fall into the error of believing that human beings adopt the right and wrong paths, not on the basis of their free will but because it is so willed for them by God. This means pure Determinism. But when we read the above verse, or any other verse of similar import, in conjunction with other relevant verses, we find that to deduce determinism from such verses is absolutely baseless.

The question is: Does God leave straying anyone for no fault of his, and does He guide anyone for no merit on his part? The Qur'ãnic answer is: No. It says clearly:

---

33 Commenting on this verse, Abdullah Yusuf Ali says: "*Kafara, Kufr, Ḳãfir* and other derivative forms of the word, imply a deliberate rejection of Faith as opposed to a mistaken idea of God or faith, which is not inconsistent with an earnest desire to see the truth. Where there is such desire, the grace and mercy of God gives the guidance. But that guidance is not efficacious when it is deliberately rejected, and the possibility of rejection follows from the grant of free will. The consequence of rejection is that the spiritual faculties become dead or impervious to better influences." (*op.cit.*, p. 18, n. 30).

34 For the Divine Wisdom in not willing it, refer to the author's forthcoming book on the "*Dynamics of Moral Revolution*".

35 Some translators have wrongly translated the word as "leads astray". Commenting on this verse, Abdullah Yusuf Ali says: "God's Will and Plan, in allowing limited free will to man, is, not to force man's will, but to give all guidance, and leave alone those who reject the guidance, in case they should repent and come back into Grace. But in all cases, in so far as we are given the choice, we shall be called to account for all our actions. 'Leaving to stray' does not mean that we can do what we please. Our personal responsibility remains." (*op.cit.*, p. 682, n. 2133).

36 There are some other verses of similar import, e.g., VI:88; XIV:4; XXIV:35; LXXIV:31.

"And Allah will leave to stray the wrongdoers (in consequence of their misuse of free will); and Allah does what He wills (i.e., His Will is not in subjection to the will of anybody)". (XIV:27)[37]

It means that, inspite of being All-Powerful, God leaves straying only those who earn it through their transgression, which is based on their free will.

Then we are told:

"And He (i.e., Allah) guides unto Himself (i.e., to the Right Path) those who turn to Him in penitence". (XIII:27).

Coming now to forgiveness and punishment by God, we are told thus:

"And Allah's is the dominion of the heavens and the earth. He forgives whomsoever He will and torments whom He will; and Allah is ever Forgiving, Merciful." (XLVIII:14).[38]

Now God's will to forgive is for the righteous: the Believers:[39]

"Allah has promised those who believe and practise righteousness that for them shall be forgiveness and a mighty reward".

(V:10).

"O ye who believe! if ye are careful of your duty to Allah (of which righteousness is an integral part), He will bless you with a Criterion (to judge between right and wrong), and will rid you of your evil thoughts and deeds, and will *forgive you*. For Allah is the Lord of Abounding Grace." (VIII:29)

And God's will to punish is for the wrongdoers: i.e., those who commit *zulm*, whether spiritually or morally:

"Verily the wrongdoers! for them is grievous Penalty".

(XIV:22).[40]

---

38 There are several other verses also of the same import.

39 There are numerous verses in the Holy Qur'ãn which bear out this fact. We have quoted here only two.

40 Ref: several other verses of similar import.

Consider also the verse: "....nor is Allah going to punish them while they ask forgiveness." (VIII.33).

"....and unto the Rejectors of Truth shall be grievous Penalty." (II:104).

It means that reward and punishment come to human beings on the basis of their own free will and not because of any arbitrary attitude on the part of God.

It is Man's nature, however, that he would like to avoid the responsibility for evil, unless his will has been purified. That is why the idol-worshippers of Arabia said:

"....If it had been the Will of (God) Most Gracious, we would not have worshipped these (idols)". (XLIII:20)

But God refused to accept this plea, because in spite of the supremacy of Divine Will, He does not force the will of anyone into any channel—i.e., He does not interfere with anyone's free will. Hence, in the next part of the above-quoted verse, it has been said:

"They have no knowledge thereof (i.e., of the working of the Divine Will in the universe); they are only guessing. Have We vouchsafed to them any Book[41] before this, so that they are holding fast thereto?" (XLIII:20, 21)

In other words, they have neither rational nor scriptural basis for the denial of their free will and responsibility.

The upshot of the entire foregoing discussion is that the Holy Qur'ãn affirms freedom of will for Man in the moral domain. It is limited freedom, of course,—namely, it is limited to the choice of the motive and does nor extend to the consequences of an action; but it is freedom all the same. And the Divine Will, which is supreme in the universe, sustains the human will but does not interfere in its working. The Divine Knowledge and Power arranges the consequences in the earthly life of Man in accordance with the Divine Plan, wherein the world is a Moral Order. Man shall, however, be rewarded and punished on the Day of Judgement

---

41 Here the emphasis is on the truth that the *knowledge* of the ultimate facts, of which the relation between God's Will and the human will is one, belongs only to God, Who alone can enlighten human beings about them; and as for the human efforts, even of philosophers, to unveil them through speculative endeavour, their resultant opinions can never consistently claim the status of *knowledge*, and should therefore, be rightfully termed as *conjectures*.

(or, Final Accountability) in the measure and on the basis of his freedom of will. Says the Holy Qur'ãn:

"On no soul does Allah place a burden except according to its capacity. For it shall be the Good it earns (through the exercise of free will) and against it the evil it earns (—again through free will) (—all non-voluntary states of mind and actions being excluded from accountability)."[42] (II:286).

X. Life After Death:

We have seen that Freedom of Will is a necessary condition for the realisation of morality and the moral ideal. We have also seen that the Holy Qur'ãn affirms Freedom of Will.

But, although affirmation of the Freedom of Will, taken by itself, may render morality possible, the realisation of the moral ideal remains inconceivable without, among other verities[43], belief in Life after Death, or Life Hereafter.

This is so, because it is common experience that virtue is not adequately rewarded during the short period of human life on earth. Nay, quite often the virtuous actually suffer. And in many cases it is observed that the evil-minded persons do not suffer the consequences of their evil acts.

Now, the appearance of incompatibility with the moral ideal which the world thus gives, especially in those instances where even the most disinterested moral efforts are frustrated by persons who possess violently devilish motives, is likely to unhinge the moral faith. But moral consciousness revolts against the very idea of virtue remaining frustrated or inadequately rewarded and evil and crime escaping their nemesis wholly or partly.

Therefore, to meet the consummation of the moral struggle and to realise the reciprocity of virtue and success, and of vice and

---

42 Mark that this verse repudiates 'original sin', 'universal redemption' and determinism; and it proclaims that every individual must, through the exercise of freedom of will conferred on him by God, work out himself the possibilities of his spiritual success.

43 The other verities are: belief in the creation of the world essentially as moral order, and belief in the existence of God.

punishment, the moral consciousness demands that man must survive after his death.[44]

Moreover, utmost effort for the realisation of the moral ideal cannot be invited from the human beings without faith in life after death. If survival after death is believed in, it will be easier not only to preserve the morals but also to lay down one's life for the sake of the ideal.

Life after death is also the requirement of human nature from four other angels:

Firstly, the love of life[45] and the yearning for self-preservation, which are ingrained in human nature, refuse to admit the cessation of life in death.

Secondly, denial of life after death engenders Nihilistic attitude, and nihilism is wedded to despair.

Thirdly, confining the reward or punishment of actions to immediate execution in this life amounts to a negation of the world being a moral order, because the individual is deprived of the chance of exhausting the possibilities of improving himself. And if the world is not accepted as a perfect moral order, moral struggle becomes a meaningless idea.

Fourthly, no human action—good or evil—can mature as regards its consequences until the present human world endures, because every action gives rise to an endless chain reaction. This renders the fulfilment

---

44 It may be observed here that life after death, or immortality, is not the condition of the realisation of the moral ideal alone but of all spiritual ideals, as affirmed by the Holy Qur'ãn. For instance, the ideal of art consists in the beautification of the self and the surroundings. According to the Holy Qur'ãn, this ideal will be realised in the form of Heavenly Bliss in the next world, as a reward of righteous life in this world. Again, the actual fact of religion consists in faith in a metaphysical outlook on the testimony of Prophetic Revelation. But there is also involved the ideal of intimate experience of religious verities, including the direct Vision of God. This ideal is to be realised, according to the Holy Qur'ãn, as a reward in the Life Hereafter. (*see*: forthcoming discussion on "Heaven").

45 This love may have roots in what is called the Unconscious and may be representative of the urge of human ego to survive to witness the transformation of the world as moral order.

of the principle of just and adequate reward and punishment in the present life impossible.

Hence final and full reward and punishment should be conceived to be deferred to the Life Hereafter, where, according to the Holy Qur'ãn, Heaven and Hell exist for this purpose[46]; thought, in this life also, virtue does bear fruit, even if not adequately and in all cases; and, as regards evil, the individuals cannot escape in acute cases the nemesis of their evil actions.

It may be observed here in passing that it is only in the *nihilistic* attitude, which emerges in the present-day *conjectures* of materialistic approach to human life, that we come across a denial of life after death. Modern Materialism objects, without any conclusive proof, to the concept of Personality, and teaches, again, without any conclusive proof, that the human being is only an embodiment of the interplay of mechanical forces—emerging as an accident and dissolving finally into oblivion. This is a subjective and fallacious judgement born of temperamental despair; and it is a challenge to human nature as well as to human history, wherein belief in survival after death has been held by almost all the human communities in one form or the other.

One of the most brilliant exponents of the philosophy of Nihilism is Bertrand Russell, who, with all his academic genius, has spoken more as a poet than as a scientific thinker. In his Essay on "*Free Man's Worship*", he projects his belief about Man thus:

> "...Man is the product of the cause which had no pre-vision of the end they were achieving, that his origin, his growth, his hopes and his fears, his loves and his beliefs are but the outcome of accidental collection of atoms; that no fire, no heroism, no intensity of thought and feeling can preserve an individual life beyond the grave, that all the labours of ages, all the devotion,

46 Here we should keep in mind the distinction in the belief of life after death imparted by the Holy Qur'ãn and the notion of Immortality presented by Kant. Kant's notion originates in *despair*, which seems to be based on the Christian dogma of sinful beginning of human life and the evil character of the earthly environment. This despair leads to the view that the present life is basically unamenable to success in the realisation of the moral ideal, and that there ought to be a Life Hereafter in order that the said ideal may be realised. The Qur'ãnic point of view is based, on the other hand, on *hope* which is enshrined in the Qur'ãnic concept of Evolution.

> all the inspiration, all the noon-day brightness of human genius are destined to extinction in the vast death of solar system, and that the whole temple of Man's achievement must inevitably be buried under a debris of ruins...."[47]

Then, side by side with that arbitrary verdict, he lands himself in contradiction when he proceeds to project, with all his poetic fancy and with passionate idealistic fervour, all the grace and beauty of *freedom* for the 'slave of blind forces' that Man is in his estimation! He says:

> "The life of Man, viewed outwardly, is but a small thing compared with the forces of Nature. The slave is doomed to worship Time and Fate and Death, because they are greater than anything he finds himself, and because all his thoughts are of things which they devour. But, great as they are, to think of them greatly, to feel their passionless splendour, is greater still. And such thought makes us free men; we no longer bow before the inevitable in Oriental subjection but we absorb it, and make it a part of ourselves. To abandon the struggle of private happiness, to expel all eagerness of temporary desire, to burn with passion for eternal things—this is emancipation, and this is free man's worship. And this liberation is effected by a contemplation of Fate; for Fate itself is subdued by the mind which leaves nothing to be purged by the purifying fire of Time.
>
> "United with his fellow-men by the strongest of all ties, the tie of a common doom, the free man finds that a new vision is with him always, shedding over every daily task the light of love. The life of Man is a long march through the night, surrounded by invisible foes, tortured by weariness and pain, towards a goal that few can hope to reach, and where none may tarry long. One by one, as they march, our comrades vanish from our sight, seized by the silent orders of omnipotent Death. Very brief is the time in which we can help them, in which their happiness or misery is decided....
>
> "Brief and powerless is Man's life; on him and on all his race the slow, sure doom falls pitiless and dark. Blind to good and evil, reckless of destruction, omnipotent matter rolls on its relentless way; for Man, condemned today to lose his dearest, tomorrow himself to pass through the gates of darkness, it remains only to

47 Bertrand Russell: *Mysticism and Logic* (London 1969), p. 41.

cherish, ere yet the blow falls, the lofty thoughts that ennoble his little day; disdaining the coward terrors of the slave of Fate, to worship at the shrine that his own hands have built; undismayed by the empire of chance, to preserve a mind free from the wanton tyranny that rules his outward life; proudly defiant of the irresistible forces that tolerate, for a moment, his knowledge and his condemnation, to sustain alone, a weary but unyielding Atlas, the world that his own ideals have fashioned despite the trampling march of unconscious power."[48]

With the above preliminary discussion, we may turn to the guidance of the Holy Qur'ãn.

Belief in Life Hereafter—an Article of Islamic Creed:

We may start by noting that belief in the Life Hereafter forms an article of Islamic Creed in the Holy Qur'ãn. Namely, it is a basic truth without active belief in which it is impossible for anyone to be a Muslim. Indeed, the Qur'ãnic Guidance can benefit only him who, among other religious verities, believes in the Life-Hereafter, as, for instance, the following verse, which is to be found in the very early part of the holy book, clearly proclaims:

"This Book, whereof there is no doubt, is a guidance unto the god-fearing (or, Pursuers of Righteousness with Faith in God)—(namely, those) who believe in the Unseen (Reality), and establish prayer, and out of what We have provided for them spend (for the well-being of others); and who believe in the Revelation sent to thee (O Muhammad!), and (sent) before thy time, *and of the (life) Hereafter they have firm conviction.* These are on the right path guided by their Lord, and these are the successful (in this life as well as in the next)."(II:2-5).

Indeed, belief in the Life Hereafter is so important in the estimation of the Holy Qur'ãn that it has been mentioned therein at many places conjoined with belief in God[49], which indicates that, according to the Qur'ãnic evaluation, it stands immediately next to belief in God in importance for human success, which depends, in its turn, on proper approach to life.

---

48 *op.cit.*, pp. 46, 47.

49 E.g: in the following verses: II:228, II:264, III:114, IV:59, IX:29, IX:44, IX:45 18:99, LXV:2.

For those who do not believe in the Life Hereafter, the Holy Qur'ãn has emphasised the wrongfulness of their attitude and its consequences thus:

"Verily thou callest them unto a Straight Way (— the Way of Balanced Life). *And verily those who believe not in the Hereafter are deviators from that Way* (and cannot, therefore, enjoy balanced life and, as a result, cannot attain genuine success). And though We have mercy on them and We may remove the distress which is on them, they would obstinately persist in their transgression, wandering perplexed. We inflicted torment on them, but they humbled not themselves to their Lord, nor do they submissively entreat (Him)! — until We open on them a gate leading to a severe torment: then lo ! they will be plunged in despair[50] therein."[51] (XXIII:73-77)

The following verses are also of similar import:

"Nay, it is those who believe not in the Hereafter, they are in a torment and error far-reaching.

"Behold they not[52] that which is before them and that which is behind them of the heaven and the earth." (XXXIV:8, 9)

Qur'ãnic Arguments in favour of Life Hereafter:

The error (referred to in verse 8 above), whose evil consequences are far-reaching in so far as it deprives human beings of genuine success in this life and brings them grievous failure in the Hereafter, is rooted in a wrong philosophy which has been referred to in the Holy Qur'ãn thus:

"And they (i.e., the deniers of Life Hereafter) say: there is naught (i.e., no other life) but our life of the world; we die and we live (of ourselves, with no reference to the Creator):[53] and naught destroys

---

50 *Cf.* our remark earlier: "....denial of life after death engenders nihilistic attitude, and nihilism is wedded to despair."

51 The verses portray the psychology of the person who disbelieves in the Life Hereafter and the evil consequences of such disbelief.

52 Commenting on it, A. Yusuf Ali says: "The men who walk in spiritual darkness and laugh at a Hereafter, have but to observe the Power of God in the nature around them. He who created the heavens and the earth and sustains them can surely make a new Creation!" (*op.cit.*, p. 1135, n. 3796).

53 As to the pagan Arabs' materialistic outlook and indifference to spiritual values Hitti observes: "The hedonistic Arabian character was too much absorbed in

us save Time.[54] And they have no knowledge thereof: they do but guess (i.e., their denial is not based on any sound logical argument or any rational facts, but on mere superstition). And when Our Clear Signs (which affirm Life Hereafter) are rehearsed to them, their argument is nothing but this: they say: 'Bring (back) our forefathers, if what ye say is true'." (XLV: 24, 25)[55]

Verse 9 of Chapter XXXIV, quoted to the above verses, gives an argument against disbelief in the Life Hereafter which is sound; but it may not be properly graspable by the common folk. On other occasions, however, the argument has been stated in simpler terms. For instance, in reply to the argument of the disbelievers in the Hereafter, in XLV: 24-25, the holy book proceeds to state the counter-argument thus:

"Say thou! 'It is Allah Who gives you life, then gives you death; then He will gather you for the Day of Judgement about which there is no doubt': but most of humankind know not." (XLV:26)[56]

At another place, the argument has been stated in terms of Evolution. Thus we read:

"Does man think that he will be left uncontrolled (without purpose and without moral responsibility)? Was he not a drop of sperm

---

the immediate issues of life to devote much thought to the Hereafter. In the words of an old bard:

'We spin about, whirl our own way through life, then, rich and poor alike, at last seek rest below the ground in hollow pits slate-covered, and there do we abide'. (*History of the Arabs*. p. 102).

54 We may quote here the *Encyclopaedia of Religion and Ethics*: "Time in the abstract was popularly imagined to be the cause of all earthly happiness, and especially of all earthly misery.....The poets are continually alluding to Time (*dahr, Zamãn*), for which they often substitute 'the days', or 'the nights'. Time is represented as bringing misfortune, causing perpetual change, as biting, weaning down, shooting arrows that never miss the mark, blowing stones and so forth. In such cases we are often obliged to render 'time' by 'fate' which is not quite correct, since time is here conceived as the determining factor, not as being itself determined by some other power, least of all by a conscious agent." (Vol. I; pp. 661, 662).

55 *Cf.* XXIII:37.

56 Other verses with similar wordings and the same import are: II:28; XXII: 66, XXX:40.

emitted (in lowly from)? Then did he become a leech-like clot; Then did (Allah) make and fashion (him) in due proportion. And of him He made two sexes, male and female. Is not That One then able to quicken the dead"? (LXXV: 36-40).[57]

Another form of the Qur'ãnic argument in support of the Hereafter is in terms of the revival of the dead earth. For instance, we read:

"Know that Allah quickeneth the earth after its death. We have made clear Our Signs to you, that haply ye may be able to understand rationally (the phenomenon of future Resurrection)". (LVII:17).

"And We send down from the sky rain charged with blessings, and We produce therewith gardens and grain for harvest; and tall (and stately) palm-trees, with shoots of fruit-stalks, piled one over another;—as sustenance for (Our) servants;—and We give new life therewith to a land that is dead: *thus will be the Resurrection*. Before them (i.e., pagan Arabs) was denied (the Hereafter) by the people of Noah, the Companions of the Rass, the *Thamûd*, the '*Ãd*, Pharaoh, the Brethren of Lot, the Companions of the Wood, and the people of *Tubba*'; each one of them rejected the Messengers, and My warning was duly fulfilled (in them). Are We then weary with the first Creation, that they should be in confusion about a new Creation (in the Hereafter)?" (L:9-15)[58]

The Qur'ãnic conception of Life Hereafter related in all its steps to the concept of the World being a Moral Order:

Having seen that the Qur'ãn affirms the Life Hereafter, we may now proceed to note that, in the Qur'ãnic system of meaning, Life-Hereafter is grounded in the Qur'ãnic teaching that the world is a Moral Order, wherein every action of man, however insignificant, is accountable and must meet its reward or punishment.

The first point that has been emphasised in this connection is that all our actions, including our most hidden thoughts and motives, are known to God at all times, and that instead of becoming relegated to oblivion—as might be thought by the ignorant, every human action, whether virtuous or vicious, is recorded and preserved by Divine Arrangement. We are told:

---

57 *Cf.* XXIII: 12-16, and other similar verses.

58 *Cf. XXX:50.*

"He (i.e., Allah) knoweth the unseen and that which is open; He is the Great, the Most High. It is the same (to Him) whether any of you conceal his speech or declare it openly; whether he lie hid by night or walk forth freely by day. For each (one) there are angels in succession, before and behind them: they guard him with Allah's command."

(XIII:9-11)

"And assuredly We have created Man and We know whatsoever his soul whispers unto him, and We are nearer to him that his jugular vein." (L:16)

"Verily We shall give life to the dead (on the Day of Resurrection), and We record that which they send before (i.e., their own deeds, good or bad), and of all things have We taken account in a clear Book (of evidence)".

(XXXVI:12)

The recording and preservation of human words and deeds is done by the angels[59] appointed by God for this purpose. Thus says the Qur'ãn:

"By no means! Aye, ye belie the Requital. But verily over you are appointed (angels) to protect you,—kind and honourable—writing down (your deeds). They know whatsoever ye do." (LXXXII: 9-12).

"Behold, two (guardian angels) appointed to learn (human doings) (and note them), one sitting on the right and one on the left. Not a word does he utter but there is a sentinel[60] by him ready (to note it)." (L:17, 18)

Man's deeds, good or evil, are not only recorded by the angels, but they also hang round his neck. Thus 'are his actions inseparable from him; and it is they that make or mar a man's fortune."[61] The Holy Qur'ãn says:

"Every man's deeds We have fastened on his own neck: and on the Day of Judgement We shall bring out for him a scroll (containing the record of all his thoughts and actions), which he will see spread open.

---

59 The personality of an angel should not be understood in the anthropomorphic sense.

60 The three together seem to constitute the honourable Recorders, *Kirãman Kãtibîn* (plural, not dual number), mentioned in LXXXII:11.

61 Abdul Majid Daryabadi (*op.cit.*, p. 460, n. 46).

And it will be said (to him) 'Read thine (own) record. Sufficient is thy soul this day to make out an account against thee'." (XVII:13,14)

Verse 14 point out that the recording of actions is done in order to produce evidence before every human being on the Day of Final Accountability on which Day God will pronounce the Judgement in order that every human action, having matured, reaches its full reward or punishment:

"Verily the Hour (of Final Accountability) is coming—My design is to keep it hidden—in order that everyone may be requited according to that which he has endeavoured[62]." (XX:15).

That every action must reach its reward or punishment is the immutable Law of God, ingrained, so to say, in the very constitution of the universe and in the very destiny of Man:

"Yea, to Allah belongs all that is in the heavens and on the earth: so that He may recompense those who do evil according to their deeds, and He may reward those who do good with 'what is best'." (LIII:31)[63]

The good and evil fruits of human deeds become manifest, in accordance with the limitations of man's earthly life, even in this world. The Holy Qur'ãn affirms this fact when it says:

"Verily, your endeavour is (directed to) diverse (ends) (which may be broadly classified as good and evil). Then as for him who gives (in charity) and keeps his duty to God, and (in all sincerity) testifies to the Good,—We will indeed make for him smooth the path to ease (by way of reward).

"And as for him who is a greedy miser and thinks himself self-sufficient (not believing in accountability in the Hereafter), and belies the Good,—We will indeed make smooth for him the path to hardship (by way of punishment)." (XCII:4-10).

On the day of Judgement in the Life Hereafter, however, every human action, however insignificant it might appear to us in this life, shall meet its full and complete recompense:

---

62 Mark the word 'endeavoured'.

63 There are numerous other verses also of the same import, e.g.,: X:4; XIV: 48-50; XXX:45; etc.

"When the earth is shaken to her (utmost) convulsion, and she throws up her burdens (from within), and Man cries (distressed): 'What is the matter with her',—on that Day will she declare her tidings (i.e., will declare all the events that ever took place on her); for that thy Lord will have given her inspiration. On that Day will humankind proceed in companies sorted out, that they may be shown their Deeds. Then whosoever has worked good of an atom's weight shall behold it; and whosoever has worked evil of an atom's weight shall behold it (i.e., the subtlest form of good and evil will then be brought to account)".

(XCIX:1-8)[64]

Virtue might give the appearance of being frustrated in this life, and vice might appear in certain circumstances to gain the upper hand, and this may cause suffering to the virtuous; but on the Day of Final Accountability in the Life Hereafter, the virtuous shall be more than fully rewarded for their righteous life, and they shall have the upper-hand. So says the Holy Qur'ãn:

"Those who are god-fearing (i.e., cultivate and practise righteousness out of respect for Divine Pleasure) shall be (triumphant) above them (i.e., the Unbelievers in Submission to God, or the unrighteous) on the Day of Resurrection." (II:212)

As we remarked before, the moral ideal consists in adequate, nay, full reward of virtue and vice. We have now seen that the Holy Qur'ãn ensures it through the affirmation of the Life Hereafter and Final Accountability, and for that purpose it affirms the existence of Heaven for the former and of Hell for the latter:

"Then, when there comes the great, overwhelming Event,—the Day when Man shall remember (all) that he strove for, and Hell-Fire shall be placed in view for (all) to see,—then, for such as had transgressed all bounds (in rebellion against Truth and Goodness) and had preferred the life of this world (in respect of *indulgence* in the satisfaction of their lower Desires), his abode shall be Hell-Fire. And for such as had entertained the fear of standing before their Lord's (tribunal) and had restrained (their) soul from (the sway of) lower Desires, their abode will be the Garden." (LXXIX: 34-41)

64 *Cf.* XXXIX: 6-7.

[Note: Basic Principle No: 11, mentioned in the beginning of this chapter, shall be taken up in Chapter II under 'Heaven and Hell'.]

Chapter II

THE WORLD

I.

Compatibility of the World with Success in the Realisation of the Moral Ideal

We have seen that the Holy Qur'ãn affirms Freedom of Will and Life after Death. But, along with the affirmation of these two verities, it is also necessary, for the realisation of the moral ideal, to affirm that the world is compatible in its origin, constitution and destiny with success in the moral struggle.

I. *Basic Questions:*

Now, the questions that emerge in that respect, and their implications, are:

A. With regard to Origin:

(a) Did the world have an origin? Namely, is the existence of the world based on *creation*?

(b) If the world had an origin, did it originate essentially as a *moral order*?

It is a necessary requirement of the realisation of the moral ideal that the answers to both the above questions should be in the affirmative.

(a) Affirmation of *creation* is necessary, because:

(i) The concept of *creation* alone involves the necessary existence of an All-Wise, All-Powerful, All-Controlling *Creator*. And His Wisdom, Power and Control are also proved in respect of being evident in the very constitution of the world as it exists.

(ii) The existence of an All-Wise, All-Powerful, All-Controlling Creator involves, in its turn, the necessary existence of a Plan and a Purpose in the working of the world.

In brief, affirmation of *creation* implies the existence of Plan and Purpose.

(b) Existence of Plan and Purpose is, however, not enough as such for ensuring the realisation of the moral ideal. What is needed is that, side by side with being a physical order, the world should also be in its Plan a moral order; and, as for its Purpose, it should refer directly to the realisation of the moral ideal.

B. *With regard to Constitution:*

(a) Is the wold real?

(b) Is the world essentially good, and is it the best possible world?

(c) Is the basis for struggle ingrained in the very constitution of the world; and, if so, how?

It is a necessary condition of the realisation of the moral ideal that the answers to the above questions should be in the affirmative, because:

(a) The affirmation of the existence of the world independently of the percipient being, which is ingrained in the realistic consciousness of man, is indispensable for the idealistic attitude, because, unless the world *exists*, neither morality, nor the unification of knowledge under systematic categories, nor the possibility of turning the ugly into beautiful, nor the need for belief in the existence of God, can ever come into being, because dissatisfaction with what exists and the aspiration to transform it according to the demands of human yearnings will lose all validity. Hence it has to be affirmed, as the necessary requirement of the realisation of the moral ideal, that human beings, society and environment do exist with reference to which the moral agent has to adopt a particular attitude and has to wage a successful struggle within his domain.

(b) The essential goodness of the world implies that it is so constituted since its very origin that it is compatible with success in the struggle for the realisation of man's ideals, including the moral ideal.

That this world is the best possible world implies the highest degree of its goodness.

This is in contradistinction to the world-view entertained by pagan cultures e.g., Hellenism, that the forces of nature are pitched in conspiracy against humanity for bringing about frustration in human struggles. Thus affirmation of the essential goodness of the world is a necessary condition for the realisation of the moral ideal.

(c) Affirmation of the existence of a basis for struggle in the very constitution of the world is a necessary requirement in that behalf, because, man being a part of the world, that alone will provide valid ground for the moral struggle. Again, that basis should be in the form of two opposing principles—one possessing positive character, the other possessing negative character; one representing the Good, the other representing Evil, existing in a state of perpetual conflict with one another—each one dominating the other by turns.

C *With Regard to Destiny:*

Is it enshrined in the very destiny of the world that, come what may, the realisation of the moral ideal—the final and total triumph of virtue over vice—is irrevocably assured?

The fact is that while the affirmative answers with respect to the previous questions envisage merely the *possibility* of the realisation of the moral ideal, that possibility is transformed into a *guarantee* through the affirmative answer to this last question—which thus forms a vital condition in that regard.

II. *In the Light of the Qur'ãn:*

Turning to the Holy Qur'ãn, we find that the different requirements affirmed in the foregoing with regard to the realisation of the moral ideal are contained explicitly in the guidance it offers. It says:

(i) The World is not Eternal but has been Created by God:

To Him is due the primal origin of the heavens and the earth: when He decreeth a matter, He saith to it: 'Be', and it is." (II:117)

'He (i.e., Prophet Abraham) said: 'Nay, your Lord is the Lord of the heavens and the earth, *He Who brought them into existence*: and I am a witness to this (truth)'." (XXI:56).

"Allah originateth the creation (—nothing existing of its own accord or fortuitously)...." (XXX: 11)[1]

1 As to the words *bada'a, fatara, bada'a* used for the act of creation in the above verses. *Bada'a* stands for the very primal beginning; *Fatara* implies, like *bada'a*, the creating of a thing out of nothing and after no pre-existing

(ii) The world has been created by the All-Wise, All-Powerful, All-Controlling God with exquisite Plan and Design:

"Blessed is He Who sent down the Criterion to His Servant (Muhammad), that he may be unto all nations a Warner—He to Whom belongs the dominion of the heavens and the earth: no son has He begotten, nor has He a partner in His dominion: It is He Who created everything, and ordained for it a measure (establishing thereby exquisite Plan and Design)". (XXV: 1, 2)

"No want of proportion wilt thou see in the Creation of (Allah) Most Gracious. So turn thy vision again. Seest thou any flaw?" (LXVII:3)

(iii) The world created for a serious and definite Purpose:

"We created not the heavens, the earth, and all between them, merely in (idle) sport: We created them not except for just ends. But most of them do not understand." (XLV: 38, 39)

(iv) Creation of the world is for a moral end—the world is a Moral Order:

"And Allah has created the heavens and the earth with purpose (and for just ends) and in order that every soul may find the recompense of what it has earned, and none of them be wronged." (XLV:22)

"Blessed is He in Whose hands (i.e., possession) is the Dominion; and He over all things has Power;—He Who created Death and Life, that He may try which of you is best in deeds: and He is the Exalted in Might, Oft-Forgiving." (LXVII:1,2)

(v) The World is real:

"And it is He Who has created the heavens and the earth in Truth (or, as real)" (VI:73)

"Not falsely and without purpose did We create the heavens and the earth and all between! That was the thought of the Rejectors of Truth." (XXXVIII:27)

---

similitude, or, the creation of primeval matter to which further process were applied later; *Bada'a* (without the '*ain*) denotes beginning the process of creation. (Ref. Lane's *Arabic English Lexicon*).

"Behold! in the constitution of the heavens and the earth, and the alternation of the Day and the Night, there are indeed Signs for those who possess and employ understanding. (They are those) who remember Allah standing, sitting and lying on their sides, and contemplate the (wonders of) Creation in the heavens and the earth (and say): 'Our Lord! Thou hast created not all this falsely (and in vain)[2]. Glory be to Thee! Preserve us from the doom of the Fire'." (III:190, 191)

Also, we have been told:

"(O Man!) pursue not that of which thou hast no knowledge (i.e., entertain no such opinion for which thou hast no sound reason to believe to be true). Verily, the hearing and the sight and the heart—each of these is accountable in respect of it." (XVII:36)

It should be noted here that if the contents of sense-experience be unreal, the accountability of the senses would become meaningless. Hence, the world, according to this verse also, is real.

(vi), (vii) The world is essentially Good and it is the Best Possible World:

"....He Who has made everything which He has created Most Good...." (XXXII:7)

(viii) Basis for struggle in the form of pairs of conflicting forces functioning under the Law of Opposites[3], is ingrained in the very constitution of the world:

"And in all things We have created pairs (—pairs of opposites and pairs of complementaries—): that haply ye may reflect (and obtain the guidance involved)". (LI:49).

(ix) Realisation of the Moral Ideal enshrined in the very Destiny of the world:

This point has been discussed and affirmed in detail in the section on "Life after Death". Here we may quote just two verses:

---

2 Here the Hindu doctrine of *Maya*, which regards the whole universe as an illusion, has been repudiated, affirming the reality of the world as we perceive it by our senses.

3 This Law has been discussed in detail in the Author's forthcoming book on the "*Dynamics of Moral Revolution*".

The following verse refers to the success of the forces of the Good and the defeat of the forces of Evil, both in the earthly career of humanity and the Life Hereafter:

"Yea, to Allah belongs all that is in the heavens and on the earth: so that He may recompense those who do evil according to their deeds, and He may reward those who do good with what is best." (LIII:31)

The following verse speaks specially of the final and total triumph of the forces of the Good and in the Life Hereafter:

"Those who are god-fearing (i.e., cultivate and practise righteousness out of respect for Divine Pleasure) shall be (triumphant) above them (i.e., the Unbelievers in the principle of Submission to God—or, the unrighteous) on the Day of the Resurrection." (II:212)

II

Conception of Heaven and Hell as Related Directly to the Moral Ideal

Having discussed 'the Man' and 'the World' in their different relevant dimensions, we are now confronted with the question: What is the Qur'ãnic conception of Heaven and Hell.

In that connection, we may consider the disparity that exists, in the earthly life of Man, between the Actual and the Ideal,—and exists as an irresolvable difficulty and an unsolvable problem, while the human heart is in dead earnest for the way out.

To elaborate:

(1) Nature of Physical Happiness: Happiness:	(1) Ideal of Physical
Only 'pleasure mixed with pain' possible.	Possession of healthy and abiding Pleasure along with total absence of pain.
(2) Nature of Moral Life: Performance of Duty under the stress of a two-fold limitation:	(2) Ideal of Morality: (a) Possession of absolute purity of the Will.
(a) want of absolute purity of	(b) Realisation of the

the will; (b) moral effort constantly frustrated by others.	perfect. Moral Order.
(3) Nature of the Pursuit of Art: Beautification of a very minute portion of Reality, and that too in imperfect manner and measure, alone possible.	(3) Ideal of Art: Comprehensive beautification of the Self and the Environment.
(4) Nature of the Pursuit of Knowledge: Knowledge of only an infinitesimally small portion of Reality, alone possible.	(4) Ideal of Knowledge: Possession of complete and direct knowledge of Reality.
(5) Nature of the Pursuit of Religion: (a) Indirect faith in religious verities on the testimony of the Prophet, or, at best, imperfect experience of those verities, and communion with God from behind the veil: alone possible. (b) Holiness acquirable only in limited measure because of the continuous existence of devilish forces in the environment.	(5) Ideal of Religion: (a) Acquiring direct and intimate experience of religious verities, including the Vision of God, the Really Real, and the Source of all-Grace. (b) Acquiring perfect holiness in accordance with human status.

Now:

Heaven is the realisation of the above ideals; while:

Hell bears reference to Evil Will, Ugliness, Deprivation of Communion with God, and Torture of different types, in consequence of the denial of the Source of Grace and of the conditions necessary for the realisation of the above mentioned ideals.

The following verses[4] of the Holy Qur'ãn concerning Heaven and Hell bear out the above statement:

---

4 Only representative verses, which depict different aspects, have been quoted.

THE HEAVEN :

(a) *Heaven as the reward of righteous life; Peace, Security, Eternal Life—nay, the realisation of all positive human yearnings and ideals (mentioned above)—and even more:*

"And the Garden will be brought nigh to the righteous,—no more a thing distant. (And they will be told:) 'This is what was promised for you,—for everyone who turned (to Allah) in sincere repentance, who kept (His Law), who feared (the Displeasure of Allah) Most Gracious unseen, and brought a heart turned in devotion (to Him)—: Enter ye therein in *Peace* and *Security*. This is the Day of *Eternal Life*!' *There will be for them therein all that they yearn*[5] *,—and more besides in Our Presence."* (L:31, 35)

(b) *Abode of Peace:*

"But Allah invites (humanity through the Holy Qur'ãn) to the *Abode of Peace* (in which there shall be no fear, frustration or sorrow, but only perfect security from evil of all types)". (X:25)

"For them (i.e., the god-fearing righteous) there will be an *Abode of Peace* in the Presence of their Lord: He will be their Patron and Friend, because they practised (righteousness)". (VI:127)

"Their salutation on the Day they meet Him will be 'Peace!', and He has prepared for them a generous reward." (XXXIII:44)

(c) *Absolute Purity of Will—Social Harmony and Love:*

The spirit of rancour and jealousy will be totally obliterated from the hearts of the righteous, giving place to absolute purity of will, on the one hand, and to love and harmony, on the other, and establishing genuine fraternal relations wherein each member of the fraternity of the righteous will enjoy his or her own dignity and will deal with others with joy and confidence. Also, the delights of Heaven will be perfect, for there will be absolute freedom from fear, frustration and sorrow and from toil and fatigue:

"The righteous (will be) amidst Gardens and springs. (And the greeting to them of the angels will be:) 'Enter ye here in peace and security'. And *We shall have removed whatsoever of rancour and*

---

5 *Cf.* XLII:22.

jealousy and sense of injury may be in their hearts. (*They will be*) *in fraternal relationship*, (joyfully) facing each other on thrones (of dignity). There no sense of toil and fatigue shall touch them, nor shall they (ever) be asked to leave." (XV:45-46)

In the perfect felicity of the righteous all lurking memories of disappointments in earthly life shall be blotted out:

"And those who believe and work righteousness,—no burden do We place on any soul, but that which it can bear,—they will be companions of the Garden, therein to dwell (for ever).

"And *We shall remove from their hearts whatsoever lurking sense of disappointment and injury there may have been,* rivers flowing beneath them; and they will say: 'All praise unto Allah Who has guided us to this (felicity)'...." (VII:42, 43)

(d) Company of the Blessed Servants of God :

"And whosoever obeys Allah and the Messenger (Muhammad), then *those shall be in the company of those whom Allah has blessed,*— of the Prophets (who teach the Truth), the Sincere (who are lovers of Truth), the Witnesses (who testify to Truth through martyrdom), and the Righteous (who do good normally). Ah! What an Excellent (and Exalted) Fellowship! That is the Grace from Allah, and Allah sufficeth as Knower." (IV:69, 70)[6]

(e) Light will run before the inmates of Heaven and by their right hands:

"(Mention the) Day whereon thou (O Prophet!) shall see the believing men and the believing women, their Light running before them and by their right hand......" (LVII: 12).

(f) Light of Beauty and Blissful Joy:

"But Allah will deliver them from the evil of that Day, and will shed over them a *Light of Beauty and a (Blissful) Joy.*" (LXXVI:11)

6 This verse refers to spiritual fellowship with members of the Righteous Hierarchy of four types of the Blessed Servants of God in the earthly life also. That fellowship will assume concrete shape in the Life Hereafter as Grace from God. (Hierarchy=a body classified in successively subordinate grades. Ref: *Chambers's Twentieth Century Dictionary, section 'H'*).

(g) *Assembly of Truth in the Presence of God:*

"As to the god-fearing righteous, they will be in the midst of Gardens and Rivers, in an *Assembly of Truth*, in the Presence of the Sovereign Omnipotent." (LIV: 54, 55).

(h) *Direct Knowledge of the Cosmos:*

"Truly the Pious will be in Bliss: on thrones (of Dignity) will they command a sight (of all things): Thou wilt recognise in their faces the brightness of Bliss (as a result of the attainment of complete satisfaction at the realisation, among other ideals, of the ideal of Knowledge)". (LXXXIII: 22-24)

(i) *Stabilisation in the state of Absolute Purity of the Will; Acquisition of Holiness; Attainment of complete peace and satisfaction; well-pleased with and well-pleasing to God; company of the righteous servants of the Lord[7]; entry into God's 'own' Heaven—the highest stage of Bliss:*

"(God will address the righteous thus:) O (thou) sould that has attained complete peace and satisfaction! Come back thou to thy Lord,—wel-pleased (thyself) and well-pleasing unto Him! Enter thou, then, among My Devotees! Yea, enter thou My Heaven!"

(LXXXIX: 27-30)[8]

"Allah will say: This is a Day whereon their *truthfulness will benefit the truthful*. Theirs are Gardens beneath which rivers flow; (they shall be) abiders therein for ever: Allah well-pleased with them and they well-pleased with Him: that is the achievement supreme." (V:122)

(j) *Angels' salutation of Peace to the entrants; thanks-giving to God by the inmates; angels hymning praise of the Lord:*

---

7 *Cf.* IV: 69, 70.

---

8 *Cf.* XCVIII: 7, 8.

Mark that this verse states the stabilisation of harmony between the human will and the perfectly Holy Will, i.e., the Will of God. It is this harmony whereby alone Man attains absolute and abiding purity of the will and genuine human holiness. This state of blessed life is fed perennially through constant communion with God and is stabilised through direct Vision of Him. That has been mentioned in the verse that follow.

"And those who were careful of duty to their Lord will be led to the Garden in troops till, when they arrive there, and the portals thereof will be opened, the *keepers thereof will say unto them: 'peace be unto you!* well have ye done! enter ye here to dwell therein for ever'[9]. They will say: 'Praise be unto Allah, Who has truly fulfilled His promise to us, and has given us (this) land in heritage for (eternity), so that we may dwell in the Garden wherever we will: how excellent a reward for those who work (righteousness)'. And thou (O Prophet!) wilt see the *angels surrounding the Throne (Divine) on all sides, singing Glory and Praise to their Lord.* The Decision between them (at Judgement) will be in (perfect) justice, and the cry (on all sides) will be: 'Praise be to Allah, Cherisher and Sustainer of the Worlds'."

(XXXIX: 73-75)

(k) *Realisation of the highest Ideal in obtaining the Supreme Blessing of the Vision of God:*

"Faces (of the Righteous Servants of God) will, on that Day, beam (in brightness and beauty),—*looking towards their Lord.*"

(LXXV:22, 23).

(l) *Peace with God, Peace with Fellow-beings, Peace with the rest of God's Creation, will be attained in the highest degree:*

"Those who believe and work righteousness,—their Lord will guide them because of their Faith: beneath them will flow rivers in Gardens of Bliss. Their cry of (adoration to God, i.e., their loud chanting of hymn of prayer) therein will be 'Glory to Thee, O Allah!' and 'Peace' will be their greeting therein! And the close of their cry will be: 'Praise be to Allah, the Cherisher and Sustainer of the Worlds'." (X: 9, 10)

(m) *Garden in nearness to God, eternal home; companions pure and holy; cool shades; highest satisfaction of the sentient aspect of the self in its transcendental transformation:*

"For the righteous are *Gardens in nearness to their Lord....*"

(III: 15)

"But give glad tidings to those who believe and work righteousness, that their portion is *Gardens, beneath which rivers flow.* Everything they are *fed with fruits therefrom*, they say: 'Why, this is what

9 *Cf.* XVI:32.

we were fed with before'. *For they are given things in similitude*: and they have therein companions pure (and holy)[10] and they *abide therein (for ever)*." (II:25)

(n) Happily employed, with the highest enjoyment suited to the heavenly life of the righteous; Greeting of 'Peace' from God:

"Verily the Companions of the Garden *shall that Day be happily employed.* They and their spouses will be in groves of (cool) shade, reclining on thrones (of dignity); every fruit[11] (i.e., highest enjoyment) will be there for them; *and they shall have whatever they call for*[12]; 'Peace'—a Word (of greeting) from the Lord Merciful."[13] (XXXVI: 55-58).

(o) Enduring delights:

"Their Lord gives them glad tidings of Mercy from Himself, of His Good Pleasure, and of Gardens for them, wherein are *Delights that endure*: they will dwell therein for ever. Verily in Allah's Presence is a reward, the greatest (of all)." (IX: 21, 22).

---

10 The participants in this 'companionship' will be men as well as women, and as emphasised in this verse, this companionship will be based on purity and holiness and without any earthly grossness. Also, all objects of beauty and enjoyment, which have been mentioned symbolically in connection with the heavenly life, here and at different other places in the Qur'ãn, will belong *equally* to men and women: both. (XXXIII: 35).

11 As to the word *fãkihatun*, employed in the Arabic original of the Qur'ãnic text for the word 'fruit', it refers actually to an inner quality of heavenly life, because, its root-word stands for: 'to rejoice greatly', 'to be full of merriment', Thus what it actually emphasises is the notion of the 'highest enjoyment'. Even in its literal sense, it should be taken to mean 'fruit' as possessing not earthly but transcendental nature.

12 According to A. Yusuf Ali, "using the language of this life, the musician's heaven will be full of music; the mathematician's will be full of mathematical symmetry and perfection; the artist's will be full of beauty of form, and so on." (*op.cit.*, p. 1183). The fact that heavenly life will not be a static life—a life of idle duration, but a dynamic life—a life full of *activity* and *achievement*, as the statement in the verse under comment about being "happily employed" affirms, should be given due importance in this connection. (It will be a 'life of achievement' with reference to itself, and a 'life of reward' with reference to the earthly life lived previously).

13 *Cf.* LVI: 26.

(p) *Beautiful Mansions in Gardens:*

"Allah has promised to the Believers, man and women, Gardens under which rivers flow, to dwell therein, and *beautiful mansions*[14] in Gardens of everlasting bliss. *But the greatest bliss is the Good Pleasure of Allah. That is the achievement supreme.*"[15] (IX:72).

(q) *Costly Adornments:*

"As to those who believe and work righteousness, verily We shall not suffer to perish the reward of any who do a (single) righteous deed.

"For them will be *Gardens of Eternity*[16], beneath which rivers flow: they will be adorned therein with *bracelets of gold*[17] and they will wear green garments of *fine silk*[18] *and heavy brocade*: they will recline therein on *raised thrones*[19]. How good the recompense! How beautiful a couch to recline on!" (XVIII: 30, 31).[20]

(r) *Hospitable homes:*

"For those who believe and work righteousness, are Gardens as *hospitable homes* (where they will be entertained as honourable guests), for their (good) deeds". (XXXII:19).

---

14 *Cf.* "loftly mansions one above another", in description of Heaven in XXXIX: 20.

15 Mark that the blessing of "Beautiful Mansions in Gardens" has been contrasted in this verse with the "Good Pleasure of Allah", emphasising about the latter that it is "the achievement supreme". Thus, it is plain that not only is the Qur'ãnic ideal of heavenly life not anthropomorphic, as we shall discuss later, but even such enjoyments which bear affinity with the earthly enjoyments—of course, only nominally—do not constitute the real ideal but are only ancillary. In other words, *holiness* permeates the entire Qur'ãnic concept of Heaven.

16 and not the gardens of this world.

17 *Cf.* "bracelets of gold and pearls" in XXII:23.

18 *Cf.* LXXVI: 12.

19 *Cf.* LXXVI:13.

20 All the blessings mentioned in verse 31 should be understood only in respect on their transcendental nature and form. The "Garden" as well as the adornments signify comfort, dignity and beauty. So also the things mentioned in the forthcoming verses.

(s) *No sorrow, no dull happiness:*

"Gardens of Eternity will they enter: therein will they be adorned with bracelets of gold and pearls; and their garments there will be of silk; And they will say: 'Praise be to Allah, Who *has removed us from (all) sorrow*: for our Lord is indeed Oft-Forgiving, ready to appreciate (service): Who has, out of His Bounty, settled us in the abode of permanence: no toil *nor sense of monotony* and weariness (in the enjoyment of perpetual happiness) shall touch us in it'." (XXXV: 33-35)

(t) *Enjoyment of honour and dignity; passing round of the social cup; company of chaste women:*

"But the sincere servants of Allah,—for them is a sustenance determined, fruits (or Delights); and they (shall enjoy) honour and dignity, in Gardens of Felicity, facing each other on thrones (of dignity); around will be passed to them *a Cup*[21] *from a clear-flowing fountain,* crystal-white, of a taste delicious to those who drink (thereof), free from headiness, nor will they suffer intoxication therefrom[22]. And besides them shall be *chaste women, restraining their glances*[23], with large eyes (having grace and beauty) as though they were delicate eggs closely guarded[24]."

(XXXVII: 40-49)[25]

(u) *Complete happiness and perfect realisation of spiritual and aesthetic ideals:*

"(It will be said unto the righteous): 'Enter ye the Garden, ye and your spouses, in (beauty and) rejoicing.' To them will be passed round dishes and goblets of gold[26]: and therein will be whatsoever souls

---

21 *Cf.* "vessels of silver and goblets of crystal" (LXXVI: 15, 16). Also: "a Cup (full to the brim)" (LXXVIII:34).

22 Mark that the evil accompaniments of earthly sensate pleasure have been negated here totally, although such pleasures have been mentioned here as types.

23 Mark the emphasis on chastity and lack of boldness. These characteristics relate to *moral purity*, which is an integral part of *holiness*.

24 The implication is of natural beauty, innocence and grace.

25 *Cf.* XXXVIII: 49-54; VII: 42-46; LVI: 10-12, 22-24, 32, 33, 34-40; LXXXVIII: 12-16.

26 A very important fact is worthy of notice here. The Islamic view of righteousness is built up on the concept of simplicity—nay, even austerity, in

desire and eyes delight in; and ye will be therein abiders. Such will be the Garden of which ye are made heirs for your (good) deeds (in earthly life). Ye shall have therein abundance of fruit, from which ye shall have satisfaction." (XLIII:70-73)

(v) *No further death:*

"As to the Righteous (they will be) in a position of Security, among Gardens and Springs; dressed in fine silk and in rich brocade[27], they will face each other. Thus it shall be; and We shall join them to Companions with beautiful and lustrous eyes (*Hûr*[28] *'în*). They will call therein for every kind of fruit in peace and security[29]; and *they will not taste Death therein*, except the first death (which removed them from their earthly life); and He will preserve them from the torments of the Flaming Fire,—as Bounty of Grace from thy Lord! That (Bounty of Grace) will be the Supreme Achievement!" (XLIV: 51-57).

(w) *Delicious drinks; Grace from the Lord; no vain discourse; Salutations of Peace; Sustenance:*

---

life. Thus, self-control and self-sacrifice are its watchwords, and the Path of Righteousness cannot be travelled, according to the Holy Qur'ãn, without avoiding indulgence in luxuries (LXXIX: 40, 41). This fact is thoroughly exemplified in the personality of the Holy Prophet Muhammad and of every other Prophet of God—Jesus, Moses, Abraham, etc., and in the personalities of all the exemplary followers of Islam, like the Righteous Caliphs, the illustrious Imams, and the great Sufis.

Now, the heavenly ideal consists in the attainment of perfection adequate to human personality in respect of the rational, moral and spiritual values. The luxuries denied to themselves by the righteous in the earthly life will, however, be compensated in a *transcendental and hallowed form*, in keeping with the holiness of Heaven, as a further reward implying the perfection also of the sentient dimension of human personality which it lived in its earthly life.

27 *Cf.* LXXVI: 21.

28 The word *Hûr* implies the following ideas: "(1) *purity*: possibly the word *Hawãriyyûn*, as applied to the first Disciples of Jesus, is connected with this root; (b) *beauty*, especially of eyes, where the intense white of the eye-balls stands out against the intense black of the pupil, thus giving the appreance of lustre, and intense feeling, as opposed to dullness or want of expression; and (3) *truth* and *goodwill*." (A. Yusuf Ali, *op.cit.*, p. 1352, n. 4729).

29 *Cf.* LXIX: 21-24.

"*(Here is) a Parable*[30] *of the Garden* which the (god-fearing) righteous are promised: in it are *rivers of water* incorruptible; *rivers of milk* of which the taste never changes; *rivers of wine,* a joy to those who drink; and *river of honey* pure and clear. In it there are for them all kinds of fruits; and *Grace from their Lord*[31]." (XLVII: 15)

"Gardens of Eternity, those which the Most Gracious (Allah) has promised to His servants in the Unseen; for His promise must (necessarily) come to pass.

"They *will not hear any vain discourse therein*[31], but only *salutation of Peace*[33] and therein they will have their *sustenance*[34], morning and evening (i.e., always)[35]. Such is the Garden which We

---

30 Note the word 'parable', The water, the milk, the wine, the honey, the fruits as also all other things which bear reference to earthly life but have been mentioned in connection with the life in Heaven, are symbolism, whose true nature is known to God alone, and the words used denote the heavenly blessings metaphorically only: and they are meant to convey to us the truth that the heavenly blessings are real and meaningful.

Thus, the four drinks mentioned in this verse refer to those heavenly blessings which will refresh the spirits, nourish the personalities, warm up the heart and sweeten the live of the righteous.

31 Mark the mention of bestowal of 'Grace from the Lord', which represents all *spiritual delights,* after the mention of such blessings as bear reference to earthly life—in this verse, as well as in other verses of the Holy Qur'ãn.

32 *Cf.* "No vanity shall they hear therein, nor untruth." (LXXVIII:35). Also: LXXXVIII:11.

33 "*Salãm,* translated 'Peace', has a much wider signification. It includes: (1) a sense of security and permanence, which is unknown in this life; (2) soundness, freedom from defects, perfection, as in the word *sãlim*; (3) preservation, salvation, deliverance, as in the word *sallama;* (4) salutation accorded with those around us; (5) resignation, in the sense that we are satisfied and not discontented; beside (6) the ordinary meaning of Peace, i.e., freedom from any jarring element. All these shades of meaning are implied in the word *Islãm*. Heaven therefore is the perfection of Islam." (A. Yusuf Ali, *op.cit.*, p. 780, n. 2512).

34 Namely, provision of all the requirements for the fulfilment of human destiny in the transcendental dimension of existence in Heaven.

35 According to Abdul Majid Daryabadi, "....'morning' and 'evening' are only used in relative sense, so as to be comprehended by us, as there will be no actual sunset in the Paradise." (*op.cit.*, p. 500). But, in the view of the present

will give as an inheritance to those of Our servants who guard against evil[36]." (XIX: 61-63)[37]

(x) *Social bliss; Family re-union; Fruits and meat; No frivolity, nor taint of ill; Service:*

"As to the god-fearing righteous, they will be in Gardens and in Happiness,—enjoying the (Bliss) which their Lord has bestowed on them, and their Lords shall deliver them from the torment of the Fire. (To them will be said:) ' Eat and drink ye with profit and health, because of your good deeds'. They will recline (in comfort) on thrones (of dignity) arranged in ranks, and We shall join them to Companions with beautiful big and lustrous eyes. *And those who believe and whose families follow them in Faith,—to them We shall join their families:* nor shall We deprive them (of the fruit) of aught of their works: (yet) is each individual in pledge for his deeds. And *We shall bestow on them of fruit and meat*—anything they shall desire. They shall there exchange, one with another, a (loving) *cup*[38] free of frivolity, free of all taint of ill. Round about will serve, (devoted) to them, youths (handsome) as pearls well-guarded (i.e., of exquisite beauty)[39]."

(LII:17-24)

---

writer, there is a possibility of some phenomena of transcendental or metaphysical nature In Heaven akin in some sense to morning and evening in our present dimension of existence.

36 Note the emphasis on all such occasions on moral merit, which should, of course, be combined with true relationship with God.

37 *Cf.* LVI: 25-33.

38 *Cf.* "As to the *abrãr* (i.e., those perfect in Piety), they shall drink of a cup whereof the admixture (or, odour) is (like unto) camphor." (LXXVI:5).

Also: "And they will be given therein to drink of a cup the admixture (or, odour) whereof is (like unto) ginger,—from a fountain therein named *salsabîl*." (LXXVI:17, 18).

Also: "Their thirst will be slaked with Pure Wine sealed: the seal thereof will be Musk: and for this (i.e., the blessings of heaven described in verses 22-24 and in this verse) let those aspire, who have aspiration (for eternal happiness): with it will be given a mixture of *Tasnîm*: a spring from (the waters) whereof drink those Nearest to God (*muqarrabûn*)." (LXXXIII:25-28).

39 *Cf.* LXXVI:19.

(y) *Fragrance for the 'Nearest-to-God' and mutual greetings of Peace among the Companions of the Right Hand:*

"Thus, then, if he be of the 'Nearest-to-God' (*muqarrabûn*), (there is for him) *comfort* and *fragrance* and a Garden of Delights. And if he be of the Companions of the Right Hand, (for him is the salutation:) '*Peace be unto thee*', *from the Companions of the Right Hand.*" (LVI:88-91).

(z) *Realm magnificent:*

"And when thou lookest (at the Heaven), it is there thou wilt see a Bliss and a Realm Magnificent." (LXXVI:20)

Two Important Points:

There are two important points which must be kept in view while considering the Qur'ãnic conception of Heaven and trying to understand the real implication of the verses relating thereto. The points are:

(1) Before the Day of Judgement, the world will be destroyed and re-created in a new form:

"One day the earth will be changed into a different earth, and so will be the heavens...." (XIV:48)

As for the human beings, they also will be re-created in a new form:

"We have decreed death to be your common lot, and We are not to be frustrated from changing your *forms* and *creating you* (*again*) *in* (*forms*) *that ye know not*. And ye certainly know already the first form of (your) creation Why then ye heed not?" (LVI:60-62).

Thus the conditions of life and nature of experience in the next world will be so different from what we know and experience now in the phenomenal world that presently we can only imagine it and must find it impossible to comprehend it truly:

"Now no person knows what delights of the eyes[40] are kept hidden (in reserve) for them (in Heaven)—as a reward for their (good) Deeds." (XXXII:17).

---

40 "delights of the eyes" in an idiom for that which gives the highest satisfaction. It should not be taken to mean sensuous pleasure.

(2) Now life and experience in Heaven (as also in Hell) being on a different plane, it can be described to us here only by symbols and metaphors. And this is what the Holy Qur'ãn has itself plainly affirmed; as, for instance, when it gives the description of delicious drinks in Heaven, it starts that description with the worlds:

"(Here is) a *parable* of the Garden which the righteous are promised." (XLVII:15)

Thus *the entire Qur'ãnic description of Heaven and Hell is symbolical*, and it would be the greatest intellectual dishonesty on the part of anyone to try to understand it in the literal sense.

The critics of Islam have stumbled especially in connection with the description of the delights of Heaven. But, as explained, the description there has been given through the medium of symbols and metaphors which actually have very profound and rich spiritual connotation.

Recapitulation:

Having made the above clarification, we may now state that the description of Heaven in the Holy Qur'ãn contains the following basic elements:

1. Immortality:
2. Peace;
3. Absolute Purity of the Will enjoyed by all:
4. Social Harmony and Love;
5. Companionship of the Blessed Servants of God;
6. Light;
7. Beauty;
8. Truth;
9. Direct Experience of Reality;
10. Holiness;
11. Happiness.

No. 1 forms the basic human yearning in connection with the realisation of all human ideals.

Nos. 2 to 5 form the ideal of Morality.

Nos. 6 and 7 form the ideal of Aesthetic Enjoyment.

Nos. 8 and 9 form the ideal of Knowledge.

No. 10 forms the ideal of Religion.

No. 11 forms the ideal of the Sentient Self.

Thus the realisation of all healthy human yearnings and ideals has been affirmed in the Qur'ãnic conception of Heaven.

Re-stating this fact in other words: The form of human personality—its constitution—will be changed in the next world. It will exist in a different dimension—on a different plane—, with all the grossness and carnality of its earthly physical existence removed. Thus the individual will enjoy all that he desires here in respect of physical happiness, but he will enjoy it in a sublimated form, i.e., without the grossness and other limitations of physical existence. *It will not be physical happiness but beatitude, i.e., heavenly happiness—happiness of the highest kind, all spiritual delights having been figured forth from parallel experiences in our present life.*

He will also enjoy the aesthetic pleasures, but those pleasures shall be free of all morbidity and grossness, experienced as they will be on the non-physical plane.

Thus the ideals of physical happiness and aesthetic enjoyment will be realised in Heaven to the full but on a higher level—the level of *holiness*—, and all that as a reward of moral effort and the maintenance of true relationship with God in this earthly life.[41]

And not only that. Man's moral effort and his trials and sufferings in the Way of God—in the Path of God-orientated Righteousness—shall culminate in Heaven in the perfect realisation of the moral ideal, i.e., the attainment of Moral Bliss and Social Bliss.

The reward, however, will not end there. The recipients of heavenly life shall be blessed with the direct knowledge of the Reality of

---

41 The Holy Qur'ãn has stated this fact clearly and beautifully in verses III:14-17.

the Cosmos. Then, even beyond that; they will be blessed with the direct Vision of God, the Really-Real, the Source of all that exists.

And they will be blessed not only with the direct Vision of God, but will live in Divine Presence and will be fed by Divine Pleasure eternally—increasing qualitatively in holiness and employed happily all the time, each individual in accordance with his individual taste, calibre and destiny[42].

The Hell

As regards Hell, it has been mentioned in the Holy Qur'ãn as punishment for the rejectors of Truth (II:24; etc.) and the wrongdoers (L:25; etc.), wherever Heaven has been mentioned as a reward for the righteous,—and it has been described as a contrast of Heaven. Its symbol is the Fire (II:24; etc.), in contrast to the Garden, which is the symbol of Heaven. "(It is) the *Fire* of God (namely, having come into existence under the command of God) kindled (to a blaze), which *rises above the hearts*: It *shall be made into a vault over them, in columns outstretched.*" (CIV:6-9). In other words, the hell-fire originates within the hearts of those who reject the Source of Goodness, namely, God, and the Pattern of Goodness, namely, the Prophet of God, and nurture evil in their breasts. They will be those "to whom God will not speak, nor will He look at them on the Day of Judgement; nor will He purify them (on that Day)" (III:77). And because on the hearts of those who earn Hell in this life "is the stain of the (evil) which they do, verily, from (the Light of) their Lord, that Day, will they be veiled" (LXXXIII:14, 15), becoming thus deprived of all the Blessings which will flow to the inmates of Heaven from the Bounties of God. The life of the inmates of Hell will, indeed, be a life of roasting in agony (IV:56; XIV: 17; XXV:13, 14; LIV:48; XXXII:20). They will be held in bondage to the punishment brought on them by their evil beliefs and evil deeds (XXXII:19-22; LXIX:30-37). Their faces will be covered with humiliation (LXXX:40, 41), and their surroundings will be pervaded by ugliness and darkness "in the shades of Black Smoke: nothing will there be to refresh, nor to please: for that they

---

42 That there are numerous degrees in good and evil, in respect of the deeds and motives of human beings, and that, consequently, there will be degrees in respect of rewards and the respective spiritual positions of the recipients of heavenly life, has been affirmed in the following verse of the Holy Qur'ãn: "For all (moral responsible beings) will be degrees (of reward) in accordance with that which they did". (VI:132).

were wont to be indulged, before that, in wealth (and luxury), and persisted obstinately in wickedness supreme!" (LVI:43-46). Their life will be a life of horrible misery, even in respect of their "foods" and "drinks" which will be of the most painful type (XIV: 17; XIV:49-50; XXXVII:62-67; XLIV: 43-48; LV: 43-44; LVI:52-55; LXXVIII: 21-25). In short, the conditions of life in Hell shall be the exact opposite of those we have described in detail in connection with Heaven. Life in Heaven being the life of Fulfilment, life in Hell will reflect the Agony attendant on Frustration, in the onward march towards the realisation of Human Destiny. The nature and the measure of punishment will vary in respect of the denizens of Hell, even as reward will vary in the case of the inmates of Heaven. (VI:132)

Chapter III

THE GOD (ALLAH)

Although morality may be regarded as conceivable in spite of disbelief in God's existence, moral consciousness is denuded on all enthusiasm for moral struggle without a dynamic faith in God.

Moreover, the appearance of incompatibility with the realisation of the moral ideal which the world gives, and the imperfections from which Man suffers, on the one hand, and Man's state of dissatisfaction with the Actual and his yearning to transform it into the Ideal, on the other, form a source of agony for him; and the human soul yearns for an all-Perfect Being Who, through His interference, and out of sheer Grace, may guide him on the *straight path* to success in the realisation of his ideal, in spite of the internal and external obstacles.[1]

Also: Creation, which has been already proved to be the necessary requirement of the realisation of the moral ideal, implies necessarily the existence of an All-Powerful, All-Wise, All-Controlling Creator, Who is also the Moral Ruler of the universe.

Thus the affirmation of the existence of God from the point of view of moral consciousness is a necessity.

The question now arises: It being so, what are the Divine Attributes that are indispensable in respect of Man's success in his moral struggle.

---

1 *Cf.* The prayer that the Holy Qur'ãn has taught—a prayer for beseeching Divine Guidance, a prayer obligatory for a Muslim to recite in all the institutional Prayers that he has been commanded to offer: "Guide us Thou (O Lord!) unto the Straight Path—the path of those on whom Thou hast bestowed Thy Grace, not of those whose portion is Wrath nor of those who go astray." (I:6,7).

Through this prayer a Muslim aspires for guidance in order to bring about, preserve and promote the Islamic social order—a social order which is meant to be constituted of spiritually and morally integrated individuals. Such individuals, it may be emphasised, cannot be evolved except through intensive and extensive moral struggle, wherein success can be possible only through Divine Guidance and Grace: "And whosoever has faith in Allah, He guideth his heart (to the path of success)." (LXIV:11).

Such Attributes Are:

(i) God should be the *Creator* of every thing in the world, in order that the world and every thing belonging to it may be amenable to His interference.

(ii) He should be *Eternal,* in order to be capable of functioning and interfering at all stages in the life of the universe.

(iii), (iv), (v) He should be *Omnipotent* (Almighty), *Omnipresent* and *Omniscient*, in order to have *perfect control* not only over the universe as a system but also over discreet events and objects.

(vi) He should be the *Possessor of Perfect Wisdom*, in order that He may be capable of acting unerringly in guiding Man in his struggles, including the moral struggle.

(vii) He should be *the Guide*, i.e., the possessor of the Will to guide human beings in their moral struggle.

(viii) He should be the *Possessor of Mercy and Love*, in order that help to human beings may be the inherent demand of His nature.

(ix) He should be *Capable of Response*, in order that human beings may approach Him with confidence in times of need and may commune with Him.

(x), (xi) Since it is possible that Man may remain, at some stage of his life, indifferent to the demands of his moral nature and subsequently he may have the despair that the wrongs and the evil deeds committed by him cannot be undone, and that therefore their evil effects cannot be avoided—a despair that must kill the enthusiasm to lead a morally good life—, God should be the *Forgiver of sins* and the *Acceptor of Repentance*; thereby ensuring the possibility of acquiring enthusiasm for participation in the moral struggle even for the worst evil-doer.

(xii) The duality of human nature and the conflict thereof form a hindrance in respect of Man's rising to his full moral stature, and it is difficult for him to stick in his actions to the purest moral standard as regards the motive. Hence, *God should be the possessor of the Will to remove the deficiencies in the consequences of the morally good actions* through His unbounded Grace. In other words, He should be the *Possessor of Unbounded Grace.*

(xiii) He should be the *Debaser of Evil* and the *Avenger of Wrongs* in order to assist the righteous in their moral struggle.

(xiv) Since the consequence of good and evil do not mature during the earthly life of the individual, He should be the *Sovereign of the Day of Judgement*, in order to act as the *Judge Supreme* for recompensing good and evil in the requisite measure, whereby alone the moral ideal can be realised.

(xv) He should be '*Above-every-want*', i.e., independent of everyone else and every thing, in order that His own wants may never stand in the way of His creatures, and, also, He may be capable of fulfilling every conceivable need of everyone.

(xvi) He *should not suffer from any infirmities*, in order that His relation with the world and Man remains immune from all deviational defects.

(xvii) He should be *al-Rabb* (i.e., *the Evolver* and *the Perfector*), in order that human beings can be successful with certainty, through Him, in their struggle for moral and spiritual perfection.

(xviii) He should be positively *Righteous* in all His actions, in order to be the Helper of the righteous unflinchingly.

(xix) He should be *Perfectly Holy*, i.e., *Possessor* of *Absolute Good,* in order that His relationship with His creatures may not be tainted with evil even in the smallest measure.

(xx) He should be *the One* and *the Unique*, with no compeer who may challenge His authority in any manner and in any respect whatsoever.

(xxi) He should be *the Perfect Being*, in order that human beings may be able to attain perfection adequate to their nature, including moral perfection—through His Grace.

The Holy Qur'ãn affirms all the above-mentioned Attributes of God:

(i) *He is the Creator of everything, having originated the existence of everything:*

"The Originator (*Badî'*) of the heavens and the earth." (II:117)

"Say : O Allah! Creator (*Fãtir*) of the heavens and the earth (*ab novo*)!...." (XXXIX:46).

"Allah is the Creator (*Khãliq*) of all things, and He is the Guardian and Disposer of all affairs." (XXXIX:62)

"He is Allah, the Creator (*Khãliq*), the Evolver (*Bãrî*), the Bestower of Forms (*Musawwir*). To Him belong the Most Excellent Names." (LIX:24)

(ii) He is the Self-Existent, the Eternal:

"Allah! There is no God save He,—*the Ever-Living, the Self-Existent, the Eternal*. No slumber can seize Him nor sleep. Unto Him belongeth whatsoever is in the heavens and whatsoever is in the earth. Who is he that can intercede with Him save by His leave? He knoweth what (appeareth to His creatures as) Before or After or Behind. Nor shall they encompass of His knowledge except as He willeth. His Throne doth extend over the heavens and the earth, and the guarding of the twain weareth Him not. For He is the Sublime, the Supreme." (II:255)

(iii), (iv), (v) He is Omnipotent, Omnipresent and Omniscient:

(a) As to His *Omnipotence*[2] :

"To Allah belongeth the dominion of the heavens and the earth; and Allah hath Power over all things." (III:189).

"(Allah is) the Doer of all that He intends." (LXXXV:16).

(b) As to His *Omnipresence*:

"....and He it is that encompasseth all things." (IV:126).

"....and whithersoever ye turn, there is Allah's countenance. Lo! Allah is All-Embracing, All-Knowing." (II:115).

"He is with you wheresoever ye may be. And Allah is Seer of what ye do." (LVII:4).

---

2 Besides the Attributes contained in III:189 and LXXXV:16, there are, in the Holy Qur'ãn, several others also which bear reference to God's Greatness, Majesty and Omnipotence. For instance: the Sublime, the Most High, the Exalted, the Supreme, the Great, the Most Great, the Exalted in Might, the Strong, the Prevailer, the Irresistible, the Almighty, the Lord of Majesty and Honour.

(c) As to *Omniscience*:

"....and He is All-Hearing, All-Seeing." (XLII:11)

"Verily Allah has perfect knowledge of all things." (XXIX:62)

"(Allah is) Knower of the Invisible[3] and the Visible[4], and He is All-Wise (and) the Perfectly Informed (of all events and things)." (VI:73)

"And Allah is ever Watcher over all things." (XXXIII:52)

"Verily Allah is over everything a Witness."[5] (XXII:17)

"....and that Allah comprehends all things in (His) Knowledge." (LXV:12)

(vi) He is the Possessor of Perfect Wisdom:

"And unto Him (alone) belongeth Majesty in the heavens and on the earth; and He is Exalted in Power Possessor of Perfect Wisdom." (XLV:37)

(vii) He Possesses the Will to Guide:

"And thine Lord sufficeth as Guide and Helper." (XXV:31).

"....for verily Allah is the Guide of those who believe (in His guidance), to the Straight Way." (XXII:54)

"Glorify the name of thy Guardian-Lord Most High, Who created, and bestowed order and proportion; Who hath ordained laws and hath guided (all things to their goal)...." (LXXXVII:1-3)

(viii) He is the Possessor of Mercy and Love:

"All Praise unto Allah, the Cherisher, Sustainer, Evolver and Perfector of (all) the Worlds, the Compassionate, the merciful[6]." (I: 2, 3).

---

3 i.e., whatever is kept secret, whatever has happened in the past or is to happen in future.

4 i.e., whatever is open and public, whatever is happening at a given moment.

5 (so He will requite everyone according to his deeds).

6 Commenting on Allah's Attribute of Mercy, Abdul Majid Daryabadi says: "Both words *Rahmãn* and *Rahîm* are derived from *Rahmat* which signifies

"He is the One that sends down the saving rain after they have despaired, and scatters His Mercy (far and wide). He is the Protecting Friend, the Praiseworthy." (XLII:28)

"....and He is the Forgiving, the Loving." (LXXXV:14)

(ix) He is Responsive to Supplications:

"(Says Allah:) When My servants ask thee (O Muhammad!) concerning Me, then surely I am near (to them). In answer the prayer of the suppliant when he crieth unto Me...." (II:186)

"....then ask forgiveness of Him, and turn to Him (in repentance): for my Lord is (always) near, Responsive (unto those who supplicate Him)." (XI:61)

(x), (xi) He is the Forgiver of Sins and Acceptor of Repentance:

(*a*) *As Forgiver of Sins*:

"And Allah knows (all) that is in your hearts: and Allah is All-knowing, Most Forbearing." (XXXIII:51)

"Verily He is the benign (or Beneficent), the Merciful." (LII:28)

"Verily, Allah is Most Kind and Most Merciful to human beings. (XXII:65)

"Verily, Allah is One that blots out (sins) and forgives again and again." (XXII:60)

"....the Lord of the heavens and the earth, and all between,—the Exalted in Might, Able to enforce His Will, Most Forgiving." (XXXVIII:66)

---

tenderness, requiring the exercise of beneficence and thus comprising the idea of love and mercy. Both are intensive forms. The former denotes tenderness towards all His creatures in general, and the latter towards His worshippers in particular. The Divine attribute of *Rahmãt* may on analysis be found to have the following as its components:— (1) His provision of everything beforehand that could be needed by man in the world: (2) His concern for the well-being of man, both in life and death; (3) His tenderness for man's helplessness; and (4) a disposition on His part to deal kindly and generously with man." (*op.cit*., p. 2, n. 15).

(*b*) *As Acceptor of Repentance*:

"Know they not that Allah doth accept repentance from His votaries and receives their gifts of charity, and that Allah is surely Oft-Returning (in accepting repentance), Most Merciful." (IX:104)

(xii) He is the Possessor of Unbounded Grace:

"....and Allah is the Possessor of Unbounded Grace."
(VIII:29)

(xiii) He is theDebaser of Evil and the Avenger of Wrongs:

"And those who earn evil deeds, (for them) the requital of each evil deed is by the like thereof; and ignominy overtaketh them...."
(X:28)

"And who among you does wrong, We shall make him taste great torment (unless he repents and adopts the path of Righteousness)."
(XXV:19)

(xiv) He is the Sovereign of the Day of Judgement and the Judge Supreme:

"(All) Praise unto Allah, the Evolver and the Perfector of (all) the Worlds; the Compassionate, the Merciful; *Sovereign of the Day of Judgement*." (I:2-4)

"And He is the Supreme over His creatues, and He sendeth guardians over you until when death cometh unto (any) one of you, Our messengers (i.e., angels) take his soul, and they fail not. Then they all shall be taken back unto Allah, their true Master. Lo! *His shall be the judgement*. And He is Most Swift in taking account." (VI: 61, 62)

(xv) He is 'Above-every-want', while all depnd on him:

"O ye men! It is ye that have the need of Allah: but Allah is the One Free of all wants, Worthy of all praise." (XXXV:15).

"And whosoever disbelieveth, (let him know that) lo! Allah is Independent of (all) the creatures." (III:97)

(xvi) He does not suffer from any infirmities, emotional or otherwise:

"Verily Allah! He is the Great Provider of Sustenance, Lord of Power, Steadfast (for ever)." (LI:58)

(xvii) He is al-Rabb, i.e., the Evolver and the Perfector:

"All praise is due to Allah, the *Rabb*, i.e., the Sustainer, the Nourisher, the Evolver, the Perfector, of all the Worlds." (I:2)

"Say, 'Shall I seek for my *Rabb* other than Allah, while He is the *Rabb* of all things (that exist)?'" (VI:164)

"(Allah is the) *Rabb* of the heavens and the earth, and of all that is between them: so worship Him, and be constant and patient in His worship: Knowest thou of any who is worthy of the same name (and status) as he?" (XIX:65)

(xviii) He is positively Righteous:

"Lo my Lord is on the Straight Path." (XI:56)

(xix) He is perfectly Holy and the Possessor of all Good:

"Allah is He, than Whom there is no other God;—the Sovereign, *the all-Holy*, the Source of Peace (and Perfection), the Guardian of Faith, the Protector, the Exalted in Might, the Irresistible, the Supreme. Glory to Allah! (High is He) above all that they associate (with Him)." (LIX:23)

"....O Allah!.....In Thine hand is all Good." (III:26)

(xx) He is the One and the Unique:

"....and He is the One (or, the Sole God) the Almighty." (XIII:16)

"Say: He is Allah, the One! Allah, the Absolute, the Perfect. He begetteth not, nor was He begotten. And there hath never been co-equal with Him anyone (and, as such, He is the Unique)." (CXII:1-4)

"....Not like unto Him is aught...." (XLII:11)

(xxi) He is the Absolute, the Perfect:

"Allah (is) the Absolute, the Perfect." (CXII:2)

The Qur'ãnic Foundations and Structure of Muslim Society

The Qur'ãnic Foundations and Structure of Muslim Society

By

Dr. Muhammad Fazl-ur-Rahman Ansari

B. Th., M.A., Ph.D.

President

World Federation of Islamic Missions

Volume II

KITAB BHAVAN

NEW DELHI-110002

Kitab Bhavan
Publishers, Distributors, Exporters & Importers
1784, Kalan Mahal, Darya Ganj
New Delhi-110002 (India)

Phone : (91-11) 3277392/93, 3274686
Web Site: www.kitabbhavan.com
E-mail : nasri@vsnl.com
Fax : (91-11) 3263383

Edition ... 2002

ISBN : 81-7151-319-0
Book Code :

Laser Typesetting at:
Laser Track
Darya Ganj, New Delhi-2

Published in India by:
Nusrat Ali Nasri for Kitab Bhavan
1784, Kalan Mahal, Darya Ganj
New Delhi-110002 [India]

Printed in India at:
Nice Printing Press
Khureji Khas, Delhi-110051

CONTENTS

Volume II

Preamble

Book I
DUTIES TO SELF

Part I. Duties as Spiritual Being

Part II. Duties as Physical Being

Part III. Duties as Rational Being

Part IV. Duties as Aesthetical Being

Part V. Duties as Moral Being

Book II
DUTIES TO OTHER INDIVIDUALS

Part I. Fundamental Duties Towards All Human Beings

Part II. Duties of Condition Towards Other Individuals

PREAMBLE

Chapter I

THE MORAL CODE: WHY AND HOW?

Chapter II

CLASSIFICATION OF DUTIES

Chapter I

THE MORAL CODE: WHY AND HOW?

I. Need for a Comprehensive Code of Life

Human life moves under the impact of different types of conflicts. To start with: there exists a conflict between the individual's theoretical yearnings, and that to an extent that the fulfilment of one implies the frustration of another. For instance, in the field of Ethics, the yearning for Knowledge implies 'causality' and 'necessity', while the yearning for Morality affirms 'freedom'; and, in the domain of Metaphysics, the yearning for Knowledge demands the affirmation of the principles of 'unfolding' and 'immanence', while the yearning for Religion insists on accepting the validity of the principles of 'creation' and 'transcendence'. Secondly, there is the problem of the emergence of conflicts in the life of the individual at the instinctive level. For instance, the parental instinct which forces the parents to behave tenderly and affectionately towards the offspring stands in direct conflict with the instinct of self-assertion which requires the adoption of a stern attitude when the offspring commits an act of disobedience. Thirdly, the instinctive nature of the individual comes into conflict with his rational nature. Fourthly, the ideals embedded in the individual's rational nature may—and, in fact, do—come into conflict with one another. Fifthly, every individual is unique in respect of his or her past experiences and environmental factors, and this uniqueness becomes the breeding ground of conflicts between individual and individual. Then, beyond the individual level, existence of conflicts between the individual and the society is a fact of human life. Lastly, the narrow racial, territorial and ideological loyalties and economic interests of different communities and nations become sources of conflicts which threaten the very existence of humanity, as they are doing nowadays,—not to speak of the realisation of the spiritual and moral ideals.

In such a situation of manifold conflicts and of the dangers involved in respect of realisation of the highest human ideals, the question emerges in the mind of every thoughtful and conscientious person: "How ought I to behave to realise my ideals?" In other words: "What should be the Code for determining my conduct?"

The Holy Qur'ãn provides the answer to that all-important question by imparting sure[1] and complete[2] guidance in all the different problems of

1. XVI:9.

2. XVI:89.

human life, including the metaphysical and ethical problems with which philosophy deals, and a comprehensive and genuine Moral Code.

Viewing the problem of the need for a Code from another angle: It is the Code which imparts *uniform pattern of behaviour* and the *bond of community* to the group. It also creates optimistic outlook on life and forms the sure ground for progress. Because, if the individuals who constitute a group have a Code to govern their modes of behaviour, they will always have a genuine and firm basis for reciprocal social responses.[3] On the contrary, if a human group is devoid of a Code with social reference, as we find in respect of the Christian and the Greek pagan outlooks, the consequence shall be the emergence of a pessimistic view of life along with all its resultant evils.

II. Basis of Systematisation of the Qur'ãnic Moral Code—the Qur'ãnic Ideal

The effort to systematise the Moral Code has passed through several stages in the history of human thought. Among the ancients, it was Aristotle who gave a classification that is based on the main psychological aspects of human nature *viz.*, Knowing, Feeling and Willing. The highest virtue pertaining to Knowing is Wisdom, pertaining to Feeling is Temperance, and pertaining to Willing is Courage, while Justice governs them all. But the Greek mind does not seem to have developed its moral consciousness properly[4], and that because of the

---

3. It may be remarked here in passing that it is the radical conflict in outlooks because of which Islam does not permit marriage between a Believer and a *mushrikah* (pagan woman), while it allows marriage between a Believer and a *Kitãbiyah* (i.e., a woman professing faith in some revealed religion), because the *Kitãbiyah* has an avenue, however imperfect, through which an appeal can be made to her personality. (See: The Holy Qur'ãn, II:221; V:6).

4. Speaking of that period in the life of humanity as a whole, Illingworth observes: ".....as a rule it is beyond dispute that neither the *universality* nor the *unity* of personality, its two most important features were adequately understood...." (*Personality: Human and Divine*, p. 8).

Commenting on the deficiencies in Greek moral thought, D. M. Donaldson says: "As evidence of Aristotle's unwillingness to grant the benefits of his conception of personality universally we may instance the facts that he was ready to rule out some men on the ground that they were of barbarous origin, others because they were of slave origin, and women he regarded 'as nature's failures in the attempt to produce men.' That he was likewise unable to unify

fact that, as the historical account of Greek civilisation available today shows, it was pagan in character and possessed no proper conception of 'personality'; whereas morality is inseparably related to 'personality' and seems to have developed under the impact of the teachings of revealed religions and not otherwise[5].

Among the philosophers of the modern age, it is Kant who has made an important contribution. But his emphasis on the form of the Moral Law as the standard of morality and his attitude of leaving the contents of that Law to be traced from the established morality and the moral situation did not provide much lead in respect of the Moral Code, though the importance of his contribution to Moral Philosophy cannot be denied without injustice. Kant did furnish us with a classification of duties in order to complete his ethical system. But, the Code prescribed by him is through and through ideational and individualistic in character, because it does not attach importance to the duties of the moral agent towards the societal whole, nor is there any reference to the duties of the societal whole to its parts. This appears to be due to his limitation that he was born and lived in Christian environment,—the Christian point of view being that man's socio-cultural yearnings are inherently incompatible with his spirituo-moral yearnings.

What, then is the basis of systematisation of the Qur'ãnic Moral Code? Answer to this question necessitates the statement of the Qur'ãnic Ideal, which emerges in the following terms:

The Qur'ãn places equal emphasis on the sensate and the transcendental yearnings of man[6] and harmonises them; and thus it lays down for humanity a comprehensive Ideal, which consists in the cultivation of: (i) Holiness based on a dynamic, vibrant and living faith in

---

human nature is clear from his 'unsolved dualism between the soul and its organism', and from the fact that he had 'no clear conception of the will, and hardly any of the conscience'." (*Studies in Muslim Ethics*, p. 274).

5. *Cf.* The role of religions which claim to be revealed, i.e., Judaism, Christianity and Islam; as also of other and earlier religions of the world, including those of primitive peoples, in which the idea of personality with reference to the Supreme Being has found emphasis,—their monotheism providing the clue to their revealed origin. (*Ref.*. among other works, Wilhelm Schmidt's book, entitled: *Der Ursprung der Gottesidee*: *Eine historisch - Kritische und positive Studie*. 12 vols. Munster in Westfalen, Germany, 1912—1955).

6. *Cf.* Along with other references, the prayer taught by the Qur'ãn in II : 201.

God, an earnest and courageous pursuit of Truth, and an ever-present consciousness of Final Accountability; (ii) sound and comprehensive Morality; (iii) social, economic and political Justice; (iv) Knowledge in all its dimensions; and (v) Aesthetic Grace,—all of these resulting in the conquest of harmful propensities within the individual, the conquest of evil within the society, and the conquest of the physical environment, or, Nature. In the pursuit of this Ideal, Holiness, Love for Humanity, Truth, Justice, Beauty, Discipline and Progress are the watchwords, while the concept of Unity[7] permeates the entire movement towards the Ideal, and the motto of 'simple living, hard labour and high thinking' forms the wheel of progress.

7. *Ref:* Vol. I, Book I, Part IV, Chapter VI: "The Philosophy of Unity".

Chapter II

CLASSIFICATION OF DUTIES

I. Preliminary Observations

The function of the Code should be the realisation of the Ideal and the actualisation of the norms that it implies.

Before we proceed to the structural constituents of systematisation, however, it is necessary to establish the Qur'ãnic point of view with respect to the concepts of 'Duty' and 'Right'.

Duty and Right:

The Qur'ãnic moral code is based on the emphasis on 'obligation' or 'duty' in contrast to the emphasis on 'right' (v:44; etc.). Now, the implications of the emphasis respectively on duty and right are:

Right is a right *against* someone. Duty is a duty *towards* someone. Right means that someone else owes something to us. For, when we say: 'it is our right', it means that someone has to perform a duty to us. On the contrary, when we say: 'it is our duty', it means that someone has a right against us.

The emphasis on duty creates *harmony* in social life, because if everyone were to concentrate on his or her duty, the emphasis on grumbling for rights will naturally vanish. On the contrary, the emphasis on rights creates *strife*, because if everyone were to think about his rights on others, he would hardly have the mind to think of his duties towards others. The immense increase in quarrels and strifes between the different classes of human beings, as for instance, between labourers and capitalists, and between races and nations, which we find in the world today, is the direct outcome of the emphasis on rights. As regards the political life in different countries, the subjects or citizens clamour for their rights more than taking pains for fulfilling their duties towards their fellow-beings, the state and the country. Everyone tries thus to transfer blame to the shoulders of others, and the confusion gets worse confounded. This state of affairs will not improve unless the world adopts the Qur'ãnic emphasis on duty.

Then, the emphasis on duty creates *unity* among human beings, because it is built up on the idea and the sentiment of sympathy,—sympathy in the sense that in fulfilling our duty we have always to do some positive good to someone in the world. On the contrary, the emphasis on rights is conducive to disintegration and *disunity* among human beings, because it is based on the idea of demanding something from others. We all know that we feel happy when anyone *gives* something to us, and most people feel unhappy and miserably when anyone *demands* anything from them.

The Empire of Duties:

As to the classification of Duties: Since, according to the Holy Qur'ãn, man is not merely being but also a spiritual, physical, rational and aesthetical being, as we shall shortly see, the fulfilment of duties relating to all those aspects of the human personality is necessary for the realisation of the Qur'ãnic moral Ideal.

Now, since morality originates in the attitude that man takes towards personality in his own being or in the being of others, the moral duties should be classified basically as: (*i*) *Duties to Self,* and (*ii*) *Duties to Others*. And since the person who is nearest to the moral agent in his own person, Duties to Self should come first and the Duties to Others thereafter.

The question may now be raised: What is the relation between Duties to Self and Duties to Others?

If the problem is viewed in the light of the ideational cultural philosophy, the two duties remain unconnected; because the point of view there is individualistic. Their relationship can be affirmed only on the basis of the Qur'ãnic philosophy of idealistic, or integralistic, culture which is based on the synthesis of the ideational and the sensate, and which, consequently, stands for interdependent relationship between morality and social life. Thus moral perfection of the moral agent is conceived there with reference to the happiness of others, which, in its turn, is possible only in terms of social welfare.

II. Duties to Self

Human Personality and its Functions:

According to the Holy Qur'ãn, humanity emerged in Creation primarily in the transcendental dimension of existence:

"We (God) said: 'O Adam! dwell thou and thy wife in the Garden; and eat of the bountiful things therein as ye wish; but approach not this tree, or else ye run into harm and transgression." (II:35).[1]

1. That the "Garden" did not belong to the earth is borne out by the next verse which tells us unambiguously that the Divine decree in respect of "getting down" and "dwelling on the earth" was pronounced afterwards, i.e., after Adam's and Eve's Deception.

At that stage of existence itself, they possessed not only the spiritual but also the rational and the aesthetical dimensions of personality.

The spiritual dimension was there because of the very fact of the transcendental nature of their existence.

The existence of the rational dimension has been affirmed thus:

"And He (i.e., God) taught Adam the nature of all things." (II:31).

The existence of the aesthetical dimension is established in the very concept of the "Garden" where Adam and Eve lived in innocent enjoyment.

Subsequently they fell victim to the Devil's Deception. After that they appeared in the physical world, which is spatio-temporal, as physical and moral beings:

"Then Satan caused them both (i.e., Adam and Eve) to deflect therefrom and expelled them from that in which they had been. We (God) said: 'Get ye down *all* (i.e., let entire humanity commence its descent from the then transcendental stage towards the spatio-temporal, or, the physical, stage of existence[1]), with the spirit of clash between yourselves (that being the condition of all struggle, including the moral). On earth (where you will stay with physical qualities required for a physical environment) will be your dwelling place and provision for a time (i.e., for the duration of each individual's earthly sojourn)". (II:36).

Hence, the human personality and its functions are to be understood in the following terms:

1. The Real Human Personality is Spiritual in Nature

Besides the above reference (II:35), this fact is also corroborated by the following verse, which speaks, not only of the existence of all human beings—from the first to the last—at the dawn of Creation, but also of the possession of Consciousness—self-consciousness as well as consciousness of the Personality of God—and hence of personality, which is based and built up on conscious, appreciative and non-mechanical response to other personality or personalities:

"And recall what time (at the dawn of Creation and in the 'world of spirits') thy Lord took from the children of Adam[2] their

---

1. The emergence of individual human beings on the earth seems to have been designed to take place through a process of evolution covering countless stages of transformation and in the form of a series spread over a vast span of time, as different Qur'ãnic verses and the verdict of Muslim thinkers like Rumi affirms. (See: Iqbal's *Reconstruction of Religious Thought in Islam*, p. 115).

2. Adam and Eve have not been mentioned here, because they had already experienced intimate relation with God (II:31 ff).

posterity from their backs[3], and made them testify as to themselves, saying: 'Am I not your Lord?' They said: 'Yea we testify'[4]. (Thus was the Covenant of Monotheism inscribed on every human Soul). That was lest ye should say on the Day of Resurrection: verily of this we have been unaware." (VII:172).

Thus, because this event relates to the transcendental world and conditions of transcendental existence, the transcendental, or spiritual, nature of the original, *i.e.*, the real, human personality is thereby established.

This fact is further affirmed by the following verses:

"And they ask thee regarding the (human) Soul. Say thou: the Soul proceeds from my Lord's *Amr*, (or Command, Created by Him, like other things); and of knowledge ye have been vouchsafed but little. (Therefore, in spite of its intangibility, or non-physical character, do not doubt its reality)". (XVII:85).

"Surely there came over Man a period of Time when he was not a *thing that could be spoken of* (i.e., a thing tangible)". (LXXVI:1).

2. The earthly existence of every human being commences when the human Soul, whose original abode is the transcendental world, projects itself into spatio-temporal dimensions and takes on the physical form, even as the personalities of Adam and Eve were projected into the material world (II:36).[5]

The assumption, under the Command of God, of tangibility, *i.e.*, physical form and function, after passing through different stages of evolution, has been directly referred to thus:

"O Man! what hath made thee careless concerning thy Lord, the Bountiful?—Him Who created thee, then fashioned thee in due proportion, then wrought thee in symmetry: (then) into whatever *form* (*or, figure*) He willed, He constituted thee."[6] (LXXXII:6-8).

---

3. The world 'backs' should be understood in terms of transcendental existence.

4. Here, the fact should be kept in mind that in Qur'ãnic view of life, it is the Soul, and not any physiological mechanism, which is the real repository of Consciousness and they dynamo for Activity. Hence in respect of the verse under reference, the postulation of anything beside the Soul stands ruled out.

5. Quoted already.

6. There is a Qur'ãnic statement: "When I have made him and have breathed into him of My spirit...." (XV:29). It should be noted that the spirit mentioned here

3. Then, the human Soul, while retaining its transcendental dimension, *viz*., function and activity, and centred in devotion to its Source of Existence and Capabilities, namely God, of Whom it is the vicegerent (II:30), functions in four other dimensions also: namely, physical, rational, moral and aesthetical.

4. Thus: the spiritual, the physical, the rational, the moral and the aesthetical constitute the *five* dimensions of human personality, and activity relating to all these five *should be pursued in a balanced and integrated manner*, in order that the human personality may evolve and function in a healthy form on the basis of healthy activity (*al-'amal al-sãleh*):

"O ye who believe! enter into Submission *wholly* (*i.e*., adopt the Way of Life consisting of total submission to the Will of God with the totality of your life)." (II:208).

"For those who believe and practise *al-sãlihãt* (*i.e*., engage in healthy activity according to God's Law and with comprehensiveness and integration) is a reward that will never fail." (XLI:8).

"....and healthy (or, righteous) activity doth He exalt (thereby raising the practiser of healthy activity, or, righteousness, to higher and higher levels of his personality)". (XXXV:10)[7].

5. Moral activity being thus a part of an empire of Activity, which forms an organic Whole, it cannot be taken up with genuine and rational enthusiasm, and cannot be pursued consequentially—namely, cannot lead to the proper enrichment of the human personality—, unless it is grounded in the very foundation of human personality, which is spiritual in nature and transcendental in its reach and scope, and also unless all the other aspects of human activity are properly co-ordinated with it.

Such being the Qur'ãnic view, it is necessary that the Qur'ãnic Moral Code should be viewed not only in the essentially moral perspective but also in the background of those spiritual, physical, intellectual and aesthetical duties that have a direct or indirect bearing on the moral life of

---

is 'God's spirit', and not the human soul; and consequently this verse should not be understood as saying that God perfected first a soulless physical structure and then placed the soul in it. And 'the breathing of God's spirit' seems to stand for the bestowal of those extraordinary qualities that relate to the earthly and the cosmic mission of the human being in terms of the vicegerency of God.

7. *Cf.* Other Qur'ãnic verses relating to the importance of *healthy activity*.

a human being—moral life as it is conceived in the strict sense.

The above discussion leads us to the following five categories of Duties to Self:

A. Duties as Spiritual Being

1. *Duties with reference to God:*

(i) Duties of Commission; (ii) Duties of Omission.

2. *Duties with reference to the Holy Prophet (in whom God's Blessing and Peace abide!)*

(i) Duties of Commission; (ii) Duties of Omission.

3. *Duties with reference to the Angels:*

(i) Duties of Commission; (ii) Duties of Omission.

B. Duties as Physical Being

(a) Duties of Commission; (b) Duties of Omission.

C. Duties as Rational Being

(a) Duties of Commission; (b) Duties of Omission.

D. Duties as Aesthetical Being

(a) Duties of Commission; (b) Duties of Omission.

E. Duties as Moral Being

(a) Duties of Commission; (b) Duties of Omission.

The Spirituo-Moral Duties—Some Vital Facts

Among the Duties to Self, besides the duties based on the earthly environment of Man, the Holy Qur'ãn has explicitly prescribed certain duties which bear reference to the transcendental dimension of his personality and may, therefore, be termed as spirituo-moral, or, ethico-religious duties. It says, for instance:

"Virtue does not consist in turning your faces towards the east and the west (in direction-worship, which has formed part of the practices of superstitious nations, including the Greeks, the Hindus and the Christians), but virtue is of him who believes in Allah and the Last Day and the Angels and the Book (*i.e.*, the Divine Scriptures) and the Prophets; and gives of his wealth, for love of Him (*i.e.*, from the purest selfless motive), unto kindred and orphans and the needy and the wayfarer and those who ask and for the emancipation of slaves; and establishes Prayer; and pays the Poor-rate; and is of those who perform their covenants when they have covenanted; and is of the patient in adversity and affliction and time of violence. Such are those who have proved themselves true (in their Faith). Such are the god-fearing". (II:177).

Besides the essentially moral duties, this verse bears reference to the spirituo-moral duties also; which, though they appear to stand in the category of duties to Others, are actually duties to Self—as we shall shortly observe.

The function of such duties is to nourish the faith that the world is a Moral Order, thereby continuously reinforcing the moral fibre of human beings and furnishing the ground for moral struggle—indeed, *the sure* ground; and they are to three types of personalities, *viz.*, (i) God, (ii) the Holy Prophet Muhammad (Peace be on him!)[8], and (iii) the Angels. With them may also be mentioned the duties of belief in Divine Guidance and in the Life Hereafter.

Now, since the Holy Qur'ãn affirms the existence of the personal God, Who is the Possessor of all Perfection and Who undertakes to lead His creatures to perfection adequate to them, duties to Him become the foremost duties. However, those duties are, in the final analysis, duties to Self, because God being *al-samad* (CXII:2), He dose not stand in need of anything from anyone while the entire Creation depends on Him for everything. Moreover, God being the ultimate condition of the realisation of Man's moral ideal, every duty to God is really duty to Self.

Duties to the Holy Prophet Muhammad (the Divinely-Blessed) originate, like the duties to God, in the Islamic Article of Faith itself, and they have been laid down by the Qur'ãn in the interest of the Muslims themselves, because:

8. The Holy Qur'ãn has ordained that Muslim should *affirm* the Blessings of God on the Holy Prophet and should salute him (XXXIII:56). Hence, while mentioning his sacred name, a Muslim may proclaim the affirmation as, for instance, has been done on page xi, or may salute him—the standard form of Islamic salutation being in terms of the prayerful expression: 'Peace be on you', or, 'Peace be on him!' etc.

Firstly, he *alone* is the Leader who is to be followed *unconditionally*. Thus *the bond of loyalty to him is the bond of integrity of the Islamic world-community*.

[In that connection, it is necessary to emphasise that the 'bond of loyalty' to the Holy Prophet Muhammad (Peace be on him!) resides in *absolute allegiance* to him, which means that the association of anyone else in that allegiance as a condition of faith in Islam—in terms of conferring upon anyone, or accepting anyone's claim to, divinely bestowed Authority, on the basis of prophetic status or any status akin to it, in any sense whatsoever, so that disbelief in that person's status is regarded as disbelief in Islam itself, and that in spite of otherwise absolute allegiance to the Holy Prophet Muhammad (Peace be on him!)—expels a person from the fold of Islam in the same way as when he associates anyone in any manner in the Godhood of Allah.]

Secondly, he is the Model of Perfection whom every Muslim is under obligation to imitate for advancement in his spiritual and moral life. But to imitate him consequentially is not possible without practising love and respect for him, which has been prescribed as duty.

Thirdly, he is the Medium through whom Divine Grace flows to his followers[9] in respect of their spiritual and moral purification. (LXII:3-4).

---

9. In fact, as "Mercy unto the worlds" (XXI:107), he has been exalted by God to be the Medium of His Blessings in an immeasurably wider perspective. The unique position which he holds among all creatures has been unambiguously affirmed also in *hadîth* reported by the Holy Prophet's Companions Jãbir and upheld as authentic in Islamic history by eminent authorities, among whom may be mentioned, by way of example, one of the classical Qur'ãnic commentators, Allãma Alusi (*vide* his classical *Tafsîr*, the *Rûh al-Ma'ãnî*, vol. I, p. 51). It is to the effect: "Jãbir (Allah be pleased with him!) reports: I said: 'O Messenger of Allah! Inform me about the thing which Allah created before all (other) things. He replied: 'Verily, Allah, the Almighty, created before all (other) things the Light of thine Prophet through His Light....." [Quoted on the authority of *muhaddith* 'Abd al-Razzãq, (the eminent forerunner of Imam Bukhari and author of *Al-Musannaf*) by Allãma Yusuf b. Ismã'il al-Nabhãni, in *Al-Anwãr al-Muhammadiyyah min Mawãhib al-Ludunniyah*, p., 12 Beirut, 1310 A.H.]. The *hadîth* then proceeds to inform that the entire universe was created by God from the original created Light, which the luminaries of Islam have named as the '*Light of Muhammad*'. It may be pointed out that the statement made on the basis of the Qur'ãn on p. 289 (footnote) of the present volume, is corroborated by this *hadîth* (Relevant discussions in volume I in respect of the Holy Prophet's personality may also be referred to).

These facts necessitate the maintenance of a constant dutiful attitude in terms of love and respect for him.

However, just as duties to God are really duties to Sefl, because they involve the self-perfection of the moral agent, in the same manner duties to the Holy Prophet (Peace be on him!) are really duties to Self, because of the benefits that accrue to the person who fulfils them.

As regards the Angels, they are, according to the Holy Qur'ãn, possessors of the attribute of personality[10] (III:39; etc.). Also, they are sinless (=holy) beings and function as executors of Divine Will in the universe (LXVI:6). Thus, duties towards them[11] appear to stand under three categories, *viz.*, (i) duty of belief in their existence; (ii) duty of love for their sinlessness; and (iii) duty of respect for them as functionaries of the Divine Order.

The duty of belief in the existence of the angels forms a part of the Islamic Creed, which means that it has a basic significance in the Islamic system. The question might arise here, however, that moral duty is duty of action and not of belief, and hence the duty of belief should not be included here. But the fact is that the duty of belief in the angels is a duty of attitude and is actually a necessary prerequisite to the cultivation of purity in moral outlook on the basis of which alone moral life can be Islamically pursued. Thus it comes under the duty of the Moral Perfection of the Self. Also, this duty has a reference to Divine Control in the life of humanity, which highlights God's function as the Moral Ruler of the world.

We learn from the Holy Qur'ãn about two functions of the angels which bear a direct reference to our *moral* life, *viz.*, bringing the Revelations to the Prophets from God for the guidance of man—archangel Jibreel (Peace be on him!) being the chief functionary in this respect (XXII:75; II:97); and recording the deeds of human beings for presentation to them on the Day of Judgment (LXXXII:10-12), when virtue and vice shall be finally and comprehensively recompensed by God.

---

10. Mark that this bears reference to moral relationship, because morality consists in the attitude of one personality towards another. Also, it should be noted that the affirmation of personality in the angels does not imply anthropomorphism.

11. It may be emphasised that they are basically duties of attitude, and are not meant to be institutionalised.

It may be observed here in passing that belief in the Divine Messengers and the Divine Scriptures, mentioned in the above-quoted verse (II:177), and forming part of the Islamic Creed, bears reference to the existence of the Law concerning the Guidance of Man as a spiritual and moral being. Similarly, belief in the Life Hereafter has a bearing on the moral life of man, as also on his spiritual life, being the prerequisite to the performance of the moral action with the purest motive wherein all earthly considerations are transcended.

Before closing the discussion on the spirituo-moral duties, we might discuss the question, which can possibly arise in certain minds: Are those duties real and meaningful?

At the very outset, the answer is: They are, because, in the Qur'ãnic view of the cosmos, the transcendental plane of existence, or, the Spiritual Realm of the Cosmos, is not a fantasy, or jus a regulative Idea, but a fact—and, for that matter, *the basic fact*.

The materialists hold to a naturalistic view of the universe. The idealists affirm what might be termed as a psychicalistic view. The Holy Qur'ãn, in harmony with its integralistic approach and its philosophy of *Unity*, affirms the reality of both the realms of the cosmos, namely: (i) the realm governed by the Natural Law, or, the Spatio-Temporal level of Reality;—we may also call it the phenomenological level; (ii) the realm governed by the Metaphysical Law, or, the Spaceless-Timeless level of Reality. And it integrates both through the bond of the Unitary Divine Plan and Purpose, which has brought into existence both of them and maintains them within the framework of *Unity*.

Without going into the details of Qur'ãnic cosmology: God's relationship with the cosmos as its Creator emerges in the Qur'ãn at two levels, i.e., the levels of *al-Amr* and *al-Khalaq*,—both established and united under that Attribute of God which relates to cherishing, nourishing, evolving and perfecting, i.e., *al-Rubb*: ".....Lo! His is *al-Khalq* and *al-Amr*. Blessed is Allah the *Rabb* of the worlds (i.e., the entire cosmos.)". (VII:54).

Thus, the Creation began with God's *Amr*: "The Originator of the heavens and the earth; and whensoever He decrees an affair (*Amr*), He only says to it 'Be' and it *becomes*. (Hence the origination of the cosmos also took place as a result of Allah's Command 'Be')". (II:117). "His *Amr* (i.e., law of bringing something into existence is that when He intends a thing , He only says to it (by way of Command, or, *Amr*): 'Be'; and it *becomes*." (XXXVI:82).

Hence, the first stage in the creation of the cosmos should be affirmed in terms of 'Becoming'. We may also call it the stage of subtle existence, intangibility (as opposed to the tangibility of Matter), and spacelessness-cum-timelessness.

Looking at the process of creation in the background of the concept of evolution projected explicitly in the Qur'ãn, we arrive at the view of evolutionary creation, wherein—like the evolutionary hypothesis in modern Science—we are led to the affirmation of the '*Primeva Atom*' as the starting point, which functioned as the *nucleus* and out of which grew the entire cosmos through an evolutionary process;—even as we find it mentioned in the *hadîth* quoted in the foregoing page xx, wherein the concept of the 'First Created Light functioning as Nucleus' has been projected.

As for the nature of the evolutionary process, it should be conceived, in the very nature of the case, in terms of progressive decrease in subtlety, refinement, intangibility and qualitativeness, and progressive increase in respect of concreteness, crystallisation, tangibility and quantitativeness; on the basis of a progressive crystallisation of the process of *al-Khalaq*, which implies the creation of new objects from the existing materials. In other words, it must have been a progress towards more and more profound 'expression'. This is what we understand from the Qur'ãn as well as from Science.

Indeed, different things appear in the Qur'ãn to have emerged into dynamic existence at different stages of the evolutionary process. Thus, there existed the angels, the *jinns* and the human beings in that pre-physical, or, transcendental, dimension of existence; and, among them, the angels and the *jinns* were there prior to the existence of the human beings, as the Holy Qur'ãn testifies (II:30-34). Then, according to what we read in the holy book in plain terms, humanity was made to appear before God in her transcendental, or, pre-earthly, dimension of existence, to proclaim the Covenant of Monotheism (VII:172),—which means that human beings existed at that stage of Creation. Similarly, the event of the 'Covenant of the Prophets' has been mentioned therein to have occurred in that stage of Creation (III:81),—which proves the existence of the Prophets at that stage.

All this means that a Realm of Created Beings and Things became gradually established in respect of their essential or ideal nature, even in the first stage of creation. But evolution was to continue, and has continued, according to God's Plan. However, because "Allah has set a measure (or, a scale of growth and maturity—which enshrines its destiny) for every thing," (LXV:3), certain things that had emerged from potentiality into actuality, had to stay in the state they had acquired:—the angels, for instance; while others had to continue their evolutionary journey, finally emerging in the Spatio-Temporal Order of Existence:—the human beings, for instance.

However, we are not actually concerned here with the elaboration of the Qur'ãnic cosmology. Rather, the above discussion has been undertaken to emphasise the following facts:

(i) For the *formalistic* religious outlook, the world-view consists of certain dogmas, which are there to be believed in dogmatically, rather than to provide a dynamic, meaningful and comprehensive approach to the Spiritual Reality. Such an outlook is barren, and the Qur'ãn does not endorse it.

(ii) The *naturalistic* outlook confines itself to the Physical Reality, and it leads, even in the case of a believer in religion, to a materialistic approach to life and its problems—at least, for all practical purposes. The Qur'ãn also affirms the Physical Reality, giving a coherent and illuminating view of it—a view which is receiving increasing support from the world of Science as knowledge is advancing. However, it is conjoined therein to a clear-cut view of the Transcendental Reality—both the views forming thus one organic Whole.

(iii) The Qur'ãnic view that emerges thereby is an *Integralistic Spiritual View of the Universe*, wherein the spiritual, or, the transcendental, has primacy over the physical, or, the spatio-temporal, and which provides not merely a formal ground for religious life but a sound vision as well as philosophy for meaningfully *cultivating* a life dedicated to God and directed to the realisation of the ultimate human destiny, which is essentially spiritual,—that being the mission of Islam.

(iv) The essential human personality (*al-Rûh*), called 'the Soul' in common usage, belongs originally and basically to the Transcendental Realm of Existence.

The human being is, therefore, essentially a spiritual being, and should behave as such for his success.

(v) Not only God, but the entire spiritual world created by Him, is *responsive* to human spiritual quest. The spiritual quest, in its turn, is of vital importance for the human being because of the fact that he is *essentially* a spiritual being and, as such, *can build up his essential personality only through exercise in that response.*

(vi) The spiritual world plays the same role in the preservation and development of the essential human personality (which has been already emphasised time and again to be spiritual) as the physical world plays in respect of the physical aspect of human existence.

There are numerous things in the physical environment of the human being which contribute to his physical preservation and development,—they being of *different grades*, with the planet sun fulfilling the most basic role, and the others standing next in importance in a descending order of merit. Human beings have to remain in a state of contact and communication with them in order to benefit from them, or, in other words, to obtain the physical blessings placed in them by God.

Similarly, there are things of *different grades* in the spiritual world, on the Transcendental Realm, out of which the physical world has emerged and through which it is controlled by God. Those things contribute to the spiritual preservation and development of the human being,—and, because the spiritual is the essential, to his *essential* preservation and development. Among them, the role of the Holy Prophet's personality is most basic in respect of a Muslim's spiritual preservation and development; while the roles of the angels and the other spiritual things in Creation stand thereafter. Contact with the spiritual Blessings placed by God in the Holy Prophet's personality is obtained through the imitation of his *Sunnah*, with the ideal of acquiring greater and greater spiritual and moral purity, and the exercise in *Salãt* and *Salãm* with intense devotion; while contact with the Spiritual Blessings placed by God in the angels is obtained through leading a life of spiritual and moral purity and recitation of the Qur'ãn.

Then, just as in the physical world there are forces of physical destruction, or, forces of physical evil, similarly there are forces of spiritual destruction, or, forces of spiritual evil, that influence the spiritual life of human beings. The Qur'ãn has commanded the Muslims to avoid the former in the interest of their physical preservation, and to shun the latter for ensuring their spiritual preservation.

It is to be vehemently emphasised that Allah—and *none else*—is the Creator and the Bestower of all Blessings, whether physical or spiritual. But, *His Blessings flow to the human beings, not in a vacuum, but through the physical and the spiritual objects that He has created for that purpose.*

To confer divinity on any of those objects, even indirectly, is the worst form of infidelity to God; while to refuse to benefit from them is the worst form of ungratefulness to Him.

(vii) Communion with God, and communication, in terms of the establishment of spiritual contact, with the Holy Prophet (Peace be on him!), with the angels and with the spiritual verities in general, emerge, in the final analysis, as active sources of light and energy for the meaningful pursuit of Religion, in contrast to adherence to religious verities in lifeless formalism. In consequence, 'Duties to the Holy Prophet' and 'Duties to the Angels' assume vital importance for the spiritual development of a Muslim's personality.

Finally, we may recall what Dr. Sir Muhammad Iqbal, the Rumi of the modern age and the greatest Islamic thinker of the present century of Islamic era, said more than four decades ago: "Humanity needs three things today—a spiritual interpretation of the universe, spiritual emancipation of the individual, and basic principles of a universal import directing the evolution of human society on a spiritual basis. Modern Europe has, no doubt, built idealistic systems on these lines; but experience shows that truth revealed through pure reason is incapable of bringing that fire of living conviction which personal revelation alone can bring. This is the reason why pure thought has so little influenced men while religion has always elevated individuals, and transformed whole societies. The idealism of Europe never became a living factor in her life, and the result is a perverted ego seeking itself through mutually intolerant democracies whose sole function is to exploit the poor in the interests of the rich. Believe me, Europe today is the greatest hindrance in the way of man's ethical development."

Unfortunately, the formalistic religious outlook that has emerged among the Muslims in the present age of their spiritual, moral and overall degeneration, has been progressively leading to the unconscious acceptance of the naturalistic and, for all practical purposes, materialistic, view of the human being as a mere 'superior animal', to the forgetfulness of the fact that he is essentially—namely, in his origin, being and destiny—a 'spiritual being, whose nature was created by God, according to the explicit and unambiguous verdict of the Qur'ãn, in terms of His vicegerency through the infusion of what He names as 'My spirit' (*rûh*) (XV:29; etc.), and to the view of the angels as mere "forces of Nature"—in the sense of naturalistic forces. In such a view of the human being and of the angels, very naturally the Holy Prophet is also regarded as nothing more than a 'good man', a 'great leader' and a 'divine postman'; and any description of the transcendental dimension of his august personality appears to the upholders of that view as nothing less than superstition, even though they overthrow in this process of thinking the spiritual foundations of the Qur'ãnic world-view which the profoundest Islamic theological thinkers down to Shah Waliullah took the greatest pains to preserve during the ages that have elapsed since the Qur'ãnic Revelation.

Duties to Animals, Plants and Things—as Duties to Self:

We may also refer here to duties towards animals, plants, and things, to which the Holy Qur'ãn has referred implicitly while in the *Hadith* they have been mentioned explicitly. They seem to fall under the category of duties to Others. But they are basically duties to Self in so far as they relate to the maintenance of the purity of our moral tone. They have, therefore, been dealt with in the Appendix to the 'Duties to Self'.

III. Duties to Others

The obligatoriness of duties to Others is to be conceived in their two-fold origin: (i) in human shortcomings at the different stages of life, which necessitate assistance by other human beings; and (ii) in the inherent social nature of human life[12]. Indeed, the individual and the society are

12. Says Aristotle: "He who is unable to live in society, or who has no need because he is sufficient for himself, must be either a beast or a god." (*Politics*, Bk. 1, Ch. 2).

mutually related and interdependent, and the individual's realisation of moral good is not conceivable, according to the Qur'ãnic view, without reference to the societal whole.

Now, viewing the human personality in its two basic aspects, *i.e.*, the empirical and the rational, duties to Others split up into two categories *with regards to the ends that they should serve*,—namely: (i) Duties relating to 'Happiness', or, Material Well-being; (ii) Duties relating to 'Moral Perfection'—meant actually to ensure Spiritual and Moral Preservation and Advancement.

Viewed with reference to those who are to be served by these duties, two basic categories emerge, namely: (i) Individualistic duties, or, duties to other individuals as individuals; (ii) Collectivistic duties, or, duties relating to the Societal Whole.

As regards 'Duties to Other Individuals', they may be viewed basically in two perspectives: (i) other individuals in general, and (ii) other individuals as related to the moral agent through specified functional relationships. Then, the other individuals may be Muslims—and that would form the primary reference—, and as such they have to be treated as members of the Islamic social order. Also, there may be—in fact, there are—the non-Muslims who, in the first instance, cannot be regarded properly as members of the Islamic social order, even though they may be living in an Islamic state; and, secondly, there may be among them persons belonging to different categories: for example: (i) non-Muslims who are friendly towards Muslims and tolerent towards Islam; (ii) non-Muslims who are simply indifferent to Muslims and Islam; and (iii) non-Muslims who are hostile to Muslims and Islam.

Islam prescribes duties towards all the above categories of other individuals, laying down certain duties that are based on the concept that all human beings have ertain inviolable rights as human beings and that absolute justice must be practised towards all; and giving another set of duties, in addition, relating to the specified areas of relationships.

IV. Duties Relating to the Societal Whole

Duties relating to the Societal Whole split up into two categories, namely: (i) Duties *to* the Societal Whole; and (ii) Duties *of* the Societal Whole.

With reference to *Duties to the Societal Whole*, the Holy Qur'ãn has commanded thus:

"And hold fast, all together, by the Convenant of Allah (*habl-Allah*), and be not split up among yourselves". (III:103).

The word *habl*, translated here as Covenant, means primarily a rope or a cord, and hence a cause of union or a Covenant which renders one responsible for the safety of a person or a thing. (Lane's *Lexicon*).

The *habl-Allah* (Covenant with God) is, abstractly, allegiance to the objectives of *al-Din*, or, the Way of Collective Obedience to God, and, concretely, loyalty to the Islamic Society through loyalty and devotion to its Founder and Leader, the Holy Prophet Muhammad (Peace be on him!), which loyalty should manifest itself basically in doing utmost to preserve the unity, the solidarity and the social, moral and spiritual health of the Islamic society. Hence the *Duties to the Societal Whole*.

Similarly, the *Duties of the Societal Whole* towards the Individual have been emphasised in the Holy Qur'ãn; for instance, in the following verse which bears comprehensive reference to the spiritual, economic, moral and social welfare of the individuals:

"(Mulsims are) those who, if We establish them in the land, set up regular Prayer and give regular charity, enjoin what is right and forbid what is wrong...." (XXII:41).

Now, every organised Societal Whole takes, whenever and wherever possible, the form of the State, which, as an institution, is an indispensable means for the realisation of the social ideal. As regards its structural ethics, the following observations may be made.

Organisation of the Societal Whole as a state gives rise to subordination and superordination, wherein the foremost duty of the subordinate becomes obedience to the superordinate (IV:59) and of the superordinate to administer the state through coercive authority, or, *al-Amãrah* (mentioned in IV:59),—and that in the interest of the subordinate.[13] Also, besides the multifarious dimensions of positive administration, the duty of punishing offenders for all cognisable

13. It may be emphasised here that the greater the selflessness and sacrifice which the super-ordinate imposes on itself, the stronger will it be in wielding its authority; and the more the vested interests it creates, the weaker will be its authority. The Holy Prophet (Peace be on him!) set a perfect example of selflessness and the elimination of all forms of vested interests by: (1) banning the payment of *Zakãt* to his progeny; (ii) avoiding the giving of key posts to his kith and kin during his regime as head of the Islamic state; and (iii) keeping open to all Muslims the office of the head of the state for all time after his demise.

offences against life, honour, property, and ensuring the spiritual, moral and economic well-being of the people, also devolves on the superordinate. Then, a further duty of the superordinate is that of preserving or reclaiming, as the case may be, the autonomy of the state against internal turmoil and external aggression, and for that purpose to wage war against all hostile forces.

An important fact should be noted here with respect to the State Authority. The Holy Prophet Muhammad (Peace be on him!) is the founder of the Islamic society, as also of the Islamic state. As such, and as the Medium of Obediecne to God—indeed, as the representative *par excellence* of the Authority of God on earth, he is the Super-Leader of the Islamic state *for all time* (IV:80; etc.). Hence no State Authority can claim Islamically the right of obedience to itself except as the *representative* of the Holy Prophet (Peace be on him!)[14]

Note on Penal Code:

In the perspective of the superordinate's duty of punishing offenders of the Law, mentioned in the foregoing, emerges the *Penal Code*, to which we have devoted a separate section. As to the Qur'ãnic *Philosophy of Punishment*, readers should refer to Volume I, Book II, Chapter IV, of the present book, where we have come to the following conclusion:

"Viewing the Qur'ãnic punishments in the light of ethics, the punishments relating to fornication, adultery and homosexuality are reformative in the sense that they imply the spiritual purification of the offenders; the punishments prescribed for theft, dacoity and treason are of deterrent character; and the punishment in respect of murder is based on retribution which is tempered with mercy (II:178). The guiding light in all cases, however, is the procurement of spiritual good of the individuals concerned and of the society."

Note on Tabligh[15]:

The word *tabligh* means 'to reach out the Message' As a term it means 'propagation of the Message of Islam'.

The Holy Qur'ãn has given to it the status of an institution (III:104; etc.) and has ordained it as an important *societal duty*.

---

14. This truth is borne out by the fact that the first Caliph, Abu Bakr, and all other Caliphs after him, have called themselves *Khalîfatur-Rasûlillãh* (Vicegerent of the Messenger of God) and not *Khalifatillãh* (Vicegerent of God).

15. Also written as '*tableegh*'.

This duty has been conceived to function at two levels, *i.e.*, within the Islamic social order, and outside the Islamic social order, where entire humanity comes under its purview.

The ends it serves are: (i) preservation, (ii) development, and (iii) perpetuation of the Islamic Community—and that in service to the cause of humanity (III:110).

The dimension of this duty are:

(i) education of new generations of Muslims in Islam;

(ii) improvement in Islamic knowledge and inspiration of the grown-up Muslims;

(iii) dissemination of the knowledge of Islam among non-Muslims—all the non-Muslims of the world wherever they may be found—in order that they may know the Divine Message that has come for them, and those among them who are seriously dedicated to Truth may accept it for their own good; while, in the case of others, correct knowledge about Islam may dissipate their ignorance and the consequent misunderstandings, finally bringing about among them goodwill for Islam—which, in itself, forms a genuine contribution to the promotion of intercommunal and international goodwill.

Thus, *tabligh* stands out as a duty towards other individuals in respect of their spiritual and moral progress.

Also, it contributes simultaneously to the spiritual and moral development of the persons who undertake it, and thus it becomes a duty to Self.

Its role, however, as a collectivistic or societal duty, remains supreme. Indeed, from that point of view, it stands out as the foremost duty without which the very existence of Islam becomes jeopardised.

As the Holy Qur'ãn affirms, the Islamic Community is meant to continue to exist for all time—up to the Last Day. This is in the very nature of the case, because the Holy Prophet Muhammad (Peace be on him!) is the last and final Divine Messenger, and the Muslims are the last divinely raised religious Group. As such, disappearance of the Islamic Community at any time in human history is not conceivable. But, the dissipation of the energies of communities and nations—both ideological and non-ideological—being the Law of History, one of the most important instruments for keeping the Islamic community alive and functioning genuinely and truly is the repeated infusion of fresh blood into the body politic of Islam. This has already happened in Islamic history, as, for instance, when towards the end of the Abbaside period, the Muslim world began to show signs of lassitude and weakness, the conversion of the Turko-Tartars revitalised the Islamic community to an extent that it could maintain its glory for several centuries more. The same seems to be the crying need today. But this need cannot be fulfilled without resort to an *enlightened, dynamic and multidimensional* movement in the field of *tabligh,* and *not just a ritualistic or professional performance.*

V. Manners[16]

Manners may be defined as apparent modes of behaviour in relation to others, and may be evaluated as small coins of virtue.

The Qur'ãnic point of view, as emphasised already, is social. Consequently, in the Qur'ãnic moral code we find as much emphasis on manners as on morals; perhaps more, because indifference to manners may nullify a virtue itself. This is evident from the Qur'ãnic emphasis on the manners to be observed in the performance of one of the highest virtues in relation to others, *viz.*, charity:

"O ye who believe! make not your charity worthless by laying obligation and by hurt..." (II:264).

It is also evident from what has been said in connection with the manners to be observed in the presence of the Holy Prophet Muhammad (Peace be on him!):

"O ye who believe! raise not your voices above the voice of the Prophet, nor speak aloud to him in talk as ye may speak aloud to one another, lest your (good) deeds becomes vain and ye perceive not". (XLIX:2).

Coming to classification: In conformity with the comprehensive nature of the Qur'ãnic moral code, the Qur'ãnic duties in respect of manners belong to two categories: (i) those relating to religious manners, and (ii) those relating to social manners.

---

16. "Conduct may include inward activities like motives and desires as well as outward activities like speech and movements of the doer's limbs, and so these also will fall within the sphere of ethics. We so commonly think of these as causing outward bodily movements that we forget that they too are activities and liable to be judged good or bad even apart from the outward movements they produce." (W. Lillie: *Introduction to Ethics*, p. 4).

Book I

DUTIES TO SELF

Part I

DUTIES AS SPIRITUAL BEING

Part II

DUTIES AS PHYSICAL BEING

Part III

DUTIES AS RATIONAL BEING

Part IV

DUTIES AS AESTHETICAL BEING

Part V

DUTIES AS MORAL BEING

Part I

DUTIES AS SPIRITUAL BEING

Chapter I

DUTIES WITH REFERENCE TO GOD

(1) Duties of Respect; (2) Duties of Love

END:

(a) *Objective:*

Maintenance of a constant attitude of Respect and Love towards God for acquiring the Blessings of Divine Pleasure (*Ridwãn Allah*) and Divine Love (*Hubb Allah*).

as it has been said in the Holy Qur'ãn:

يَبْتَغُونَ فَضْلًا مِّنَ اللّٰهِ وَرِضْوَانًا

"....seeking Grace from Allah and (His) Good Pleasure...."
(XLVIII:29).

Also:

يُحِبُّهُمْ وَيُحِبُّونَهُ

"....whom He will love and they will love Him....." (V:57).

(b) *Subjective:*

Creating in the moral agent:

(i) purity of will, leading to possible 'holiness' in the measure it may relate to human personality, as it has been said:

وَمَنْ يُّؤْمِنْ بِاللّٰهِ يَهْدِ قَلْبَهٗ

" And whosoever believeth in Allah, He guideth his heart (aright)." (LXIV:11).

(ii) stability in, and enthusiasm for, the pursuit of moral

struggle, as we are told:

فَمَنْ يَّكْفُرْ بِالطَّاغُوْتِ وَيُؤْمِنْ بِاللّٰهِ فَقَدِ اسْتَمْسَكَ بِالْعُرْوَةِ الْوُثْقٰى
لَا انْفِصَامَ لَهَا ۚ وَاللّٰهُ سَمِيْعٌ عَلِيْمٌ ۝

".....And he who rejecteth false deities and believeth in Allah hath grasped a firm handhold which will never break. Allah is Hearer, Knower." (II:256).

(1) Duties of Respect

(a) *Duties of Commission*

(i) Cultivation of genuine and complete Faith in God and its inner realisation enjoined:

يٰٓاَيُّهَا الَّذِيْنَ اٰمَنُوْٓا اٰمِنُوْا بِاللّٰهِ وَرَسُوْلِهٖ وَالْكِتٰبِ الَّذِيْ نَزَّلَ عَلٰى
رَسُوْلِهٖ وَالْكِتٰبِ الَّذِيْٓ اَنْزَلَ مِنْ قَبْلُ ۚ وَمَنْ يَّكْفُرْ بِاللّٰهِ وَمَلٰٓئِكَتِهٖ وَكُتُبِهٖ
وَرُسُلِهٖ وَالْيَوْمِ الْاٰخِرِ فَقَدْ ضَلَّ ضَلٰلًا بَعِيْدًا ۝

"O ye who believe! believe (with all the richness of belief) in Allah[1] and His Messenger, and the Scripture which He hath sent to His Messenger and the Scripture which He sent to those before (him). And who denieth Allah, His Angels, His Books, His Messengers and the Day of Judgment, hath gone far far astray."[2] (IV:136).

(ii) Faith in the Unity of God—perfect monotheism—implying indivisible

---

1. The word "Allah", which is employed for the 'One True God' in Islamic terminology, is regarded as untranslatable in orthodox Muslim thought. Hence, while using the word God normally, I have avoided substituting it for "Allah" in quoting the Qur'ānic verses.

2. Mark that belief in God is meaningless without:

(a) having faith in Him in accordance with what He has revealed about His Essence and His Attributes; and

(b) having faith in all the verities implied by the belief in Him.

It may also be noted that, according to the Holy Qur'ān, belief in religious verities mentioned in the above verse is fruitless unless the possessor of that belief earns good by performing deeds of righteousness. (VI:158).

loyalty to Him, enjoined:

ذٰلِكُمُ اللّٰهُ رَبُّكُمْ ۚ لَآ اِلٰهَ اِلَّا هُوَ ۚ خَالِقُ كُلِّ شَيْءٍ فَاعْبُدُوْهُ ۚ

"That is Allah, your Lord! There is no God but He, the Creator of all things: then worship ye Him (alone)." (VI:102).

فَاِلٰهُكُمْ اِلٰهٌ وَّاحِدٌ فَلَهٗٓ اَسْلِمُوْا ۗ

".....and your God is One God, so unto Him submit (wholly and solely)." (XXII:34).

(iii) Maintenance of the attitude of respect for God enjoined:

اِنَّ الَّذِيْنَ اٰمَنُوْا وَعَمِلُوا الصّٰلِحٰتِ وَاَخْبَتُوْٓا اِلٰى رَبِّهِمْ ۙ اُولٰٓئِكَ اَصْحٰبُ
الْجَنَّةِ ۚ هُمْ فِيْهَا خٰلِدُوْنَ ○

"Verily those who believe and work righteousness, and *humble themselves before their Lord,* they will be Companions of the Garden, to dwell therein for aye." (XI:23).

(iv) Cultivation of the fear of Displeasure of God and of the Final Accountability by Him, enjoined:

يٰٓاَيُّهَا الَّذِيْنَ اٰمَنُوا اتَّقُوا اللّٰهَ حَقَّ تُقٰتِهٖ وَلَا تَمُوْتُنَّ اِلَّا وَاَنْتُمْ
مُّسْلِمُوْنَ ○

"O ye who believe! fear Allah[3] as He should be feared, and die not save as those who have surrendered (unto Him)." (III:102).

---

3. Fear of God is a necessary condition of our spiritual and moral development because fear is a vital element of respect. Again, fear of God does not relate to any inimical revenge from His side, but it is fear of being disowned by Him, as we read in the Holy Qur'ãn:

وَقِيْلَ الْيَوْمَ نَنْسٰىكُمْ كَمَا نَسِيْتُمْ لِقَآءَ يَوْمِكُمْ هٰذَا

"It will be said (on the Day of Judgment): 'This Day We will forget you as ye forgot the meeting of this Day of yours!' (XLV:34).

Still again, it is the fear of Him who is 'Most Beneficent' and 'Most Merciful' (1:1, etc., etc.).

إِنَّمَا ذَٰلِكُمُ الشَّيْطَٰنُ يُخَوِّفُ أَوْلِيَآءَهُۥ فَلَا تَخَافُوهُمْ وَخَافُونِ إِن كُنتُم مُّؤْمِنِينَ ۝

"It is only the devil that suggests to you the fear of his votaries: Be ye not afraid of them, but fear Me, if ye have faith." (III:175).

إِلَّا الَّذِينَ ظَلَمُوا مِنْهُمْ فَلَا تَخْشَوْهُمْ وَاخْشَوْنِي

".....except those that are bent on wickedness; so fear them not, but fear Me....." (II:150).

وَأَمَّا مَنْ خَافَ مَقَامَ رَبِّهِۦ وَنَهَى النَّفْسَ عَنِ الْهَوَىٰ ۝ فَإِنَّ الْجَنَّةَ هِيَ الْمَأْوَىٰ ۝

"And for such as had entertained the fear of standing before their Lord's (tribunal) (on the Day of Judgment)[4] and had restrained (their) souls from lower Desires, their Abode will be the Garden." (LXXIX:40, 41).

(v) Cultivation of Obedience to God enjoined:

يَٰٓأَيُّهَا الَّذِينَ آمَنُوٓا أَطِيعُوا اللَّهَ

"O ye who believe! Obey Allah...."[5] (IV:59).

يَٰٓأَيُّهَا الَّذِينَ آمَنُوا اسْتَجِيبُوا لِلَّهِ وَلِلرَّسُولِ إِذَا دَعَاكُمْ لِمَا يُحْيِيكُمْ

"O ye who believe! Give your response to (i.e., obey) Allah and His Messenger, when He calleth you to that which will give you life;...."[6] (VIII:24).

وَقُومُوا لِلَّهِ قَٰنِتِينَ ۝

".....and stand before Allah in a devout (frame of mind)."[7] (II:238).

---

4. This is connected with the Islamic article of faith relating to belief in the Last Day—the Day of Final Accountability and of receiving final reward and punishment—emphasised over and again in the Holy Qur'ãn.

5,6,7. The words *tã'ah* and *istijãbah* and *qanût* used in the first, second and third verses respectively—all of them denote obedience. But *tã'ah* and *istijãbah* seem to emphasise *external* conformity to God's commands, while *qanût* seems to emphasise the *inwardness*, the purity of the heart—the Will—in submission to God.

وَأَنِيبُوا إِلَىٰ رَبِّكُمْ وَأَسْلِمُوا لَهُ مِنْ قَبْلِ أَنْ يَأْتِيَكُمُ الْعَذَابُ ثُمَّ لَا تُنْصَرُونَ ۝

"Turn unto your Lord repentant, and *surrender* unto *Him*, before there cometh unto you the torment, and then ye shall not be helped."[8] (XXXIX:54).

يَا أَيُّهَا النَّاسُ اعْبُدُوا رَبَّكُمُ الَّذِي خَلَقَكُمْ وَالَّذِينَ مِنْ قَبْلِكُمْ لَعَلَّكُمْ
تَتَّقُونَ ۝

"O mankind! worship your Lord,[9] Who hath created you and those before you, so that ye may ward off (evil)."[10] (II:21).

(vi) Cultivation of trust in God's goodness, mercy and help enjoined:

أَمَّنْ هُوَ قَانِتٌ آنَاءَ اللَّيْلِ سَاجِدًا وَقَائِمًا يَحْذَرُ الْآخِرَةَ وَيَرْجُو رَحْمَةَ
رَبِّهِ ۗ قُلْ هَلْ يَسْتَوِي الَّذِينَ يَعْلَمُونَ وَالَّذِينَ لَا يَعْلَمُونَ ۗ إِنَّمَا يَتَذَكَّرُ
أُولُو الْأَلْبَابِ ۝

Mark also that the "devout frame of mind" should be eternally maintained by every Muslim. (III:17; XXXIII:35).

8. In another verse total submission to Allah has been emphasised:

بَلَىٰ مَنْ أَسْلَمَ وَجْهَهُ لِلَّهِ وَهُوَ مُحْسِنٌ فَلَهُ أَجْرُهُ عِنْدَ رَبِّهِ وَلَا خَوْفٌ عَلَيْهِمْ وَلَا هُمْ
يَحْزَنُونَ ۝

"Nay,—whoever submits his whole self to Allah and is a doer of good, he will get the reward with his Lord; on such shall be no fear nor shall they grieve." (II:112).

9. and Him alone:

وَقَضَىٰ رَبُّكَ أَلَّا تَعْبُدُوا إِلَّا إِيَّاهُ

"Thy Lord hath decreed that ye worship none but Him,...." (XVII:23).

10. The Holy Qur'ān demands not merely formal obedience but obedience with all one's heart and it demands not obedience in certain matters only—as is demanded in the Christian maxim: "Give unto God what is God's and unto Caesar what is Caesar's"—but total surrender, surrender of the whole self and surrender with indivisible loyalty to God. Indeed, a Muslim's attitude towards God should be that of worship, in which his role is that of a humble slave only.

"Is one who worships devoutly during the hours of night prostrating himself or standing (in adoration), who takes heed of the Hereafter, and who places his hope in the Mercy of his Lord—(like one who does not)? Say: 'Are those equal, those who know and those who do not know? It is those who are endued with understanding that receive admonition."
(XXXIX:9).

إِنَّ الَّذِينَ آمَنُوا وَالَّذِينَ هَاجَرُوا وَجَاهَدُوا فِي سَبِيلِ اللَّهِ أُولَٰئِكَ
يَرْجُونَ رَحْمَتَ اللَّهِ ۚ وَاللَّهُ غَفُورٌ رَحِيمٌ ○

"Lo! those who believe and those who suffer exile (in defence of Truth) and strive struggle in the path of Allah, they (i.e., such true Muslims) have hope of Allah's mercy; and Allah is Oft - Forgiving, Most Merciful."
(II:218).

Then, there is the command:

وَعَلَى اللَّهِ فَتَوَكَّلُوا إِنْ كُنْتُمْ مُؤْمِنِينَ ○

".....and on Allah (i.e., in Allah's goodness, mercy and help) put your trust if ye are believers."
(V:26).

(vii) Affirmation of one's dependence on God: Prayer to Him, enjoined:

وَقَالَ رَبُّكُمُ ادْعُونِي أَسْتَجِبْ لَكُمْ ۚ إِنَّ الَّذِينَ يَسْتَكْبِرُونَ عَنْ عِبَادَتِي
سَيَدْخُلُونَ جَهَنَّمَ دَاخِرِينَ ○

"And your Lord hath said: Call on Me, I will answer your prayer. Verily those who are stiff-necked against My worship (i.e., against acknowledging Me as their Lord and Benefactor), will enter hell in humiliation."
(XL:60).

ادْعُوا رَبَّكُمْ تَضَرُّعًا وَخُفْيَةً ۚ إِنَّهُ لَا يُحِبُّ الْمُعْتَدِينَ ○

"Call on your Lord with humility and in secret: Lo! Allah loveth not those who trespass beyond (rational and respectful) limits." (VII:55).

وَادْعُوهُ خَوْفًا وَطَمَعًا ۚ إِنَّ رَحْمَتَ اللَّهِ قَرِيبٌ مِنَ الْمُحْسِنِينَ ○

".....and call on Him with fear and longing (in your hearts): for the Mercy of Allah is (always) near to those who do good (to others)."
(VII:56).

(viii) Seeking Help and Grace from God, the Possessor and the Source of all Power, enjoined:

Says the Holy Qur'ãn:

اسْتَعِينُوا بِاللَّهِ

".....seek help from Allah....." (VII:128).

Now, help should be sought basically from God alone. Muslims have been commanded to pray to God in these words:

إِيَّاكَ نَعْبُدُ وَإِيَّاكَ نَسْتَعِينُ ۝

"Thee (alone) do we worship, and of Thee (alone) do we seek help." (I:5).

Again:

وَسْئَلُوا اللَّهَ مِنْ فَضْلِهِ

"And ask Allah of His Grace....." (IV:32).

And this seeking of Grace from God is a constant attribute of the life of a Muslim:

تَرَاهُمْ رُكَّعًا سُجَّدًا يَبْتَغُونَ فَضْلًا مِّنَ اللَّهِ وَرِضْوَانًا

"Thou will see them bow and prostrate themselves (in prayer) seeking Grace from Allah and (His) Good pleasure....." (XLVIII:29).

(ix) Seeking Guidance from God, the Possessor and Source of all Knowledge, enjoined:

It is a duty of every Muslim to pray to God for guidance in the following words:

اهْدِنَا الصِّرَاطَ الْمُسْتَقِيمَ ۝

"Guide us Thou (O Allah) unto the path straight....." (I:6).

(x) Following the Divine Guidance revealed in the Holy Qur'ãn, enjoined:

اتَّبِعُوا مَا أُنْزِلَ إِلَيْكُمْ مِّنْ رَّبِّكُمْ

"Follow the Revelation given unto you (in the Holy Qur'ãn) from your Lord....." (VII:3).

(xi) Showing respect to God by believing in all the Messengers and all the Scriptures sent by Him for the guidance of man, enjoined:

فَاٰمِنُوْا بِاللّٰهِ وَرُسُلِهٖ

"So believe in Allah and (all) His Messengers." (III:179).

وَالَّذِيْنَ يُؤْمِنُوْنَ بِمَآ اُنْزِلَ اِلَيْكَ وَمَآ اُنْزِلَ مِنْ قَبْلِكَ

"(Muslims are those) who believe in the Revelation sent to thee (O Muhammad), and that which was sent before thee....." (II:4).

(b) <u>*Duties of Omission*</u>:

(i) Attributing any quality to God which is profane and blasphemous, prohibited:

وَلِلّٰهِ الْاَسْمَآءُ الْحُسْنٰى فَادْعُوْهُ بِهَا ۖ وَذَرُوا الَّذِيْنَ يُلْحِدُوْنَ
فِيْٓ اَسْمَآئِهٖ ۗ سَيُجْزَوْنَ مَا كَانُوْا يَعْمَلُوْنَ ۝

"The most excellent Names belong to Allah: so call on Him by them; and shun the company[11] (and the blasphemies) of those who use profanity in His names. They will be requited what they do." (VII:180).

(ii) Associating any partner with God and limiting His uniqueness and supremacy in any manner, prohibited:

وَاعْبُدُوا اللّٰهَ وَلَا تُشْرِكُوْا بِهٖ شَيْـًٔا

"And worship Allah and associate not aught with Him (either in His Person or in His Attributes). (IV:36).

وَلَا تَدْعُ مَعَ اللّٰهِ اِلٰهًا اٰخَرَ ۘ لَآ اِلٰهَ اِلَّا هُوَ

"And call not, besides Allah, on another god. There is no god but He....." (XXVIII:88).

---

11. Mark here that not only their blasphemies but even their company is to be shunned.

(iii) Saying anything concerning God without the authority of Revelation, prohibited:

قُلْ إِنَّمَا حَرَّمَ رَبِّيَ الْفَوَاحِشَ مَا ظَهَرَ مِنْهَا وَمَا بَطَنَ وَالْإِثْمَ وَالْبَغْيَ
بِغَيْرِ الْحَقِّ وَأَنْ تُشْرِكُوا بِاللَّهِ مَا لَمْ يُنَزِّلْ بِهِ سُلْطَانًا وَأَنْ تَقُولُوا عَلَى اللَّهِ
مَا لَا تَعْلَمُونَ ○

"Say: The things that my Lord hath indeed forbidden are: shameful deeds, whether open or secret; sins and trespasses against truth or reason; assigning of partners to Allah, for which ye are given no authority: and *saying about Allah of which ye have no knowledge*."
(VII:33).

(iv) Disobedience to and arrogance in respect of God, prohibited:

وَهُمْ لَا يَسْتَكْبِرُونَ ○

".....and they (i.e., the Believers) are not arrogant (in respect of worshipping Allah)." (XXXII:15).

وَأَمَّا مَنْ بَخِلَ وَاسْتَغْنَىٰ ○ وَكَذَّبَ بِالْحُسْنَىٰ ○ فَسَنُيَسِّرُهُ لِلْعُسْرَىٰ ○

"But he who is a greedy miser and *deemeth himself free from need* (*of Allah*), and gives the lie to the Best (i.e., dishonours Truth), We will indeed make for him smooth the Path to Misery." (XCII:8-10).

Again:

وَمَنْ يَعْصِ اللَّهَ وَرَسُولَهُ فَقَدْ ضَلَّ ضَلَالًا مُبِينًا ○

"If anyone disobeys (the Commands of) Allah and His Messenger, he is indeed on a clearly wrong Path." (XXXIII:36).

(v) Despairing of the Mercy of God prohibited:

وَلَا تَيْأَسُوا مِنْ رَوْحِ اللَّهِ ۖ إِنَّهُ لَا يَيْأَسُ مِنْ رَوْحِ اللَّهِ
إِلَّا الْقَوْمُ الْكَافِرُونَ ○

".....and *never give up hope of Allah's Soothing Mercy*: truly no one despairs of Allah's Soothing Mercy except those who have no Faith."
(XII:87).

قُلْ يٰعِبَادِيَ الَّذِينَ أَسْرَفُوا عَلٰى أَنْفُسِهِمْ لَا تَقْنَطُوا مِنْ رَحْمَةِ اللّٰهِ ۚ إِنَّ اللّٰهَ
يَغْفِرُ الذُّنُوبَ جَمِيعًا ۚ إِنَّهُ هُوَ الْغَفُورُ الرَّحِيمُ ○

"Say: 'O My Servants who have transgressed against their souls! despair not of the Mercy of Allah, for Allah forgiveth all sins: verily He is Oft-Returning, Most Merciful." (XXXIX:53).

(vi) Believing in superstitions and seeking help from superstitious objects, thereby indirectly insulting God,[12] prohibited:

فَاجْتَنِبُوا الرِّجْسَ مِنَ الْأَوْثَانِ

".....so shun the abomination of idols (i.e., evils of idolatrous practices)....." (XXII:30).

يٰٓأَيُّهَا الَّذِينَ آمَنُوٓا إِنَّمَا الْخَمْرُ وَالْمَيْسِرُ وَالْأَنْصَابُ وَالْأَزْلَامُ رِجْسٌ
مِنْ عَمَلِ الشَّيْطٰنِ فَاجْتَنِبُوهُ لَعَلَّكُمْ تُفْلِحُونَ ○

"O ye who believe! Intoxicants and games of chance (i.e., all forms of gambling), *and stone altars*[13] *and* (*divination by*) *arrows*[14], are an abomination,—of Satans' handiwork: shun it therefore, that ye may prosper." (V:93).

---

12. It may be noted that anyone who indulges in superstitions insults also his own dignity as a human being.

13. The stone altars were objects of superstitious worship in pre-Islamic Arabia. Oil was poured on them for consecration. They were also used for sacrifices to idols. Says Robertson Smith: "In Arabia, where sacrifice by fire is almost unknown, we find no proper altar, but in its place a rude pillar or heap of stones, besides which the victim is slain, the blood being poured out over the stone or its base.....The sacred stones.....are called *ansãb*, i.e., stones set up, pillars." (*Religion of the Semites*, p. 281).

14. Divination by arrows was a superstitious practice prevalent among the pre-Islamic Arabs. *Zalam* is "an arrow without a head and without feather: plural *Azlãm*, which was applied to those arrows by means of which the Arabs in the time of ignorance sought to know that which was allotted to them; .....and they put them in a receptacle, and when any of them desired to make a journey, or to accomplish a want, or when he desired to perform some affairs, he put his hand into that receptacle, and took forth an arrow; and if the arrow upon which was

مَا جَعَلَ اللّٰهُ مِنْ بَحِيْرَةٍ وَّلَا سَآئِبَةٍ وَّلَا وَصِيْلَةٍ وَّلَا حَامٍ ۙ وَّلٰكِنَّ
الَّذِيْنَ كَفَرُوْا يَفْتَرُوْنَ عَلَى اللّٰهِ الْكَذِبَ ۗ وَاَكْثَرُهُمْ لَا يَعْقِلُوْنَ ۝

"It is not Allah Who hath instituted (superstitions like those of) a slit-ear she-camel, or a she-camel let loose for free pasture, or idol sacrifices for twin-births in animals, or stallion-camels freed from work. It was blasphemers who invented a lie against Allah, and most of them lack wisdom."[15] (V:106).

(vii) Magic, being evil practice and opposed to godliness, condemned; hence to abstain from it is duty:

Speaking of the practice of magic by the Jews, the Holy Qur'ãn says:

وَمَا هُمْ بِضَآرِّيْنَ بِهٖ مِنْ اَحَدٍ اِلَّا بِاِذْنِ اللّٰهِ ۗ وَيَتَعَلَّمُوْنَ مَا يَضُرُّهُمْ
وَلَا يَنْفَعُهُمْ ۗ وَلَقَدْ عَلِمُوْا لَمَنِ اشْتَرٰىهُ مَا لَهٗ فِى الْاٰخِرَةِ مِنْ خَلَاقٍ ۟

".....and they could harm none thereby (i.e., with their Magic) save by Allah's Will (i.e., in accordance with His laws). And they (i.e., the Jews) have learnt that which harmeth them (spiritually and morally), and profiteth them not; and assuredly they knew (from their Scripture) that the buyers of Magic would have no share in the happiness of the Hereafter." (II:102).

(2) Duties of Love

(a) *Duties of Commission:*

(i) Seeking in all actions the Pleasure of God, Who is the Moral Sovereign of the Universe, enjoined:

'Command' came forth, he went to accomplish his purpose, but if that upon which was 'Prohibition' came forth, he refrained; and if the blank came forth, they shuffled them a second time." (Lane's *Lexicon*).

15. This verse condemns four superstitions that were prevalent among the pagan Arabs. There are other superstitious notions and practices of the pagan Arabs also which have been condemned by the Holy Prophet Muhammad (Peace be on him) in his Sayings. Thus Islam has actually condemned all types of superstitions.

وَمِنَ النَّاسِ مَنْ يَّشْرِىْ نَفْسَهُ ابْتِغَآءَ مَرْضَاتِ اللّٰهِ ؕ
وَاللّٰهُ رَءُوْفٌۢ بِالْعِبَادِ ○

"And of mankind is he (i.e., the true Muslim) who would sell (even) his life to earn the Pleasure of Allah. And Allah is full of kindness to His devotees." (II:207).

Nay: a true Muslim, in his highest spiritual effort, goes even beyond, and seeks God Himself:

وَمَا لِاَحَدٍ عِنْدَهٗ مِنْ نِّعْمَةٍ تُجْزٰٓى ○ اِلَّا ابْتِغَآءَ وَجْهِ رَبِّهِ
الْاَعْلٰى ○

".....and (the righteous) have in their minds no favour from anyone for which a reward is expected in return but only the yearning to seek the Countenance of their Lord Most High." (XCII:19, 20).

(ii) Cultivation of Gratefulness to God enjoined:

وَ اشْكُرُوْا لِلّٰهِ اِنْ كُنْتُمْ اِيَّاهُ تَعْبُدُوْنَ ○

".....and express gratefulness to Allah, if it is (indeed) He Whom ye worship." (II:172).

وَاشْكُرُوْا نِعْمَتَ اللّٰهِ

".....and be grateful for the favour of Allah....." (XVI:114).

(iii) Cultivation of sincere devotion to God enjoined:

فَاعْبُدِ اللّٰهَ مُخْلِصًا لَّهُ الدِّيْنَ ○

".....so serve Allah offering Him sincere devotion." (XXXIX:2).

(iv) Steadfastness in devotion to God enjoined:

وَاعْتَصِمُوْا بِاللّٰهِ ؕ هُوَ مَوْلٰىكُمْ ۚ فَنِعْمَ الْمَوْلٰى وَنِعْمَ النَّصِيْرُ ○

".....and hold fast by Allah (without swerving)! He is your Patron: an excellent Patron and an excellent Helper." (XXII:78).

اِلٰهُكُمْ اِلٰهٌ وَّاحِدٌ فَاسْتَقِيْمُوْٓا اِلَيْهِ

".....Your God is One God: so stand true to Him....." (XLI:6).

إِنَّ الَّذِينَ قَالُوا رَبُّنَا اللَّهُ ثُمَّ اسْتَقَامُوا فَلَا خَوْفٌ
عَلَيْهِمْ وَلَا هُمْ يَحْزَنُونَ ۝

"Verily those who say: 'Our Lord is Allah', and remain steadfast thereto, on them shall be no fear, nor shall they grieve." (XLVI:13).

(v) Seeking nearness to God, the Source of all Goodness and Holiness, enjoined:

(a) *Through turning penitently unto Him:*

وَأَنِيبُوا إِلَىٰ رَبِّكُمْ وَأَسْلِمُوا لَهُ مِن قَبْلِ أَن يَأْتِيَكُمُ الْعَذَابُ ثُمَّ لَا تُنصَرُونَ ۝

"*And turn penitently unto your Lord and submit unto Him* before there cometh unto you the torment, and then ye shall not be succoured."[16] (XXXIX:54).

(b) *Through seeking ardently the means of approach:*

يَا أَيُّهَا الَّذِينَ آمَنُوا اتَّقُوا اللَّهَ وَابْتَغُوا إِلَيْهِ الْوَسِيلَةَ وَجَاهِدُوا فِي
سَبِيلِهِ لَعَلَّكُمْ تُفْلِحُونَ ۝

"O ye who believe! fear Allah and *seek the means of approach unto Him* and strive with might and main in His cause: that ye may prosper."[17] (V:38).

---

16. *Cf.* the Qur'ãnic verse:

مَّنْ خَشِيَ الرَّحْمَٰنَ بِالْغَيْبِ وَجَاءَ بِقَلْبٍ مُّنِيبٍ ۝ ادْخُلُوهَا بِسَلَامٍ ۖ ذَٰلِكَ
يَوْمُ الْخُلُودِ ۝

"....who feareth (Allah) Most Gracious in secret and cometh with a heart penitent (turned to Him): enter it (*i.e.*, Heaven) in Peace and Security. This is the Day of Eternal Life." (L:33, 34).

17. Mark that God is such an object of fear that, instead of being avoided, He is to be approached by us with all our Love. 'Fear of Allah' is thus the fear of our own deprivation of Divine Blessings which occurs when we remove ourselves away from Him.

Also mark that the way of approach lies in striving with might and main in His cause, something which even the pious Muslims of today seems to have forgotten, and hence the degeneration of the Muslim community everywhere.

(c) *Through detaching from wordly things and engaging in remembrance of and communion with Him:*

واذكر اسم ربك وتبتل إليه تبتيلا ۝ رب المشرق والمغرب لا إله إلا هو فاتخذه وكيلا ۝

"And remember thou the name of thy Lord, and devote thyself to Him with an *exclusive* devotion.[18] Lord of the East and the West! No God is there but He. Take Him therefore for (thy) Disposer of Affairs." (LXXIII:8, 9).

فاذكروني أذكركم

"Therefore remember Me, I will remember you....." (II:152).

يا أيها الذين آمنوا اذكروا الله ذكرا كثيرا ۝ وسبحوه بكرة وأصيلا ۝

"O ye who believe! Remember Allah with much remembrance and glorify Him early and late." (XXXIII:41, 42).

وسبح بحمده

".....and celebrate His praise." (XXV:58).

واذكر ربك في نفسك تضرعا وخيفة ودون الجهر من القول بالغدو والآصال ولا تكن من الغافلين ۝

"And remember thou thy Lord in thy (very) soul, with humility and in reverence, without loudness in word, in the mornings and evenings; and be not thou of those who are neglectful (of Allah's remembrance)."[19] (VII:205)

---

18. *tabattala il-allah* means: "He detached himself from wordly things and devoted himself to God;.....or he forsook every other thing, and applied himself to the service of God." (Lane's *Lexicon*).

19. Indeed, God's remembrance should be constant. *Cf.* the Qur'ãnic verse which says that the wise are "those who remember Allah standing, sitting and reclining" (III:191), because: "Lo! in the remembrance of Allah hearts do find serene tranquillity and steady peace." (XIII:28).

This remembrance should take the form of regular prayers also:

إِنَّنِيٓ أَنَا اللّٰهُ لَآ إِلٰهَ إِلَّآ أَنَا فَاعْبُدْنِيْ وَأَقِمِ الصَّلٰوةَ لِذِكْرِيْ ۝

"Verily I! I am Allah! no God there is but I; so worship Me and *establish regular prayer for My remembrance.*" (XX:14).

These regular, or, obligatory, prayers should be performed punctually at the appointed times:[20]

إِنَّ الصَّلٰوةَ كَانَتْ عَلَى الْمُؤْمِنِيْنَ كِتٰبًا مَّوْقُوْتًا ۝

"Verily regular prayers are enjoined on the Believers at fixed times." (IV:103).

The regular prayers are to be followed (and preceded) by as much remembrance of God as possible and practicable:

فَإِذَا قَضَيْتُمُ الصَّلٰوةَ فَاذْكُرُوا اللّٰهَ قِيٰمًا وَّقُعُوْدًا وَّعَلٰى جُنُوْبِكُمْ

"Then when ye have finished the prayer, remember Allah, standing and sitting and lying on your sides....." (IV:103).

Also, besides the regular and repeated daily communion and constant remembrance of Allah during the normal waking hours of the day and the night, devoted Muslims should sacrifice their comfort during the sleeping hours of the night, according to their individual capacity, for communion with their Lord:

إِنَّمَا يُؤْمِنُ بِاٰيٰتِنَا الَّذِيْنَ إِذَا ذُكِّرُوْا بِهَا خَرُّوْا سُجَّدًا وَّسَبَّحُوْا بِحَمْدِ رَبِّهِمْ وَهُمْ لَا يَسْتَكْبِرُوْنَ ۝ تَتَجَافٰى جُنُوْبُهُمْ عَنِ الْمَضَاجِعِ يَدْعُوْنَ رَبَّهُمْ خَوْفًا وَّطَمَعًا وَّمِمَّا رَزَقْنٰهُمْ يُنْفِقُوْنَ ۝

"Only those believe in Our revelations, who, when they are recited to them, fall down in adoration and celebrate the praises of their Lord, and they are not puffed up with pride. Their limbs do forsake their beds of sleep (while yet there is night), the while they call on their Lord, in Fear and Hope, and of that wherewith We have provided them they

20. Five times a day: at dawn, immediately afternoon, late afternoon, immediately after sunset, and before retirement to bed (in the first quarter of the night).

expend (for the welfare of others)." (XXXII:15, 16).

Indeed, the 'Servants of God' are:

وَالَّذِينَ يَبِيتُونَ لِرَبِّهِمْ سُجَّدًا وَقِيَامًا ۝

".....those who spend the night in adoration of their Lord, prostrate and standing....." (XXV:64).

(vi) Cultivation of love[21] *for God enjoined:*

Allah is the loving One (*al-Wadûd*)[22] and the cultivation of, and absorption in, His love forms the highest pursuit of a Muslim. The Holy Qur'ãn speaks of the true Believers as "a people whom Allah loves and they love Him." (V:57).

It is a relationship which is cultivated through right belief and right conduct:

إِنَّ الَّذِينَ آمَنُوا وَعَمِلُوا الصَّٰلِحَٰتِ سَيَجْعَلُ لَهُمُ الرَّحْمَٰنُ وُدًّا ۝

"Verily those who believe and work deeds of righteousness, for them (Allah) Most Gracious will appoint (in this world as well as in the next) Love (i.e., His own love and the love of fellow-creatures)." (XIX:96).

This relationship is consciously and assiduously cultivated at a level where it surpasses a Muslim's love for everything else:

وَالَّذِينَ آمَنُوا أَشَدُّ حُبًّا لِلَّهِ ۗ

".....but the Believers are strongest in love for Allah." (II:165).

It forms the highest achievement for a Muslim, gives the direction to his will, and functions as the motivating force—equally with 'fear of God'—for all the actions of his life.

---

21. The Qur'ãnic concept of love for God has no affinity whatsoever with sensuous love. God is Most Sublime, according to the Holy Qur'ãn. As such, love for Him should be of sublime nature—namely, love modified by extreme respect. That is why the Qur'ãnic teaching combines 'Love for Allah' with 'fear of Allah'.

22. LXXXV:14.

(b) <u>*Duties of Omission*</u>:

(i) Following lusts of the heart, thereby incurring God's Displeasure, prohibited:

وَلَا تَتَّبِعِ الْهَوٰى فَيُضِلَّكَ عَنْ سَبِيْلِ اللّٰهِ ۭ اِنَّ الَّذِيْنَ يَضِلُّوْنَ عَنْ سَبِيْلِ اللّٰهِ
لَهُمْ عَذَابٌ شَدِيْدٌۢ بِمَا نَسُوْا يَوْمَ الْحِسَابِ ○

".....and follow not the lusts (of thy heart) that it beguile thee from the Way of Allah. Lo! those who wander from the Way of Allah have an awful doom, for as much as they forgot the Day of Reckoning."
(XXXVIII:26).

(ii) Ungratefulness to God, prohibited:

وَاشْكُرُوْا لِيْ وَلَا تَكْفُرُوْنِ ○

".....and unto Me give thanks, and *be not ungrateful* to Me."
(II:152).

(iii) Behaving disloyally (as opposed to, sincere devotion) to God, prohibited:

يٰٓاَيُّهَا الَّذِيْنَ اٰمَنُوْا لَا تَخُوْنُوا اللّٰهَ

"O ye who believe! be not disloyal to (or, betray not the trust of) Allah....."
(VIII:27).

(iv) Worshipping false gods, whether those of the polytheists and idol-worshippers or those that reside within the human self, prohibited:

وَلَقَدْ بَعَثْنَا فِيْ كُلِّ اُمَّةٍ رَّسُوْلًا اَنِ اعْبُدُوا اللّٰهَ وَاجْتَنِبُوا الطَّاغُوْتَ ۚ

"And assuredly We sent among every people a Messenger (with the Command:) 'Serve God, and eschew Evil and shun false gods'[23]."
(XVI:36).

(v) Fickle-mindedness in respect of faith in God's Goodness, condemned: hence to abstain from it is duty:

---

23. *ijtanibu al-tāgūt* implies both meanings. Abdullah Yusuf Ali's version is: 'eschew evil', while Marmaduke Pickthall's version is: 'shun false gods'.

al-tāgūt is "whatever is worshipped instead, or to the exclusion, of God". (Lane's *Lexicon*).

وَمِنَ النَّاسِ مَن يَعْبُدُ اللَّهَ عَلَىٰ حَرْفٍ ۖ فَإِنْ أَصَابَهُ خَيْرٌ
اطْمَأَنَّ بِهِ ۖ وَإِنْ أَصَابَتْهُ فِتْنَةٌ انقَلَبَ عَلَىٰ وَجْهِهِ خَسِرَ الدُّنْيَا
وَالْآخِرَةَ ۚ ذَٰلِكَ هُوَ الْخُسْرَانُ الْمُبِينُ ۝

"And of mankind is he who worshippeth Allah, as it were, on the verge: if there befalleth him good, he is contented therewith; but if there befalleth him a trial, he turneth round on his face; he loseth the world and the Hereafter: that indeed is a loss manifest." (XXII:11).

(vi) Allowing preoccupation with and engrossment in worldly things to stand in the way of God's remembrance, prohibited:

يَا أَيُّهَا الَّذِينَ آمَنُوا لَا تُلْهِكُمْ أَمْوَالُكُمْ وَلَا أَوْلَادُكُمْ عَن ذِكْرِ اللَّهِ ۚ وَمَن
يَفْعَلْ ذَٰلِكَ فَأُولَٰئِكَ هُمُ الْخَاسِرُونَ ۝

"O ye who believe! let not your riches or your children (—the two worldly things having a wide range of engrossment—) divert you from the remembrance of Allah. And whosoever doth that, the loss is their own". (LXIII:9).

(vii) Lack of earnestness in prayer and in the remembrance of God in general, condemned as the way of the Hypocrites: hence abstinence from it is duty:

وَإِذَا قَامُوا إِلَى الصَّلَاةِ قَامُوا كُسَالَىٰ يُرَاءُونَ النَّاسَ وَلَا يَذْكُرُونَ
اللَّهَ إِلَّا قَلِيلًا ۝

".....(The Hypocrites) when they stand up in prayer, stand without earnestness, making a show to the people, and they remember not Allah but little." (IV:142).

(viii) Befriending the forces of evil, thereby violating our duty of love for God, condemned:

وَمَن يَتَّخِذِ الشَّيْطَانَ وَلِيًّا مِّن دُونِ اللَّهِ فَقَدْ خَسِرَ خُسْرَانًا مُّبِينًا ۝

"Whosoever befriends Satan (who represents all the forces of evil), instead of Allah, hath of a surety suffered a loss that is manifest". (IV:119).

This is so because:

يُرِيْدُ الشَّيْطٰنُ اَنْ يُّضِلَّهُمْ ضَلٰلًا بَعِيْدًا ○

".....Satan's wish is to lead them astray far away (from the Right)." (IV:60).

(ix) Loving any object of wordly life in preference to love for God, severely condemned: hence abstinence from it is duty.

قُلْ اِنْ كَانَ اٰبَآؤُكُمْ وَ اَبْنَآؤُكُمْ وَ اِخْوَانُكُمْ وَ اَزْوَاجُكُمْ وَ عَشِيْرَتُكُمْ
وَ اَمْوَالُ اِقْتَرَفْتُمُوْهَا وَ تِجَارَةٌ تَخْشَوْنَ كَسَادَهَا وَ مَسٰكِنُ
تَرْضَوْنَهَآ اَحَبَّ اِلَيْكُمْ مِّنَ اللّٰهِ وَ رَسُوْلِهٖ وَ جِهَادٍ فِيْ سَبِيْلِهٖ
فَتَرَبَّصُوْا حَتّٰى يَاْتِيَ اللّٰهُ بِاَمْرِهٖ ۗ وَاللّٰهُ لَا يَهْدِي الْقَوْمَ الْفٰسِقِيْنَ ○

"Say (O Muhammad! to the Muslims): If your fathers, and your sons, and your brothers, and your mates, and your kindred, and the wealth ye have acquired, and the commerce in which ye fear a decline, and the dwellings in which ye delight—(these) are dearer to you than Allah, or His Messenger, or the striving in His cause: then wait until Allah brings about His decision: and Allah guideth not the rebellious." (IX:24).

Chapter II

DUTIES TO THE HOLY PROPHET[1] MUHAMMAD (PEACE BE ON HIM)

(1) Duties of Respect; (2) Duties of Love

END:

(a) *Objective:*

Maintenance of the attitude of obedience and loyalty through the constant cultivation of respect and love for the Teacher and Exemplar of Qur'ãnic morals, in order to be able to act enthusiastically on the Qur'ãnic Moral Code.

(b) *Subjective:*

Maintenance of assurance, through the remembrance of the Example of the Holy Prophet (Peace be on him), in respect of his personal conduct and his achievements in the moral domain, that the moral idea set forth by the Holy Qur'ãn is realisable.

We have seen in the foregoing that Love for God is a Muslim's highest pursuit and the highest duty. In that connection, the Holy Qur'ãn states further that this love should manifest itself in loyalty following and imitating the communicator and exemplar of God's Guidance for mankind, namely, the Holy Prophet Muhammad (Peace be on him). It says:

قُلْ إِنْ كُنْتُمْ تُحِبُّوْنَ اللّٰهَ فَاتَّبِعُوْنِيْ يُحْبِبْكُمُ اللّٰهُ وَيَغْفِرْ لَكُمْ ذُنُوْبَكُمْ ط
وَاللّٰهُ غَفُوْرٌ رَّحِيْمٌ ○

---

1. According to the Holy Qur'ãn, the status of the Holy Prophet Muhammad (Peace be on him) is that of *nabî* and *rasûl*. Unfortunately, there is no English word capable of conveying the connotation of these terms properly. As regards the word "Prophet", it means, according to English lexicon, "a spokesman of the deity, one who proclaims a divine message, a preacher, a foreteller whether claiming to be inspired or not." Thus it can be adopted as an Islamic term only in a qualified manner—signifying there: "a spokesman of the One True God, who receives the Message from Him through Revelation, and proclaims and preaches it as a divinely appointed Teacher and as the possessor of flawless, sublime and extra-ordinary spiritual and moral personality".

In the Qur'ãnic verses quoted in this book, the words *nabî* and *rasûl* have been translated as "Prophet" and "Messenger" respectively.

"Say thou (O Muhammad)! If ye do love Allah, follow me (and build up your moral and spiritual life on my model): Allah will love you and forgive you your sins: For Allah is Oft-Forgiving, Most merciful." (III:31).

Following and imitating the Holy Prophet (Peace be on him) is not possible, however, without maintaining the attitudes of respect and love towards him,—these, in their turn, giving rise respectively to obedience and absolute loyalty. Thus we arrive at four duties relating to our relation with the Holy Prophet (Peace be on him), namely:

(1) to respect him above all created beings;

(2) to love him above all created beings;

(3) to obey him without demur;

(4) to be absolutely loyal to him.

Starting from the side of man, these four duties form the *essential condition* of the moral agent's Moral Perfection and of the Moral Perfection and Happiness of others—humanity at large, because true Guidance in that connection is available only through the Holy Prophet (Peace be on him) and that Guidance cannot be truly accepted and enthusiastically followed without maintaining the attitude implied in those duties.

We may now state the duties in the language of the Qur'ãn:

(1) Duties of Respect

(a) Subjective:

To regard the Holy Prophet with respect.

(i) Duty of Commission:

Maintaining the attitude of positive respect enjoined:

فَالَّذِينَ آمَنُوا بِهِ وَعَزَّرُوهُ وَنَصَرُوهُ وَاتَّبَعُوا النُّورَ الَّذِي أُنزِلَ
مَعَهُ ۙ أُولَٰئِكَ هُمُ الْمُفْلِحُونَ ۝

".....So it is those who believe in him (i.e., Muhammad), and *honour him*, and help him, and follow the Light which is sent down with him,—it is they who will prosper." (VII:157).

(ii) Duty of Omission:

Directly or indirectly insulting the Holy Prophet prohibited:

وَمَا كَانَ لَكُمْ أَنْ تُؤْذُوا رَسُولَ اللهِ

"And it is not right for you to insult[2] Allah's Messenger (Muhammad)....." (XXXIII:53).

Worthy of note in this respect is the following stern commands of God given to the Muslims of the Holy Prophet's time:

يَا أَيُّهَا الَّذِينَ آمَنُوا لَا تُقَدِّمُوا بَيْنَ يَدَيِ اللهِ وَرَسُولِهِ وَاتَّقُوا اللهَ ۚ
إِنَّ اللهَ سَمِيعٌ عَلِيمٌ ○ يَا أَيُّهَا الَّذِينَ آمَنُوا لَا تَرْفَعُوا أَصْوَاتَكُمْ فَوْقَ
صَوْتِ النَّبِيِّ وَلَا تَجْهَرُوا لَهُ بِالْقَوْلِ كَجَهْرِ بَعْضِكُمْ لِبَعْضٍ أَنْ تَحْبَطَ
أَعْمَالُكُمْ وَأَنْتُمْ لَا تَشْعُرُونَ ○ إِنَّ الَّذِينَ يَغُضُّونَ أَصْوَاتَهُمْ عِنْدَ
رَسُولِ اللهِ أُولَٰئِكَ الَّذِينَ امْتَحَنَ اللهُ قُلُوبَهُمْ لِلتَّقْوَىٰ ۚ لَهُمْ مَغْفِرَةٌ
وَأَجْرٌ عَظِيمٌ ○

"O ye who believe! put not yourselves forward[3] before Allah and His Messenger; and fear Allah: for Allah hears and knows all things.

"O ye who believe! raise not your voice above the voice of the Prophet (Muhammad), nor speak aloud to him in talk as ye may speak aloud to one another, lest your deeds (of righteousness) be rendered vain (thereby) and ye perceive not (the loss).

"Verily those who lower their voice in the presence of Allah's Messenger—these are they whose hearts Allah hath disposed unto Piety: For Them is Forgiveness and a great Reward." (XLIX:1-3).

Also: the following guidance to the socially uncouth people of those days:

إِنَّ الَّذِينَ يُنَادُونَكَ مِنْ وَرَاءِ الْحُجُرَاتِ أَكْثَرُهُمْ لَا يَعْقِلُونَ ○ وَلَوْ أَنَّهُمْ
صَبَرُوا حَتَّىٰ تَخْرُجَ إِلَيْهِمْ لَكَانَ خَيْرًا لَهُمْ ۚ وَاللهُ غَفُورٌ رَحِيمٌ ○

2. Insult: *'Azã*, the Arabic word used here, may equally mean: to annoy, to vex, to cause hurt or injury, to ill-treat by slander or unseemly conduct, or hurt the feelings.

3. i.e., do not attempt to give your advice in any matter before you are asked to do so by the Holy Prophet himself.

"Verily those who shout out to thee (O Muhammad) from without the inner apartments—most of them lack proper sense. If only they had patience until thou couldst come out to them, it would be best for them: but Allah is Oft-Forgiving, Most-Merciful." (XLIX:4, 5).

(b) Objective:

To obey the Holy Prophet without demur.

(i) <u>Duty of Commission</u>:

Practising positive obedience enjoined:

وَأَطِيعُوا الرَّسُولَ

".....and obey the Messenger (Muhammad)....." (IV:59).

إِنَّمَا كَانَ قَوْلَ الْمُؤْمِنِينَ إِذَا دُعُوا إِلَى اللَّهِ وَرَسُولِهِ لِيَحْكُمَ بَيْنَهُمْ أَنْ
يَقُولُوا سَمِعْنَا وَأَطَعْنَا ۚ وَأُولَٰئِكَ هُمُ الْمُفْلِحُونَ ○

"The answer of the Believers, when summoned to Allah and His Messenger, in order that he may judge between them, is no other than this: they say, 'we hear and we obey': It is such as these that will attain felicity." (XXIV:51).

(ii) Duty of Omission:

Disobedience in any manner whatsoever, prohibited:

وَمَنْ يَعْصِ اللَّهَ وَرَسُولَهُ فَقَدْ ضَلَّ ضَلَالًا مُبِينًا ○

".....and whosoever disobeys Allah and His Messenger, he verily goeth astray in error manifest." (XXXIII:36).

وَمَنْ يُشَاقِقِ الرَّسُولَ مِنْ بَعْدِ مَا تَبَيَّنَ لَهُ الْهُدَىٰ وَيَتَّبِعْ غَيْرَ
سَبِيلِ الْمُؤْمِنِينَ نُوَلِّهِ مَا تَوَلَّىٰ وَنُصْلِهِ جَهَنَّمَ ۖ وَسَاءَتْ مَصِيرًا ○

"And whosoever opposeth the Messenger even after Guidance hath been plainly conveyed unto him, and follows a path other than that becoming to men of Faith, We shall leave him in the path he hath chosen, and land him in Hell,—what an evil refuge!" (IV:115).

(2) Duties of Love

(a) Subjective:

To regard the Holy Prophet with love.

(i) *Duty of Commission:*

Maintaining the attitude of positive love—a love which transcends the love for any other created being, emphasised; hence it is duty:

اَلنَّبِيُّ اَوْلٰى بِالْمُؤْمِنِيْنَ مِنْ اَنْفُسِهِمْ

"The Prophet is closer to the Believers than their own selves (—this spiritual relationship entitling him to more love and respect from the Believers than for any created being related in any way)."[4] (XXXIII:6).

This personal spiritual love for the Holy Prophet (on whom be Peace and the Blessings of Allah) is to be cultivated, besides obeying him in all things with overflowing love, through forming spiritual contact with him by reciting *salãt* and *salãm*, as commanded by God in the following verse:

إِنَّ اللّٰهَ وَمَلٰٓئِكَتَهٗ يُصَلُّوْنَ عَلَى النَّبِيِّ ۚ يٰٓاَيُّهَا الَّذِيْنَ اٰمَنُوْا صَلُّوْا عَلَيْهِ وَسَلِّمُوْا تَسْلِيْمًا

"Lo! Allah and His angels shower blessings on the Prophet. O ye who believe! Send your benedictions on him (i.e., ask Allah for His blessings on him) and salute him with a worthy salutation (i.e., with respect and love.)"[5] (XXXIII:56)

---

4. Cf. the Saying of the Holy Prophet (Peace be on him):

لا يؤمن احدكم حتى اكون احب اليه من والده وولده والناس اجمعين

"None of you can have Faith unless I become to him dearer than his parents, his offspring and (in fact) all human beings." (Bukhãrî: *Sahîh*); Chapter on: *Hubb al Rasûl min al-Imãn.*

5. The shortest formula in this connection is:

صلى الله عليه وسلم

i.e., "Allah has bestowed on him His Blessings and Peace". This formula has

(b) Objective:

To foster absolute loyalty to the Holy Prophet (Peace be on him).

(i) Duty of Commission:

To be positively loyal to him emphasised as a condition of Faith; hence it is duty:

فَلَا وَرَبِّكَ لَا يُؤْمِنُونَ حَتَّىٰ يُحَكِّمُوكَ فِيمَا شَجَرَ بَيْنَهُمْ ثُمَّ لَا يَجِدُوا
فِي أَنفُسِهِمْ حَرَجًا مِّمَّا قَضَيْتَ وَيُسَلِّمُوا تَسْلِيمًا ○

"But nay, by thy Lord, they can have no (real) Faith, until they make thee judge in all dispute between them, and find in their souls no resistance against thy decisions, but accept them with the fullest submission." (IV:65).

وَمَا كَانَ لِمُؤْمِنٍ وَلَا مُؤْمِنَةٍ إِذَا قَضَى اللَّهُ وَرَسُولُهُ أَمْرًا أَن يَكُونَ لَهُمُ
الْخِيَرَةُ مِنْ أَمْرِهِمْ

"And it becometh not a believing man or a believing woman, when Allah and His Messenger have decided an affair (for them), that they should (after that) claim any say in their affair;....." (XXXIII:36).

(ii) Duty of Omission:

Being disloyal to him in any manner, prohibited:

يَا أَيُّهَا الَّذِينَ آمَنُوا لَا تَخُونُوا اللَّهَ وَالرَّسُولَ

"O ye who believe! *be not disloyal to* Allah and *His Messenger.....*" `(VIII:27).

---

been further condensed in the form: "Peace is with him", and is employed in the form of prayer: "Peace be on him."

These words should be repeated whenever a Muslim hears or mentions his sacred name.

Chapter III

DUTIES TO THE ANGELS

END:

(a) *Objective:*

Maintenance of the attitude of respect and love for purity of will and holiness wherever found in God's creatures.

(b) *Subjective:*

Constant consciousness of the fact that the world is a moral order, the angels being the functionaries of God's moral scheme.

(i) Nature and Functions of the Angels:

The angels, according to the Holy Qur'ãn, are neither impersonal forces in the sense of physical science, nor gods or demi-gods or sons or daughters of God, as some of the old mythologies conceived them to be. They are celestial beings endowed with personality[1] having been created[2] by God to act as His functionaries in the universe.[3]

The establishment of relation with the spiritual world, which is a vital condition of the spiritual development of a human being, is not conceivable without faith in the existence of the angels (—which, therefore, forms one of the cardinal articles of Islamic Belief—) and without a proper attitude towards them.

The angels are sinless beings—incapable of committing any sin—and as such possessors of purity, because their function is only to behave as God's absolutely obedient servants:

وَالْمَلٰٓئِكَةُ وَهُمْ لَا يَسْتَكْبِرُوْنَ ○ يَخَافُوْنَ رَبَّهُمْ مِّنْ فَوْقِهِمْ وَيَفْعَلُوْنَ
مَا يُؤْمَرُوْنَ ○

".....and the angels; they are not arrogant (before their Lord). (Rather,) they fear their Lord, High above them, and they do whatever they are commanded." (XVI:49, 50).

They are honoured servants of God:

1,2,3. XXXV:1.

بَلْ عِبَادٌ مُّكْرَمُونَ ۝ لَا يَسْبِقُونَهُ بِالْقَوْلِ وَهُم بِأَمْرِهِ يَعْمَلُونَ ۝

"They (*i.e.*, the angels) are (but) servants raised to honour. They precede Him not in word and they act (in all things) by His command." (XXI:26, 27).

Besides their numerous functions mentioned in the Holy Qur'ãn, they, out of love for the Believers, ask for God's blessings on them:

هُوَ الَّذِي يُصَلِّي عَلَيْكُمْ وَمَلَائِكَتُهُ لِيُخْرِجَكُم مِّنَ الظُّلُمَاتِ إِلَى النُّورِ
وَكَانَ بِالْمُؤْمِنِينَ رَحِيمًا ۝

"He it is Who sends blessings on you, *as do His angels*, that He may bring you out from the depths of Darkness into Light: and He is Full of Mercy for the Believers." (XXXIII:43).

Also, they pray to God for forgiveness for all beings on the earth:

وَالْمَلَائِكَةُ يُسَبِّحُونَ بِحَمْدِ رَبِّهِمْ وَيَسْتَغْفِرُونَ لِمَن فِي الْأَرْضِ

".....and the angels celebrate the praises of their Lord, and ask forgiveness for those on the earth." (XLII:5).

(ii) Duties

Thus, because they are honoured beings, they deserve respect; and because they are noble and pure, they deserve love. They deserve love and respect specially from the Believers, whom they love and for whom their solicitude is great.

Part II

DUTIES AS PHYSICAL BEING

I. Duties of Omission:

(or, Duties of Respect for the Self).

END:

Natural Self-Preservation—as the Holy Qur'ãn commands:

وَلَا تُلْقُوا بِأَيْدِيكُمْ إِلَى التَّهْلُكَةِ

".....and be not cast by your own hands to ruin..."[1] (II:195).

(i) All things which harm physical health, prohibited:

يَا أَيُّهَا النَّاسُ كُلُوا مِمَّا فِي الْأَرْضِ حَلَالًا طَيِّبًا وَلَا تَتَّبِعُوا خُطُوَاتِ الشَّيْطَانِ ۚ إِنَّهُ لَكُمْ عَدُوٌّ مُبِينٌ ○

"O mankind! eat of whatsoever is on the earth, lawful and wholesome, and *follow not the footsteps of Satan* (*by using unlawfully acquired and unclean and unwholesome foods*[2]). Lo! he is to you an avowed enemy". (II:168).

---

1. This verse has the context of participation in collective welfare. But it also lays down a general principle which covers all situations and aspects of life.

2. Some of the unclean and unwholesome foods expressly mentioned in the Holy Qur'ãn are:

حُرِّمَتْ عَلَيْكُمُ الْمَيْتَةُ وَالدَّمُ وَلَحْمُ الْخِنْزِيرِ وَمَا أُهِلَّ لِغَيْرِ اللَّهِ بِهِ وَالْمُنْخَنِقَةُ وَالْمَوْقُوذَةُ وَالْمُتَرَدِّيَةُ وَالنَّطِيحَةُ وَمَا أَكَلَ السَّبُعُ إِلَّا مَا ذَكَّيْتُمْ وَمَا ذُبِحَ عَلَى النُّصُبِ

"Forbidden unto you (for food) are carrion, and blood, and swineflesh, and that over which is invoked the name of other than Allah, and the strangled, the felled (*i.e.*, killed by a blow), and the dead through falling from a height, and that which hath been killed by (the goring of) horns, and that which hath been (partly) eaten by wild beasts—saving that which ye make lawful (by the death-stroke), and that which hath been slaughtered on the altars (according to the

(ii) Self-stupefaction, gluttony and intoxication, prohibited:

يَٰٓأَيُّهَا الَّذِينَ آمَنُوا لَا تُحَرِّمُوا طَيِّبَٰتِ مَآ أَحَلَّ اللَّهُ لَكُمْ وَلَا تَعْتَدُوا ۚ
إِنَّ اللَّهَ لَا يُحِبُّ الْمُعْتَدِينَ ○

"O ye who believe! Make not unlawful the good things (whether they be foods or drinks or any other lawful pleasures) which Allah hath made lawful for you, nor transgress (in respect of your physical, mental, moral, spiritual and social health by making lawful for yourselves harmful foods, drinks, etc.); verily Allah loveth not the transgressors."[3] (V:90).

وَكُلُوا وَاشْرَبُوا وَلَا تُسْرِفُوا ۚ إِنَّهُ لَا يُحِبُّ الْمُسْرِفِينَ ○

".....and eat and drink, but *be not immoderate and intemperate*: verily He loveth not those who are immoderate and intemperate." (VII:31).

كُلُوا مِن طَيِّبَٰتِ مَا رَزَقْنَٰكُمْ وَلَا تَطْغَوْا فِيهِ فَيَحِلَّ عَلَيْكُمْ غَضَبِى ۖ وَمَن
يَحْلِلْ عَلَيْهِ غَضَبِى فَقَدْ هَوَىٰ ○

"Eat of the good things We have provided for your sustenance, but *commit no excess therein*, lest My wrath should justly descend on you; and those on whom descends My wrath do perish indeed." (XX:81).

يَٰٓأَيُّهَا الَّذِينَ آمَنُوٓا إِنَّمَا الْخَمْرُ وَالْمَيْسِرُ وَالْأَنصَابُ وَالْأَزْلَٰمُ رِجْسٌ
مِّنْ عَمَلِ الشَّيْطَٰنِ فَاجْتَنِبُوهُ لَعَلَّكُمْ تُفْلِحُونَ ○

"O ye who believe! Intoxicants[4] and gambling, (dedication of) stones, and divination by arrows, (all these) are an abomination,—of

---

custom of pagan Arabs)...." (V:4).

وَلَا تَأْكُلُوا مِمَّا لَمْ يُذْكَرِ اسْمُ اللَّهِ عَلَيْهِ وَإِنَّهُ لَفِسْقٌ ۗ

"And eat not of that whereon Allah's name hath not been mentioned, for lo! it is abomination." (VI:121).

3. This verse forbids:—(i) self-mortification, upheld by asceticism; (ii) self-indulgence, and the consequent self-stupefaction, upheld by the hedonistic attitude.

4. The word *Khamr* used in the Arabic text stands, according to Lane, for "any intoxicating thing that clouds or obscures (lit. covers) the intellect." (*Arabic-English Lexicon*). Thus the Prohibition here relates to all intoxicants.

Of course, the most immediate reference here is to alcohol, or, wine, which was used as an intoxicant by the Arabs of those days and which is the scourge of the modern civilisation also.

The total prohibition of wine by the Qur'ãn is a fact of history, to which all historians of Islam, including its worst critics, have borne testimony. For instance, D.S. Margoliouth says: "When the revelation came, zealous followers went round the houses of the Muslims and emptied their vessels of all liquor which was supposed to be intoxicating, in many cases breaking the vessels themselves.....The prohibition was extended to vinegar made of wine and a categorical denial was given to the suggestion that wine had medicinal value." (*Muhammad*, p. 283).

Still there are some "Muslims" today who, under the impact of the irreligious and the hedonistic influences of Western culture, not only drink wine but try to believe themselves and make others believe that, according to the Holy Qur'ãn, wine is not something totally evil,—wrongly taking shelter in the Qur'ãnic verse which says:

يَسْـَٔلُونَكَ عَنِ الْخَمْرِ وَالْمَيْسِرِ قُلْ فِيهِمَآ إِثْمٌ كَبِيرٌ وَمَنَافِعُ لِلنَّاسِ
وَإِثْمُهُمَآ أَكْبَرُ مِن نَّفْعِهِمَا

"They ask thee (O Prophet) about wine and gambling. Tell (them): in both is a great sin, and *some benefit, for men,* but the sin of them is (far) greater than their benefit...." (II:219).

The vehement condemnation of wine even in this verse is very definite. However, coming to the words 'some benefits', what has been really affirmed is not any benefit in respect of human consumption but the other benefits to which a scientist refers thus: "Alcohol's most useful sphere of action is as a solvent in industrial concerns. (Dastur, *Alcohol: Its Use and Misuse*, p. 109).

The truth, based on all available evidence, is that all intoxicants, including alcohol, are among the greatest enemies of mankind. As the medical scientist whom we have just quoted says: "Alcohol belongs to a family of poisonous chemicals. Its theoretic food-value is of no value in practical dietics. It is never a stimulant. It has a sedative drug-action in moderate doses, and a narcotic poison-action in excess.....Its use as a beverage is physiologically unsound, economically disastrous, socially disruptive, and materially poisonous." (*op.cit.*, pp. 108, 109). As regards the social evils promoted by alcohol, the *Encyclopaedia of Religion and Ethics* pronounces the verdict that: "There is universal testimony as to the close relationship between excessive drinking the breaches of the moral law and the laws of the State. This is a direct consequence of the paralysis of the higher faculties, intellectual and moral, and the resulting free-play given to the

Satan's handiwork: shun such (abomination), therefore, that ye may prosper." (V:93).

(iii) Considering lawful pleasures relating to natural appetites as illegitimate, prohibited:[5]

يَآيُّهَا الَّذِيْنَ اٰمَنُوْا لَا تُحَرِّمُوْا طَيِّبٰتِ مَآ اَحَلَّ اللّٰهُ لَكُمْ

---

lower inclinations." (vol. I, p. 301). This verdict is confirmed by the *Jewish Encyclopaedia*, which says (I; p. 333): ".....the statistics of Baer, Kurella, Gallavandis, and Sichart show that from 25 to 85 percent of all malefactors are drunkards."

We may observe here in passing the very unfortunate fact that certain religious groups, which have wielded a tremendous influence in human history, should have been responsible for patronising an evil that has engulfed a large part of mankind today. We may refer, for instance, to the Jews and the Christians. In the estimation of the Bible, wine 'cheereth God and man'. (*Judg*. 9:14). As for the Jewish religious practice, Friendler says in *The Jewish Religion* that: "it has been ordered (in the Jewish religion) that our meal on the eve of Sabbath and Festival should begin with a cup of wine in the honour of the day..... The *kidduah* consists of two blessings: one over the wine, one that refers to the holiness of the day." (p. 341). Coming to the Christian Church and clergy, the use of alcohol "was never absent from the Church nor from its clergy." (Smith and Cheetam's *Dictionary of Christian Antiquities*, I, p. 585). According to Cheyne and Black's *Encyclopaedia Biblica* (c. 1569), in the case of fire on the Sabbath day, only three necessaries of life are to be rescued by the good Christians, viz., "a basket of loaves, a cake of dried figs and a jar of wine."

5. The following verse is more explicit in disapproving Asceticism as a philosophy of life:

وَرَهْبَانِيَّةَ ۨ ابْتَدَعُوْهَا مَا كَتَبْنٰهَا عَلَيْهِمْ اِلَّا ابْتِغَآءَ رِضْوَانِ اللّٰهِ فَمَا رَعَوْهَا حَقَّ رِعَايَتِهَا ۚ فَاٰتَيْنَا الَّذِيْنَ اٰمَنُوْا مِنْهُمْ اَجْرَهُمْ ۚ وَكَثِيْرٌ مِّنْهُمْ فٰسِقُوْنَ ○

"But (the institution of) Asceticism (Monasticism) which they (i.e., the early Christians) invented for themselves, We prescribed it not for them: (We commanded) only the seeking of Divine Pleasure; but that they did not foster as they should have done. Yet We bestowed, on those among them who believed, their (due) reward, but many of them are transgressors." (LVII:27).

That the unnatural suppression of sexual appetite by the institution of Asceticism promotes sexual vice, rather than cubring it, is borne out by the history of Christianity. As Scott says: "With the passing of the concubine, the nuns in the convents provided the 'holy men' with the means of satisfying their sexual cravings." (*History of Prostitution*, p. 112).

"O ye who believe! Make not unlawful (for yourselves) the good things (relating to lawful pleasures) which Allah hath made lawful for you....." (V:90)

(iv) Abusing or damaging any limb of one's body, including Castration, prohibited:

The Holy Qur'ãn says:

لَا ..... تَخُوْنُوْٓا اَمٰنٰتِكُمْ

".....and defraud not your trusts....." (VIII:27).

The various limbs of the body, and the talents of a Muslim, are the "property" of God and he possesses them in "trust" for Him. A Muslim should not, therefore, abuse or damage any limb of his body[6].

(v) Committing suicide prohibited:

وَلَا تَقْتُلُوْٓا اَنْفُسَكُمْ ۭ اِنَّ اللّٰهَ كَانَ بِكُمْ رَحِيْمًا ۝

"And kill not (or, destroy not) yourselves; verily Allah is unto you ever Merciful."[7] (IV:29).

(2) <u>Duties of Commission</u>:

(or, Duties of Love for the Self).

***<u>END</u>*:**

Happiness of the moral agent through the maintenance and promotion of his physical well-being:

(i) Proper satisfaction of natural appetites enjoined:

(a) *Satisfaction of Hunger and Thirst:*

---

6. Those spiritualists who have regarded the body as an impediment in the way of their so-called spiritual progress have practised, as among a sect of the Hindus, the "drying up", or deliberate emaciation, of the limbs. Similarly, castration has been considered a means of curbing the sexual appetite and thereby acquiring the freedom to pursue "spirituality".

7. Speaking of this Qur'ãnic injunction, which prohibits suicide in all its forms, Professor Lecky says: "Suicide, which is never expressly condemned in the Bible, is more than once forbidden in the Koran." (*History of European Morals*, II, p. 23).

وَكُلُوا وَاشْرَبُوا وَلَا تُسْرِفُوا

".....and eat and drink, but be not immoderate and intemperate....." (VII:31).

يَسْـَٔلُونَكَ مَاذَآ أُحِلَّ لَهُمْ ۖ قُلْ أُحِلَّ لَكُمُ الطَّيِّبَاتُ

"They ask thee (O Muhammad!) what is lawful to them (as food). Say: Lawful unto you are all things good and pure." (V:5).

(b) *Satisfaction of sexual appetite:*

Satisfaction of sexual appetite has been permitted by the Holy Qur'ãn through lawful marriage *only*, and marriage has been enjoined:

وَأَنكِحُوا الْأَيَامَىٰ مِنكُمْ

"Marry those among you who are single."[8] (XXIV:32).

A very important point should be noted here. Although the union of man and woman in marriage involves the satisfaction of sexual appetite, it is *not*, in the view of the Qur'ãn, the end of marriage—the end being spiritual companionship and mutual love to which the sexual union itself should contribute, but which is marked off distinctly from mere sexual pleasure. The Holy Qur'ãn says:

وَمِنْ آيَاتِهِ أَنْ خَلَقَ لَكُم مِّنْ أَنفُسِكُمْ أَزْوَاجًا لِّتَسْكُنُوا إِلَيْهَا وَجَعَلَ
بَيْنَكُم مَّوَدَّةً وَرَحْمَةً ۚ إِنَّ فِي ذَٰلِكَ لَآيَاتٍ لِّقَوْمٍ يَتَفَكَّرُونَ ○

"And among His Signs is this, that He created for you mates from among yourselves, that ye might obtain tranquillity and solace in them, and He hath ordained between you love and mercy. Verily in that are Signs for those who reflect." (XXX.21).

(c) Rest and Sleep:

وَمِن رَّحْمَتِهِ جَعَلَ لَكُمُ اللَّيْلَ وَالنَّهَارَ لِتَسْكُنُوا فِيهِ وَلِتَبْتَغُوا مِن
فَضْلِهِ وَلَعَلَّكُمْ تَشْكُرُونَ ○

---

8. i.e., not in the bond of wedlock: they may be those who are unmarried, or those who have been lawfully divorced, or those who have been widowed.

"It is of His Mercy that he hath made for you Night and Day, *that therein* (*i.e., in the night*) *ye may enjoy rest*, and that ye may seek of His Grace (during the day);—and in order that ye may be grateful (to Him)." (XXVIII:73).

(ii) *Physical cleanliness*[9] *enjoined:*

فَاطَّهَّرُوْا

".....then purify (yourselves) (with physical cleanliness)....." (V:7).

مَا يُرِيْدُ اللّٰهُ لِيَجْعَلَ عَلَيْكُمْ مِّنْ حَرَجٍ وَّلٰكِنْ يُّرِيْدُ لِيُطَهِّرَكُمْ
وَلِيُتِمَّ نِعْمَتَهٗ عَلَيْكُمْ لَعَلَّكُمْ تَشْكُرُوْنَ ۝

"Allah intendeth not to lay upon you a hardship, but intendeth to purify you (with physical cleanliness) and to complete His favour to you, ye may be grateful (for His bounties)." (V:7).

---

9. The Holy Qur'ãn emphasis on physical cleanliness stands in sharp contrast with the "merit of uncleanliness" emphasised in the life of the followers of certain other religions, *e.g.*, Christianity. Writing of the medieval Christian aspirants of holiness, Professor Licky says: "The cleanliness of the body was regarded as a pollution of the soul, and the saints who were most admired had become one hideous mass of clotted filth. St. Athanasius relates with enthusiasm how St. Anthony, the patriarch of monarchism, had never, to extreme old age, been guilty of washing his feet....St. Euphraxia joined a convent of one hundred and thirty nuns, who never washed their feet, and who shuddered at the mention of a bath." (*op.cit.*, II, p. 47). Of a Christian pilgrim of the 4th century, the *Encyclopaedia Britannica* informs: "(she) boasted that she had not washed her face for 18 years for fear of removing the baptismal chrism." (I, p. 49).

"Dirt and disease became (in Christendom) the honourable insignia of saintship; loathsome fakirs exhibited their filth and their sores for the veneration of the faithful." (Hammerton: *Universal History of the World*, IV, p. 2333).

"Certainly," says another Western scholar, "the maxim which places cleanliness next to godliness, has no place in the biographies of the saints and heroes of monasticism even in climates where bathing would seem almost one of the necessities of life. Jerome warns ascetics against warm bath as morally enervating, and in a letter to one of his female disciples denounces every sort of bathing for women. Augustine allows a bath once a month only." (*Dictionary of Christian Antiquities,* II, p. 939).

وَ يُنَزِّلُ عَلَيْكُمْ مِّنَ السَّمَآءِ مَآءً لِّيُطَهِّرَكُمْ بِهٖ وَ يُذْهِبَ عَنْكُمْ رِجْزَ الشَّيْطٰنِ

".....and He sent down water upon you from heaven that He might cleanse you thereby and remove from you the stain of Satan (—dirt being physically a symbol of evil)....." (VIII:11).

إِنَّ اللّٰهَ يُحِبُّ التَّوَّابِيْنَ وَ يُحِبُّ الْمُتَطَهِّرِيْنَ ○

"Verily Allah loveth those who turn to him constantly, and He loveth those who practise cleanliness (in body, mind and spirit)." (II:222).

وَاللّٰهُ يُحِبُّ الْمُطَّهِّرِيْنَ ○

"And Allah loveth those who always keep themselves clean." (IX:108).

(iii) Physical development enjoined:

وَ أَعِدُّوْا لَهُمْ مَّا اسْتَطَعْتُمْ مِّنْ قُوَّةٍ

"Against them (i.e., the enemies of Islam, or, the forces of evil) prepare your Power (as individuals and as a community) to the utmost of your capacity....." (VIII:60).

Development of power by an individual includes the building up of a powerful physique. Hence, the command for the physical development of the individual is contained in the above comprehensive verse. This fact is corroborated by a *hadîth* of the Holy Prophet (Peace be on him), reported by Muslim in his *Sahîh* in the following words:

المؤمن القوىّ خير واحب الى الله من المؤمن الضعيف وفى كل خير
احرص على ما ينفعك واستعن بالله ولا تعجز

"A physically strong Believer is better and more loved by Allah than a physically weak Believer. And there is good in either of them. Be enthusiastic for everything which brings thee good, and seek therein Divine Help, and do not lose heart in thine endeavour....." (*Kitãb al-Qadr*).

Part III

DUTIES AS RATIONAL BEING

END:

(*i*) *Subjective:*

Balanced and healthy development of human knowledge in all dimensions.

(*ii*) *Objective:*

Service to humanity in terms of correct and comprehensive Guidance.

(*1*) *Duty of Commission:*

Pursuit of knowledge enjoined, with emphasis on:

(i) *its sublimity and unavoidable necessity—basically and for proper moral life.*

(ii) *its importance for spiritual development:*

(iii) *its role in conferring greatness on individuals and communities:*

(iv) *its compatibility with Faith;*

(v) *the principles of observation and research;*

(vi) *the principle of continuous and ceaseless endeavour for rising to higher and higher levels of knowledge;*

(vii) *the principle of Objectivity;*

(viii) *the principle of Comprehensiveness;*

(ix) *the attainment of the stage* of al-Hikmah, *or, the Wisdom;*

(x) *the technique of attaining all Higher Knowledge.*

Thus:

(*i*) *Sublimity of the pursuit of Knowledge and its unavoidable necessity—basically as also for proper moral life, emphasised:*

The Holy Qur'ān says:

وَعَلَّمَ آدَمَ الْأَسْمَاءَ كُلَّهَا

"And He imparted to Adam knowledge of the nature of all things....." (II:31).

The story of Adam given in the Holy Qur'ãn (II:30-39) reveals that knowledge was imparted to him by God:

(a) at the transcendental or spiritual stage of his existence, —when his life was sublime because of the innocence and the serene tranquillity that he enjoyed, together with his wife, in the "Presence of God";

(b) before he embarked on his earthly career, i.e., before he had the occasion to engage himself in wordly pursuits,—nay, before he had acquired any wordly interests;

(c) before he was confronted with the moral struggle.

All this means that, in the estimation of the Holy Qur'ãn:

(*a*) Acquisition of knowledge is a sublime and a spiritual pursuit;

(*b*) Cultivation of knowledge is one of the most basic needs and, hence, one of the most basic duties of a human being;

(*c*) Proper knowledge forms one of the most basic requirements of proper moral life.

(ii) Spiritual achievement through Knowledge, especially of empirical Reality, emphasised:

The Hoy Qur'ãn says:

إِنَّمَا يَخْشَى اللَّهَ مِنْ عِبَادِهِ الْعُلَمَاءُ

".....Those only among His Servants who are learned (i.e., possessors and pursuers of knowledge) truly fear Allah." (XXXV:28).

Here possession and pursuit of knowledge—all true knowledge[1]—has been mentioned as the condition for true fear of God,

1. It is necessary to note here that the theme which is sealed by this verse, being contained in the verses immediately preceding and joining it, relates to the study of natural phenomena—the theme of physical science—, which means that the knowledge which has been commended here so highly comprehends within itself the cultivation of knowledge of God's creation and through that

which, in its turn, is, together with the love for God, the motivating force in the life of every true Muslim. Thus pursuit of knowledge becomes a duty from the point of view of leading a good spiritual and moral life.

(iii) Acquisition of greatness through Knowledge emphasised:

The Holy Qur'ãn says:

يَرْفَعِ اللَّهُ الَّذِينَ آمَنُوا مِنكُمْ وَالَّذِينَ أُوتُوا الْعِلْمَ دَرَجَاتٍ

"Allah will exalt those who have Faith among you, and those who have knowledge to high ranks"[2]. (LVIII:11).

According to this verse, basis for exaltation in the estimation of God is not only Faith in God and all spiritual verities, which is the highest theme of Religion, but also Knowledge, which forms as high a theme in the religion presented by the Holy Qur'ãn. This honoured place given to knowledge makes it obligatory for a Muslim to devote himself to it whole-heartedly.

(iv). Compatibility of Knowledge and Faith emphasised.

A very important point should be noted here. Faith and Knowledge, in the view of the Holy Qur'ãn, are compatible with each other. Indeed they are complementary—wedded to one another, as another verse clearly establishes:

---

the realisation of the greatness and the majesty of God. The immediately preceding verses are:

أَلَمْ تَرَ أَنَّ اللَّهَ أَنزَلَ مِنَ السَّمَاءِ مَاءً فَأَخْرَجْنَا بِهِ ثَمَرَاتٍ مُّخْتَلِفًا أَلْوَانُهَا ۚ
وَمِنَ الْجِبَالِ جُدَدٌ بِيضٌ وَحُمْرٌ مُّخْتَلِفٌ أَلْوَانُهَا وَغَرَابِيبُ سُودٌ ۝ وَمِنَ
النَّاسِ وَالدَّوَابِّ وَالْأَنْعَامِ مُخْتَلِفٌ أَلْوَانُهُ كَذَٰلِكَ

"Seest thou not that Allah sends down rain from the sky? With it We then bring out produce of various colours. And in the mountains are tracts white and red, of various shades of colour, and black intense in hue. And so amongst men and crawling creatures and cattle, are they of various colours....." (XXXV:27, 28).

2. This verse lays down clearly the Divine law for all human communities that one of the major factors which can make them great and powerful in the world is the cultivation of knowledge.

وَالرّٰسِخُوْنَ فِي الْعِلْمِ يَقُوْلُوْنَ اٰمَنَّا بِهٖ ۙ كُلٌّ مِّنْ عِنْدِ رَبِّنَا ۚ
وَمَا يَذَّكَّرُ اِلَّآ اُولُوا الْاَلْبَابِ ○

"And those who are firmly grounded in knowledge say: 'We believe in the Book; the whole of it is from our Lord': and none will grasp the Message except men of understanding." (III:7).

This is a unique feature of the Qur'ãnic philosophy.

Thus, the Holy Qur'ãn demands acceptance and adherence to its teachings on rational basis. It proclaims most emphatically:

لِيَهْلِكَ مَنْ هَلَكَ عَنْ بَيِّنَةٍ وَّيَحْيٰى مَنْ حَيَّ عَنْ بَيِّنَةٍ

"So that he who perisheth (spiritually) should perish by indisputable (rational) evidence (or, proof) and he who surviveth (spiritually) should survive by indisputable (rational) evidence (or, proof)". (VIII:42).

It challenges its opponents on the basis of reason and knowledge in these words:

قُلْ هَلْ عِنْدَكُمْ مِّنْ عِلْمٍ فَتُخْرِجُوْهُ لَنَا ۭ اِنْ تَتَّبِعُوْنَ اِلَّا الظَّنَّ وَاِنْ
اَنْتُمْ اِلَّا تَخْرُصُوْنَ ○ قُلْ فَلِلّٰهِ الْحُجَّةُ الْبَالِغَةُ ۚ

"Say: 'Have ye any (certain) knowledge? If so, produce it before us. Lo! ye follow naught but opinion. Lo! ye do but guess".

"Say: With Allah is the argument that reaches home'." (VI:148, 149).

Again:

اَفَلَا يَتَدَبَّرُوْنَ الْقُرْاٰنَ ۭ

"Will they not then ponder on the Qur'ãn (i.e., examine its teachings rationally)." (IV:82; XLVII:24).

In fact, the Holy Qur'ãn appeals to humanity not less than forty-eight times—and at numerous places on the basis of the physical, the psychical and the social phenomena—to employ reason, emphasising regarding the truth of its teaching that:

وَتِلْكَ الْأَمْثَالُ نَضْرِبُهَا لِلنَّاسِ ۚ وَمَا يَعْقِلُهَا إِلَّا الْعَالِمُونَ ۝

"And these similitudes We set forth for mankind. But their import is grasped by the reason of only those who possess knowledge."
(XXIX:43).

(v) Observation and Research emphasised:

Similarly, the Holy Qur'ãn appeals not less than seventeen times to contemplate and meditate on the natural phenomena as well as on the truth of its own teachings. In that connection, it emphasises also the joint exploration of truth:

قُلْ إِنَّمَا أَعِظُكُمْ بِوَاحِدَةٍ ۚ أَنْ تَقُومُوا لِلَّهِ مَثْنَىٰ وَفُرَادَىٰ ثُمَّ تَتَفَكَّرُوا

"Say: I admonish you on one point: that ye awake, for Allah's sake, by twos and singly, and then contemplate." (XXXIV:46).

This contemplation is to be pursued in the form of search and *research* for arriving at the truth:

مَا تَرَىٰ فِي خَلْقِ الرَّحْمَٰنِ مِنْ تَفَٰوُتٍ ۖ فَارْجِعِ الْبَصَرَ هَلْ تَرَىٰ مِنْ فُطُورٍ ۝
ثُمَّ ارْجِعِ الْبَصَرَ كَرَّتَيْنِ

"Thou shalt not behold want of proportion in the Creation of (Allah) Most Gracious. So turn thy vision again: seest thou any flaw? Then respect thy look twice over....." (LXVII:3, 4).

(vi) Endeavour to rise higher and higher in knowledge emphasised:

The Holy Qur'ãn has taught the prayer:

وَقُلْ رَّبِّ زِدْنِي عِلْمًا ۝

".....and say: O my Lord! advance me in knowledge." (XX:114).

It is evident that to pray for advance in knowledge and not to strive for it with might and main would be the height of irrationality. Therefore, this prayer implies the Divine Command for striving after knowledge. Hence, the duty to strive with a devoted and sincere heart for continuous progress in knowledge.

(vii) Objectivity in Knowledge emphasised:

But this duty has to be pursued, as the wordings of the above verse establish clearly, with reference to God, Who is the Source of all Truth. In other words, quest for knowledge should be based on unflinching faith in God and in His Guidance, and should be inspired purely by the motive of search for Reality and love for Truth. All preconceived notions, superficial opinions and conjectures should be avoided. In other words, the pursuit should be based on *objectivity*. Persons undertaking this pursuits should strive to be, as the Holy Qur'ãn states:

أُولُوا الْعِلْمِ قَآئِمًا بِالْقِسْطِ

"Those possessing knowledge with devotion to justice (or, objectivity in knowledge)"—in other words, "the learned who are balanced (in their view of Reality)", being spiritually as well as rationally illumined. (III:18).

According to the Holy Qur'ãn this is rationally possible only for a devotee of God, Who is the Source of all Knowledge. It says:

إِنَّ فِي خَلْقِ السَّمٰوٰتِ وَالْأَرْضِ وَاخْتِلَافِ الَّيْلِ وَالنَّهَارِ لَاٰيٰتٍ لِّأُولِي
الْأَلْبَابِ ۝ الَّذِيْنَ يَذْكُرُوْنَ اللّٰهَ قِيٰمًا وَّقُعُوْدًا وَّعَلٰى جُنُوْبِهِمْ
وَيَتَفَكَّرُوْنَ فِيْ خَلْقِ السَّمٰوٰتِ وَالْأَرْضِ ۚ رَبَّنَا مَا خَلَقْتَ هٰذَا
بَاطِلًا ۚ سُبْحٰنَكَ فَقِنَا عَذَابَ النَّارِ ۝

"Behold! in the constitution of the heavens and the earth, and in the alternation of the Day and the Night,—there are indeed Signs for the possessors of understanding (i.e., the wise),—such as celebrate the praises of Allah, standing, sitting, and reclining, and reflect on (the problems relating to) the constitution of the heavens and the earth (finally) acquiring that stage of understanding the Reality where the conviction bursts out from them): 'Our Lord! Thou createst not (all) this in vain? Glory be to Thee! Give us salvation from the Penalty of the Fire'." (III:190, 191).

Thus the pursuit of knowledge should have, as its technique, non-capricious penetrating observation of the universe and man.

(viii) Comprehensive pursuit of Knowledge emphasised:

Observation relating to the Universe as a whole has been emphasised, among other verses, in III:191 quoted above. Observation of man's immediate environment—natural as well as social—and of his inner self has been emphasised in the following verses:

وَفِي الْأَرْضِ آيَاتٌ لِّلْمُوقِنِينَ ۝ وَفِي أَنفُسِكُمْ ۚ أَفَلَا تُبْصِرُونَ ۝

"On the earth are Signs for those who have sure faith (in the meaningfulness of all things), as also (there are Signs) in your own selves: will ye not, then, observe?" (LI:20, 21).

(ix) Quest for the stage of 'Wisdom' emphasised:

Such quest for knowledge will bear the fruit of *al-Hikmah*, or the Wisdom, about which the Holy Qur'ãn says:

وَمَن يُؤْتَ الْحِكْمَةَ فَقَدْ أُوتِيَ خَيْرًا كَثِيرًا ۗ وَمَا يَذَّكَّرُ إِلَّا أُولُو الْأَلْبَابِ ۝

".....and whoso is granted the Wisdom, receives indeed abundant Good, but none receives admonition save those possessing understanding." (II:269).

They will finally be blessed with guiding mankind aright on the basis of sure knowledge contained in the Divine Guidance, even as the Holy Prophet (Peace be on him) has been asked by God to declare:

قُلْ هَٰذِهِ سَبِيلِي أَدْعُو إِلَى اللَّهِ ۚ عَلَىٰ بَصِيرَةٍ أَنَا وَمَنِ اتَّبَعَنِي ۖ وَسُبْحَانَ
اللَّهِ وَمَا أَنَا مِنَ الْمُشْرِكِينَ ۝

"Say: 'This is my Way. I call to Allah with sure knowledge, I and whoever follows after me. To Allah be glory! And I am not among the idolaters'." (XII:108).

(x) The correct technique of attaining Higher Knowledge:

The process of education for acquiring higher knowledge, deducible from the Holy Qur'ãn, may also be mentioned here for further edification. Speaking of the functions of the Holy Prophet (Peace be on him) as Divine *Teacher*, the holy book informs us:

هُوَ الَّذِي بَعَثَ فِي الْأُمِّيِّينَ رَسُولًا مِّنْهُمْ يَتْلُو عَلَيْهِمْ آيَاتِهِ وَيُزَكِّيهِمْ وَيُعَلِّمُهُمُ
الْكِتَابَ وَالْحِكْمَةَ

"It is He Who has sent among the Unlettered a Messenger (Muhammad) from among them, to rehearse His revelations to them, to purify them, and to teach them the Book and the Wisdom...." (LXII:2).

Thus, we are given three stages of education for the acquisition of higher knowledge:

(1) The stage of basic and general education, represented in the Holy Prophet's mission by communicating Divine Revelations to the people;

(2) The stage of spiritual and moral purification for the sake of eradicating all subjective perversions and acquiring absolute devotion to truth, even as it was ordained in the Holy Prophet's mission;

(3) The stage of pursuing knowledge at the higher level where research is undertaken on the different facets of Reality and direct conviction is acquired on the basis of personal observation and insight, represented in the Holy Prophet's mission by 'teaching the Book and the Wisdom'.

The sum up: Cultivation of all knowledge, employing the method laid down for ensuring the service to truth, is a duty, according to the Holy Qur'ãn, commanded by the Holy Prophet Muhammad (Peace be on him) in the following words:

طلب العلم فريضة على كل مسلم ومسلمة

"Quest for knowledge is a duty for every Muslim man and woman." (Muslim's *Sahîh, Kitãb al-'Ilm*, p. 34).

(2) Duty of Omission:

Subjectivity and capriciousness in the pursuit of knowledge, as also lack of the spirit of observation and open-minded understanding to Truth, condemned:

According to the Holy Qur'ãn, those who employ subjectivity and caprice in the domain of knowledge remain misguided, in spite of the apparent scholarly tone of their endeavour:

أَفَرَءَيْتَ مَنِ اتَّخَذَ إِلٰهَهُ هَوٰىهُ وَأَضَلَّهُ اللّٰهُ عَلٰى عِلْمٍ وَّخَتَمَ عَلٰى
سَمْعِهٖ وَقَلْبِهٖ وَجَعَلَ عَلٰى بَصَرِهٖ غِشٰوَةً ۚ فَمَنْ يَّهْدِيْهِ مِنْ بَعْدِ
اللّٰهِ ۚ أَفَلَا تَذَكَّرُوْنَ ۝

"Hast thou seen him who has taken his caprice to be his god, and Allah has left him astray despite his knowledge, and has sealed up his hearing and his heart (and understanding), and has set on his sight a covering? Who, then, will guide him after Allah (has withdrawn guidance)? Will ye not receive admonition?" (XLV:23).

This is so because:

وَمَا لَهُم بِهِۦ مِنْ عِلْمٍ ۖ إِن يَتَّبِعُونَ إِلَّا ٱلظَّنَّ ۖ وَإِنَّ ٱلظَّنَّ
لَا يُغْنِى مِنَ ٱلْحَقِّ شَيْـًٔا ○

".....they have no knowledge therein. They follow nothing but conjecture; and conjecture avails nothing against Truth." (LIII:28).

As to those who lack the spirit of observation and open-minded understanding of the Truth, they are led to, or remain in, nothing less than infidelity. We are told:

وَكَأَيِّن مِّنْ ءَايَةٍ فِى ٱلسَّمَٰوَٰتِ وَٱلْأَرْضِ يَمُرُّونَ عَلَيْهَا وَهُمْ عَنْهَا
مُعْرِضُونَ ○ وَمَا يُؤْمِنُ أَكْثَرُهُم بِٱللَّهِ إِلَّا وَهُم مُّشْرِكُونَ ○

"How many a Sign there is in the heavens and in the earth that they pass by, turning away from it. And most of them believe not in God without associating other gods with Him!" (XII:105, 106).

This is so, because:

لَهُمْ قُلُوبٌ لَّا يَفْقَهُونَ بِهَا وَلَهُمْ أَعْيُنٌ لَّا يُبْصِرُونَ بِهَا وَلَهُمْ
ءَاذَانٌ لَّا يَسْمَعُونَ بِهَا ۚ أُو۟لَٰٓئِكَ كَٱلْأَنْعَٰمِ بَلْ هُمْ أَضَلُّ ۚ أُو۟لَٰٓئِكَ هُمُ
ٱلْغَٰفِلُونَ ○

"...They have hearts, but understand not with them (*i.e.*, do not exert their will to understand); they have eyes, but perceive not with them; they have ears, but hear not with them. They are like cattle; nay, they are worse (in their listlessness). They are heedless." (VII:179).

Part IV

DUTIES AS AESTHETICAL BEING

Chapter I

PRELIMINARY OBSERVATIONS

The Holy Qur'ãn has given to humanity a theory of Aesthetics of its own. The present is not, however, the proper occasion to expound it. Only the following five points may be mentioned here:

(1) The Qur'ãnic concept of Beauty is wedded to spirituality or godliness.

(2) According to the Qur'ãnic teaching, the essential attributes of Beauty are:

Piety, Purity, Sublimity, Harmony, Balance, Proportion, Order and Perfection.

(3) The Holy Qur'ãn upholds only that Art which is noble and sublime, both in its conception and its goal, and it regards as vulgar and inadmissible all those forms of Art which do not enshrine the essential attributes of Beauty, as it understands and acknowledges.

(4) According to the Holy Qur'ãn, the spiritual value, or, religion, is the highest, and below it stand in serial order the moral, the intellectual and the physical values.

(5) As regards the aesthetic value, it should permeate and pervade all the aspects of human life: physical intellectual, moral, spiritual and social.

Our concern in the present discourse being the duties of man as the possessor of aesthetic consciousness, however, we may first of all observe with advantage the emphasis on aesthetic value found in the Holy Qur'ãn in respect of God, universe and man.

We find in the Holy Writ as follows:

(1) *GOD*:

God is the Possessor of Absolute Beauty:

The Holy Qur'ãn says:

اَللّٰهُ نُوْرُ السَّمٰوٰتِ وَالْاَرْضِ ط

"Allah is the Light of the heavens and the earth." (XXIV:35).

This is one of the most profound verses, endowed with depths of meaning that are unfathomable. In understanding its implication from the point of view of the problem before us, however, the guidance for us lies in the fact that, according to the Holy Qur'ãn, darkness is ugliness, as the following verse denotes:

وَالَّذِيْنَ كَسَبُوا السَّيِّاٰتِ جَزَآءُ سَيِّئَةٍۭ بِمِثْلِهَا ۙ وَتَرْهَقُهُمْ ذِلَّةٌ ؕ مَا لَهُمْ مِّنَ اللّٰهِ مِنْ عَاصِمٍ ۚ كَاَنَّمَآ اُغْشِيَتْ وُجُوْهُهُمْ قِطَعًا مِّنَ الَّيْلِ مُظْلِمًا ؕ اُولٰٓئِكَ اَصْحٰبُ النَّارِ ۚ هُمْ فِيْهَا خٰلِدُوْنَ ○

"But those who have earned evil will have a reward (in the Hereafter) of like evil: ignominy will cover them: no protector they shall have from (the wrath of) Allah: (*ugliness will be their lot*) *as if their faces had been covered with a cloak of darkest night*. Such are the Companions of the Fire; they will abide therein." (X:27).

Now, if darkness relates to ugliness, light relates to beauty,— and thus the transcendental Light of God implies the possession of transcendental Beauty by Him.

Again, God is the Absolute, as we have seen elsewhere. Hence His beauty is Absolute Beauty.

The Holy Prophet (Peace be on him) has, as the expounder of the Holy Qur'ãn *par excellence*, made a very explict and direct statement in this regard. He says:

الله جميل ويحب الجمال

"Allah is Beautiful and He loves Beauty." (Muslim's *Sahîh, Bãb Tahrîm al-Kibr,* p. 65).

(2) *UNIVERSE*:

Being the Possessor of Absolute Beauty, God has very naturally created everything of the world in the frame of beauty, as the following verse says:

الَّذِىٓ أَحْسَنَ كُلَّ شَىْءٍ خَلَقَهُ

".....He Who has made everything which He has created most Good and Beautiful." (XXXII:7).

This is a statement about the universe as a whole and covers all things in the heavens and on the earth.

The Holy Qur'ãn goes, however, beyond this universal statement and embarks, in order to emphasise the existence of beauty further, on certain details with reference to: (i) the earth, its plant life and animal life, (ii) the heavenly bodies that surround the earth, and (iii) Heaven in the World Hereafter, or, what is called, the next world.

(i) *The earth, its plant life and animal life:*

The Holy Qur'ãn says:

(a) in respect of *all things*:

إِنَّا جَعَلْنَا مَا عَلَى الْأَرْضِ زِينَةً لَّهَا

"That which is on the earth We have made but as an adornment[1] for it...." (XVIII:7).

(b) in respect of *minerals and plants:*

وَأَنۢبَتْنَا فِيهَا مِن كُلِّ شَىْءٍ مَّوْزُونٍ

".....and We produced therein (i.e., in the earth) all kinds of things in due balance.[2]" (XV:19).

(c) in respect of *plants only:*

حَتَّىٰٓ إِذَآ أَخَذَتِ الْأَرْضُ زُخْرُفَهَا وَازَّيَّنَتْ

"(vegetation grows) till the earth is clad with its golden ornaments and is decked out in beauty......" (X:24).

(d) in respect of *animals:*

---

1. Mark that 'adorn' means 'add beauty to'.

2. Mark that 'balance' is an essential attribute of beauty.

وَالْأَنْعَامَ خَلَقَهَا ۗ لَكُمْ فِيهَا دِفْءٌ وَمَنَافِعُ وَمِنْهَا تَأْكُلُونَ ۝ وَلَكُمْ فِيهَا جَمَالٌ حِينَ تُرِيحُونَ وَحِينَ تَسْرَحُونَ ۝

"And cattle He hath created for you (O mankind): from them ye derive warmth, and numerous benefits, and of their (meat) ye eat. And *therein is beauty of you as* ye drive them home in evening, and as ye lead them forth to pasture in the morning." (XVI:5, 6).

وَالْخَيْلَ وَالْبِغَالَ وَالْحَمِيرَ لِتَرْكَبُوهَا وَزِينَةً ۚ وَيَخْلُقُ مَا لَا تَعْلَمُونَ ۝

"And (God hath created) horse, mules, and donkeys, that ye may ride them, and as *adornment;* and He will create (in future, through the mind and ingenuity of man, other vehicles) that ye know not (at the time of the revelation of the Qur'ãn)". (XVI:8).

فَاقِعٌ لَوْنُهَا تَسُرُّ النَّاظِرِينَ ۝

"(The sacrificial cow, ordered by Moses, was to be) bright in her colour, providing pleasure to the beholders." (II:69).

(ii) The heavenly bodies that surround the earth:

In this respect, the Holy Qur'ãn says:

وَلَقَدْ جَعَلْنَا فِي السَّمَاءِ بُرُوجًا وَزَيَّنَّاهَا لِلنَّاظِرِينَ ۝

"And assuredly We have set constellations in the heaven and We have beautified it for beholders." (XV:16).

إِنَّا زَيَّنَّا السَّمَاءَ الدُّنْيَا بِزِينَةٍ الْكَوَاكِبِ ۝

"We have indeed decked the lower heaven with beauty (in) the stars....." (XXXVII:6).

(iii) Heaven in the World Hereafter:

The Holy Qur'ãn says about Heaven:

حَسُنَتْ مُسْتَقَرًّا وَمُقَامًا ۝

".....how beautiful an abode and place of rest!" (XXV:76).

وَحُسْنَ مَاٰبٍ ۝

".....beautiful Place of (final) Return." (XXXVIII:25).

فَلَا تَعْلَمُ نَفْسٌ مَّآ اُخْفِيَ لَهُمْ مِّنْ قُرَّةِ اَعْيُنٍ ۚ جَزَآءًۢ بِمَا كَانُوْا يَعْمَلُوْنَ ۝

"Now no person knows what delight of the eyes (—what aesthetic satisfaction—) is kept hidden (in reserve) for them (in Heaven)—as a reward for their (good) deeds." (XXXII:17).

فَوَقٰىهُمُ اللّٰهُ شَرَّ ذٰلِكَ الْيَوْمِ وَلَقّٰىهُمْ نَضْرَةً وَّسُرُوْرًا ۝

"But Allah will deliever them from the evil of that Day, and will shed over them a Light of Beauty and a (blissful) Joy." (LXXVI:11).

وُجُوْهٌ يَّوْمَئِذٍ نَّاضِرَةٌ ۝ اِلٰى رَبِّهَا نَاظِرَةٌ ۝

"Some faces, that Day, will beam (in brightness and beauty), looking towards their Lord (Who is the Source of all Beauty and the Bestower of all Blessings)." (LXXV:22, 23).

(3) *MAN*:

According to the Holy Qur'ãn, human beings are possessors of Beauty, both outwardly and inwardly. It says:

لَقَدْ خَلَقْنَا الْاِنْسَانَ فِيْٓ اَحْسَنِ تَقْوِيْمٍ ۝

"We have indeed created man in the best and the most beautiful[3] constitution.[4]"[5] (XCV:4)

وَصَوَّرَكُمْ فَاَحْسَنَ صُوَرَكُمْ

---

3. *Ahsan* means: the best, the most beautiful.

4. *Taqwîm* means: constitution, mould, form, nature, symmetry.

5. Man is, therefore, "the comeliest specimen of God's handiwork", according to Maulana Abdul Majid Daryabadi (*English Translation and Commentary of the Holy Qur'ãn*, p. 956, n. 438); and, according to Allama Abdullah Yusuf Ali (*English Translation and Commentary of the Holy Qur'ãn*, p. 1759, n. 6199), "to man God gave the purest and the best nature." Mark here that symmetry and purity are the attributes of beauty.

"And (it is Allah Who hath) given you shape (O mankind!), and made your shapes beautiful...." (XL:64).

وَنَفْسٍ وَمَا سَوّٰىهَا

"By the Soul and Him Who endowed it with proportion and order[6]...." (XCI:7).

The above discussion proves that the Holy Qur'ãn is vehemently emphatic on the aesthetic value, affirming as it does, beauty in God, universe and man.

6. Mark that proportion and order are attributes of Beauty. Hence this verse refers definitely to the beauty of the inner personality of the human being.

Chapter II
DUTIES

The facts stated in the preceding chapter being what they are, the question is: Has the Holy Qur'ãn prescribed any duties relating to the aesthetic aspect of human life?

The answer is: yes.

Let us look into the details.

1. *The Holy Qur'ãn wants its followers to beautify their Faith and their actions,* and strive to obtain beautiful reward from God, as the following verses reveal:

وَمَنْ أَحْسَنُ دِينًا مِّمَّنْ أَسْلَمَ وَجْهَهُ لِلَّهِ وَهُوَ مُحْسِنٌ

"Who can be more beautiful in religion (—Faith and Action—) than one who surrendereth his whole self to Allah while doing good (to mankind)....." (IV:125).

وَأَنِ اسْتَغْفِرُوا رَبَّكُمْ ثُمَّ تُوبُوا إِلَيْهِ يُمَتِّعْكُم مَّتَاعًا حَسَنًا إِلَىٰ أَجَلٍ مُّسَمًّى

".....and that, seek the forgiveness of your Lord, and turn to Him in repentance, He will grant you enjoyment, good and beautiful, for a term appointed." (XI:3).

لِّلَّذِينَ أَحْسَنُوا الْحُسْنَىٰ وَزِيَادَةٌ ۖ وَلَا يَرْهَقُ وُجُوهَهُمْ قَتَرٌ وَلَا ذِلَّةٌ ۚ أُولَٰئِكَ أَصْحَابُ الْجَنَّةِ ۖ هُمْ فِيهَا خَالِدُونَ

"Those who do good (beautifying their deeds) obtain a (like) beautiful (reward)—and more (through Divine Grace). No darkness (of ugliness and sorrow) nor shame shall cover their faces (on the Day of Judgment)! They are Companions of the Garden: therein they will abide." (X:26).

وَمَن يَقْتَرِفْ حَسَنَةً نَّزِدْ لَهُ فِيهَا حُسْنًا ۚ

"And if anyone earns any good, We shall give him an increase in beauty (or, of good) in respect thereof." (XLII:23).

مَنْ ظَلَمَ ثُمَّ بَدَّلَ حُسْنًا بَعْدَ سُوٓءٍ فَإِنِّي غَفُورٌ رَّحِيمٌ ○

"But if any have done wrong and have thereafter substituted beauty (in conduct) to take the place of evil, truly, I am Oft-Forgiving, Most Merciful." (XXVII:11).

2. *In respect of beauty in conduct*, the Qur'ãnic verses bear reference in the form of command to certain specific situations also. For instance:

(i) Beauty in Speech:

وَقُولُوا لِلنَّاسِ حُسْنًا

"Speak to people employing beauty (in your speech)." (II:83).

(ii) Beauty in behaviour towards Parents:

وَوَصَّيْنَا الْإِنسَانَ بِوَالِدَيْهِ حُسْنًا

"We have enjoined on man beauty (in conduct) in respect of his parents." (XXIX:8).

(iii) Beauty in Preaching and Argument:

ادْعُ إِلَىٰ سَبِيلِ رَبِّكَ بِالْحِكْمَةِ وَالْمَوْعِظَةِ الْحَسَنَةِ وَجَادِلْهُم بِالَّتِي
هِيَ أَحْسَنُ ۚ

"Invite (all to the Way of thy Lord with wisdom and beautiful preaching; and argue with them in ways that are best and most beautiful." (XVI:125).

3. *As regards physical life*, the following emphatic verse refers to the duty of beautifying it in all manner, of course, in harmony with the Qur'ãnic norms and principles:

قُلْ مَنْ حَرَّمَ زِينَةَ اللَّهِ الَّتِي أَخْرَجَ لِعِبَادِهِ وَالطَّيِّبَاتِ مِنَ
الرِّزْقِ ۚ قُلْ هِيَ لِلَّذِينَ آمَنُوا فِي الْحَيَاةِ الدُّنْيَا خَالِصَةً يَوْمَ
الْقِيَامَةِ ۗ كَذَٰلِكَ نُفَصِّلُ الْآيَاتِ لِقَوْمٍ يَعْلَمُونَ ○

"Say: Who hath forbidden[1] things of beauty which Allah hath brought forth for His servants, and the things, clean and pure, which He hath provided for sustenance? Say: They are, in the life of this world, for those who believe (and) purely for them on the Day of Judgment. Thus do We explain the Signs in detail for those who have knowledge." (VII:32).

4. *In respect of dress*, we are told first that one of the functions of dress is beautification of the human personality:

يٰبَنِیۡۤ اٰدَمَ قَدۡ اَنۡزَلۡنَا عَلَیۡکُمۡ لِبَاسًا یُّوَارِیۡ سَوۡاٰتِکُمۡ وَ رِیۡشًا ؕ وَلِبَاسُ التَّقۡوٰی ۙ ذٰلِکَ خَیۡرٌ ؕ ذٰلِکَ مِنۡ اٰیٰتِ اللّٰہِ لَعَلَّہُمۡ یَذَّکَّرُوۡنَ ○

"O children of Adam! We have bestowed upon you raiment to cover your shame[2] and as a means of beautification[3]; and the raiment of piety (which covers and beautifies the inner self) is the best.[4] That is of the Signs of Allah that haply they may be admonished." (VII:26).

Then, as if to emphaise the element of *sanctity* in beautification through dress, and to emphasise it for rectifying the wrong notion

---

1. The religious view of life has often been based on asceticism which stands for the negation of beauty. According to the Holy Qur'ãn, it is a wrong view of sanctity.

2. Here the Holy Qur'ãn condemns the cult of nudism, which is a product of the psychological perversions of modern times.

3. (*a*) Note here a relevant *hadîth* the Holy Prophet (Peace be on him) used to praise God when putting on a new dress in these words:

الحمد للہ الذی کسانی ما اواری بہ عورتی واتجمل بہا فی حیوتی

"Praise be to Allah who gave me to wear that which covers the part of the body that should remain hidden, and whereby I acquire beauty in my life." (Tirmizi: *Jãme'*). (*Al-Tãj al-Jãme' lî al-Usûl, fi Ahadîth al-Rusûl, Kitãb al-Libãs*, p. 174).

(*b*) Dress, according to Westermarck, "owes its origin, at least in great many cases, to the desire of men and women to make themselves mutually attractive". (Quoted in *Ency., Br.* VII, p. 649).

4. Here we obtain the principle that the garments we wear should never transgress the bounds of piety; otherwise, they will become source of ugliness.

Thus, the Holy Qur'ãn voices a masculine protest against those perversions in dress which have plagued modern womanhood in the West and in the countries coming under the influence of the West.

preached by certain other religions, it says, referring to worship, and, because a Muslim must compulsorily pray five times during the day and the night, referring, actually to all the twenty-four hours of one's daily life, as follows:

يٰبَنِيْٓ اٰدَمَ خُذُوْا زِيْنَتَكُمْ عِنْدَ كُلِّ مَسْجِدٍ وَّكُلُوْا وَاشْرَبُوْا وَلَا تُسْرِفُوْا ۚ اِنَّهٗ لَا يُحِبُّ الْمُسْرِفِيْنَ ۝

"O Children of Adam! look to your adornment[1] at every time and place of prayer: eat and drink: (Enjoy) but waste not by excess;[2] for Allah loveth not the wasters." (VII:31).

5. To conclude: *The Holy Qur'ãn demands and commands positive beautification of every aspect of human life*: spiritual, moral, intellectual and physical. Its teaching in this respect has been beautifully summed up by the Holy Prophet (Peace be on him) in these words:

إن الله كتب الإحسان على كل شيئ

"Verily Allah hath made obligatory the employment of beauty in respect of evrerything."[3] (*Sahîh al-Muslim*). (*Mishkãt al-Masãbîh, Kitãb al-Said, al-Fasl al-awwal*, p. 357).

---

1. It means not only dressing for grace and piety but also keeping the hair in proper form, and toilet and cleanliness.

   The following incident of the Holy Prophet's time may be quoted here with advantage, as it reveals the attitude of Islam in practice:

   "The Prophet (Peace be on him) was in the mosque, when a person came there with the hair of his head and beard in a dishevelled condition. The Prophet (Peace be on him) made a sign towards him which implied that he was ordering him to set his hair in order. That person (left the mosque), obeyed the command and returned. Then the Prophet (Peace be on him) remarked: 'Is it not better than that someone among you comes with dishevelled hair as if he is Satan'." (*Mishkãt al-Masãbih*, vol. I, p. 384).

2. Mark that the Holy Qur'ãn allows aesthetic fulfilment but not luxury, which is vice.

3. The Holy Prophet (Peace be on him) has commanded Muslims to fulfil aesthetic requirements even in respect of such matters as putting on the clothing over the dead body, preparing a grave, slaughtering an animal and killing an enemy soldier on the battlefield. (See: *Miskãt al-Masãbih, Bãb Ghusl al-Mayyit*, p. 143; and *Kitãb al-Said*, p. 357).

And let every Muslim artist and artisan remember the following Prophetic exhortation:

إنّ العبد اذا عمل عملا احبّ الله أن يتقنه

"Verily, when a servant (of Allah) executes any task, Allah loves that he executes it with thorough skill and for stability and perfection."[4] (*Kanz al-'Ummãl*).

4. Mark that 'perfection' is the attribute of beauty.

Part V

DUTIES AS MORAL BEING

(*or, Duties to Self Relating Strictly to Morality*)

I. Duties of Omission

(Duties of Respect for the Self)

2. Duties of Commission

(Duties of Love for the Self)

Chapter I

Duties of Omission

END :

Moral Self-Preservation.

(i) *Lying, or false speech, prohibited:*

وَاجْتَنِبُوا قَوْلَ الزُّورِ ۝

".....and shun the word that is false." (XXII:30).

إِنَّ اللَّهَ لَا يَهْدِي مَنْ هُوَ كَاذِبٌ كَفَّارٌ ۝

"Verily Allah guideth not those who are false and ungrateful." (XXXIX:3).

هَلْ أُنَبِّئُكُمْ عَلَىٰ مَنْ تَنَزَّلُ الشَّيَاطِينُ ۝ تَنَزَّلُ عَلَىٰ كُلِّ أَفَّاكٍ أَثِيمٍ ۝

"Shall I inform you (O people!) on whom it is that the evil ones descend? They descend on every sinful liar."[1] (XXVI:221, 222).

(ii) Mixing up truth with falsehood prohibited:

وَلَا تَلْبِسُوا الْحَقَّ بِالْبَاطِلِ

"And confound not truth with falsehood." (II:42).

---

1. Cf. XLV:7.

(iii) Concealing truth prohibited:

لَا ..... تَكْتُمُوا الْحَقَّ وَأَنْتُمْ تَعْلَمُونَ ○

"And conceal not the truth while ye know (it)". (II:42).

(iv) Concealing evidence prohibited:

وَلَا تَكْتُمُوا الشَّهَادَةَ ۚ وَمَنْ يَكْتُمْهَا فَإِنَّهُ آثِمٌ قَلْبُهُ ۗ وَاللَّهُ بِمَا تَعْمَلُونَ عَلِيمٌ ○

"Conceal not evidence; for whoever conceals it,—his heart is tainted with sin. And Allah knoweth all that ye do." (II:283).

(v) Aversion to truth (—a state of mental perversion—a moral disease—) condemned:

لَقَدْ جِئْنَاكُمْ بِالْحَقِّ وَلَٰكِنَّ أَكْثَرَكُمْ لِلْحَقِّ كَارِهُونَ ○

"Verily We have brought the Truth to you: But most of you have hatred for truth (—truth being always bitter for those who become accustomed to living on and benefitting from falsehoods)." (XLIII:78).

(vi) Assisting falsehood or fraud, and giving false evidence, ruled out from Islamic conduct: hence abstinence from it is duty:

وَالَّذِينَ لَا يَشْهَدُونَ الزُّورَ

"....and (the servants of the Most Gracious are those) who witness no falsehood." (XXV:72).

Note: 'Witnessing no falsehood' implies in the wordings of the Arabic text: (1) 'do not give false evidence'; and (2) 'do not assist falsehood or fraud'.

(vii) Spirit of hypocrisy condemned: hence abstinence from it is duty:

وَمِنَ النَّاسِ مَنْ يَقُولُ آمَنَّا بِاللَّهِ وَبِالْيَوْمِ الْآخِرِ وَمَا هُمْ بِمُؤْمِنِينَ ○
يُخَادِعُونَ اللَّهَ وَالَّذِينَ آمَنُوا وَمَا يَخْدَعُونَ إِلَّا أَنْفُسَهُمْ وَمَا يَشْعُرُونَ ○ فِي قُلُوبِهِمْ
مَرَضٌ فَزَادَهُمُ اللَّهُ مَرَضًا ۖ وَلَهُمْ عَذَابٌ أَلِيمٌ بِمَا كَانُوا يَكْذِبُونَ ○

"And of the people there are some who say: 'We believe in Allah and the Last Day'; but they do not (really) believe. Fain would they deceive Allah and those who believe, but they only deceive themselves, and how little they perceive! In their hearts is a disease, so Allah hath increased unto them (that) disease; and grievous is the penalty they (incur), because they have been lying." (II:8-10).

These verses speak of the hypocrites of the Holy Prophet's time, who were practising deception in respect of the Muslims. They, however, lay down the moral principle that practising deception in human relations is strongly condemnable, and he who practises it becomes morally diseased. Thus, it is duty not only to others, but also to one's own self, to abstain from adopting hypocritical attitude in any matter whatsoever.

(viii) Deeds not conforming to words condemned: hence abstinence from the same is duty:

يٰٓاَيُّهَا الَّذِيْنَ اٰمَنُوْا لِمَ تَقُوْلُوْنَ مَا لَا تَفْعَلُوْنَ ۝ كَبُرَ مَقْتًا عِنْدَ اللّٰهِ
اَنْ تَقُوْلُوْا مَا لَا تَفْعَلُوْنَ ۝

"O ye who believe! why say ye that which ye do not? Grievously odious is it in the sight of Allah that ye say that which ye do not". (LXI:2, 3).

Disparity between word and the deed of a person may bring harm to others who may repose confidence in him in any matter, but it damages that person also, because: (1) he loses the capacity to stick to truth; and (2) he loses the confidence of his fellow-beings and, hence his prestige.

(ix) The spirit of duplicity condemned: hence abstinence from it is duty.

وَاِذَا لَقُوا الَّذِيْنَ اٰمَنُوْا قَالُوْٓا اٰمَنَّا ۚ وَاِذَا خَلَوْا اِلٰى شَيٰطِيْنِهِمْ ۙ قَالُوْٓا اِنَّا
مَعَكُمْ ۙ اِنَّمَا نَحْنُ مُسْتَهْزِءُوْنَ ۝ اَللّٰهُ يَسْتَهْزِئُ بِهِمْ وَيَمُدُّهُمْ فِيْ طُغْيَانِهِمْ
يَعْمَهُوْنَ ۝ اُولٰٓئِكَ الَّذِيْنَ اشْتَرَوُا الضَّلٰلَةَ بِالْهُدٰى ۠ فَمَا رَبِحَتْ تِّجَارَتُهُمْ
وَمَا كَانُوْا مُهْتَدِيْنَ ۝.

"When they (*i.e.*, the Hypocrites) meet those who believe, they say: 'We believe'; but when they are alone with their evil ones, they say: 'We are really with you: we were only jesting'. Allah will throw back their mockery on them and give them rope in their trespasses; so they will wander like blind ones (to and fro). These are they who have bartered guidance for error: but their traffic is profitless, and they have lost true direction." (II:14-16).

Although these verses refer to the Hypocrites of Madinah, they lay down a universal principle, namely, that duplicity, which is a deeper phase of hypocrisy, corrupts a person's moral tone, on the one hand, and brings loss of face to him, on the other. Thus, side by side with being unjust to others, he who practise duplicity also damages himself. Hence it is a 'duty to self' to abstain from it completely.

(x) Making a show of hollow acts of goodness, devotion and charity, condemned; hence abstinence from that is duty:

Making a show of hollow acts of goodness, devotion and charity is a form of hypocrisy and, as such has been condemned by the Holy Qur'ãn:

فَوَيْلٌ لِّلْمُصَلِّينَ ۝ الَّذِينَ هُمْ عَن صَلَاتِهِمْ سَاهُونَ ۝ الَّذِينَ هُمْ
يُرَاءُونَ ۝ وَيَمْنَعُونَ الْمَاعُونَ ۝

"So woe to the worshippers who are neglectful of their Prayers, *those who do (good) to be seen*, but refuse (to supply) (even) small kindnesses (or, neighbourly needs)." (CVII:4-7).

(xi) Oath-mongering condemned; hence abstinence from it is duty:

All habitual liars lose the faith of their fellow-beings and hence resort to habitual and false swearing in order to create belief and confidence in their word: while "the true man's word is as good as his bond". Oath-mongering is thus related to evil character and a false personality, and is disapproved by the Holy Qur'ãn:

وَلَا تُطِعْ كُلَّ حَلَّافٍ مَّهِينٍ ۝

"Heed not the type of despicable man,—ready with oaths...."
(LXVIII:10).

(xii) Following one's lusts of the heart prohibited:

The Holy Qur'ãn enjoins:

فَلَا تَتَّبِعُوا الْهَوَىٰ أَنْ تَعْدِلُوا

"So follow not lusts of the heart[2] lest ye lapes (from truth)...."
(IV:135).

(xiii) Desiring false appreciation and being pleased with flattery condemned; hence abstinence from it is duty:

The Holy Qur'ãn says:

لَا تَحْسَبَنَّ الَّذِينَ يَفْرَحُونَ بِمَا أَتَوا وَّيُحِبُّونَ أَنْ يُحْمَدُوا بِمَا لَمْ يَفْعَلُوا
فَلَا تَحْسَبَنَّهُمْ بِمَفَازَةٍ مِّنَ الْعَذَابِ وَلَهُمْ عَذَابٌ أَلِيمٌ ۝

"Think not that those who exult in what they have brought about, and *love to be praised for what they have not done*,—think not that they can escape the penalty. For them is a penalty grievous indeed." (III:188).

(xiv) Flattery, as embodying self-debasement of the flatterer[3] ruled out in Islamic conduct; hence abstinence from it is duty:

The Holy Qur'ãn says:

يَا أَيُّهَا الَّذِينَ آمَنُوا اتَّقُوا اللَّهَ وَقُولُوا قَوْلًا سَدِيدًا ۝ يُصْلِحْ لَكُمْ أَعْمَالَكُمْ

"O ye who believe! Guard your duty to Allah and speak a straight speech: He will (on that account) make your conduct whole and sound....."
(XXXIII:70, 71).

The Arabic word *Sadîd*, used in this verse, when applied to speech, means[4] 'true' and 'directed to the right point'. Now true speech is 'statement according to fact', as also 'sincere speech'. Moreover, a speech which is according to fact and sincere shall be a dignified speech. As for 'directed to the right point', it connotes a 'speech which has no

2. The word *Hawã* used in the Arabic text does not mean simple desire but "blameable or evil inclination". (Lane's *Arabic-English Lexicon*). It is "lusts of the heart" when related to morality; and "caprice" when related to knowledge.

3. It damages morally the other party also. We shall deal with it in "duties to others".

4. Lane's *Lexicon*. It also means: correct, right, relevant, pertinent.

exaggeration or its opposite'. It also contains the sense of straightforwardness[5].

The English word 'flattery' means: 'treating with insincere and exaggerated praise and servile attentions'.[6]

Flattery is, therefore, the very opposite of the 'straight speech' mentioned in the above verse.

Moreover, according to the above verse, 'straight speech' renders one's conduct whole and sound, which means that flattery renders conduct unsound.

Therefore, viewing it in the light of the Qur'ãnic teaching, flattery is immoral, and a Muslim should abstain from it totally. Condemning this vice, the Holy Prophet (Peace be on him) says:

اذا رأيتم المدّاحين فاحثوا فى افواههم التراب

"When you meet the flatterers, throw dust into their mouths." (Muslim's *Sahîh*; Abû Dã'ûd's *Sunan*, Chap. on "Disapprobation of Flattery").

(xv) Love for pomp and show—ostentation[7], prohibited:

وَلَا تَكُونُوا كَالَّذِينَ خَرَجُوا مِن دِيَارِهِم بَطَرًا وَرِئَاءَ النَّاسِ

"And be not like those who started from their homes insolently and to be seen of men (i.e., in vainglory and ostentation)." (VIII:47).

Referring to the unseemly conduct of the enemies of Islam at the battle of Badr, this verse lays down the moral injunction that a Muslim should always abstain from vainglory and ostentation.

(xvi) Conceit condemned; hence abstinence from it is duty:

The Holy Qur'ãn disapproves conceit in the following reference:

وَيَوْمَ حُنَيْنٍ إِذْ أَعْجَبَتْكُمْ كَثْرَتُكُمْ فَلَمْ تُغْنِ عَنكُمْ شَيْئًا وَضَاقَتْ
عَلَيْكُمُ الْأَرْضُ بِمَا رَحُبَتْ ثُمَّ وَلَّيْتُم مُّدْبِرِينَ

---

5. The other implications of 'straight speech' shall be dealt with in connection with the duty of truthfulness.

6. See Chambers, *Twentieth Century Dictionary*.

7. i.e., display to draw attention or admiration.

".....and on the day of (the battle of) Hunain: Behold! your superiority in numbers elated you; then it availed you naught, and the earth, for all that it is wide, straitened unto you; then ye turned back in retreat." (IX:25).

This verse relates to the battle of Hunain, in which for the first time the Muslim army outnumbered the enemy forces; yet it was in this battle that the Muslim forces suffered a severe set-back first, which has been ascribed to the spirit of elation, as opposed to the spirit of faith in God, which overtook the minds of a part of them, i.e., the new converts and the less disciplined.

The moral principle contained in that event is that God disapproves and punishes conceit and self-elation. Hence the duty to abstain from the same.

(xvii) Exultation in one's achievements condemned; hence abstinence from it is duty:

لَا تَحْسَبَنَّ الَّذِينَ يَفْرَحُونَ بِمَآ أَتَوْا وَّيُحِبُّونَ أَنْ يُّحْمَدُوْا بِمَا لَمْ يَفْعَلُوْا
فَلَا تَحْسَبَنَّهُمْ بِمَفَازَةٍ مِّنَ الْعَذَابِ ۚ وَلَهُمْ عَذَابٌ أَلِيْمٌ ○

"Think not that *those who exult in what they have brought about*, and love to be praised for what they have not done,—think not that they can escape the penalty. For them is a penalty grievous indeed." (III:188).

Exultation in one's achievements has been condemned here because it breeds pride which leads to a person's ruin at least in damaging his character. In fact, it also blocks further progress.

A Muslim should always attribute his achievements to the favour of God and maintain the state of mind known as humility.

(xviii) Self-goodness—self-piousness (piety-complex) condemned; hence abstinence from it is duty:

The Holy Qur'ãn lays down the rule:

فَلَا تُزَكُّوْٓا أَنْفُسَكُمْ ۖ هُوَ أَعْلَمُ بِمَنِ اتَّقٰى ○

"Therefore ascribe not purity (i.e., goodness and righteousness) unto yourselves. He is Best Aware of him who wardeth off evil.[8]" (LIII:32).

---

8. *zakã'un*, i.e., purity, goodness, righteousness....and *zakã nafsahu*: "He praised himself." (Lane's *Lexicon*).

Many of those who are strict in conformity to external religious behaviour, without imbibing thoroughly the inner spirit of religious life, develop consciously or unconsciously, what may be termed as 'piety-complex', which is actually a form of self-esteem culminating in contempt for others.

Many others who strive to be morally good develop a feeling of self-esteem in that respect.

Both of those wrong attitudes have been disapproved by the Holy Qur'ãn and should be shunned by every Muslim.

(xix) Haughtiness prohibited:

Haughtiness in all forms has been regarded as a basic evil by the Holy Qur'ãn. *Iblîs*, who enjoyed the prerogative of the holy company of angels, became Devil because he compared himself with Adam and said:

أَنَا خَيْرٌ مِّنْهُ ؕ

".....I am better that he." (XXXVIII:76).

and thus:

اِسْتَكْبَرَ وَكَانَ مِنَ الْكٰفِرِيْنَ ۝

"he was haughty, and became one of those who reject Faith (—indeed, became the Devil)." (XXXVIII:74).

As regards mankind:

اِنَّهٗ لَا يُحِبُّ الْمُسْتَكْبِرِيْنَ ۝

"Verily He (i.e., God) loveth not those who are haughty." (XVI:23).

and:

فَلَبِئْسَ مَثْوَى الْمُتَكَبِّرِيْنَ ۝

"....evil indeed is the abode of those who are haughty." (XVI:29).

Hence, it is a Qur'ãnic moral duty to abstain from haughtiness in all forms. It should be shunned in thought, word and deed. The Holy

Qur'ãn lays down the rules:

لَا تُصَعِّرْ خَدَّكَ لِلنَّاسِ وَلَا تَمْشِ فِي الْأَرْضِ مَرَحًا ۖ إِنَّ اللَّهَ لَا يُحِبُّ كُلَّ
مُخْتَالٍ فَخُورٍ ○ وَاقْصِدْ فِي مَشْيِكَ وَاغْضُضْ مِنْ صَوْتِكَ ۚ إِنَّ أَنْكَرَ
الْأَصْوَاتِ لَصَوْتُ الْحَمِيرِ ○

"Swell not thy cheek (for pride) at the people, and walk not in insolence through the earth[9]; for Allah loveth not any vainglorious[10] boastful[11] (person). And be modest in thy gait, and lower thy voice (in humility)[12]; for the harshest of sounds without doubt is the braying of an ass." (XXXI:18, 19).

Another verse which condemns the demonstration of haughtiness in very strong terms may also be quoted:

وَلَا تَمْشِ فِي الْأَرْضِ مَرَحًا ۖ إِنَّكَ لَنْ تَخْرِقَ الْأَرْضَ وَلَنْ تَبْلُغَ الْجِبَالَ طُولًا ○

"And walk not in insolence through the earth. Verily, thou wilt by no means rend the earth, nor canst thou attain to the mountains in stature." (XVII:37).

(xx) Obstinacy, perverseness, self-righteousness ruled out; hence abstinence from the same is duty:

In emphasising the qualities of the righteous, the Holy Qur'ãn says:—

وَلَمْ يُصِرُّوا عَلَىٰ مَا فَعَلُوا وَهُمْ يَعْلَمُونَ ○

".....and they are never obstinate in persisting knowingly in (the wrong) they have done." (III:135).

It is thus a duty to abstain from obstinancy, perverseness and self-righteousness in all the situations of life.

---

9. These injunctions relate to behaviour in general.

10. Vainglorious; i.e., proud in the heart. This emphasises condemnation of haughtiness as it is to be found in the haughty person's thought.

11, 12. The reference here is to abstain from employing haughty tone in talk.

(xxi) Quarrelsomeness prohibited:

The Holy Qur'ãn has mentioned quarrelsomeness as the opposite of righteousness:—

فَإِنَّمَا يَسَّرْنَٰهُ بِلِسَانِكَ لِتُبَشِّرَ بِهِ ٱلْمُتَّقِينَ وَتُنذِرَ بِهِۦ قَوْمًا لُّدًّا ○

"So have We made the (Qur'ãn) easy in thine own tongue, that with it thou mayest give glad tidings to the righteous, and warn therewith the vehemently quarrelsome folk." (XIX:97).

The holy book also says about true Muslims:—

وَإِذَا خَاطَبَهُمُ ٱلْجَٰهِلُونَ قَالُوا۟ سَلَٰمًا ○

"....and when the ignorant address them (in arrogance and lack of culture), they say, 'Peace! (avoiding thus all quarrel with them)...." (XXV:63).

Finally, there is the command, given to the Holy Prophet (Peace be on him), but meant to be obeyed by all Muslims, according to their situation:—

وَأَعْرِضْ عَنِ ٱلْجَٰهِلِينَ ○

".....and keep away from the (disputations raked up by the) ignorant."[13] (VII:199).

It is, therefore, a duty for everyone who aims at righteousness, i.e., every true follower of the Qur'ãn, to abstain completely from quarrelsomeness.

(xxii) Being overpowered by wrath ruled out; hence abstinence from it is duty:

In emphasising the qualities of the righteous, the Holy Qur'ãn says:—

---

13. It should be noted that in its relation to the Holy Prophet (Peace be on him), which forms its real context, this command has a more comprehensive implication. He was commanded not to engage in fruitless controversies with his ignorant strong-headed opponents, nor to conciliate them, but to ignore them; "holding to forgiveness and commanding what was right." (VII: 199, first part of the verse).

وَالْكٰظِمِيْنَ الْغَيْظَ

".....and (those) who control their wrath...." (III:134).

Hence, it is a Qur'ãnic duty of omission not to permit oneself under any circumstance to be overpowered by wrath.

(xxiii) Light-heartedness prohibited:

The Holy Qur'ãn says:

... وَلَا تَفْرَحُوْا بِمَآ اٰتٰىكُمْ ؕ

".....and (in order that) ye may not (lose the balance of your mind in) joy because of that (wordly good) which hath been given (to you)...." (LVII:23).

Exultation over the good things of the world is wedded to light-heartedness. The man of God should regard all wordly good fortune as illusory (LVII:20)[14]. Hence he should not suffer from emotional disturbance on such occasions, and should maintain his serenity, knowing, as he does, its true value. In other words, he should avoid light-heartedness.

(xxiv) Pessimism, i.e., being overpowered by despair, prohibited:

The Holy Qur'ãn says:

لِكَيْلَا تَاْسَوْا عَلٰى مَا فَاتَكُمْ

"That ye may not despair over matters which have escaped you...." (LVII:23).

Elsewhere, the exhortation is in the form of the emphatic command:

وَلَا تَايْـَٔسُوْا مِنْ رَّوْحِ اللّٰهِ ؕ اِنَّهٗ لَا يَايْـَٔسُ مِنْ رَّوْحِ اللّٰهِ اِلَّا الْقَوْمُ الْكٰفِرُوْنَ ○

---

14. The verse reads:

وَمَا الْحَيٰوةُ الدُّنْيَآ اِلَّا مَتَاعُ الْغُرُوْرِ ○

"What is the life of this world but a matter of illusion."

"and never give up hope of Allah's Soothing Mercy: Truly no one despairs of Allah's Soothing Mercy except those who have no faith." (XII:87).

This should be so, because every true Muslim is a man of God and devotion to Him is the end-all and be-all of his life:

قُلْ إِنَّ صَلَاتِي وَنُسُكِي وَمَحْيَايَ وَمَمَاتِي لِلَّهِ رَبِّ الْعَالَمِينَ ۝ لَا شَرِيكَ لَهُ ۚ

"Say: 'Truly, my prayer and my service of sacrifice, my life and my death are (all) for Allah, the Cherisher of the Worlds: No partner hath He." (VI:162, 163).

It is through this intense devotion that the light of Faith and Hope continues to burn constantly in his heart, and despair can never overtake him. Indeed, he is, in his religious make-up, out and out an optimist, and pessimism is the very negation of his Faith.

Hence the Qur'ãnic duty of shunning Pessimism completely and thoroughly.

(xxv) Being overpowered by fear ruled out; hence the effort to eradicate it is duty:

Fear is one of the greatest scourges of human life, and he who can overcome it is really a fortunate man. The Holy Qur'ãn has given a teaching which ensures this merit thoroughly.

According to the holy book, a true Muslim is he who has absolute faith in God and cultivates true devotion to Him. (VI:162)[15]. This faith and this devotion lend a strength to his will, a balance to his emotions and a grace to the personality which never fail him in life, because God's help and protection is unfailingly and always available to him:

فَمَنْ يَكْفُرْ بِالطَّاغُوتِ وَيُؤْمِنْ بِاللَّهِ فَقَدِ اسْتَمْسَكَ بِالْعُرْوَةِ الْوُثْقَىٰ لَا انْفِصَامَ لَهَا ۗ

"So whoever rejects Evil and believes in Allah hath grasped the most trustworthy hand-hold that never breaks". (II:256).

Thus a true Muslim is never afraid of anything of this world. He

---

15. Quoted above.

leads a life free of fear in proportion to the strength of his faith and trust in God:

أَلَآ إِنَّ أَوْلِيَآءَ اللّٰهِ لَا خَوْفٌ عَلَيْهِمْ وَلَا هُمْ يَحْزَنُونَ ۝ الَّذِينَ ءَامَنُوا
وَكَانُوا يَتَّقُونَ ۝ لَهُمُ الْبُشْرَىٰ فِي الْحَيَوٰةِ الدُّنْيَا وَفِي الْآخِرَةِ ۚ لَا تَبْدِيلَ
لِكَلِمَٰتِ اللّٰهِ ۚ ذَٰلِكَ هُوَ الْفَوْزُ الْعَظِيمُ ۝

"Behold! verily on the friends of Allah there is no fear, nor shall they grieve; those who believe and (constantly) guard against evil; for them are Glad Tidings in the life of the Present and in the Hereafter: No change can there be in the Words of Allah. This is indeed the supreme Felicity." (X:62-64).

For them, the Comforting Message and the Command is:

وَلَا تَحْزَنُوا

"Entertain no fear!" (XLI:30).

Because: all things and the consequences of all events are under the control and command of the All-Powerful, the All-Just and Most Merciful God:

تَبَٰرَكَ الَّذِي بِيَدِهِ الْمُلْكُ وَهُوَ عَلَىٰ كُلِّ شَيْءٍ قَدِيرٌ ۝

"Blessed be He in Whose hands is Dominion; and He over all things hath Power...." (LXVII:1).

وَلِلّٰهِ عَٰقِبَةُ الْأُمُورِ ۝

".....and with Allah rests the end of (all) affairs". (XXII:41).

It is thus the duty of a Muslim not to allow himself to be overpowered by fear.

(xxvi) Cowardice on the battlefield prohibited:

A true Muslim develops the strength of his heart through a dynamic and vibrant faith in God to such an extent that cowardice on the battlefield is inconceivable in his case:

وَالصَّٰبِرِينَ فِي الْبَأْسَآءِ وَالضَّرَّآءِ وَحِينَ الْبَأْسِ ۗ أُولَٰٓئِكَ الَّذِينَ صَدَقُوا ۖ
وَأُولَٰٓئِكَ هُمُ الْمُتَّقُونَ ۝

".....and those who are firm and patient, in pain (or suffering) and adversity, and throughout all periods of panic and violence.[16] These are they who are proven true (in their faith in God); and these are they who are (truly) righteous". (II:177).

Therefore, the Holy Qur'ãn lays down the command:

يَٰٓأَيُّهَا ٱلَّذِينَ ءَامَنُوٓا۟ إِذَا لَقِيتُمُ ٱلَّذِينَ كَفَرُوا۟ زَحْفًا فَلَا تُوَلُّوهُمُ ٱلْأَدْبَارَ ۝ وَ
مَن يُوَلِّهِمْ يَوْمَئِذٍ دُبُرَهُۥٓ إِلَّا مُتَحَرِّفًا لِّقِتَالٍ أَوْ مُتَحَيِّزًا إِلَىٰ فِئَةٍ
فَقَدْ بَآءَ بِغَضَبٍ مِّنَ ٱللَّهِ وَمَأْوَىٰهُ جَهَنَّمُ ۖ وَبِئْسَ ٱلْمَصِيرُ ۝

"O ye who believe! When ye meet the Unbelievers[17] in hostile array, *never turn your backs to them.*

"If any do turn his back to them on such a day, unless it be in a stratagem of war or to retreat to a troop (of his own), he draws on himself the wrath of Allah, and his abode is Hell,—an evil refuge (indeed)!" (VIII:15, 16).

Thus, to abstain from cowardice is a duty.

(xxvii) Fear of opponents of truth and justice ruled out; hence abstinence from it is duty:

The Holy Qur'ãn mentions it as one of the essential qualities of a true Muslim that, in upholding truth and justice, he is never afraid of those who may be opposed to him:

وَلَا يَخَافُونَ لَوْمَةَ لَآئِمٍ ۚ

"and (they are) never afraid of the reproaches of such as find fault....." (V:57).

Thus, to abstain from fear of opposition in respect of upholding truth and justice is a duty.

(xxviii) Cultivation of sadness, anxiety and worry in respect of worldly events and things prohibited:

---

16. i.e., in war.

17. War between Muslim states is inconceivable in Islam.

A true Muslim is, as we have already noted, a man of God, and his motto in life is to commit all his affairs to His care:

وَأُفَوِّضُ أَمْرِيٓ إِلَى ٱللَّهِ ۚ إِنَّ ٱللَّهَ بَصِيرٌۢ بِٱلْعِبَادِ ○

"(He said:) and I commit my affair to Allah: for Allah (ever) watches over His Servants." (XL:44).

This motto, taught by the Holy Qur'ãn, cuts at the very root of that attitude of mind which subjects a person to indulge irrationally in sadness, anxiety and worry, thereby damaging him in many ways.

Speaking directly of the problem, the holy book says:

لِّكَيْلَا تَحْزَنُوا۟ عَلَىٰ مَا فَاتَكُمْ وَلَا مَآ أَصَٰبَكُمْ ۗ

"....that (He might teach) you not to grieve for that which ye missed or for that which befell you...." (III:153).

Thus it is the duty of every true Muslim not to cultivate sadness, anxiety and worry in respect of what happens to him in his life.

(xxix) (a) *Capriciousness,*

(b) *indulgence in fancies and phantasms divorced from the realities of life,*

and (c) *harbouring evil thoughts,*

—all ruled out in Islamic conduct; hence abstinence from them is duty:

The Holy Qur'ãn regards *waswãs* as a great evil, so much so that it teaches a definite prayer for seeking God's protection against it. The prayer is:

قُلْ أَعُوذُ بِرَبِّ ٱلنَّاسِ ○ مَلِكِ ٱلنَّاسِ ○ إِلَٰهِ ٱلنَّاسِ ○ مِن شَرِّ
ٱلْوَسْوَاسِ ۥ ٱلْخَنَّاسِ ○ ٱلَّذِى يُوَسْوِسُ فِى صُدُورِ ٱلنَّاسِ ○ مِنَ ٱلْجِنَّةِ
وَٱلنَّاسِ ○

"Say: I seek refuge with the Lord and Cherisher of Mankind, the King (or Ruler) of Mankind, the God (or Judge) of Mankind from the evil of the *waswãs* of (or caused by) the slinking (devil), who whispereth in the hearts of Mankind,—among jinns and among men." (CXIV).

The word *'waswãs'* which has been left untranslated by the present writer comprehends within it several meanings that relate to different aspects of evil in the thoughts and feelings of human beings. The "*Dictionary of Modern Written Arabic*" gives the following meanings:

"devilish insinuation, temptation, wicked thoughts, doubt, misgiving, suspicion; delusion, fixed idea; uneasiness, anxiety, concern, melancholy."

The word '*waswãs*' covers, therefore: (*i*) depression of spirits through thoughts of sadness (—melancholy): (*ii*) anxiety; worry (—uneasiness and concern); (*iii*) capriciousness (—doubt, misgiving, suspicion); (*iv*) indulgence in delusions; (*v*) harbouring of evil thoughts.

Thus, the above prayer, while it emphasises the duty of abstaining from cultivation of sadness, anxiety and worry—stated in the immediately preceding section, also emphasises the duty of (*i*) shunning of capriciousness, and (*ii*)[18] abstaining from indulgence in delusions, namely, in fancies and phantasms divorced from the realities of life and consequently living in an imaginary world of one's own making, and (*iii*) guarding oneself against harbouring evil thoughts.

(xxx) Perversion—straying, and leading others, into evil courses condemned; hence abstinence from it is duty:

The Holy Qur'ãn condemns perversion in all its forms in the following verses:

وَاتْلُ عَلَيْهِمْ نَبَأَ الَّذِيٓ اٰتَيْنٰهُ اٰيٰتِنَا فَانْسَلَخَ مِنْهَا فَاَتْبَعَهُ
الشَّيْطٰنُ فَكَانَ مِنَ الْغٰوِيْنَ ۝

"And relate to them the story[19] of the man to whom We sent Our Signs, but he passed them by: So Satan followed him up, and he became of the perverted". (VII:175).

18. With regard to this duty, refer also to XXVI:225 where the word *wahm* has been employed.

19. "The story is preferably to be taken in a general sense, and not with reference to any particular individual." (Abdul Majid Daryabadi, *op.cit*, p. 298, n. 295).

وَبُرِّزَتِ الْجَحِيمُ لِلْغَاوِينَ ۝

"And the Fierce Fire shall be placed in full view before the perverted ones." (XXVI.91).

Hence, it is a duty to abstain from perversion in all its forms.

(xxxi) Indulgence in everything vain ruled out; hence abstinence from it is duty:

Emphasising certain essential attributes of Islamic conduct, the Holy Qur'ãn says:

وَالَّذِينَ هُمْ عَنِ اللَّغْوِ مُعْرِضُونَ ۝

".....and those (Believers) who from (everything) vain keep away....." (XXIII:3).

At another place, the same trait of Muslim character has been mentioned in these words:

وَإِذَا مَرُّوا بِاللَّغْوِ مَرُّوا كِرَامًا ۝

".....and when they pass by some vanity (like vain random talk, unedifying jokes, vain 'recreations', etc.), they pass by it with dignified (avoidance[20])". (XXV:72).

(xxxii) Idle discourse disapproved; hence abstinence from it is duty:

The following verse of the Holy Qur'ãn, though it relates to a particular event, also lays down a general rule of conduct:

وَمِنَ النَّاسِ مَنْ يَشْتَرِي لَهْوَ الْحَدِيثِ لِيُضِلَّ عَنْ سَبِيلِ اللَّهِ بِغَيْرِ عِلْمٍ وَيَتَّخِذَهَا هُزُوًا ۚ أُولَٰئِكَ لَهُمْ عَذَابٌ مُهِينٌ ۝

"And of mankind are those who purchase (i.e., are occupied with) idle discourse[21], to mislead (men) from Allah's Way (—which is

20. i.e., neither indulging in it nor being fussy about it.

21. "Life is taken seriously by men who realize the issues that hang upon it. But there are men of a frivolous turn of mind who prefer idle tales to true Realities and they are justly rebuked here". (A. Yusuf Ali, *op.cit.*, p. 1080).

the way of beneficial spending of time and energy) without knowledge (i.e., on the basis of vain fanciful stories), and throw ridicule on it: for such there will be a humiliating Penalty." (XXXI:6).

It is, therefore, duty to abstain from wasting time and energy in vain talks, frivolous discourses and idle tales.

(xxxiii) Recklessness prohibited:

One of the attributes of the unrighteous mentioned by the Holy Qur'ãn is that of being '*musrif*' (XL:28), which word comprehends 'recklessness' in its meanings.

Also, the injunction has been laid down:

وَلَا تُسْرِفُوا

".....Do not practice recklessness....." (VII:31).

(xxxiv) Abstinence enjoined in respect of:

(*i*) Idle curiosity;

(*ii*) Believing in unfounded reports;

(*iii*) Spreading unfounded reports;

(*iv*) Entering into discussions without correct knowledge of the problem;

(*v*) Entertaining opinions for which no strong reason to believe exists;

(*vi*) Proffering uncertain opinion;

(*vii*) Tendering uncertain advice.

In the following pithy verse, whose Arabic text can be but poorly translated into English, the Holy Qur'ãn lays down a comprehensive duty of omission which covers all the above vices:

وَلَا تَقْفُ مَا لَيْسَ لَكَ بِهِ عِلْمٌ

"Pursue not and follow not that whereof thou hast no knowledge." (XVII:36).

(xxxv) Idleness ruled out; hence abstinence from it is duty:

The Holy Qur'ãn commands the Muslims in these words:

يَٰٓأَيُّهَا الَّذِيْنَ اٰمَنُوا اصْبِرُوْا وَصَابِرُوْا وَرَابِطُوْا وَاتَّقُوا اللّٰهَ لَعَلَّكُمْ تُفْلِحُوْنَ ۝

"O ye who believe! persevere, and excel in perseverance, and be (always) in a state of readiness, and observe your duty to Allah that haply ye may prosper." (III:200).

Idleness, or aversion to labour, is possible in a physically normal person only when: (*a*) he has no serious end in view, and (*b*) he possesses a tone of mind whereby he suffers from lack of perseverance.

The Holy Qur'ãn cuts at the root of both of these shortcomings when it commands the Muslims, in the above verse, to develop the very opposite character, namely, maximum of perseverance and the most serious end, *i.e.,* making observance of the duty to God the goal of life.

Thus, idleness is definitely a vice in the Qur'ãnic moral system and should, as such, be shunned by every Muslim.

Expounding this Qur'ãnic teaching, the Holy Prophet (Peace be on him) has taught the Muslims to seek God's refuge from idleness. The wordings of the prayer are:

اللّٰهم إني أعوذ بك من الهمّ والحزن والعجز والكسل والبخل وضلع الدّين
وغلبة الرّجال

"O Allah! I seek refuge with Thee from worry and grief and incompetence (in the performance of duties) and *idleness* and cowardice and miserliness and the burden of debt and the tyranny of the people." (Bukhãrî's *Sahîh*).

(xxxvi) Abstinence enjoined in respect of false endeavour in earning livelihood:

(a) through beggary;

(b) through acquiring money falsely by religious pretences and superstitious practices;

(c) through gambling.

(a) Beggary:

The qualities of the needy person who deserves financial help have been laid down thus:

لِلْفُقَرَآءِ الَّذِينَ أُحْصِرُوا فِي سَبِيلِ اللهِ لَا يَسْتَطِيعُونَ ضَرْبًا فِي الْأَرْضِ يَحْسَبُهُمُ الْجَاهِلُ أَغْنِيَآءَ مِنَ التَّعَفُّفِ تَعْرِفُهُم بِسِيمَٰهُمْ لَا يَسْـَٔلُونَ النَّاسَ إِلْحَافًا

"(Voluntary financial help is[22]) for those in need, who, in Allah's cause[23], are restricted, and cannot move about in the land (seeking for trade or work). The ignorant man thinks because of their modesty (in respect of asking for help), that they are free from want. Thou shalt know them from their (unfailing) mark. They beg not importunately from all and sundry....." (II:273).

Thus: the person who deserves help should fulfil the following conditions:

(*i*) his need for money should be genuine;

(*ii*) it should arise from some honourable or acceptable cause, including inability to work due to physical ailments or non-availability of employment;

(*iii*) he should be respectable in his demeanour;

(*iv*) he should not beg from all and sundry, namely, should not adopt beggary as a profession.

Professional beggary, which is a debasing form of acquiring easy money, is, therefore, completely ruled out by the Holy Qur'ãn. Indeed, it has no place in Muslim society[24].

(b) Acquiring money falsely through religious pretences and superstitious practices:

---

22. (Primarily).

23. All genuine service to mankind, specially religious service, is included here.

24. The fact is affirmed further by the uncompromising verdict of the Holy Prophet (Peace be on him) against beggary. (See: e.g., Abû Dã'ûd: *Sunan*, Vol. I, pp. 232, 247).

The Holy Qur'ãn points out condemningly another false means of earning money which damages both the recipient and the giver of money,—the means, namely, of employing religious pretences and superstitions, or, so-called "spiritual" practices. It says:

يَا أَيُّهَا الَّذِينَ آمَنُوا إِنَّ كَثِيرًا مِّنَ الْأَحْبَارِ وَالرُّهْبَانِ لَيَأْكُلُونَ
أَمْوَالَ النَّاسِ بِالْبَاطِلِ

"O ye who believe! verily many of the priests and the monks devour the substances of the people in falsehood (i.e., on false pretences)....." (IX:34).

This verse refers to the Jewish priest and divines and the Christian monks and clergy. The false pretences consisted in that the Jewish priests used to misinterpret the law for the benefit of obtaining money from the interested parties[25], and the Christian monks and clergy used to issue indulgences and dispensations and had made the shrines of their saints a source of revenue for themselves.[26]

The condemnation by the Holy Qur'ãn means that it is the duty of a Muslim to abstain from acquiring money from all types of false pretences and practices in the name of spirituality and religion.

(c) *Gambling, as embodying the spirit of earning wealth without labour, prohibited:*

Another way of acquiring easy money is through the different forms of gambling. The Holy Qur'ãn commands the Muslims to shun all those forms of false earning, when it says:

يَا أَيُّهَا الَّذِينَ آمَنُوا إِنَّمَا الْخَمْرُ وَالْمَيْسِرُ وَالْأَنصَابُ وَالْأَزْلَامُ رِجْسٌ
مِّنْ عَمَلِ الشَّيْطَانِ فَاجْتَنِبُوهُ لَعَلَّكُمْ تُفْلِحُونَ ۝

"O ye who believe! intoxicants and *gambling*[27], (dedication of)

---

25. Cf. *Is.* 1:23, *Je.* 6:13; *Mi.* 3:11.

26. See: Prof. Lecky's *History of European Morals.*

27. Gambling: the word *maisir*, used in the Arabic text, denotes literally: a means of getting something too easily—getting profit without labour and on the basis of chance. Finally, it is 'any game of hazard, or play of stakes, or wagers, so that even the game of children with walnut is included under this name by Mujahid'. (Lane's *Arabic-English Lexicon*). The most familiar form of gambling

stones, and (divination by) arrows, are *an abomination*—of *Satan's handiwork: Shun it, therefore,* that ye may prosper.[28]" (V:93).

Thus, it is a duty to abstain totally from all forms of gambling.

(xxxvii) Love of wealth for its won sake[29] *vehemently condemned; hence abstinence from it is duty:*

The Holy Qur'ãn, while condemning unrighteousness, recounts love of wealth as one of the vices:

وَتُحِبُّونَ الْمَالَ حُبًّا جَمًّا

".....and ye love wealth with inordinate love." (LXXXIX:20).

وَإِنَّهُ لِحُبِّ الْخَيْرِ لَشَدِيدٌ

---

among the Arabs was based on the principle of lottery through the employment of arrows. The Greeks used knuckle-bones. The Roman children employed 'head-or-tail' system with the coins. The Israelites used to draw lots. Certain other communities, like the Aryans, used dice. (*Encyclopaedia of Religion and Ethics*, VI, pp. 163, 164).

28. The total abolition of this evil practise in Muslim society by the Holy Prophet (Peace be on him) has been admitted even by his worst critics as one of the "most celebrated" reforms accomplished by him. (See: D.S. Margoliouth in: *Encyclopaedia Brit.*, XVII, p. 407, 11th Ed.). As for the non-Muslim communities, even of the present 'age of enlightenment': "The extent to which gambling prevails at the present time is difficult to assess.....Most of it is centered in the horse-racing....On the whole, it may safely be asserted that little short of £100,000,000 changes hands every year in England in connection with gambling transactions.....Side by side with the betting odds and betting tips, the newspapers record the tragic results on those who yield to the temptation. In 13 years (1895-96 to 1906-7) there were 156 suicides in England assigned to this cause, as well as 719 cases of theft on embezzlement, and 442 bankruptcies". (*Encyclopaedia of Religion and Ethics*, VI, pp. 164, 168). Indeed, the close relationship between gambling and crime, including sexual crime and crime against life and property, is an established fact of human history and can be perused in the cultural histories of the different communities who have indulged in this devastating vice.

29. It should be noted that the verses which voice condemnation of love for wealth are all to be found in the closing part of the Holy Qur'ãn. This fact seems to emphasize that love for wealth may damage even an otherwise virtuous life. Hence, the greatest caution is necessary in that respect.

"and lo! in the love of wealth the (i.e., the unregenerate man who is ungrateful to God) is violent." (C:8).

أَلْهٰكُمُ التَّكَاثُرُ ۝ حَتّٰى زُرْتُمُ الْمَقَابِرَ ۝

"The emulous desire for abundance and increase (in wealth, status and other wordly possessions) distracts you (from the more serious and higher things), until ye visit the graves (*i.e.,* ye die)." (CII:1, 2).

وَيْلٌ لِّكُلِّ هُمَزَةٍ لُّمَزَةٍ ۝ الَّذِىْ جَمَعَ مَالًا وَّعَدَّدَهٗ ۝ يَحْسَبُ اَنَّ مَالَهٗٓ اَخْلَدَهٗ ۝
كَلَّا لَيُنْۢبَذَنَّ فِى الْحُطَمَةِ ۝

"Woe to every kind of scandal-monger and backbiter, who amasseth wealth and counteth it (often out of love for it), thinking his wealth would make him last for ever. By no means! He will surely be thrown into that (Hell) which breaks to pieces." (CIV:1-4).

It is, therefore, the duty of a Muslim to shun love for wealth totally, regarding wealth only as a means to virtue.

(xxxviii) Abstinence enjoined in respect of Covetousness[30] *or, the spirit of Greed, which expresses itself in:*

(a) *Covetous Selfishness, or, withholding from others the goods possessed by one's own self (=miserliness);*

and (b) *Coveting other's goods.*

(a) *Covetous Selfishness*:

The Holy Qur'ãn has laid down the rule:

وَمَنْ يُّوْقَ شُحَّ نَفْسِهٖ فَاُولٰٓئِكَ هُمُ الْمُفْلِحُوْنَ ۝

"And those saved from the covetousness[31] of their own souls,—they are the ones that achieve prosperity." (LIX:9; LXIV:16).

Thus it is duty to abstain from harbouring the spirit of covetousness—covetous selfishness—in all things that we possess.

---

30. Synonymous words are: Avarice, avidity, cupidity, greed, greediness.

31. The word used here in the Arabic text is *shuhh*, which means 'covetousness combined with stinginess'. We may call it 'covetous selfishness'.

(b) Coveting other's goods prohibited:

By coveting others' goods:

(i) one damages his spirit of contentment and, as a consequence, his peace of mind; and

(*ii*) he cultivates the spirit of jealousy.

Both of these are vices.

The Holy Qur'ãn, therefore, says:

وَلَا تَتَمَنَّوْا مَا فَضَّلَ اللّٰهُ بِهٖ بَعْضَكُمْ عَلٰى بَعْضٍ

"And in no wise covet those things in which Allah hath made some of you excel others." (IV:32).

It is, thus, a duty to abstain from coveting the goods that others possess.

(xxxix) Permitting oneself the very Spirit of Miserliness, prohibited:

The Holy Qur'ãn commands:

وَلَا تَجْعَلْ يَدَكَ مَغْلُوْلَةً اِلٰى عُنُقِكَ

"Make not thy hand tied (in miserliness) to thy neck....."
(XVII:29).

Because, the true Muslims are those who:

وَلَمْ يَقْتُرُوْا

"are not niggardly". (XXV:67).

And every Muslim should always remember that :

وَالَّذِيْنَ يَكْنِزُوْنَ الذَّهَبَ وَالْفِضَّةَ وَلَا يُنْفِقُوْنَهَا فِيْ سَبِيْلِ اللّٰهِ فَبَشِّرْ
هُمْ بِعَذَابٍ اَلِيْمٍ ۝ يَوْمَ يُحْمٰى عَلَيْهَا فِيْ نَارِ جَهَنَّمَ فَتُكْوٰى بِهَا
جِبَاهُهُمْ وَجُنُوْبُهُمْ وَظُهُوْرُهُمْ هٰذَا مَا كَنَزْتُمْ لِاَنْفُسِكُمْ فَذُوْقُوْا
مَا كُنْتُمْ تَكْنِزُوْنَ ۝

"....there are those who bury gold and silver and spend it not in the Way of Allah: announce unto them a most grievous penalty—on the Day when heat will be produced out of that (wealth) in the fire of Hell, and with it will be branded their foreheads, their flanks, and their backs: (And it will be said to them:) 'This is the (treasure) which ye buried for yourselves: taste ye, then, the (treasure) ye buried'." (IX: 34, 35).

and:

وَلَا يَحْسَبَنَّ الَّذِينَ يَبْخَلُونَ بِمَا آتَاهُمُ اللَّهُ مِنْ فَضْلِهِ هُوَ خَيْرًا لَهُمْ ۖ بَلْ هُوَ
شَرٌّ لَهُمْ ۖ سَيُطَوَّقُونَ مَا بَخِلُوا بِهِ يَوْمَ الْقِيَامَةِ ۗ وَلِلَّهِ مِيرَاثُ السَّمَاوَاتِ
وَالْأَرْضِ ۗ وَاللَّهُ بِمَا تَعْمَلُونَ خَبِيرٌ ۝

"Let not those who are niggardly in respect of the gifts which Allah hath given of His Grace, think it is good for them: nay! it is bad for them. Soon shall the things withheld in niggardliness be tied to their necks like a collar (—the callar of agonising misery—) on the Day of Judgment. To Allah belongs the heritage of the heavens and earth; and Allah is well acquainted with what ye do." (III:180).

It is, therefore, a duty to self to keep one's heart absolutely clear of the spirit of miserliness.

(xl) Practising miserliness in respect of one's self specifically condemned; hence abstinence from it is duty:

People are generally miserly in respect of others. But there are those also who are miserly, not only towards others, but even towards themselves. Namely, they deprive themselves of rationally and justly benefiting from those means of healthy living which God bestows on them. Such persons have been condemned by the Holy Qur'ãn:

إِنَّ اللَّهَ لَا يُحِبُّ مَنْ كَانَ مُخْتَالًا فَخُورًا ۝ الَّذِينَ يَبْخَلُونَ
وَيَأْمُرُونَ النَّاسَ بِالْبُخْلِ وَيَكْتُمُونَ مَا آتَاهُمُ اللَّهُ مِنْ
فَضْلِهِ ۗ وَأَعْتَدْنَا لِلْكَافِرِينَ عَذَابًا مُهِينًا ۝

"Verily, Allah loveth not the arrogant, the vainglorious;—nor those who are niggardly and command mankind to niggardliness and *hide the bounties which Allah hath bestowed on them*; and We have prepared for the ungrateful a punishment that steeps them in contempt...." (IV:36, 37).

"Hiding the bounties which Allah hath bestowed on them" implies:

(*i*) Withholding bounties from others;

(*ii*) Disallowing those bounties from manifesting themselves on one's person and in the different aspects of one's personal life.

There is a *hadith* which clarifies the duty in respect of the second implication directly:

إِنَّ اللّٰهَ يُحِبُّ أَنْ يَرٰى أَثَرَ نِعْمَتِهٖ عَلٰى عَبْدِهٖ

"Allah loves to see the effects of His bounties on the person of His Servant." (Tirmizi).

It is, therefore, the duty of a Muslim to abstain from practising miserliness towards his own self.

(xli) (a) Squandering—Vain Spending, prohibited:

The Holy Qur'ãn says:

وَلَا تُبَذِّرْ تَبْذِيْرًا ۝ إِنَّ الْمُبَذِّرِيْنَ كَانُوْٓا إِخْوَانَ الشَّيٰطِيْنِ ۖ وَكَانَ الشَّيْطٰنُ لِرَبِّهٖ كَفُوْرًا ۝

"....but squander not (your wealth) in the manner of a spendthrift. Verily spendthrifts are associates of (*i.e.*, of the same family as) the Evil Ones; and the Evil One is to his Lord (Himself) ungrateful'[32]."[33] (XVII:26, 27).

It is, therefore, a duty to abstain totally from squandering one's wealth, whether of one's own self and defendants or for others.

---

32. Hence those who squander their wealth commit no less a sin than that of being ungrateful to God by misusing His bounty.

33. Cf. another verse:

وَلَا تَبْسُطْهَا كُلَّ الْبَسْطِ فَتَقْعُدَ مَلُوْمًا مَّحْسُوْرًا ۝

".....nor open it (*i.e.*, the hand) with a complete opening lest thou become blameworthy and destitute." (XVII:29).

(b) *Insincerity in acts seemingly of charity and spending one's wealth for show in general, condemned:*

إِنَّ اللّٰهَ لَا يُحِبُّ مَنْ كَانَ مُخْتَالًا فَخُوْرًا ۝ .... وَالَّذِيْنَ يُنْفِقُوْنَ أَمْوَالَهُمْ رِئَآءَ النَّاسِ

"Verily Allah loveth not the arrogant, the vainglorious.....those who expend their substance to show off to men...." (IV: 36, 38).

(xlii) *Impatience, or want of calm endurance and perseverance, disapproved; hence abstinence from it is duty;*

وَلَوْ أَنَّهُمْ صَبَرُوْا حَتّٰى تَخْرُجَ إِلَيْهِمْ لَكَانَ خَيْرًا لَّهُمْ ۚ

"If only they had patience until thou (O Prophet) could come out to them, it would have been good for them. (That they behaved impatiently was bad for them)". (XLIX:5).

This verse indicates that impatience, namely, want of calm endurance and perseverance, is bad for one's self. Hence to abstain from it is duty to self.

(xliii) *Spirit of Ungratefulness condemned; hence abstinence from it is duty:*

The Holy Qur'ãn says:

إِنَّ اللّٰهَ لَا يُحِبُّ كُلَّ خَوَّانٍ كَفُوْرٍ ۝

"Verily, Allah loveth not any treacherous, ungrateful (person)." (XXII:38).

This verse emphasises basically the *spirit* of ungratefulness. Of Course, active ungratefulness, whether towards God or towards fellow-beings, is also definitely included.

It is, therefore, duty to eschew the spirit of ungratefulness and to abstain from being ungrateful to anyone, whereby the moral purity of one's own inner personality is damaged.

(xliv) *Indecency, lewdness and everything abominable in thought and word and deed, prohibited:*

The Holy Qur'ãn has commanded:

وَلَا تَقْرَبُوا الْفَوَاحِشَ مَا ظَهَرَ مِنْهَا وَمَا بَطَنَ ۚ

"....and draw not nigh to indecencies, whether open or secret...."[34] (VI:151).

Again:

وَيَنْهَىٰ عَنِ الْفَحْشَاءِ وَالْمُنكَرِ وَالْبَغْيِ ۚ

"....and He forbidden lewdness and abomination and wickedness...."[35] (XVI:90).

It is, thus, duty to abstain totally from indecency, lewdness and everything abominable in thought, in speech and in action.

(xlv) *The very Spirit of Sexual Immodesty prohibited:*

The Holy Qur'ãn says:

وَلَا تَقْرَبُوا الزِّنَىٰ ۖ إِنَّهُ كَانَ فَاحِشَةً وَسَاءَ سَبِيلًا ○

"And come not nigh to adultery: for it is a shameful (deed) and an evil, opening the road (to other evils)." (XVII:32).

The words "come not nigh to" imply abstinence from the very *spirit* of sexual immodesty, as also the attitude and the behaviour in which it manifests itself. Thus it is a duty to shun[36] they very spirit of sexual

---

34, 35. The words *fawãhish* and *fahshã'* used in the above verses for shameful things are very rich in their meanings and cannot be translated into English.

36. This stern moral attitude of Islam may be compared with the spirit, the attitude, and the consequent behaviour, nurtured in the Western communities, where, because of freedom of promiscuity, adultery "has become fashionable in both England and America" and elsewhere. (Scott: *History of Prostitution*, p. 226). Indeed, because of the absence of the spirit of sexual modesty and of the cultivation of general licence in respect of sexual manners, sexual morality has been damaged to such an extent that: "The old type of prostitute who pranced about gaudily and drunkenly in the Strand, Leicester Square, Piccadily and Regent Street, is a thing of the past..... There has been a huge increase in promiscuity among men and even greater increase among women....The results are that more and more every year is man turning to so-called girls of respectability in order to satisfy his sexual appetite.... Virginity among women is becoming something to sneer at.... Where all the practising what is virtually prostitution there can be no such thing as prostitution." (*Ibid.*, pp. 224, 225, 228). There is a lesson in this for all those Muslims who advocate the adoption

immodesty, as also the immodest attitudes and behaviour that cause temptation in relations between the sexes.

(xlvi) *Defiling one's spiritual and moral purity through illicit sexual gratification, including homosexuality and self-abuse, prohibited:*

Abstinence from lewdness has already been included in the duty mentioned in the previous section. Here we may quote the verse where the command has been given with particular reference to sexual appetite. The Holy Qur'ãn says:

قُلْ لِّلْمُؤْمِنِيْنَ يَغُضُّوْا مِنْ اَبْصَارِهِمْ وَ يَحْفَظُوْا فُرُوْجَهُمْ ؕ ذٰلِكَ اَزْكٰى لَهُمْ ؕ اِنَّ اللّٰهَ خَبِيْرٌ ۢ بِمَا يَصْنَعُوْنَ ۝ وَ قُلْ لِّلْمُؤْمِنٰتِ يَغْضُضْنَ مِنْ اَبْصَارِهِنَّ وَ يَحْفَظْنَ فُرُوْجَهُنَّ

"Say thou (O Prophet!) to the believing men that they should lower their gaze (in the spirit of sexual modesty) and guard their private parts (against misuse): that will make for greater purity for them. And Allah is well acquainted with all that ye do.

"And say to the believing women that they should lower their gaze and guard their private parts (against misuse)." (XXIV:30, 31).

These verse lay down the duty of abstaining from defiling one's purity by illicit sexual relations and sexual self-abuse.[37]

(xlvii) *Indifference to self-reform condemned; hence abstinence from it is duty:*

The greatest of moral diseases consists in the attitude of indifference to self-reform. The Holy Qur'ãn takes full cognizance of it and, in order to warn the Muslims of its evil implications and consequences, condemns the presence of this disease among the clergy and the people of a previous religious community.

Addressing their clergy, it says:

---

of western culture. Alas! the social evils of the West are only too fast penetrating the Muslim communities also under the spell of modernisation!

37. The only way of satisfying the sexual appetite recognised by the Holy Qur'ãn as legitimate and chaste is that of marriage between man and woman duly solemnised. (XXIII: 5-7; LXX:29-31). All other ways are totally prohibited.

أَتَأْمُرُونَ النَّاسَ بِالْبِرِّ وَتَنْسَوْنَ أَنْفُسَكُمْ وَأَنْتُمْ تَتْلُونَ الْكِتَٰبَ ۚ أَفَلَا تَعْقِلُونَ ۝

"Do ye enjoin right conduct on the people, and forget (to practise it) yourselves, and yet ye study the Scripture? Will ye not understand?" (II:44).

ثُمَّ قَسَتْ قُلُوبُكُمْ مِنْ بَعْدِ ذَٰلِكَ فَهِيَ كَالْحِجَارَةِ أَوْ أَشَدُّ قَسْوَةً ۚ وَإِنَّ
مِنَ الْحِجَارَةِ لَمَا يَتَفَجَّرُ مِنْهُ الْأَنْهَٰرُ ۚ وَإِنَّ مِنْهَا لَمَا يَشَّقَّقُ فَيَخْرُجُ مِنْهُ الْمَاءُ ۚ
وَإِنَّ مِنْهَا لَمَا يَهْبِطُ مِنْ خَشْيَةِ اللَّهِ ۗ وَمَا اللَّهُ بِغَٰفِلٍ عَمَّا تَعْمَلُونَ ۝

"Thenceforth your hearts hardened: they became like a rock and even worse in hardness. For among rocks there are some from which rivers gush forth; others there are which when split asunder send forth water; and others which sink for fear of Allah: and Allah is not unmindful of your actions." (II:74).

It is, therefore, the duty of a Muslim to abstain from cultivating or retaining an attitude which may disable him from reforming himself in respect of his weaknesses and deficiencies.

Chapter II

DUTIES OF COMMISSION

END :

Moral Development ensuring Moral Perfection.

(i) Cultivation and practice of Truthfulness enjoined:

The Holy Qur'ãn lays down the command in the following two verses:

يَاأَيُّهَا الَّذِينَ آمَنُوا اتَّقُوا اللَّهَ وَكُونُوا مَعَ الصَّادِقِينَ ۝

"O ye who believe! Guard your duty to Allah (in respect of truthfulness) and be with those who are true (in thought, word and deed.)" (IX:119).

يَاأَيُّهَا الَّذِينَ آمَنُوا اتَّقُوا اللَّهَ وَقُولُوا قَوْلًا سَدِيدًا ۝ يُصْلِحْ لَكُمْ أَعْمَالَكُمْ وَيَغْفِرْ لَكُمْ ذُنُوبَكُمْ ۗ وَمَنْ يُطِعِ اللَّهَ وَرَسُولَهُ فَقَدْ فَازَ فَوْزًا عَظِيمًا ۝

"O ye who believe! Guard your duty to Allah and speak words (that are) true and directed to the right point: that He may make your conduct whole and sound and forgive you your sins. He that obeys Allah and His Messenger, hath indeed attained the highest achievement." (XXXIII:70, 71).

The first commands the Muslims:

(a) to be most conscientiously truthful, namely, through guarding their duty of obedience to God Who is all time a witness even to their innermost thoughts and feelings, not to speak of speech and action;

(b) to be comprehensively truthful, because conscientious truthfulness means truthfulness in every respect, namely, in thought, word and deed;

(c) to develop the spirit and activity of truthfulness by upholding the cause of truthfulness and by loving the company of those who are genuinely truthful.

The second verse commands, not only conscientious truthfulness in speech, but also guarding against even unconscious slip from truth by making the speech "directed to the right point."[1]

Truthfulness in thought, word and deed is, therefore, a duty. Indeed, it is such an important duty that it forms one of essential attributes of righteousness (III:14-16), and Heaven has been promised to those who uphold truth in their hearts and practise it in their actions (XXXIII:35). In Heaven itself, the righteous will enjoy their blissful life in "*an Assembly of Truth* in the Presence of the Sovereign Omnipotent." (LIV:55).

(ii) Guarding of Oaths enjoined:

Taking lightly one's oaths is the quality of the person who is deficient in moral earnestness and lacks in true devotion to truthfulness. Hence, in order to maintain sound moral outlook and character, it is a duty to guard one's oaths, i.e., to be true to one's oaths; and this is what the Holy Qur'ãn has commanded:

وَاحْفَظُوٓا اَيْمَانَكُمْ

".....and guard your oaths." (V:92).

(iii) Cultivation of the spirit of Sincerity and Uprightness enjoined:

Sincerity means freedom from pretence. Uprightness (or, *honesty*) means freedom from fraud. Both these qualities are actually forms of truthfulness, implying that there should be sameness in reality as in appearance. In other words, what we express in words should be the same as we feel in our hearts, and in no way should we do injustice to our speech by making it immoral through making it discordant with what we believe to be true. The Holy Qur'ãn has thus commanded sincerity and uprightness (side by side with truthfulness in giving evidence and with justice in pronouncing judgment), in the following verse:

وَإِذَا قُلْتُمْ فَاعْدِلُوا

".....and when ye utter a word, do justice thereunto...."
(VI:152).

---

1. "Directed to the right point" also means employing accuracy in expression, which is a part of wisdom—another great excellence upheld by the Holy Qur'ãn. (II:269).

(iv) Steadfastness in everything good and true enjoined:

The Holy Qur'ãn has commanded the Muslims to be steadfast in the cause of Truth:

وَرَابِطُوا

".....and be ever ready (*i.e.,* fixed in your resolve)...." (III:200).

Again:

يٰٓاَيُّهَا الَّذِيْنَ اٰمَنُوْٓا اِذَا لَقِيْتُمْ فِئَةً فَاثْبُتُوْا

"O ye who believe! when ye meet a (hostile) force, stay firm...." (VIII:45).

This should be so, because firmness is one of the basic qualities of true Believers:

يُثَبِّتُ اللّٰهُ الَّذِيْنَ اٰمَنُوْا بِالْقَوْلِ الثَّابِتِ فِى الْحَيٰوةِ الدُّنْيَا وَفِى الْاٰخِرَةِ

"Allah keepeth firm those who believe, with the Word that stands firm, in this world and in the Hereafter..." (XIV:27).

Hence, steadfastness in all that is good and true is duty.

(v) Modesty enjoined:

Modesty, which means "restraint by a sense of seemliness" and which implies spiritual purity and moral decency in one's inner attitudes and outward behaviour *in respect of moral decorum*, has been emphasised in a beautiful manner in the following Qur'ãnic verses:

يٰبَنِيْٓ اٰدَمَ قَدْ اَنْزَلْنَا عَلَيْكُمْ لِبَاسًا يُّوَارِيْ سَوْاٰتِكُمْ وَرِيْشًا ؕ وَلِبَاسُ التَّقْوٰى ۙ ذٰلِكَ خَيْرٌ ؕ ذٰلِكَ مِنْ اٰيٰتِ اللّٰهِ لَعَلَّهُمْ يَذَّكَّرُوْنَ ۝ يٰبَنِيْٓ اٰدَمَ لَا يَفْتِنَنَّكُمُ الشَّيْطٰنُ كَمَآ اَخْرَجَ اَبَوَيْكُمْ مِّنَ الْجَنَّةِ يَنْزِعُ عَنْهُمَا لِبَاسَهُمَا لِيُرِيَهُمَا سَوْاٰتِهِمَا ؕ

"O ye children of Adam! We have bestowed raiment upon you to conceal your shame, and as an adornment. But *the raiment of piety, that is the best*. Such are among the Signs of Allah, that ye may be admonished.

"O ye children of Adam! *Let not Satan seduce you,* in the same manner as he got your parents out of the Garden (of felicity), stripping them of the raiment (of innocence and purity), that he might manifest their shame to them....." (VII:26, 27).

'Raiment of piety', in verse 26, emphasises the observance of modesty in the inner attitude as well as outward behaviour; while the words: 'let not Satan seduce you' in verse 27, proclaim the duty of the observance of modesty.[2]

(vi) Marriage enjoined for providing the protection of the moral fortress of married life to the individual:

The law has been laid down:

وَأَنْكِحُوا الْأَيَامٰى مِنْكُمْ وَالصّٰلِحِيْنَ مِنْ عِبَادِكُمْ وَإِمَآئِكُمْ ؕ إِنْ يَّكُوْنُوْا
فُقَرَآءَ يُغْنِهِمُ اللّٰهُ مِنْ فَضْلِهٖ ؕ وَاللّٰهُ وَاسِعٌ عَلِيْمٌ ○

"Marry those among you who are single, or the virtuous ones among your slaves, male or female: If they are in poverty Allah will give them Means out of His Grace: for Allah encompasseth all, and He knoweth all things." (XXIV:32).

That marriage provides a moral fortress, a fortress of chastity, has been emphasised by the Holy Qur'ãn in the word *muhsin—hisn* meaning fortess—employed in the verse which points out the true motive with which a Muslim should marry:

مُحْصِنِيْنَ غَيْرَ مُسٰفِحِيْنَ ؕ

".....desiring chastity, not lust....." (IV:24).

(vii) Chastity under all conditions: Preservation of sexual sanctity enjoined:

Chastity implies maintenance of purity in thought, word and deed, and in respect of the sexual passion. The Holy Qur'ãn makes it a duty when it commands:

2. The Holy Qur'ãn has not only laid down this duty in fundamental terms, but has also given certain rules in that respect. We shall state those rules in the section on "Manners."

وَلْيَسْتَعْفِفِ الَّذِينَ لَا يَجِدُونَ نِكَاحًا

"Those who find not the wherewithal of marriage shall keep themselves chaste (in thought, word and deed)...." (XXIV:33).

Elsewhere, the womenfolk have been specifically commanded:

وَأَنْ يَسْتَعْفِفْنَ خَيْرٌ لَّهُنَّ ط

".....and that they shall observe the principle of chastity (even in respect of the most distantly related aspects of attitude and behaviour), that is best for them...." (XXIV:60).

(viii) Labouring for earning one's livelihood enjoined:

The Holy Qur'ãn has commanded:

وَابْتَغُوا مِنْ فَضْلِ اللهِ وَاذْكُرُوا اللهَ كَثِيرًا لَّعَلَّكُمْ تُفْلِحُونَ○

".....*and seek of* (*i.e., strive and labour for*) *Allah's bounty* (*i.e., means of livelihood*): and remember Allah much, that ye may prosper." (LXII:10).

The above command to strive and labour for earning one's livelihood has actually been given in the context of the observance of special weekly congregational worship on Fridays. This does not mean, however, that the command is confined only to Fridays. On the contrary, the Holy Qur'ãn has emphasised the virtue of labouring for earning one's livelihood by repudiating the Jewish-Christian notion of the Sabbath—of the false belief as to the sanctity of idleness and abstinence from work—and asserting that labour for honest earning is most definitely a part of worship.

Expounding the Qur'ãnic view, the Holy Prophet (Peace be on him) says:

طلب كسب الحلال فريضة ....

"To engage in labour for honest livelihood is duty...." (*Mishkãt al-Masabîh*, vol. II., p. 7).

(ix) Earning livelihood through honest means enjoined:

The verse quoted in the preceding injunction[3] implies one more

3. LXII:10.

command also: namely, to earn one's livelihood by honest means and in honest manner, because it has to be earned as "God's Bounty" and not as Satan's favour. Moreover, the command to earn has been combined with the command to "remember Allah much, that ye may prosper", thereby commanding spiritualisation of the effort for earning, which alone can truly guarantee the maintenance of one's conscience as sound and unblemished.

(x) Benefiting oneself from only that which has been lawfully acquired, enjoined:

The most basic need of man is food, and hence it is hunger in respect of which it is most difficult to observe lawfulness. Even an honest person finds it most difficult to abstain from employing debasing or illegitimate means, like theft, when he is confronted with death by starvation. Hence, the Holy Qur'ãn has mentioned food when laying down the duty of benefiting oneself from only that which has been lawfully acquired. It says:

يَٰٓأَيُّهَا ٱلنَّاسُ كُلُوا۟ مِمَّا فِى ٱلْأَرْضِ حَلَٰلًا طَيِّبًا

"O mankind! eat of whatsoever is on the earth (provided it is) lawfully acquired, and good (*i.e.*, lawful for your health)...." (II:168).

Then the Holy Qur'ãn goes beyond food and lays down the general law:

يَٰٓأَيُّهَا ٱلَّذِينَ ءَامَنُوٓا۟ أَنفِقُوا۟ مِن طَيِّبَٰتِ مَا كَسَبْتُمْ وَمِمَّآ أَخْرَجْنَا لَكُم مِّنَ ٱلْأَرْضِ

"O ye who believe! Spend out of the good things which ye have lawfully earned and out of that which We have brought forth for you from the earth...." (II:267).

According to Qur'ãnic commentators, this verse relates to spending in charity for others[4], from which a person benefits spiritually. But, spending on one's personal needs should all the more strictly be based on what one has lawfully earned, because in that way alone can the spiritual health—the integrity of personality—be properly maintained.

---

4. Actually speaking, there is nothing in the wordings of the verse whereby personal expenditure should be excluded.

(xi) Virtue of industry enjoined:

To lead a hard life, to engage in perpetual endeavour for the flowering up of one's talents and faculties, to struggle incessantly through honest labour for higher and higher achievement: that is the law of life in Islam, emphasised time and again in the Holy Qur'ãn and enshrined in the life of the Holy Prophet (Peace be on him). Emphasising this law, the Holy Qur'ãn says:

وَاَنْ لَّيْسَ لِلْاِنْسَانِ اِلَّا مَا سَعٰى ○ وَاَنَّ سَعْيَهٗ سَوْفَ يُرٰى ○

".....and that for man shall be naught (*i.e.,* no man deserves) save that wherefor he maketh effort, and that (the fruit of) his effort will soon come in sight." (LIII:39, 40).

Again:

وَلِكُلٍّ دَرَجٰتٌ مِّمَّا عَمِلُوْا ؕ وَمَا رَبُّكَ بِغَافِلٍ عَمَّا يَعْمَلُوْنَ ○

"For each (human being) is a rank according to the *deeds* which he doth: for thy Lord is not unaware of what they do". (VI:132).

The first verse says that no human being deserves any success in life except what he labours for. The second verse emphasises progress on the basis of genuine, practical endeavour.

Industry is, therefore, an important duty to self, according to the Holy Qur'ãn.

(xii) Virtue of pursuing stable and sound Progress in life, through:

(i) Planning one's life and activity soundly;

(ii) Aiming at consequential (as opposed to wasteful) activity;

(iii) Aiming at the highest and the soundest productivity in one's activity,

enjoined:

The Holy Qur'ãn commands:

يٰۤاَيُّهَا الَّذِيْنَ اٰمَنُوا اتَّقُوا اللّٰهَ وَلْتَنْظُرْ نَفْسٌ مَّا قَدَّمَتْ لِغَدٍ ۚ وَ
اتَّقُوا اللّٰهَ ؕ اِنَّ اللّٰهَ خَبِيْرٌۢ بِمَا تَعْمَلُوْنَ ○

"O ye who believe! Fear Allah (in wasting your life and talents in vain or wrong pursuits and through unsound planning and execution), and (in all types of actions) let every soul look to what (resulting good and worthiness for success and progress) he has sent forth for the morrow. Yea, fear Allah (for making your activity positive, planned, consequential and progressive, thereby manifesting your true and active thankfulness to Him for His bounties): for Allah is well acquainted with (all) that ye do." (LIX:18).

That the human outlook should be progressive, which necessitates aiming at the highest and the soundest productivity, is borne out by the fact that man, according to the Holy Qur'ãn, is an evolutionary being and the character of human life is evolutionary:[5]

فَلَآ أُقْسِمُ بِالشَّفَقِ ۝ وَالَّيْلِ وَمَا وَسَقَ ۝ وَالْقَمَرِ إِذَا اتَّسَقَ ۝ لَتَرْكَبُنَّ
طَبَقًا عَنْ طَبَقٍ ۝

"So I do call to witness the ruddy glow of Sunset; the Night and its Homing; and the Moon in her Fulness: Ye shall surely travel from stage to stage." (LXXXIV:16-19).

(xiii) Cultivation and maintenance of Optimism enjoined:

Optimism, or maintaining an unflinching attitude of hope, is based, in a Muslim's life, on his unswerving faith in, and sincere reliance on, God, and has been mentioned in the Holy Qur'ãn as an essential attribute of Islamic life:[6]

أَمَّنْ هُوَ قَانِتٌ آنَاءَ الَّيْلِ سَاجِدًا وَقَائِمًا يَحْذَرُ الْآخِرَةَ وَيَرْجُوا
رَحْمَةَ رَبِّهِ ؕ

"Is one who worships devoutly during the hours of the night prostrating himself and standing (in adoration), who takes heed of the

---

5. A critical study of the Holy Qur'ãn reveals that it is not only the human personality which is evolutionary but also the universe wherein humanity originated and has to fulfil its destiny.

6. That Pessimism, as mentioned before (on page 71), amounts to infidelity (*Kufr*) also shows that, according to the Holy Qur'ãn, the Faithful is he for whom Optimism is an inseparable quality of character.

Hereafter, and *who places his hope in the Mercy of his Lord* (like one who does not)?...." (XXXIX:9).

To maintain optimistic attitude in life, is, therefore, duty.

(xiv) Cultivation and maintenance of the spirit of and the attitude of Generosity (or, Spirit of Benevolence) enjoined:

Actual generosity is a duty to others. But the cultivation and maintenance of the spirit and the attitude of generosity is a duty towards self because of the purity and enrichment that it acquires thereby. It is this spirit and this attitude that have been emphasised together with actual generosity, as essential attributes of righteousness, in the following verses:

وَسَارِعُوٓا إِلَىٰ مَغْفِرَةٍ مِّن رَّبِّكُمْ وَجَنَّةٍ عَرْضُهَا السَّمٰوٰتُ وَالْأَرْضُ
أُعِدَّتْ لِلْمُتَّقِينَ ۝ الَّذِينَ يُنفِقُونَ فِى السَّرَّآءِ وَالضَّرَّآءِ

"And view with one another, hastening to forgiveness from your Lord, and to a Garden whose breadth is that (of the whole) of the heavens and of the earth, prepared for the righteous,—those who spend (freely), whether in prosperity or in adversity....." (III:133, 134).

اَلَّذِينَ يُنفِقُونَ أَمْوٰلَهُم بِالَّيْلِ وَالنَّهَارِ سِرًّا وَعَلَانِيَةً فَلَهُمْ أَجْرُهُمْ
عِندَ رَبِّهِمْ وَلَا خَوْفٌ عَلَيْهِمْ وَلَا هُمْ يَحْزَنُونَ ۝

"Those who spend (in Charity) of their goods by night and by day, in secret and in public, have their reward with their Lord; on them shall be no fear, nor shall they grieve." (II:274).

(xv) Constancy in Life commanded; hence its observance is duty:

Success and productivity in life demands constancy in our effort, and hence devotion to the principle of constancy is a duty to self. The Holy Qur'ãn enjoins it in respect of Prayer, saying that life is truly and ultimately successful of those "who," besides possessing other virtues, "are constant at their worship."[7] (LXX:23).

Now, Prayer being the most basic character-building exercise according to the Holy Qur'ãn, the above verse refers indirectly to the

---

7. الَّذِينَ هُمْ عَلَىٰ صَلَاتِهِمْ دَآئِمُونَ ۝

merit of cultivation and maintenance of the principle of constancy in respect of all virtues. This fact has been directly emphasised by the Holy Prophet (Peace be on him) when he says:

إِنَّ أَحَبَّ الْعَمَلِ إِلَى اللهِ أَدْوَمُهُ

"The action (of goodness) most loved by God is that in which the principle of Constancy is observed most." (Bukhãri: *Sahîh*, Vol. II., p. 957).

(xvi) Punctuality and Regularity in life enjoined:

The Holy Qur'ãn has enjoined punctuality in respect of Prayer:

إِنَّ الصَّلٰوةَ كَانَتْ عَلَى الْمُؤْمِنِيْنَ كِتٰبًا مَّوْقُوْتًا ۝

"Verily the Prayer is prescribed unto the Believers at definite times (or, at appointed hours)". (IV:103).

In this manner the Holy Qur'ãn trains and accustoms the Muslims to punctuality in all the affairs of life.

Moreover, the holy book appeals repeatedly to the Believers to observe the principle of regularity found in Nature and within their own selves, and take lesson from it all. For instance:

وَفِي الْأَرْضِ اٰيٰتٌ لِّلْمُوْقِنِيْنَ ۝ وَفِيْٓ أَنْفُسِكُمْ ۚ أَفَلَا تُبْصِرُوْنَ ۝

"On the earth are Signs for those of assured Faith, as also in your own selves: will ye not then observe?" (LI:20, 21).

إِنَّ فِيْ خَلْقِ السَّمٰوٰتِ وَالْأَرْضِ وَاخْتِلَافِ الَّيْلِ وَالنَّهَارِ لَاٰيٰتٍ لِّأُولِي الْأَلْبَابِ ۝

"Behold! In the constitution of the heavenly bodies and the earth, and the alternation of the Day and the Night, there are indeed Signs for the possessors of understanding...." (III:190).

Such being the importance of punctuality and regularity according to the Holy Qur'ãn, it is a duty to observe them in life to the best of one's ability.

(xvii) Observance of the principle of Moderation enjoined:

According to the Holy Qur'ãn, conformity to the just mean in all things of life is one of the basic distinguishing marks of Islamic conduct. God says:

وَكَذٰلِكَ جَعَلْنٰكُمْ أُمَّةً وَّسَطًا

"Thus We have exalted you as a community (*ummah*) conforming to the just mean...." (II:143).

Having laid down the principle basically and for universal application in life, the holy book also refers to certain concrete instances of its application. For instance:

(a) Concerning prayer:

وَلَا تَجْهَرْ بِصَلَاتِكَ وَلَا تُخَافِتْ بِهَا وَابْتَغِ بَيْنَ ذٰلِكَ سَبِيلًا ○

"Neither speak the Prayer aloud, nor speak it in a low tone, but seek a middle course between." (XVII:110).

(b) Concerning spending:

The true servants of God are:

وَالَّذِينَ إِذَآ أَنفَقُوا لَمْ يُسْرِفُوا وَلَمْ يَقْتُرُوا وَكَانَ بَيْنَ ذٰلِكَ قَوَامًا ○

"those who, when they spend[8] (their wealth, talents, time, energy, etc.), are neither extravagant nor sparing, but hold a just (balance) between those (extremes)." (XXV:67).

(c) Concerning walking:

وَاقْصِدْ فِي مَشْيِكَ

"And be moderate in thy pace....." (XXXI:19).

Thus, observance of the principle of moderation in all things is a duty.

(xviii) Observance and maintenance of Discipline enjoined:

A true Muslim's life is a disciplined life. It is hedged in by

8. Here there is no specific mention of wealth. Hence the reference is general.

principles, rules and laws from all sides, named by the Holy Qur'ãn as 'limits ordained by God', and it is a duty to maintain life strictly within those limits. Discipline is thus the hallmark of Islamic life. Speaking of the true Believers the Holy Qur'ãn says:

وَالْحٰفِظُوْنَ لِحُدُوْدِ اللّٰهِ ؕ وَبَشِّرِ الْمُؤْمِنِيْنَ ۝

"....and those who keep the limits ordained by Allah. So proclaim the glad tidings to the Believers." (IX:112).

As regards those who are undisciplined and violate those limits, we are told:

تِلْكَ حُدُوْدُ اللّٰهِ فَلَا تَعْتَدُوْهَا ۚ وَمَنْ يَّتَعَدَّ حُدُوْدَ اللّٰهِ فَاُولٰٓئِكَ هُمُ الظّٰلِمُوْنَ ۝

"These are the limits (ordained by) Allah. Transgress them not. For whoso transgresses Allah's limits: such are wrongdoers." (II:229).

Again:

وَمَنْ يَّتَعَدَّ حُدُوْدَ اللّٰهِ فَقَدْ ظَلَمَ نَفْسَهٗ ؕ

".....and any who transgresses the limits ordained by Allah, does verily wrong his own soul....." (LXV:1).

Observance of strict discipline in life is, therefore, duty to self.

(xix) *Cultivation and Practice of Moral Courage enjoined:*

Moral courage consists in upholding and advocating truth without fear.

According to the Holy Qur'ãn, it forms one of the essential attributes of Islamic conduct. For, the true Believers are those who are:

لَا يَخَافُوْنَ لَوْمَةَ لَآئِمٍ ؕ

".....never afraid (in upholding Truth) of the reproaches of such as find fault." (V:57).

Hence, cultivation and maintenance of moral courage is duty.

(xx) *Remaining pitched in battle against the forces of evil enjoined:*

A true Muslim is a man of God and, as such, his function is to enjoin what is right and to forbid what is wrong[9]. He cannot perform this function, however, unless he remains pitched in battle against the forces of evil. And this he has been commanded by the Holy Qur'ãn:

إِنَّ الشَّيْطَٰنَ لَكُمْ عَدُوٌّ فَاتَّخِذُوهُ عَدُوًّا

"Verily Satan is an enemy to you: so treat him (constantly) as an enemy (remaining engaged in perpetual fight with him)." (XXXV:6).

Shaitãn or, Satan, is according to Lane's *Arabic-English Lexicon*, not only 'the devil', but 'any that is exceedingly, or inordinately, proud or corrupt or unbelieving or rebellious.' As such, Satan represents all evils, whatever their form, wherever they are found, and whenever they manifest themselves. Used as a proper noun, i.e., as 'the Satan', the word signifies the personification of Evil. In any case, the promptings to evil are there all the time: the forces of evil, in their multifarious forms, are perpetually at work. Those who do not treat evil as their enemy fall a victim to it. But every Muslim is, so to say, born to destroy evil and to establish the good. He cannot treat evil even with indifference, not to speak of befriending it. He must fight, fight continuously and with all his might, against evil, wherever it is within his reach and whatever its form. It is his unavoidable duty.

Expounding this duty, the Holy Prophet (Peace be on him) says:

من رأى منكم منكرا فليغيّره بيده ومن لم يستطع فبلسانه ومن لم يستطع فبقلبه وذالك اضعف الإيمان

"Whoever observe evil it is his duty to eradicate it with his hand (or, power of authority). But he who is unable to do that, let him employ (the power of) his tongue. In case there is one who is unable even to do that, let him (at least detest it) with his heart. This last, however, is the weakest degree of Faith". (Muslim: *Sahîh*, vol. I, p. 51).

(xxi) Cultivation and Practice of Bravery enjoined:

True Muslims, according to the Holy Qur'ãn, are those who face all hardships and trials, and the forces of the enemy at the battlefield, bravely:

---

9. III:110; IX:71; IX:112; etc.

وَالْمُوْفُوْنَ بِعَهْدِهِمْ اِذَا عٰهَدُوْا ۚ وَالصّٰبِرِيْنَ فِى الْبَاْسَآءِ وَالضَّرَّآءِ
وَحِيْنَ الْبَاْسِ ۗ اُولٰٓئِكَ الَّذِيْنَ صَدَقُوْا ۗ وَاُولٰٓئِكَ هُمُ الْمُتَّقُوْنَ ۝

".....and those who observe firmness and calmness in pain (or suffering) and adversity, and throughout all periods of panic and violence (i.e., in war): Such are they who are true (in their Faith[10]). Such are the God-fearing." (II:177).

Muslims have been, therefore, commanded:

يٰٓاَيُّهَا الَّذِيْنَ اٰمَنُوْٓا اِذَا لَقِيْتُمْ فِئَةً فَاثْبُتُوْا وَاذْكُرُوا اللّٰهَ كَثِيْرًا
لَّعَلَّكُمْ تُفْلِحُوْنَ ۝

"O ye who believe! When ye meet a force (of the enemy on the battlefield), hold firm (i.e., face the enemy bravely), and call Allah in remembrance much[11] (and often), that ye may be successful). (VIII:45).

Again:

يٰٓاَيُّهَا الَّذِيْنَ اٰمَنُوْٓا اِذَا لَقِيْتُمُ الَّذِيْنَ كَفَرُوْا زَحْفًا فَلَا تُوَلُّوْهُمُ الْاَدْبَارَ ۝

"O ye who believe! When ye meet the Unbelievers in battle, never turn your backs to them." (VIII:15).

(xxii) Observance of Self-Respect, Magnanimity and Sobriety enjoined:

It is the duty of every Muslim to cultivate and observe self-respect, side by side with humility; because the very fact that he is a Muslim makes every true follower of Islam honourable. The Holy Qur'ãn says:

كُنْتُمْ خَيْرَ اُمَّةٍ

10. Mark that bravery belongs to the heart and not to the body. It is the true faith and the true spirit (i.e., true devotion to an ideal) that makes a man brave. In the case of a Muslim, it is Faith in God in all its aspects which is the only motivating force in his life; and Faith in God is the highest and the most unfailing source of strength.

11. Mark that bravery is cultivated at higher and higher levels through devotion to God.

"Ye are the best community (in respect of your ideology and your mission)....." (III:110).

وَلِلّٰهِ الْعِزَّةُ وَلِرَسُوْلِهٖ وَلِلْمُؤْمِنِيْنَ

"Honour belongs to Allah and His Messenger (Muhammad) and the (true) Believers;...." (LXIII:8).

That is why God has commended the self-respecting attitude of the *Ashãb-us-Suffah* (People of the Platform) in II:273, already quoted[12], and has referred to the virtues of self-respect, magnanimity and sobriety as the virtues which should be practised by all of His true Servants:

وَإِذَا مَرُّوْا بِاللَّغْوِ مَرُّوْا كِرَامًا ۝

".....and when they pass by what is nonsense, they pass by it observing self-respect, magnanimity and sobriety." (XXV:72).

(xxiii) Self-defence against wrong enjoined:

Self-respect makes self-defence necessary, wherever required. Of course, all mischief is to be avoided (VII:56; XXVIII:77, etc.) and nothing should be done which violates any of the virtues that have been enjoined (II:208). With these precautions, self-defence is a duty, because it has been mentioned by the Holy Qur'ãn as a quality of the Believer's conduct:

وَالَّذِيْنَ إِذَآ أَصَابَهُمُ الْبَغْيُ هُمْ يَنْتَصِرُوْنَ ۝

"and those who, when an oppressive wrong is inflicted on them, help and defend themselves."[13] (XLII:39).

(xxiv) Observance of the spirit of Contentment enjoined:

Discontentment can be in respect of:

(a) one's resources, or, (b) one's possessions.

(a) As to the first one may feel that if he is able to acquire the patronage of the high-ups, he can increase his resourcefulness for

12. See page 80.

13. This verse relates to individual as well as collective action, according to the form of the wrong inflicted.

increasing his possessions: wealth, prestige, power, etc. Such an ambition leads almost always to debasement of the self, and consequently to the violation of the virtue of self-respect. Hence, a Muslim has been commanded to direct all his needs and all his ambitions to God and God alone, as, for instance, in the basic Muslim prayer:

إِيَّاكَ نَعْبُدُ وَإِيَّاكَ نَسْتَعِينُ ۝

"Thee alone (O Allah) do we worship and Thine help alone we seek." (I:5).

The Holy Qur'ãn wants a Muslim to be absolutely contented with the Patronage of God, Who is the Source of all Good, when it asks emphatically:

أَلَيْسَ اللَّهُ بِكَافٍ عَبْدَهُ ۝

"Is not Allah enough for His servant?" (XXXIX:36).

(b) The usual form of discontentment is in respect of what one possesses, and it becomes more damaging morally when one starts cultivating jealousy in relation to what others possess. The Holy Qur'ãn has forbidden it outright:

وَلَا تَتَمَنَّوْا مَا فَضَّلَ اللَّهُ بِهِ بَعْضَكُمْ عَلَىٰ بَعْضٍ لِلرِّجَالِ نَصِيبٌ مِمَّا اكْتَسَبُوا وَلِلنِّسَاءِ نَصِيبٌ مِمَّا اكْتَسَبْنَ وَسْئَلُوا اللَّهَ مِنْ فَضْلِهِ إِنَّ اللَّهَ كَانَ بِكُلِّ شَيْءٍ عَلِيمًا ۝

"And covet not the thing in which Allah hath made some of you excel others (but cultivate the spirit of contentment). Unto men a fortune from that which they have earned, and unto women a fortune from that which they have earned. (Be not jealous of one another) but ask Allah of his bounty (through positive, rational effort and the fulfilment of your genuine needs). Lo! Allah is ever Knower of all things (including your innermost feelings; so be careful)." (IV:32).

Cultivation and maintenance of the spirit of contentment[14] is, therefore, a duty to self for keeping it morally healthy.

---

14. Contentment should be clearly distinguished from want of effort for improving one's life in all those things which have been approved or commended by God, including rational possession of the goods of this world.

(xxv) Practice of Selflessness in doing good enjoined:

The Prophets of God, who have embodied service to humanity at its highest, were asked by God to proclaim in unequivocal terms that they did not want any reward for it. The Holy Qur'ãn has mentioned this time and again[15], thus laying down the principle that it is a duty to observe selflessness in doing a duty to others.

In fact, all good to others should be done purely out of love for God[16], and therefore, never, never for any selfish end. Or else, the merit of the otherwise virtuous deed will become null and void, as the Holy Qur'ãn warns:

يٰٓاَيُّهَا الَّذِيْنَ اٰمَنُوْا لَا تُبْطِلُوْا صَدَقٰتِكُمْ بِالْمَنِّ وَالْاَذٰى

"O ye who believe! Render not vain your charity by reminders of your generosity or by injury..." (II:264).

On the positive side, the following motto of selflessness has been laid down as the guiding light for all true Muslims. Their attitude, whenever they do any good to others, should invariably be:

لَا نُرِيْدُ مِنْكُمْ جَزَآءً وَّلَا شُكُوْرًا ۝

".....No reward do we desire from you, nor thanks." (LXXVI:9).

(xxvi) Soft-heartedness, gentleness and kindness enjoined:

A Muslim, while he has been commanded to be stiff and mighty against evil[17], has to be, in his basic character, soft-hearted. This is what the Holy Qur'ãn has taught. A Muslim should practise humility (XXXIII:35) which means showing respect to others. That makes it

---

15. VI:90; XI:29; XI:51; XXV:57; XXVI:109; XXVI:127; XXVI:145; XXVI:164; XXVI:180; XXXVIII:86; XLII:23; etc. The words mentioned in connection with the Holy Prophet Muhammad (Peace be on him) are:

قُلْ لَّآ اَسْئَلُكُمْ عَلَيْهِ اَجْرًا ۝

".....Say: No reward for this (i.e., my service to humanity as Prophet of God) do I ask of you...." (VI.90).

16. II:177; etc.

17. See page 103. Also: XLVIII:29.

impossible for him to be of harsh temperament. Then, he is to be the pursuer of "compassion and kindness" (XC:17). Taking both of these qualities into consideration, the basic tone of his character should not but be that of soft-heartedness, gentleness and kindness, unless any exceptional situation justly demands otherwise.

Moreover, he has to follow the examples of the Prophets whose conduct has been set for him as a pattern. Now, the Holy Qur'ãn says, on the one hand, that: "there is for you an excellent pattern (of conduct) in Abraham and those with him...." (LX:4); and on the other hand, it informs us: "Lo! Abraham was soft-hearted, long-suffering." (IX:114). Therefore, to cultivate and maintain soft-heartedness is duty.

Concerning the Holy Prophet Muhammad (Peace be on him) the Holy Qur'ãn emphasises his soft-heartedness in these words:

فَبِمَا رَحْمَةٍ مِّنَ اللَّهِ لِنتَ لَهُمْ

"It is part of the Mercy of Allah that thou dost deal soft-heartedly with them...." (III:159).

Indeed, he is:

رَحْمَةً لِّلْعٰلَمِينَ ۝

"Mercy (and Blessing) unto all the worlds." (XXI:107).

And:

بِالْمُؤْمِنِينَ رَءُوفٌ رَّحِيمٌ ۝

".....To the Believers he is most kind, merciful." (IX:128).

".....To follow the Holy Prophet Muhammad (Peace be on him) is duty[18]. To cultivate and maintain soft-heartedness, gentleness and kindness is, therefore, also duty.

(xxvii) Patience, Forbearance, Perseverance, Composure, Equanimity, Steadfastness, Self-control and Hardiness enjoined:

The virtues mentioned above are very closely related to one another and are included in the Arabic word *sabr*[19], which has been

---

18. III:31; XXXIII:21.

19. See: *A Dictionary of Modern Written Arabic*, published by Cornell University Press, U.S.A.

repeatedly emphasised by the Holy Qur'ãn in different contexts and has been enjoined forcefully.

The Holy Book says:

يٰٓاَيُّهَا الَّذِيْنَ اٰمَنُوا اسْتَعِيْنُوْا بِالصَّبْرِ وَالصَّلٰوةِ ۭ اِنَّ اللّٰهَ مَعَ الصّٰبِرِيْنَ ○....
وَلَنَبْلُوَنَّكُمْ بِشَيْءٍ مِّنَ الْخَوْفِ وَالْجُوْعِ وَنَقْصٍ مِّنَ الْاَمْوَالِ وَالْاَنْفُسِ وَ
الثَّمَرٰتِ ۭ وَبَشِّرِ الصّٰبِرِيْنَ ○ الَّذِيْنَ اِذَآ اَصَابَتْهُمْ مُّصِيْبَةٌ ۙ قَالُوْٓا اِنَّا لِلّٰهِ وَ
اِنَّآ اِلَيْهِ رٰجِعُوْنَ ○ اُولٰۗىِٕكَ عَلَيْهِمْ صَلَوٰتٌ مِّنْ رَّبِّهِمْ وَرَحْمَةٌ ۣ وَاُولٰۗىِٕكَ
هُمُ الْمُهْتَدُوْنَ ○

"O ye who believe! seek help in *sabr* and prayer; verily Allah is with those who practise *sabr*.....

"Be sure We shall test you with something of fear and hunger, some loss in goods or lives or the fruits (of your toil), but give glad tidings to those who practise *sabr*,—who say, when afflicted with calamity: 'To Allah we belong and to Him is our return': They are those on whom (descend) the Blessings and the Mercy of Allah; and they are the rightly guided." (II:153, 155-157).

وَالصّٰبِرِيْنَ فِي الْبَاْسَاۗءِ وَالضَّرَّاۗءِ وَحِيْنَ الْبَاْسِ ۭ اُولٰۗىِٕكَ الَّذِيْنَ
صَدَقُوْا ۭ وَاُولٰۗىِٕكَ هُمُ الْمُتَّقُوْنَ ○

".....and those who practise *sabr* in pain (or suffering) and adversity, and throughout all periods of panic and violence. Such are the people of truth, the God-fearing." (II:177).

وَاللّٰهُ يُحِبُّ الصّٰبِرِيْنَ ○

".....and Allah loveth those who practise *sabr*." (III:146).

الصّٰبِرِيْنَ وَالصّٰبِرٰتِ . . . اَعَدَّ اللّٰهُ لَهُمْ مَّغْفِرَةً وَّاَجْرًا عَظِيْمًا ○

".....the men and the women who practise *sabr*,.....for them Allah hath prepared forgiveness and great reward." (XXXIII:35).

وَالَّذِيْنَ صَبَرُوا ابْتِغَاۗءَ وَجْهِ رَبِّهِمْ . . . اُولٰۗىِٕكَ لَهُمْ عُقْبَى الدَّارِ ○

"Those who observe *sabr*, seeking their Lord's Countenance (i.e., Divine Pleasure).....for such there is the final attainment of the (Eternal) Home." (XIII:22).

It is, therefore, the duty of every Muslim to practise *sabr* with a view to attain perfection in it:

يٰٓاَيُّهَا الَّذِيْنَ اٰمَنُوا اصْبِرُوْا وَصَابِرُوْا وَرَابِطُوْا ۗ وَاتَّقُوا اللّٰهَ لَعَلَّكُمْ تُفْلِحُوْنَ ۝

"O ye who believe! practise *sabr*, vie in the practise of *sabr* and be (ever) ready (in the cause of Truth); and be careful of your duty to Allah; that ye may succeed and prosper." (III:200).

(xxviii) Cultivating the spirit of Humility and Modesty enjoined:

The Holy Qur'ãn refers to, and enjoins the duty of, cultivating and observing humility and modesty in the following verses:

وَالْخٰشِعِيْنَ وَالْخٰشِعٰتِ ... اَعَدَّ اللّٰهُ لَهُمْ مَّغْفِرَةً وَّاَجْرًا عَظِيْمًا ۝

"......the men and the women who posses the spirit of humility..... for them Allah hath prepared forgiveness and mighty reward." (XXXIII:35).

وَعِبَادُ الرَّحْمٰنِ الَّذِيْنَ يَمْشُوْنَ عَلَى الْاَرْضِ هَوْنًا وَّاِذَا خَاطَبَهُمُ الْجٰهِلُوْنَ
قَالُوْا سَلٰمًا ۝

"And the servants of (God) Most Gracious are those who walk on the earth with humility, and when the ignorant address them (in arrogance), they (do not insult them or engage with them, but) say (or, wish them) 'Peace!' (separating themselves from them calmly)[20]. (XXV:63).

وَلَا تُصَعِّرْ خَدَّكَ لِلنَّاسِ وَلَا تَمْشِ فِى الْاَرْضِ مَرَحًا ۗ اِنَّ اللّٰهَ لَا يُحِبُّ
كُلَّ مُخْتَالٍ فَخُوْرٍ ۝ وَاقْصِدْ فِيْ مَشْيِكَ وَاغْضُضْ مِنْ صَوْتِكَ ۗ
اِنَّ اَنْكَرَ الْاَصْوَاتِ لَصَوْتُ الْحَمِيْرِ ۝

---

20. *i.e.*, "Peace, and Good-bye; let me leave you." (Abdullah Yusuf Ali, *op.cit.*, p. 941, n. 3123).

"And swell not thy cheek (for pride) at the fellow-beings,[21] nor walk in insolence through the earth[22]; for Allah loveth not any arrogant boaster. And be moderate in thy pace, and lower thy voice[23]; for the harshest of sounds without doubt is the braying of the ass."

(XXXI:18, 19).

(xxix) Observance of the spirit of Thankfulness[24] enjoined:

The Holy Qur'ãn contains the command, originally given by God to the Holy Prophet Moses (Peace be on him) but meant to be obeyed by every Muslim:

وَكُن مِّنَ الشَّٰكِرِينَ ○

"..... and be of those who are thankful." (VII:144).

Speaking directly to its addresses, the holy book has commanded:

وَاشْكُرُوا نِعْمَتَ اللَّهِ إِن كُنتُمْ إِيَّاهُ تَعْبُدُونَ ○

"....and be thankful for the favours of Allah, if it is He Whom ye serve." (XVI:114).

It should be noted here that all the goods that a man receives in his life, through whatever medium they might be delivered to him, are God's favours according to the Qur'ãnic teaching. When a person bestows his favours on anyone, not only the thing that he bestows, but he himself becomes God's favour in that respect. It is thus a duty to thank God for every good that one receives, as also to thank him who acts as the agency for obtaining that good.[25]

---

21. This is the command to observe humility in one's behaviour in general.

22. This is the command to observe humility in walking.

23. This is the command to observe humility in the tone of one's talk.

24. Thankfulness comes into operation with regard to others, and as such it is a duty to others. But the spirit of thankfulness enriches the inner personality of the moral agent himself. Hence it forms a duty to self also.

25. This has been emphasised in direct terms by the Holy Prophet (Peace be on him) when he says:—

لا يشكر الله من لا يشكر الناس

"He who does not express thankfulness to human beings is not (really) thankful to Allah (also)." (Bukhãrî: *Adab al-Mufrad*, p. 34).

(xxx) Struggle to achieve Self-Purification, along with its Qur'ãnic technique, enjoined:

(1) According to the Holy Qur'ãn, the servants of God, namely, true Muslims, are those who not only practise righteousness but constantly yearn for perfection in it:

وَالَّذِينَ يَقُولُونَ رَبَّنَا هَبْ لَنَا مِنْ أَزْوَاجِنَا وَذُرِّيَّاتِنَا قُرَّةَ أَعْيُنٍ وَّاجْعَلْنَا لِلْمُتَّقِينَ إِمَامًا

"And those who pray, 'Our Lord! bestow on us coolness of eyes from our wives and our offspring, and make us (so perfect in virtue that we may be) unto the righteous a pattern (to be followed)." (XXV:74).

And this yearning becomes a reality in the case of those who strive for it truly:

وَمِنْهُمْ سَابِقٌ بِالْخَيْرَاتِ بِإِذْنِ اللَّهِ ذَٰلِكَ هُوَ الْفَضْلُ الْكَبِيرُ

".....and among them (i.e., the followers of the Qur'ãn) there are those who, by Allah's leave, are foremost in virtues. That is the great Grace (i.e., the most honourable achievement)." (XXXV:32).

For that achievement, however, it is necessary to purify the self. Hence, true Muslims are those who:

الَّذِينَ هُمْ لِلزَّكَاةِ فَاعِلُونَ

"act aiming at (self-) purification." (XXIII:4).

And, thereby they develop:

قَلْبٍ سَلِيمٍ

"a sound heart." (XXVI:89).

Hence, Self-purification and development of Conscientiousness is duty.

(2) But the human heart cannot be developed into a morally sound heart without:

(a) Constant self-examination; and

(b) The consequent struggle directed at abstaining from evil of every type and practising good in every way.

The Holy Qur'ãn commands its followers in respect of both:

(a) As to constant self-examination:

يَٰٓأَيُّهَا ٱلَّذِينَ ءَامَنُوا ٱتَّقُوا ٱللَّهَ وَلْتَنظُرْ نَفْسٌ مَّا قَدَّمَتْ لِغَدٍ ۖ وَٱتَّقُوا
ٱللَّهَ ۚ إِنَّ ٱللَّهَ خَبِيرٌۢ بِمَا تَعْمَلُونَ ۝

"O ye who believe! Fear Allah, and let every soul look to (i.e., examine) what it has sent forth for the morrow. Yea! fear Allah: for Allah is well acquainted with what ye do." (LIX:18).

(b) As regards the struggle:

(i) against all evil within and without the self:

إِنَّ ٱلشَّيْطَٰنَ لَكُمْ عَدُوٌّ فَٱتَّخِذُوهُ عَدُوًّا

"Verily Satan (who represents and prompts all evils within and without the self) is an enemy to you: so treat him (constantly) as an enemy (remaining engaged in perpetual fight with him)." (XXXV:6).

(ii) in favour of all that is good;

وَجَٰهِدُوا فِى ٱللَّهِ حَقَّ جِهَادِهِۦ ۚ هُوَ ٱجْتَبَىٰكُمْ

"And strive for Allah (i.e., for the establishment of the highest good within and without the self) as is due unto Him, hard striving. He has chosen you (for it).... (XXII:78).

Thus, constant Self-examination and the Struggle to destroy evil and to establish the good are Qur'ãnic duties to self.

(3) But the Struggle (*Jihãd*) mentioned above is not possible without a living and dynamic faith in God and devotion[26] to Him, i.e., without maintaining the heart as:

قَلْبٍ مُّنِيبٍ ۝

"a heart turned in devotion to God." (L:33).

---

26. Duty in this respect has been mentioned on pp. 3-8.

For that, however, it is necessary:

(a) to conscientiously and devotedly practise:

(i) Communion with God;

(ii) Fasting; and

(iii) Charity; —and

(b) to fulfil all duties rigorously, whether they are to self or to others.

The Holy Qur'ãn has enjoined all the above as duty:

(a) (i) As to communion with God, it has prescribed three forms and has enjoined their observance:

(*i*) Constant remembrance of God:

يٰاَيُّهَا الَّذِيْنَ اٰمَنُوا اذْكُرُوا اللّٰهَ ذِكْرًا كَثِيْرًا ۝ وَّسَبِّحُوْهُ بُكْرَةً وَّاَصِيْلًا ۝

"O ye who believe! Celebrate the remembrance of Allah, remembring (Him) much (in word and in thought), and glorify Him morning and evening." (XXXIII:41, 42).

(*ii*) Observance of Regular Prayer, in congregation and otherwise.

وَاَقِيْمُوا الصَّلٰوةَ

"And establish regular prayer....."[27] (II:110).

(*iii*) Congregational worship at the highest level:

وَلِلّٰهِ عَلَى النَّاسِ حِجُّ الْبَيْتِ مَنِ اسْتَطَاعَ اِلَيْهِ سَبِيْلًا

"And pilgrimage to the House (i.e., the *Ka'bah* at Makkah) (for congregational worship at world-level) is a duty unto Allah for mankind,— for him who can afford the journey...." (III:97).

(ii) As to fasting, which is the most potent exercise for the practise of self-control, the Holy Qur'ãn orders it in these words:

يٰاَيُّهَا الَّذِيْنَ اٰمَنُوْا كُتِبَ عَلَيْكُمُ الصِّيَامُ كَمَا كُتِبَ عَلَى الَّذِيْنَ مِنْ
قَبْلِكُمْ لَعَلَّكُمْ تَتَّقُوْنَ ۝

27. This command has been repeated at numerous places in the Holy Qur'ãn.

"O ye who believe! Fasting is prescribed to you, even as it was prescribed to those before you, that ye may (learn) self-restraint." (II:183).

(iii) As to charity, the Holy Qur'ãn enjoins:

(a) compulsory charity (*Zakat*, etc.),

as well as

(b) optional charity.

It says:

وَاٰتُوا الزَّكٰوةَ ط

".....and pay the poor-due....."[28] (II:110).

يٰٓاَيُّهَا الَّذِيْنَ اٰمَنُوْٓا اَنْفِقُوْا مِنْ طَيِّبٰتِ مَا كَسَبْتُمْ وَمِمَّآ اَخْرَجْنَا لَكُمْ مِّنَ الْاَرْضِ

"O ye who believe! Spend (for helping those in need) but of the good things which ye have (honourably) earned, and of that which We bring forth from the earth for you....[29] (II:267).

(b) As regards fulfilment of all duties rigorously, whether they are to self or to others, the Holy Qur'ãn lays down the command:

يٰٓاَيُّهَا الَّذِيْنَ اٰمَنُوا ادْخُلُوْا فِى السِّلْمِ كَآفَّةً

"O ye who believe! Enter into Islam wholly (i.e., fulfil all the duties prescribed by Islam, including those related to apparently trivial issues of life)." (II:208).

28. This command has been repeated at numerous places in the Holy Qur'ãn. It shall be properly referred to in the "Duties to Others."

29. This command has been repeated at numerous places in the holy book.

Appendix

DUTIES TO ANIMALS AND THINGS

Note: Duties to animals and things are really duties to Self, because in the final analysis, they form part of "duty of Conscientiousness". Hence they have been included as appendix to "Duties to Self."

God says in the Holy Qur'ãn:

(1)

وَبِالْوَالِدَيْنِ إِحْسَانًا . . . وَمَا مَلَكَتْ أَيْمَانُكُمْ

".....and do good to parents....and to what your right hands own...." (IV:36).

According to the celebrated commentator Imam Fakhr al-Din al-Razi[1], the expression "what your right hands own," stands for all those that have no civil rights, including the dumb animals. Thus this verse lays down the duty[2] of being good towards, and doing good to, the animals.

(2)

هُوَ الَّذِي خَلَقَ لَكُمْ مَا فِي الْأَرْضِ جَمِيعًا

"It is He Who hath created for you all things that are on the earth....." (II:29).

All things having been created for our benefit, it becomes our natural duty:

(i) to protect everything from damage;

(ii) to employ it for our benefit in keeping with its dignity as God's creation;

---

1. See *al-Tafsir al-Kabir*, vol. III, p. 323.

2. This duty has been taught in an elaborate form in the *Hadîth*.

(iii) to promote its well-being, as far as possible, thereby establishing our thankfulness to God for His Blessing in a practical manner.

Book II

DUTIES TO OTHER INDIVIDUALS

Part I

FUNDAMENTAL DUTIES TOWARDS ALL HUMAN BEINGS

Part II

DUTIES OF CONDITION TOWARDS OTHER INDIVIDUALS

Part III

DUTIES IN RESPECT OF MANNERS

Part I

FUNDAMENTAL DUTIES TOWARDS ALL HUMAN BEINGS

I. Duties Relating to the Happiness of Others.

II. Duties Relating to the Moral Perfection of Others.

Chapter I

DUTIES RELATING TO THE HAPPINESS OF OTHERS

(1) Duties of Omission (2) Duties of Commission

(I) DUTIES OF OMISSION

END: Abstinence from ill-wishing and ill-doing to fellow-beings:

(A) Comprehensive Commands;

(B) Specific Commands:

I. Duties of Love. II. Duties of Respect.

(A) *Comprehensive Commands relating to the duty of abstaining from all evil against fellow-beings:*

(i) *With regard to the duties of omission pertaining to the happiness of other individuals, in their capacity basically and purely as human beings, the Holy Qur'ãn has laid down certain comprehensive commands through which Muslims have been ordered to abstain from committing every conceivable form of evil against them. For instance:*

وَيَنْهٰى عَنِ الْفَحْشَآءِ وَالْمُنْكَرِ وَالْبَغْيِ يَعِظُكُمْ لَعَلَّكُمْ تَذَكَّرُوْنَ ○

".....and He (i.e., God) forbiddeth lewdness and wickedness (i.e., all evil conduct) and infringement (of the rights of others). He exhorteth you that haply ye may be admonished." (XVI:90).

وَلَا تَبْخَسُوا النَّاسَ اَشْيَآءَهُمْ

"....and wrong not mankind in their things[1]....." (VII:85).

وَالَّذِينَ يَنقُضُونَ عَهْدَ اللَّهِ مِن بَعْدِ مِيثَاقِهِ وَيَقْطَعُونَ مَا أَمَرَ اللَّهُ بِهِ
أَن يُوصَلَ وَيُفْسِدُونَ فِي الْأَرْضِ ۙ أُولَٰئِكَ لَهُمُ اللَّعْنَةُ وَ
لَهُمْ سُوءُ الدَّارِ ۝

"And those who break the Covenant of Allah after having plighted their world thereto, and sever that which Allah hath commanded should be joined[2], and work mischief (i.e., cause moral corruption and material disorder) in the land: on them is the Curse and for them is the terrible Abode (i.e., Hell)." (XIII:25).

قُلْ إِنَّمَا حَرَّمَ رَبِّيَ الْفَوَاحِشَ مَا ظَهَرَ مِنْهَا وَمَا بَطَنَ وَالْإِثْمَ
وَالْبَغْيَ بِغَيْرِ الْحَقِّ

"Say (O Muhammad): my Lord forbiddeth only indecencies, such of them as are open and such as are secret, and sin, and infringement (of the rights of others) without justice....." (VII:33).

وَلَا تُفْسِدُوا فِي الْأَرْضِ بَعْدَ إِصْلَاحِهَا وَادْعُوهُ خَوْفًا وَطَمَعًا ۚ
إِنَّ رَحْمَتَ اللَّهِ قَرِيبٌ مِّنَ الْمُحْسِنِينَ ۝

"Work not confusion in the earth after the fair ordering (thereof), and call on Him in fear and hope. Lo! the Mercy of Allah is (always) near to those who do right." (VII:56).

وَوَضَعَ الْمِيزَانَ ۝ أَلَّا تَطْغَوْا فِي الْمِيزَانِ ۝

".....and He hath set up the Balance, that ye transgress not the balance (of justice in your actions)" (LV: 7,8).

---

1. According to Baidawi, things imply 'rights' of human beings. (See his *Tafsir*, p. 300).
2. According to the commentators of the Holy Qur'ãn, it refers to the non-fulfilment of duties which men owe to God and to parents, family, neighbours, community, country and fellow-creatures in general. (See Abdul Majid Daryabadi, *op.cit.*, Vol. I, n. 118).

لَا تَظْلِمُونَ وَلَا تُظْلَمُونَ ○

"....ye shall neither wrong nor be wronged." (II:279).

(ii) Wrongdoing has not been allowed even against worst enemics :

وَلَا يَجْرِمَنَّكُمْ شَنَآنُ قَوْمٍ عَلَىٰ أَلَّا تَعْدِلُوا ۚ

"....and let not the hatred of others to you make you swerve to wrong and depart from justice.... (V:9).

(iii) Wrongdoing to anyone is so severely abhorred that even befriending the wrongdoer is most severely condemned:

وَلَا تَرْكَنُوا إِلَى الَّذِينَ ظَلَمُوا فَتَمَسَّكُمُ النَّارُ وَمَا لَكُمْ مِنْ دُونِ اللَّهِ
مِنْ أَوْلِيَاءَ ثُمَّ لَا تُنْصَرُونَ ○

"And incline not to those who do wrong, or else the Fire will scize you—ye have no protectors other than Allah,—and ye shall not be succoured." (XI:113).

(B) <u>*Specific Commands relating to specific duties of commission*</u>:

I. Duties of Love:

(i) Violating others' right to life prohibited:

(*a*) *The Holy Qur'ãn commands the Muslims never to commit murder*:

وَلَا تَقْتُلُوا النَّفْسَ الَّتِي حَرَّمَ اللَّهُ إِلَّا بِالْحَقِّ ۚ ذَٰلِكُمْ وَصَّاكُمْ
بِهِ لَعَلَّكُمْ تَعْقِلُونَ ○

"....Take not life, which Allah hath made sacred, except by way of justice and law: Thus doth He command you, that ye may learn wisdom." (VI:151).

وَلَا تَقْتُلُوا النَّفْسَ الَّتِي حَرَّمَ اللَّهُ إِلَّا بِالْحَقِّ ۗ وَمَنْ قُتِلَ مَظْلُومًا فَقَدْ جَعَلْنَا
لِوَلِيِّهِ سُلْطَانًا فَلَا يُسْرِفْ فِي الْقَتْلِ ۖ إِنَّهُ كَانَ مَنْصُورًا ○

"And take not life, which Allah hath made sacred, except by way of justice and law. And if anyone is slain wrongfully, We have given his heir authority (to demand redress through law or to forgive): but let him not exceed bounds in the matter of taking life; for he is helped (by the law)[3]." (XVII:33).

(b) *The following verse stresses the gravity of the crime of murder in the strongest possible terms*:

مَنْ قَتَلَ نَفْسًا بِغَيْرِ نَفْسٍ أَوْ فَسَادٍ فِي الْأَرْضِ فَكَأَنَّمَا قَتَلَ
النَّاسَ جَمِيعًا

".....if anyone killeth a human being—unless it be for murder or for spreading mischief in the land—it shall be as if he killed all mankind....." (V:35).

(c) *The Holy Qur'ãn condemns not only murder in general but also human sacrifice to idols and false deities, and the custom of female infanticide, practised by the pagan communities, including the pre-Islamic Arabs*[4]:

وَكَذَٰلِكَ زَيَّنَ لِكَثِيرٍ مِّنَ الْمُشْرِكِينَ قَتْلَ أَوْلَادِهِمْ شُرَكَاؤُهُمْ لِيُرْدُوهُمْ
وَلِيَلْبِسُوا عَلَيْهِمْ دِينَهُمْ

"Even so, in the eyes of many of the Pagans, their (so-called) 'partners' (of God) made alluring the slaughter of their offspring, in order to lead them to their own destruction, and cause confusion in their religion." (VI:137).

وَلَا تَقْتُلُوا أَوْلَادَكُمْ خَشْيَةَ إِمْلَاقٍ نَّحْنُ نَرْزُقُهُمْ وَإِيَّاكُمْ إِنَّ
قَتْلَهُمْ كَانَ خِطْئًا كَبِيرًا

---

3. In this respect, there is no discrimination in Islam. "According to *Hanafis*, the life of a slave stands on equal footing with that of a free-man, of a woman with that of a man, of a non-Muslim with that of a Muslim." (Abdur Rahim: *Muhammadan Jurisprudence*, p. 359).

4. For the wide-spread practice of infanticide among different ancient nations, including the Greeks and the Romans, see *Encyclopaedia Britannica*, XII, p. 332. The Qur'ãnic law in respect of this almost universal evil is actually a world-reform.

"Kill not your children for fear of want: We shall provide sustenance for them as well as for you. Verily killing of them is a great sin." (XVII:31).

(ii) Violating the Rights of Others in respect of wealth prohibited:

(*a*) *The Holy Qur'ãn forbids all illegal methods, including dishonesty, theft, dacoity, etc., in acquiring what belongs to others:*

وَلَا تَبْخَسُوا النَّاسَ أَشْيَاءَهُمْ

".....and wrong not mankind in their goods....." (VII:85).

يَا أَيُّهَا الَّذِينَ آمَنُوا لَا تَأْكُلُوا أَمْوَالَكُمْ بَيْنَكُمْ بِالْبَاطِلِ

"O ye who believe! devour not your property among yourselves (i.e., consume not one another's belongings) unlawfully....." (IV:29).

It is generally the demands of one's family for higher standard of living which induce a person to acquire wealth by unlawful means. The Holy Qur'ãn makes a pointed reference to it and asks the Muslims not to succumb to their wives' and children's wrong requests or desires—though treating them with affection—and to stick to absolute honesty in respect of one's earnings:

يَا أَيُّهَا الَّذِينَ آمَنُوا إِنَّ مِنْ أَزْوَاجِكُمْ وَأَوْلَادِكُمْ عَدُوًّا لَكُمْ
فَاحْذَرُوهُمْ ۚ وَإِنْ تَعْفُوا وَتَصْفَحُوا وَتَغْفِرُوا فَإِنَّ اللَّهَ غَفُورٌ
رَحِيمٌ ○ إِنَّمَا أَمْوَالُكُمْ وَأَوْلَادُكُمْ فِتْنَةٌ ۚ وَاللَّهُ عِنْدَهُ
أَجْرٌ عَظِيمٌ ○ فَاتَّقُوا اللَّهَ مَا اسْتَطَعْتُمْ

"O ye who believe! Truly, among your wives and children are (some that are) enemies to yourselves: so beware of them! But if ye forgive and overlook and cover up (their faults), verily Allah is Forgiving, Merciful. Your wealth and your children may be but a trial, whereas Allah! with Him is an immense Reward. So keep your duty to Allah as best as ye can....." (LXIV:14-16).

(*b*) *Loot and arson have been specifically condemned and prohibited:*

وَإِذَا تَوَلَّىٰ سَعَىٰ فِي الْأَرْضِ لِيُفْسِدَ فِيهَا وَيُهْلِكَ الْحَرْثَ وَالنَّسْلَ ۗ
وَاللَّهُ لَا يُحِبُّ الْفَسَادَ ○

"And when he (i.e., the enemy of Truth) turneth away, he speedeth through the land that he may act corruptly therein and destroy the crops and the cattle. And Allah approveth not mischief." (II:205).

وَلَا تَقْعُدُوا بِكُلِّ صِرَاطٍ

"Beset not the highways menacing (wayfarers)...." (VII:86).

(*c*) *With regard to theft, its prohibition is covered fully in* IV: 29. *It has, however, been specifically prohibited also in the following verse:*

وَلَا يَسْرِقْنَ

"(that).....they will not steal....."[5] (LX:12).

The stern view that the Holy Qur'ãn takes in respect of theft is evident from the punishment it has prescribed in V:38. We shall mention it at its suitable place.

(*d*) *Depriving other persons of their inheritance condemned:*

In counting the vices which shall lead human beings to Hell, the Holy Qur'ãn says:

وَتَأْكُلُونَ التُّرَاثَ أَكْلًا لَّمًّا ۝

"And ye devour Inheritance (of the weak), devouring greedily." (LXXXIX:19).

(*e*) *To take by deceit more than one's share out of a thing jointly deserved or owned by several persons, condemned:*

وَمَنْ يَغْلُلْ يَأْتِ بِمَا غَلَّ يَوْمَ الْقِيٰمَةِ ۚ ثُمَّ تُوَفّٰى كُلُّ نَفْسٍ مَّا كَسَبَتْ
وَهُمْ لَا يُظْلَمُونَ ۝

".....whosoever is false to his trust (as a co-sharer), he shall restore on the Day of Resurrection (and Judgment) what he misappropriated.

---

5. This verse forms part of the pledge which the women converts from paganism took at the hands of the Holy Prophet (Peace be on him). It applies, however, equally to men. (Ref: *Tafsir al-Jalãlain*, p. 458).

Then every soul will receive its due, whatever (good or evil) it earned, and none shall be dealt with unjustly." (III:161).

(*f*) *Defrauding in general in mutual relations of business prohibited:*

وَلَا تُخْسِرُوا الْمِيزَانَ ۝

"....and make not deficient the balance (by diminishing what is due to the buyer)". (LV:9).

وَلَا تَكُونُوا مِنَ الْمُخْسِرِينَ ۝

"....and cause no loss (to others in trade through fraud)". (XXVI:181).

وَلَا تَنقُصُوا الْمِكْيَالَ وَالْمِيزَانَ

"....And give not short measure or weight....." (XI:84).

وَيْلٌ لِّلْمُطَفِّفِينَ ۝ الَّذِينَ إِذَا اكْتَالُوا عَلَى النَّاسِ يَسْتَوْفُونَ ۝ وَإِذَا كَالُوهُمْ
أَو وَّزَنُوهُمْ يُخْسِرُونَ ۝

"Woe to those that deal in fraud,—those who, when they have to receive by measure from men, exact full measure, but when they have to give by measure or weight to men, give less than due."(LXXXIII:1-3).

(g) *Misappropriating things entrusted, prohibited:*

يَا أَيُّهَا الَّذِينَ آمَنُوا لَا تَخُونُوا اللَّهَ وَالرَّسُولَ وَتَخُونُوا أَمَانَاتِكُمْ
وَأَنتُمْ تَعْلَمُونَ ۝

"O ye who believe! Betray not the trust of Allah and the Messenger, *nor misappropriate knowingly things entrusted to you."* (VIII:27).

Also, *favouring and supporting the misappropriator is prohibited:*

وَلَا تَكُن لِّلْخَائِنِينَ خَصِيمًا ۝

"....and be not thou an advocate for those who betray their trust...." (IV:105).

(*h*) *Hoarding commodities and withholding them from free circulation for exploiting fellow-beings through the creation of artificial scarcity and the consequent shooting up of prices, condemned.*

In counting the vices that will lead human beings to Hell, the Holy Qur'ãn says:

وَجَمَعَ فَأَوْعٰى ○

"He hoarded and withheld it (from circulation)." (LXX:18).

(*i*) *Exploiting the needs of others by lending money on interest*[6] *vehemently condemned and prohibited:*

اَلَّذِيْنَ يَاْكُلُوْنَ الرِّبٰوا لَا يَقُوْمُوْنَ اِلَّا كَمَا يَقُوْمُ الَّذِيْ يَتَخَبَّطُهُ
الشَّيْطٰنُ مِنَ الْمَسِّ ؕ ذٰلِكَ بِاَنَّهُمْ قَالُوْٓا اِنَّمَا الْبَيْعُ مِثْلُ الرِّبٰوا ۘ وَ
اَحَلَّ اللّٰهُ الْبَيْعَ وَحَرَّمَ الرِّبٰوا ؕ فَمَنْ جَآءَهٗ مَوْعِظَةٌ مِّنْ رَّبِّهٖ فَانْتَهٰى
فَلَهٗ مَا سَلَفَ ؕ وَاَمْرُهٗٓ اِلَى اللّٰهِ ؕ وَمَنْ عَادَ فَاُولٰٓئِكَ اَصْحٰبُ النَّارِ ۚ
هُمْ فِيْهَا خٰلِدُوْنَ ○ يَمْحَقُ اللّٰهُ الرِّبٰوا وَيُرْبِي الصَّدَقٰتِ ؕ وَاللّٰهُ لَا يُحِبُّ
كُلَّ كَفَّارٍ اَثِيْمٍ ○

"Those who devour *ribã*[7] (usury and interest) will not stand (on the Day of Resurrection) except as stands one whom the Evil One by his touch hath driven to madness. That is because they say: 'Trade is like *ribã*'. But Allah hath permitted trade and forbidden *ribã.* Those who after receiving direction from their Lord desist, shall be pardoned for the past; their case is for Allah (to Judge); but those who repeat the offence are Companions of the Fire: they will abide therein.

"Allah will deprive *ribã* of all blessings, but will give increase for deeds of charity: For He loveth not creatures ungrateful and wicked." (II:275, 276).

---

6. The economy which Islam offers is interest-free economy, and therefore, Islam condemns not only usury but all forms of interest-bearing transactions.

7. *Ribã* means "any addition, however slight, over and above the principal," and thus includes both usury and interest. (See: Lane's *Arabic-English Lexicon.*)

يٰۤاَيُّهَا الَّذِيْنَ اٰمَنُوْا لَا تَاْكُلُوا الرِّبٰوٓا اَضْعَافًا مُّضٰعَفَةً ۖ وَّاتَّقُوا اللّٰهَ
لَعَلَّكُمْ تُفْلِحُوْنَ ۝

"O ye who believe! Devour not *ribã*, doubled and multiplied, but fear Allah that ye may (really) prosper." (III:130).

(iii) Corrupting others in respect of wealth, prohibited:

(a) Through Bribery:

وَلَا تَاْكُلُوْٓا اَمْوَالَكُمْ بَيْنَكُمْ بِالْبَاطِلِ وَتُدْلُوْا بِهَآ اِلَى الْحُكَّامِ لِتَاْكُلُوْا فَرِيْقًا
مِّنْ اَمْوَالِ النَّاسِ بِالْاِثْمِ وَاَنْتُمْ تَعْلَمُوْنَ ۝

"Do not consume your property among yourselves iniquitously; neither proffer it to the judges, that you may sinfully consume a portion of other men's goods, and that wittingly." (II:188).

In the *Hadith* we find that the Holy Prophet (Peace be on him) has very strongly condemned the acceptor of bribe, the giver of bribe and the middleman. (See: *Mishkãt al-Masãbîh, Bãb a'-Rizq al-Wulãt*, p. 326).

(b) Through Gambling:

يٰۤاَيُّهَا الَّذِيْنَ اٰمَنُوْٓا اِنَّمَا الْخَمْرُ وَالْمَيْسِرُ وَالْاَنْصَابُ وَالْاَزْلَامُ رِجْسٌ
مِّنْ عَمَلِ الشَّيْطٰنِ فَاجْتَنِبُوْهُ لَعَلَّكُمْ تُفْلِحُوْنَ ۝

"O ye who believe! Intoxicants and gambling, and (dedication of) stones, and divination by arrows, are an abomination,—of Satan's handiwork: Eschew such (abomination), that ye may prosper." (V:93).

(iv) Want of Helpfulness and Charitableness towards others condemned; hence abstinence from it is duty:

(a) *Hoarding gold and silver, thereby keeping it out of circulation and thus damaging collective economy, on the one hand, and abstaining from rendering economic assistance in deserving individual cases, on the other, vehemently condemned:*

وَالَّذِيْنَ يَكْنِزُوْنَ الذَّهَبَ وَالْفِضَّةَ وَلَا يُنْفِقُوْنَهَا فِيْ سَبِيْلِ اللّٰهِ ۙ
فَبَشِّرْهُمْ بِعَذَابٍ اَلِيْمٍ ۝ يَّوْمَ يُحْمٰى عَلَيْهَا فِيْ نَارِ جَهَنَّمَ فَتُكْوٰى
بِهَا جِبَاهُهُمْ وَجُنُوْبُهُمْ وَظُهُوْرُهُمْ ۗ هٰذَا مَا كَنَزْتُمْ لِاَنْفُسِكُمْ
فَذُوْقُوْا مَا كُنْتُمْ تَكْنِزُوْنَ ۝

".....those who hoard up gold and silver and spend it not in the Way of Allah (i.e., for the welfare of fellow-beings), announce to them (O Muhammad) a most grievous penalty—on the day when heat will be produced out of that (wealth) in the fire of Hell, and with it will be branded their foreheads (representing human thinking) and their flanks (which support the seat of greed, i.e., the stomach) and their backs (as symbolising stability and strength)—(and it will be said unto them:) Here is that which ye hoarded for yourselves. Now taste of what ye used to hoard."

(IX:34, 35).

(b) Practising niggardliness and promoting it as a creed condemned:

وَلَا تَجْعَلْ يَدَكَ مَغْلُولَةً إِلَىٰ عُنُقِكَ

"Make not thy hand tied (in niggardliness) to thy neck....."

(XVII:29).

إِنَّ اللَّهَ لَا يُحِبُّ مَن كَانَ مُخْتَالًا فَخُورًا ۝ الَّذِينَ يَبْخَلُونَ وَ
يَأْمُرُونَ النَّاسَ بِالْبُخْلِ وَيَكْتُمُونَ مَا آتَاهُمُ اللَّهُ مِن فَضْلِهِ ۗ
وَأَعْتَدْنَا لِلْكَافِرِينَ عَذَابًا مُّهِينًا ۝

"Verily Allah loveth not such as are vainglorious, boasters—those who are niggardly and command mankind to niggardliness and hide that which Allah hath vouchsafed to them of His Bounty; and We have prepared for the infidels torment ignominious." (IV:36, 37).[8]

(c) Refusing small kindness to Others condemned:

فَوَيْلٌ لِّلْمُصَلِّينَ ۝ الَّذِينَ هُمْ عَن صَلَاتِهِمْ سَاهُونَ ۝ الَّذِينَ هُمْ
يُرَاءُونَ ۝ وَيَمْنَعُونَ الْمَاعُونَ ۝

"Ah, woe unto the worshippers, who are heedless of their Prayers; who would be seen (at worship) *yet refuse small kindnesses* to (others)."

(CVII:4-7).

(d) Well-doing to Others with a view to getting more in return disapproved as worthless act of goodness:

---

8. Cf. LVII: 23, 24.

وَمَآ اٰتَيْتُمْ مِّنْ رِّبًا لِّيَرْبُوَا۟ فِىٓ اَمْوَالِ النَّاسِ فَلَا يَرْبُوْا عِنْدَ اللّٰهِ ۚ وَمَآ اٰتَيْتُمْ
مِّنْ زَكٰوةٍ تُرِيْدُوْنَ وَجْهَ اللّٰهِ فَاُولٰٓئِكَ هُمُ الْمُضْعِفُوْنَ ۝

"And whatsoever ye give in gift[9] in order that it may increase among the substance of men (and return to you augmented) increaseth not with Allah (i.e., is not accepted as virtue and blessed by Allah); but that which ye give out for charity, seeking the Countenance (i.e., Pleasure) of Allah, (will increase): it is these who will get a recompense multiplied." (XXX:39).

(e) *Charity with laying obligation on the recipient and/or, hurting him in any way, prohibited:*

يٰٓاَيُّهَا الَّذِيْنَ اٰمَنُوْا لَا تُبْطِلُوْا صَدَقٰتِكُمْ بِالْمَنِّ وَالْاَذٰى ۙ

"O ye who believe! Render not vain your charity by reminders of your generorsity or by injury....." (II:264).

(v) Want of Goodwill towards Others prohibited:

(a) *Breaking promises, pledges and covenants and violating oaths taken in mutual dealings prohibited:*

وَلَا تَنْقُضُوا الْاَيْمَانَ

".....And break not your oaths (when ye pledge your word in any matter)....." (XVI:91).

اِنَّمَا يَتَذَكَّرُ اُولُوا الْاَلْبَابِ ۝ الَّذِيْنَ يُوْفُوْنَ بِعَهْدِ اللّٰهِ وَلَا
يَنْقُضُوْنَ الْمِيْثَاقَ ۝

".....It is those who are endued with understanding that receive admonition;—those who fulfil the Covenant of Allah and fail not in their plighted word." (XIII:19, 20).

(b) *Abstaining from giving false evidence made a condition of Faith, and thereby a duty:*

Recounting the fundamental virtues of true Muslims, the Holy Qur'ãn says:

---

9. This is the rendering of the word *ribã* here by Maulana Abdul Majid Daryabadi. (See in *English Translation of the Holy Qur'ãn*, p. 651).

وَالَّذِيْنَ لَا يَشْهَدُوْنَ الزُّوْرَ

".....and those who witness no falsehood (i.e., do not give false evidence)[10]...." (XXV:72).

(c) Concealing evidence prohibited:

وَلَا تَكْتُمُوا الشَّهَادَةَ ، وَمَنْ يَّكْتُمْهَا فَإِنَّهٗ اٰثِمٌ قَلْبُهٗ ، وَاللّٰهُ بِمَا تَعْمَلُوْنَ عَلِيْمٌ ○

"Conceal not evidence; for whoever conceals it, his heart is tainted with sin. And Allah knoweth all that ye do." (II:283).

(d) Treachery condemned; hence abstinence from it is duty:

The Holy Qur'ãn says:

إِنَّ اللّٰهَ لَا يُحِبُّ كُلَّ خَوَّانٍ كَفُوْرٍ ○

"Verily, *Allah loveth not any that is treacherous,* or shows ingratitude." (XXII:38).

Also:

وَالَّذِيْنَ لَا يَشْهَدُوْنَ الزُّوْرَ

"(The servants of God are)....those who witness no falsehood (i.e., deal not falsely or treacherously with anyone)...." (XXV:72).

(e) Ingratitude for the good received from others condemned; hence abstinence from it is duty:

The Holy Qur'ãn says:

إِنَّ اللّٰهَ لَا يُحِبُّ كُلَّ خَوَّانٍ كَفُوْرٍ ○

"Verily, Allah loveth not any that is treacherous, or *shows ingratitude.*" (XXII:38).

II. Duties of Respect:

(i) (*a*) *Showing contempt for others; and*

10. The other meaning of this verse has been quoted below 142.

(b) *Oppressing others,*

prohibited:

وَلَا تُصَعِّرْ خَدَّكَ لِلنَّاسِ وَلَا تَمْشِ فِي الْأَرْضِ مَرَحًا ۖ إِنَّ اللَّهَ لَا يُحِبُّ
كُلَّ مُخْتَالٍ فَخُورٍ ۝

"And swell not thy cheek at human beings (i.e., do not treat others contemptuously and do not oppress them), nor walk in insolence through the earth; for Allah loveth not any vainglorious, boaster."
(XXXI:18).

Arrogance and oppression are such grave vices that the hearts of those who indulge in them are sealed up to influences for good:

كَذَٰلِكَ يَطْبَعُ اللَّهُ عَلَىٰ كُلِّ قَلْبِ مُتَكَبِّرٍ جَبَّارٍ ۝

"Thus doth Allah seal up every heart—of (him who is) stiff-necked, oppressor." (XL:35).

Indeed, they alone who abstain from belittling and oppressing others will go to Heaven:

تِلْكَ الدَّارُ الْآخِرَةُ نَجْعَلُهَا لِلَّذِينَ لَا يُرِيدُونَ عُلُوًّا فِي الْأَرْضِ
وَلَا فَسَادًا ۚ وَالْعَاقِبَةُ لِلْمُتَّقِينَ ۝

"That Home of the Hereafter We shall give to those who intend not high-handedness or mischief (i.e., evil in general) on earth: And the End is (best) for the righteous." (XXVIII:83).

(ii) Damaging the honour of Others through defaming them in any way, even though the defamatory remarks are based on truth, prohibited:

(a) Defamation in general forbidden:

وَلَا تَلْمِزُوا أَنْفُسَكُمْ

"....and defame not (nor be sarcastic to) each other...." (XLIX:11).

The only exception in speaking ill of others is where a person has been wronged mischievously and he has to defend his honour by exposing his wicked enemy. Even in that case, however, such a wronged person has been advised to practise forgiveness and to abstain from exposing the evils of his enemy—leaving the affair to God and hoping for His Reward—because God is 'Forgiving, Powerful'.

The Holy Qur'ãn says:

لَا يُحِبُّ اللَّهُ الْجَهْرَ بِالسُّوءِ مِنَ الْقَوْلِ إِلَّا مَن ظُلِمَ ۚ وَكَانَ اللَّهُ سَمِيعًا عَلِيمًا ۝
إِن تُبْدُوا خَيْرًا أَوْ تُخْفُوهُ أَوْ تَعْفُوا عَن سُوءٍ فَإِنَّ اللَّهَ كَانَ عَفُوًّا قَدِيرًا ۝

"Allah approveth not the utterance of evil speech (directed at defaming others), unless by one who hath been wronged; and Allah is ever Hearing, Knowing.

"If ye do good openly or keep it secret, or cover evil with pardon, lo! Allah is ever Forgiving, Powerful." (IV:148, 149).

(b) Scandalmongering specifically condemned; hence abstinence from it is duty:

وَيْلٌ لِّكُلِّ هُمَزَةٍ لُّمَزَةٍ ۝

"Woe to every (kind of) scandalmonger[11], backbiter...." (CIV:1).

وَلَا تُطِعْ كُلَّ حَلَّافٍ مَّهِينٍ ۝ هَمَّازٍ مَّشَّاءٍ بِنَمِيمٍ ۝

"Heed not thou any (who is) ready with oaths, (is) a slanderer, (and) goes about with calumnies...." (LXVIII:10, 11).

(c) Fabrication of lies against Others condemned; hence abstinence from it is duty:

وَيْلٌ لِّكُلِّ أَفَّاكٍ أَثِيمٍ ۝

"Woe to every sinful fabricator of falsehoods." (XLV:7).

(d) Transferring one's guilt to Others condemned; hence abstinence from it is duty:

وَمَن يَكْسِبْ خَطِيئَةً أَوْ إِثْمًا ثُمَّ يَرْمِ بِهِ بَرِيئًا فَقَدِ احْتَمَلَ بُهْتَانًا
وَإِثْمًا مُّبِينًا ۝

"But if anyone earns a fault or a sin and throws it on to one that

---

11. The vice of scandalmongering covers "talking or suggesting evil of men or women by word, or innuendo, or behaviour, or mimicry, or sarcasm, or insult."

is innocent, he carries (on himself) (both) a falsehood and a flagrant sin."
(IV:112).

(e) *Attacking the honour of chaste women through slandering them condemned vehemently; hence abstinence from it is duty:*

إِنَّ الَّذِينَ يَرْمُونَ الْمُحْصَنَٰتِ الْغَٰفِلَٰتِ الْمُؤْمِنَٰتِ لُعِنُوا فِي الدُّنْيَا وَالْآخِرَةِ
وَلَهُمْ عَذَابٌ عَظِيمٌ ۝ يَوْمَ تَشْهَدُ عَلَيْهِمْ أَلْسِنَتُهُمْ وَأَيْدِيهِمْ وَأَرْجُلُهُمْ
بِمَا كَانُوا يَعْمَلُونَ ۝ يَوْمَئِذٍ يُوَفِّيهِمُ اللَّهُ دِينَهُمُ الْحَقَّ وَيَعْلَمُونَ أَنَّ
اللَّهَ هُوَ الْحَقُّ الْمُبِينُ ۝

"Those who slander chaste women, indiscreet but believing, are cursed in this life and in the Hereafter; for them is a grievous Penalty,—on the day when their tongues, their hands, and their feet will bear witness against them as to their actions. On that Day Allah will pay them back (all) their just dues, and they will realize that Allah is the (very) Truth that makes all things manifest." (XXIV:23-25).

(iii) *Backbiting others prohibited:*

وَلَا يَغْتَبْ بَعْضُكُمْ بَعْضًا ۚ أَيُحِبُّ أَحَدُكُمْ أَنْ يَأْكُلَ لَحْمَ
أَخِيهِ مَيْتًا فَكَرِهْتُمُوهُ ۚ وَاتَّقُوا اللَّهَ ۚ إِنَّ اللَّهَ تَوَّابٌ رَحِيمٌ ۝

"....and speak not ill of each other behind their backs. Would any of you like to eat the flesh of his dead brother? Nay, ye would abhor it. So fear Allah. Verily, Allah is Relenting, Merciful."
(XLIX:12).

(iv) *Using obscene language against anyone prohibited:*

وَيَنْهَىٰ عَنِ الْفَحْشَاءِ وَالْمُنْكَرِ وَالْبَغْيِ

"....and (God) forbiddeth all shameful, abominable deeds...."
(XVI:90).

Using obscene language is in itself shameful. To use it for insulting another person is all the more shameful, and it is, therefore, absolutely forbidden to a Muslim.

(v) Cultivation of rancour against anyone ruled out; hence abstinence from it is duty:

The Holy Qur'ãn commands in relation to the worst ideological enemies of the Muslims who were in a state of perpetual war with them, thus:

وَإِنْ جَنَحُوا لِلسَّلْمِ فَاجْنَحْ لَهَا وَتَوَكَّلْ عَلَى اللهِ ۚ إِنَّهُ
هُوَ السَّمِيعُ الْعَلِيمُ ○

"And if they (i.e., the enemies at war) incline to peace, incline thou also to it, and trust in Allah. Lo! He is the Hearer, the Knower. (VIII:61).

This command implies that a Muslim should not cultivate rancour against anyone, but should always be ready to establish peace even with his worst ideological enemies, not to speak to enemies at lower level, namely, the level of simple social relations.

(vi) Jealousy prohibited in its very basis:

Jealousy is a widely prevalent moral shortcoming of human beings. Its goal is the deprivation of others of the good things that they may have in excess of what one may possess, and it emerges and entrenches itself in the character of those who are not blessed with true faith in God and genuine moral refinement. Its roots lie in covetousness. Consequently, those who do not efface covetousness from their lives fall victim to it.

The Holy Qur'ãn mentions its evil and teaches the prayer for being saved from it. (CXIII:5). Then going to its root, it lays down the command that it is the duty of a Muslim to abstain from covetousness and the consequent jealousy under all circumstances:

وَلَا تَتَمَنَّوْا مَا فَضَّلَ اللهُ بِهِ بَعْضَكُمْ عَلَى بَعْضٍ ۚ لِلرِّجَالِ نَصِيبٌ مِمَّا
اكْتَسَبُوا ۖ وَلِلنِّسَاءِ نَصِيبٌ مِمَّا اكْتَسَبْنَ ۚ وَسْئَلُوا اللهَ مِنْ فَضْلِهِ ۗ
إِنَّ اللهَ كَانَ بِكُلِّ شَيْءٍ عَلِيمًا ○

"And in no wise covet those things in which Allah hath bestowed His gifts more freely on some of you than on others. Unto men a fortune from that which they have earned, and unto women a fortune from that which they have earned. (All this is with Allah's permission. Therefore, never wish or try that the good things which others have may be diminished for them), but ask (for yourselves) Allah of His Bounty (with a positive healthy outlook). Lo! Allah is ever Knower of all things." (IV:32).

(vii) Observance of Duplicity[12] *condemned; hence abstinence from it is duty:*

Duplicity is a deeper phase of insincerity, which has its roots in hypocrisy. The Holy Qur'ãn condemns it in very strong terms:

وَإِذَا لَقُوا الَّذِينَ آمَنُوا قَالُوا آمَنَّا وَإِذَا خَلَوْا إِلَىٰ شَيَاطِينِهِمْ قَالُوا إِنَّا مَعَكُمْ
إِنَّمَا نَحْنُ مُسْتَهْزِئُونَ ○ اللَّهُ يَسْتَهْزِئُ بِهِمْ وَيَمُدُّهُمْ فِي طُغْيَانِهِمْ
يَعْمَهُونَ ○ أُولَٰئِكَ الَّذِينَ اشْتَرَوُا الضَّلَالَةَ بِالْهُدَىٰ فَمَا رَبِحَتْ تِجَارَتُهُمْ
وَمَا كَانُوا مُهْتَدِينَ ○

"When they meet those who believe, they say: 'We believe'. But when they are alone with their evil ones, they say: 'We are really with you; we were only jesting'.

"Allah will throw back their mockery on them, and give them rope in their trespasses; so they will wander like blind ones (to and fro).

"These are they who bartered Guidance for error; but their traffic is profitless, and they have lost true direction." (II:14-16).

It should be noted that, though the particular reference in these verses is to the Hypocrites of Madinah, they contain the general law that duplicity, wherever practised, is a grave vice, and it is the duty of a Muslim to abstain from it totally if he has to be true to his Faith.

(viii) Cultivating the habit of suspecting the motives of Others prohibited:

يَا أَيُّهَا الَّذِينَ آمَنُوا اجْتَنِبُوا كَثِيرًا مِّنَ الظَّنِّ إِنَّ بَعْضَ
الظَّنِّ إِثْمٌ

"O ye who believe! Shun as much suspicion (as possible); for lo! some suspicion is a crime (because it involves cruel injustice to innocent

11. We have mentioned this vice in connection with 'Duties to Self' also. This is so because duplicity is a two-edged vice. It injures, on the one hand, the moral tone of him who indulges in it; and, on the other hand, the interests of him against whom it is practised.

and well-meaning people)....." (XLIX:12).

(ix) Spying, i.e., probing into the affairs of Others, prohibited:

وَلَا تَجَسَّسُوْا

".....and spy not (into the affairs of others for fault-finding)...." (XLIX:12).

(x) Deriding and ridiculing Others prohibited:

يٰٓاَيُّهَا الَّذِيْنَ اٰمَنُوْا لَا يَسْخَرْ قَوْمٌ مِّنْ قَوْمٍ

"O ye who believe! let not a folk deride a folk...." (XLIX:11).

(xi) Giving offensive nicknames to Others prohibited:

وَلَا تَنَابَزُوْا بِالْاَلْقَابِ ؕ

"And offend not others by nicknames....." (XLIX:11).

(xii) Corrupting others through flattery to be avoided:

The Holy Qur'ãn condemns those who love to be flattered and warns them of grievous consequences. (III:188). Now, to be the cause of the commission of sin by someone else is also a sin. Thus to flatter anyone and thereby corrupt his mentality is a sin, and hence to abstain from it is duty.

(ii) Duties of Commission

END:

Positive well-wishing and well-doing to fellow-beings.

(A) *Comprehensive command relating to the duty of practising well-wishing and well-doing towards fellow-beings, enjoined:*

The Holy Qur'ãn says:

يٰٓاَيُّهَا الَّذِيْنَ اٰمَنُوا ارْكَعُوْا وَاسْجُدُوْا وَاعْبُدُوْا رَبَّكُمْ وَافْعَلُوا الْخَيْرَ لَعَلَّكُمْ تُفْلِحُوْنَ ۚ

"O ye who believe! Bow down, prostrate yourselves and adore

your Lord, and (always) do good (to others), that ye may prosper."

(XXII:77).

(B) <u>*Specify Commands relating to specific Duties of Commission*</u>*:*

(a) Duties of Love;

(b) Duties of Respect.

(*a*) *Duties of Love*:

(i) <u>*Duties relating to life*</u>*:*

(a) Protecting and preserving human life: an act of sublime goodness; hence, an important duty:

The Holy Qur'ãn says:

وَمَنْ أَحْيَاهَا فَكَأَنَّمَا أَحْيَا النَّاسَ جَمِيعًا ۚ

"....and whoso saveth (i.e., protects and preserves) the life of one, it shall be as if he had saved the life of all mankind...." (V:35).

(b) The Qur'ãnic law of Equality, combining permission for blood-wit, in cases of murder, also directed to saving of human lives as far as equitable:

يٰٓأَيُّهَا الَّذِيْنَ اٰمَنُوْا كُتِبَ عَلَيْكُمُ الْقِصَاصُ فِي الْقَتْلٰى ۖ اَلْحُرُّ بِالْحُرِّ وَ
الْعَبْدُ بِالْعَبْدِ وَالْاُنْثٰى بِالْاُنْثٰى ۚ فَمَنْ عُفِيَ لَهٗ مِنْ اَخِيْهِ شَيْءٌ فَاتِّبَاعٌ ۢ
بِالْمَعْرُوْفِ وَاَدَاۗءٌ اِلَيْهِ بِاِحْسَانٍ ۚ

"O ye who believe! the law of Equality is prescribed to you in cases of murder: the free for the free, the slave for the slave, the woman for the woman. But if any remission is made by the brother (i.e., the heirs of the murdered person), then grant any reasonable demand, and compensate him (in the form of blood-money) with handsome gratitude....." (II:178).[13]

(c) Active sympathy with Others for the amelioration and removal of their sufferings in respect of their health—as also in other respects—, enjoined:

---

13. The legal implications of this verse have been discussed in Penal Ethics.

Recounting the moral qualities of true Muslims, the Holy Qur'ãn says:

ثُمَّ كَانَ مِنَ الَّذِينَ آمَنُوا وَتَوَاصَوْا بِالصَّبْرِ وَتَوَاصَوْا بِالْمَرْحَمَةِ ۝

"Then will he be of those who believe, and enjoin patience (i.e., constancy and self-restraint), and enjoin compassion and active sympathy (with others for the amelioration and removal of their sufferings and misfortunes)". (XC:17).

Thus visiting the sick, not as a mere formality but for active sympathy in their suffering, and participation, according to one's capacity, in all collective efforts directed at the preservation and promotion of human health is a duty, without the fulfilment of which no one can aspire to be a true Muslim.

(ii) *Duties in respect of wealth of Others:*

To regard the weaith of others as absolutely inviolable, enjoined:

(a) *Only that which has been acquired by a Muslim lawfully can be owned and utilized by him:*

يَا أَيُّهَا النَّاسُ كُلُوا مِمَّا فِي الْأَرْضِ حَلَالًا طَيِّبًا وَلَا تَتَّبِعُوا خُطُوَاتِ الشَّيْطَانِ إِنَّهُ لَكُمْ عَدُوٌّ مُبِينٌ ۝ إِنَّمَا يَأْمُرُكُمْ بِالسُّوءِ وَالْفَحْشَاءِ

"O humankind! consume, out of that which is (found) on the earth, (only) that which is lawful and good; and do not follow the footsteps of the devil, for he is to you an avowed enemy. He enjoineth upon you only the evil and the foul....."[14] (II:168, 169).

(b) *Protecting the wealth of Others entrusted to one's custody, enjoined:*

إِنَّ اللَّهَ يَأْمُرُكُمْ أَنْ تُؤَدُّوا الْأَمَانَاتِ إِلَىٰ أَهْلِهَا

"Lo! Allah commandeth you to render back your Trusts to those to whom they are due....." (IV:58).[15]

---

14. Cf. XVI:90; XXIV:21.

15. Cf. II;283.

(c) Complete honesty in commercial transactions enjoined:

وَاَوْفُوا الْكَيْلَ اِذَا كِلْتُمْ وَزِنُوْا بِالْقِسْطَاسِ الْمُسْتَقِيْمِ ؕ ذٰلِكَ خَيْرٌ وَّ اَحْسَنُ تَاْوِيْلًا ○

"Give full measure when ye measure, and weigh with an even balance, (in short, be fully honest in all your commercial dealings): That is most fitting and most advantageous in the final determination".

(XVII:35).

وَاَوْفُوا الْكَيْلَ وَالْمِيْزَانَ بِالْقِسْطِ ۚ

".....Give measure and weight with full justice....." (VI:152).[16]

(iii) *Duty in respect of spending one's wealth for Others:*

(A) Charitableness and generosity towards Others enjoined:

(a) All that belongs to a Muslim belongs actually to God and is, therefore, meant to be generously spent for the benefit of God's creatures:

اِنَّ اللّٰهَ اشْتَرٰى مِنَ الْمُؤْمِنِيْنَ اَنْفُسَهُمْ وَاَمْوَالَهُمْ بِاَنَّ لَهُمُ الْجَنَّةَ ؕ

"Allah hath purchased of the Believers their persons and their wealth because the Garden (of Paradise) will be theirs." (IX:111).

(b) The basis of a Muslim's charity and generosity is purely "love for God" and "fear of the Hereafter" and hence the economic assistance which he renders to anyone is to be from the highest motive and without the least tinge of worldliness:

وَاٰتَى الْمَالَ عَلٰى حُبِّهٖ

".....(but it is righteousness).....to spend wealth (in charity) *out of love for Him* (i.e., God) (alone)....." (II:177).

. . . . . الَّذِىْ يُؤْتِىْ مَالَهٗ يَتَزَكّٰى ○ وَمَا لِاَحَدٍ عِنْدَهٗ مِنْ نِّعْمَةٍ تُجْزٰٓى ○ اِلَّا ابْتِغَآءَ وَجْهِ رَبِّهِ الْاَعْلٰى ○ وَلَسَوْفَ يَرْضٰى ○

16. Cf. XXVI:181, 182.

".....(the righteous) who spend their wealth (on others) for increase in self-purification, and have in their minds no favour from anyone for which a reward is expected in return, but only the desire to seek for the countenance of their Lord Most High; and soon will they attain (complete) satisfaction." (XCII:18-21).

وَالَّذِينَ يُؤْتُونَ مَا آتَوا وَّقُلُوبُهُمْ وَجِلَةٌ أَنَّهُمْ إِلَىٰ رَبِّهِمْ رَاجِعُونَ ○
أُولَٰئِكَ يُسَارِعُونَ فِي الْخَيْرَاتِ وَهُمْ لَهَا سَابِقُونَ ○

"And those who dispense their charity with their hearts full of fear, because they will return to their Lord;—it is these who hasten in every good work, and these who are foremost in them." (XXIII:60-61).

(c) Charity—a Basic Virtue:

لَن تَنَالُوا الْبِرَّ حَتَّىٰ تُنفِقُوا مِمَّا تُحِبُّونَ ۚ وَمَا تُنفِقُوا مِن شَيْءٍ
فَإِنَّ اللَّهَ بِهِ عَلِيمٌ ○

"By no means shall ye attain righteousness unless ye give (freely) of that which ye love; and whatever ye give, of a truth Allah knoweth it well." (III:92).

(d) Measure of charity defined: To spend what is superfluous from one's rational needs:

وَيَسْأَلُونَكَ مَاذَا يُنفِقُونَ ۚ قُلِ الْعَفْوَ ۗ كَذَٰلِكَ يُبَيِّنُ اللَّهُ لَكُمُ الْآيَاتِ
لَعَلَّكُمْ تَتَفَكَّرُونَ ○ فِي الدُّنْيَا وَالْآخِرَةِ ۗ

"They ask thee (O Muhammad!) how much they are to spend; say: 'What is beyond your needs.' Thus Allah maketh clear to you His signs: in order that ye may consider (their bearings) on this life and the Hereafter." (II:219, 220).

(e) Mode of giving charity defined:

إِن تُبْدُوا الصَّدَقَاتِ فَنِعِمَّا هِيَ ۖ وَإِن تُخْفُوهَا وَتُؤْتُوهَا
الْفُقَرَاءَ فَهُوَ خَيْرٌ لَّكُمْ ۚ وَيُكَفِّرُ عَنكُم مِّن سَيِّئَاتِكُمْ ۗ وَاللَّهُ بِمَا تَعْمَلُونَ
خَبِيرٌ ○

"If ye disclose (acts of) charity, even so it is well, but if ye conceal them, and make them reach those (really) in need, that is best for you. It will atone for some of your evil deeds. And Allah is well acquainted with what ye do." (II:271).

(f) Blessings of charity emphasised through parables:

مَثَلُ الَّذِيْنَ يُنْفِقُوْنَ اَمْوَالَهُمْ فِيْ سَبِيْلِ اللّٰهِ كَمَثَلِ حَبَّةٍ اَنْۢبَتَتْ
سَبْعَ سَنَابِلَ فِيْ كُلِّ سُنْۢبُلَةٍ مِّائَةُ حَبَّةٍ ؕ وَاللّٰهُ يُضٰعِفُ لِمَنْ
يَّشَآءُ ؕ وَاللّٰهُ وَاسِعٌ عَلِيْمٌ ۝ اَلَّذِيْنَ يُنْفِقُوْنَ اَمْوَالَهُمْ فِيْ سَبِيْلِ اللّٰهِ ثُمَّ
لَا يُتْبِعُوْنَ مَآ اَنْفَقُوْا مَنًّا وَّلَآ اَذًى ۙ لَّهُمْ اَجْرُهُمْ عِنْدَ رَبِّهِمْ ۚ وَلَا
خَوْفٌ عَلَيْهِمْ وَلَا هُمْ يَحْزَنُوْنَ ۝

"The parable of those who spend their substance in the Way of Allah is that of a grain of corn: it groweth seven ears, and each ear hath a hundred grains. Allah giveth manifold increase to whom He pleaseth: for Allah careth for all, and He knoweth all things. Those who spend their substance in the cause of Allah, and follow not up their gifts with reminders of their generosity or with injury,—their reward is with their Lord: on them shall be no fear, nor shall they grieve." (II:261, 262).

وَمَثَلُ الَّذِيْنَ يُنْفِقُوْنَ اَمْوَالَهُمُ ابْتِغَآءَ مَرْضَاتِ اللّٰهِ وَتَثْبِيْتًا مِّنْ اَنْفُسِهِمْ
كَمَثَلِ جَنَّةٍ بِرَبْوَةٍ اَصَابَهَا وَابِلٌ فَاٰتَتْ اُكُلَهَا ضِعْفَيْنِ ۚ فَاِنْ لَّمْ
يُصِبْهَا وَابِلٌ فَطَلٌّ ؕ وَاللّٰهُ بِمَا تَعْمَلُوْنَ بَصِيْرٌ ۝

"And the likeness of those who spend their substance, seeking to please Allah and to strengthen their souls, is as a garden, high and fertile: heavy rain makes it yield a double increase of harvest, and if it receives not heavy rain, light moisture sufficeth it. Allah seeth well whatever ye do." (II:265).

(g) Charity should be practised at all times and under all circumstances:

اَلَّذِيْنَ يُنْفِقُوْنَ اَمْوَالَهُمْ بِالَّيْلِ وَالنَّهَارِ سِرًّا وَّعَلَانِيَةً فَلَهُمْ اَجْرُهُمْ
عِنْدَ رَبِّهِمْ ۚ وَلَا خَوْفٌ عَلَيْهِمْ وَلَا هُمْ يَحْزَنُوْنَ ۝

"Those who (in charity) spend of their goods by night and by day, in secret and in public, have their reward with their Lord: on them shall be no fear, nor shall they grieve." (II:274).

وَسَارِعُوٓا إِلَىٰ مَغْفِرَةٍ مِّن رَّبِّكُمْ وَجَنَّةٍ عَرْضُهَا ٱلسَّمَٰوَٰتُ وَٱلْأَرْضُ
أُعِدَّتْ لِلْمُتَّقِينَ ۝ ٱلَّذِينَ يُنفِقُونَ فِى ٱلسَّرَّآءِ وَٱلضَّرَّآءِ وَٱلْكَٰظِمِينَ
ٱلْغَيْظَ وَٱلْعَافِينَ عَنِ ٱلنَّاسِ ۗ وَٱللَّهُ يُحِبُّ ٱلْمُحْسِنِينَ ۝

"Be quick in race for forgiveness from your Lord, and for a Garden whose width is that (of the whole) of the heavens and of the earth, prepared for the righteous,—those who spend (freely), whether in prosperity, or in adversity; who restrain anger, and pardon (all) men;—for Allah loves those who do good". (III:133, 134).

(h) A very forceful appeal made for practising charity:

أَيَوَدُّ أَحَدُكُمْ أَن تَكُونَ لَهُۥ جَنَّةٌ مِّن نَّخِيلٍ وَأَعْنَابٍ تَجْرِى مِن تَحْتِهَا
ٱلْأَنْهَٰرُ لَهُۥ فِيهَا مِن كُلِّ ٱلثَّمَرَٰتِ وَأَصَابَهُ ٱلْكِبَرُ وَلَهُۥ ذُرِّيَّةٌ ضُعَفَآءُ
فَأَصَابَهَآ إِعْصَارٌ فِيهِ نَارٌ فَٱحْتَرَقَتْ ۗ كَذَٰلِكَ يُبَيِّنُ ٱللَّهُ لَكُمُ ٱلْءَايَٰتِ
لَعَلَّكُمْ تَتَفَكَّرُونَ ۝

"Does any of you wish that he should have a garden with date-palms and vines and streams flowing underneath, and all kinds of fruit, while he is stricken with old age, and his children are not strong (enough to look after themselves)—that it should be caught in a whirlwind with fire therein, and be burnt up? Thus doth Allah make clear to you His Sings (in respect of possible economic misery and the way to remedy it through the universal practise of economic well-doing to others), that they may consider." (II:266).

(i) Specific categories of those who deserve charitable economic assistance, mentioned:

The following categories have been specified:

The kinsfolk, the orphans, the needy; 'those who ask'; the poverty-stricken persons in general; those in bondage (as slaves or as prisoners of war), (including the task of their emancipation through payment of ransom); those suffering from the burden of debt (and have to be relieved through the payment of that debt); the wayfarers; and recent converts to Islam." (II:177; IX:60).

(j) Command given to use one's talents and possessions for, and practise assistance of all kinds to, all:

يَٰٓأَيُّهَا ٱلَّذِينَ ءَامَنُوٓا۟ أَنفِقُوا۟ مِمَّا رَزَقْنَٰكُم مِّن قَبْلِ أَن يَأْتِىَ يَوْمٌ لَّا بَيْعٌ فِيهِ وَلَا خُلَّةٌ وَلَا شَفَٰعَةٌ ۗ وَٱلْكَٰفِرُونَ هُمُ ٱلظَّٰلِمُونَ ۝

"O ye who believe! spend out of (the bounties) We have provided for you, before the Day comes when no bargaining (will avail), nor friendship nor intercession. Those who reject Faith injure (only themselves)."[17] (II:254).

(B) Charitableness towards one's debtor enjoined:

وَإِن كَانَ ذُو عُسْرَةٍ فَنَظِرَةٌ إِلَىٰ مَيْسَرَةٍ ۚ وَأَن تَصَدَّقُوا۟ خَيْرٌ لَّكُمْ ۖ إِن كُنتُمْ تَعْلَمُونَ ۝

"If the debtor is in a difficulty, grant him time till it is easy for him to repay. But if ye remit it by way of charity, that is best for you if ye only knew." (II:280).

(C) Giving of free gifts to cultivate and to enhance love enjoined:

The Holy Qur'ãn says:

وَلَا تَنسَوُا۟ ٱلْفَضْلَ بَيْنَكُمْ ۚ

"....and do not forget grace amongst yourselves...." (II:237).

The Arabic word used here for 'grace' means, according to Lane's *Lexicon*, "a free gift, or favour, a benefit, and bounty". Thus this verse includes the command of giving free gifts for cultivating generosity and for enhancing love.

(iv) <u>Maintenance of goodwill towards Others</u>:

(a) Absolute injustice enjoined, even though it means any amount of personal suffering for the moral agent, or the interests of those

17 Besides this verse, there are numerous other verses where the merit of helping others has been mentioned e.g., LVI:7, LXIII:10.

nearest and dearest to him are sacrificed, and even though the other party is his or Islam's worst enemy:

إِنَّ اللّٰهَ يَأْمُرُ بِالْعَدْلِ

"Verily, Allah enjoineth justice (to all and under all circumstances)....." (XVI:90).

يَاَيُّهَا الَّذِيْنَ اٰمَنُوْا كُوْنُوْا قَوّٰمِيْنَ بِالْقِسْطِ شُهَدَآءَ لِلّٰهِ وَلَوْ عَلٰٓى اَنْفُسِكُمْ
اَوِ الْوَالِدَيْنِ وَالْاَقْرَبِيْنَ ۚ اِنْ يَّكُنْ غَنِيًّا اَوْ فَقِيْرًا فَاللّٰهُ اَوْلٰى بِهِمَا ۫ فَلَا
تَتَّبِعُوا الْهَوٰٓى اَنْ تَعْدِلُوْا ۚ وَاِنْ تَلْوٗٓا اَوْ تُعْرِضُوْا فَاِنَّ اللّٰهَ كَانَ بِمَا
تَعْمَلُوْنَ خَبِيْرًا ۝

"O ye who believe! Be ye staunch in justice, witnesses for Allah, even though it be against yourselves or (your) parents or (your) kindred, whether (the case be of) a rich man or a poor man, for Allah is nearer unto both (than ye are). So follow not passion lest ye lapse (from truth); and if ye lapse or fall away, then lo! Allah is ever informed as to what ye do." (IV:135).

يَاَيُّهَا الَّذِيْنَ اٰمَنُوْا كُوْنُوْا قَوّٰمِيْنَ لِلّٰهِ شُهَدَآءَ بِالْقِسْطِ ۫ وَلَا يَجْرِمَنَّكُمْ
شَنَاٰنُ قَوْمٍ عَلٰٓى اَلَّا تَعْدِلُوْا ۚ اِعْدِلُوْا ۫ هُوَ اَقْرَبُ لِلتَّقْوٰى ۫ وَاتَّقُوا اللّٰهَ ۚ
اِنَّ اللّٰهَ خَبِيْرٌۢ بِمَا تَعْمَلُوْنَ ۝

"O ye who believe! Be steadfast witnesses for Allah in equity, and let not the hatred of any people seduce you that ye deal not justly. Deal justly, that is nearer to your duty. Observe your duty to Allah. Lo! Allah is informed of what ye do." (V:9).

(b) *Bearing witness firmly and without fear or favour and thereby assisting those who are in the right made a basic virtue and, hence, duty:*

وَالَّذِيْنَ هُمْ بِشَهٰدٰتِهِمْ قَآئِمُوْنَ ۝

"And those who stand firm in their testimonies." (LXX:33).

(c) *Fulfilling all promises, agreements, pledges, covenants, contracts, engagements and treaties, enjoined:*

وَ اَوْفُوْا بِالْعَهْدِ ۚ اِنَّ الْعَهْدَ كَانَ مَسْـُٔوْلًا

".....and fulfil (every) promise (and engagement); for (every) promise (and engagement) will be enquired into (on the Day of Reckoning)." (XVII:34).

يٰٓاَيُّهَا الَّذِيْنَ اٰمَنُوْٓا اَوْفُوْا بِالْعُقُوْدِ ۚ

"O ye who believe! Fulfil (all) obligations (or compacts)[18]." (V:1).

(d) Sincerity and straightforwardness in general towards Others enjoined:

As we have already seen, a Muslim is required to do good to others purely for the sake of God, which alone is virtue according to the Holy Qur'ãn. But that is impossible without cultivating and maintaining absolute sincerity for God, as demanded in the Holy Qur'ãn:

وَادْعُوْهُ مُخْلِصِيْنَ لَهُ الدِّيْنَ ۚ

".....and call upon Him, making your devotion sincere as in His sight...." (VII:29).

But genuine sincerity for God is impossible to maintain unless one possesses sincerity essentially. Hence cultivation and maintenance of essential sincerity, one channel of which is sincerity towards fellow-beings, is duty.

Thus the Holy Qur'ãn commands the Muslims to be sincere and straightforward in all their dealings with everyone:

وَ اَنَّ هٰذَا صِرَاطِيْ مُسْتَقِيْمًا فَاتَّبِعُوْهُ ۚ

"And (He commandeth you, saying): This is My straight Way (—the Way of Truth, Justice, Sincerity and Straightforwardness—): follow it....." (VI:153).

---

18. The Arabic word '*aqd*, used there, means literally: a contract, a compact, a covenant, and an engagement. Finally, it comprehends all duties towards God and man. (See: Lane's *Arabic-English Lexicon*).

(e) *Cultivating and maintaining the attitude of compassionate kindness towards others emphasized as one of the basic qualities of a true Muslim's character:*

وَتَوَاصَوْا بِالْمَرْحَمَةِ ۝

"....and enjoin on each other practice of compassionate kindness (towards all)....." (XC:17).

(f) *Gracefulness and liberality in dealing with Others enjoined:*

وَلَا تَنسَوُا الْفَضْلَ بَيْنَكُمْ ۚ

".....and forget not gracefulness and liberality in your mutual dealings....." (II:237).

(g) *Positive effort for the creation and maintenance of harmony and peace among human beings, emphasized as a great virtue which should never be avoided:*

لَا خَيْرَ فِي كَثِيرٍ مِّن نَّجْوَاهُمْ إِلَّا مَنْ أَمَرَ بِصَدَقَةٍ أَوْ مَعْرُوفٍ أَوْ
إِصْلَاحٍ بَيْنَ النَّاسِ ۚ وَمَن يَفْعَلْ ذَٰلِكَ ابْتِغَاءَ مَرْضَاتِ اللَّهِ فَسَوْفَ
نُؤْتِيهِ أَجْرًا عَظِيمًا ۝

"In most of their secret talks there is no good; but if one exhorts to a deed of charity or justice or conciliation between human beings, (secrecy is permissible). To him who does this, seeking the good pleasure of Allah, We shall soon give a reward of the highest (value)." (IV:114).

وَلَا تَجْعَلُوا اللَّهَ عُرْضَةً لِّأَيْمَانِكُمْ أَن تَبَرُّوا وَتَتَّقُوا وَتُصْلِحُوا بَيْنَ النَّاسِ ۗ
وَاللَّهُ سَمِيعٌ عَلِيمٌ ۝

"And make not Allah's (name) an excuse in your oaths against doing good, or acting rightly, or making peace between human beings; for Allah is He Who heareth and knoweth all things." (II:224).

إِنَّا لَا نُضِيعُ أَجْرَ الْمُصْلِحِينَ ۝

"....never shall We suffer the reward of the reformers to perish." (VII:170).

(h) Judging Others' motives in the best light, except when a definite reasonable cause exists, enjoined:

As we have already seen, the Holy Qur'ãn forbids guessing about others' motives:

يَآيُّهَا الَّذِيْنَ اٰمَنُوا اجْتَنِبُوْا كَثِيْرًا مِّنَ الظَّنِّ اِنَّ بَعْضَ
الظَّنِّ اِثْمٌ

"O ye who believe! Shun as much suspicion as possible; for lo! some suspicion is a crime....." (XLIX:12).

It means that a Muslim should cultivate basically the attitude of initially judging other's motives in the best light, except when a definite reasonable cause exists to the contrary.

(i) Speaking good of Others, while paying due regard to truth and justice, enjoined:

The Holy Qur'ãn says:

وَقُلْ لِّعِبَادِيْ يَقُوْلُوا الَّتِيْ هِيَ اَحْسَنُ اِنَّ الشَّيْطٰنَ يَنْزَغُ بَيْنَهُمْ اِنَّ الشَّيْطٰنَ
كَانَ لِلْاِنْسَانِ عَدُوًّا مُّبِيْنًا ۝

"Say to My servants that they should (only) say (in general and about others) those things that are best; for Satan doth sow dissensions among them: lo! Satan is to man an avowed enemy." (XVII:53).

(j) Speaking to Others with courtesy and politeness enjoined:

وَقُوْلُوْا لِلنَّاسِ حُسْنًا

".....and speak unto mankind with courtesy and politeness (according to best standards of human speech)...." (II:83).

(k) Gratefulness to Others for any good that one may receive from them, enjoined:

In asking the questions:

هَلْ جَزَآءُ الْاِحْسَانِ اِلَّا الْاِحْسَانُ ۝

"Is the reward of goodness aught save goodness?" (LV:60), the Holy Qur'ãn emphasises the principle that a Muslim should always reward goodness with goodness, and the least that he can do is to sincerely thank him who does him any good. And gratefulness brings reward from God:

وَسَنَجْزِي الشّٰكِرِيْنَ ○

"We (i.e., God) shall reward the thankful." (III:145).

(*l*) *The most rational behaviour upheld and the highest moral standard enjoined in respect of evil emanating from Others:*

(*i*) *The Holy Qur'ãn permits equal redress of wrongs done to a Muslim by Others, at the same time commending forgiveness:*

وَإِنْ عَاقَبْتُمْ فَعَاقِبُوا بِمِثْلِ مَا عُوقِبْتُمْ بِهِ ۖ وَلَئِنْ صَبَرْتُمْ لَهُوَ
خَيْرٌ لِّلصّٰبِرِيْنَ ○

"If you punish (him who has wronged you) then punish with the like of that wherewith ye were afflicted. But if ye show patience, that is indeed the best (course) for those who are patient." (XVI:126).

وَجَزٰٓؤُا سَيِّئَةٍ سَيِّئَةٌ مِّثْلُهَا ۚ فَمَنْ عَفَا وَأَصْلَحَ فَأَجْرُهُ عَلَى اللّٰهِ ۚ إِنَّهُ
لَا يُحِبُّ الظّٰلِمِيْنَ ○ وَلَمَنِ انْتَصَرَ بَعْدَ ظُلْمِهِ فَأُولٰٓئِكَ مَا عَلَيْهِمْ مِّنْ سَبِيْلٍ ○
إِنَّمَا السَّبِيْلُ عَلَى الَّذِيْنَ يَظْلِمُوْنَ النَّاسَ وَيَبْغُوْنَ فِي الْأَرْضِ بِغَيْرِ
الْحَقِّ ۚ أُولٰٓئِكَ لَهُمْ عَذَابٌ أَلِيْمٌ ○ وَلَمَنْ صَبَرَ وَغَفَرَ إِنَّ ذٰلِكَ لَمِنْ عَزْمِ
الْأُمُوْرِ ○

"The recompense for an injury is an injury equal (in degree) thereto; (i.e., when anyone is wronged and he stands up for his rights, the most he can claim is equal redress): but if a person (prefers the saintly character to that of the wordly-wise man, and) forgives (the offender) and makes reconciliation (in the interests of morality), his reward is due from Allah: Lo! He loveth not those who do wrong. And whosoever vindicateth himself (without transgressing limits of justice) after he hath suffered wrong—for such there is no way (of blame) against them. The way (of blame) is only against those who oppress mankind and insolently transgress beyond bounds through the land, defying right and justice. For such there will be a painful doom. And verily whoso showeth patience and forgiveth—lo! that (voluntary forbearance and clemency) would truly be an exercise of courageous will and solution in the conduct of affairs." (XLII:40-43).

(ii) *Nay, the Holy Qur'ãn goes further. It enjoins repelling evil with goodness as the highest moral ideal—as a necessary condition of moral perfection:*

وَلَا تَسْتَوِي الْحَسَنَةُ وَلَا السَّيِّئَةُ ۚ اِدْفَعْ بِالَّتِي هِيَ أَحْسَنُ فَإِذَا الَّذِي بَيْنَكَ وَ
بَيْنَهُ عَدَاوَةٌ كَأَنَّهُ وَلِيٌّ حَمِيمٌ ○ وَمَا يُلَقَّاهَا إِلَّا الَّذِينَ صَبَرُوا ۚ وَمَا يُلَقَّاهَا
إِلَّا ذُو حَظٍّ عَظِيمٍ ○ وَإِمَّا يَنْزَغَنَّكَ مِنَ الشَّيْطٰنِ نَزْغٌ فَاسْتَعِذْ بِاللهِ ۖ إِنَّهُ هُوَ
السَّمِيعُ الْعَلِيمُ ○

"Nor can Goodness and Evil be equal. Repel (Evil) with what is better (i.e., Goodness): Then will he between whom and thee was hatred become as it were thy friend and intimate! And no one will be granted such goodness except those who exercise patience and self-restraint,—none but persons of the greatest good fortune. And if (at any time) an incitement to discord is made to thee by the Evil One, seek refuge in Allah. He is the One Who hears and knows all things." (XLI:34-36).

وَإِنَّ السَّاعَةَ لَآتِيَةٌ فَاصْفَحِ الصَّفْحَ الْجَمِيلَ ○

"And the Hour (of Final Accountability and Divine Judgment) is surely coming. So overlook (any human faults) with gracious forgiveness."
(XV:85).

وَلْيَعْفُوا وَلْيَصْفَحُوا أَلَا تُحِبُّونَ أَنْ يَغْفِرَ اللهُ لَكُمْ وَاللهُ غَفُورٌ رَحِيمٌ

"....Let them forgive (those who do any injury to them) and let them overlook (the offenders' faults). Do you not wish that Allah forgive you? For Allah is Oft-Forgiving, Most Merciful." (XXIV:22).

فَاعْفُوا وَاصْفَحُوا حَتّٰى يَأْتِيَ اللهُ بِأَمْرِهِ ۚ إِنَّ اللهَ عَلٰى كُلِّ شَيْءٍ قَدِيرٌ ○

"....But forgive (the enemies of Islam) and overlook (their hostility) till Allah accomplisheth His purpose; for Allah hath power over all things." (II:109).

(*b*) *Duties of Respect*:

(*i*) *Treating with respect all human beings in their fundamental rights as fellow-beings—irrespective of differences of sex, race, colour, etc., enjoined:*

According to the Holy Qur'ãn every human being deserves respect in his capacity as a human being:

وَلَقَدْ كَرَّمْنَا بَنِيٓ اٰدَمَ

"Verily We have honoured the Children of Adam...." (XVII:70).

This aspect of the Qur'ãnic moral teaching includes:

(*a*) *respecting the rights of all human beings with regard to life, honour and property.*

Also: (*b*) *respecting every human being's equality of status as a human being;*

and, as a consequence:

(*c*) *respecting his right to freedom,*

(*d*) *and the right to fraternise with all other human beings,*

—except when a just moral cause intervenes.

The following verse of the Holy Qur'ãn prescribes it, in conjunction with other numerous relevant and connected verses that have been quoted in different contexts in the present dissertation, as a duty of all human beings to protect and promote the above human rights:

يٰٓاَيُّهَا النَّاسُ اتَّقُوْا رَبَّكُمُ الَّذِيْ خَلَقَكُمْ مِّنْ نَّفْسٍ وَّاحِدَةٍ وَّخَلَقَ
مِنْهَا زَوْجَهَا وَبَثَّ مِنْهُمَا رِجَالًا كَثِيْرًا وَّنِسَآءً ۚ وَاتَّقُوا اللّٰهَ الَّذِيْ تَسَآءَلُوْنَ
بِهٖ وَالْاَرْحَامَ ۚ اِنَّ اللّٰهَ كَانَ عَلَيْكُمْ رَقِيْبًا ۝

"O humankind! fear (in respect of the rights of fellow-beings) your Guardian-Lord (*i.e.*, Allah) Who created you from a single soul, and created, of like nature, his mate, and from them twain hath spread abroad countless men and women (everyone of whom is thus bound up in one fraternity—the human family—and possesses the birthright of basic human equality with his fellow-beings to have the freedom of equal opportunity for enjoying the blessings of life on earth). Reverence Allah, through Whom you claim your mutual (rights) (and, therefore, respect your fellow-beings' rights to life, honour, and property, as also those relating to liberty, equality and fraternity), and (reverence) the wombs (that bore you): for Allah ever watches over you." (IV:1).

Here we may also quote with advantage another important related verse which specifically repudiates the erroneous notion of inequality of human beings on physical bases—tribal, racial, etc.—and lays down the basic and the most just principle on the basis of which one human being *earns* more honour than another. God proclaims in the Holy Qur'ãn:

يٰٓاَيُّهَا النَّاسُ اِنَّا خَلَقْنٰكُمْ مِّنْ ذَكَرٍ وَّ اُنْثٰى وَ جَعَلْنٰكُمْ شُعُوْبًا وَّ
قَبَآئِلَ لِتَعَارَفُوْا ؕ اِنَّ اَكْرَمَكُمْ عِنْدَ اللّٰهِ اَتْقٰىكُمْ ؕ اِنَّ اللّٰهَ عَلِيْمٌ
خَبِيْرٌ ۝

"O humankind! We created you from a single (pair) of a male and female, and made you into nations and tribes, that you may know each other (not that ye may despise each other). Verily the most honoured of you in the sight of Allah is (he who is) the most righteous of you and Allah has full knowledge and is well acquainted (with all things.)"
(XLIX:13).

(ii) Humility, forbearance and peacefulness have been mentioned in the Holy Qur'ãn as basic virtues; hence to practise them is duty:

وَعِبَادُ الرَّحْمٰنِ الَّذِيْنَ يَمْشُوْنَ عَلَى الْاَرْضِ هَوْنًا وَّ اِذَا خَاطَبَهُمُ الْجٰهِلُوْنَ
قَالُوْا سَلٰمًا ۝

"And the servants of (Allah) Most Gracious are those who walk on the earth in humility, and when the ignorant address them, they say, 'Peace!' " (XXV:63).

وَ الْخٰشِعِيْنَ وَ الْخٰشِعٰتِ وَ الْمُتَصَدِّقِيْنَ وَ الْمُتَصَدِّقٰتِ وَ الصَّآئِمِيْنَ وَ الصّٰٓئِمٰتِ
وَ الْحٰفِظِيْنَ فُرُوْجَهُمْ وَ الْحٰفِظٰتِ وَ الذّٰكِرِيْنَ اللّٰهَ كَثِيْرًا وَّ الذّٰكِرٰتِ اَعَدَّ
اللّٰهُ لَهُمْ مَّغْفِرَةً وَّ اَجْرًا عَظِيْمًا ۝

"*.....for men and women who humble themselves*, for men and women who give in charity, for men and women who fast (and deny themselves), for men and women who guard their chastity, and for men and women who engage much in Allah's remembrance—, for them has Allah prepared forgiveness and great reward." (XXXIII:35).

The most important occasion when a person's spirit of humility is put to test is when he speaks to another person. Hence, humility in talk with others has been enjoined specifically also:

وَاغْضُضْ مِن صَوْتِكَ ۚ إِنَّ أَنكَرَ الْأَصْوَاتِ لَصَوْتُ الْحَمِيرِ

".....and lower thy voice (in humility); for the harshest of sounds without doubt is the braying of an ass." (XXXI:19).

Chapter II

DUTIES OF THE MORAL PERFECTION OF OTHERS

END:

Moral Perfection of Others.

(1) Duties of Omission;

(2) Duties of Commission.

I. Duties of Omission

END:

Abstinence from all forms of activity that might be conducive to the creation of, or might directly create, conditions of immorality.

(a) Duties of Love; (b) Duties of Respect.

(*a*) *Duties of Love*:

(*i*) *Creating conditions of moral corruption prohibited:*

وَلَا تُفْسِدُوا فِي الْأَرْضِ بَعْدَ إِصْلَاحِهَا وَادْعُوهُ خَوْفًا وَطَمَعًا ۚ
إِنَّ رَحْمَتَ اللَّهِ قَرِيبٌ مِّنَ الْمُحْسِنِينَ ۝

"Do not mischief (moral or material) on the earth, after it hath been set in order, but call on Him with fear and hope: For the Mercy of Allah is always near to those who practise virtue." (VII:56).

(*ii*) *Obstructing the path of morality, as also other paths of goodness, prohibited:*

وَلَا تَكُونُوا كَالَّذِينَ خَرَجُوا مِن دِيَارِهِم بَطَرًا وَرِئَاءَ النَّاسِ
وَيَصُدُّونَ عَن سَبِيلِ اللَّهِ ۚ

"And be not like those who started from their homes insolently and to be seen of men, and to hinder (men) from the Way of Allah (i.e., the perfect System of Goodness which alone leads to God)." (VIII:47).

أَلْقِيَا فِي جَهَنَّمَ كُلَّ كَفَّارٍ عَنِيدٍ ○ مَّنَّاعٍ لِّلْخَيْرِ

"(The sentence will be:) throw, throw into Hell every contumacious Rejector (of God)!—hinderer of good....." (L:24, 25).

وَلَا تُطِعْ كُلَّ حَلَّافٍ مَّهِينٍ ○ هَمَّازٍ مَّشَّاءٍ بِنَمِيمٍ ○ مَّنَّاعٍ لِّلْخَيْرِ

"Heed not the type of despicable man,—ready with oaths, a slanderer, going about with calumnies, hinderer of good....." (LXVIII:10-12).

(iii) Co-operating with others in sin and transgression prohibited:

وَلَا تَعَاوَنُوا عَلَى الْإِثْمِ وَالْعُدْوَانِ وَاتَّقُوا اللَّهَ إِنَّ اللَّهَ شَدِيدُ الْعِقَابِ ○

".....and help ye not one another in sin and transgression: Fear Allah: Lo! Allah is strict in punishment." (V:3).

(iv) Spreading lewdness in any form; and thereby enticing others in vice prohibited:

قُلْ إِنَّمَا حَرَّمَ رَبِّيَ الْفَوَاحِشَ مَا ظَهَرَ مِنْهَا وَمَا بَطَنَ

"Say: the things that my Lord hath indeed forbidden are: (indulging in and spreading[1], at any level and any type of,) shameful deeds (or lewdness), whether open or secret....." (VII:33).

وَيَنْهَىٰ عَنِ الْفَحْشَاءِ

"....and He forbids (indulging in and spreading, at any level and any type of,) shameful deeds (or lewdness)....." (XVI:90).

(*b*) *Duties of Respect*:

Duties in respect of illegitimate and immoral sexual relations whereby, side by side with one's own chastity, the chastity and honoūr of others as well as the sanctity of the institution of family[2], is violated:

---

1. Cf. XXIV:19.

2. It should be noted that one of the ends of "sexual duties" is the preservation and promotion of the "family" as the basic unit of society –a point which is

(i) Adultery and Fornication prohibited[3]:

وَلَا تَقْرَبُوا الزِّنٰٓى إِنَّهُ كَانَ فَاحِشَةً ۖ وَسَآءَ سَبِيلًا ۝

"And come not nigh to fornication and adultery: For it is a shameful (deed) and an evil, opening the road (to other evils)." (XVII:32).

وَلَا يَزْنُونَ

"(The true servants of God are those who).....do not commit adultery (nor fornication)...." (XXV:68).

وَلَا يَزْنِينَ

"....that they will not commit adultery (nor fornication)...." (LX:12).

(ii) Homosexuality vehemently condemned; hence abstinence from it is duty:

Speaking of the Sodomites, the Holy Qur'ãn says:

وَلُوطًا إِذْ قَالَ لِقَوْمِهِۦٓ أَتَأْتُونَ الْفَاحِشَةَ مَا سَبَقَكُم بِهَا مِنْ أَحَدٍ مِّنَ
الْعٰلَمِينَ ۝ إِنَّكُمْ لَتَأْتُونَ الرِّجَالَ شَهْوَةً مِّن دُونِ النِّسَآءِ ۚ بَلْ
أَنتُمْ قَوْمٌ مُّسْرِفُونَ ۝ . . . . وَأَمْطَرْنَا عَلَيْهِم مَّطَرًا ۖ فَانظُرْ كَيْفَ
كَانَ عَاقِبَةُ الْمُجْرِمِينَ ۝

"We also (sent) Lut: He said to his people: 'Do you commit lewdness such as no people in creation (ever) committed before you? For ye practise your lusts on men in preference to women: ye are indeed a people transgressing beyond bounds'.....And We rained down on them a shower (of brimstone): then see what was the end of those who indulged in sin and crime?" (VII:80, 81, 84).

(iii) The institution of Prostitution condemned:

Speaking of the women prisoners of war, the Holy Qur'ãn lays

---

basic to the Qur'ãnic social philosophy and which is of immense value in respect of its bearing on the moral health of human society.

3. "Polyandry" and "Noega" also come under this category. They are, therefore, prohibited. See p. 185.

down the following rule, thus promulgating the law condemning the business of prostitution in all its aspects:

وَلَا تُكْرِهُوْا فَتَيٰتِكُمْ عَلَى الْبِغَآءِ اِنْ اَرَدْنَ تَحَصُّنًا لِّتَبْتَغُوْا عَرَضَ الْحَيٰوةِ
الدُّنْيَا

"....and force not your maids to prostitution (—a custom prevalent among the pagan Arabs in respect of their slave-girls—) their desire being for chastity, in order that ye may make a gain in the goods of this life....."
(XXIV:33).

(II) Duties of Commission

END:

Active struggle for creating an atmosphere conducive to morality and awakening the moral consciousness of one's fellow-beings by word and deed.

Preliminary:

The Holy Qur'ãn says:

وَالْعَصْرِ ○ اِنَّ الْاِنْسَانَ لَفِيْ خُسْرٍ ○ اِلَّا الَّذِيْنَ اٰمَنُوْا وَعَمِلُوا الصّٰلِحٰتِ وَتَوَاصَوْا
بِالْحَقِّ ۙ وَتَوَاصَوْا بِالصَّبْرِ ○

"By Time (as it has unfolded through the ages, recording man's successes and failures), verily man is in a state of loss, but not those who have Faith and do (constantly) righteous deeds, and exhort one another to Truth and exhort one another to endurance (in the service of Truth)."
(CIII:1-3).

The Holy Qur'ãn further warns that evasion of this active struggle leads to calamities of the highest magnitude, which afflict the innocent and the guilty alike:

وَاتَّقُوْا فِتْنَةً لَّا تُصِيْبَنَّ الَّذِيْنَ ظَلَمُوْا مِنْكُمْ خَآصَّةً ۚ وَ
اعْلَمُوْٓا اَنَّ اللّٰهَ شَدِيْدُ الْعِقَابِ ○

"And fear the chastisement that shall not afflict those alone who among you do wrong; and know that verily Allah is Severe in Chastising."
(VIII:25).

DUTIES:

(a) Duty of Love; (b) Duty of Respect.

(*a*) *Duty of Love*:

Active struggle for the fullest establishment of morality enjoined:

(i) The mission which has been entrusted by God to the Muslim community is the establishment of moral order in the world as a whole—a mission the fulfilment of which is the duty of every Muslim, man and woman:

كُنْتُمْ خَيْرَ أُمَّةٍ أُخْرِجَتْ لِلنَّاسِ تَأْمُرُوْنَ بِالْمَعْرُوْفِ وَ تَنْهَوْنَ عَنِ
الْمُنْكَرِ وَ تُؤْمِنُوْنَ بِاللّٰهِ ؕ

"Ye (O Muslim!) are the best (ideological) community that hath been raised up for mankind. Ye enjoin right conduct and forbid all that is wrong (=evil); and ye believe in Allah....." (III:110).

(ii) This mission entails, however, certain difficult conditions, which cannot be possible for every Muslim to fulfil. Consequently, while it is the duty of every Muslim to co-operate[4] in it to the best of his capacity and in the manner best suited to him, it is necessary that there should be a trained, disciplined and devoted band of Muslims who should lead the struggle. And this is what the Holy Qur'ãn has enjoined:

وَلْتَكُنْ مِّنْكُمْ أُمَّةٌ يَّدْعُوْنَ إِلَى الْخَيْرِ وَيَأْمُرُوْنَ بِالْمَعْرُوْفِ وَيَنْهَوْنَ
عَنِ الْمُنْكَرِ ؕ وَأُولٰٓئِكَ هُمُ الْمُفْلِحُوْنَ ۝

"Let there arise out of you a band of people inviting to all that is good, enjoining what is right, and forbidding what is wrong: They are the ones who attain felicity." (III:104).

---

4. Co-operation is also participation according to the Holy Qur'ãn:

مَنْ يَّشْفَعْ شَفَاعَةً حَسَنَةً يَّكُنْ لَّهٗ نَصِيْبٌ مِّنْهَا ۚ وَمَنْ يَّشْفَعْ شَفَاعَةً
سَيِّئَةً يَّكُنْ لَّهٗ كِفْلٌ مِّنْهَا ؕ وَكَانَ اللّٰهُ عَلٰى كُلِّ شَيْءٍ مُّقِيْتًا ۝

"Whoever recommends and helps a good cause becomes a partner therein: and whoever recommends and helps an evil cause shares in its burden: and Allah hath power over all things." (IV:85).

(iii) The basic struggle consists, thus, in propagating among mankind the Divine Teachings which form the very foundation and the life-blood of the moral order. This struggle has, however, to be pursued in the sublimest manner. The Holy Qur'ãn says:

ادْعُ إِلَىٰ سَبِيلِ رَبِّكَ بِالْحِكْمَةِ وَالْمَوْعِظَةِ الْحَسَنَةِ وَجَادِلْهُمْ بِالَّتِي
هِيَ أَحْسَنُ ۚ إِنَّ رَبَّكَ هُوَ أَعْلَمُ بِمَنْ ضَلَّ عَنْ سَبِيلِهِ وَهُوَ أَعْلَمُ
بِالْمُهْتَدِينَ ○

"Invite (all) to the Way of thy Lord with wisdom and beautiful preaching; and argue with them in ways that are best and most gracious: For thy Lord knoweth best who have strayed from His Path and who receive guidance." (XVI:125).

(iv) The establishment of the moral order necessitates finally the employment of state authority for this purpose. The Holy Qur'ãn enjoins this function on the Islamic State:

وَلَيَنْصُرَنَّ اللّٰهُ مَنْ يَنْصُرُهُ ۗ إِنَّ اللّٰهَ لَقَوِيٌّ عَزِيزٌ ○ اَلَّذِينَ إِنْ مَّكَّنّٰهُمْ
فِي الْأَرْضِ أَقَامُوا الصَّلٰوةَ وَاٰتَوُا الزَّكٰوةَ وَأَمَرُوا بِالْمَعْرُوفِ وَنَهَوْا
عَنِ الْمُنْكَرِ ۗ وَلِلّٰهِ عَاقِبَةُ الْأُمُورِ ○

"....Allah will certainly aid those who aid His (cause)—for verily Allah is Full of Strength, exalted in Might, (able to enforce His Will) (Muslims are) those who, if We give them authority in the land, establish regular prayer and give regular charity, enjoin the right and forbid wrong; and with Allah rests the end (and decision) of (all) affairs. (XXII:40, 41).

(v) The Holy Qur'ãn condemns the establishment of secret societies for evil ends. But it permits secret activity, if absolutely necessary, for the promotion of virtue:

لَا خَيْرَ فِي كَثِيرٍ مِّنْ نَّجْوٰىهُمْ إِلَّا مَنْ أَمَرَ بِصَدَقَةٍ أَوْ مَعْرُوفٍ
أَوْ إِصْلَاحٍ بَيْنَ النَّاسِ ۚ وَمَنْ يَّفْعَلْ ذٰلِكَ ابْتِغَاءَ مَرْضَاتِ اللّٰهِ فَسَوْفَ
نُؤْتِيهِ أَجْرًا عَظِيمًا ○

"In most of their secret talks there is no good, but if one exhorts to a deed of charity or justice or conciliation between human beings, (secrecy is permissible): to him who does this, seeking the good pleasure of Allah, We shall soon give a reward of the highest (value)." (IV:114).

(*h*) *Duty of Respect*:

Marriage permitted as the only means of fulfilling sexual need and made obligatory for preserving the moral health of society:

وَ اَنْكِحُوا الْاَيَامٰى مِنْكُمْ وَالصّٰلِحِيْنَ مِنْ عِبَادِكُمْ وَ اِمَآئِكُمْ ؕ اِنْ يَّكُوْنُوْا
فُقَرَآءَ يُغْنِهِمُ اللّٰهُ مِنْ فَضْلِهٖ ؕ وَاللّٰهُ وَاسِعٌ عَلِيْمٌ ﴿۳۲﴾ وَلْيَسْتَعْفِفِ الَّذِيْنَ لَا
يَجِدُوْنَ نِكَاحًا حَتّٰى يُغْنِيَهُمُ اللّٰهُ مِنْ فَضْلِهٖ ؕ

"Marry those among you who are single, or the virtuous ones among your slaves, male or female :if they are in poverty, Allah will give them means out of His Grace: for Allah encompasseth all, and He knoweth all things. Let those who find not the wherewithal for marriage keep themselves chaste, until Allah gives them means out of His Grace."

(XXIV:32, 33).

Part II

DUTIES OF CONDITION TOWARDS OTHER INDIVIDUALS

(A) Duties to Relatives and to the non-Relatives belonging to one's home;

(B) Duties with respect to Age and Rank;

(C) Duties to Particular Categories of non-Relatives;

(D) Duties to Muslims as Muslims;

(E) Duties to non-Muslims as non-Muslims.

In part I of the "Duties of Others", we have covered those duties of omission and commission which the Holy Qur'ãn has prescribed in respect of our dealings with our fellow-beings without consideration of the nature of our relationship with them. They are duties which, according to the Holy Qur'ãn, we owe to every human being in his capacity as human being. In other words, they are duties which relate to fundamental human rights.

The Holy Qur'ãn has prescribed, however, another set of duties also, which we owe to others in consideration of their specific relations with us. They may be called: "Duties of Condition". We shall deal with them now, classifying them first into five broad sections: A, B, C, D, and E, as given above. Of course, these sections are further subdivisible, as we shall see.

Chapter I

DUTIES TO RELATIVES AND TO THE NON-RELATIVES BELONGING TO ONE'S HOME

(1) Duties towards one's Parents.

(2) Duties towards one's Offspring.

(3) Respective duties of Husband and Wife.

(4) Duties towards Relatives in General.

(5) Duties towards Domestic Servants.

(1) Duties Towards One's Parents

(*a*) Duties of Commission

(*i*) *As the following verses show,* the Holy Qur'ãn enjoins:

(*a*) *doing good to parents in every way;*
(*b*) *obeying them without demur in everything good;*
(*c*) *behaving respectfully towards them;*
(*d*) *maintaining attitude of thankfulness towards them;*
(*e*) *caring for them with mercy—*
with special regard for the mother[1].

The Holy Qur'ãn says:

وَقَضٰى رَبُّكَ اَلَّا تَعْبُدُوْٓا اِلَّآ اِيَّاهُ وَبِالْوَالِدَيْنِ اِحْسَانًا ۭ اِمَّا يَبْلُغَنَّ
عِنْدَكَ الْكِبَرَ اَحَدُهُمَآ اَوْ كِلٰهُمَا فَلَا تَقُلْ لَّهُمَآ اُفٍّ وَّلَا تَنْهَرْهُمَا وَقُلْ لَّهُمَا
قَوْلًا كَرِيْمًا ۝ وَاخْفِضْ لَهُمَا جَنَاحَ الذُّلِّ مِنَ الرَّحْمَةِ وَقُلْ رَّبِّ ارْحَمْهُمَا كَمَا
رَبَّيٰنِيْ صَغِيْرًا ۝ رَبُّكُمْ اَعْلَمُ بِمَا فِيْ نُفُوْسِكُمْ ۭ اِنْ تَكُوْنُوْا صٰلِحِيْنَ فَاِنَّهٗ كَانَ
لِلْاَوَّابِيْنَ غَفُوْرًا ۝

"Thy Lord hath decreed that ye worship none but Him, and that ye be kind to parents. Whether one or both of them attain old age in thy life, say not to them a word of contempt, nor repel them, but address them in terms of honour. And, out of kindness, lower to them the wing of humility; and say, 'My Lord! bestow on them Thy Mercy even as they

1. Ref.: Footnote on p. 176.

cherished me in childhood'. Your Lord knoweth best what is in your hearts: if ye do deeds of righteousness, verily He is Most Forgiving to those who turn to Him again and again (in true penitence)."

(XVII:23-25).

وَوَصَّيْنَا الْإِنْسَانَ بِوَالِدَيْهِ إِحْسٰنًا ۖ حَمَلَتْهُ أُمُّهُ كُرْهًا وَّوَضَعَتْهُ
كُرْهًا ۖ وَحَمْلُهُ وَفِصٰلُهُ ثَلٰثُوْنَ شَهْرًا ۖ حَتّٰى إِذَا بَلَغَ أَشُدَّهُ وَبَلَغَ أَرْبَعِيْنَ
سَنَةً ۙ قَالَ رَبِّ أَوْزِعْنِيْٓ أَنْ أَشْكُرَ نِعْمَتَكَ الَّتِيْٓ أَنْعَمْتَ عَلَيَّ وَعَلٰى
وَالِدَيَّ وَأَنْ أَعْمَلَ صٰلِحًا تَرْضٰىهُ وَأَصْلِحْ لِيْ فِيْ ذُرِّيَّتِيْ ۚ إِنِّيْ تُبْتُ
إِلَيْكَ وَإِنِّيْ مِنَ الْمُسْلِمِيْنَ ○ أُولٰٓئِكَ الَّذِيْنَ نَتَقَبَّلُ عَنْهُمْ أَحْسَنَ مَا
عَمِلُوْا وَنَتَجَاوَزُ عَنْ سَيِّاٰتِهِمْ فِيْٓ أَصْحٰبِ الْجَنَّةِ ۖ وَعْدَ الصِّدْقِ
الَّذِيْ كَانُوْا يُوْعَدُوْنَ ○

"We have enjoined on man kindness to his parents: In pain did his mother bear him, and in pain did she give him birth. The carrying of the (child) to his weaning is (a period of) thirty months. At length, when he reaches the age of full strength and attains forty years, he says, O my Lord! grant me that I may be grateful for Thy favour which Thou hast bestowed upon me, and upon both my parents, and that I may work righteousness such as Thou mayest approve; and be gracious to me in my issue. Truly have I turned to Thee and truly do I bow (to Thee) in Islam'. Such are they from whom we shall accept the best of their deeds and pass by their ill deeds: (they shall be) among the companions of the Gardenias promise of truth, which was made to them (in this life). (XLVI:15, 16).

(ii) *Doing good to parents even if they are non-Muslims, regardless of their attitude to Islam, enjoined:*

وَوَصَّيْنَا الْإِنْسَانَ بِوَالِدَيْهِ ۚ حَمَلَتْهُ أُمُّهُ وَهْنًا عَلٰى وَهْنٍ وَّفِصٰلُهُ فِيْ عَامَيْنِ
أَنِ اشْكُرْ لِيْ وَلِوَالِدَيْكَ ۗ إِلَيَّ الْمَصِيْرُ ○ وَإِنْ جَاهَدٰكَ عَلٰٓى أَنْ تُشْرِكَ بِيْ
مَا لَيْسَ لَكَ بِهٖ عِلْمٌ ۙ فَلَا تُطِعْهُمَا وَصَاحِبْهُمَا فِي الدُّنْيَا مَعْرُوْفًا ۖ وَّاتَّبِعْ
سَبِيْلَ مَنْ أَنَابَ إِلَيَّ ۚ ثُمَّ إِلَيَّ مَرْجِعُكُمْ فَأُنَبِّئُكُمْ بِمَا كُنْتُمْ تَعْمَلُوْنَ ○

"And We have enjoined on man (to be good) to his parents: In travail upon travail did his mother bear him, and in years twain was his weaning: (hear the command), 'Show gratitude to Me and to thy parents':

to Me is (thy final) Goal. But if they strive to make thee join in worship with Me things of which thou hast no knowledge, obey them not; yet bear them company in this life with justice (and consideration), and follow the way of those who turn to Me (in love): In the end the return of you all is to Me, and I will tell you (the truth and meaning of) all that ye did."

(XXXI:14, 15).

(*b*) Duty of Omission:

Abstinence from obeying non-Muslim parents in their anti-Islamic religious beliefs and practices, enjoined:

وَوَصَّيْنَا الْإِنسَانَ بِوَالِدَيْهِ حُسْنًا ۖ وَإِن جَاهَدَاكَ لِتُشْرِكَ بِي مَا لَيْسَ
لَكَ بِهِ عِلْمٌ فَلَا تُطِعْهُمَا ۚ إِلَيَّ مَرْجِعُكُمْ فَأُنَبِّئُكُم بِمَا
كُنتُمْ تَعْمَلُونَ ○

"We enjoined on man kindness to parents: but if they (either of them) strive (to force) thee to join with Me (in worship) anything of which thou hast no knowledge, obey them not. Ye have (all) to return to Me, and I will tell you (the truth) of all that ye did." (XXIX:8).

2. Duties Towards one's Offspring

A. Social and Spiritual Status of the Child:

(i) The Holy Qur'ãn teaches that the child is a respectable being:

(a) because of his humanity, concerning which it has been said:

وَلَقَدْ كَرَّمْنَا بَنِي آدَمَ

"Verily We have honoured the Children of Adam...." (XVII:70).

(b) because of his sinlessness, as it has been said:

لَقَدْ خَلَقْنَا الْإِنسَانَ فِي أَحْسَنِ تَقْوِيمٍ ○

"Assuredly We have created man in the goodliest constitution (i.e., pure and individually perfect)." (XCV:4).

وَلَا تَكْسِبُ كُلُّ نَفْسٍ إِلَّا عَلَيْهَا ۚ وَلَا تَزِرُ وَازِرَةٌ وِزْرَ أُخْرَىٰ

".....Every soul draws the need of its acts on none but itself: no bearer of burden can bear the burden of another....." (VI:164).

Thus the child is born singles, without inheriting the sins of his ancestors. And it is classed as innocent up to the age of discretion, as it has been said:

لَا يُكَلِّفُ اللّٰهُ نَفْسًا اِلَّا وُسْعَهَا ۚ

"On no soul doth Allah place a responsibility but to the extent of its ability....." (II:286).

And its categorisation as innocent makes it logically immune from receiving those punishments which are meant for adults in respect of commission of wrongs.

(ii) In its condemnation of infanticide, the Holy Qur'ãn teaches that the child is a 'gift from God'—a 'trust'[1] of God placed in the care of the child's elders, and should, therefore, be treated with love, understanding and extreme care:

قَدْ خَسِرَ الَّذِيْنَ قَتَلُوْٓا اَوْلَادَهُمْ سَفَهًاۢ بِغَيْرِ عِلْمٍ وَّ حَرَّمُوْا مَا رَزَقَهُمُ
اللّٰهُ افْتِرَآءً عَلَى اللّٰهِ ۚ قَدْ ضَلُّوْا وَ مَا كَانُوْا مُهْتَدِيْنَ ۝

"Lost are those who besottedly have murdered their children without knowledge, and forbidden (to themselves) that which Allah bestowed upon them (as gift), inventing a lie against Allah. They have indeed gone astray and heeded no guidance." (VI:140).

B. Duties

(*i*) Duties of Omission:

Infanticide had been practised by different communities of the world, including the pagan Arabs, the Hindus, the Greeks and the Romans, in the pre- Qur'ãnic era of human history.[2] When the Holy Qur'ãn came, it voiced its condemnation of that evil and inhuman practice in strong

---

1. A Muslim holds everything—his life, property, position, children, etc.—as trust from God. (IX:111).

2. See: *Encyclopaedia of Religion and Ethics* and *Encyclopaedia Britannica* (relevant portions).

terms and forbade it totally, as we have seen in verse VI:140 quoted above, and as we find in the following:

(a) *Killing of offspring for fear of poverty—before their birth: in the form of abortion, or after their birth: in the form of murder—forbidden:*

وَلَا تَقْتُلُوٓا أَوْلَادَكُمْ خَشْيَةَ إِمْلَاقٍ نَحْنُ نَرْزُقُهُمْ وَإِيَّاكُمْ إِنَّ
قَتْلَهُمْ كَانَ خِطْأً كَبِيرًا ○

"Kill not your children for fear of want: We shall provide sustenance for them as well as for you. Verily the killing of them is a great sin." (XVII:31).[3]

(b) *Killing of daughters for extra fear of dishonour specially condemned*:

وَإِذَا بُشِّرَ أَحَدُهُمْ بِالْأُنْثَىٰ ظَلَّ وَجْهُهُ مُسْوَدًّا وَهُوَ كَظِيمٌ ○
يَتَوَارَىٰ مِنَ الْقَوْمِ مِنْ سُوٓءِ مَا بُشِّرَ بِهِ أَيُمْسِكُهُ عَلَىٰ هُونٍ أَمْ يَدُسُّهُ
فِي التُّرَابِ أَلَا سَآءَ مَا يَحْكُمُونَ ○

"When news is brought to one of them, of (the birth of) a female (child), his face darkens, and he is filled with inward grief! With shame does he hide himself from his people, because of the bad news he has had! Shall he retain it on (sufferance and) contempt, or bury it in the dust! Ah! what an evil (choice) they decide on!" (XVI:58, 59).

وَإِذَا الْمَوْءُدَةُ سُئِلَتْ ○ بِأَيِّ ذَنْبٍ قُتِلَتْ ○

"When the female (infant), buried alive, is questioned (by God on the Day of Judgment)—for what crime she was killed!" (LXXXI:8, 9).

(c) *Infanticide with 'religious' motives condemned*:

وَكَذَٰلِكَ زَيَّنَ لِكَثِيرٍ مِنَ الْمُشْرِكِينَ قَتْلَ أَوْلَادِهِمْ شُرَكَآؤُهُمْ لِيُرْدُوهُمْ
وَلِيَلْبِسُوا عَلَيْهِمْ دِينَهُمْ وَلَوْ شَآءَ اللَّهُ مَا فَعَلُوهُ فَذَرْهُمْ وَمَا يَفْتَرُونَ ○

3. There is another verse also of the same import, *i.e.*, VI:151.

"Even so, in the eyes of most of the Pagans, their 'partners' made alluring the slaughter of their children, to lead them to their own destruction, and cause confusion in their religion. If Allah had willed, they would not have done so: But leave alone them and their inventions." (VI:137).

(*ii*) Duties of Commission:

Condemning contempt for one's children, forbidding their treatment as a burden, and teaching respect and love for them, the Holy Qur'ãn refers to their upbringing by their parents,—a function which all parents, including the animal parents, perform basically and naturally under the urge of the parental instinct, but wherein the outlook requires to be refined and enlightened in the interest of human well-being. In this connection:

(a) The Holy Qur'ãn commands the safeguarding of the interest of the child, in the most delicate period of his life, in respect of suckling him, which is specially jeopardised in case the parents are unfortunately separated from each other through divorce:

وَالْوَالِدٰتُ يُرْضِعْنَ اَوْلَادَهُنَّ حَوْلَيْنِ كَامِلَيْنِ لِمَنْ اَرَادَ اَنْ يُّتِمَّ الرَّضَاعَةَ ؕ
وَعَلَى الْمَوْلُوْدِ لَهٗ رِزْقُهُنَّ وَكِسْوَتُهُنَّ بِالْمَعْرُوْفِ ؕ

"The mothers shall give suck to their offspring for two whole years, if the father desires to complete the term. But he shall bear the cost of their food and clothing on equitable terms....." (II:233).

(b) Then it refers to the unselfish upbringing of the child by the parents up to the time of his maturity[4] as a virtue, in the following prayer which Muslim children are taught to make for their parents:

وَقُلْ رَّبِّ ارْحَمْهُمَا كَمَا رَبَّيٰنِيْ صَغِيْرًا ؕ

".....and say: 'My Lord! bestow on them Thy Mercy even as they (tenderly) cherished me (when I was) young." (XVII:24).

This verse refers to the fact that the parents have to look after the needs of the child until he is mature. It has been mentioned as a

4. The obligation of maintenance of the offspring upto the age of maturity is borne out by the law laid down for transferring to the orphans living in one's charge the administration of their properties. (See IV:6).

universal fact which occurs in a natural course,—namely, everyone whose outlook in respect of his children is rational and not perverted and whose circumstances do not force him to act against the true dictates of human nature[5], is bound to do it. However, although natural, it should be treated as a specific duty in the light of the general command of "doing good to all" and "taking special care of those who are related to one in blood" (XVI:90), in the interest of the moral health of human society.

(c) The Holy Qur'ãn teaches prayers which are highly instructive in guiding us to the parents' duties towards their children. The prayers are:

وَ اَصْلِحْ لِيْ فِيْ ذُرِّيَّتِيْ ؕ

".....and be Thou good unto me in my progeny (O Lord!) (i.e., cause my progeny to be good and accomplished in every way)....."

(XLVI:15).

رَبَّنَا هَبْ لَنَا مِنْ اَزْوَاجِنَا وَ ذُرِّيّٰتِنَا قُرَّةَ اَعْيُنٍ وَّ اجْعَلْنَا لِلْمُتَّقِيْنَ اِمَامًا ۝

"....Our Lord! Grant unto us the comfort of our eyes from our wives and our offspring, and give us (the grace) to lead the righteous."

(XXV:74).

Now, for the offspring to be "comfort of one's eyes" it is necessary that they should be good in every way; and they would not be normally so unless the parents exert to their full for building up their children in all aspects of their lives and to the highest stature possible.

We know that mere yearning expressed in prayer and left at that means nothing more than sheer idiocy and insult to God. Hence this verse refers to the duty of doing everything in the power of the parents to bring up their children healthy and strong physically, intellectually, morally, spiritually and economically. Of course, that would mean sacrifice for the parents. But, according to the Holy Qur'ãn, self-sacrifice is an essential quality of Muslim character (LIX:9), and it becomes a duty in the case of one's children.

---

5. In case of adverse circumstances the Qur'ãnic social philosophy makes it the duty of the state to look after the proper upbringing and development of the child, as we shall see later.

(d) Finally, the Holy Qur'ãn lays down the command:

يَٰٓأَيُّهَا ٱلَّذِينَ ءَامَنُوا۟ قُوٓا۟ أَنفُسَكُمْ وَأَهْلِيكُمْ نَارًا وَقُودُهَا ٱلنَّاسُ
وَٱلْحِجَارَةُ عَلَيْهَا مَلَٰٓئِكَةٌ غِلَاظٌ شِدَادٌ لَّا يَعْصُونَ ٱللَّهَ مَآ
أَمَرَهُمْ وَيَفْعَلُونَ مَا يُؤْمَرُونَ ۝

"O ye who believe! *protect yourselves and your wives and children from a (spiritual) Fire* whose fuel (unlike the fuel of physical fire) is human beings (who lead wrong lives) and stones (which have been worshipped as false deities by ancient communities) over which are (appointed) angels stern (and) severe, who fliench not (from executing) the Commands they receive from Allah, but do (precisely) what they are commanded." (LXVI:6).

In order to understand the implications of the above command truly and comprehensively, it is necessary to grasp deeply the constitution of the human personality and the dynamics of human activity. The fact is that the different aspects of the human personality are inter-related and, according to the Qur'ãnic concept of *tauhid*, they form an organic unity,—their inter-relationship and inter-dependence being expressible as follows:

Sound mind resides in a sound body.

Sound morality is possible only for a person of sound mind.

Sound spirituality is attainable only by a person of sound morals.

Sound economic pursuit requires at least the soundness of body and mind both.

Thus, saving one's children from the fire of Hell necessitates not only giving them formal teaching of certain religious beliefs and practices—which, if not integrated with other aspects of life, amounts for all practical purposes to a defective attempt—but taking all those steps which will make them good in every way, as taught by the Holy Qur'ãn and expounded in the present dissertation, in respect of human life, namely: *physically, intellectually, morally, spiritually and economically*: the comprehensive programme and the manner in which the Holy Prophet (Peace be on him) built up the despicable pagan Arabs into a community of righteous and progressive superhumans.[6]

---

6. Indeed, the Holy Prophet (Peace be on him) built up his followers in a most comprehensive way, as would be evident even from a perusal of the present dissertation. The same comprehensiveness should grace the programme of the parents for their children.

This means that the verse quoted above envisages the following rights of the child and their fulfilment:

(1) establishment of an atmosphere of love and understanding for the child's proper growth;

(2) protection against all evils; neglect, cruelty and exploitation;

(3) provision of adequate nutrition, proper housing, recreation, and medical service;

(4) provision of opportunities and facilities for the child's balanced development in freedom and dignity, according to the Qur'ãnic code of life;

(5) provision of the best available formal education, in keeping with the child's aptitude and capabilities;

(6) provision of comprehensive moral education and training;

(7) Above all and running through every phase of the child's life, there should be the provision of spiritual education and training—of as high an order as possible—for making him truly God-fearing: which is the most basic and the highest virtue that a Muslim should possess.

3. Respective Duties of the Husband and the Wife

For a proper understanding of the mutual rights and duties of the husband and the wife as taught by the Holy Qur'ãn, it is necessary to begin with a basic evaluation of woman's position in that teaching.[7]

---

7. It may be observed at the very outset that the Qur'ãnic teaching on this problem is in sharp contrast with the point of view of other religions. We may mention here the teaching of the Bible. "According to the Old Testament, woman is responsible for the fall of man, and this became the cornerstone of Christian teaching....It is a remarkable fact that the gospels (barring divorce, Matt. 19:9) contain not a word in favour of woman....The epistles of St. Paul definitely insist that no change can be permitted in the position of woman...St Jerome has aught but good to say of woman....'Woman is the gate of the devil, the road of evil, the sting of the scorpion'. Canon law declares: 'Man only is created to the image of God, not woman: therefore woman shall serve him and be his hand-maid'. The Provincial Council of Macon (sixth century) seriously discussed the question 'whether woman had a soul at all'." (Krafft-Ebing: *Psychopathia Sexualis*, p. 4. n.).

(A) Basic Guidance Constituting the Background of Duties

1. Position of Woman:

We have already seen that the Holy Qur'ãn makes no distinction between man and woman as regards the fundamental human rights. Here we may specifically state that:

Woman, like man, is the possessor of free personality, and enjoys equality with man, in respect of:

(a) Her spiritual and moral status:

لِلرِّجَالِ نَصِيبٌ مِّمَّا اكْتَسَبُوا ۖ وَلِلنِّسَاءِ نَصِيبٌ مِّمَّا اكْتَسَبْنَ ۚ

".....Unto men the benefit of what they earn (of virtue), and unto women the benefit of what they earn (of virtue) (i.e., in matters of spiritual grace both, man and woman, enjoy equal status and are independent of one another)." (IV:32).

إِنَّ الْمُسْلِمِينَ وَالْمُسْلِمَاتِ وَالْمُؤْمِنِينَ وَالْمُؤْمِنَاتِ وَالْقَانِتِينَ وَالْقَانِتَاتِ
وَالصَّادِقِينَ وَالصَّادِقَاتِ وَالصَّابِرِينَ وَالصَّابِرَاتِ وَالْخَاشِعِينَ وَ
الْخَاشِعَاتِ وَالْمُتَصَدِّقِينَ وَالْمُتَصَدِّقَاتِ وَالصَّائِمِينَ وَالصَّائِمَاتِ وَالْحَافِظِينَ
فُرُوجَهُمْ وَالْحَافِظَاتِ وَالذَّاكِرِينَ اللَّهَ كَثِيرًا وَالذَّاكِرَاتِ أَعَدَّ اللَّهُ لَهُم
مَّغْفِرَةً وَأَجْرًا عَظِيمًا ﴿٣٥﴾

"Lo! men who surrender (unto Allah) and women who surrender, and men who believe and women who believe, and men who obey and women who obey, and men who speak the truth and women who speak the truth, and men who persevere (in righteousness) and women who persevere, and men who are humble and women who are humble, and men who give alms and women who give alms, and men who fast and women who fast, and men who guard their modesty and women who guard (their modesty), and men who remember Allah much and women who remember—Allah hath prepared for them forgiveness and vast reward." (XXXIII:35).

As regards the point of view of other religions, primitive as well as civilised, reference may be made to: *Encyclopaedia of Religion and Ethics*.

(b) Her economic rights:

لِلرِّجَالِ نَصِيبٌ مِّمَّا اكْتَسَبُوا ۖ وَلِلنِّسَاءِ نَصِيبٌ مِّمَّا اكْتَسَبْنَ ۚ

".....Unto men a fortune from what they have earned (of wealth), and unto women a fortune from what they have earned (of wealth) (both being free and equal with regard to the possession of their economic rights)....." (IV:32).[8]

لِلرِّجَالِ نَصِيبٌ مِّمَّا تَرَكَ الْوَالِدَانِ وَالْأَقْرَبُونَ وَلِلنِّسَاءِ نَصِيبٌ
مِّمَّا تَرَكَ الْوَالِدَانِ وَالْأَقْرَبُونَ مِمَّا قَلَّ مِنْهُ أَوْ كَثُرَ ۚ نَصِيبًا
مَّفْرُوضًا ○

"Unto the men (of a family) belongeth a share of that which parents and near kindred leave, and unto the women a share of that which the parents and near kindred leave, whether it be little or much—a legal share." (IV:7).

(c) Her legal rights:

وَلَهُنَّ مِثْلُ الَّذِي عَلَيْهِنَّ بِالْمَعْرُوفِ ۚ

".....And they (women) have rights similar to those (of men) over them, according to what is equitable...." (II:228).

لَا تُضَارَّ وَالِدَةٌ بِوَلَدِهَا وَلَا مَوْلُودٌ لَّهُ بِوَلَدِهِ ۚ

"A mother should not be made to suffer because of her child, nor he to whom the child is born (be made to suffer) because of his child (because both are equal before the law)...." (II:233).

2. Inequalities of Condition:

Indeed, as a *human being*, woman enjoys equality of status with man. With this, however, there are also "inequalities of condition" which have been necessitated by the differences in her physical constitution, mental make-up and her distinct roles in society as mother and as wife. Thus:

(a) as mother:

In the verses we have quoted concerning the duties to parents we find that the Holy Qur'ãn lays special emphasis on the role of the mother, thereby pointing to the superiority of her role in respect of the

8. It should be noted that this verse applies to worldly wealth as well as to virtue.

child—as a consequence of which she deserves devotion grater, and honour higher, than the father.[9]

(b) as wife:

As a wife, side by side with enjoying equal fundamental human rights, she has been placed one degree below the husband in the matter of administering the affairs of the family:

وَلِلرِّجَالِ عَلَيْهِنَّ دَرَجَةٌ ۗ

"....but men have a degree (of advantage) over them[10]...." (II:228).

---

9. This implication has been stated by the Holy Prophet (Peace be on him) in concrete terms when he singles out the mother and says:

ان الجنة عند رجليها

"Verily Paradise is by the side of her feet." (Mishkãt al-Masãbih, p. 421)

Also in the *hadith* where he (Peace be on him) emphasised service to the mother thrice and thereafter mentioned service to the father. (*Riyãd al-Sãlihîn*, p. 163).

10. Compare this with the following verdicts of the exponents of modern scientific thought on this problem:

Says Nemilov: "Man, perhaps even down to the protein molecules of his tissue cells, is biologically different from woman. From the very moment of sex formation in the embryo, the biological ducting of the sexes develops along entirely divergent paths..... We must recognize the unquestionable existence of the biological inequality of the sexex. It goes deeper and is of far greater import than it would appear to those not familiar with natural science."

(*Biological Tragedy of Woman*, pp. 75-78).

"The desires and conduct of the two sexes", says Mercier, "are not similar but are complementary and reciprocal. In courtship the male is active: his role is to court, to pursue, to possess, to control, to protect, to love. The role of the female is passive.....Consequent on this fundamental difference are certain others. For pursuit, greater ardour is necessary than for mere reception; and the courting activity of the male is, throughout the whole animal kingdom, more ardent than that of the female; and this greater ordour is connected with certain other differences." (*Conduct and its Disorders Biologically Considered*, pp. 289-290).

Julian Huxley observes: "I venture to prophesy not only that the inherent differences between the sexes will not tend to diminish in the course of evolution but that man will continue, as now and in the past, to emphasise them by custom and convention." (*Essays in Popular Science*, p. 63).

It should, however, be clearly kept in mind that, in the Qur'ãnic teaching, the husband and the wife stand in complementary relation to each other, and never in the relation of the ruler and the ruled (II:187).

In the presence of the husband, the Holy Qur'ãn has not chosen her to function as the head of the family, because owing to his masculine constitution and appropriate mental make-up, the husband is better equipped to earn livelihood for the family, to bear the physical strains, and to avert dangers to the family in general. The Holy Qur'ãn refers to these functions of the husband when, speaking of his role for the wife, it says:

اَلرِّجَالُ قَوّٰمُوْنَ عَلَى النِّسَآءِ بِمَا فَضَّلَ اللّٰهُ بَعْضَهُمْ عَلٰى بَعْضٍ وَّبِمَآ اَنْفَقُوْا مِنْ اَمْوَالِهِمْ

"Men are the protectors and maintainers of women, because Allah hath given the one more (strength) than the other, and because they spend of their wealth (for supporting them and other members of the family)....." (IV:34).

Of course, the husband has to administer the family jointly with the wife, according to the Qur'ãnic law:

وَاَمْرُهُمْ شُوْرٰى بَيْنَهُمْ

"....(Believers are those) who conduct their affairs by mutual consultation (and not arbitrarily)...." (XLII:38).

As a follower of the Qur'ãn, it is only in extreme cases that the husband may differ irreconcilably with the wife. But then too he cannot transgress the bounds of justice and mercy; for the Holy Qur'ãn commands him to be always just, merciful and considerate[12].

The second position of the wife as administrator is, thus, not a source of suffering for her but a source of strength and a blessing.

(c) as sharer in inheritance:

In respect of inheritance, the Holy Qur'ãn has laid down the law:

---

12. See references on absolute justice to all and mercifulness towards all (p. 156, 158).

يُوصِيكُمُ اللَّهُ فِي أَوْلَادِكُمْ لِلذَّكَرِ مِثْلُ حَظِّ الْأُنثَيَيْنِ

"Allah (thus) directeth you as regards your children's inheritance: to the male a portion equal to that of two females...." (IV:11).

This, however, has nothing to do with the inferiority of woman, the real reason behind this inequality in share being that the male has been given the role of the bread-winner for the family and, as such, entrusted with the financial burden of himself and his wife and children, while the female has not been given the role of bread-winner and, as such, has not been entrusted with any financial obligations towards anyone, including her husband and children; indeed, not even her own, because that has been made the obligation of the husband. Thus, although getting half of the male's share, she, in most cases, remains at an advantage as compared with the male, rather than suffering loss.

(d) as giver of evidence in lawsuits:

In its law of evidence, the Holy Qur'ãn had laid down:

وَاسْتَشْهِدُوا شَهِيدَيْنِ مِن رِّجَالِكُمْ فَإِن لَّمْ يَكُونَا رَجُلَيْنِ فَرَجُلٌ
وَامْرَأَتَانِ مِمَّن تَرْضَوْنَ مِنَ الشُّهَدَاءِ أَن تَضِلَّ إِحْدَاهُمَا
فَتُذَكِّرَ إِحْدَاهُمَا الْأُخْرَىٰ

".....and get two witnesses out of your own men, and if there are not two men, then a man and two women, such as ye chose for witnesses, so that if one of them errs (in her judgment or in her memory), the other can remind her...." (II:282).

This law is based on the fact that unlike man, whose sphere of activity is mostly outside the home and who thereby gains a rich experience of and a sharp judgment about men and things, the natural sphere of activity for the woman is the home, which does not allow her to acquire the same richness of experience and sharpness of judgment regarding the affairs of the outside world. Hence, she is not likely to hold her own under the severe strain of cross-examination, because of which any possible short coming on her part as a witness to a case is required to be made up through a second woman's evidence.

This is the Muslim point of view, deducible from the above verse itself. And it bears no insult for womanhood.

The non-Muslim point of view with respect to woman's evidence is, however, harsh and insulting to her.

In the Judaic law, woman is completely debarred from giving evidence. We are told in the *Jewish Encyclopaedia*, (V, p. 177) that: "The witness must be a man and not woman." Indeed, "let not the testimony of women be admitted, on account of the levity and boldness of their sex." (Josephus: *Antiquities of the Jews*, v, 8:15).

The verdict of the sages of the modern age of enlightenment—of a civilisation that is referred to as "Christian", is:

The fact that women are difficult to deal with under cross-examination is well-known among lawyers, and their skill in drawing red herrings across the path of any enquiry directed against themselves, makes them stubborn and evasive witnesses at all times when they have anything to conceal". (Ludovici: *Woman*, p. 320).

"We are again and again forced to admit", says Bauer, "that a woman is not in a position to judge objectively, without being influenced by her emotions". (*Woman and Love*, I, p. 289).

In the view of Havelock Ellis: "In women deception is almost physiological....in some countries it has led to the legal testimony of women being placed on a lower footing than that of men". (*Man and Woman*, p. 196).

3. The Institution of Marriage.

The Qur'ãnic point of view with regard to the institution of Marriage is based on the following principles and laws:

(i) Interdependence of man and woman in ensuring fullness of life for each other through mutual affection, mutual confidence and mutual protection as husband and wife has been stressed by using a metaphor of profound beauty:

هُنَّ لِبَاسٌ لَّكُمْ وَأَنتُمْ لِبَاسٌ لَّهُنَّ

"....They are a garment unto you, and ye are a garment unto them...." (II:187).

(ii) For those who can afford it, marriage is an obligation:

وَأَنكِحُوا الْأَيَامَىٰ مِنكُمْ وَالصَّالِحِينَ مِنْ عِبَادِكُمْ وَإِمَائِكُمْ ۚ إِن يَكُونُوا فُقَرَاءَ
يُغْنِهِمُ اللَّهُ مِن فَضْلِهِ ۗ وَاللَّهُ وَاسِعٌ عَلِيمٌ

"Marry[13] those among you who are single, and the pious among your slaves, male or female: if they are in poverty, Allah will give them means out of His grace: Allah is of ample means, and He knoweth all things." (XXIV:32)[14]

(iii) Marriage is a social contract:

The word *nikãh*, used for marriage in the Holy Qur'ãn, originally means *'aqd*, according to Imam Raghib (vide *Mufradãt al-Qur'ãn*); and *'aqd* means contract. Thus the very word *nikãh* implies that marriage is a social contract, and not a sacrament, although it is a sacred contract. Moreover, the Qur'ãnic permission to terminate the relation of marriage, if it becomes absolutely impossible for the husband and the wife to continue that relation, proves that the Qur'ãn regards marriage as a social contract only.

(iv) Women are not to be treated as chattels:

يَٰٓأَيُّهَا ٱلَّذِينَ ءَامَنُوا لَا يَحِلُّ لَكُمْ أَن تَرِثُوا ٱلنِّسَآءَ كَرْهًا ۖ

---

13. As to those who cannot afford married life, they have been commanded to observe absolute chastity:

وَلْيَسْتَعْفِفِ ٱلَّذِينَ لَا يَجِدُونَ نِكَاحًا حَتَّىٰ يُغْنِيَهُمُ ٱللَّهُ مِن فَضْلِهِۦ ۗ

"Let those who find not the wherewithal for marriage keep themselves chaste, until Allah gives them means out of His grace...." (XXIV:33).

14. Contrast it with the attitude of those religions which advocate celibacy and idolise it as the ideal of perfection, considering sexual satisfaction even in the bond of marriage as positive evil from the spiritual point of view. Thus, in Christianity: "As an institution, Jesus regards marriage as essentially physical and intended only for the present age. Those who were to share in the blessings of the eschatological kingdom would neither marry nor be given in marriage but would be possessed of the non-physical body in the resurrection." (Hastings' *Dictionary of the Bible*, II, p. 138). "It was this outlook on sex which led to the rule that no man or woman, married or unmarried, who had performed the sex act the previous night, should take part in a Church festival or in the Eucharist." (Scott: *History of Prostitution*, pp. 72, 73). "Christianity", writes the sociologist Ludovici "......preaches that sex is to be deplored, to be avoided, and, if possible, negatived. And the Puritan, who may be regarded as the extreme Christian, is notorious for his implacable loathing of sex". (*Woman*, p. 5). It may be observed here in passing that it is this attitude of Christianity that has been responsible for the very dirty crusade of Western writers against Islam's affirmative attitude towards sex.

"O ye who believe! You are forbidden to inherit (as chattels) the women against their will...." (IV:19).

(v) Marriage with persons of certain categories has been prohibited:

The Holy Qur'ãn has prohibited marriage with all those who may stand in the relations of consanguinity, or affinity, or fosterage, in IV:23. Abdur Rahim explains that Qur'ãnic law thus: "By reason of consanguinity a man cannot marry any female ascendant or descendant of his or the daughter of any ascendant, how high soever, or of any descendant, how low soever, or the daughter of his brother or sister or the daughter of a brother's or sister's daughter, and so on. On the ground of affinity he is debarred from marrying a woman who has been the wife of any ascendant of his, and any ascendant or descendant of the wife if marriage has been consummated, or of any woman with whom he has had unlawful connection and any woman who has been the wife of his son or grandson. Generally speaking, fosterage induces the same limits of relationship prohibitive of marriage as consanguinity". (*Muhammadan Jurisprudence*, p. 329).

(vi) Relations between husband and wife have been conceived as based on mutual co-operation, love and compassion:

وَمِنْ اٰيٰتِهٖٓ اَنْ خَلَقَ لَكُمْ مِّنْ اَنْفُسِكُمْ اَزْوَاجًا لِّتَسْكُنُوْٓا اِلَيْهَا وَجَعَلَ
بَيْنَكُمْ مَّوَدَّةً وَّرَحْمَةً ۭ اِنَّ فِيْ ذٰلِكَ لَاٰيٰتٍ لِّقَوْمٍ يَّتَفَكَّرُوْنَ ۝

"And among His Signs is this, that He created your mates from among yourselves, that ye may dwell in transquillity with them, and He has put love and mercy between your (hearts); verily in that are Signs for those who reflect." (XXX:21).

It means that:—

(*a*) marriage is essentially a spiritual bond of union, rather than a mere physical relationship;

(*b*) marriage should be contracted with the firm resolve of maintaining that relation for life;

(*c*) monogamy should be the ideal[15], because that is the ideal

---

15. Polygamy has been permitted by the Holy Qur'ãn on humanitarian grounds, under exceptional circumstances, and with restrictive conditions, as we shall see later.

condition in which mutual co-operation, harmony and love can be practised normally and smoothly by the common man.

(vii) Polygamy permitted with severe restrictions:

The only Qur'ãnic verse which contains the permission for polygamous marriage, says:

وَإِنْ خِفْتُمْ أَلَّا تُقْسِطُوا فِي الْيَتَامَىٰ فَانكِحُوا مَا طَابَ لَكُم مِّنَ النِّسَاءِ مَثْنَىٰ
وَثُلَاثَ وَرُبَاعَ ۖ فَإِنْ خِفْتُمْ أَلَّا تَعْدِلُوا فَوَاحِدَةً أَوْ مَا مَلَكَتْ أَيْمَانُكُمْ ۚ
ذَٰلِكَ أَدْنَىٰ أَلَّا تَعُولُوا ۝

"And if ye fear that ye shall not be able to deal justly with the orphans, marry of the women who seem good to you, two and three and four; and if ye fear that (in case of having more wives than one) ye shall not be able to deal justly (with them) then (marry) only one (free woman) or (a captive) that your right hands possess. That will be more suitable to prevent you from doing injustice." (IV:3).

Important points, worthy of being carefully noted, are:—

(*a*) This verse does not enjoin polygamy, but only permits it.

(*b*) Unrestricted polygamy, which had been rampant among the pre-Qur'ãnic Arabs and many other nations of the world.[16] has been restricted to the maximum of four.[17]

(*c*) The permission relates to situations of emergency[18], and not to normal conditions of life and society.

---

15. "Polygamy", says Roberts, "was the rule among the Eastern peoples before Muhammad's time." (*Social Laws of the Qur'ãn*. p. 8). As for a comprehensive discussion of the history of this institution among different nations of the world, see: *Encyclopaedia of Religion and Ethics*.

16. Fixing the maximum at four seems to be based on the natural law relating to monthly courses, whereby the husband can do justice in respect of conjugal relations even if he has the maximum of four wives.

17. This verse was revealed after the battle of Uhud, which gave rise to a situation of emergency. Appreciable number of Muslim men were killed in the battle, leaving behind orphans and widows, and giving to the preponderance of adult females. Also there were some women captives of war. Polygamy was prescribed for those who were God-fearing and whose sole mission in life was spiritual refinement and pursuit of Divine Pleasure.

(*d*) The permission is based, not on considerations of lust, nor on any benefit accruing to the marrying male, but on the principle of sacrifice—of providing protection and support to orphans, while undergoing a severe tension of dealing with all the wives.

(*e*) The permission is conditioned by one's ability to deal equitably with his wives, which even at the formal level is an extremely difficult condition to fulfil except for those who are thoroughly disciplined, stick to spiritual and moral values above everything else, and enter into marriage for spiritual considerations—for the sake of obtaining Divine Pleasure.

(*f*) Thus this verse, instead of inducing the men to practise polygamy, recommends to them monogamy.

(*g*) Finally, looking at the Qur'ãnic permission for polygamy with an unbiased mind, every rational person is bound to be convinced that in situations of emergency, namely, whenever there is a preponderance of females—as it happens after the wars—and wherever there is the problem of the uncured for and unsolicited widows and orphans, it becomes a moral duty of God-fearing people to practise polygamy, whereby alone the individuals can be saved from disaster and the community can escape the horrors of prostitution.

The verdict of human history in this behalf, coming down to the year 1970, is indisputable.

The *Natal Mercury* (Durban, Sept. 10, 1970) reports thus:—

"The people of a strongly Christian town near Calabar, capital of Nigeria's South-Eastern State, have agreed to relax the one-man-one-wife rule. At a mass meeting recently they decided that every man was free to marry from two to six women at the drastically reduced

---

A. Yusuf Ali says: "Notice the conditional clause about orphans, introducing the rules about marriage. This reminds us of the immediate occasion of the promulgation of this verse. It was after Uhud, when the Muslim community was left with many orphans and widows, and some captives of war. Their treatment was to be governed by principles of the greatest humanity and equity. The occasion is past, but the principles remain. Marry the orphans if you are quite sure that you will in that way protect their interests and their property, with perfect justice to them and to your own dependants, if you have any. If not, make other arrangements for the orphans." (*op.cit.*, p. 179).

price of R 10 a wife. Bride price in the area used to be between R 100 and R 300.

"The reason for the move is that the town has been swarming with unmarried girls and widows since the end of the Nigerian civil war. The town's elders believe that a general return to polygamy will help to keep women from turning to prostitution for a living.

"The decision, almost certain to be approved by the State's military Government, highlights one of the serious social problems now confronting Nigeria in the aftermath of the 30-month civil war.

"Japan and most of Europe faced similar situations after World War II....

"West Germany, which suffered most and made the most rapid post-war economic recovery, is still faced with the problem of surplus women. And the same is true today of Japan and Italy.

"For Nigeria the problem will be especially difficult to solve. The country is still underdeveloped. The surplus women are mostly illiterate.

"The matter is further complicated by the fact that most ex-soldiers now joining the ranks of the unemployed have no other professional training or skills.

"Federal and State leaders agree that a 'liberalisation of marriage law' will go a long way to minimising the problem.

"The main difficulty is the attitude of the Church, still a very powerful influence in the three states in former Eastern Nigeria where the problem is most acute. More than 75 per cent of the population is Christian.

"An Ibo leader told me: 'We would like our people to follow the example of the Calabar people because the problem is really serious in our area. One difficulty, of course, will be economic....But our main difficulty may be with the Christian missions, especially the Roman Catholic Church which still exercises a strong influence on our people. But we hope the Church will close its eyes, so that Christians can marry as many wives as they can afford just as the Muslims and pagans do. I can see no other way out'."

"There is", wrote Dr. Mrs. Annie Besant, the renowned English leader of the Theosophical Movement, "pretended monogamy in the West, but there is really polygamy without responsibility; the 'mistress' is cast out to be the 'woman of the street', for the first lover has no responsibility for her future and she is a hundred times worse off than the sheltered wife and mother in the polygamous home. When we see thousands of miserable women who crowd the streets of Western towns during the night, we must surely feel that it does not lie in the Western mouth to reproach Islam for polygamy. It is better for woman, happier for woman, more respectable for woman, to live in polygamy, united to one man only, with the legitimate child in her arms, and surrounded with respect, than to be seduced, cast out into the street—perhaps with an illegitimate child outside the pale of law—unsheltered and uncared for, to become the victim of any passerby, night after night, rendered incapable of motherhood, despised by all".

(Annie Besant, *The Life and Teachings of Muhammad*, p. 3).

(viii) Polyandry and Neoga ruled out:

Recounting the categories of women with whom marriage is forbidden, the Holy Qur'ãn says:

وَالْمُحْصَنٰتُ مِنَ النِّسَآءِ

"....and (forbidden also) are wedded women (i.e., women having husbands)....." (IV:24).

Thus the holy book repudiates polyandry (or, plurality of husbands) and the Hindu custom of *Neoga* (or, loaning the wife to another person for getting an issue), and the custom of exchanging wives practised by certain savage tribes[18].

(ix) Temporary and 'companionate' marriage prohibited:

Temporary conjugal relations are prompted purely by lust, and in no case for establishing that sublime spiritual relation between man and woman which alone can form the basis for building up the family. Therefore, the Holy Qur'ãn disallows temporary and 'companionate' marriages. It says:

وَأُحِلَّ لَكُمْ مَّا وَرَآءَ ذٰلِكُمْ أَنْ تَبْتَغُوْا بِأَمْوَالِكُمْ مُّحْصِنِيْنَ غَيْرَ مُسٰفِحِيْنَ

".....Except for these (prohibited relations), all others (i.e., other women) are lawful, provided ye seek (them in marriage) with gifts from

18. Refer to *Encyclopaedia of Religion and Ethics*, Vol. I., p. 125.

your property (as dower-money), desiring chastity (in permanent companionship), not lust (in any form of temporary marriage)....''[19] (IV:24).

(x) Dowry enjoined out of regard for woman's dignity[20] *and her economic interest:*

وَآتُوا النِّسَآءَ صَدُقٰتِهِنَّ نِحْلَةً ؕ

"And give the woman[21] (on marriage) their dower as a free gift...." (IV:4).

(B) Duties of Husband and Wife Towards One Another

1. *Duties of the Husband*:

Preliminary:

The Holy Qur'ãn stresses the extraordinary importance of, and hence the duty of extreme carefulness about, the relationship of marriage:

وَاتَّقُوا اللّٰهَ الَّذِي تَسَآءَلُونَ بِهٖ وَالْاَرْحَامَ ؕ اِنَّ اللّٰهَ كَانَ عَلَيْكُمْ رَقِيْبًا ۝

"....and be careful of your duty to Allah, through Whom ye demand (your mutual rights), and to the wombs. Verily Allah ever watches over you." (IV:1).

It should be noted here that in the Arabic text the word 'womb' has been coupled grammatically with the word 'Allah' in respect of the observance of carefulness in duty, thus highlighting the position of the mother and the wife in the Qur'ãnic teaching.

19. "Real satisfaction", says Pollens, "Come not from mere sexual experience but from a relationship which is lasting and continuous and which is built on feelings of affection, devotion and tenderness." (*The Sex Criminal*, p. 196).

20. Says Abdur Rahim: "It is not a consideration proceeding from the husband for the contract of marriage, but it is an obligation imposed by the law on the husband as a mark of respect for the wife, as is evident from the fact that the non-specification of the dower at the time of marriage does not affect the validity of the marriage." (*Muhammadan Jurisprudence*, p. 334).

21. This should be clearly distinguished from the evil custom of paying the price of the bride to her parents, a custom prevalent in ancient times in many communities of the world, for which refer to Westermarck's *Short History of Marriage*, pp. 166-169.

(i) <u>Duties of Commission</u>:

(a) Protecting and maintaining the wife stressed as an unavoidable function of the husband; hence fulfilments of this function is duty:

اَلرِّجَالُ قَوّٰمُوْنَ عَلَى النِّسَآءِ بِمَا فَضَّلَ اللّٰهُ بَعْضَهُمْ عَلٰى بَعْضٍ وَّبِمَآ
اَنْفَقُوْا مِنْ اَمْوَالِهِمْ ؕ

"Men are the protectors and maintainers of women, because Allah has given the one more (strength) than the other, and because they support them from their means....." (IV:34).

(b) Treating the wife with kindness and equity enjoined:

وَعَاشِرُوْهُنَّ بِالْمَعْرُوْفِ ۚ

"....and (O Believers!) live with them (*i.e.*, the wives) on a footing of kindness and equity......" (IV:19).

(c) Toleration of the faults and the shortcomings[22] of the wife, enjoined:

فَاِنْ كَرِهْتُمُوْهُنَّ فَعَسٰٓى اَنْ تَكْرَهُوْا شَيْئًا وَّيَجْعَلَ اللّٰهُ فِيْهِ خَيْرًا كَثِيْرًا

".....If ye take a dislike to them (i.e., the wives), it may be that ye dislike a thing, and Allah brings about through it a great good."(IV:19).

(d) Spiritualisation of physical relation, abstaining from damaging wife's dignity through unnatural offence, and keeping the duty of parenthood in view with due regard to wife's health enjoined:

نِسَآؤُكُمْ حَرْثٌ لَّكُمْ ۪ فَاْتُوْا حَرْثَكُمْ اَنّٰى شِئْتُمْ ۫ وَقَدِّمُوْا لِاَنْفُسِكُمْ ؕ وَاتَّقُوا
اللّٰهَ وَاعْلَمُوْٓا اَنَّكُمْ مُّلٰقُوْهُ ؕ وَبَشِّرِ الْمُؤْمِنِيْنَ ۝

"Your wives are a tilth unto you (like the soil which accepts the seed and brings forth the plants). So go in unto your tilth (and not anywhere

---

22. According to Nemilov: "Anyone familiar with the physiology and biology of woman will be less annoyed and irritated at her sudden change of mood, allegedly unreasonable flares of temper, her unmotivated acts. Understanding this, man will deeply sympathise with the bearers of the egg cells who, having the same aspirations and claims upon life, are burdened with more difficult biological tasks." (*Biological Tragedy of Woman*: pp. 187, 188).

else) when and in what manner ye like; but send (good deeds) before you for your souls; and fear Allah (in respect of your moral and spiritual obligations towards your wife, towards yourselves and towards the offspring that you may beget as a consequence); and know that ye will (one day) meet Him. And give (O Muhammad) glad tidings to the Believers (i.e., those who, as believers in the Qur'ãnic Guidance, remain devoted to spiritual and moral values even in carnal pleasures)." (II:223).

A commentator of the Holy Qur'ãn comments on this verse thus:—

"Sex is not a thing to be ashamed of, or to be treated lightly, or to be indulged to excess. It is as solemn a fact as any in life. It is compared to a husbandman's tilth; it is a serious affair to him: he sows the seed in order to reap the harvest. But he chooses his own time and mode of cultivation. He does not sow out of season nor cultivate in a manner which will injure or exhaust the soil. He is wise and considerate and does not run riot. Coming from the simile to human beings, every kind of mutual consideration is required, but above all, we must remember that even in these matters there is a spiritual aspect. We must never forget our souls, and that we are responsible to God.

"It was carnal-minded men who invented the doctrine of original sin: 'Behold', says the Psalmist, 'I was shapen in iniquity, and in sin did my mother conceive me' (*Psalms*, li:5). This is entirely repudiated by Islam, in which the office of father and mother is held in the highest veneration. Every child of pure love is born pure. Celibacy is not necessarily a virtue, and may be a vice". (A. Yusuf Ali, *op.cit.*, p. 88).

(e) *Concern for the welfare of the wife in all respects, specially the spiritual, stressed, and hence looking after the physical, mental, moral, spiritual and economic welfare of the wife is duty:*

The Holy Qur'ãn has taught the prayer:

رَبَّنَا هَبْ لَنَا مِنْ أَزْوَاجِنَا وَذُرِّيَّاتِنَا قُرَّةَ أَعْيُنٍ وَّاجْعَلْنَا لِلْمُتَّقِينَ إِمَامًا ۝

"....Our Lord! *Grant to us the comfort of our eyes from our wives* and our offspring, and give us (the grace to lead the righteous." (XXV:74).

Moreover, the Muslim husband and fathers have been entrusted with the following duty:

يَاَيُّهَا الَّذِيْنَ اٰمَنُوْا قُوْٓا اَنْفُسَكُمْ وَ اَهْلِيْكُمْ نَارًا

"O ye who believe! protect yourselves and *your wives* and children from a (spiritual) Fire...." (LXVI:6).

While expounding the teaching contained in these verses with respect to "duties", in the section on "Duties to the Offspring", we have already seen that these verses relate to the duty of ensuring the physical, mental, moral, spiritual and economic welfare. (See. p. 172).

(ii) Duty of Omission:

There are several duties of omission which are directly and indirectly contained in the foregoing and the forthcoming discussions relating to the "Position of Woman" and the "Husband-Wife relation". One specific duty, which is not contained there, may, however, be mentioned here.

Accusing the wife falsely, or without proper evidence, has been regarded as a heinous crime; hence to abstain from it is duty[23]:

The Holy Qur'ãn says:

وَالَّذِيْنَ يَرْمُوْنَ الْمُحْصَنٰتِ ثُمَّ لَمْ يَاْتُوْا بِاَرْبَعَةِ شُهَدَآءَ فَاجْلِدُوْهُمْ
ثَمٰنِيْنَ جَلْدَةً وَّلَا تَقْبَلُوْا لَهُمْ شَهَادَةً اَبَدًا ۚ وَاُولٰٓئِكَ هُمُ الْفٰسِقُوْنَ ۙ

"And those who accuse clean women (of unchastity) and then produce not four (eye) witnesses, scourge them with eighty stripes and accept not their testimony for ever. And these! they are the transgressors." (XXIV:4).[24]

2. *Duties of the Wife:*

Of Commission and Omission:

(a) *Submissiveness to the husband as the head of the family—not in servile manner but with the spirit of dignified maintenance of harmony;*

(b) *guarding the conjugal rights of the husband through*

---

23. It is also a duty of all men towards all women.

24. The procedure of law in case of accusation of the wife by the husband of adultery, has been mentioned in the verses that follow. We shall deal with it when discussing punishments.

abstaining from doing anything that may, in the least measure, violate her chastity;

(c) *protecting the prestige and the property of her husband:*

The above three virtues form the unavoidable functions of the righteous wife, according to the Holy Qur'ãn; and hence constitute the basic duties of the wife.

The Holy Qur'ãn says:

فَالصّٰلِحٰتُ قٰنِتٰتٌ حٰفِظٰتٌ لِّلْغَيْبِ بِمَا حَفِظَ اللّٰهُ ؕ

"....So the righteous women are obedient (to God and submissive to their husbands), and guard in (the husband's) absence what Allah would have them guard (i.e., their chastity and the prestige and property of the husband)...." (IV:34).

(C) Laws Relating to Abnormal Situations and the Respective Duties:

1. *Efforts of the husband, in case of wife's refractoriness and fear of desertion, to bring her to the path of rectitude:*

وَالّٰتِيْ تَخَافُوْنَ نُشُوْزَهُنَّ فَعِظُوْهُنَّ وَاهْجُرُوْهُنَّ فِي الْمَضَاجِعِ وَ اضْرِبُوْهُنَّ ۚ فَاِنْ اَطَعْنَكُمْ فَلَا تَبْغُوْا عَلَيْهِنَّ سَبِيْلًا ؕ اِنَّ اللّٰهَ كَانَ عَلِيًّا كَبِيْرًا ۝

".....As to those (wives) on whose part ye fear rebellion and desertion admonish them (first); (in case that does not reform their conduct) banish them to beds apart; (lastly, if they still prove to be incorrigible, ye are permitted to) beat them (with a tooth-brush or something like it, in order to awaken in them the sentiment of self-respect and the consciousness of the seriousness of their guilt in itself and in respect of its consequences for the family-life, and in a manner which causes no injury or pain to them). Then if they obey you (by returning to the path of rectitude), seek not a way (of harassment or ill-treatment) against them. Verily, Allah is Most High, Great (wherefore it does not behove you to tyrannise over your wives)." (IV:34).

This verse speaks of serious breach in loyalty to the marital bond on the part of the wife. Now, there can be three ways: (1) to divorce the wife offhand; (2) to take the matter to a court of law; (3) to deal with it at personal level. The Holy Qur'ãn prefers the last, and that for obvious reasons. The first is an extreme measure, and its consequences may be very damaging for the wife or for the family as a whole. The second alternative is scandalous and means 'washing dirty linen' in public. It invites accusations and counter-accusations, and it is specially damaging for the wife. It is the third alternative only, the one prescribed by the Holy Qur'ãn, which is the best in the interest of the wife and of public morality.

In connection with beating the rebellious wife, there are certain important facts which should be borne in mind:

Firstly, to resort to it as a last remedy has been merely *permitted, and not made obligatory.*

Secondly, although permitted in theory, it has been positively discouraged in practice, as, for instance, the Holy Prophet (Peace be on him), who alone has the original right to interpret the teachings of the Qur'ãn and whose interpretation alone can be absolutely correct, says: "You will not find these men (who beat their wives) as the good ones among you."[25] Again: "No one should ever beat his wife with a whip like a slave (who was beaten with the whip by non-Muslim masters)."[26] Still again: "The best of you is he who is best to his wife."[27]

Thirdly, it has been made absolutely clear by the Holy Prophet (Peace be on him) that the beating should be of a symbolic or norminal type. It should be "striking without injury of pain",[28] and it should be "with a tooth-brush or something like it."[29]

Fourthly, the function of the Holy Qur'ãn is to provide guidance to human beings belonging to all stages of social evolution. Consequently, this remedy, while it may be unthinkable in respect of people belonging to the higher stages of social evolution, may yet form the only proper and 'natural' corrective instrument in the case of those who stand at the lower ladders of social and psychological refinement. In fact, it has not only formed a vital part of marital life but has been regarded as a positive

---

25. Abû Dã'ûd: *Sunan*, vol. I, p. 292; etc.

26. Bukhãrî: *Sahîh*, vol. II, p. 784.

27. Ibn Mãjah: *Sunan; Bãb Husn ma'ãshrat al-Nisã*, p. 142.

28. Ibn Mãjah: Sunan, p. 133. Muslim: *Sahîh*, vol. I, p. 291.

29. See Tabarî's *Tafsir*, vol. V, p. 41, Egyptian edition.

contribution to marital success among many a community of the world, who have believed in the eminent philosopher Nietzsche's verdict: "When you go to a woman forget not your whip." And the testimony in this behalf is irrefutable.

Krafft-Ebing says: "Among peoples of a lower class of culture the subjection of woman is extended even to brutality. This flagrant proof of dependence is felt by woman even with sexual pleasure and accepted as a token of love". (*Psychopathia Sexualis*, p. 211).

" Among the Slaves of the lower class the wives feel hurt if they are not beaten by their husbands; the peasant women in some parts of Hungary do not think they are loved by their husbands until they have received the first box on the ear; among the Italian community a wife, if not beaten by her husband, regards him as a fool." (*Encyclopaedia of Religion and Ethics*, VIII: p. 156).

"The Englishman's privilege of beating his wife with a stick not thicker than his thumb, has become rather favourite." (Ludovici: *Woman*, p. 13).

According to the school of thought founded by Freud, the scientist, the father of Psychoanalysis, and the idol of the rebels against religion: "Helence Dentach has elaborated Freud's assumption and generalised it in calling masochism the elemental power in feminine mental life. She contends that what woman ultimately wants in intercourse is to be raped and violated, what she wants in mental life is to be humiliated: menstruation is significant to woman because it feeds masochistic fantasies: childbirth represents the climax of masochistic satisfaction." (Horney: *New Ways in Psychoanalysis*, p. 110).

2. *Procedure in case of serious disagreement and conflict between the husband and the wife:*

(i) Effort at reconciliation through arbitration by a Family Council composed of one representative from each side[30], enjoined:

وَإِنْ خِفْتُمْ شِقَاقَ بَيْنِهِمَا فَابْعَثُوا حَكَمًا مِّنْ أَهْلِهِ وَحَكَمًا مِّنْ
أَهْلِهَا ۚ إِن يُرِيدَا إِصْلَاحًا يُوَفِّقِ اللَّهُ بَيْنَهُمَا ۗ إِنَّ اللَّهَ كَانَ عَلِيمًا
خَبِيرًا ۝

"And if ye (O Muslims) fear a breach between them twain (i.e.,

30. Mark the healthy nature of this prescription, wherein scandal as well as chicaneries of the law have been avoided and the sanctity of the husband-wife relation has been fully maintained.

the husband and the wife), appoint two arbiters, one from his family, and the other from hers (—the two knowing the mentalities, the faults and the merits of both—); then if the two (arbiters) wish for rectification (i.e., strive for reconciliation earnestly and justly), Allah shall bring about harmony between the twain: For Allah hath full knowledge, and is acquainted with all things." (IV:35).

(ii)

(*a*) While lending its weight to the sanctity of the marriage-relation, the Holy Qur'ãn gives due consideration to the weaknesses and aberrations of human nature. Therefore, it allows divorce as a necessary evil[31], when that becomes the only remedy for rectifying a situation of irreconcilable incompatibility.

(*b*) In allowing the divorce, however, the Holy Qur'ãn prescribes a procedure which aims at eliminating the evils of idiosyncrasy and availing every possible opportunity and means for reconciliation before the final repture,—the procedure consisting in abstention from pronouncing divorce during the menstrual period, which is the period of least mutual husband-wife attraction, and pronouncing it in three stages at intervals of one month each, thereby preventing hasty step and providing the parties repeated opportunity for cool deliberation.

(*c*) Though pronouncement of divorce has been placed in the hands of the husband, the wife has also been given the right to sue for, and obtain, divorce.[32]

(*d*) In case of divorce, again the Holy Qur'ãn emphasises with full force the safeguarding of the welfare of the wife and treatment of the wife with generosity.

(*e*) The Qur'ãnic teachings is also emphatic in safeguarding the welfare of the unborn child, if that may be the case.

(*f*) When the marriage tie has been *finally* dissolved, the husband is not permitted to take back his wife, until she has married someone else sincerely and has thereafter become a widow or a divorce. This injunction is meant to check husbands from making fun of marriage, which is a

31. Cf. The Holy Prophet's exposition of the Qur'ãnic standpoint: "Of all things permitted by law, divorce is the most hateful in the sight of God." (Abu Dã'ûd: *Sunan*, XIII:3).

32. Marriage being a social contract, the Islamic law gives to the wife also the right to deprive the husband of the prerogative of pronouncing the divorce at his will. Says Abdur Rahim: "It is open to a woman at the time of marriage or subsequently thereto to stipulate for their (*i.e.*, husband's rights) curtailment or to get some of them transferred to herself, such as the right to dissolve the marriage." (*Muhammadan Jurisprudence*, p. 328).

serious affair according to the Holy Qur'ãn.

(*g*) A period of waiting or probation, has been prescribed for the divorced women as a healthy gap in their sexual life, and for saving them from taking any hasty step in connection with their next marriage (which is necessary after the emotional disturbance caused by the shock of divorce), and for safeguarding the interests of the unborn child, if any.

(*h*) Cessation of relations with the wife without freeing her from the marriage-tie has been prohibited.

The following verses of the Holy Qur'ãn contain injunctions in respect of the above:

يَٰٓأَيُّهَا ٱلنَّبِيُّ إِذَا طَلَّقْتُمُ ٱلنِّسَآءَ فَطَلِّقُوهُنَّ لِعِدَّتِهِنَّ وَأَحْصُوا
ٱلْعِدَّةَ ۚ وَٱتَّقُوا ٱللَّهَ رَبَّكُمْ ۖ لَا تُخْرِجُوهُنَّ مِنۢ بُيُوتِهِنَّ وَلَا يَخْرُجْنَ
إِلَّآ أَن يَأْتِينَ بِفَٰحِشَةٍ مُّبَيِّنَةٍ ۚ وَتِلْكَ حُدُودُ ٱللَّهِ ۚ وَمَن
يَتَعَدَّ حُدُودَ ٱللَّهِ فَقَدْ ظَلَمَ نَفْسَهُۥ ۚ لَا تَدْرِى لَعَلَّ ٱللَّهَ يُحْدِثُ
بَعْدَ ذَٰلِكَ أَمْرًا ۝ فَإِذَا بَلَغْنَ أَجَلَهُنَّ فَأَمْسِكُوهُنَّ بِمَعْرُوفٍ
أَوْ فَارِقُوهُنَّ بِمَعْرُوفٍ وَأَشْهِدُوا ذَوَىْ عَدْلٍ مِّنكُمْ وَأَقِيمُوا
ٱلشَّهَٰدَةَ لِلَّهِ ۚ ذَٰلِكُمْ يُوعَظُ بِهِۦ مَن كَانَ يُؤْمِنُ بِٱللَّهِ وَٱلْيَوْمِ
ٱلْءَاخِرِ ۚ وَمَن يَتَّقِ ٱللَّهَ يَجْعَل لَّهُۥ مَخْرَجًا ۝ وَيَرْزُقْهُ مِنْ حَيْثُ
لَا يَحْتَسِبُ ۚ وَمَن يَتَوَكَّلْ عَلَى ٱللَّهِ فَهُوَ حَسْبُهُۥٓ ۚ إِنَّ ٱللَّهَ بَٰلِغُ أَمْرِهِۦ ۚ قَدْ
جَعَلَ ٱللَّهُ لِكُلِّ شَىْءٍ قَدْرًا ۝ وَٱلَّٰٓـِٔى يَئِسْنَ مِنَ ٱلْمَحِيضِ مِن نِّسَآئِكُمْ
إِنِ ٱرْتَبْتُمْ فَعِدَّتُهُنَّ ثَلَٰثَةُ أَشْهُرٍ وَٱلَّٰٓـِٔى لَمْ يَحِضْنَ ۚ وَأُولَٰتُ
ٱلْأَحْمَالِ أَجَلُهُنَّ أَن يَضَعْنَ حَمْلَهُنَّ ۚ وَمَن يَتَّقِ ٱللَّهَ يَجْعَل لَّهُۥ
مِنْ أَمْرِهِۦ يُسْرًا ۝ ذَٰلِكَ أَمْرُ ٱللَّهِ أَنزَلَهُۥٓ إِلَيْكُمْ ۚ وَمَن يَتَّقِ ٱللَّهَ
يُكَفِّرْ عَنْهُ سَيِّـَٔاتِهِۦ وَيُعْظِمْ لَهُۥٓ أَجْرًا ۝ أَسْكِنُوهُنَّ مِنْ حَيْثُ
سَكَنتُم مِّن وُجْدِكُمْ وَلَا تُضَآرُّوهُنَّ لِتُضَيِّقُوا عَلَيْهِنَّ ۚ وَإِن كُنَّ
أُولَٰتِ حَمْلٍ فَأَنفِقُوا عَلَيْهِنَّ حَتَّىٰ يَضَعْنَ حَمْلَهُنَّ ۚ فَإِنْ أَرْضَعْنَ
لَكُمْ فَـَٔاتُوهُنَّ أُجُورَهُنَّ ۖ وَأْتَمِرُوا بَيْنَكُم بِمَعْرُوفٍ ۖ وَإِن تَعَاسَرْتُمْ
فَسَتُرْضِعُ لَهُۥٓ أُخْرَىٰ ۝ لِيُنفِقْ ذُو سَعَةٍ مِّن سَعَتِهِۦ ۖ وَمَن قُدِرَ عَلَيْهِ
رِزْقُهُۥ فَلْيُنفِقْ مِمَّآ ءَاتَىٰهُ ٱللَّهُ ۚ لَا يُكَلِّفُ ٱللَّهُ نَفْسًا إِلَّا مَآ ءَاتَىٰهَا ۚ
سَيَجْعَلُ ٱللَّهُ بَعْدَ عُسْرٍ يُسْرًا ۝

" O Prophet! When ye (the Muslims) do divorce women, divorce them at their prescribed periods, and count (accurately) their prescribed periods; and fear Allah your Lord: and turn them not out of their houses, nor shall they (themselves) leave, except in case they are guilty of some open lewdness; those are the limits set by Allah: and any who transgresses the limits of Allah, does verily wrong his (own) soul: thou knowest not if perchance Allah will bring about thereafter some new situation.

"Thus when they fulfil their term appointed, either take them back on equitable terms or part with them on equitable terms; and take for witness two persons from among you, endued with justice, and establish the evidence (as) before Allah. Such is the admonition given to him who believes in Allah and the Last Day. And for those who fear Allah, He (ever) prepares a way out.

"And He provides for him from (sources) he never could imagine. And if anyone puts his trust in Allah, sufficient is (Allah) for him. For Allah will surely accomplish His purpose. Verily, for all things has Allah appointed a due proportion.

"Such of your women as have passed the age of monthly courses, for them the prescribed period, if ye have any doubt, is three months, and for those who have no courses (it is the same): For those who carry (life within their wombs), their period is until they deliver their burdens: and for those who fear Allah, He will make their path easy.

"That is the Command of Allah, which He has sent down to you: and if anyone fears Allah, He will remove his ills from him and will enlarge his reward.

"Let the women live (in *'Iddat*), in the same style as ye live, according to your means: Annoy them not, so as to restrict them. And if they carry (life in their wombs), then spend (your substance) on them until they deliver their burden: and if they suckle your (offspring), give them their recompense: And take mutual counsel together, according to what is just and reasonable, And if ye find yourselves in difficulties, let another woman suckle (the child) on the (father's) behalf.

"Let the man of means spend according to his means: and the man whose resources are restricted, let him spend according to what Allah has given him. Allah puts no burden on any person beyond what He has given him After a difficulty, Allah will soon grant relief." (LXV:1-7).

وَالْمُطَلَّقٰتُ يَتَرَبَّصْنَ بِاَنْفُسِهِنَّ ثَلٰثَةَ قُرُوْٓءٍ ؕ وَلَا يَحِلُّ لَهُنَّ اَنْ يَّكْتُمْنَ
مَا خَلَقَ اللّٰهُ فِيْٓ اَرْحَامِهِنَّ اِنْ كُنَّ يُؤْمِنَّ بِاللّٰهِ وَالْيَوْمِ الْاٰخِرِ ؕ وَ بُعُوْلَتُهُنَّ
اَحَقُّ بِرَدِّهِنَّ فِيْ ذٰلِكَ اِنْ اَرَادُوْٓا اِصْلَاحًا ؕ وَلَهُنَّ مِثْلُ الَّذِيْ عَلَيْهِنَّ
بِالْمَعْرُوْفِ ۪ وَلِلرِّجَالِ عَلَيْهِنَّ دَرَجَةٌ ؕ وَاللّٰهُ عَزِيْزٌ حَكِيْمٌ ○ اَلطَّلَاقُ مَرَّتٰنِ
فَاِمْسَاكٌۢ بِمَعْرُوْفٍ اَوْ تَسْرِيْحٌۢ بِاِحْسَانٍ ؕ وَلَا يَحِلُّ لَكُمْ اَنْ تَاْخُذُوْا مِمَّآ
اٰتَيْتُمُوْهُنَّ شَيْئًا اِلَّآ اَنْ يَّخَافَآ اَلَّا يُقِيْمَا حُدُوْدَ اللّٰهِ ؕ فَاِنْ خِفْتُمْ اَلَّا
يُقِيْمَا حُدُوْدَ اللّٰهِ ۙ فَلَا جُنَاحَ عَلَيْهِمَا فِيْمَا افْتَدَتْ بِهٖ ؕ تِلْكَ حُدُوْدُ
اللّٰهِ فَلَا تَعْتَدُوْهَا ۚ وَمَنْ يَّتَعَدَّ حُدُوْدَ اللّٰهِ فَاُولٰٓئِكَ هُمُ الظّٰلِمُوْنَ ○
فَاِنْ طَلَّقَهَا فَلَا تَحِلُّ لَهٗ مِنْۢ بَعْدُ حَتّٰى تَنْكِحَ زَوْجًا غَيْرَهٗ ؕ فَاِنْ طَلَّقَهَا
فَلَا جُنَاحَ عَلَيْهِمَآ اَنْ يَّتَرَاجَعَآ اِنْ ظَنَّآ اَنْ يُّقِيْمَا حُدُوْدَ اللّٰهِ ؕ وَتِلْكَ
حُدُوْدُ اللّٰهِ يُبَيِّنُهَا لِقَوْمٍ يَّعْلَمُوْنَ ○ وَاِذَا طَلَّقْتُمُ النِّسَآءَ فَبَلَغْنَ اَجَلَهُنَّ
فَاَمْسِكُوْهُنَّ بِمَعْرُوْفٍ اَوْ سَرِّحُوْهُنَّ بِمَعْرُوْفٍ ۪ وَلَا تُمْسِكُوْهُنَّ ضِرَارًا
لِّتَعْتَدُوْا ۚ وَمَنْ يَّفْعَلْ ذٰلِكَ فَقَدْ ظَلَمَ نَفْسَهٗ ؕ وَلَا تَتَّخِذُوْٓا اٰيٰتِ اللّٰهِ
هُزُوًا ۫ وَّاذْكُرُوْا نِعْمَتَ اللّٰهِ عَلَيْكُمْ وَمَآ اَنْزَلَ عَلَيْكُمْ مِّنَ الْكِتٰبِ وَ
الْحِكْمَةِ يَعِظُكُمْ بِهٖ ؕ وَاتَّقُوا اللّٰهَ وَاعْلَمُوْٓا اَنَّ اللّٰهَ بِكُلِّ شَيْءٍ عَلِيْمٌ ○
وَاِذَا طَلَّقْتُمُ النِّسَآءَ فَبَلَغْنَ اَجَلَهُنَّ فَلَا تَعْضُلُوْهُنَّ اَنْ يَّنْكِحْنَ
اَزْوَاجَهُنَّ اِذَا تَرَاضَوْا بَيْنَهُمْ بِالْمَعْرُوْفِ ؕ ذٰلِكَ يُوْعَظُ بِهٖ مَنْ كَانَ مِنْكُمْ
يُؤْمِنُ بِاللّٰهِ وَالْيَوْمِ الْاٰخِرِ ؕ ذٰلِكُمْ اَزْكٰى لَكُمْ وَاَطْهَرُ ؕ وَاللّٰهُ يَعْلَمُ وَ
اَنْتُمْ لَا تَعْلَمُوْنَ ○

"Divorced women shall wait concerning themselves for three monthly periods. Nor is it lawful for them to hide what Allah hath created in their wombs, if they have faith in Allah and the Last Day. And their husbands have the better right to take them back in that period, if they wish for reconciliation. And women shall have rights similar to the rights against them, according to what is equitable; but men have a degree (of advantage) over them. And Allah is Exalted, Wise.

"A divorce is only permissible twice: After that, the parties should either hold together on equitable terms, or separate with kindness. It is not lawful for you (men) to take back any of your gifts (from your wives), except when both parties fear that they would be unable to keep the limits ordained by Allah. If ye (judges) do indeed fear that they would be unable to keep the limits ordained by Allah, there is no blame on either of them if she gives something for her freedom. These are the limits ordained by Allah; so do not transgress them. If any do transgress the limits ordained by Allah, such persons wrong (themselves as well as others).

"So if a husband divorce his wife (irrevocably), he cannot, after that, re-marry her until after she has married another husband and he has divorced her. In that case there is no blame on either of them if they re-unite, provided they feel that they can keep the limits ordained by Allah. Such are the limits ordained by Allah, which He makes plain to those who understand.

"When ye divorce women, and they fulfil their term, either take them back on equitable terms or set them free with kindness; but do not take them back to injure them, or to take undue advantage; if anyone does that, he wrongs his own soul. Do not treat Allah's Signs as a jest, but solemnly rehearse Allah's favours on you, and the fact that He sent down to you the Book and the Wisdom for your instruction. And fear Allah, and know that Allah is well acquainted with all things.

"When ye divorce women, and they fulfil their term, do not prevent them from marrying their (former) husbands, if they mutually agree on equitable terms. This instruction is for all amongst you, who believe in Allah and the Last Day. That is (the course making for) most virtue and purity amongst you. And Allah knows, and ye know not."

(II:228-232).

وَلِلْمُطَلَّقٰتِ مَتَاعٌۢ بِالْمَعْرُوْفِ ؕ حَقًّا عَلَى الْمُتَّقِيْنَ ○

"For divorced women maintenance (should be provided) on a reasonable (scale). This is a duty on the righteous." (II:241).

لَا جُنَاحَ عَلَيْكُمْ اِنْ طَلَّقْتُمُ النِّسَآءَ مَا لَمْ تَمَسُّوْهُنَّ اَوْ تَفْرِضُوْا لَهُنَّ فَرِيْضَةً ۚۖ
وَّمَتِّعُوْهُنَّ ۚ عَلَى الْمُوْسِعِ قَدَرُهٗ وَعَلَى الْمُقْتِرِ قَدَرُهٗ ۚ مَتَاعًاۢ بِالْمَعْرُوْفِ ۚ
حَقًّا عَلَى الْمُحْسِنِيْنَ ○ وَاِنْ طَلَّقْتُمُوْهُنَّ مِنْ قَبْلِ اَنْ تَمَسُّوْهُنَّ وَقَدْ
فَرَضْتُمْ لَهُنَّ فَرِيْضَةً فَنِصْفُ مَا فَرَضْتُمْ اِلَّآ اَنْ يَّعْفُوْنَ اَوْ يَعْفُوَا
الَّذِىْ بِيَدِهٖ عُقْدَةُ النِّكَاحِ ؕ وَاَنْ تَعْفُوْٓا اَقْرَبُ لِلتَّقْوٰى ؕ وَلَا
تَنْسَوُا الْفَضْلَ بَيْنَكُمْ ؕ اِنَّ اللّٰهَ بِمَا تَعْمَلُوْنَ بَصِيْرٌ ○

"There is no blame on you if ye divorce women before consummation or the fixation of their dower; but bestow on them (a suitable gift), the wealthy according to his means, and the poor according to his means;—a gift of a reasonable amount is due from those who wish to do the right thing.

"And if ye divorce them before consummation, but after the fixation of a dower for them, then the half of the dower (is due to them), unless they remit it or the man's half is remitted by him in whose hands is the marriage tie; and the remission (of the man's half) is nearest to righteousness. And do not forget liberality between yourselves. For Allah sees well all that ye do." (II:236, 237).

وَإِنْ أَرَدتُّمُ اسْتِبْدَالَ زَوْجٍ مَّكَانَ زَوْجٍ وَآتَيْتُمْ إِحْدَاهُنَّ قِنطَارًا
فَلَا تَأْخُذُوا مِنْهُ شَيْئًا ۚ أَتَأْخُذُونَهُ بُهْتَانًا وَإِثْمًا مُّبِينًا ○ وَكَيْفَ
تَأْخُذُونَهُ وَقَدْ أَفْضَىٰ بَعْضُكُمْ إِلَىٰ بَعْضٍ وَأَخَذْنَ مِنكُم مِّيثَاقًا غَلِيظًا ○

"But if ye decide to take one wife in place of another, even if ye had given the latter a whole treasure for dower, take not the least bit back: would ye take it by slander and a manifest wrong?

"And how could ye take it when ye have gone in unto each other, and they have taken (from you) a solemn covenant?" (IV:20-21).

وَإِنِ امْرَأَةٌ خَافَتْ مِن بَعْلِهَا نُشُوزًا أَوْ إِعْرَاضًا فَلَا جُنَاحَ عَلَيْهِمَا
أَن يُصْلِحَا بَيْنَهُمَا صُلْحًا ۚ وَالصُّلْحُ خَيْرٌ ۗ وَأُحْضِرَتِ الْأَنفُسُ الشُّحَّ ۚ وَإِن
تُحْسِنُوا وَتَتَّقُوا فَإِنَّ اللَّهَ كَانَ بِمَا تَعْمَلُونَ خَبِيرًا ○ وَلَن تَسْتَطِيعُوا أَن
تَعْدِلُوا بَيْنَ النِّسَاءِ وَلَوْ حَرَصْتُمْ ۖ فَلَا تَمِيلُوا كُلَّ الْمَيْلِ فَتَذَرُوهَا
كَالْمُعَلَّقَةِ ۚ وَإِن تُصْلِحُوا وَتَتَّقُوا فَإِنَّ اللَّهَ كَانَ غَفُورًا رَّحِيمًا ○ وَ
إِن يَتَفَرَّقَا يُغْنِ اللَّهُ كُلًّا مِّن سَعَتِهِ ۚ وَكَانَ اللَّهُ وَاسِعًا حَكِيمًا ○

"If a wife fears cruelty or desertion on her husband's part, there is no blame on them if they arrange an amicable settlement between themselves; and such settlement is best; even though men's souls are swayed by greed. And if ye do good and practise self-restraint, Allah is well acquainted with all that ye do.

"Ye are never able to be fair and just as between women even if it is your ardent desire: But turn not away (from a woman) altogether, so as to leave her (as it were) hanging (in the air).[33] If ye come to a friendly understanding and practise self-restraint, Allah is Oft-Forgiving, Most Merciful.

"If they disagree (and must part), Allah will provide abundance for all from His all-reaching bounty: For Allah careth for all and is Wise." (IV:128-130).

(4) Duties Towards Relatives in General

(*i*) <u>*Duties of Commission*</u> :

The Holy Qur'ãn has enjoined looking after the well-being of one's relatives—sisters, brothers, aunts, uncles, cousins, nieces, nephews, grandparents, grandsons, grand daughters, etc.,—and rendering to them all possible assistance with the purest of motives. In that connection:

(a) It emphasises through conscientiousness in respect of the ties of kinship:

وَاتَّقُوا اللَّهَ الَّذِي تَسَاءَلُونَ بِهِ وَالْأَرْحَامَ

"....and reverence Allah in Whom ye claim (your rights) and (reverence) the wombs (i.e., the ties of kinship)...." (IV:1)

(b) It places the duty of doing good to one's kith and kin immediately next to the duty of doing good to parents—which stands at the highest in the category of social duties—, thus highlighting the great importance of the duty of kith and kin.

---

33. We may refer here also to the customs of *'Ilã* and *Zihãr*, mentioned in the Holy Qur'ãn in II:226 and in XXXIII:4; LVIII:2-4 respectively. They were practised by the pagan Arabs and were repudiated by Islam.

'Ilã is the 'vow of abstinence from one's wife'. "It was a recognised pre-Islamic form of repudiating one's wife and a denial of her rights for a period, definite or indefinite. In Islam the legal effect of such conduct amounts to a single irrevocable divorce". (Abdul Majid Daryabadi, *op.cit.*, p. 71).

Zihãr "was ane evil Arab custom, by which the husband selfishly deprived his wife of her conjugal rights and yet kept her tied to himself like a slave without freeing her to remarry. He pronounced words importing that she was like his mother. After that she could not demand conjugal rights but was not free from his control and could not contract another marriage. See also LVIII:1-5, where this is condemned in the strongest terms and punishment is provided for it. A man sometimes said such words in a fit of anger: they did not affect him, but they degraded her position." (A. Yusuf Ali, *op.cit.*, p. 1103).

وَبِالْوَالِدَيْنِ إِحْسَانًا وَبِذِي الْقُرْبَىٰ

".....and do good to parents and to the kinsfolk...." (IV:36).

(c) It makes economic assistance to the kinsfolk, with the noblest motive, one of the basic ingredients of practical piety:

وَآتَى الْمَالَ عَلَىٰ حُبِّهِ ذَوِي الْقُرْبَىٰ

"....(it is true righteousness) to spend of your substance, out of love for Him (i.e., God), for your kith and kin....." (II:177).

(d) And not only that. Doing good to one's relatives and assisting them in their needs, is not just an optional act of goodness but an unavoidable duty; because the relatives have a definite *right* whose fulfilment a Muslim owes to them:

فَآتِ ذَا الْقُرْبَىٰ حَقَّهُ

"So give what is due to kindred[34]...." (XXX:38).

Again:

إِنَّ اللَّهَ يَأْمُرُ بِالْعَدْلِ وَالْإِحْسَانِ وَإِيتَاءِ ذِي الْقُرْبَىٰ

"Verily Allah enjoineth justice, the doing of good (to others in general), and giving to kinsfolk (their due)....." (XVI:90).

Thus: *Duties of Commission* towards the kinsfolk may be broadly classified into:

(a) Maintaining cordial relations with them, and cultivating love for them;

(b) Rendering economic assistance to them, whenever necessary;

(c) Doing good to them in every other way.

(*ii*) Duty of Omission:

The Holy Qur'ãn condemns in strong terms the damaging of the ties of relationship with one's kith and kin; hence to abstain from it is duty:

34. Cf. Similar command in XVII:26.

الْفَٰسِقِينَ ۝ الَّذِينَ يَنقُضُونَ عَهْدَ اللَّهِ مِن بَعْدِ مِيثَٰقِهِۦ وَيَقْطَعُونَ مَآ أَمَرَ اللَّهُ
بِهِۦٓ أَن يُوصَلَ وَيُفْسِدُونَ فِي الْأَرْضِ ۚ أُو۟لَٰٓئِكَ هُمُ الْخَٰسِرُونَ ۝

"....The transgressors, who break the Covenant of Allah after ratifying it, and sever that which Allah ordered to be joined (i.e., damage the relationship with, the violate the duties they owe to, among others, the kinsfolk), and act corruptly on the earth, these are they who are the losers."[35] (II:26, 27).

(5) Duties Towards Domestic Servants

The Qur'ãnic doctrine of love for God and man is so thorough and comprehensive in its scope that it transforms the formal, and often temporary, relationship of "give and take" between the employer and the servant into a relationship of liberality and love, giving to the domestic servant virtually the role of a part and parcel of the family.[36] In any case the Holy Qur'ãn has made it a duty for every Muslim to do good to all those who are under his control and in subjection to him, including the domestic servants,—and to treat it as one of his basic duties:

وَبِالْوَٰلِدَيْنِ إِحْسَٰنًا . . . وَمَا مَلَكَتْ أَيْمَٰنُكُمْ ۗ

"....and do good to parents....and to those whom your right hands possess (i.e., those who are subject to your authority)...." (IV:36).

---

35. Ref. also: XIII:25.

36. This aspect of relationship has been explicitly propounded by the Holy Prophet (Peace be upon him). He says in connection with the prisoners of war, who, so long as they do not obtain their freedom, are to be distributed in Muslim families to serve them and who stand below the ordinary free domestic servants and, as enemies, hardly deserve any privilege according to the canons of pre-Qur'ãnic laws and, for all practical purposes, of the post-Qur'ãic laws:

"....Whoever has his brother (human being) under him, he should feed him with the food that he himself eats, and clothe him with such clothing as he himself wears. And do not impose upon him a duty which is beyond his power to perform; if, however, you command them to do what they are unable to do, assist them in that affair." (Bukhãrî: *Sahîh*, vol. II, *Kitãb al-Adãb*).

Chapter II

DUTIES IN RESPECT OF AGE AND RANK

The Holy Qur'ãn says:

وَهُوَ الَّذِي جَعَلَكُمْ خَلَٰٓئِفَ الْأَرْضِ وَرَفَعَ بَعْضَكُمْ فَوْقَ بَعْضٍ دَرَجَٰتٍ
لِّيَبْلُوَكُمْ فِي مَآ ءَاتَىٰكُمْ ۗ إِنَّ رَبَّكَ سَرِيعُ الْعِقَابِ وَإِنَّهُۥ لَغَفُورٌ
رَّحِيمٌ ۝

"He it is Who hath placed you as vicegerents on the earth and hath raised some of you above others in degrees that He may try you by (the test of) that (position and rank) which He hath given you. Lo! thy Lord is swift in prosecution: yet He is Oft-Forgiving, Most Merciful."
(VI:165).

This verse refers to the fact that there have always existed and will always exist gradations in human society in respect of seniority and superiority, giving rise to:

(i) Seniors in age, on the one hand, and juniors in age, on the other;

(ii) Superiors in talents and accomplishments (with respect to piety, knowledge, etc.,), on the one hand, and those inferior to them, on the other;

(iii) Employers and officers, on the one hand, and the employees and the subordinates, on the other.

This social phenomenon has, however, a moral implication according to this verse, as is clearly affirmed by the words: "that He may try you by (the test of) that (position and rank) which He hath given you". This trial consists in the proper and improper moral behaviour in the situations contained in this phenomenon.

There are two attitudes which seem to be ingrained in every healthy and balanced human personality—as is evident from a study of classical morally elevated human personalities in history, to whom the Holy Qur'ãn refers—the attitudes, namely, of:

(i) Respect for everyone who excels in anything of life as compared to one's self; and

(ii) compassionate kindness towards everyone who is deficient in anything of life.

In this respect, the Holy Qur'ãn has commanded its followers to behave in requisite goodness and beauty towards fellow-beings (XVI:90). Moreover, it has enjoined respect for one's parents (XVII:23), on the one hand, and compassionate kindness as a general rule of life, on the other. (XC:17).

Thus, the duty towards those who are one's senior in age, or superior in talents or accomplishments, or one's employers or officers, would be that of showing respect to them; while the duty to those who are one's juniors in age, or inferior to him in talents or accomplishments, or they are one's employees of subordinates, would be that of compassionate kindness.

We find these duties specified in the following words in the Holy Prophet's exposition of the Qur'ãnic Teaching:

ليس منّا من لم يرحم صغيرنا ولم يوقّر كبيرنا

"Whoever does not show compassionate kindness to him who is small (as compared to him in age or rank), or does not observe respect towards him who is big (as compared to him in age or rank), is not one of us (i.e., is not a Muslim)." (Tirmizi: *Jãme*', vol. II, p. 14).

Chapter III

DUTIES TO PARTICULAR CATEGORIES OF NON-RELATIVES

---

(1) Duty towards Neighbours.

(2) Duty towards Friends and Associates.

(3) Duties towards Orphans.

(4) Duties towards Widows.

(5) Duties towards the Needy and the Destitute.

(6) Duties towards Guests and Wayfarers.

(7) Duties towards Slaves.

---

(1) Duty Towards Neighbours

Concerning one's neighbours, the Holy Qur'ãn has classified them into two categories, namely:

(a) *Neighbours who are near*. Nearness includes here nearness in residence as well as nearness in relationship,—the relationship may be of any sort: family ties, religion, etc. Those who enjoy nearness in both ways have a double right on a Muslim.

(b) *Neighbours who are strangers*, i.e., those with whom we have no relationship, and those who reside at some distance from us, and those who belong to a different religion. Their rights would be naturally less than the rights of category (a).

For all of them, *the comprehensive duty of doing good has been enjoined,* as the following verse says:

وَاعْبُدُوا اللّٰهَ وَلَا تُشْرِكُوْا بِهٖ شَيْـًٔا وَّبِالْوَالِدَيْنِ اِحْسَانًا وَّبِذِى الْقُرْبٰى
وَالْيَتٰمٰى وَالْمَسٰكِيْنِ وَالْجَارِ ذِى الْقُرْبٰى وَالْجَارِ الْجُنُبِ وَالصَّاحِبِ
بِالْجَنْۢبِ وَابْنِ السَّبِيْلِ ۙ وَمَا مَلَكَتْ اَيْمَانُكُمْ ۗ اِنَّ اللّٰهَ لَا يُحِبُّ مَنْ
كَانَ مُخْتَالًا فَخُوْرًا ۙ

"Serve Allah, and join not equals with Him; and do good—to parents, kinsfolk, orphans, those in need, *neighbours who are near, neighbours who are strangers,* the companion by your side, the wayfarer (ye meet), and what your right hands possess: for Allah loveth not the arrogant, the vainglorious;...." (IV:36)[1]

(2) Duty Towards Friends and Associates

Doing good to friends and associates enjoined:

The verse quoted in connection with 'duty to neighbours' (IV:36) speaks of the 'companion by your side' and *enjoins the duty of doing good to him.*

The words 'companion by your side' mean:

(a) a close friend, and

(b) he with whom one may be associated in any sphere of activity, *e.g.,* a fellow-worker.

(3) Duties Towards Orphans

The Holy Qur'ãn assigns an important place in its system of duties to the doing of good to orphans, so much so that caring for the orphans has assumed the form of a sacred institution in Islam—and that for the first time in the known history of mankind.

The holy book divides the orphans into two categories, namely, (1) those who are destitute; and (2) those who inherit means of subsistence and are under one's care; and it condemns the malpractices of the people in respect of both, and lays down duties of omission and commission with regard to both.

I. Duties Relating to those Orphans who are Destitute and to Orphans in General:

---

1. In respect of this duty, the Holy Prophet (Peace be on him) has given the following stern warning:-

لا يؤمن عبدٌ حتى يحب لجاره ما يحب لنفسه

"None of you will be (counted) a Believer unless he loves for his neighbour what he loves for himself." (Tirmizi: *Jãme'*, vol. II, p. 16).

(a) *Duty of Omission:*

Treating the orphan with harshness prohibited:

فَأَمَّا الْيَتِيمَ فَلَا تَقْهَرْ ۝

"Therefore, treat not the orphan with harshness." (XCIII:9).

Because, treating the orphans with harshness should be possible only for him who belies religion and not for a believer in Divine Guidance:

أَرَأَيْتَ الَّذِي يُكَذِّبُ بِالدِّينِ ۝ فَذَٰلِكَ الَّذِي يَدُعُّ الْيَتِيمَ ۝

"Hast thou observed him who belieth religion? That is he who repelleth the orphan (with harshness)." (CVII:1, 2).

(b) *Duties of Commission:*

(i) Doing good to the orphan in every way, enjoined:

وَاعْبُدُوا اللَّهَ وَلَا تُشْرِكُوا بِهِ شَيْئًا وَبِالْوَالِدَيْنِ إِحْسَانًا وَبِذِي الْقُرْبَىٰ
وَالْيَتَامَىٰ

"Serve Allah, and join not equals with Him; and do good—to parents, kinsfolk, *orphans*...." (IV:36).[2]

(ii) Spending one's wealth with the highest motive for the welfare of the orphans emphasised as an act of true righteousness and as one of the acid tests of one's Faith; hence its observance is duty:

لَيْسَ الْبِرَّ أَنْ تُوَلُّوا وُجُوهَكُمْ قِبَلَ الْمَشْرِقِ وَالْمَغْرِبِ وَلَٰكِنَّ الْبِرَّ مَنْ
آمَنَ بِاللَّهِ وَالْيَوْمِ الْآخِرِ وَالْمَلَائِكَةِ وَالْكِتَابِ وَالنَّبِيِّينَ وَآتَى الْمَالَ عَلَىٰ
حُبِّهِ ذَوِي الْقُرْبَىٰ وَالْيَتَامَىٰ

"It is not righteousness that ye turn your faces towards East or West; But it is righteousness—to believe in Allah and the Last Day, and the Angels, and the Book, and the Messengers; to spend of your substance, out of love for Him, for your kin, *for orphans*...." (II:177).

---

2. Cf. II:83; II:215.

(iii) *The difficult path of duty which brings the highest rewards from God emphasised, among other things, in terms of feeding the orphans in times of distress:*

وَمَا أَدْرَاكَ مَا الْعَقَبَةُ ۝ فَكُّ رَقَبَةٍ ۝ أَوْ إِطْعَامٌ فِي يَوْمٍ ذِي
مَسْغَبَةٍ ۝ يَتِيمًا ذَا مَقْرَبَةٍ ۝ أَوْ مِسْكِينًا ذَا مَتْرَبَةٍ ۝

"Ah, what will convey unto thee what the Ascent is: —(it is) to free a slave, and *to feed in a day of privation an orphan near of kin*, or some poor wretch in misery." (XC:12-16).[3]

It may be noted here that, besides the 'orphan near of kin' who has naturally a special claim, orphans in general are included in the category of 'some poor wretch in misery'

(iv) *To set aside a portion of one's wealth for the benefit of orphans when inheritance is divided, enjoined:*

وَإِذَا حَضَرَ الْقِسْمَةَ أُولُوا الْقُرْبَىٰ وَالْيَتَامَىٰ وَالْمَسَاكِينُ فَارْزُقُوهُم مِّنْهُ
وَقُولُوا لَهُمْ قَوْلًا مَّعْرُوفًا ۝

"But if, at the time of division, other relatives, or orphans, or the poor are present, give them something also, and speak to them words of kindness and justice." (IV:8).

(v) *Besides voluntary help from the Muslims, making the orphans beneficiaries in the spoils of war and in enemy property acquired otherwise by the Islamic State, enjoined:*

وَاعْلَمُوا أَنَّمَا غَنِمْتُم مِّن شَيْءٍ فَأَنَّ لِلَّهِ خُمُسَهُ وَلِلرَّسُولِ وَلِذِي الْقُرْبَىٰ وَالْيَتَامَىٰ
وَالْمَسَاكِينِ وَابْنِ السَّبِيلِ إِن كُنتُمْ آمَنتُم بِاللَّهِ وَمَا أَنزَلْنَا عَلَىٰ عَبْدِنَا يَوْمَ
الْفُرْقَانِ يَوْمَ الْتَقَى الْجَمْعَانِ ۗ وَاللَّهُ عَلَىٰ كُلِّ شَيْءٍ قَدِيرٌ ۝

"And know that of all the booty that ye may acquire (in war), a fifth share is assigned to Allah,—and to the Messenger, and to near relatives, (and to) the orphans, the needy, and the wayfarer,—if ye do

---

3. Cf. LXXVI:8.

believe in Allah and in the revelation We sent down to Our Servant on the Day of Testing,—the Day of the meeting of the two forces; for Allah hath power over all things." (VIII:41).

مَآ أَفَآءَ اللّٰهُ عَلٰى رَسُوْلِهٖ مِنْ أَهْلِ الْقُرٰى فَلِلّٰهِ وَلِلرَّسُوْلِ وَلِذِى الْقُرْبٰى وَ
الْيَتٰمٰى وَالْمَسٰكِيْنِ وَابْنِ السَّبِيْلِ كَىْ لَا يَكُوْنَ دُوْلَةً بَيْنَ الْأَغْنِيَآءِ مِنْكُمْ ؕ
وَمَآ اٰتٰكُمُ الرَّسُوْلُ فَخُذُوْهُ وَمَا نَهٰكُمْ عَنْهُ فَانْتَهُوْا ۚ وَاتَّقُوا اللّٰهَ ؕ إِنَّ
اللّٰهَ شَدِيْدُ الْعِقَابِ ۝

"What Allah has bestowed on His Messenger (and taken away) from the people of the townships,—belongs to Allah,—to His Messenger and to kindred and orphans, the needy and the wayfarer; in order that it may not (merely) make a circuit between the wealthy among you. So take what the Messenger assigns to you, and deny yourselves that which he withholds from you. And fear Allah; for Allah is strict in Punishment." (LIX:7).

2. Duties Relating to those Orphans who Inherit Means of Subsistence and are under one's Care:

(a) *Duties of Omission:*

To start with: the Holy Qur'ãn condemns very strongly the practice of the pagan Arabs who used to misappropriate the helpless orphan's inheritance.

Taking up the problem of the orphans who may come under a Muslim's care, and for whose property he may be the custodian, *the holy book prohibits all such acts whereby even the slightest injustice may accrue to an orphan—and that in the following terms:*

(i) *It enjoins abstinence from interfering with—nay, even coming near—the orphan's property except when it becomes necessary in the interest of the latter's welfare*:

وَلَا تَقْرَبُوْا مَالَ الْيَتِيْمِ إِلَّا بِالَّتِىْ هِىَ أَحْسَنُ حَتّٰى يَبْلُغَ أَشُدَّهٗ ۪ وَأَوْفُوْا بِالْعَهْدِ ۚ إِنَّ
الْعَهْدَ كَانَ مَسْئُوْلًا ۝

"Come not nigh to the orphan's property except to improve it, until he attains the age of full strength; and fulfil (every) engagement, for (every) engagement will be enquired into (on the Day of Reckoning)." (XVII:34).

إِنَّ الَّذِينَ يَأْكُلُونَ أَمْوَالَ الْيَتٰمٰى ظُلْمًا إِنَّمَا يَأْكُلُونَ فِي بُطُونِهِمْ نَارًا ۖ
وَسَيَصْلَوْنَ سَعِيرًا ۝

"Those who unjustly eat up the property of orphans, eat up a Fire into their own bellies: they will soon be enduring a blazing Fire!" (IV:10).

(ii) *It enjoins abstinence from employing deceptive measures for misappropriating the orphans's property*:

وَاٰتُوا الْيَتٰمٰى أَمْوَالَهُمْ وَلَا تَتَبَدَّلُوا الْخَبِيثَ بِالطَّيِّبِ ۖ وَلَا تَأْكُلُوا أَمْوَالَهُمْ
إِلَىٰ أَمْوَالِكُمْ ۚ إِنَّهُ كَانَ حُوبًا كَبِيرًا ۝

"To orphans restore their property (when they reach their age), and do not substitute (your) worthless things for (their) good ones; and devour not their substance (by mixing it up) with your own. For this is indeed a great sin." (IV:2).

(iii) *It enjoins abstinence from marrying the orphan-girls with the motive of exploiting their wealth thereby*:

وَإِنْ خِفْتُمْ أَلَّا تُقْسِطُوا فِي الْيَتٰمٰى فَانْكِحُوا مَا طَابَ لَكُمْ مِنَ النِّسَاءِ مَثْنٰى
وَثُلٰثَ وَرُبٰعَ ۖ فَإِنْ خِفْتُمْ أَلَّا تَعْدِلُوا فَوَاحِدَةً أَوْ مَا مَلَكَتْ أَيْمَانُكُمْ ۚ ذٰلِكَ
أَدْنٰى أَلَّا تَعُولُوا ۝

And if ye apprehend that ye may not deal justly with the orphan-girls, then marry such as please you, of other women, by twos and threes or fours, but if ye apprehend that ye shall not act justly, then marry one only, or that which your right hands own, that will be more suitable that ye may swerve not." (IV:3)[4]

(iv) *It enjoins abstinence from wasteful spending of the orphan's property out of dishonest selfish consideration*:

4. This verse embraces two implications. One of them has been mentioned in connection with "polygamy". The other one has been given here.

وَلَا تَأْكُلُوهَا إِسْرَافًا وَبِدَارًا أَنْ يَكْبَرُوا ۚ

".....And consume it not wastefully, not in haste against their growing up...." (IV:6).

(v) *It enjoins abstinence from carelessness in safeguarding the interests of the orphans in respect of restoration of the orphan's property to them*:

وَلَا تُؤْتُوا السُّفَهَاءَ أَمْوَالَكُمُ الَّتِي جَعَلَ اللَّهُ لَكُمْ قِيَامًا وَارْزُقُوهُمْ فِيهَا
وَاكْسُوهُمْ وَقُولُوا لَهُمْ قَوْلًا مَعْرُوفًا ۝

"And give not unto the weak of understanding (what is in) your (keeping of their) wealth, which Allah hath given you to maintain, but feed and clothe them out of it, and speak to them words of kindness and justice." (IV:5).

(vi) *Finally, it makes a touching appeal and registers a stern warning in these words*:

وَلْيَخْشَ الَّذِينَ لَوْ تَرَكُوا مِنْ خَلْفِهِمْ ذُرِّيَّةً ضِعَافًا خَافُوا عَلَيْهِمْ فَلْيَتَّقُوا اللَّهَ
وَلْيَقُولُوا قَوْلًا سَدِيدًا ۝ إِنَّ الَّذِينَ يَأْكُلُونَ أَمْوَالَ الْيَتَامَىٰ ظُلْمًا إِنَّمَا
يَأْكُلُونَ فِي بُطُونِهِمْ نَارًا ۖ وَسَيَصْلَوْنَ سَعِيرًا ۝

"Let those (disposing of an estate) have the same fear in their minds as they would have for their own if they had left a helpless family behind: Let them fear Allah, and speak words of appropriate (comfort). Those who unjustly eat up the property of orphans, eat up a Fire into their bellies; they will soon be enduring a blazing Fire!" (IV.9, 10).

(b) *<u>Duties of Commission</u>*:

(i) Loving care for, and conscientious service to, the orphans living under one's guardianship, and honest protection of their property, with permission for reasonable remuneration to the manager of orphan's property, in case of his poverty, enjoined:

وَابْتَلُوا الْيَتٰمٰى حَتّٰى إِذَا بَلَغُوا النِّكَاحَ ۚ فَإِنْ اٰنَسْتُمْ مِّنْهُمْ رُشْدًا فَادْفَعُوْٓا إِلَيْهِمْ
أَمْوَالَهُمْ ۚ وَلَا تَأْكُلُوْهَآ إِسْرَافًا وَّبِدَارًا أَنْ يَّكْبَرُوْا ۚ وَمَنْ كَانَ غَنِيًّا
فَلْيَسْتَعْفِفْ ۚ وَمَنْ كَانَ فَقِيْرًا فَلْيَأْكُلْ بِالْمَعْرُوْفِ ۚ فَإِذَا دَفَعْتُمْ إِلَيْهِمْ
أَمْوَالَهُمْ فَأَشْهِدُوْا عَلَيْهِمْ ۚ وَكَفٰى بِاللّٰهِ حَسِيْبًا ۝

"And test the orphans (in respect of their capacity to handle their affairs independently) until they reach the marriageable age (i.e., age of majority)[5]; then if ye find them of sound judgment, hand over unto them their property; and consume it not wastefully, nor in haste against their growing up. If the guardian is well off, let him claim no remuneration (for service to an orphan). But if he is poor, let him have for himself (as remuneration) what is just and equitable. When ye release their property to them, take witness in their presence. But all-sufficient is Allah in taking account." (IV:6).

(ii) Co-partnership with the orphans, for better management of their property and their affairs, permitted:

وَيَسْـَٔلُوْنَكَ عَنِ الْيَتٰمٰى ۚ قُلْ إِصْلَاحٌ لَّهُمْ خَيْرٌ ۚ وَإِنْ تُخَالِطُوْهُمْ فَإِخْوَانُكُمْ ۚ وَ
اللّٰهُ يَعْلَمُ الْمُفْسِدَ مِنَ الْمُصْلِحِ ۚ وَلَوْ شَآءَ اللّٰهُ لَأَعْنَتَكُمْ ۚ إِنَّ اللّٰهَ عَزِيْزٌ
حَكِيْمٌ ۝

"They ask thee concerning the orphans. Say: The best thing to do is what is for their good: if ye mix their (financial) affairs with yours (as co-partners), they are your brethren (and as such entitled to all generosity and love). But Allah knoweth the man who means mischief from the man who means good. An if Allah had wished, He could have put you into difficulties: He is indeed Exalted, Wise." (II:220).

(iii) The principle of the Court of Wards for protecting people of "weak understanding", including minor orphans, through the institution of guardianship, laid

---

5. According to the Hanafi school of Islamic Law, the age of majority is 18 years for boys and 17 years for girls. (See: Mustafā Ahmad al-Zarqā: *al-Madkhal al-Fiqhī al-'Ām*, vol. II, p. 779).

down. Also, permission given to invest the capital of the orphans in trade with a view to benefit them:

وَلَا تُؤْتُوا السُّفَهَاءَ أَمْوَالَكُمُ الَّتِي جَعَلَ اللَّهُ لَكُمْ قِيَامًا وَارْزُقُوهُمْ فِيهَا
وَاكْسُوهُمْ وَقُولُوا لَهُمْ قَوْلًا مَعْرُوفًا ۝

"Give not unto the weak of understanding (what is in) your (keeping of their) wealth[6], which Allah hath given you to maintain; but feed and clothe them out of (the profits of) it[7], and speak to them words of kindness and justice". (IV:5).

(iv) Finally, the Holy Qur'ãn enjoins absolute justice in all respects towards the orphans:

وَيَسْتَفْتُونَكَ فِي النِّسَاءِ ۖ قُلِ اللَّهُ يُفْتِيكُمْ فِيهِنَّ وَمَا يُتْلَىٰ عَلَيْكُمْ فِي
الْكِتَابِ فِي يَتَامَى النِّسَاءِ اللَّاتِي لَا تُؤْتُونَهُنَّ مَا كُتِبَ لَهُنَّ وَتَرْغَبُونَ أَنْ
تَنْكِحُوهُنَّ وَالْمُسْتَضْعَفِينَ مِنَ الْوِلْدَانِ وَأَنْ تَقُومُوا لِلْيَتَامَىٰ بِالْقِسْطِ ۚ
وَمَا تَفْعَلُوا مِنْ خَيْرٍ فَإِنَّ اللَّهَ كَانَ بِهِ عَلِيمًا ۝

"They ask thee concerning the Women. Say: Allah doth instruct you about them: and (remember) what hath been rehearsed unto you in the Book, concerning (justice to) the orphans of women to whom ye give not the portions prescribed, and yet whom ye desire to marry, as also concerning the children who are weak and oppressed: that ye shall stand firm for justice to orphans. There is not a good deed which ye do, but Allah is well acquainted therewith." (IV:127).

(4) Duties Towards Widows

Basic Observations:

The position of the widows had been miserable even in certain advanced and civilised communities of the world before the advent of the

---

6. Here the verse lays down the rule of guardianship for all those owners of property who are weak of understanding, thereby establishing the institution of Court of Wards.

7. According to the Qur'ãnic commentary, *Bahr al-Muhît*, it means: "Make it a means of maintaining them so that you invest it in trade and earn profit, and so that you may be able to meet their expenses from the profit and not from the capital". (Vol. III, p. 179).

Holy Qur'ãn. Among the Jews and Christians, they enjoyed no prerogatives, because of the Biblical dogma which affirms woman's responsibility for the Oriential Sin[8], so much so that she could not even benefit from her husband's wealth as an inheritor[9]. Among the Hindus, it was not considered appropriate for her even to remain alive,—it being a virtue for the widow to burn herself alive in the funeral pyre of the husband; and, even when she chose to abstain from suicide, it was her most sacred duty to regard all her remaining life as a period of mourning and to pass it, therefore, in wretchedness and misery—as a mark of devotion to her deceased husband: remarriage being considered a heinous crime. This was so, because "widowhood, according to Hindu doctrine is the penalty incurred for the sins committed in a previous incarnation, entailing hopeless drudgery for the rest of life."[10] In the Greco-Roman culture, "the dying husband could leave her by will to a friend, with his goods and by the same title."[11]

As regards the pagan Arabs themselves, who were the first addressees of the Holy Qur'ãn: "The widows....were regarded as part of the estate, and as such passed ordinarily into the hands of their husband's heirs."[12]

Of course, the widow's right to property was unthinkable in any community of the world, because "women appear to have been *universally and in every respect* regarded as minors so far as rights of property went....Only sons, not daughters, still less wives, can inherit."[13]

It was in this background that the Holy Qur'ãn introduced the following thoroughgoing reforms in respect of the widows, and made it an obligation on the Muslims to practise them:

(i) *The period of mourning has been restricted to four mounts and ten days.* It has been actually called 'period

---

8. According to Lecky, the havoc that this dogma created for a woman among the Jews and Christians was that "woman was represented as the door of hell, as the mother of all human ills. She should be ashamed at the very thought that she is a woman." (*History of European Morals*, II, p. 142).

9. Letourneau: *Evolution of Marriage*, p. 261.

10. Hammerton's *Encyclopaedia of Modern Knowledge*, IV, p. 1927.

11. Letourneau: *Evolution of Marriage*, p. 261.

12. Roberts: *Social Laws of the Qur'ãn*, pp. 62, 63.

13. Cheyne and Black's *Encyclopaedia Biblica*, cc. 2724, 2728.

of waiting', and, as such, it is not a period for imposing wretchedness and misery on the widow but a period prescribed in the interest of her biological preparation for re-marriage and in the interest of finding out if she is with an unborn child by her deceased husband,—all this being for the promotion of human welfare.

The Holy Qur'ãn says:

وَالَّذِيْنَ يُتَوَفَّوْنَ مِنْكُمْ وَيَذَرُوْنَ اَزْوَاجًا يَّتَرَبَّصْنَ بِاَنْفُسِهِنَّ
اَرْبَعَةَ اَشْهُرٍ وَّعَشْرًا ۚ فَاِذَا بَلَغْنَ اَجَلَهُنَّ فَلَا جُنَاحَ عَلَيْكُمْ فِيْمَا فَعَلْنَ
فِيْٓ اَنْفُسِهِنَّ بِالْمَعْرُوْفِ ۗ وَاللّٰهُ بِمَا تَعْمَلُوْنَ خَبِيْرٌ ۝

"If any of you die and leave widows behind, they (the widows) shall wait, keeping themselves apart (i.e., in restricted social intercourse), four months and ten days. Then when they have fulfilled their (prescribed) terms, there is no blame on you if they (as independent dispensers of their future) dispose of themselves in a just and reasonable manner (in the enjoyment of social life and in connection with their re-marriage)[14]. And Allah is well acquainted with what ye do." (II:234).

(ii) *In case the dower-money has not been already paid by the husband, or has not been written off by the wife, it shall be treated as debt and shall be paid to the wife after the death of her husband before any share is delivered to any inheritor,—this, according to the Qur'ãnic law:*

مِنْۢ بَعْدِ وَصِيَّةٍ يُّوْصِىْ بِهَآ اَوْ دَيْنٍ ۗ

"....(The distribution of inheritance in all cases is) after the payment of legacies and debts...." (IV:11).

---

14. In case it is proved that there is unborn issue, a widow will not re-marry until it is born and for a reasonable time thereafter—in which case, the terms may be more or less than four months and ten days; and during the entire period her maintenance is the liability of her late husband and shall be chargeable to whatever assets he leaves behind. (See: *al-Hedãya*, Vol. II, pp. 33, 34., Egyptian edition).

(iii) The widow shall receive her fixed share in inheritance from her husband's estate, according to circumstances:

وَلَهُنَّ الرُّبُعُ مِمَّا تَرَكْتُمْ إِنْ لَمْ يَكُنْ لَكُمْ وَلَدٌ ۚ فَإِنْ كَانَ لَكُمْ وَلَدٌ
فَلَهُنَّ الثُّمُنُ مِمَّا تَرَكْتُمْ ۚ مِنْ بَعْدِ وَصِيَّةٍ تُوصُونَ بِهَا أَوْ دَيْنٍ ۗ

"....In what ye leave, their (i.e., the wives') share is a fourth, if ye leave no child; but if ye leave a child, they get an eighth; after payment of legacies and debts...." (IV:12).

(iv) Re-marriage of widows has been strongly advocated for providing them enjoyment of fullness of life:

The Holy Qur'ãn says:

وَأَنْكِحُوا الْأَيَامَىٰ مِنْكُمْ

"(O Muslims!) Wed those among you who are single (i.e., those who are not already in the bond of wedlock, whether they are unmarried, or lawfully divorced, or widowed)[15]." (XXIV:32).

(v) Abstinence from treating the widow as a chattel, enjoined:

يَا أَيُّهَا الَّذِينَ آمَنُوا لَا يَحِلُّ لَكُمْ أَنْ تَرِثُوا النِّسَاءَ كَرْهًا ۖ

"O ye who believe! It is not lawful for you forcibly to inherit the women (of your deceased kinsmen)...." (IV:19).

(a) Duties of Commission:

Among the above injunctions, numbers (i), (ii), (iii) and (iv) relate serially to the following *three duties of commission:*

(1) *Duty of permitting a period of consolation and readjustment to the widow:*

(2) *Duty of strengthening the widow financially;*

(3) *Duty of encouraging the widow to re-enjoy fullness of life through suitable re-marriage, in case she desires it and consider it conducive to her over-all welfare.*

---

15. See for this denotation of the Arabic word for 'single': Rãghib Isfahãnî *Mufradãt al-Qur'ãn*, p. 31; and *'Alûsî's Rûh al-Ma'ãnî*. Vol. VI, p. 147.

(b) <u>*Duty of Omission*</u>:

Injunction (v), on the other hand, relates to the *duty of omission—the duty, namely, of abstaining from damaging her personality and her human dignity.*

Indeed, according to the Qur'ãnic teaching, a widow possesses a free and independent personality, and anyone who subjects her to humiliation or loss is a sinner.

(5) Duties Towards the Destitute and the Needy

As we have already noticed in the sections on "duties to self" and "duties to others—I (general)", the Holy Qur'ãn lays great emphasis on the cultivation of fellow-felling and maximum assistance to fellow-beings for ensuring their welfare and happiness in all respects, and it regards the economic welfare of the people as a thing of vital import. Here we may take note of such Qur'ãnic statements and injunctions as deal with the service of fellow-beings with specific reference to the destitute and the needy,—statements and injunctions which relate not only to economic assistance but to help in all possible respects.

(a) <u>*Duties of Commission*</u>:

(i) *Food being the most primary and most basic physical need of a human being, feeding the indigent has been classed as one of the outstanding virtues; hence it is duty:*

وَيُطْعِمُونَ الطَّعَامَ عَلَىٰ حُبِّهِ مِسْكِينًا وَيَتِيمًا وَأَسِيرًا ۝ إِنَّمَا نُطْعِمُكُمْ لِوَجْهِ
اللَّهِ لَا نُرِيدُ مِنكُمْ جَزَاءً وَلَا شُكُورًا ۝

"(As to the righteous)....they feed, for the love of Allah, *the indigent*, the orphan, and the captive,—(saying), 'We feed you for the sake of Allah alone: no reward do we desire from you, nor thanks'."
(LXXVI:8-9).

وَمَا أَدْرَاكَ مَا الْعَقَبَةُ ۝ فَكُّ رَقَبَةٍ ۝ أَوْ إِطْعَامٌ فِي يَوْمٍ ذِي
مَسْغَبَةٍ ۝ يَتِيمًا ذَا مَقْرَبَةٍ ۝ أَوْ مِسْكِينًا ذَا مَتْرَبَةٍ ۝

"And what will explain to thee the path that is steep?—(It is) freeing the bondman; or the giving of food in a day of privation to the orphan with claims of relationship, or *to the indigent* (*down*) *in the dust.*" (XC:12-16).

(2)(i) Again, not only feeding those who need it, but all economic assistance to the economically distressed people has been enjoined as the duty of a Muslim, emphasising that it is the fulfilment of a right:

فَاٰتِ ذَا الْقُرْبٰى حَقَّهٗ وَالْمِسْكِيْنَ وَابْنَ السَّبِيْلِ ؕ ذٰلِكَ خَيْرٌ لِّلَّذِيْنَ
يُرِيْدُوْنَ وَجْهَ اللّٰهِ ؗ وَاُولٰٓئِكَ هُمُ الْمُفْلِحُوْنَ ○

"So give what is due to kindred, the *needy*, and the wayfarer. That is best for those who seek the Countenance of Allah, and it is they who will prosper." (XXX:38).

وَفِيْٓ اَمْوَالِهِمْ حَقٌّ لِّلسَّآئِلِ وَالْمَحْرُوْمِ ○

"And in their wealth and possessions (was remembered) the right of the (*needy*), him who asked, and him who (for some reason) was prevented (from asking)." (LI:19).[16]

(ii) Continuing economic assistance to a needy person, even though he gives cause for personal anger through some misbehaviour, enjoined:

وَلَا يَاْتَلِ اُولُوا الْفَضْلِ مِنْكُمْ وَالسَّعَةِ اَنْ يُّؤْتُوْٓا اُولِي الْقُرْبٰى وَالْمَسٰكِيْنَ
وَالْمُهٰجِرِيْنَ فِيْ سَبِيْلِ اللّٰهِ ۪ۖ وَلْيَعْفُوْا وَلْيَصْفَحُوْا ؕ اَلَا تُحِبُّوْنَ اَنْ يَّغْفِرَ
اللّٰهُ لَكُمْ ؕ وَاللّٰهُ غَفُوْرٌ رَّحِيْمٌ ○

"Let not those among you who are endued with grace and amplitude of means resolve by oath against helping their kinsmen, *those in want*, and those who have left their homes in Allah's cause: let them forgive and overlook; do you not wish that Allah should forgive you? For Allah is Oft-Forgiving, Most Merciful." (XXIV:22).

(iii) Kind treatment of the needy person, in case of one's inability in rendering economic assistance, enjoined:

وَاِمَّا تُعْرِضَنَّ عَنْهُمُ ابْتِغَآءَ رَحْمَةٍ مِّنْ رَّبِّكَ تَرْجُوْهَا فَقُلْ لَّهُمْ قَوْلًا مَّيْسُوْرًا ○

---

16. Cf. XVII:26; II:177; II:215; IV;8,

"And even if thou hast to turn away from them in pursuit of the Mercy of thy Lord which thou dost expect, yet speak to them a word of easy kindness." (XVII:28).

(3) The above refers to economic assistance by individuals. The Holy Qur'ãn takes care, however, to make it also *a collective obligation of the Muslims to provide for the economic needs of the economically distressed people out of compulsory charitable taxes:*

وَالَّذِيْنَ فِيْٓ اَمْوَالِهِمْ حَقٌّ مَّعْلُوْمٌ ۝ لِّلسَّآئِلِ وَالْمَحْرُوْمِ ۝

"...and those in whose wealth is a *recognized right for the* (*needy*) who asks and him who is prevented (for some reason from asking)...." (LXX:24, 25).

اَلصَّدَقٰتُ لِلْفُقَرَآءِ وَالْمَسٰكِيْنِ

"Alms are for *the poor and the needy....*" (IX:60)[17].

(4) The Holy Qur'ãn then goes beyond mere economic assistance and enjoins the comprehensive duty of *doing good to the needy in all respects*:

وَبِالْوَالِدَيْنِ اِحْسَانًا . . . وَالْمَسٰكِيْنِ

"....and do good to the parents....and to *those in need....*" (IV:36).

(5) In case a Muslim is not in a position to help someone in need, the Holy Qur'ãn has advocated indirect assistance through recommending and pleading the needy person's case with those who may be capable of solving his difficulty. *Such indirect assistance also is meritorious in the sight of God and to render it, therefore, is duty.*[18]

مَنْ يَّشْفَعْ شَفَاعَةً حَسَنَةً يَّكُنْ لَّهٗ نَصِيْبٌ مِّنْهَا ۚ وَمَنْ يَّشْفَعْ شَفَاعَةً
سَيِّئَةً يَّكُنْ لَّهٗ كِفْلٌ مِّنْهَا ۗ وَكَانَ اللّٰهُ عَلٰى كُلِّ شَيْءٍ مُّقِيْتًا ○

---

17. Cf. VIII:41; LIX:7. It may be noted that in these verses the duty of helping the destitute and the needy has been placed on the Islamic State.

18. It becomes duty under the general duty of "doing good" referred to in the foregoing.

"Whoever recommends and helps a good cause becomes a partner therein: and whoever recommends and helps an evil cause, shares in its burden: and Allah hath power over all things." (IV:85).

(b) *Duties of Omission:*

(i) Not feeding the poverty-stricken people, if one possesses the means to do so, is a grave sin according to the Holy Qur'ān, to avoid which is a duty for all those who wish to escape the terrible punishment mentioned therein:

Condemning the evils of the pagan Arabs, the holy book says:

كَلَّا بَلْ لَّا تُكْرِمُوْنَ الْيَتِيْمَ ۝ وَلَا تَحَضُّوْنَ عَلٰى طَعَامِ الْمِسْكِيْنِ ۝

"Nay, nay! But ye honour not the orphans! Nor do ye urge upon one another to feed the poor!—" (LXXXIX:17, 18).

اَرَءَيْتَ الَّذِيْ يُكَذِّبُ بِالدِّيْنِ ۝ فَذٰلِكَ الَّذِيْ يَدُعُّ الْيَتِيْمَ ۝ وَلَا يَحُضُّ عَلٰى طَعَامِ الْمِسْكِيْنِ ۝

"Hast thou observed him who belieth religion (or, Requital)? That is he who repelleth the orphan, and urgeth not the feeding of the needy." (CVII:1-3).

اِنَّهٗ كَانَ لَا يُؤْمِنُ بِاللّٰهِ الْعَظِيْمِ ۝ وَلَا يَحُضُّ عَلٰى طَعَامِ الْمِسْكِيْنِ ۝ فَلَيْسَ لَهُ الْيَوْمَ هٰهُنَا حَمِيْمٌ ۝

"Lo! he (i.e., the one condemned to Hell) used not to believe in Allah the Mighty, and urged not on the feeding of the indigent; wherefore hath he no friend here this day...." (LXIX:33-35).

قَالُوْا لَمْ نَكُ مِنَ الْمُصَلِّيْنَ ۝ وَلَمْ نَكُ نُطْعِمُ الْمِسْكِيْنَ ۝

"They (i.e., those condemned to Hell) will say, 'We were not of those who prayed, nor were we of those who fed the indigent'." (LXXIV:43-44).

(ii) Abstinence from ill-treating anyone who asks for help, enjoined:

وَاَمَّا السَّآئِلَ فَلَا تَنْهَرْ ۝

"And as to him who solicits help (of any type), scold him not."
(XCIII:10).

(6) Duties of Hospitality

I. Duties relating to:

(a) the Guest: and (b) the Host.

II. Duties relating to the Stranded Stranger (Wayfarer).

(I) Duties Relating to the Guest and The Host:

The basic duties towards others which the Holy Qur'ãn has taught and which we have expounded in the foregoing are fully exhaustive for guidance in respect of the highest principles concerning the duties of the guest and the host. These duties have, however, been given explicitly and specifically by the Holy Prophet (Peace be on him) in his Sayings; and because those Sayings form an exposition and explanation of the Qur'ãnic code of life itself, it is necessary to trace them in the Holy Qur'ãn. In doing so we find the problem of guest-host duties contained in the stories of two Prophets, Abraham and Lot (Peace be on them), whose conduct is the standard for a Muslim, and to follow whom is a duty.

Speaking of the guests of Prophet Abraham (Peace be on him), the Holy Qur'ãn says:

هَلْ أَتٰىكَ حَدِيثُ ضَيْفِ إِبْرٰهِيمَ الْمُكْرَمِينَ ۝ إِذْ دَخَلُوا عَلَيْهِ فَقَالُوا سَلٰمًا ۖ
قَالَ سَلٰمٌ ۚ قَوْمٌ مُّنكَرُونَ ۝ فَرَاغَ إِلٰىٓ أَهْلِهِۦ فَجَآءَ بِعِجْلٍ سَمِينٍ ۝ فَقَرَّبَهُۥٓ
إِلَيْهِمْ قَالَ أَلَا تَأْكُلُونَ ۝ فَأَوْجَسَ مِنْهُمْ خِيفَةً ۖ قَالُوا لَا تَخَفْ ۖ
وَبَشَّرُوهُ بِغُلٰمٍ عَلِيمٍ ۝

"Hast the story reached thee, of the honoured guests of Abraham (who were angels). Behold, they entered His presence, and said: 'Peace!' He said: 'Peace!' (and thought, 'These seem) unusual people'. Then he (remarked nothing at their being unusual strangers and) turned quickly to his household (to arrange for hospitality), and brought out a calf fatted (and roasted) (to honour them with the best food). And he set it before them and (seeing that they touched it not) said: 'Will ye not eat?' (When they did not eat and thus appeared to refuse his hospitality,) he conceived a fear of them. They said: 'Fear not', and they gave him glad tidings of a son endowed with knowledge." (LI:24-28).

Again, the holy book says in respect of the guests of Prophet Lot (Peace be on him):

وَجَآءَ أَهْلُ الْمَدِينَةِ يَسْتَبْشِرُونَ ○ قَالَ إِنَّ هَٰٓؤُلَآءِ ضَيْفِي فَلَا تَفْضَحُونِ ○ وَاتَّقُوا اللَّهَ وَلَا تُخْزُونِ ○

"The inhabitants of the City (who were addicted to unnatural crime) came in (mad) joy (at the news of the arrival of handsome young guests, who were actually angels). Lot said (to them): 'These are my guests: disgrace me not: fear Allah, and shame me not'." (XV:67-69).

(a) *Duties of the host deducible from the above are:*

(*i*) He should wish Peace to his guests, even though they are strangers.

(*ii*) He should make haste with a generous and loving heart to provide comfort for them.

(*iii*) He should defend and protect them against all wrongs.

(b) *Duties of the guest deducible from the above are:*

(*i*) He should wish Peace to the host.

(*ii*) He should demonstrate his goodwill towards the host.

(*iii*) He should behave considerately towards the host.

(II) Duties Towards the Stranded Stranger (Wayfarer).

The stranded strangers constitute actually a category of guests,— of course, guests of the community or the country as a whole.

The general attitude of the human beings is that they regard their relatives and friends only as deserving their altruistic courtesy and hospitality. For, it is innate in man to bestow courtesy without effort on those for whom he cultivates love. But very few are those who may have the same feelings and attitude towards strangers that may be in need of their help and hospitality, although moral goodness manifest itself more positively and more strongly in their case.

The Holy Qur'ãn has taken up their cause, affirming service to them as their right, and has prescribed duties whereby their welfare and comfort has been genuinely and comprehensively ensured.

(i) Concerning economic assistance to them, it has preserved duties on the individual as well as on the collective level:

(a) *Individual level:*

The Holy Qur'ãn says:

فَآتِ ذَا الْقُرْبٰى حَقَّهٗ وَالْمِسْكِيْنَ وَابْنَ السَّبِيْلِ ۚ ذٰلِكَ خَيْرٌ لِّلَّذِيْنَ
يُرِيْدُوْنَ وَجْهَ اللّٰهِ ۖ وَاُولٰٓئِكَ هُمُ الْمُفْلِحُوْنَ ۝

"So give what is due to kindred, the needy, and *the wayfarer*. That is best for those who seek the Countenance of Allah, and it is they who will prosper." (XXX:38).

يَسْـَٔلُوْنَكَ مَاذَا يُنْفِقُوْنَ ۗ قُلْ مَآ اَنْفَقْتُمْ مِّنْ خَيْرٍ فَلِلْوَالِدَيْنِ وَالْاَقْرَبِيْنَ
وَالْيَتٰمٰى وَالْمَسٰكِيْنِ وَابْنِ السَّبِيْلِ ۗ وَمَا تَفْعَلُوْا مِنْ خَيْرٍ فَاِنَّ اللّٰهَ بِهٖ
عَلِيْمٌ ۝

"They ask thee what they should spend (in charity). Say: 'Whatever ye spend that is good, is for parents and kindred and orphans and those in want and for *wayfarers.* And whatever ye do that is good,—Allah knoweth it well." (II:215).[19]

(b) *Collective level, namely, on the basis of charitable taxes:*

One of the fixed items on which the Compulsory Welfare Tax (*Zakãt*) it to be spent is the welfare of the stranded stranger:

الصَّدَقٰتُ لِلْفُقَرَآءِ وَالْمَسٰكِيْنِ . . . وَابْنِ السَّبِيْلِ ۗ

"Alms are only for the poor and the needy....and (for) *the wayfarers....*" (IX:60).

Also, one of the items on which a fixed portion of war booty and of enemy property acquired otherwise by the Islamic state, is the welfare of the stranded stranger. (Ref: VIII:41 and LIX:7).

In this connection the Muslim jurists have made it clear that besides personal help to the stranded stranger, or the wayfarer, in respect

19. Cf. XVII:26; II:177.

of his needs, the Islamic state may also, if need arises, spend a part of the amount meant for the welfare of the wayfarers on the construction and repairs of roads and highways, bridges and rest-houses.[20]

(ii) Then, going beyond economic assistance and physical comfort, the Holy Qur'ãn has enjoined doing of good to the stranded strangers in all respects. It says:

وَبِالْوَالِدَيْنِ إِحْسَانًا وَّبِذِى الْقُرْبٰى .... وَابْنِ السَّبِيْلِ

"....and do good—to parents, the kinsfolk....and (to) *the wayfarer....*" (IV:36).

(7) Duties Towards Slaves

(A) The Qur'ãnic Stand Concerning Slavery and Prisonership of War:

We have seen in the section on basic duties towards others that the Holy Qur'ãn promulgates and upholds most ardently and without reserve the ideals of human equality, liberty and fraternity, and bestows a most comprehensive system of rights and duties based not only on absolute justice but, beyond that, on liberality, graciousness and compassion.

All rights are, however, always subject to curtailment if the interests of human society or even of the individual so demand, because of the unhealthy and injurious attitude or action on the part of anyone. This is a principle which has been universally accepted by mankind, and its validity is ingrained in the very concept of social justice. As such, it has received sanction in the Qur'ãnic moral code also.

Viewing this principle in the perspective of human freedom, we find that the mission of the Holy Qur'ãn is to establish and promote conditions in which the ideal of human freedom thrives and prospers and all forms of cruel subjection and exploitation of man by man and all types of misery which a human being may be capable of bringing about for any of his fellow-beings, are eliminated.

Thus the Holy Qur'ãn refuses to endorse the different forms of genuine slavery and serfdom practised unblushingly by the ancient primitive communities as well as by such civilised communities as the

---

20. See: Qãdi Abû Yûsuf's *Kitãb al-Kharãj, Bãb al-Sadqãt.*

Greeks, the Romans, the Christians and the Hindus[21], rcognising *only* prisonership of war, and that too under unavoidable circumstances.

It is essential for every student of the Qur'ãnic teaching to remember that the Holy Qur'ãn came into a world wherein slavery had been practised as a normal pursuit of the powerful since times immemorial; and consequently it had taken deep roots in the socio-economic life of numerous human communities spread all over the world, including the Arabs.

The Holy Qur'ãn had, therefore, to tackle not only time-honoured evil custom but also a deep-rooted economic institution. As such, it adopted a gradual programme for its total abolition, in the meantime laying down moral principles and statutory laws whereby the evils connected with slavery were totally eliminated from the Muslim society during the period of its revelation itself.

We may now examine the Qur'ãnic teachings concerning male and female slaves and the problem of prisonership of war and evaluate them:—

(*i*) The first great truth that reveals itself to a student of the Holy Qur'ãn is that making slaves of human beings has not been *enjoined* anywhere even indirectly. And not only is there no command, even an indirect recommendation does not exist.

(*ii*) Taking prisoners of war as a war-strategy has been, of course, permitted in conformity with the practice of all the nations of the world. The Holy Qur'ãn says:

فَإِذَا لَقِيتُمُ الَّذِينَ كَفَرُوا فَضَرْبَ الرِّقَابِ حَتَّىٰ إِذَا أَثْخَنتُمُوهُمْ
فَشُدُّوا الْوَثَاقَ

"Therefore, when ye meet in battle the Unbelievers (*i.e.,* non-Muslim enemies), then it is smiting of the necks; at length when ye have thoroughly routed them, bind a bond firmly (*i.e.*, make them prisoners of war):...." (XLVII).:4).

---

21. For details of the cruel principles and practices of these communities concerning slavery refer, among other scholarly works, to *Encyclopaedia of Religion and Ethics*, vol. II, Art. "Slavery", pp. 595-631.

Again:

مَا كَانَ لِنَبِيٍّ أَنْ يَكُونَ لَهُ أَسْرَىٰ حَتَّىٰ يُثْخِنَ فِي الْأَرْضِ ۚ

"It is not for a Prophet (and similarly for any of his followers) to have captives unless he has fought and triumphed in the land." (VIII:67).

This verse goes on further, however, to condemn worldly motives in respect of prisoners of war—the motive of benefiting for their services, or the motive of acquiring money in case they are ransomed,—a Muslim's motive for fighting in a war being only the triumph of the Divine Order of Truth and Justice: thus discouraging even retaining prisoners of war:

تُرِيدُونَ عَرَضَ الدُّنْيَا ۖ وَاللَّهُ يُرِيدُ الْآخِرَةَ ۗ وَاللَّهُ عَزِيزٌ حَكِيمٌ ۝

"Ye (O Muslims) desire the temporal goods of this world,[22] while Allah desireth (for you) the (blessings of the) Hereafter (which are attainable only through rising above wordly passions): and Allah is Mighty, Wise." (VIII:67).

(*iii*) As to slavery proper, namely, acquiring men and women in bondage without a just war, there is not even a permission. Rather, the above quoted verse (VIII:67) makes it positively illegal.

(*iv*) As we have already noted, the institution of slavery formed a vital part of Arab life, with all its economic implications, at the time of the advent of the Holy Qur'ãn. The Qur'ãnic method of reform in respect of such complicated evil institutions being their gradual elimination[23], the Holy Qur'ãn began with emphasising the evil nature of that institution through exhortations to Muslims to emancipate the slaves, placing that act in the list of the highest virtues and announcing for it the highest reward to which a Muslim can and should aspire, namely, earning the Divine Pleasure. In the very earliest revelations belonging to the first year of the Call, we find the following historic declaration:—

وَمَا أَدْرَاكَ مَا الْعَقَبَةُ ۝ فَكُّ رَقَبَةٍ ۝

22. This reference is not to Muslims as such but to some of the Muslims of the time when the Qur'ãnic guidance had not yet been completely revealed.

23. Cf. the gradual Qur'ãnic respect of intoxicants.

"Ah, what will convey to thee what the Ascent (i.e., the high and difficult path of Duty) is? (It is) to free a slave." (XC:12, 13).

The exhortation was repeated at Madinah in the following words:—

وَلَٰكِنَّ الْبِرَّ مَنْ . . . آتَى الْمَالَ عَلَىٰ حُبِّهِ . . . فِي الرِّقَابِ ۚ

"....but righteous is he who.... giveth his wealth for love of Him (i.e., God)...." to set free slaves....." (II:177)[24].

(*v*) When the Holy Prophet (Peace be on him) had established the Islamic state at Madinah, the problem of the prisoners of war arose in consequence of the battles waged by the enemies of Islam, giving birth to another category of bondmen and bondwomen,—the only category permitted by the Holy Qur'ãn, as we have seen above.

Prisonership of war is, like war, a necessary evil, and humanity has never been and can never be immune from it. The Holy Qur'ãn has, however, tried to mitigate this evil to the utmost rational limit.

We have seen above that it has condemned coveting prisoners of war. It being, however, unavoidable to have prisoners of war, the holy book has laid down most humane laws in that respect, giving due weight at the same time to avoidance of positive harm to the Muslims through any politically unrealistic approach—specially in the case when the enemy has also acquired Muslim prisoners of war, takes up an unjust stand concerning them and closes doors on the Islamic state in respect of awarding freedom to the prisoners of war in its hands. For, the Holy Qur'ãn, while preaching forgiveness and compassion, has also permitted the Muslims to retaliate if the enemy continues to stick to mischief and injustice:—

---

24. This clarion call did not go unheeded. Rather, the response was most enthusiastic. According to a conservative estimate, the number of slaves who received their freedom at the hands of the Companions of the Holy Prophet (Peace be on him) reached a total of thirty-nine thousand, two hundred and fifty-nine. (*Fath al-'Allãm*, commentary on *Bulûgh al-Marãm*, p. 332). It may also be pointed out that this estimate does not include many more whose references are found in other books.

As regards the Holy Prophet himself, it has been recorded that he emancipated sixty-three slaves. (*Ibid*).

وَإِنْ عَاقَبْتُمْ فَعَاقِبُوا بِمِثْلِ مَا عُوقِبْتُمْ بِهٖ ۚ وَلَئِنْ صَبَرْتُمْ لَهُوَ
خَيْرٌ لِّلصّٰبِرِينَ ○

"If you punish, then punish with the like of that wherefore ye were afflicted (by the enemies of Islam). But if you endure patiently, verily it is better for the patient." (XVI:126).

Thus, the Qur'ãnic teaching is fundamentally aimed at the elimination of this form of bondage also, and the Islamic state has been exhorted by the Holy Qur'ãn to adopt, according to the exigencies of the situation, either of the following courses for setting free the prisoners of war:—

(*a*) setting free as a favour and out of sheer grace;

(*b*) setting free in return for ransom.

The injunction reads:—

فَإِذَا لَقِيتُمُ الَّذِينَ كَفَرُوا فَضَرْبَ الرِّقَابِ ۭ حَتّٰىٓ إِذَآ أَثْخَنْتُمُوهُمْ
فَشُدُّوا الْوَثَاقَ ۙ فَإِمَّا مَنًّاۢ بَعْدُ وَإِمَّا فِدَآءً حَتّٰى تَضَعَ الْحَرْبُ
أَوْزَارَهَا ۛ ذٰلِكَ ۛ

"Therefore, when ye meet in battle the Unbelievers (i.e., the non-Muslim enemies), then it is smiting of necks; at length when ye have thoroughly routed them, bind a bond firmly (i.e., make them prisoners of war); thereafter either (setting them free as a matter of) grace[25] or (freeing

25. It is worthy of being remembered that in most cases when the Muslim army captured prisoners of war in the battle fought during the regime of the Holy Prophet (Peace be on him), those captives were awarded their freedom as a mark of sheer grace, in conformity with the alternative permitted in this verse. Thus, several of those who had been taken prisoners after the first battle of Islam, namely, the battle of Badr, were granted freedom without ransom. Similarly, the six thousand prisoners connected with the Banû Mustãlaq expedition, the inveterate enemies of Islam captured after the fall of Makkah, the captives obtained after the siege of Ta'if, and the prisoners captured on some other occasions of warfare, were set free by the Holy Prophet (Peace be on him) by way of grace. (See: Muslim: *Sahîh*, Vol. II, p. 93; Bukhãri: *Sahîh*, Vol. II, pp. 376, 593; Ibn Athîr: *al-Tãrikh*, vol. II, p. 92.

them in return for) ransom; until the war lays down its burdens (i.e., peace returns, after which no one can be made captive). That (is the ordinance)...." (XLVII:4).

In case, however, the Islamic state does not find itself strategically in a position where it may adopt the first alternative with justice to the Cause of Truth, nor are the prisoners in a position to take benefit of the permission to ransom themselves, they must naturally remain captives.

But, then, the Holy Qur'ãn lays down the third ordinance whereby the captives can obtain their freedom in due course. It says:—

وَالَّذِيْنَ يَبْتَغُوْنَ الْكِتٰبَ مِمَّا مَلَكَتْ اَيْمَانُكُمْ فَكَاتِبُوْهُمْ اِنْ عَلِمْتُمْ فِيْهِمْ
خَيْرًا ۖ وَّاٰتُوْهُمْ مِّنْ مَّالِ اللّٰهِ الَّذِيْٓ اٰتٰىكُمْ ؕ

"....And if any of those whom your right hands possess ask for a deed in writing (to enable them to earn their freedom for a certain sum) gave them (as your bounden duty) such a deed if ye know in them any good (i.e., fitness for earning their livelihood through some work and thus bettering their position), and (for helping them to freedom) bestow upon them of the wealth of Allah which He hath bestowed upon you....." (XXIV:33).

This actually terminates, from the side of the Holy Qur'ãn, that form of bondage which is incidental to prisonership of war and which concerns Islam's bloodthirsty enemies. Of course, the very creation of every other form of bondage is out of the question, as we have already seen. Thus, there should be no bondsmen and bondswomen of any category in an Islamic state.

Indeed the Holy Qur'ãn is so vehemently opposed to slavery in all its forms that it has ordained redemption of prisoners of war and emancipation of slaves as a collective duty of the Muslims in respect of the definite and permanent functions of the perpetual compulsory Welfare Tax, i.e., *Zakãt* which every Muslim of means has been ordered to pay yearly for planned spending on welfare projects. The holy book says:

اِنَّمَا الصَّدَقٰتُ لِلْفُقَرَآءِ وَالْمَسٰكِيْنِ ...... وَفِي الرِّقَابِ

"Alms (i.e., compulsory Welfare Tax meant to be collected and spent by the communal treasury or by the Islamic state) are for the poor, and the needy.... (and) *for those in bondage*...." (IX:60).

Thus: (*a*) prisoners of war should be redeemed, and (*b*) slaves should be helped to freedom. This injunction forms, indeed, a charter for the Muslims to eradicate slavery from the world on an organized scale.

Here we may refer also to another channel adopted by the Holy Qur'ãn for the emancipation of slaves. That is the channel of recommending to, or commanding, the Muslims to expiate for certain sins through setting slaves free or purchasing for their freedom.

Thus:

(*i*) if a Muslim killed another Muslim by mistake, it was made obligatory for him to emancipate a slave:

وَمَنْ قَتَلَ مُؤْمِنًا خَطَـًٔا فَتَحْرِيرُ رَقَبَةٍ مُّؤْمِنَةٍ

"He who killeth a Believer by mistake must set free a believing slave....." (IV:92).

(*ii*) It was, however, not only in case the person killed was a Muslim, but also when he was a non-Muslim and belonged to a community with whom Muslims had a treaty of mutual alliance:—

وَإِنْ كَانَ مِنْ قَوْمٍ بَيْنَكُمْ وَبَيْنَهُمْ مِّيثَاقٌ فَدِيَةٌ مُّسَلَّمَةٌ إِلَىٰٓ
أَهْلِهِ وَتَحْرِيرُ رَقَبَةٍ مُّؤْمِنَةٍ ج

"...If he belonged to a people with whom you have a treaty of mutual alliance, compensation should be paid to his family, and a believing slave be freed...." (IV:92).

(*iii*) For those who had separated from their wive through *Zihãr*, to which a reference has already been made[26], and desired re-union, the first alternative given to them in respect of expiation was that of setting free a slave:—

وَالَّذِينَ يُظٰهِرُونَ مِنْ نِّسَآئِهِمْ ثُمَّ يَعُودُونَ لِمَا قَالُوا فَتَحْرِيرُ رَقَبَةٍ مِّنْ
قَبْلِ أَنْ يَّتَمَآسَّا ۚ ذٰلِكُمْ تُوعَظُونَ بِهِ ۚ وَاللّٰهُ بِمَا تَعْمَلُونَ خَبِيرٌ ۝

"As to those who divorce their wives by *Zihãr*, then wish to go back on the words uttered,—(it is ordained that such a one) should free a

26. See page 199.

slave before they touch each other. This are ye admonished to perform and Allah is well acquainted with (all) that ye do". (LVIII:3).

(*iv*) Failure in keeping to one's solemn oath was ordained to be expiated, among other alternatives, by freeing a slave:—

لَا يُؤَاخِذُكُمُ اللّٰهُ بِاللَّغْوِ فِيْٓ اَيْمَانِكُمْ وَلٰكِنْ يُّؤَاخِذُكُمْ بِمَا عَقَّدْتُّمُ الْاَيْمَانَ ۚ
فَكَفَّارَتُهٗٓ اِطْعَامُ عَشَرَةِ مَسٰكِيْنَ مِنْ اَوْسَطِ مَا تُطْعِمُوْنَ اَهْلِيْكُمْ اَوْ كِسْوَتُهُمْ
اَوْ تَحْرِيْرُ رَقَبَةٍ ط

"Allah will not take you to task for that which is unintentional in your oaths, but He will take you to task for the oaths which ye swear in earnest. The expiation thereof is the feeding of ten of the needy with the average of that wherewith ye feed your own folk, or the clothing of them, or the emancipation of a slave....[27]" (V:92)[28].

We should now take note of those verses of the Holy Qur'ãn which speak of the relations of Muslims with slaves and prisoners of war. The question may be asked: If the Holy Qur'ãn stands firmly for the abolition of bondage and slavery in all its forms, why those injunctions? The plain reply is: The Holy Qur'ãn, as we have already noted, came into a world wherein slavery was so deep-rooted that to uproot it at a stroke was to bring into existence some other intolerable evils. Hence, while giving that ethical teaching and laying down those laws whereby this institution was to completely wither away in due course, it tolerated the presence of the pre-existing slaves and of the prisoners of war who could not tread the paths of freedom opened out for them by it and chose to stay in the Muslim community,—laying down, however, definite laws for the eradication of the tortures of slavery. In fact, there have been prisoners of

---

27. In the *Hadîth* we find that if any Muslim terminates his fast deliberately before time, one of the alternatives laid down for him by the Holy Prophet (Peace be on him) for expiating his sin is to free a slave. (Bukhãri: *Sahîh*; vol. I, p. 259). Similarly, if a person slaps or beats his slave, the expiation of that sin is to free the slave. (Abû Dã'ûd: *Sunan*, vol. I., p. 466).

28. Besides the channel of expiation of sins, another channel, which has been mentioned in the *Hadîth*, has also been fixed. The Holy Prophet (Peace be on him) enjoined at Madinah that, on the occasion of the solar eclipse, Muslims of means should not only engage in extra devotions like other Muslims, but should also emancipate slaves. (Muslim: *Sahîh*; vol. I, p. 291).

war even afterwards who did not avail of the opportunity for freedom offered by the Holy Qur'ãn. And the same situation can repeat itself in the future. That, however, has been and would be, not because the Holy Qur'ãn enjoins it or desires it but because of the failure on the side of Islam's enemies.

We may now consider this part of the Qur'ãnic teaching.

(B) Duties:

(a) Duties of Commission:

(i) *Doing good to slaves and prisoners of war enjoined:*

The first and foremost teaching of the Holy Qur'ãn in this connection is the promulgation of *the duty of doing good* in all respects to "those whom the right hands possess",—doing good positively as well as negatively; positively, in the sense of doing all positive good possible; and, negatively, in the sense of refraining from all injury:—

وَبِالْوَالِدَيْنِ إِحْسَانًا . . . وَمَا مَلَكَتْ أَيْمَانُكُمْ ۗ إِنَّ اللَّهَ لَا يُحِبُّ
مَنْ كَانَ مُخْتَالًا فَخُورًا ۝

"....and do good to parents.... and to those whom your right hands own[29]. Lo! Allah approveth not the arrogant, the vainglorious". (IV:36).

(ii) Enabling the male and female slaves to enjoy healthy married life, enjoined:

وَأَنْكِحُوا الْأَيَامَىٰ مِنْكُمْ وَالصَّالِحِينَ مِنْ عِبَادِكُمْ وَإِمَائِكُمْ ۚ إِنْ يَكُونُوا
فُقَرَاءَ يُغْنِهِمُ اللَّهُ مِنْ فَضْلِهِ ۗ وَاللَّهُ وَاسِعٌ عَلِيمٌ ۝

"And wed the single among you and the fit ones among your male and female slaves (both of whom to become free by marriage); if they be poor, Allah will give them means out of His grace. For Allah encompasseth all, and He knoweth all things." (XXIV:32).

---

29. "What your right hands own". This includes prisoners of war, slaves, people in one's power and the animals which might belong to a person. (See A. Yusuf Ali, *op.cit.*, p. 191 n. 553).

(iii) Marriage with female slaves advocated and recommended:

فَإِنْ خِفْتُمْ أَلَّا تَعْدِلُوا فَوَاحِدَةً أَوْ مَا مَلَكَتْ أَيْمَانُكُمْ ذَٰلِكَ أَدْنَىٰ أَلَّا تَعُولُوا ۝

"....But if ye fear that ye shall not be able to deal justly (with wives more than one), then (marry) only one (free woman), or (marry) what your right hands possess (i.e., a prisoner of war or a slave). That will be more suitable, to prevent you from injustice." (IV:3).

(b) *Duties of Omission:*

(i) *Compelling slave-girls to prostitution, prohibited:*

وَلَا تُكْرِهُوا فَتَيَاتِكُمْ عَلَى الْبِغَاءِ إِنْ أَرَدْنَ تَحَصُّنًا لِّتَبْتَغُوا عَرَضَ الْحَيَاةِ
الدُّنْيَا ۚ

"And compel not your slave-girls to prostitution (—a custom practised by the pagan Arabs and certain other pagan communities—), they being desirous of keeping chaste, in order that ye may seek the frail goods of this world's life...." (XXIV:33).

(ii) *Promiscuous relations with female slaves, prohibited:*

وَالْمُحْصَنَاتُ مِنَ النِّسَاءِ إِلَّا مَا مَلَكَتْ أَيْمَانُكُمْ ۖ كِتَابَ اللَّهِ عَلَيْكُمْ ۚ وَأُحِلَّ لَكُم مَّا
وَرَاءَ ذَٰلِكُمْ أَن تَبْتَغُوا بِأَمْوَالِكُم مُّحْصِنِينَ غَيْرَ مُسَافِحِينَ ۚ فَمَا اسْتَمْتَعْتُم بِهِ
مِنْهُنَّ فَآتُوهُنَّ أُجُورَهُنَّ فَرِيضَةً ۚ وَلَا جُنَاحَ عَلَيْكُمْ فِيمَا تَرَاضَيْتُم بِهِ مِن
بَعْدِ الْفَرِيضَةِ ۚ إِنَّ اللَّهَ كَانَ عَلِيمًا حَكِيمًا ۝ وَمَن لَّمْ يَسْتَطِعْ مِنكُمْ طَوْلًا أَن
يَنكِحَ الْمُحْصَنَاتِ الْمُؤْمِنَاتِ فَمِن مَّا مَلَكَتْ أَيْمَانُكُم مِّن فَتَيَاتِكُمُ الْمُؤْمِنَاتِ ۚ وَ
اللَّهُ أَعْلَمُ بِإِيمَانِكُم ۚ بَعْضُكُم مِّن بَعْضٍ ۚ فَانكِحُوهُنَّ بِإِذْنِ أَهْلِهِنَّ وَآتُوهُنَّ
أُجُورَهُنَّ بِالْمَعْرُوفِ مُحْصَنَاتٍ غَيْرَ مُسَافِحَاتٍ وَلَا مُتَّخِذَاتِ أَخْدَانٍ ۚ فَإِذَا أُحْصِنَّ
فَإِنْ أَتَيْنَ بِفَاحِشَةٍ فَعَلَيْهِنَّ نِصْفُ مَا عَلَى الْمُحْصَنَاتِ مِنَ الْعَذَابِ ۚ
ذَٰلِكَ لِمَنْ خَشِيَ الْعَنَتَ مِنكُمْ ۚ وَأَن تَصْبِرُوا خَيْرٌ لَّكُمْ ۗ وَاللَّهُ غَفُورٌ
رَّحِيمٌ ۝

"Also (forbidden unto you for marriage are) women already in wedlock, except[30] those whom your right hands possess. Thus hath Allah ordained (prohibitions) against you. Except for these, all others (including those whom your right hands possess) are lawful (for marriage), *so that ye seek them with your wealth in honest wedlock, not debauchery.* Seeing that ye derive benefit from them, give them their dowers (at least) as prescribed; but if, after a dower is prescribed, ye agree mutually on aught. Lo! Allah is ever Knower, Wise.

"And whoso is not able to afford to marry free, believing women, let them marry from the believing maids whom your right hands possess. Allah knoweth best (concerning) your faith. Ye (i.e., the free and those in bondage) are one from another (i.e., equals in human status). So (without entertaining the false notion of loss of dignity) wed them by permission of their folk, and give unto them their dowers in kindness (as properly) wedded women, *not (as) fornicatresses, nor as those taking to themselves secret paramours.* When they are taken into wedlock, if they fall into lewdness, their punishment is half that for free women. *This (permission to marry female captives and slaves) is for those among you who fear sin. But is better for you that you practise self-restraint.* And Allah is Oft-Forgiving, Most Merciful." (IV:24, 25).

The above discussion shows that prisonership of war, as also the "slavery" of those whom the early converts to Islam possessed as a pre-Islamic legacy and whom they retained thereafter, is actually "controlled freedom",—the basic human rights, i.e., rights to proper food, clothing, shelter, health, marriage, education, etc., having been ensured with the exception of what falls under the proprietary rights of the guardian in the services of the prisoner of war of his so-called slave. And these proprietary rights in services have been retained, in respect of the prisoner of war, as atonement for his or her crime in engaging in war against the Cause of God, and the restrictions on freedom that have been prescribed are solely with reference to the protection of the Islamic state and of the Muslim community from the harm that he may likely inflict otherwise as an active enemy. It is, thus, not slavery in the sense in which, for instance, the Greeks, the Romans, the Hindus and the Christians have practised it by

30. The reason for this exception is that the Holy Qur'ān places a married female prisoner of war whose husband has not been captured along with her, and who is therefore alone, in the category of a divorced woman. Marriage with her in case her husband has also been captured, is illegal. (See Abdul Majid Daryabadi, *op.cit.*, p. 154, n. 3).

treating their slaves as something sub-human or even non-human. The Holy Qur'ãn, and its exposition: the *Hadîth*, have commanded the Muslims to treat them just like servants and that too with affection and full regard for their welfare.

(C) The Problem of Concubinage:

Concubinage may be defined as the establishment and maintenance of sexual relations between a man and a woman outside the marriage bond. As such, it has been widely practised by human communities, which include not only primitive tribal groups[31] but also civilised peoples like the Japanese, the Chinese, the Hindus, the Greeks, the Romans, the Jews and the Christians[32]. As for the Arabs, they lagged behind none in that respect when the Holy Qur'ãn came.

We have already noted that the Qur'ãnic reform in respect of slavery was of a gradual nature. But the question is: Does the Holy Qur'ãn sanction concubinage?

The reply to this question necessitates certain observations:—

(i) We have already noted that the Holy Qur'ãn prohibits promiscuity and debauchery in relations with those "whom the right hands possess."

(ii) We have also noted that the holy book upholds, advocates and enjoins marriage with them.

(iii) If it is said that marriage with polytheists has been forbidden by the Holy Qur'ãn (II:221), and most of the female captives of war obtained during the period of Qur'ãnic revelation were polytheists, and that, therefore, the Qur'ãn injunction concerning marriage with female captives does not include them; and if the inference is made that the Holy Qur'ãn sets aside that category for being used as concubines, it would be, in the first instance, a fallacious inference, and, secondly, it would go against

31. *Encyclopaedia of Religion and Ethics,* vol. 3, pp. 809-811, 813.

32. *Ibid.*, pp. 812-814, 817-820.

We might note here the verdict of a modern English Sociologist also: "Wherever possible, the man should, of course, have a concubine of some sort." (Ludovici: *Woman*, p. 172.

the explicit Qur'ãn injunction which forbids extra-marital relations in an unqualified manner (XVII:32)[33].

Moreover, as we have already noted[34], the Holy Qur'ãn forbids Muslims from employing their female captives for prostitution. Can it be conceivable that a Muslim would be free to establish extra-marital relations with her himself?

(*iv*) There are certain verses in the Holy Qur'ãn wherein those with whom a Muslim can have legitimate sexual relations have been classed separately as 'spouses' and 'those whom their right hands possess'[35]. But this distinction does not imply, even according to the most anti-modernistic, conservative and literatlistic exponents of the Holy Qur'ãn[36], that the expression "those whom their right hands possess" refers to concubines. Rather, the word "spouses" denotes "free women joined to them by regular marriage bond"[37] and the expression: "those whom their right hands possess" stands for "women taken as captives in war and raised to the status of wives"[38].

(v) There is no doubt that, although "those whom the right hands posses" enjoy all the rights as wives, they are distinguishable from those wives who are from among the free women, and hence their separate mention as wives. This distinction of the 'free' and the 'captive' is there even when they are not wives of anyone but merely servants in the household. And this distinction has a natural and rational basis. For, the captive belongs originally to the enemy camp where her original mission was to destroy Islam and Muslims, while the free woman belongs solely to the fold of Islam. The loyalty to Islam and to the Islamic state of the latter cannot be normally doubtful; while in respect of the former's loyalty great precautions are necessary; because even when a captive embraces Islam, it is possible that he or she may have

33. Also note IV:24, 25, quoted on p. 251.

34. See p. 250.

35. XXIII:5, 6; XXXIII:50; XXXIII:52; LXX:30.

36. See Abdul Majid Daryabadi, *op.cit.*, vol. 4, p. 477.

37, 38. See: *Ibid.*, Commentary notes on verses 5 and 6 of Chap. XXIII.

done so to be able to do greater injury to the Muslim community under the mask of conversion. Of course, if he or she is sincere, the devotion from the Muslim community is bound to come to him or her gradually but definitely, to which Muslim history bears ample testimony.

That distinction is there not only with regard to their position in society but also in respect of punishment for crimes, wherein they have been placed at an advantage out of regard for their lesser infusion into Islamic culture. Their punishment is half of that of a free person:[39]—

فَإِذَآ أُحْصِنَّ فَإِنْ أَتَيْنَ بِفَٰحِشَةٍ فَعَلَيْهِنَّ نِصْفُ مَا عَلَى ٱلْمُحْصَنَٰتِ مِنَ ٱلْعَذَابِ ۚ

".....When they (i.e., "those whom the right hands possess") are taken in wedlock, if they fall into shame, their punishment is half that of free women...." (IV:25).

To sum up: a critical study of the relevant verses proves that the Holy Qur'ãn does not sanction the institution of Concubinage.

39. Contrast it with the outlook of non-Qur'ãnic ideologies where the punishment of those in bondage was higher, often to a most cruel extent, than that of the free persons. (See: *Encyclopaedia of Religion and Ethics*. Art., Slavery").

Chapter IV

DUTIES TOWARDS MUSLIMS AS MUSLIMS

(1) Duties of Commission;

(2) Duties of Omission

(1) *Duties of Commission*

***END*:**

Promotion of the Happiness and Moral Perfection of the Muslims.

(i) *Respecting the sanctity of life, honour and property of other Muslims enjoined:*

This duty is contained in the following directives:—

(*a*) Cultivation and maintenance of genuine brotherly relations have been enjoined:

إِنَّمَا الْمُؤْمِنُونَ إِخْوَةٌ فَأَصْلِحُوا بَيْنَ أَخَوَيْكُمْ وَاتَّقُوا اللّٰهَ لَعَلَّكُمْ
تُرْحَمُونَ ۝

"The Believers are but a single Brotherhood[1]: So make peace and reconciliation between your two (contending) brothers; and be careful

---

1. It is a Brotherhood in which:

(*a*) the odious distinctions of caste and colour, and of tribe and race, have been totally eliminated. (See XLIX:13, quoted on p. 165).

(*b*) even the worst enemy of Islam is accepted as a full brother, if he chooses genuinely to be a Muslim:

لَا يَرْقُبُوْنَ فِيْ مُؤْمِنٍ إِلًّا وَّلَا ذِمَّةً ۚ وَأُولٰٓئِكَ هُمُ الْمُعْتَدُوْنَ ۝
فَإِنْ تَابُوْا وَأَقَامُوا الصَّلٰوةَ وَاٰتَوُا الزَّكٰوةَ فَإِخْوَانُكُمْ فِي الدِّيْنِ ۗ
وَنُفَصِّلُ الْاٰيٰتِ لِقَوْمٍ يَّعْلَمُوْنَ ۝

"In a Believer they (*i.e.*, the enemies of Islam respect not either the ties of kinship or of covenant! It is they who have transgressed all bounds. But (even so), if they repent, establish regular prayers, and practise regular charity,—they are your brethren in Faith: Thus do We explain the Sings in detail for those who understand." (IX:10, 11)

of your duty towards Allah (in respect of safeguarding these brotherly relations), that ye may receive Mercy." (XLIX:10).

To maintain the integrity of this world Brotherhood[2] forms one of the highest duties of a Muslim, as we shall note elsewhere.

That cannot be possible, however, without constantly maintaining the attitude of respecting the sanctity of the life, honour and property of individual Muslims. Hence the same is duty.

(*b*) Mercifulness towards Muslims has been proclaimed as one of the basic virtues of Islamic life:

مُحَمَّدٌ رَّسُولُ اللَّهِ ۚ وَالَّذِينَ مَعَهُ أَشِدَّاءُ عَلَى الْكُفَّارِ رُحَمَاءُ بَيْنَهُمْ

"Muhammad is the Messenger of Allah; and those who are with him are strong against (hostile) Disbelievers, and merciful amongst each other...." (XLVIII:29).

(*c*) Observing respectfulness towards other Muslims has been proclaimed as one of the basic virtues which should be possessed by every Muslim:

أَذِلَّةٍ عَلَى الْمُؤْمِنِينَ

"....humble (or, respectful) toward Believers...." (V:57).

(*d*) Absolute honesty in respect of other Muslims' trusts has been enjoined:

فَإِنْ أَمِنَ بَعْضُكُم بَعْضًا فَلْيُؤَدِّ الَّذِي اؤْتُمِنَ أَمَانَتَهُ
وَلْيَتَّقِ اللَّهَ رَبَّهُ ۗ

(*c*) even a human being with practically no social standing, including the humblest slave, who may belong to any race or colour or country, can enter as a full brother by mere acceptance of Islam:

فَإِن لَّمْ تَعْلَمُوا آبَاءَهُمْ فَإِخْوَانُكُمْ فِي الدِّينِ وَمَوَالِيكُمْ ۚ

"....But if ye know not their fathers, they are your Brothers in Faith and your friends...." (XXXIII:5).

2. Having a membership today of seven hundred million souls.

"....And if one of you deposits a thing on trust with another, let the trustee (faithfully) discharge his trust, and let him fear his Lord...."
(II:283).

(*e*) Finally: keeping straight the relations with other Muslims, has been enjoined:

فَاتَّقُوا اللّٰهَ وَ اَصۡلِحُوۡا ذَاتَ بَيۡنِكُمۡ

"....so fear Allah, and keep straight the relations between yourselves (i.e., preserve the sanctity of life, honour and property between yourselves)...."
(VIII:1).

(ii) Endeavour to ensure peace and justice among Muslims, whether the moral agent is involved in it or not, enjoined:

This duty is contained in the following directives:

(*a*) In case quarrel or fight takes place between two Muslim parties, all possible effort for bringing about just peace between them, and, in case of failure, assisting the wronged party, has been commanded:

وَ اِنۡ طَآئِفَتٰنِ مِنَ الۡمُؤۡمِنِيۡنَ اقۡتَتَلُوۡا فَاَصۡلِحُوۡا بَيۡنَهُمَا ۚ فَاِنۡۢ بَغَتۡ اِحۡدٰىهُمَا عَلَى الۡاُخۡرٰى فَقَاتِلُوا الَّتِىۡ تَبۡغِىۡ حَتّٰى تَفِىۡٓءَ اِلٰٓى اَمۡرِ اللّٰهِ ۚ فَاِنۡ فَآءَتۡ فَاَصۡلِحُوۡا بَيۡنَهُمَا بِالۡعَدۡلِ وَ اَقۡسِطُوۡا ؕ اِنَّ اللّٰهَ يُحِبُّ الۡمُقۡسِطِيۡنَ ۝

"If two parties among the Believers fall into a quarrel, make ye peace between them: But if one of them transgreses beyond bounds against the other, then fight ye against the one that transgresses until it complies with the command of Allah; but if it complies, then make peace between them with justice, and be fair. For Allah loves those who are just."
(XLIX:9).

(*b*) In case of one's personal dispute, rising above self and settling all differences with brother Muslims on the basis of Divine Guidance given in the Holy Qur'ān and in the *Sunnah* (Way of the Prophet), has been enjoined:

فَإِنْ تَنَازَعْتُمْ فِي شَيْءٍ فَرُدُّوهُ إِلَى اللَّهِ وَالرَّسُولِ إِنْ كُنْتُمْ تُؤْمِنُونَ
بِاللَّهِ وَالْيَوْمِ الْآخِرِ ۚ ذَٰلِكَ خَيْرٌ وَأَحْسَنُ تَأْوِيلًا ○

"....and if ye dispute in aught (do not try to settle your dispute on the basis of any subjective considerations but purely on the objective grounds of justice, and for that) refer to Allah and His Messenger (Muhammad), if ye (indeed) believe in Allah and the Last Day. That is the best and fairest (course) for final determination." (IV:59).

(*c*) Such an attitude being impossible without the spirit of absolute selflessness, sacrificing personal interests and comforts for other Muslims has been commanded and emphasised as one of the virtues of true Muslims:

وَيُؤْثِرُونَ عَلَىٰ أَنْفُسِهِمْ وَلَوْ كَانَ بِهِمْ خَصَاصَةٌ ۚ

"....and they give preference to (the interests and the needs of others) above themselves, though poverty become their lot...." (LIX:9).

(*d*) The spirit of selflessness cannot be maintained without the constant cultivation of the attitude of goodwill towards all Muslims. This has been taught in the following prayer:

رَبَّنَا اغْفِرْ لَنَا وَلِإِخْوَانِنَا الَّذِينَ سَبَقُونَا بِالْإِيمَانِ وَلَا تَجْعَلْ فِي
قُلُوبِنَا غِلًّا لِلَّذِينَ آمَنُوا رَبَّنَا إِنَّكَ رَءُوفٌ رَحِيمٌ ○

"....Our Lord! forgive us and our brethren who have preceded us in the Faith, and permit not in our hearts rancour towards the Believers. Our Lord! verily Thou art Kind, Merciful." (LIX:10).

(iii) Ensuring and promoting the moral and spiritual welfare of Muslims, enjoined:

Enjoining right conduct and forbidding all evil ways has been proclaimed as the mission of every Muslim:

Also: constantly exhorting one another to truth, perseverance in the way of truth, and the practice of compassion, have been declared as the basic conditions for the spiritual and moral progress of the Muslims:

Hence to strive for the moral and spiritual perfection of other Muslims in the above ways, is duty.

The Holy Qur'ãn says:

كُنتُمْ خَيْرَ أُمَّةٍ أُخْرِجَتْ لِلنَّاسِ تَأْمُرُونَ بِالْمَعْرُوفِ وَتَنْهَوْنَ عَنِ الْمُنكَرِ وَتُؤْمِنُونَ بِاللَّهِ ط

"Ye are the best community that hath been raised up for mankind. Ye enjoin right conduct and forbid what is wrong: and ye believe in Allah...." (III:110).

وَتَوَاصَوْا بِالْحَقِّ وَتَوَاصَوْا بِالصَّبْرِ ۝

"....and (those who) exhort one another to truth and exhort one another to perseverance (in the cause of truth)." (CIII:3).

وَتَوَاصَوْا بِالْمَرْحَمَةِ ۝

"....and (those who) exhort one another to compassion...." (XC:17).

(2) <u>*Duties of Omission*</u>:

<u>END</u>:

Preservation of the Happiness and the Moral Health of the Muslims.

(i) *Killing a Muslim most severely condemned and prohibited:*

وَمَا كَانَ لِمُؤْمِنٍ أَن يَقْتُلَ مُؤْمِنًا إِلَّا خَطَأً ۚ . . . . . . وَمَن يَقْتُلْ مُؤْمِنًا مُّتَعَمِّدًا فَجَزَاؤُهُ جَهَنَّمُ خَالِدًا فِيهَا وَغَضِبَ اللَّهُ عَلَيْهِ وَلَعَنَهُ وَأَعَدَّ لَهُ عَذَابًا عَظِيمًا ۝

"It is not for a Believer to kill a Believer unless (it be) by mistake...."

"Whoso slayeth a Believer of set purpose, his reward is Hell for ever. Allah is worth against him and He hath cursed him and prepared for him an awful doom." (IV:92, 93).

(ii) *Damaging the honour of other Muslims in any form, prohibited:*

(*a*) Insulting in any manner, defaming and backbiting has been ruled out:

يَا أَيُّهَا الَّذِينَ آمَنُوا لَا يَسْخَرْ قَوْمٌ مِنْ قَوْمٍ عَسَىٰ أَنْ يَكُونُوا خَيْرًا
مِنْهُمْ وَلَا نِسَاءٌ مِنْ نِسَاءٍ عَسَىٰ أَنْ يَكُنَّ خَيْرًا مِنْهُنَّ ۖ وَلَا تَلْمِزُوا
أَنْفُسَكُمْ وَلَا تَنَابَزُوا بِالْأَلْقَابِ ۖ بِئْسَ الِاسْمُ الْفُسُوقُ بَعْدَ الْإِيمَانِ ۚ
وَمَنْ لَمْ يَتُبْ فَأُولَٰئِكَ هُمُ الظَّالِمُونَ ○ . . . .
وَلَا يَغْتَبْ بَعْضُكُمْ بَعْضًا ۚ أَيُحِبُّ أَحَدُكُمْ أَنْ يَأْكُلَ لَحْمَ
أَخِيهِ مَيْتًا فَكَرِهْتُمُوهُ ۚ وَاتَّقُوا اللَّهَ ۚ إِنَّ اللَّهَ تَوَّابٌ رَحِيمٌ ○

"O ye who believe! Let not a folk deride a folk, belike they may be better than they are, not let (some) women (deride) (other) women, belike they may be better than they are; neither defame one another, nor insult one another by nicknames. Ill is the name of sin after belief. And whoso turneth not in repentance, such are evil-doers.

".....nor backbite one another. Would anyone of you love to eat the flesh of his dead brother? Ye abhor that (so abhor the other)! And keep your duty to Allah. Lo! Allah is Relenting, Merciful."

(XLIX:11, 12).

(*b*) Slandering the Muslims has been very severely condemned:

وَالَّذِينَ يُؤْذُونَ الْمُؤْمِنِينَ وَالْمُؤْمِنَاتِ بِغَيْرِ مَا اكْتَسَبُوا فَقَدِ احْتَمَلُوا بُهْتَانًا
وَإِثْمًا مُبِينًا ○

"And those who hurt (through slander) the believing men and the believing women undeservedly, they bear the guilt of slander and manifest sin." (XXXIII:58).

(iii) *Raking up disputes with other Muslims prohibited, with warning of very serious consequences:*

وَلَا تَنَازَعُوا فَتَفْشَلُوا وَتَذْهَبَ رِيحُكُمْ

"(O ye who believe!)....rake up no disputes (with one another), lest ye lose heart and your power depart...." (VIII:46).

One of the factors which lends ugliness to disputes is rancour. The Holy Qur'ãn deprecates rancour also, and teaches the following prayer:

وَلَا تَجْعَلْ فِي قُلُوبِنَا غِلًّا لِّلَّذِينَ آمَنُوا رَبَّنَا إِنَّكَ رَءُوفٌ رَّحِيمٌ ○

"(The true Muslims pray[3]: Our Lord)....permit not our hearts to suffer from rancour against the Believers. Our Lord! Thou art indeed Kind, Merciful." (LIX:10).

(iv) *Damaging the just interest of other Muslims, prohibited:*

(*a*) In respect of defrauding them in matters pertaining to wealth:

يَا أَيُّهَا الَّذِينَ آمَنُوا لَا تَأْكُلُوا أَمْوَالَكُم بَيْنَكُم بِالْبَاطِلِ

"O ye who believe! Eat up not your wealth among yourselves (i.e., do not consume one another's wealth) unlawfully...." (IV:29).

(*b*) In respect of concealing evidence:

وَلَا تَكْتُمُوا الشَّهَادَةَ ۚ وَمَن يَكْتُمْهَا فَإِنَّهُ آثِمٌ قَلْبُهُ ۗ وَاللَّهُ بِمَا تَعْمَلُونَ
عَلِيمٌ ○

"Conceal not evidence; for whoever conceals it,—his heart is tainted with sin. And Allah knoweth all that ye do." (II:283).

(v) *Damaging the moral tone of the social environment of Muslims prohibited:*

Propagating indencecies, including scandalous gossip, among the Muslims has been condemned very severely; hence, abstinence from the same is duty.

The Holy Qur'ãn says:

إِنَّ الَّذِينَ يُحِبُّونَ أَن تَشِيعَ الْفَاحِشَةُ فِي الَّذِينَ آمَنُوا لَهُمْ عَذَابٌ أَلِيمٌ ۙ فِي
الدُّنْيَا وَالْآخِرَةِ ۚ وَاللَّهُ يَعْلَمُ وَأَنتُمْ لَا تَعْلَمُونَ ○

3. "They pray", says A. Yusuf Ali, "not only for themselves, but for all their brethren, and above all, they pray that their hearts may be purified of any desire or tendency to disparage the work or virtues of other Muslims or to feel any jealousy on account of their success or good fortune." (*Op.cit.*, p. 1524).

"Verily those who love that indecency (and scandalous gossip) should be propagated among, and regarding, those who believe, for them shall be a torment afflictive in the (present) world and the Hereafter. And Allah knoweth (what terrible harm accrues to human society through such acts), and ye know not." (XXIV:19).

Chapter V

DUTIES TOWARDS NON-MUSLIMS[1] AS NON-MUSLIMS

(1) Duties towards all non-Muslims irrespective of their being friendly or inimical.

(2) Particular attitude towards those non-Muslims who are either friendly or neutral.

(3) Particular attitude towards those non-Muslims who are active enemies of Islam and Muslims.

(1) Duties Towards all Non-Muslims Irrespective of their being Friendly or Inimical

END:

(1) Ensuring justice to, and co-operation in goodness with, the non-Muslims;

(2) Active sympathy with non-Muslims in rescuing them from spiritual and moral evils.

(1) Ensuring justice to, and co-operation in Goodness with, the Non-Muslims:

(a) Duties of Commission:

(i) *Absolute justice under all circumstances enjoined:*

يَاأَيُّهَا الَّذِينَ آمَنُوا كُونُوا قَوَّامِينَ لِلَّهِ شُهَدَاءَ بِالْقِسْطِ ز وَلَا يَجْرِمَنَّكُمْ
شَنَآنُ قَوْمٍ عَلَىٰ أَلَّا تَعْدِلُوا ط اعْدِلُوا قف هُوَ أَقْرَبُ لِلتَّقْوَىٰ ز وَاتَّقُوا اللَّهَ ط
إِنَّ اللَّهَ خَبِيرٌ بِمَا تَعْمَلُونَ ○

"O ye who believe! be ye maintainers of your pact with Allah (stand out firmly for Allah), as witnesses to fair dealing, and let not the hatred of others to you make you swerve to wrong and depart from justice. Be just: that is nearer to Duty: and fear Allah. For Allah is well acquainted

1. Refer also to Duties to Human Beings in general, from page 199 onwards.

with all that ye do." (V:9).

(ii) *Fulfilment of pacts, contracts and treaties enjoined:*

يَـٰٓأَيُّهَا الَّذِينَ آمَنُوٓا أَوْفُوا بِالْعُقُودِ

"O ye who believe! fulfil the compacts (with whomsoever you may make them)...." (V:1).

(iii) *Forgiveness, in case of personal injuries from non-Muslims, enjoined:*

قُل لِّلَّذِينَ آمَنُوا يَغْفِرُوا لِلَّذِينَ لَا يَرْجُونَ أَيَّامَ اللَّهِ لِيَجْزِيَ
قَوْمًا بِمَا كَانُوا يَكْسِبُونَ ○

"Tell those who believe, to forgive those who do not look forward to the Days of Allah (i.e., the non-Muslims); it is for Him to recompense (for good or ill) each People according to what they have earned." (XLV:14).

(iv) *Granting protection to non-Muslims, even from amongst enemies, if they so desire, enjoined:*

وَإِنْ أَحَدٌ مِّنَ الْمُشْرِكِينَ اسْتَجَارَكَ فَأَجِرْهُ حَتَّىٰ يَسْمَعَ كَلَامَ اللَّهِ
ثُمَّ أَبْلِغْهُ مَأْمَنَهُ ۚ ذَٰلِكَ بِأَنَّهُمْ قَوْمٌ لَّا يَعْلَمُونَ ○

"If one amongst the Pagans asks thee for asylum, grant it to him, so that he may hear the Word of Allah; and then escort him to where he can be secure. That is because they are men without knowledge." (IX:6).

(b) *<u>Duties of Omission</u>:*

(i) *Transgressing the limits of justice in respect of non-Muslims and persecuting even the enemies of Islam among them, prohibited:*

وَلَا يَجْرِمَنَّكُمْ شَنَآنُ قَوْمٍ أَن صَدُّوكُمْ عَنِ الْمَسْجِدِ الْحَرَامِ أَن تَعْتَدُوا ۘ

".....And let not the hatred of some people—because they shut you out from the Sacred Mosque—incite you to transgress (the limits of justice and humanity in respect of them)...." (V:3).

(ii) *Co-operation in sin and transgression prohibited:*

وَلَا تَعَاوَنُوا عَلَى الْإِثْمِ وَالْعُدْوَانِ ۚ وَاتَّقُوا اللَّهَ ۖ إِنَّ اللَّهَ شَدِيدُ الْعِقَابِ ○

"....and co-operate not in sin and transgression, but keep your duty to Allah. Lo! Allah is strict in punishment." (V:3).

(2) ***Active Sympathy with non-Muslims in Rescuing them from Spiritual and Moral Evils, Enjoined:***

(a) *Duties of Commission:*

(i) *Duty of reaching out the Message of Islam to non-Muslims enjoined:*

Inviting fellow-beings to Truth, and, for that purpose, the dissemination and propagation of the eternal Message of Islam, constitutes one of the noblest tasks, as the Holy Qur'ãn says:

وَمَنْ أَحْسَنُ قَوْلًا مِّمَّنْ دَعَا إِلَى اللّٰهِ وَعَمِلَ صَالِحًا وَقَالَ إِنَّنِي مِنَ
الْمُسْلِمِينَ ○

"Who is better in speech than one who calls (men) to Allah, works righteousness, and says: 'I am of those who bow in Islam'?" (XLI:33).

This task has been made the obligation of every Muslim, because it has devolved on the Muslim community as a whole:

كُنْتُمْ خَيْرَ أُمَّةٍ أُخْرِجَتْ لِلنَّاسِ تَأْمُرُونَ بِالْمَعْرُوفِ وَتَنْهَوْنَ عَنِ
الْمُنْكَرِ وَتُؤْمِنُونَ بِاللّٰهِ

"Ye are the best of Peoples, evolved for (the service of) mankind, enjoining what is right, forbidding what is wrong, and believing in Allah...." (III:110).

Reaching out the Message of Islam successfully is, however, a difficult and highly specialised task—a task for which God raised the Prophets. It, therefore, necessitates high-class organization and highly qualified and superbly trained missionaries. The Holy Qur'ãn is fully alive to it and mikes it a duty of the Muslims to provide both:

وَلْتَكُنْ مِّنْكُمْ أُمَّةٌ يَّدْعُونَ إِلَى الْخَيْرِ وَيَأْمُرُونَ بِالْمَعْرُوفِ وَيَنْهَوْنَ
عَنِ الْمُنْكَرِ وَأُولٰٓئِكَ هُمُ الْمُفْلِحُونَ ○

"Let there arise out of you (O Muslims!) a band (of missionaries) inviting to all that is good, enjoining what is right, and forbidding what is wrong: They are the ones to attain felicity." (III:104).

The necessity of the creation of a high-class missionary organization as well as of superb accomplishments of those who might undertake to serve as missionaries of Islam, have both been emphasised in the following verse—the former in the word "wisdom", the latter in the verse as a whole:

ادْعُ إِلَىٰ سَبِيلِ رَبِّكَ بِالْحِكْمَةِ وَالْمَوْعِظَةِ الْحَسَنَةِ وَجَادِلْهُم بِالَّتِي
هِيَ أَحْسَنُ ۚ إِنَّ رَبَّكَ هُوَ أَعْلَمُ بِمَن ضَلَّ عَن سَبِيلِهِ ۖ وَهُوَ أَعْلَمُ
بِالْمُهْتَدِينَ ۝

"Invite (all) to the Way of thy Lord with wisdom and beautiful preaching; and argue with them in ways that are best and most gracious: For thy Lord knoweth best, who have strayed from His Path, and who receive guidance."[2] (XVI:125).

All in all, reaching out the Message of the Holy Qur'ãn—the message of Islam—to every human being, and to exert to the utmost in that way, is the bounden duty of the Muslims towards God, towards themselves and towards the non-Muslims.

The Holy Qur'ãn enjoins:

وَجَاهِدُوا فِي اللَّهِ حَقَّ جِهَادِهِ ۚ هُوَ اجْتَبَاكُمْ وَمَا جَعَلَ عَلَيْكُمْ فِي
الدِّينِ مِنْ حَرَجٍ ۚ مِّلَّةَ أَبِيكُمْ إِبْرَاهِيمَ ۚ هُوَ سَمَّاكُمُ الْمُسْلِمِينَ ۝
مِن قَبْلُ وَفِي هَٰذَا لِيَكُونَ الرَّسُولُ شَهِيدًا عَلَيْكُمْ وَتَكُونُوا
شُهَدَاءَ عَلَى النَّاسِ ۚ

"And strive hard for (the Cause of) Allah (i.e., reaching out to

---

2. The comments of Abdullah Yusuf Ali on this verse are very edifying. He says:

"In this wonderful passage are laid down principles of religious teaching, which are good for all time. But where are the Teachers with such qualifications? We must invite all to the Way of God, and expound His Universal Will; we must do it with wisdom and discretion, meeting people on their own knowledge and experience, which may be very narrow, or very wide. Our preaching must be, not dogmatic, not self-guarding, not offensive, but gentle, considerate, and such as would attract their attention. Our manner and arguments should not be acrimonious, but modelled on the most courteous and the most gracious example, so that the hearer may say to himself; 'This man is not dealing merely with dialectics; he is not trying to get a rise out of me; he is sincerely expounding the faith that is in him, and his motive is the love of man and love of God." (*Op.cit.*, p. 689, n. 2161).

all mankind the Religion of Allah and consolidating it all over the earth[3]) with the (sincere, disciplined and hard) striving which is His right.

"He hath chosen you (for this), and hath not laid upon you in Religion any hardship (but only blessing); it is the Faith of your father Abraham. It is He Who hath named you Muslims (lit. 'those who have surrendered to God'), both (in the Revelation that came) before (since the time of Adam) and in this (Revelation), that the Messenger (Muhammad) may be a witness for you, and ye be (by word and deed) witnesses (of the truth of Islam) for (all) mankind." (XXII:78).

(ii) *Co-operation in deeds of righteousness enjoined:*

وَتَعَاوَنُوا عَلَى الْبِرِّ وَالتَّقْوَىٰ

"....and co-operate in righteousness and pious duty". (V:3).

(*b*) Duties of Omission:

(i) *Forced conversion of non-Muslims prohibited:*

The Holy Qur'ãn says:

لَا إِكْرَاهَ فِي الدِّينِ قَد تَّبَيَّنَ الرُّشْدُ مِنَ الْغَيِّ

"Let there be no compulsion in (respect of adoption of the) religion (of Islam): Truth stands out clear from error[4]...." (II:256).

Note: This verse also rules out persectuion of non-Muslims on religious basis.

---

3. Ref:

هُوَ الَّذِي أَرْسَلَ رَسُولَهُ بِالْهُدَىٰ وَدِينِ الْحَقِّ لِيُظْهِرَهُ عَلَى الدِّينِ كُلِّهِ وَلَوْ كَرِهَ الْمُشْرِكُونَ

"It is He Who has sent His Messenger with Guidance and the Religion of Truth, that He may proclaim it (make it triumph) (as the supreme spiritual force) over all religion (i.e., overall systems of belief and action), even though the Pagans may detest (it)." (LXI:9).

4. Cf. VIII:42:-

لِيَهْلِكَ مَنْ هَلَكَ عَنْ بَيِّنَةٍ وَيَحْيَىٰ مَنْ حَيَّ عَنْ بَيِّنَةٍ

"....so that he who was to perish (spiritually), should perish by a clear proof (of the Truth of Islam); and he who was to remain alive (spiritually) may remain alive by a clear proof...."

(ii) *Hurting the religious feelings through hurtful language, even when it relates to pure and simple superstitions, prohibited:*

وَلَا تَسُبُّوا الَّذِينَ يَدْعُونَ مِنْ دُونِ اللَّهِ

"Revile not ye (O Muslims!) those (false deities) whom they call upon besides Allah...." (VI:108).

It may, however, be noted that, in controversies with the non-Muslims, if they attack Islam maliciously, a Muslim has been permitted to retort but with the condition of sticking to strictest equity. At the same time, however, the Holy Qur'ãn wants the Muslim debater and controversialist to restrain himself, not losing temper and not forgetting his religion's sublime principles of conduct. We are told:

وَإِنْ عَاقَبْتُمْ فَعَاقِبُوا بِمِثْلِ مَا عُوقِبْتُمْ بِهِ ۖ وَلَئِنْ صَبَرْتُمْ لَهُوَ خَيْرٌ لِلصَّابِرِينَ ○

"And if ye catch them out (in a controversy), catch them out no worse than they catch you out: But if ye show forbearance, that is indeed the best (i.e., the most appropriate course) of those who are forbearing." (XVI:126).

(2) Particular Attitude Towards those Non-Muslims who are either Friendly or Neutral

(*a*) *Duty of Commission:*

Social Intercourse and Benevolence permitted:

(*i*) The Holy Qur'ãn says:

لَا يَنْهَاكُمُ اللَّهُ عَنِ الَّذِينَ لَمْ يُقَاتِلُوكُمْ فِي الدِّينِ وَلَمْ يُخْرِجُوكُمْ مِنْ دِيَارِكُمْ أَنْ تَبَرُّوهُمْ وَتُقْسِطُوا إِلَيْهِمْ ۚ إِنَّ اللَّهَ يُحِبُّ الْمُقْسِطِينَ ○

"Allah forbiddeth you not that ye should deal benevolently and equitably with those who fought not against you on account of religion nor drove you out from your homes; verily Allah loveth those who are just." (LX:8).

(*ii*) The Holy Qur'ãn permits the extension of social relations with non-Muslims in proportion to the affinity which they may have with the Qur'ãnic moral and spiritual values. Thus, it permits marriage with the women who follow some revealed religion and have thus affinity with Islam. It also allows partaking of their lawful food:

الْيَوْمَ أُحِلَّ لَكُمُ الطَّيِّبٰتُ ۖ وَطَعَامُ الَّذِينَ أُوتُوا الْكِتٰبَ حِلٌّ لَّكُمْ ۠
وَطَعَامُكُمْ حِلٌّ لَّهُمْ ۖ وَالْمُحْصَنٰتُ مِنَ الْمُؤْمِنٰتِ وَالْمُحْصَنٰتُ مِنَ الَّذِينَ
أُوتُوا الْكِتٰبَ مِن قَبْلِكُمْ إِذَا آتَيْتُمُوهُنَّ أُجُورَهُنَّ مُحْصِنِينَ غَيْرَ مُسٰفِحِينَ
وَلَا مُتَّخِذِي أَخْدَانٍ ۗ وَمَن يَكْفُرْ بِالْإِيمَانِ فَقَدْ حَبِطَ عَمَلُهُ ۠ وَهُوَ فِي
الْآخِرَةِ مِنَ الْخٰسِرِينَ ۝

"This day are (all) good things made lawful for you. The food of those who have received the Scripture is lawful for you (provided it consists of lawful things), and your food is lawful for them And so are the virtuous women of the believers and the virtuous women of those who received the Scripture before you (lawful for you) when ye give them their marriage portions and live with them in honour, not in fornication, nor taking them as secret concubines. Whoso denieth the faith, his work is vain and he will be among the losers in the Hereafter." (V:6)[5].

---

5. "The question is for food generally, such as is ordinarily 'good and pure': in the matter of meat it should be killed with some sort of solemnity analogous to that of the *Kalima*. The rules of Islam in this respect being analogous to those of the People of the Book, there is no objections to mutual recognition, as opposed to meat killed by Pagans with superstitious rites. In this respect the Christian rule is the same: 'That ye abstain from meats offered to idols, and from blood, and from things strangled, and from fornication.' (*Acts*, XV:29). Notice the bracketing of fornication with things unlawful to eat.

"Islam is not exclusive. Social intercourse, including intermarriage, is permitted with the People of the Book. A Muslim man may marry a woman from their ranks on the same terms as he would marry a Muslim woman, i.e., he must give her an economic and moral status, and must not be actuated merely by motives of lust or physical desire. A Muslim woman may not marry a non-Muslim man, because her Muslim status would be affected: the wife ordinarily takes the nationality and status given by her husband's law. A non-Muslim woman marrying a Muslim husband would be expected eventually to accept Islam. Any man or woman, of any race or faith, may, on accepting Islam, freely marry any Muslim woman or man, provided it be from motives of purity and chastity and not of lewdness." (A. Yusuf Ali, *op.cit.*, p. 241).

(*b*) <u>*Duty of Omission*</u>:

Marriages with : (a) polytheistic and idolatrous women or men, or (b) men belonging to the 'People of the Book', even when they are friendly or neutral, prohibited:

As to (a):

وَلَا تَنكِحُوا الْمُشْرِكَاتِ حَتَّىٰ يُؤْمِنَّ ۚ وَلَأَمَةٌ مُّؤْمِنَةٌ خَيْرٌ مِّن مُّشْرِكَةٍ
وَلَوْ أَعْجَبَتْكُمْ ۗ وَلَا تُنكِحُوا الْمُشْرِكِينَ حَتَّىٰ يُؤْمِنُوا ۚ وَلَعَبْدٌ مُّؤْمِنٌ
خَيْرٌ مِّن مُّشْرِكٍ وَلَوْ أَعْجَبَكُمْ ۗ أُولَٰئِكَ يَدْعُونَ إِلَى النَّارِ ۖ وَاللَّهُ يَدْعُو إِلَى
الْجَنَّةِ وَالْمَغْفِرَةِ بِإِذْنِهِ ۖ وَيُبَيِّنُ آيَاتِهِ لِلنَّاسِ لَعَلَّهُمْ
يَتَذَكَّرُونَ ۝

"And do not marry the idolatresses until they believe, and certainly a believing slave woman is better than an idolatress woman, even though she should please you; and do not give (believing women) in marriage to idolaters until they believe, and certainly a believing male slave is better than an idolater even though he should please you; these invite to the Fire, and Allah invites to the Garden (of Bliss) and forgiveness by His will, and makes clear His Signs to human beings, that they might be mindful." (II:221).

As to (b):

Verse 6 of Chapter V, quoted above, confines the permission of marriage with the 'People of the Book' to their women only, thus definitely excluding their males whom, therefore, a Muslim woman is not allowed to marry.

(3) Particular Attitude towards those Non-Muslims who are active enemies of Islam and Muslims:

(*a*) <u>*Duties of Omission*</u>:

<u>***END***</u>:

Preservation of Islam and Muslims.

(*i*) *Befriending active enemies, who are devoted to the destruction of Islam and Muslims, and establishing with them intimate relations, even though they are near relatives, prohibited:*

There are several verses in the Holy Qur'ãn which bear reference to this problem. We quote all the important ones herein below: Every such verse relates, without exception, only to those non-Muslims of the days of Qur'ãnic Revelation—Pagans, Jews and Christians who were sworn enemies of Islam and whose active hostility towards Muslims had reached the highest limits[6]. They had it as their permanent mission to do all in their power for destroying and annihilating Islam and Muslims. It was, thus, for protecting Islam and Muslims against their enemies and not out of spite for non-Muslims as such, that the following verses were revealed, and they hold good wherever and whenever similar situation arises. The rationality and justice of laying down this duty is obvious and must be accepted by every reasonable human being.

The Holy Qur'ãn says:

لَا يَتَّخِذِ الْمُؤْمِنُونَ الْكٰفِرِينَ أَوْلِيَآءَ مِنْ دُونِ الْمُؤْمِنِينَ ۚ وَمَنْ
يَفْعَلْ ذٰلِكَ فَلَيْسَ مِنَ اللّٰهِ فِي شَيْءٍ إِلَّآ أَنْ تَتَّقُوا مِنْهُمْ تُقٰىةً ۗ

"Let not the Believers take for friends or helpers infidels[7] rather than believers: if ye do that, in nothing will there be help from Allah: except (entering into some no-war pact with them) by way of precaution, that ye may guard yourselves from them...." (III:28).

يٰٓأَيُّهَا الَّذِينَ آمَنُوا لَا تَتَّخِذُوا بِطَانَةً مِنْ دُونِكُمْ لَا يَأْلُونَكُمْ خَبَالًا ۖ
وَدُّوا مَا عَنِتُّمْ قَدْ بَدَتِ الْبَغْضَآءُ مِنْ أَفْوَاهِهِمْ ۖ وَمَا تُخْفِي صُدُورُهُمْ
أَكْبَرُ ۚ قَدْ بَيَّنَّا لَكُمُ الْآيٰتِ إِنْ كُنْتُمْ تَعْقِلُونَ ۝ هٰٓأَنْتُمْ أُولَآءِ تُحِبُّونَهُمْ
وَلَا يُحِبُّونَكُمْ وَتُؤْمِنُونَ بِالْكِتٰبِ كُلِّهِ ۚ وَإِذَا لَقُوكُمْ قَالُوٓا آمَنَّا ۚ وَإِذَا
خَلَوْا عَضُّوا عَلَيْكُمُ الْأَنَامِلَ مِنَ الْغَيْظِ ۚ قُلْ مُوتُوا بِغَيْظِكُمْ ۗ إِنَّ اللّٰهَ
عَلِيمٌ بِذَاتِ الصُّدُورِ ۝ إِنْ تَمْسَسْكُمْ حَسَنَةٌ تَسُؤْهُمْ ۖ وَإِنْ تُصِبْكُمْ
سَيِّئَةٌ يَفْرَحُوا بِهَا ۖ وَإِنْ تَصْبِرُوا وَتَتَّقُوا لَا يَضُرُّكُمْ كَيْدُهُمْ شَيْئًا ۗ
إِنَّ اللّٰهَ بِمَا يَعْمَلُونَ مُحِيطٌ ۝

---

6. This can be verified from the historical records, for which any detailed and proper book on Islamic history will suffice.

7. (actively hostile to Islam).

"Oh ye who believe! take not into your intimacy those outside your ranks. They will not fail to corrupt you. *They only desire your ruin: Rank hatred has already appeared from their mouths: Something far worse is hidden in their hearts.* We have made plain to you to the Signs, if ye have wisdom. Ah! ye are those who love them, but they love you not,—though ye believe in the whole of the Book. When they meet you, they say, 'We believe'; but when they are alone, they bite off the very tips of their fingers at you in their rage. Say: 'Perish in your rage; Allah knoweth well all the secrets of the heart'. If aught that is good befalls you, it grieves them; but if some misfortune overtakes you, they rejoice at it. But if ye are constant and do right, not the least harm will their cunning do to you; for Allah compasseth round about all that they do." (III:118-120).

وَدُّوا لَوْ تَكْفُرُونَ كَمَا كَفَرُوا فَتَكُونُونَ سَوَآءً فَلَا تَتَّخِذُوا مِنْهُمْ أَوْلِيَآءَ حَتّٰى
يُهَاجِرُوا فِي سَبِيلِ اللّٰهِ ۚ فَإِنْ تَوَلَّوْا فَخُذُوهُمْ وَاقْتُلُوهُمْ حَيْثُ وَجَدْتُّمُوهُمْ ۖ
وَلَا تَتَّخِذُوا مِنْهُمْ وَلِيًّا وَّلَا نَصِيرًا ۝

"*They but wish that ye should reject Faith, as they do, and be on the same footing* (*as they*): but take not friends from their ranks until they flee in the Way of Allah (from what is forbidden). But if they turn renegades seize them and slay them; and (in any case) take no friends or helpers from their ranks:...." (IV:89).

وَقَدْ نَزَّلَ عَلَيْكُمْ فِي الْكِتٰبِ أَنْ إِذَا سَمِعْتُمْ آيٰتِ اللّٰهِ يُكْفَرُ بِهَا وَ
يُسْتَهْزَأُ بِهَا فَلَا تَقْعُدُوا مَعَهُمْ حَتّٰى يَخُوضُوا فِي حَدِيثٍ غَيْرِهِ ۚ إِنَّكُمْ
إِذًا مِّثْلُهُمْ ۗ إِنَّ اللّٰهَ جَامِعُ الْمُنٰفِقِينَ وَالْكٰفِرِينَ فِي جَهَنَّمَ جَمِيعًا ۝

"Already have We sent you word in the Book, that when ye hear *the Signs of Allah held in defiance and ridicule*, ye are not to sit with them unless they turn to a different theme; if ye did, ye would be like them. For Allah will collect the Hypocrites and those who defy Faith—all in Hell;...." (IV:140).

يٰٓأَيُّهَا الَّذِينَ آمَنُوا لَا تَتَّخِذُوا الْيَهُودَ وَالنَّصٰرٰٓى أَوْلِيَآءَ ۘ بَعْضُهُمْ أَوْلِيَآءُ
بَعْضٍ ۚ وَمَنْ يَّتَوَلَّهُمْ مِّنْكُمْ فَإِنَّهُ مِنْهُمْ ۗ إِنَّ اللّٰهَ لَا يَهْدِي الْقَوْمَ
الظّٰلِمِينَ ۝

"Oh ye who believe! take not the Jews and the Christians for your friends and protectors: They are but friends and protectors to each other[8]. And he amongst you that turn to them (for friendship) is of them. Verily Allah guideth not a people unjust." (V:54).

يَاأَيُّهَا الَّذِينَ آمَنُوا لَا تَتَّخِذُوا الَّذِينَ اتَّخَذُوا دِينَكُمْ هُزُوًا وَلَعِبًا
مِنَ الَّذِينَ أُوتُوا الْكِتَابَ مِنْ قَبْلِكُمْ وَالْكُفَّارَ أَوْلِيَاءَ ۚ وَاتَّقُوا اللَّهَ
إِنْ كُنْتُمْ مُؤْمِنِينَ ۝

"Oh ye who believe! take not for friends and protectors those who take your religion for a mockeiy or sport,—whether amongst those who received the Scripture before you, or among those who reject Faith; But fear ye Allah, if ye have Faith (indeed)." (V:60).

وَإِذَا رَأَيْتَ الَّذِينَ يَخُوضُونَ فِي آيَاتِنَا فَأَعْرِضْ عَنْهُمْ حَتَّىٰ يَخُوضُوا فِي
حَدِيثٍ غَيْرِهِ ۚ وَإِمَّا يُنْسِيَنَّكَ الشَّيْطَانُ فَلَا تَقْعُدْ بَعْدَ الذِّكْرَىٰ مَعَ
الْقَوْمِ الظَّالِمِينَ ۝

"When thou seest men engaged in vain discourse about Our Signs, turn away from them unless they turn to a different theme. If Satan even makes thee forget, then after recollection, sit not thou in the company of the ungoldly." (VI:68).

فَإِذَا انْسَلَخَ الْأَشْهُرُ الْحُرُمُ فَاقْتُلُوا الْمُشْرِكِينَ حَيْثُ وَجَدْتُمُوهُمْ
وَخُذُوهُمْ وَاحْصُرُوهُمْ وَاقْعُدُوا لَهُمْ كُلَّ مَرْصَدٍ ۚ فَإِنْ تَابُوا وَ
أَقَامُوا الصَّلَاةَ وَآتَوُا الزَّكَاةَ فَخَلُّوا سَبِيلَهُمْ ۚ إِنَّ اللَّهَ غَفُورٌ رَحِيمٌ ۝

"But when the forbidden months are past, then fight and slay the Pagans[9] wherever ye find them, or seize them, beleaguer them, and lie in wait for them in every stratagem (of war); but if they repent, and establish regular prayers and practise regular charity, then open the way for them; for Allah is Oft-Forgiving, Most Merciful." (IX:5).

---

8. The Holy Qur'ān refers to a well attested historical fact.

9. (of Arabia, who were in a state of pitched war with Islam and Muslims).

يَٰٓأَيُّهَا ٱلَّذِينَ ءَامَنُوا لَا تَتَّخِذُوٓا ءَابَآءَكُمْ وَإِخْوَٰنَكُمْ أَوْلِيَآءَ إِنِ ٱسْتَحَبُّوا
ٱلْكُفْرَ عَلَى ٱلْإِيمَٰنِ ۚ وَمَن يَتَوَلَّهُم مِّنكُمْ فَأُولَٰٓئِكَ هُمُ ٱلظَّٰلِمُونَ ○

"Oh ye who believe! Take not for protectors your fathers and your brothers if they love infidelity above Faith: If any of you do so, they do wrong." (IX:23).

يَٰٓأَيُّهَا ٱلنَّبِىُّ جَٰهِدِ ٱلْكُفَّارَ وَٱلْمُنَٰفِقِينَ وَٱغْلُظْ عَلَيْهِمْ ۚ وَمَأْوَىٰهُمْ
جَهَنَّمُ ۖ وَبِئْسَ ٱلْمَصِيرُ ○

"Oh Prophet! Strive hard against the Rejecters and the Hypocrites (to combat the evils of their hostility). And be firm against them. Their abode is Hell,—an evil refuge indeed." (IX:73).

يَحْلِفُونَ بِٱللَّهِ مَا قَالُوا وَلَقَدْ قَالُوا كَلِمَةَ ٱلْكُفْرِ وَكَفَرُوا بَعْدَ
إِسْلَٰمِهِمْ وَهَمُّوا بِمَا لَمْ يَنَالُوا ۚ وَمَا نَقَمُوٓا إِلَّآ أَنْ أَغْنَىٰهُمُ ٱللَّهُ وَرَسُولُهُۥ
مِن فَضْلِهِۦ ۚ فَإِن يَتُوبُوا يَكُ خَيْرًا لَّهُمْ ۖ وَإِن يَتَوَلَّوْا يُعَذِّبْهُمُ ٱللَّهُ عَذَابًا
أَلِيمًا فِى ٱلدُّنْيَا وَٱلْءَاخِرَةِ ۚ وَمَا لَهُمْ فِى ٱلْأَرْضِ مِن وَلِىٍّ وَلَا نَصِيرٍ ○

"They (i.e., the Hypocrites) swear by Allah that they said nothing (evil), but indeed they uttered blasphemy, and they did it after accepting Islam; and they meditated a plot which they were unable to carry out: this revenge of theirs was (their) only return for the bounty with which Allah and His Messenger had enriched them! If they repent, it will be best for them. But if they turn back (to their evil ways), Allah will punish them with a grievous penalty in this life and in the Hereafter: they shall have none on earth to protect or help them." (IX:74).

يَٰٓأَيُّهَا ٱلَّذِينَ ءَامَنُوا قَٰتِلُوا ٱلَّذِينَ يَلُونَكُم مِّنَ ٱلْكُفَّارِ وَلْيَجِدُوا فِيكُمْ
غِلْظَةً ۚ وَٱعْلَمُوٓا أَنَّ ٱللَّهَ مَعَ ٱلْمُتَّقِينَ ○

"O ye who believe! Fight the (hostile) infidels who gird you about, and let them find firmness in you: and know that Allah is with those who fear Him". (IX:123).

لَا تَجِدُ قَوْمًا يُؤْمِنُونَ بِاللّٰهِ وَالْيَوْمِ الْآخِرِ يُوَادُّونَ مَنْ حَادَّ اللّٰهَ وَرَسُولَهُ
وَلَوْ كَانُوا آبَاءَهُمْ أَوْ أَبْنَاءَهُمْ أَوْ إِخْوَانَهُمْ أَوْ عَشِيرَتَهُمْ ؕ

"Thou wilt not find any people who believe in Allah and the Last Day, befriending those who oppose Allah and His Messenger, even though they were their fathers or their sons, or their brothers, or their kindred...." (LVIII:22).

يَا أَيُّهَا الَّذِينَ آمَنُوا لَا تَتَّخِذُوا عَدُوِّي وَعَدُوَّكُمْ أَوْلِيَاءَ تُلْقُونَ إِلَيْهِمْ
بِالْمَوَدَّةِ وَقَدْ كَفَرُوا بِمَا جَاءَكُمْ مِنَ الْحَقِّ ۚ يُخْرِجُونَ الرَّسُولَ وَإِيَّاكُمْ
أَنْ تُؤْمِنُوا بِاللّٰهِ رَبِّكُمْ ؕ إِنْ كُنْتُمْ خَرَجْتُمْ جِهَادًا فِي سَبِيلِي وَابْتِغَاءَ
مَرْضَاتِي ۚ تُسِرُّونَ إِلَيْهِمْ بِالْمَوَدَّةِ ۖ وَأَنَا أَعْلَمُ بِمَا أَخْفَيْتُمْ وَمَا أَعْلَنْتُمْ ؕ وَ
مَنْ يَفْعَلْهُ مِنْكُمْ فَقَدْ ضَلَّ سَوَاءَ السَّبِيلِ ۝ إِنْ يَثْقَفُوكُمْ يَكُونُوا لَكُمْ
أَعْدَاءً وَيَبْسُطُوا إِلَيْكُمْ أَيْدِيَهُمْ وَأَلْسِنَتَهُمْ بِالسُّوءِ وَوَدُّوا لَوْ
تَكْفُرُونَ ۝ لَنْ تَنْفَعَكُمْ أَرْحَامُكُمْ وَلَا أَوْلَادُكُمْ ۚ يَوْمَ الْقِيَامَةِ ۚ يَفْصِلُ بَيْنَكُمْ ؕ
وَاللّٰهُ بِمَا تَعْمَلُونَ بَصِيرٌ ۝

"O ye who believe! take not My enemies and yours as friends (or protectors),—offering them (your) love, even though they have rejected the Truth that has come to you, and *have driven out the Prophet and yourselves* (*from your homes*), (*simply*) *because ye believe in Allah your Lord!* If ye have come out to strive in My Way and to seek My Good Pleasure (take them not as friends), holding secret converse of love (and friendship) with them: for I know full well all that ye reveal. And any of you that does this has strayed from the Straight Path. *If they were to get the better of you, they would behave to you as enemies, and stretch forth their hands and their tongues against you for evil; and they desire that ye should reject the Truth.* Of no profit to you will be your relatives and your children on the Day of Judgment: He will judge between you: For Allah sees well all that ye do." (LX:1-3).

إِنَّمَا يَنْهَاكُمُ اللّٰهُ عَنِ الَّذِينَ قَاتَلُوكُمْ فِي الدِّينِ وَأَخْرَجُوكُمْ مِنْ
دِيَارِكُمْ وَظَاهَرُوا عَلَىٰ إِخْرَاجِكُمْ أَنْ تَوَلَّوْهُمْ ۚ وَمَنْ يَتَوَلَّهُمْ فَأُولٰئِكَ
هُمُ الظّٰلِمُونَ ۝

"*Allah only forbids you with regard to those who fight you for (your) Faith, and drive you out of your homes, and support (others) in driving you out, from turning to them (for friendship and protection).* It is such as turn to them (in the circumstances), that do wrong." (LX:9).

(ii) Firmness against the enemies of Islam enjoined:

مُحَمَّدٌ رَّسُولُ اللَّهِ ۚ وَالَّذِينَ مَعَهُ أَشِدَّاءُ عَلَى الْكُفَّارِ

"Muhammad is the Messenger of Allah; and those who are with him are strong against (the evils of) the Rejectors...." (XLVIII:29).

(iii) Mightiness against the enemies of Islam enjoined:

أَعِزَّةٍ عَلَى الْكَافِرِينَ

"....(The quality of true Muslims should be that they should be) mighty against the (hostile) Rejectors...." (V:57).

(iv) Building up military strength in the highest possible measure, as a safeguard against dangers from the side of the enemies of Islam, enjoined:

وَأَعِدُّوا لَهُم مَّا اسْتَطَعْتُم مِّن قُوَّةٍ وَمِن رِّبَاطِ الْخَيْلِ تُرْهِبُونَ بِهِ
عَدُوَّ اللَّهِ وَعَدُوَّكُمْ وَآخَرِينَ مِن دُونِهِمْ لَا تَعْلَمُونَهُمُ اللَّهُ
يَعْلَمُهُمْ ۚ وَمَا تُنفِقُوا مِن شَيْءٍ فِي سَبِيلِ اللَّهِ يُوَفَّ إِلَيْكُمْ وَأَنتُمْ
لَا تُظْلَمُونَ ○

"Against them (i.e., your enemies) make ready your Power to the utmost of your strength, including steeds of war, to strike terror into (the hearts of) the enemies of Allah and your enemies, and others besides, whom ye know not, but whom Allah doth know. Whatever ye shall spend in the Cause of Allah, shall be repaid unto you, and ye shall not be treated unjustly." (VIII:60).

(v) Fighting against the enemies with the fullest enthusiasm and to the finish, in order to defend Islam and Muslims and make them safe, in case the non-Muslims create a state of war, enjoined:

يَا أَيُّهَا النَّبِيُّ حَرِّضِ الْمُؤْمِنِينَ عَلَى الْقِتَالِ ۚ إِن يَكُن مِّنكُمْ
عِشْرُونَ صَابِرُونَ يَغْلِبُوا مِائَتَيْنِ ۚ وَإِن يَكُن مِّنكُم مِّائَةٌ يَغْلِبُوا
أَلْفًا مِّنَ الَّذِينَ كَفَرُوا بِأَنَّهُمْ قَوْمٌ لَّا يَفْقَهُونَ ۝

"Oh Messenger! rouse the Believers to the fight. If there are twenty among you, patient and persevering, they will conquer two hundred: if a hundred, they will conquer a thousand of the Rejectors: for these are a people without understanding." (VIII:65).

أُذِنَ لِلَّذِينَ يُقَاتَلُونَ بِأَنَّهُمْ ظُلِمُوا ۚ وَإِنَّ اللَّهَ عَلَىٰ نَصْرِهِمْ
لَقَدِيرٌ ۝ الَّذِينَ أُخْرِجُوا مِن دِيَارِهِم بِغَيْرِ حَقٍّ إِلَّا أَن يَقُولُوا
رَبُّنَا اللَّهُ ۗ وَلَوْلَا دَفْعُ اللَّهِ النَّاسَ بَعْضَهُم بِبَعْضٍ لَّهُدِّمَتْ صَوَامِعُ وَبِيَعٌ
وَصَلَوَاتٌ وَمَسَاجِدُ يُذْكَرُ فِيهَا اسْمُ اللَّهِ كَثِيرًا ۗ

"*To those against whom war is made, permission is given* (*to fight*)*, because they are wronged;—and verily Allah is Most Powerful for their aid;*—(*they are*) *those who have been expelled from their homes in defiance of right,*—(*for no cause*) *except that they say, 'Our Lord is Allah',* Did not Allah check one set of people by means of another, there would surely have been pulled down monasteries, churches, synagogues, and mosques, in which the name of Allah is commemorated in abundant measure...." (XXII:39, 40)[10].

(*b*) Duties of Commission:

END:

Promotion of Peace, Justice and Goodwill among mankind.

(i) Maintaining the attitude of readiness for making peace with the

---

10. "Several translators have failed to notice the *yuqãtalûna* (in the best approved texts) is in the passive voice, 'against whom war is made'....not 'who take arms against the unbelievers' as Sale translates it. The cause 'and verily....their aid' is parenthetical. Verse 40 connects on with 'they are wronged'. The wrong is indicated. 'driven by persecution from their home, for no other reason than that they worshipped the One True God'. This was the first occasion on which fighting—in self defence—was permitted. This passage therefore undoubtedly dates from Madinah." (Abdullah Yusuf Ali, *op.cit.*, p. 86).

enemies of Islam in the interest of human welfare, enjoined:

وَإِن جَنَحُوا لِلسَّلْمِ فَاجْنَحْ لَهَا وَتَوَكَّلْ عَلَى اللَّهِ ۚ إِنَّهُ هُوَ السَّمِيعُ
الْعَلِيمُ ۝ وَإِن يُرِيدُوا أَن يَخْدَعُوكَ فَإِنَّ حَسْبَكَ اللَّهُ ۚ

"But if the enemy incline towards peace, do thou (also) incline towards peace, and trust in Allah: for He is the One who heareth and knoweth (all things). Should they intend to deceive thee,—verily Allah sufficeth thee...." (VIII:61, 62).

(ii) Finally, observing absolute justice in all respects and in all dealings with the enemies of Islam enjoined as bounden duty:

يَا أَيُّهَا الَّذِينَ آمَنُوا كُونُوا قَوَّامِينَ لِلَّهِ شُهَدَاءَ بِالْقِسْطِ ۖ وَلَا يَجْرِمَنَّكُمْ
شَنَآنُ قَوْمٍ عَلَىٰ أَلَّا تَعْدِلُوا ۚ اعْدِلُوا هُوَ أَقْرَبُ لِلتَّقْوَىٰ ۖ وَاتَّقُوا اللَّهَ ۚ إِنَّ
اللَّهَ خَبِيرٌ بِمَا تَعْمَلُونَ ۝

"Oh ye who believe! be maintainers of your pact with Allah (i.e., stand out firmly for Allah) as witnesses to fair dealing, and let not the hatred of others to you make you swerve to wrong and depart from justice. Be just: that is nearer to Duty: and fear Allah. For Allah is well acquainted with all that ye do." (V:9).

(iii) In the case of non-Muslim parents, continued service to them enjoined, even when they exert to turn a Muslim away from Islam:

وَإِن جَاهَدَاكَ عَلَىٰ أَن تُشْرِكَ بِي مَا لَيْسَ لَكَ بِهِ عِلْمٌ فَلَا تُطِعْهُمَا ۖ وَ
صَاحِبْهُمَا فِي الدُّنْيَا مَعْرُوفًا ۖ وَاتَّبِعْ سَبِيلَ مَنْ أَنَابَ إِلَيَّ ۚ ثُمَّ إِلَيَّ
مَرْجِعُكُمْ فَأُنَبِّئُكُم بِمَا كُنتُمْ تَعْمَلُونَ ۝

"But if they (i.e., the non-Muslim parents) strive to make thee join in worship with Me things of which thou hast no knowledge, obey them not; yet bear them company in this life with justice (and consideration) and follow the way of those who turn to Me (in love). In the end the return of you all is to Me, and I will tell you the truth (and meaning) of all that ye did." (XXXI:15).

Part III

DUTIES IN RESPECT OF MANNERS

END:

Practical demonstration, in terms of etiquette, of the Qur'ãnic spiritual, moral and social ideals in life, with a view to refinement of culture.

I. Religious Manners. II. Personal and Social Manners.

Chapter I

RELIGIOUS MANNERS

(1) **In respect of beginning an act: To say at the beginning of every act**:

بِسْمِ اللّٰهِ الرَّحْمٰنِ الرَّحِيْمِ ۝

(Bismillãhir-Rahmãnir-Rahîm)

"In the name of Allah, Most Gracious, Most Merciful."[1]

This 'manner' is contained in the following Qur'ãnic references:

(*i*) *In respect of seeking knowledge and guidance:*

اِقْرَاْ بِاسْمِ رَبِّكَ الَّذِيْ خَلَقَ ۝

"Read in the name of thy Lord and Cherisher Who created." (XCVI:1).

(*ii*) *In respect of beginning a communication or discourse:*

اِنَّهٗ مِنْ سُلَيْمٰنَ وَاِنَّهٗ بِسْمِ اللّٰهِ الرَّحْمٰنِ الرَّحِيْمِ ۝

1. All the chapters of the Holy Qur'ãn, except one, begin with this spiritual formula, which fact highlights its importance in Muslim life.

"It (i.e., this communication) is from Solomon, and is (as follows): 'In the name of Allah, Most Gracious, Most Merciful."

(XXVII:30).

(*iii*) *In respect of riding a vehicle and beginning a journey:*

وَقَالَ ارْكَبُوْا فِيْهَا بِسْمِ اللّٰهِ مَجْرٖىهَا وَمُرْسٰىهَا

"So he (Noah) said: 'Embark ye thereon (i.e., on the Ark)!' 'In the name of Allah be its course and its mooring'." (XI:41).

(*iv*) *In respect of slaughtering animals:*

وَلِكُلِّ اُمَّةٍ جَعَلْنَا مَنْسَكًا لِّيَذْكُرُوا اسْمَ اللّٰهِ عَلٰى مَا رَزَقَهُمْ مِّنْ بَهِيْمَةِ الْاَنْعَامِ

"To every people did We appoint rites (of sacrifice), that they might celebrate the name of Allah[2] over the sustenance He gave them from animals (fit for food.)..." (XXII:34).

(2) **<u>In respect of Praise to God: the Holy Qur'ān's first chapter opens with the words</u>**:

اَلْحَمْدُ لِلّٰهِ

(Alhamdo-lillāh)

"Praise be to Allah." (I:2).

Muslim writings and speeches may begin with these words.

Also, a Muslim should utter them whenever he is delivered from evil (XXIII:28) or sorrow (XXXV:34), or he is blessed with God's Grace in any way (XXVII:19).

Indeed, the accomplishment of every good and beneficial act should be followed by these words as expression of thankfulness, as it has been commanded:

قُلِ الْحَمْدُ لِلّٰهِ

"Say: 'Praise be to Allah'...." (XVII:111).

2. A Muslim should say: "*Bismillāhe Allāho-Akbar*" ("In the name of Allah: Allah is Possessor of all Greatness").

Thus, these words should be uttered after enjoying food or drink and when putting on new clothes.

(3) **<u>In respect of affirming the Glory of God</u>**:

The Holy Qur'ãn says:

سَبِّحِ اسْمَ رَبِّكَ الْأَعْلَى ۝

"Glorify the name of thy Lord, Most High." (LXXXVII:1).

Hence, on all occasions when God's Glory is to be proclaimed, a Muslim should say:

سُبْحٰنَ اللّٰهِ

(Subhân-Allah)

"Glory to Allah". (XII:108).

Or,

سُبْحَانَ رَبِّي

(Subhãna-Rabbî)

"Glory to my Lord!" (XVII:93)

(4) **<u>In respect of affirming the Greatness of God</u>**:

A Muslim derives all his strength from faith in God. Hence, he has been commanded to affirm constantly, through his attitude, and through words, whenever occasion arises, the greatness of God, as the Holy Qur'ãn says:

وَكَبِّرْهُ تَكْبِيرًا ۝

"Yea, magnify Him for His Greatness and Glory."

(XVII:111).

The standard expression in this respect is:

اَللّٰهُ أَكْبَرُ

(Allãho-Akbar)

"Allah is Possessor of all Greatness."

(5) **In respect of affirming God's excellence as Creator**:

Admiring anything in God's creation, a Muslim should say:

فَتَبَارَكَ اللّٰهُ أَحْسَنُ الْخَالِقِينَ ۝

(Fa tabãrak-Allaho ahsan-ul-Khãliqin)

"So blessed be Allah, the Best to create!" (XXIII:14).

(6) **In respect of God's Forgiving and Mercy**:

On occasions of consciousness of one's error or guilt, a Muslim should say:

أَسْتَغْفِرُ اللّٰهَ

(Astaghfirullãh)

"I ask the forgiveness of Allah."

Because, the Holy Qur'ãn says:

وَالَّذِينَ إِذَا فَعَلُوا فَاحِشَةً أَوْ ظَلَمُوٓا أَنفُسَهُمْ ذَكَرُوا اللّٰهَ فَاسْتَغْفَرُوا لِذُنُوبِهِمْ ۖ وَمَن يَغْفِرُ الذُّنُوبَ إِلَّا اللّٰهُ ۚ

"And those who, having done something to be ashamed of, or having wronged their own souls, earnestly bring Allah to mind, and ask for forgiveness for their sins,—and who can forgive sins except Allah?...." (III:135).

He may also say, when the consciousness of the violation of Divine Law deepens:

لَّا إِلٰهَ إِلَّآ أَنتَ سُبْحَانَكَ إِنِّي كُنتُ مِنَ الظَّالِمِينَ ۝

(Lã ilãha illã anta Subhãnaka inni kuntu min-az-Zãlimîn)

".....There is no God but Thou: Glory to Thee: I was indeed wrong!" (XXI:87)[3]

---

3. He should pray to God in these words:

رَّبِّ اغْفِرْ وَارْحَمْ وَأَنتَ خَيْرُ الرَّاحِمِينَ ۝

(Rabbighfir warham wa anta khair-ur-Rahîmin)

"O my Lord! Grant Thou forgiveness and mercy! For Thou art the best of those who show mercy!" (XXIII:118).

(7) **In respect of guarding against evil in general**:

When an evil is imputed to a Muslim, or he is invited to evil, he should say:

مَعَاذَ اللهِ

(Ma'āz-Allah)

"I seek refuge in Allah." (XII:23).

(8) **In respect of guiding against Satan**:

For keeping evil thoughts away, or for casting them off, a Muslim has been commanded:

وَإِمَّا يَنْزَغَنَّكَ مِنَ الشَّيْطٰنِ نَزْغٌ فَاسْتَعِذْ بِاللهِ ۚ إِنَّهُ سَمِيعٌ عَلِيمٌ ○

"If a suggestion from Satan assail thy (mind), seek refuge with Allah; for He heareth and knoweth all things." (VII:200).

Its usual form, based on this verse, is:

اعوذ بالله من الشيطٰن الرجيم

(A'ûzo billāhi min-ash-Shaitān-ir-Rajîm)

"I seek refuge in Allah from the accursed Devil."

Its other form, mentioned in the Holy Qur'ān, is:

وَقُلْ رَّبِّ أَعُوذُ بِكَ مِنْ هَمَزٰتِ الشَّيٰطِينِ ○ وَأَعُوذُ بِكَ رَبِّ أَنْ يَحْضُرُونِ ○

(Rabbe a-'ûzo bika min hamazāt-ish Shayātine wa a'ûzo bika Rabbe anyyahdurûn)

"O my Lord! I seek refuge with Thee from the suggestions of the Evil Ones. And I seek refuge with Thee O my Lord! lest they should come near me." (XXIII:97, 98).[4]

(9) **In respect of guarding serenity in afflictions**:

When confronted with any calamity or saddening news, a Muslim has been guided thus:

إِذَآ أَصٰبَتْهُمْ مُّصِيبَةٌ ۙ قَالُوٓا إِنَّا لِلّٰهِ وَإِنَّآ إِلَيْهِ رٰجِعُونَ ○

---

4. Prayers contained in chapters CXIII and CXIV are also recited on such occasions.

"They say, when afflicted with calamity: 'To Allah we belong, and to Him is our return'[5]". (II:156).

(10) **In respect of thoughts of elation and pride**:

When there is occasion for elation and pride, in respect of oneself or someone else, a Muslim, suppressing pride and attributing all achievements to the Power of God, should say:

مَا شَآءَ اللّٰهُ ، لَا قُوَّةَ اِلَّا بِاللّٰهِ

(Mãshã-Allah Lã quwwata illã billãh)

".....'Allah's Will (be done)! There is no power but with Allah!'....." (XVIII:39).

(11) **In respect of making a promise**:

When a Muslim makes a promise, he should on the one hand make a firm resolve to carry out his promise at all cost, and on the other hand say, seeking the help of God:

اِنْ شَآءَ اللّٰهُ

(Inshã-Allah)

"If Allah wills." (XLVIII:27)[6].

Similarly, he should say these words when he anticipates something. Because the Holy Qur'ãn has commanded the Muslims to do so:

وَلَا تَقُوْلَنَّ لِشَايْءٍ اِنِّيْ فَاعِلٌ ذٰلِكَ غَدًا ۙ اِلَّآ اَنْ يَّشَآءَ اللّٰهُ

"Nor say of anything, I shall be sure to do so and so tomorrow without adding, 'So please Allah!'....." (XVIII:23, 24).

(12) **In respect of recalling something forgotten**:

The Holy Qur'ãn says:

وَاذْكُرْ رَّبَّكَ اِذَا نَسِيْتَ وَقُلْ عَسٰٓى اَنْ يَّهْدِيَنِ رَبِّيْ لِاَقْرَبَ مِنْ هٰذَا رَشَدًا ۝

---

5. (Innã lillãhi wa innã ilaihi rãje'ûn).

6. These words have been used not only by the Holy Prophet Muhammad (Peace be on him), as in this verse, but by other Prophets also. Ref: XII:99; XVIII:69; XXVIII:27; XXXVIII:102.

".....and call thy Lord to mind when thou forgettest, and say, 'I hope that my Lord will guide me ever closer (even) than this to the right road"[7]." (XVIII:24).

(13) **In respect of safeguarding devotion to the Holy Prophet (Peace be on him)**:

Affirming, and invoking increase in, Divine Blessings and Peace on the Holy Prophet Muhammad (Divinely Blessed is he and in eternal Peace) whenever his name is mentioned,—doing this with all respect and as a mark of gratitude for his suffering in the cause of the service of mankind, and in obedience to the command of God given in the Holy Qur'ãn:

إِنَّ اللَّهَ وَمَلَٰٓئِكَتَهُۥ يُصَلُّونَ عَلَى النَّبِيِّ ۚ يَٰٓأَيُّهَا الَّذِينَ ءَامَنُوا صَلُّوا عَلَيْهِ وَسَلِّمُوا تَسْلِيمًا

"Lo! Allah and His angels shower Blessings (always) on the Prophet. O ye who believe! Ask blessings on him and salute him with a worthy salutation (i.e., with all respect)." (XXXIII:56)[8].

The shortest and the most generally used expression for affirming Divine Blessings and Peace on him is:

صلى الله عليه وسلم

(Sallallãho 'alaihe wa sallam)

i.e., "Allah has bestowed upon him His Blessings and Peace."[9]

---

7. ('Asa anyyahdiyane Rabbî li aqraba min hãzã rashadã).

8. This verse has a profound spiritual implication. We are, however, concerned here only with its implication in respect of manners.

9. It is necessary to point out here the grave mischief of those non-Muslim scholars who translate the expression in question as: "God bless him and grant him salvation." (*A Dictionary of Modern Written Arabic*, edited by J. Milton Cowan, p. 425). As regards salvation, every Prophet of God was born with his salvation ensured, because he was the Messenger of God and, as such, remained all his life, under Divine Protection, immune from sins. And this is perfectly logical, because he came to lead others into salvation. With reference to Muhammad, this fact has been clearly affirmed by the Qur'ãn in several contexts, e.g., in XLVIII:2. My rendering is according to the classical commentators of the Qur'ãn. (See *Tafsir al-Jalãlain*, p. 357).

The shortest comprehensive expression for invoking increase[10]—infinite increase—in God's Blessings and Peace for him, is:

اللّٰهمّ صلّ على محمّد وبارك وسلّم

(Allãhumma Salle'alã Muhammadin wa bãrik wa sallim)

"O Allah! shower Thine Mercy, Thine Benediction and Thine Peace on Muhammad."

In English, the words "Peace be on him" have been used by Muslim writers. These words form the translation of:

عليه السّلام

('Alaihis-Salãm)

That expression, however, also means:

"He is blessed with Peace."

(14) **<u>In respect of revering the Holy Prophet's memory, and hence, his grave at Madinah</u>:**

The Holy Qur'ãn says:

لِتُؤْمِنُوا بِاللّٰهِ وَرَسُولِهِ وَتُعَزِّرُوهُ وَتُوَقِّرُوهُ

"....in order that ye (O mankind) may believe in Allah and His Messenger (Muhammad) and may assist and *honour* him....." (XLVIII:9).

Moreover, the Holy Qur'ãn lays down:

إِنَّ أَكْرَمَكُمْ عِنْدَ اللّٰهِ أَتْقٰكُمْ

"Verily the most honourable among you is he who excels in Piety." (XLIX:13).

---

10. The Holy Prophet's entire life, since the very first day of his existence, has been, and is, and will be, under Divine Blessings and Peace. It is, therefore, increase which is invoked, and not mere bestowal. And this invoking for increase, again, is actually for getting blessings ourselves and not because the Holy Prophet needs it from us,—the continuous and abiding evolution of his personality in Beauty, Grace and Perfection having been already ensured by God (XCIII:4, 5).

And the Holy Prophet, according to Islamic theology, excels all human beings is Piety. He is, therefore, not only honourable but the most honourable in entire creation.

Besides that, he is the first Muslim among God's creatures (VI:163); hence he deserves honour foremost in God's creation.[11]

Thus, when a Muslim visits Madinah, he should treat the Holy Prophet's Mausoleum with deep and unstinted reverence, stand before his grave most respectfully while paying homage to him and seeking God's Blessings for himself.

(15) **<u>In respect of revering the Holy Ka'bah at Makkah</u>**:

The Holy *Ka'bah* is one of the 'Symbols of God'; and the Holy Qur'ãn teaches:

وَمَنْ يُعَظِّمْ شَعَآئِرَ اللّٰهِ فَاِنَّهَا مِنْ تَقْوَى الْقُلُوْبِ ۝

".....whoever holds in honour the Symbols of Allah, it surely is from piety of the hearts." (XXII:32).

Hence, when a Muslim visits the Holy *Ka'bah* and looks at it, he should do so with a deep reverential attitude and even his formal behaviour there should be such as to be entirely based on its sacredness.

(16) **<u>In respect of revering the Holy Qur'ãn</u>**:

(*a*) The Holy Qur'ãn says about itself:

لَّا يَمَسُّهٗٓ اِلَّا الْمُطَهَّرُوْنَ ۝

"which none shall touch but those who are clean." (LVI.79).

Hence, a Muslim should handle it only when he is in a state of formal purity with *wudû* and his total personality is in a state of communion with God.

(*b*) We are also told:

وَاِذَا قُرِئَ الْقُرْاٰنُ فَاسْتَمِعُوْا لَهٗ وَاَنْصِتُوْا لَعَلَّكُمْ تُرْحَمُوْنَ ۝

---

11. He is the first in Creation. This is borne out by the facts that:-

(1) everything in the universe is Muslim (III:83); and (2) the Holy Prophet is the first Muslim (VI:163).

"When the Qur'ãn is read, listen to it with attention, and hold your peace: that ye may receive Mercy." (VII:204).

Hence, when the Holy Qur'ãn is read loudly, a Muslim should not only concentrate his mind on it but should also adopt the attitude of reverence.

(17) **<u>In respect of venerating the mosque</u>**:

The Holy Qur'ãn says:

يَٰبَنِيٓ ءَادَمَ خُذُوا۟ زِينَتَكُمْ عِندَ كُلِّ مَسْجِدٍ

"O Children of Adam! Wear your beautiful apparel (adornment) at every (time and) place of prayer:....." (VII:31).

Hence, when a Muslim visits the mosque, he should go there properly dressed and with respectful attitude.

And as long as he stays there, he should observe the most dignified manners, in accordance with the advice given in XXII:32, quoted in the text of "manner 15"

Chapter II

PERSONAL AND SOCIAL MANNERS

(1) **In respect of employing the concept of "Rightism"**:

The Holy Qur'ãn designates the Muslims as "the Companions of the Right Hand", and "those on the right hand" (LVI:8). From here emerges the concept of "Rightism" which projects itself in the domain of manners and is employed in all acts involving cleanliness, beneficiality, sanctity, and the like.

The *Hadîth* supplies the details in this respect, which have been incorporated in the book of *Fiqh* (Islamic Law).[1]

(2) **In respect of greeting one another**:

The Holy Qur'ãn says:

وَإِذَا حُيِّيتُم بِتَحِيَّةٍ فَحَيُّوا بِأَحْسَنَ مِنْهَا أَوْ رُدُّوهَا ۗ إِنَّ اللَّهَ كَانَ عَلَىٰ كُلِّ شَيْءٍ حَسِيبًا ۝

"When a (courteous) greeting is offered to you, meet it with a greeting still more courteous, or (at least) of equal courtesy. Allah takes

---

1. Such laws relating to manners are:

The right hand should be used for: (*a*) eating and drinking, (*b*) putting on clothes on the upper part of the body, and (*c*) giving and réceiving gifts and washing hands.

The left hand should be used for: (*a*) cleansing the nose and (*b*) washing soiled part of the body after the call of nature.

The right foot should be: (*a*) placed first in entering the mosque, (*b*) used in putting on trousers, pants, socks and shoes, (*c*) employed in coming out of the toilet; and (*d*) handled first when washing the feet.

The left foot should be: (*a*) employed in coming out of the mosque, (*b*) entered first into the toilet, and (*c*) used in putting off clothes, etc., from the lower part of the body.

When a person lies down to take rest, he should rest on his right side first.

These manners are not based on any superstition, but are meant to form the symbolic reminders of the fact that a Muslim has to build up his life as one of the "Companions of the Right Hand." The other end is the creation of the sense of discipline and of uniformity of behaviour among Muslims. (For references, see: *Kitãb al-Adãb* in the Compendiums of *Hadîth* and the relevant sections in the books on Islamic Law.

careful account of all things." (IV:86).

The basic form of greeting has been given in the Holy Qur'ãn at several places, as for instance in the following verse:

وَإِذَا جَآءَكَ الَّذِينَ يُؤْمِنُونَ بِـَٔايَـٰتِنَا فَقُلْ سَلَـٰمٌ عَلَيْكُمْ ۖ كَتَبَ رَبُّكُمْ عَلَىٰ نَفْسِهِ الرَّحْمَةَ ۖ

"When those come to thee who believe in Our Sings, say: 'Peace be on you: your Lord hath prescribed for Himself (the rule of) Mercy....." (VI:54).

سَلَـٰمٌ عَلَيْكُم بِمَا صَبَرْتُمْ ۚ فَنِعْمَ عُقْبَى الدَّارِ ۝

"Peace unto you for that ye persevered in patience! Now how excellent is the final Home!" (XIII:24).

وَالسَّلَـٰمُ عَلَىٰ مَنِ اتَّبَعَ الْهُدَىٰٓ ۝

".....and peace to all who follow the Guidance." (XX:47).

The Islamic *Sharî'ah* has prescribed the following standard form:

السّلام علیکم

(Assalãmo 'alaikum)

"Peace be on (or, with) you",

which, as a reply, take the form:

وعلیکم السّلام

(Wa 'alaikum-us-Salãm)

"and on you (also) be Peace."

To it can be added:

ورحمة الله

(Wa Rahmatullãh)

"and the Mercy of Allah."

And after that, also:

وبركاته

(Wa Barakātuhū)

"and His Blessings."

These additions are meant to raise the standard of greeting in the expression of love.

(3) **In respect of dignified bearing in life**:

A Muslim should keep aloof from all unedifying things in word and deed, not to speak of indulging in them. (XXIII:3). In spite of that, however, if he is ever confronted with an unedifying situation or thing, it is his duty to withdraw in an honourable and dignified manner. The Holy Qur'ān says:

وَإِذَا مَرُّوا بِاللَّغْوِ مَرُّوا كِرَامًا ○

"....and when they pass by any senseless thing, they pass by it with dignified (avoidance)." (XXV:72).

(4) **In respect of dealing with unreasonable people**:

With aggressive, unreasonable people who dispute merely for the sake of disputing, a Muslim should deal in a dignified manner, courteously withdrawing from their wranglings. The Holy Qur'ān says:

وَإِذَا خَاطَبَهُمُ الْجَاهِلُونَ قَالُوا سَلَامًا ○

"....and when the ignorant address them, they say, 'Peace'." (XXV:63).

(5) **In respect of talking to people**:

A Muslim's manner of talk should contain the elements of courtesy, serenity and dignity.

The Holy Qur'ān says:

وَقُولُوا لِلنَّاسِ حُسْنًا

".....and speak in goodly (i.e., courteous and dignified) manner to mankind...." (II:83).

وَاغْضُضْ مِنْ صَوْتِكَ ط

".....and lower thy voice (i.e., speak to people with serenity)...." (XXXI:19).

(6) **In respect of avoidance of ostentation and haughtiness and observance of humility**:

A Muslim's manners should always reflect the above virtues. The Holy Qur'ãn says:

وَلَا تَمْشِ فِي الْأَرْضِ مَرَحًا ۚ إِنَّكَ لَنْ تَخْرِقَ الْأَرْضَ وَلَنْ تَبْلُغَ الْجِبَالَ طُولًا ۝

"Nor walk on the earth with insolence: For thou canst not rend the earth asunder, nor reach the mountains in height." (XVII:37).

وَاقْصِدْ فِي مَشْيِكَ وَاغْضُضْ مِنْ صَوْتِكَ ۚ إِنَّ أَنْكَرَ الْأَصْوَاتِ لَصَوْتُ الْحَمِيرِ ۝

"And be moderate in thy pace, and lower thy voice; for the harshest of sounds without doubt is the braying of the ass." (XXXI:19).

وَعِبَادُ الرَّحْمٰنِ الَّذِينَ يَمْشُونَ عَلَى الْأَرْضِ هَوْنًا

"And the servants of (Allah) Most-Gracious are those who walk on the earth in humility....." (XXV:63).

(7) **In respect of avoidance of light-heartedness**:

A Muslim's manner's should always be based on avoidance of light-heartedness and vainglory and should reflect dignified bearing, because, according to the Holy Qur'ãn.

إِنَّ اللّٰهَ لَا يُحِبُّ الْفَرِحِينَ ۝

"Verily Allah approveth not those who exult in vanity." (XXVIII:76).

(8) **In respect of being thankful**:

The Holy Qur'ãn has repeatedly emphasised thankfulness as one of the basic qualities of Islamic character and has condemned ungratefulness[2],—thankfulness benefiting not only the personality of the moral agent in respect of its harmonious build-up but also bringing reward from God in the Hereafter:

وَسَنَجْزِى الشّٰكِرِيْنَ ۝

"....and Allah will reward those who give thanks (to God and man)." (III:145).

Hence, a Muslim should always thank in suitable word everyone who does any good to him.

(9) **In regard to demonstration of respect towards the elders**:

A Muslim should always maintain a respectful attitude towards his elders and demonstrate this attitude even in his manners, as it has been commanded in the case of one's parents:

وَاخْفِضْ لَهُمَا جَنَاحَ الذُّلِّ مِنَ الرَّحْمَةِ

"And, out of kindness, lower unto them the wing of humility—" (XVII:24).

(10) **In respect of compassion**:

A Muslim should not only maintain in his heart but also demonstrate through his manners compassionate kindness for all those who are weaker than him in any way or junior to him in age or rank, because the Holy Qur'ãn has laid down this virtue as one of the qualities of Muslim character. It says:—

ثُمَّ كَانَ مِنَ الَّذِيْنَ اٰمَنُوْا وَتَوَاصَوْا بِالصَّبْرِ وَتَوَاصَوْا بِالْمَرْحَمَةِ ۝

"...and to be of those who believe and exhort one another to perseverance and exhort one another to compassionate kindness." (XC:17).

(11) **In respect of treating those who seek help**:

A Muslim should treat politely and nor rudely everyone who ask for his help, because the Holy Qur'ãn says:

وَاَمَّا السَّآئِلَ فَلَا تَنْهَرْ ۝

2. As recorded in the foregoing.

"And as to one who asks (for thine help) scold (him) not".
(XCIII:10).

(12) **In respect of visiting the people**:

(i) Respect for each other's privacy with a view to maintain personal and family privacy and to avoid social scandal to which its non-observance is likely to give rise, enjoined:

يٰۤاَيُّهَا الَّذِيْنَ اٰمَنُوْا لِيَسْتَاْذِنْكُمُ الَّذِيْنَ مَلَكَتْ اَيْمَانُكُمْ وَالَّذِيْنَ لَمْ يَبْلُغُوا الْحُلُمَ
مِنْكُمْ ثَلٰثَ مَرّٰتٍ ؕ مِنْ قَبْلِ صَلٰوةِ الْفَجْرِ وَحِيْنَ تَضَعُوْنَ ثِيَابَكُمْ مِّنَ الظَّهِيْرَةِ
وَمِنْ بَعْدِ صَلٰوةِ الْعِشَآءِ ؕ ثَلٰثُ عَوْرٰتٍ لَّكُمْ ؕ لَيْسَ عَلَيْكُمْ وَلَا عَلَيْهِمْ
جُنَاحٌۢ بَعْدَهُنَّ ؕ طَوّٰفُوْنَ عَلَيْكُمْ بَعْضُكُمْ عَلٰى بَعْضٍ ؕ كَذٰلِكَ يُبَيِّنُ اللّٰهُ
لَكُمُ الْاٰيٰتِ ؕ وَاللّٰهُ عَلِيْمٌ حَكِيْمٌ ۝ وَاِذَا بَلَغَ الْاَطْفَالُ مِنْكُمُ الْحُلُمَ فَلْيَسْتَاْذِنُوْا
كَمَا اسْتَاْذَنَ الَّذِيْنَ مِنْ قَبْلِهِمْ ؕ كَذٰلِكَ يُبَيِّنُ اللّٰهُ لَكُمْ اٰيٰتِهٖ ؕ وَاللّٰهُ
عَلِيْمٌ حَكِيْمٌ ۝ وَالْقَوَاعِدُ مِنَ النِّسَآءِ الّٰتِيْ لَا يَرْجُوْنَ نِكَاحًا فَلَيْسَ عَلَيْهِنَّ
جُنَاحٌ اَنْ يَّضَعْنَ ثِيَابَهُنَّ غَيْرَ مُتَبَرِّجٰتٍۭ بِزِيْنَةٍ ؕ وَاَنْ يَّسْتَعْفِفْنَ خَيْرٌ
لَّهُنَّ ؕ وَاللّٰهُ سَمِيْعٌ عَلِيْمٌ ۝

"O ye who believe! let those whom your right hands own and those of you who have not attained puberty ask leave of you three times, before the dawn-prayer, and when ye lay aside your garments at noonday, and after the night-prayer: three times of privacy for you. No fault there is upon them beyond these times going round upon you, some of you upon some other. In this wise Allah expoundeth unto you the commandments: and Allah is Knowing, Wise.

"And when the children among you attain puberty, then let them ask leave even as those befor them asked leave. In this wise Allah expoundeth unto you His commandments; and Allah is Knowing, Wise.

"And past child-bearing women who have no hope of wedlock—upon them it is no fault that they lay aside their outer garments, not flaunting their adornment. And that they should restrain themselves is better for them; Allah is Hearing, Knowing." (XXIV:58-60).

(ii) *Soliciting permission before entering another person's house, enjoined:*

(iii) *Respect for the inmate's decision in refusing permission, enjoined:*

In connection with these two manners, the Holy Qur'ãn says:—

يٰٓاَيُّهَا الَّذِيْنَ اٰمَنُوْا لَا تَدْخُلُوْا بُيُوْتًا غَيْرَ بُيُوْتِكُمْ حَتّٰى تَسْتَاْنِسُوْا وَتُسَلِّمُوْا
عَلٰٓى اَهْلِهَا ۭ ذٰلِكُمْ خَيْرٌ لَّكُمْ لَعَلَّكُمْ تَذَكَّرُوْنَ ۝ فَاِنْ لَّمْ تَجِدُوْا فِيْهَآ اَحَدًا
فَلَا تَدْخُلُوْهَا حَتّٰى يُؤْذَنَ لَكُمْ ۚ وَاِنْ قِيْلَ لَكُمُ ارْجِعُوْا فَارْجِعُوْا هُوَ اَزْكٰى لَكُمْ ۭ
وَاللّٰهُ بِمَا تَعْمَلُوْنَ عَلِيْمٌ ۝ لَيْسَ عَلَيْكُمْ جُنَاحٌ اَنْ تَدْخُلُوْا بُيُوْتًا غَيْرَ
مَسْكُوْنَةٍ فِيْهَا مَتَاعٌ لَّكُمْ ۭ وَاللّٰهُ يَعْلَمُ مَا تُبْدُوْنَ وَمَا تَكْتُمُوْنَ ۝

"O ye who believe enter not houses other than your own until ye have asked leave and invoked peace on the inmates thereof. That is better for you, haply ye may take heed.

"Then if ye find no one therein, enter not until leave hath been given you. And if it is said unto you, go back, then go back. It is cleaner for you, and Allah is of that which ye work Knower.

"No fault it is upon you that ye enter houses uninhabited wherein there is some property for you, and Allah knoweth that what ye disclose and that which ye hide." (XXIV:27-29).

(iv) *Greeting the inmates on entering a house, enjoined:*

فَاِذَا دَخَلْتُمْ بُيُوْتًا فَسَلِّمُوْا عَلٰٓى اَنْفُسِكُمْ تَحِيَّةً مِّنْ عِنْدِ اللّٰهِ مُبٰرَكَةً طَيِّبَةً ۭ

"....Then when ye enter houses, salute one another with a greeting from Allah, blessed and sweet." (XXIV:61).

(v) *Obtaining permission from the host before leaving him, enjoined:*

The Holy Qur'ãn says:—

اِنَّمَا الْمُؤْمِنُوْنَ الَّذِيْنَ اٰمَنُوْا بِاللّٰهِ وَرَسُوْلِهٖ وَاِذَا كَانُوْا مَعَهٗ عَلٰٓى اَمْرٍ
جَامِعٍ لَّمْ يَذْهَبُوْا حَتّٰى يَسْتَاْذِنُوْهُ ۭ

"The Believers are those alone who have believed in Allah and His Messenger, and when they are with him on (some) affair collecting (people together) they depart not until they have asked his leave...."
(XXIV:62).

This verse, although particular in its reference, contains the general principle of Muslim conduct and manners.

(13) **In respect of dining at other persons' homes**:

(i) Coming to dine without invitation deprecated.

(ii) Coming to dine before the appointed time deprecated.

(iii) Seeking to stay after dining for indulging in idle talk deprecated

All these there injunctions are contained in the following verse, in its general application:—

يَٰٓأَيُّهَا الَّذِينَ اٰمَنُوا لَا تَدْخُلُوا بُيُوتَ النَّبِيِّ إِلَّآ أَنْ يُؤْذَنَ لَكُمْ إِلَىٰ طَعَامٍ
غَيْرَ نٰظِرِينَ إِنٰهُ وَلٰكِنْ إِذَا دُعِيتُمْ فَادْخُلُوا فَإِذَا طَعِمْتُمْ فَانْتَشِرُوا
وَلَا مُسْتَأْنِسِينَ لِحَدِيثٍ

"O ye who believe! enter not the Prophet's houses,—until leave is given you,—for a meal, (and then) not (so early as) to wait for its preparation; but when ye are invited, enter; and when ye have taken your meal, disperse without seeking familiar talk......." (XXXIII:53).

(14) **In respect of assemblies**:

(i) Considerateness for others in accommodating them, enjoined:

يَٰٓأَيُّهَا الَّذِينَ اٰمَنُوٓا إِذَا قِيلَ لَكُمْ تَفَسَّحُوا فِي الْمَجٰلِسِ فَافْسَحُوا يَفْسَحِ اللّٰهُ
لَكُمْ وَإِذَا قِيلَ انْشُزُوا فَانْشُزُوا

"O ye who believe! When it is said, make room! in assemblies, then make room. Allah will make way for you (hereafter). And when it is said, Come up higher! go up higher." (LVIII:11).

(ii) Engaging in whispers with someone to the annoyance of others while participating in an assembly, deprecated:

إِنَّمَا النَّجْوٰى مِنَ الشَّيْطٰنِ لِيَحْزُنَ الَّذِينَ اٰمَنُوا

"Secret counsels are from Satan that he may cause grief to the Believers". (LVIII:10).

(15) **<u>In respect of modesty in relation with members of the opposite sex</u>:**

Note.— Injunctions under this head, together with those relating to privacy (quoted in the foregoing), lay down the basis of domestic peace and happiness and form a preventive measure against sexual vices and slander. They are meant to promote purity of the heart and chastity.

These injunctions may be divided into two categories, namely:—

(*a*) those relating to men; and

(*b*) those relating to women.

(*a*) <u>*Relating to men*</u>:

When meeting those women who are categorised as strangers by Islam:—

(i) *Lowering the gaze out of respect for modesty, enjoined:*

(ii) *Guarding modesty through proper covering of the body,*[3] *enjoined:*

The Holy Qur'ān says:

قُلْ لِّلْمُؤْمِنِيْنَ يَغُضُّوْا مِنْ اَبْصَارِهِمْ وَ يَحْفَظُوْا فُرُوْجَهُمْ ؕ ذٰلِكَ اَزْكٰى
لَهُمْ ؕ اِنَّ اللّٰهَ خَبِيْرٌۢ بِمَا يَصْنَعُوْنَ ۝

"Say to the believing men that they should lower their gaze and guard their modesty: that will make for greater purity for them: and Allah is well acquainted with all that they do." (XXIV:30).

(*b*) <u>*Relating to women*</u>:

When meeting those men who are categorised as strangers by Islam:—

(*i*) *Lowering the gaze out of modesty, enjoined:*

(*ii*) *Guarding modesty through proper covering of the body, enjoined:*

(*iii*) *Use, in public appearance, of long gowns covering the whole body, enjoined:*

---

3. This rules out nudism, and even semi-nudism.

(*iv*) *Display of beauty and ornaments, except what must appear thereof, prohibited:*

(*v*) *Thinking the ankle ornaments, thereby attracting the attention of male passers-by,*[4] *prohibited:*

All these injunctions are covered by the following two verses:—

وَقُلْ لِّلْمُؤْمِنٰتِ يَغْضُضْنَ مِنْ اَبْصَارِهِنَّ وَ يَحْفَظْنَ فُرُوْجَهُنَّ وَلَا يُبْدِيْنَ
زِيْنَتَهُنَّ اِلَّا مَا ظَهَرَ مِنْهَا وَلْيَضْرِبْنَ بِخُمُرِهِنَّ عَلٰى جُيُوْبِهِنَّ

"And say to the believing women that they should lower their gaze and guard their modesty; that they should not display their beauty and ornaments except what (must ordinarily) appear thereof; that they should draw their scarves over their bosoms—" (XXIV:31).

يٰۤاَيُّهَا النَّبِيُّ قُلْ لِّاَزْوَاجِكَ وَبَنٰتِكَ وَنِسَآءِ الْمُؤْمِنِيْنَ يُدْنِيْنَ عَلَيْهِنَّ
مِنْ جَلَابِيْبِهِنَّ ذٰلِكَ اَدْنٰۤى اَنْ يُّعْرَفْنَ فَلَا يُؤْذَيْنَ وَكَانَ اللّٰهُ غَفُوْرًا رَّحِيْمًا

"O Prophet! Tell thy wives and daughters, and the believing women, that they should cast their outer garments over their persons (when abroad); that is better, that they should be known (as such) and not molested. And Allah is Oft-Forgiving, Most Merciful". (XXXIII:59).

---

4. Such actions are possible only for those who are inclined to unchastity.

Book III

DUTIES RELATING TO THE SOCIETAL WHOLE

Part I

DUTIES OF THE INDIVIDUAL TOWARDS THE MUSLIM SOCIETY

Part II

DUTIES OF THE MUSLIM SOCIETY TOWARDS THE INDIVIDUAL

Part III

PENAL ETHICS

Book III

DUTIES RELATING TO THE SOCIETAL WHOLE

Part I

[illegible]

Part II

[illegible]

Part I

DUTIES OF THE INDIVIDUAL TOWARDS THE MUSLIM SOCIETY

END: Creation, Preservation and Promotion of Collective Life in a manner which ensures the Spiritual, Moral and Social Progress of the Individual in a healthy manner and eliminates the contrary.

I.— Preamble:

Society *vis-a-vis* the Individual.

II.— Duties:

1. Duty relating to active struggle for the Spiritual and Moral Perfection of the Muslim society.
2. Duties relating to active struggle for ensuring and promoting the economic soundness of the Muslim society.
3. Duties relating to active struggle for ensuring and promoting the political stability of the Muslim society.

Chapter I

PREAMBLE

Society vis-a-vis the Individual:

(i) The organic nature of human society:

يَا أَيُّهَا النَّاسُ اتَّقُوا رَبَّكُمُ الَّذِي خَلَقَكُم مِّن نَّفْسٍ وَاحِدَةٍ وَخَلَقَ
مِنْهَا زَوْجَهَا وَبَثَّ مِنْهُمَا رِجَالًا كَثِيرًا وَنِسَاءً ۚ وَاتَّقُوا اللَّهَ الَّذِي تَسَاءَلُونَ
بِهِ وَالْأَرْحَامَ ۚ إِنَّ اللَّهَ كَانَ عَلَيْكُمْ رَقِيبًا ۝

"O mankind! reverence your Guardian-Lord, Who created you from a single soul, created, of like nature, his mate, and from them twain scattered (like seeds) countless men and women;—Reverence Allah through Whom ye demand your mutual (rights), and (reverence) the wombs (that bore you): for Allah ever watches over you." (IV:1).

يَا أَيُّهَا النَّاسُ إِنَّا خَلَقْنَاكُم مِّن ذَكَرٍ وَأُنثَىٰ وَجَعَلْنَاكُمْ شُعُوبًا وَقَبَائِلَ
لِتَعَارَفُوا ۚ إِنَّ أَكْرَمَكُمْ عِندَ اللَّهِ أَتْقَاكُمْ ۚ إِنَّ اللَّهَ عَلِيمٌ خَبِيرٌ ۝

"O mankind! We created you from a single (pair) of a male and a female, and made you into nations and tribes, that ye may known each other (not that ye may despise each other). Verily the most honoured of you in the sight of Allah is (he who is) the most righteous of you. And Allah has full knowledge and is well acquainted (with all things)."

(XLIX:13).

مَّا خَلْقُكُمْ وَلَا بَعْثُكُمْ إِلَّا كَنَفْسٍ وَاحِدَةٍ ۗ إِنَّ اللَّهَ سَمِيعٌ بَصِيرٌ ۝

"And your creation and your resurrection is in no wise but as an individual soul: for Allah is He Who hears and sees (all things)."

(XXXI:28).

(ii) The organic nature of Muslim society as coming into existence by a "Contract":

إِنَّ اللَّهَ اشْتَرَىٰ مِنَ الْمُؤْمِنِينَ أَنفُسَهُمْ وَأَمْوَالَهُم بِأَنَّ لَهُمُ الْجَنَّةَ ۚ يُقَاتِلُونَ
فِي سَبِيلِ اللَّهِ فَيَقْتُلُونَ وَيُقْتَلُونَ ۖ وَعْدًا عَلَيْهِ حَقًّا فِي التَّوْرَاةِ وَالْإِنجِيلِ

وَالْقُرْآنِ ۚ وَمَنْ أَوْفَىٰ بِعَهْدِهِ مِنَ اللَّهِ فَاسْتَبْشِرُوا بِبَيْعِكُمُ الَّذِي بَايَعْتُمْ
بِهِ ۚ وَذَٰلِكَ هُوَ الْفَوْزُ الْعَظِيمُ ۝

"Allah hath purchased of the Believers their persons and their goods; for theirs (in return) is the Garden (of Paradise): They fight in His Cause, and slay and are slain: a promise binding on Him in Truth, through the *Taurãt*, the *Injîl*, and the Qur'ãn: and who is more faithful to his Covenant than Allah? Then rejoice in the bargain which ye have concluded: That is the achievement supreme." (IX:111).

(iii) *The manifoldness of social life as the natural condition of the progress of human civilisation:*

وَاللَّيْلِ إِذَا يَغْشَىٰ ۝ وَالنَّهَارِ إِذَا تَجَلَّىٰ ۝ وَمَا خَلَقَ الذَّكَرَ وَالْأُنْثَىٰ ۝
إِنَّ سَعْيَكُمْ لَشَتَّىٰ ۝

"By the Night as it conceals (the light); by the Day as it appears in glory; by (the mystery of) the creation of male and female;—verily (the ends) ye strive for are diverse." (XCII:1-4).

(iv) *The importance of social environment for the development of the individual:*

وَاتَّقُوا فِتْنَةً لَا تُصِيبَنَّ الَّذِينَ ظَلَمُوا مِنْكُمْ خَاصَّةً ۚ وَاعْلَمُوا
أَنَّ اللَّهَ شَدِيدُ الْعِقَابِ ۝

"And fear tumult (or oppression), which affecteth not in particular (only) those of you who do wrong: and know that Allah is strict in punishment." (VIII:25).

(v) *Treating the demands of society above the demands of self, i.e., subordinating personal interests to the interests of the Social Whole created by Islam, enjoined:*

قُلْ إِنْ كَانَ آبَاؤُكُمْ وَأَبْنَاؤُكُمْ وَإِخْوَانُكُمْ وَأَزْوَاجُكُمْ وَعَشِيرَتُكُمْ وَ
أَمْوَالٌ اقْتَرَفْتُمُوهَا وَتِجَارَةٌ تَخْشَوْنَ كَسَادَهَا وَمَسَاكِنُ تَرْضَوْنَهَا
أَحَبَّ إِلَيْكُمْ مِنَ اللَّهِ وَرَسُولِهِ وَجِهَادٍ فِي سَبِيلِهِ فَتَرَبَّصُوا حَتَّىٰ
يَأْتِيَ اللَّهُ بِأَمْرِهِ ۗ وَاللَّهُ لَا يَهْدِي الْقَوْمَ الْفَاسِقِينَ ۝

"Say: if it be that your fathers, your sons, your brothers, your mates, or your kindred; the wealth that ye have gained; the commerce in which ye fear a decline; or the dwellings in which ye delight—are dearer to you than Allah, or His Messenger, or the striving in His cause;— then wait until Allah brings about His decision: and Allah guides not the rebellious." (IX:24).

Chapter II

DUTIES

I. Duty Relating to Active Struggle for the Spiritual and Moral Perfection of the Muslim Society

Active struggle for the spiritual and moral perfection of humanity in general, and of their own community in particular, is the very mission of the Muslims:

كُنْتُمْ خَيْرَ أُمَّةٍ أُخْرِجَتْ لِلنَّاسِ تَأْمُرُونَ بِالْمَعْرُوفِ وَتَنْهَوْنَ عَنِ الْمُنْكَرِ وَتُؤْمِنُونَ بِاللّٰهِ ؕ

"Ye are the best of People, evolved for (the service of) mankind, enjoining what is right, forbidding what is wrong, and believing in Allah....." (III:110).

Indeed, it is the inseparable quality of Muslim character:

الْاٰمِرُوْنَ بِالْمَعْرُوْفِ وَالنَّاهُوْنَ عَنِ الْمُنْكَرِ

"....(it is their character that) they (always) enjoin good and (always) forbid evil....." (IX:112).

Hence, Muslims have been commanded to set aright their affairs:

فَاتَّقُوا اللّٰهَ وَاَصْلِحُوْا ذَاتَ بَيْنِكُمْ

".....So be careful of your duty to Allah and set aright matters among you (in respect of your mutual duties)....." (VIII:1).

Nay, the Holy Qur'ãn goes beyond that. It orders *all* Muslims to engage in an unceasing struggle for the promotion of the Cause of spiritual and moral perfection of Muslim society in particular and of humanity in general. It says:

يٰۤاَيُّهَا الَّذِيْنَ اٰمَنُوْا كُوْنُوْۤا اَنْصَارَ اللّٰهِ

"O ye who believe! Be ye helpers (in the Cause) of Allah (—the Cause of helping human beings to spiritual and moral perfection)....." (LXI:14).

While laying down that duty, however, the Holy Qur'ãn also guarantees success, if the struggle is pursued with the fulfilment of all the prescribed conditions:

وَلَيَنصُرَنَّ اللَّهُ مَن يَنصُرُهُ ۗ إِنَّ اللَّهَ لَقَوِيٌّ عَزِيزٌ ۝

".....Allah will certainly aid those who aid His (Cause);—for verily Allah is Full of Strength, Exalted in Might, (able to enforce His Will)." (XXII:40).

يَا أَيُّهَا الَّذِينَ آمَنُوا إِن تَنصُرُوا اللَّهَ يَنصُرْكُمْ وَيُثَبِّتْ أَقْدَامَكُمْ ۝

"O ye who believe! if ye will aid (the Cause of) Allah, He will aid you and will make your foothold firm." (XLVII:7).

One of those conditions is that the struggle has to be pursued not only as an individual responsibility but also co-operatively and collectively:

تَعَاوَنُوا عَلَى الْبِرِّ وَالتَّقْوَىٰ ۖ وَلَا تَعَاوَنُوا عَلَى الْإِثْمِ وَالْعُدْوَانِ ۚ

"....Help ye one another in righteousness and piety, but help not one another in sin and enmity....." (V:3).

2. Duties[1] Relating to Active Struggle for Ensuring and Promoting the Economic Soundness of the Muslim Society

I. The Principle of 'Wealth for Welfare':

The Holy Qur'ãn denounces inordinate love of wealth as an anti-Islamic quality of character, which leads to hell:

وَيْلٌ لِّكُلِّ هُمَزَةٍ لُّمَزَةٍ ۝ الَّذِي جَمَعَ مَالًا وَعَدَّدَهُ ۝ يَحْسَبُ أَنَّ مَالَهُ أَخْلَدَهُ ۝
كَلَّا ۖ لَيُنبَذَنَّ فِي الْحُطَمَةِ ۝

"Woe to every (kind of) scandalmonger and back-biter, who pileth up wealth and layeth it by, thinking that his wealth would make him last for ever! By no means! he will be surely thrown into 'That which Breaks to Pieces'." (CIV:1-4).

1. All those duties which relate to economic matters and which have been listed in the previous sections, are also directly related here.

Similarly, it condemns those who amass wealth, make it idle, and do not spend freely for the good of their fellow-beings:

وَالَّذِينَ يَكْنِزُونَ الذَّهَبَ وَالْفِضَّةَ وَلَا يُنفِقُونَهَا فِي سَبِيلِ اللَّهِ
فَبَشِّرْهُم بِعَذَابٍ أَلِيمٍ ۝ يَوْمَ يُحْمَىٰ عَلَيْهَا فِي نَارِ جَهَنَّمَ فَتُكْوَىٰ بِهَا
جِبَاهُهُمْ وَجُنُوبُهُمْ وَظُهُورُهُمْ ۖ هَٰذَا مَا كَنَزْتُمْ لِأَنفُسِكُمْ فَذُوقُوا
مَا كُنتُمْ تَكْنِزُونَ ۝

"....And there are those who bury gold and silver and spend it not in the Way of Allah: announce unto them a most grievous penalty—On the Day when heat will be produced out of that (wealth) in the fire of Hell, and with it will be branded their foreheads, their flanks, and their backs.—'This is the (treasure) which ye buried for yourselves: taste ye, then, the (treasure) ye buried!' " (IX:34-35).

Abstaining from spending for the promotion of truth and righteousness and the welfare of fellow-beings leads to the ruin (moral, spiritual and economic) of the individual and the cummunity:

وَأَنفِقُوا فِي سَبِيلِ اللَّهِ وَلَا تُلْقُوا بِأَيْدِيكُمْ إِلَى التَّهْلُكَةِ ۛ وَأَحْسِنُوا ۛ
إِنَّ اللَّهَ يُحِبُّ الْمُحْسِنِينَ ۝

"And spend of your substance in the cause of Allah, and make not your own hands contribute to your destruction; but do good; for Allah loveth those who do good." (II:195).

Its consequences are, indeed, grave, as exemplified in the story of Qārûn (or, Korah):

إِنَّ قَارُونَ كَانَ مِن قَوْمِ مُوسَىٰ فَبَغَىٰ عَلَيْهِمْ ۖ وَآتَيْنَاهُ مِنَ الْكُنُوزِ
مَا إِنَّ مَفَاتِحَهُ لَتَنُوءُ بِالْعُصْبَةِ أُولِي الْقُوَّةِ إِذْ قَالَ لَهُ قَوْمُهُ لَا تَفْرَحْ
إِنَّ اللَّهَ لَا يُحِبُّ الْفَرِحِينَ ۝ وَابْتَغِ فِيمَا آتَاكَ اللَّهُ الدَّارَ الْآخِرَةَ
وَلَا تَنسَ نَصِيبَكَ مِنَ الدُّنْيَا ۖ وَأَحْسِن كَمَا أَحْسَنَ اللَّهُ إِلَيْكَ
وَلَا تَبْغِ الْفَسَادَ فِي الْأَرْضِ ۖ إِنَّ اللَّهَ لَا يُحِبُّ الْمُفْسِدِينَ ۝ قَالَ
إِنَّمَا أُوتِيتُهُ عَلَىٰ عِلْمٍ عِندِي ۚ أَوَلَمْ يَعْلَمْ أَنَّ اللَّهَ قَدْ أَهْلَكَ مِن قَبْلِهِ

من القرون من هو أشد منه قوة وأكثر جمعا ۚ ولا يسئل عن
ذنوبهم المجرمون ○ فخرج على قومه في زينته ۖ قال الذين
يريدون الحيوة الدنيا يليت لنا مثل ما أوتي قارون ۙ إنه لذو حظ
عظيم ○ وقال الذين أوتوا العلم ويلكم ثواب الله خير لمن آمن و
عمل صالحا ۚ ولا يلقىها إلا الصبرون ○ فخسفنا به وبداره الأرض فما كان
له من فئة ينصرونه من دون الله وما كان من المنتصرين ○

"Qãrûn was, doubtless, of the people of Moses; but he acted insolently towards them: Such were the treasures We had bestowed on him, that their very keys would have been a burden to a body of strong men. Behold, his people said to him: 'Exult not, for Allah loveth not those who exult (in riches). But seek, with the (wealth) which Allah has bestowed on thee, the Home of the Hereafter, nor forget thy portion in this world: but do thou good, as Allah has been good to thee, and seek not (occasions for) mischief in the land: for Allah loves not those who do mischief.' He said: 'This has been given to me because of a certain knowledge which I have.' Did he not know that Allah had destroyed before him (whole) generations,—which were superior to him in strength and greater in the amount (of riches) they had collected? But the wicked are not called (immediately) to account for their sins. So he went forth among his people in the (pride of his worldly) glitter. Said those whose aim is the Life of this World: 'Oh! that we had the like of what Qãrûn has got! for he is truly a lord of mighty good fortune!' But those who had been granted (true) knowledge said: 'Alas for you! The reward of Allah (in the Hereafter) is best for those who believe and work righteousness: but this none shall attain, save those who steadfastly persevere (in good). Then, We caused the earth to swallow up him and his house; and he had not (the least little) party to help him against Allah, nor could he defend himself." (XXVIII:76-81).

Viewing the problem from the other side, we find that, according to the Holy Qur'ãn, spending freely in the service of fellow-beings[2] forms

2. Exhortations to this effect have been repeatedly and emphatically made in the Holy Qur'ãn, both in the form of injunctions and otherwise, and have been quoted in detail on pp. 217-220.

a sure guarantee for the prosperity of the individual as well as of the community. We are told:

مَثَلُ الَّذِيْنَ يُنْفِقُوْنَ اَمْوَالَهُمْ فِيْ سَبِيْلِ اللّٰهِ كَمَثَلِ حَبَّةٍ اَنْۢبَتَتْ سَبْعَ
سَنَابِلَ فِيْ كُلِّ سُنْۢبُلَةٍ مِّائَةُ حَبَّةٍ ؕ وَاللّٰهُ يُضٰعِفُ لِمَنْ يَّشَآءُ ؕ
وَاللّٰهُ وَاسِعٌ عَلِيْمٌ ○

"The parable of those who spend their substance in the Way of Allah is that of a grain of corn: it groweth seven ears, and each ear hath a hundred grains. Allah giveth manifold increase to whom He pleaseth: for Allah careth for all, and He knoweth all things." (II:261).

اِنَّ الَّذِيْنَ اٰمَنُوْا وَعَمِلُوا الصّٰلِحٰتِ وَاَقَامُوا الصَّلٰوةَ وَاٰتَوُا الزَّكٰوةَ لَهُمْ اَجْرُهُمْ
عِنْدَ رَبِّهِمْ ۚ وَلَا خَوْفٌ عَلَيْهِمْ وَلَا هُمْ يَحْزَنُوْنَ ○

"Lo! those who believe and do good works and establish worship and pay the poor-due, their reward is with their Lord and there shall no fear come upon them, neither shall they grieve." (II:277).

II. Duties:

The Holy Qur'ãn does not, however, confine itself to mere exhortation, but lays down economic duties of the individual towards the Muslim society in concrete terms.

In this respect, there are:

(*a*) Duties of Commission; and

(*b*) Duties of Omission;

We may now take up these duties.

(*a*) Duties of Commission:

(i) *An annual Welfare Tax, called al-Zakãh*[3], *enjoined:*

3. According to Islamic Law, *al-Zakãh* is leviable annually on all Muslims of means, at the rate of 2 1/2%, on all uninvested wealth like silver, gold, jewellery (in the view of Hanafi Law), cash, commercial goods and debts receivable. It is not imposed on the value of built-up houses, tools of the artisan—including industrial machinery, and agricultural implements. (For detailed laws concerning this tax, reference may be made to *Fath al-Bãrî*, the Commentary on Bukhãrî's

The Holy Qur'ãn says:

وَأَقِيمُوا الصَّلٰوةَ وَآتُوا الزَّكٰوةَ ۚ وَمَا تُقَدِّمُوا لِأَنْفُسِكُمْ مِنْ خَيْرٍ تَجِدُوهُ عِنْدَ اللّٰهِ ۗ
إِنَّ اللّٰهَ بِمَا تَعْمَلُونَ بَصِيرٌ ○

"And establish (regular) Prayer and pay *al-Zakãh* (i.e., the obligatory annual poor-rate, or, welfare tax)[4]. And whatever good ye send forth for your souls before you, ye will find it with Allah. Lo! Allah is the Seer of all that ye do." (II:110)[5].

Note 1:— There is another annual welfare tax also, which is very much like *al-Zakãh*, i.e., the *Sadaqah al-Fitr*. It becomes due every year at the end of the fasting month, i.e., *Ramadãn*, and is to be compulsorily paid, for the benefit of the poor, by every Muslim of means, on his behalf as well as on behalf of everyone of his dependants. Its rate has been fixed in terms of four pounds of wheat flour per head, and payment can be made according to its market-price. It has been prescribed

---

Sahih, vol. IV, in *Hadīth* literature, and to *Hedâya* in Hanafi law: chapters on *al-Zakãh*).

It may be noted here that the institution of *al-Zakãh*, as it exists today, is in urgent need of recasting and re-evaluation.

4. That *al-Zakãh* is a welfare-tax is borne out explicitly by verse IX:60, quoted elsewhere.

The Holy Qur'ãn further mentions the aim of this tax in terms of the "eradication of economic fear and sorrow." It says:

إِنَّ الَّذِينَ آمَنُوا وَعَمِلُوا الصّٰلِحٰتِ وَأَقَامُوا الصَّلٰوةَ وَآتَوُا الزَّكٰوةَ لَهُمْ أَجْرُهُمْ
عِنْدَ رَبِّهِمْ ۚ وَلَا خَوْفٌ عَلَيْهِمْ وَلَا هُمْ يَحْزَنُونَ ○

"Lo! those who believe and do deeds of righteousness and establish (regular) Prayer and pay *al-Zakãh*, their reward is with their Lord. On them (as a community) shall be no fear, nor shall they grieve (i.e., they shall not suffer from fear and sorrow, either in respect of their Salvation in the Hereafter as individuals, or in respect of their collective economic life on the earth)." (II:277).

5. Other verses on *al-Zakãh*, where the command has been repeated, are: XXII:78; XXIV:56; XXXIII:33; LXXIII:20.

That this has been God's Law since all time, and forms one of the bases of economic welfare, has been affirmed in the following verses: II:43; II:83; XIX:13; XIX:31; XIX:55; XXI:73; XCVIII:5.

by the Holy Prophet (Peace be on him)[6] and not by the Holy Qur'ãn. It is, however, directly covered by the following Qur'ãnic injunction:

وَآتِ ذَا الْقُرْبَىٰ حَقَّهُ وَالْمِسْكِينَ

"And render to the kindred their due rights, as (also) to those in want....." (XVII:26).

Note 2:— There is still another tax prescribed by the Holy Qur'ãn in VI:141. It is called *'Ushr* in Islamic Law, and is levied as 1/20th of the agricultural produce on artificially irrigated land, and 1/10th of the agricultural produce on land benefiting from rain or natural spring only. It gives the appearance of being a tax like *al-Zakãh*[7], but it has been regarded in Islamic Law as land-revenue, pure and simple.

(ii) *Paying honestly and cheerfully any other taxes imposed by the Islamic State on the wealthy—for the welfare of the people and defence of the state, enjoined:*

When we study the scheme of taxation given by the Holy Qur'ãn, it is revealed to us that its outlook in that respect is rational and aimed at taxing the common man as lightly as possible. Indeed, that cruel type of heavy taxation which sucks the blood out of the common man is absolutely foreign to the spirit and the letter of the holy book.

The economic ideal of the Holy Qur'ãn being, however, the eradication of poverty and of the multifaced evils to which the possession of excessive wealth by individuals leads, spending of wealth by the wealthy freely[8] and at the highest level[9] for the benefit of their unfortunate fellow-

---

6. See: *Fath al-Bãrî*, vol. IV, p. 117.

7. See: Bukhãrî's *Sahîh*, *Bãb al-Zakãh*.

8. Cf:

الَّذِينَ يُنْفِقُونَ فِي السَّرَّاءِ وَالضَّرَّاءِ

"Those who spend (freely), whether in prosperity, or in adversity." (III:134).

9. Cf:

لَنْ تَنَالُوا الْبِرَّ حَتَّىٰ تُنْفِقُوا مِمَّا تُحِبُّونَ

"By no means shall ye attain righteousness unless ye give (freely) of that which ye love;...." (III:92).

beings has been proclaimed as the characteristic and unavoidable virtue of every wealthy Muslim[10]. Indeed, the holy book regards it as the duty of a Muslim to spend all that he can save from his basic needs for the welfare of others:

وَيَسْـَٔلُونَكَ مَاذَا يُنفِقُونَ قُلِ الْعَفْوَ كَذَٰلِكَ يُبَيِّنُ اللَّهُ لَكُمُ الْآيَاتِ
لَعَلَّكُمْ تَتَفَكَّرُونَ

"They ask thee how much they are to spend (for the welfare of others). Say: 'What is beyond your needs'. Thus doth Allah make clear to you His Signs: in order that ye may consider....." (II:219).

This is so, because a Muslim is only a *trustee* of the wealth that he possesses, and not its "owner" in the sense of having the right to do with it whatever he likes:

إِنَّ اللَّهَ اشْتَرَىٰ مِنَ الْمُؤْمِنِينَ أَنفُسَهُمْ وَأَمْوَالَهُم بِأَنَّ لَهُمُ الْجَنَّةَ

"Allah hath purchased of the Believers their persons and their goods; for theirs (in return) is the Garden (of Paradise):....." (IX:111).

Moreover, the Holy Qur'ãn has emphasised that the have-nots have an inalienable *right* in the wealth of those who possess beyond their needs:

وَآتِ ذَا الْقُرْبَىٰ حَقَّهُ وَالْمِسْكِينَ وَابْنَ السَّبِيلِ

"And render to the kindred their due *rights* as (also) to *those in want*, and to the wayfarer:...." (XVII:26).

This Qur'ãnic right of the economically distressed has led eminent exponents of Islam, like Caliph 'Ali, 'Abdullah ibn 'Umar, Mujahid, Taoos, Ibn Hazm, etc., to lay down the rule that there are

10.

وَلَٰكِنَّ الْبِرَّ مَنْ . . . وَآتَى الْمَالَ عَلَىٰ حُبِّهِ . . . أُولَٰئِكَ الَّذِينَ صَدَقُوا
وَأُولَٰئِكَ هُمُ الْمُتَّقُونَ

"....but it is (true) righteousness....to spend of your wealth, out of love for Him.... Such are they who are sincere (in their Faith); such are the God-fearing." (II:177).

economic *duties* on the wealthy Muslims, in respect of those who may be in economic distress, beyond the payment of the welfare taxes prescribed by the Holy Qur'ãn[11], and that the Islamic state[12] has the right—nay, it is its duty, to impose further taxes on the wealthy, if it finds that with its normal scheme of taxation it is unable to meet the challenge of expenditure on the welfare of the people and the state.[13]

(iii) *Voluntary economic assistance to others, subject to one's ability, enjoined:*

The Holy Qur'ãn has exhorted the Muslims at numerous places and in different ways and contexts to render voluntary economic assistance to their fellow-beings.[14] The following verse, however, proclaims that virtue in the form of command:

وَأَقِيمُوا الصَّلَوٰةَ وَآتُوا الزَّكَوٰةَ وَأَقْرِضُوا اللَّهَ قَرْضًا حَسَنًا ۚ وَمَا تُقَدِّمُوا
لِأَنفُسِكُم مِّنْ خَيْرٍ تَجِدُوهُ عِندَ اللَّهِ هُوَ خَيْرًا وَأَعْظَمَ أَجْرًا ۚ وَ
اسْتَغْفِرُوا اللَّهَ ۖ إِنَّ اللَّهَ غَفُورٌ رَّحِيمٌ

".....And establish regular Prayer and give regular Charity; and loan to Allah a Beautiful Loan. And whatever good ye send forth for your souls, ye shall find it in Allah's Presence,—yea, better and greater in Reward. And seek ye the Grace of Allah: for Allah is Oft-forgiving, Most Merciful." (LXXIII:20).

Now, voluntary economic assistance to others can assume the following forms:

(1) Casual assistance:

(a) *Casual Gifts and Donations:*

(b) *Repayable interest-free monetary loans;*

(c) *Returnable rent-free loans of things.*

---

11. For reference see: Ibn Hazm's *al-Mohallã*, vol. VI, p. 156.

12. It should be clearly noted that an 'Islamic State' is only that state which is dedicated to the mission of Islam and is governed solely and comprehensively by the Islamic norms, principles and laws.

13. Ibn Hazm: *al-Mohallã*, vol. VI, p. 158.

14. Such verses have been already quoted. See pp. 234-236; etc.

(2) Permanent assistance:

(a) *Bequests for individuals or for welfare projects (orphanages, homes of the destitute, hospitals, hostels, educational institutions, etc.).*

(b) *Donating funds and creating charitable Trusts for the above purposes in one's own lifetime.*

All the above forms are comprehended by the above verse and have found their due place in their Holy Prophet's exposition of the Qur'ãnic teaching. They have been included in the Islamic Law under the names, respectively, of: *Hibah; Qard al-Hasanah*, *'Ãriyah* and *Waqf*; and rules and regulations relating to them have been laid down in full-fledged form[15].

(iv) *Research in agricultural production and cattle-breeding with a view to proper utilization and advancement in those fields and for promoting the welfare of mankind, advocated; hence a duty:*

The Holy Qur'ãn says:

إِنَّ فِي خَلْقِ السَّمٰوٰتِ وَالْأَرْضِ وَاخْتِلَافِ الَّيْلِ وَالنَّهَارِ وَالْفُلْكِ
الَّتِيْ تَجْرِيْ فِي الْبَحْرِ بِمَا يَنْفَعُ النَّاسَ وَمَآ أَنْزَلَ اللّٰهُ مِنَ السَّمَآءِ
مِنْ مَّآءٍ فَأَحْيَا بِهِ الْأَرْضَ بَعْدَ مَوْتِهَا وَبَثَّ فِيْهَا مِنْ كُلِّ دَآبَّةٍ وَّ
تَصْرِيْفِ الرِّيٰحِ وَالسَّحَابِ الْمُسَخَّرِ بَيْنَ السَّمَآءِ وَالْأَرْضِ لَاٰيٰتٍ
لِّقَوْمٍ يَّعْقِلُوْنَ ○

"Behold! In the constitution of the heavens and the earth; in the alternation of the Day and the Night; in the sailing of the ships through the Ocean for the profit of mankind; in the rain which Allah sends down from the skies, and *the life which it gives to an earth that is dead: in the beasts of all kinds that He scatters through the earth*; in the change of the winds, and the clouds which they trail like their slaves between the sky and the earth;—here indeed are Signs for (study, observation and research by) those who employ reason." (II:164).

---

15. For the *Hadîth*, refer to: Tirmizi, *Sunan*, vol. II., p. 345; Bukhãrî: *Sahîh*, vol. II, pp. 243, 541; Abu Dã'ûd: *Sunan*, vol. II., p. 501. For Islamic Law, refer to such books as *al-Hedãyã,* vol. II., p. 289, etc.

وَالْأَنْعَامَ خَلَقَهَا ۗ لَكُمْ فِيهَا دِفْءٌ وَمَنَافِعُ وَمِنْهَا تَأْكُلُونَ ○ وَلَكُمْ فِيهَا
جَمَالٌ حِينَ تُرِيحُونَ وَحِينَ تَسْرَحُونَ ○ وَتَحْمِلُ أَثْقَالَكُمْ إِلَىٰ بَلَدٍ لَمْ
تَكُونُوا بَالِغِيهِ إِلَّا بِشِقِّ الْأَنْفُسِ ۚ إِنَّ رَبَّكُمْ لَرَءُوفٌ رَحِيمٌ ○ وَ
الْخَيْلَ وَالْبِغَالَ وَالْحَمِيرَ لِتَرْكَبُوهَا وَزِينَةً ۚ وَيَخْلُقُ مَا لَا تَعْلَمُونَ ○

"And callte He has created for you (O mankind): from them ye derive warmth, and numerous benefits, and of their meat ye eat. And ye have a sense of pride and beauty in them as ye drive them home in the evening, and as ye lead them forth to pasture in the morning. And they carry your heavy loads to lands that ye could not otherwise reach except with souls distressed: for your Lord is indeed Most Kind, Most Merciful. And (He has created) horses, mules, and donkeys, for you to ride and as an adornment; and He will create (in future, other vehicles, through the ingenuity of Man) of which ye have no knowledge." (XVI:5-8).

هُوَ الَّذِي أَنْزَلَ مِنَ السَّمَاءِ مَاءً ۖ لَكُمْ مِنْهُ شَرَابٌ وَمِنْهُ شَجَرٌ فِيهِ
تُسِيمُونَ ○ يُنْبِتُ لَكُمْ بِهِ الزَّرْعَ وَالزَّيْتُونَ وَالنَّخِيلَ وَالْأَعْنَابَ وَ
مِنْ كُلِّ الثَّمَرَاتِ ۗ إِنَّ فِي ذَٰلِكَ لَآيَةً لِقَوْمٍ يَتَفَكَّرُونَ ○

"It is He Who sends down rain from the sky: from it ye drink, and out of it grows the vegetation on which ye feed your cattle. With it He produces for you corn, olives, date-palms, grapes, and every kind of fruit: verily in this is a Sign for (observation, study and research by) those who reflect (on the nature, constitution and functions of things)."

(XVI:10-11).

وَإِنَّ لَكُمْ فِي الْأَنْعَامِ لَعِبْرَةً ۖ نُسْقِيكُمْ مِمَّا فِي بُطُونِهِ مِنْ بَيْنِ
فَرْثٍ وَدَمٍ لَبَنًا خَالِصًا سَائِغًا لِلشَّارِبِينَ ○ وَمِنْ ثَمَرَاتِ النَّخِيلِ وَ
الْأَعْنَابِ تَتَّخِذُونَ مِنْهُ سَكَرًا وَرِزْقًا حَسَنًا ۗ إِنَّ فِي ذَٰلِكَ لَآيَةً لِقَوْمٍ
يَعْقِلُونَ ○ وَأَوْحَىٰ رَبُّكَ إِلَى النَّحْلِ أَنِ اتَّخِذِي مِنَ الْجِبَالِ بُيُوتًا وَمِنَ
الشَّجَرِ وَمِمَّا يَعْرِشُونَ ○ ثُمَّ كُلِي مِنْ كُلِّ الثَّمَرَاتِ فَاسْلُكِي سُبُلَ
رَبِّكِ ذُلُلًا ۚ يَخْرُجُ مِنْ بُطُونِهَا شَرَابٌ مُخْتَلِفٌ أَلْوَانُهُ فِيهِ شِفَاءٌ
لِلنَّاسِ ۗ إِنَّ فِي ذَٰلِكَ لَآيَةً لِقَوْمٍ يَتَفَكَّرُونَ ○

"And verily in the cattle will ye find an instructive Sign. From what is within their bodies, between excretions and blood, We produce, for your drink, milk, pure and agreeable to those who drink it. And from the fruit of the date-palm and the vine, ye get out wholesome drink and food: behold! in this also is a Sign for those who employ reason. And thy Lord taught the Bee to build its cells in the hills, on trees and in (Men's) habitations; then to eat of all the produce (of the earth), and find with skill the specious Paths of its Lord: there issues from within their bodies a drink of varying colours, wherein is healing for men: verily in this is a Sign for (observation, study and research by) those who reflect (on the nature, constitution and function of things)." (XVI:66-69).

الَّذِي جَعَلَ لَكُمُ الْأَرْضَ مَهْدًا وَسَلَكَ لَكُمْ فِيهَا سُبُلًا وَأَنْزَلَ مِنَ السَّمَاءِ
مَاءً فَأَخْرَجْنَا بِهِ أَزْوَاجًا مِنْ نَبَاتٍ شَتَّىٰ ۝ كُلُوا وَارْعَوْا أَنْعَامَكُمْ إِنَّ
فِي ذَٰلِكَ لَآيَاتٍ لِأُولِي النُّهَىٰ ۝

"(he said)....'He Who has made for you the earth as a bed, and has enabled you to go about therein by roads (and channels); and has sent down water from the sky'. With it have We produced divers pairs of plants, each separate from the others. Eat (for yourselves) and pasture your cattle; verily in this are Signs for (observation, study and research by) the intellectuals." (XX:53, 54).

(v) *Pursuit and promotion of commerce in general, and international commerce in particular, advocated: here a duty:*

The Holy Qur'ãn says:

(a) *legalising commerce:*

وَأَحَلَّ اللَّهُ الْبَيْعَ

"....and Allah hath permitted (i.e., hath made lawful) trade...."
(II:275).

(b) *defining the basis of commercial morality:*[16]

أَنْ تَكُونَ تِجَارَةً عَنْ تَرَاضٍ مِنْكُمْ

---

16. It may also be noted that the Holy Qur'ãn lays down the law of commercial morality in II:282.

".....let there be amongst you traffic and trade by mutual goodwill...." (IV:29).

(c) *referring to the benefits of inland commerce:*

وَلَكُمْ فِيهَا مَنَافِعُ وَلِتَبْلُغُوا عَلَيْهَا حَاجَةً فِي صُدُورِكُمْ وَعَلَيْهَا وَعَلَى
الْفُلْكِ تُحْمَلُونَ ○

"And there are other advantages in them (i.e., the cattle) for you; that you may through them attain to any need in your hearts (in respect of the provision of transport for human necessities); and on them and in the boats ye are carried (to distant places for the fulfilment of your needs)." (XL:80).

(d) *advocating advancement in commerce through technological advance based on the pursuit of physical sciences, and referring to international trade in terms of Divine Bounty:*

اللَّهُ الَّذِي سَخَّرَ لَكُمُ الْبَحْرَ لِتَجْرِيَ الْفُلْكُ فِيهِ بِأَمْرِهِ وَلِتَبْتَغُوا مِنْ فَضْلِهِ
وَلَعَلَّكُمْ تَشْكُرُونَ ○ وَسَخَّرَ لَكُمْ مَا فِي السَّمٰوٰتِ وَمَا فِي الْأَرْضِ
جَمِيعًا مِنْهُ ۚ إِنَّ فِي ذٰلِكَ لَآيٰتٍ لِقَوْمٍ يَتَفَكَّرُونَ ○

"It is Allah Who has subjected the sea to you, that ships may sail through it by His Command, that ye may seek of His Bounty, and that ye may show gratefulness (to God by developing those bounties further through the conquest of Nature spoken of in the following verse).

"And He hath subjected to you, as from Him, all that is in the heavens and on the earth: behold! in that indeed are Signs for those who reflect (on the nature, constitution and utility of things)." (XLV:12, 13).

(vi) *Pursuit and promotion of industrial technology based on steel industry prescribed as the basic material means of maintaining and advancing the mission of the Holy Qur'ãn, hence a duty:*

The Holy Qur'ãn refers to shipbuilding by the Holy Prophet Noah (Peace be on him)[17] and the steel industry pursued by the Holy Prophet David (Peace be on him),[18] thus placing industrial technology

17. XI:38.

18. XXI:80; XXXIV:10.

among holy pursuits and making its acquisition and cultivation one of the sacred duties of a Muslim.

The holy book does not stop at that, however. It emphasises the importance of iron and steel industry directly—an industry whose development led to the Industrial Revolution and which forms the foundation of power and prosperity of the advanced nations of today—and projects it as the deciding factor in respect of the dominance of Islam in the industrial age as a world-force. The Qur'ānic statement has already proved prophetic to the core. The verse reads:

لَقَدْ أَرْسَلْنَا رُسُلَنَا بِالْبَيِّنٰتِ وَأَنْزَلْنَا مَعَهُمُ الْكِتٰبَ وَالْمِيزَانَ
لِيَقُومَ النَّاسُ بِالْقِسْطِ ۚ وَأَنْزَلْنَا الْحَدِيدَ فِيهِ بَأْسٌ شَدِيدٌ وَمَنَافِعُ
لِلنَّاسِ وَلِيَعْلَمَ اللّٰهُ مَنْ يَنْصُرُهُ وَرُسُلَهُ بِالْغَيْبِ ۚ إِنَّ اللّٰهَ قَوِيٌّ
عَزِيزٌ ○

"We verily sent Our messengers (to different communities of the world) with clear proofs, and revealed with them the Scripture and the Balance that mankind may observe right measure (in all their affairs); and We sent down Iron[19], wherein is (material for) mighty war, as well as many (industrial) benefits for mankind, that Allah may test who it is that will help (the Religion of) Him and His Messengers though unseen:[20] Lo!

19. "Sending down" of iron have reference to the meteoric origin of this metal in ages gone by.

20. God is unseen. But the Messengers of God also having been referred to as "unseen", the verse seems to refer to the present industrial age which began after the last Messenger (Muhammad) had departed and had become "unseen", and which saw the enemies of Islam in such power through industrialisation that industrialisation and technological advancement on a higher scale alone could have saved the Muslims from the defeat and decline which they suffered during to nineteenth and the early twentieth centuries and which has been the source of the ruin of Islam and Muslims up to this day. Indeed, if the Muslims had maintained their lead in physical sciences and technology as wise followers of the Holy Qur'ān, they would never have fallen on evil days and would have continued to maintain their international supremacy. Their failure, however, spelled their destruction as a world-power and led ultimately to those servile conditions which have progressively assisted in the de-Islamisation of the rising generation of Muslim, until non-Islamic and even anti-Islamic ideologies are now being foisted on free Muslim countries.

Allah is full of Strength, Exalted in Might (and able to make Muslims triumphant against all odds; and promise to do so if they follow His Guidance honestly)." (LVII:25).

It may be emphasised with regard to (iv), (v), (vi) above that a categorical command is explicitly contained in the following verse in respect thereof:

وَأَعِدُّوا لَهُم مَّا اسْتَطَعْتُم مِّن قُوَّةٍ وَمِن رِّبَاطِ الْخَيْلِ تُرْهِبُونَ بِهِ
عَدُوَّ اللّٰهِ وَعَدُوَّكُمْ وَآخَرِينَ مِن دُونِهِمْ لَا تَعْلَمُونَهُمُ اللّٰهُ
يَعْلَمُهُمْ

"Against them (i.e., your enemies) make ready your Power to the utmost of your capacity, including steeds of war, to strike terror into (the hearts of) the enemies of Allah and your enemies, and others (i.e., enemies of the future) besides, whom ye know not, but whom Allah doth know." (VIII:60).

Mark how clearly God had warned the followers of Islam of those formidable enemies who rose against them after the Industrial Revolution and whose might the Muslims were, and have been so far, unable to counteract mainly because of their backwardness in respect of physical science and technology.

(*b*) Duties of Omission:

(i) *Wasting money in luxuries and unproductive pursuits, prohibited:*

The Holy Qur'ãn says:

وَلَا تُسْرِفُوا إِنَّهُ لَا يُحِبُّ الْمُسْرِفِينَ ۝

"And act not wastefully (i.e., unproductively). Lo! He approveth not the wasters." (VI:141).

وَلَا تُبَذِّرْ تَبْذِيرًا ۝ إِنَّ الْمُبَذِّرِينَ كَانُوا إِخْوَانَ الشَّيَاطِينِ وَكَانَ الشَّيْطَانُ
لِرَبِّهِ كَفُورًا ۝

".....and squander not (thy wealth) in wantonness. Lo! the squanderers were ever brothers of the devil, and the devil was ever an ingrate to his Lord." (XVII:26-27).

(ii) *Withholding money from expenditure in doing good to others and in productive pursuits, prohibited:*

وَلَا تَجْعَلْ يَدَكَ مَغْلُولَةً إِلَىٰ عُنُقِكَ

"And let not thy hand be chained to the neck (in respect of wealth)...." (XVII:29).

(iii) *Hoarding wealth and withholding it from circulation and expenditure in good causes, most vehemently condemned: hence abstinence from the same is duty:*

The Holy Qur'ãn says:

وَالَّذِينَ يَكْنِزُونَ الذَّهَبَ وَالْفِضَّةَ وَلَا يُنفِقُونَهَا فِي سَبِيلِ اللَّهِ
فَبَشِّرْهُم بِعَذَابٍ أَلِيمٍ ۝

"....And there are those who bury gold and silver and spend it not in the Way of Allah: announce unto them a most grievous penalty—" (IX:34).

(iv) *Economic exploitation of others condemned; hence abstinence from it is duty:*

The Holy Qur'ãn says, condemning the Jews of those days:

وَتَرَىٰ كَثِيرًا مِّنْهُمْ يُسَارِعُونَ فِي الْإِثْمِ وَالْعُدْوَانِ وَأَكْلِهِمُ السُّحْتَ ۚ
لَبِئْسَ مَا كَانُوا يَعْمَلُونَ ۝

"And thou shalt see many of them hastening toward sin and transgression and their devouring of ill-gotten wealth (obtained through the exploitation of others). Vile indeed is that which they have been doing." (V:65).

(v) *All types and forms of interest totally banned and abstinence from interest-bearing transactions enjoined:*

الَّذِينَ يَأْكُلُونَ الرِّبَا لَا يَقُومُونَ إِلَّا كَمَا يَقُومُ الَّذِي يَتَخَبَّطُهُ
الشَّيْطَانُ مِنَ الْمَسِّ ۚ ذَٰلِكَ بِأَنَّهُمْ قَالُوا إِنَّمَا الْبَيْعُ مِثْلُ الرِّبَا ۗ وَأَحَلَّ
اللَّهُ الْبَيْعَ وَحَرَّمَ الرِّبَا ۚ

"Those who devour *ribã* (usury and interest) will not stand except as standeth one whom the satan hath confounded with his touch. That is because they say: 'Trade is like *ribã*'. But Allah hath permitted trade and hath forbidden *ribã*....." (II:275).

يٰٓاَيُّهَا الَّذِيْنَ اٰمَنُوْا لَا تَاْكُلُوا الرِّبٰوٓا اَضْعَافًا مُّضٰعَفَةً ۪ وَّاتَّقُوا اللّٰهَ
لَعَلَّكُمْ تُفْلِحُوْنَ ۝

"O ye who believe! Devour not usury, doublign and quadrupling (the sum lent). Observe your duty to Allah that ye may be successful." (III:130).

Two important points are worthy of being noted here:

(*a*) While banning *ribã*, the Holy Qur'ãn has forbidden not only usury but also interest in other forms. Because according to the best authorities[21], the word *ribã*, which means literally 'an excess or addition', denotes as a term of economics 'any addition, however slight, over and above the principal sum lent'; and, as such, *ribã* includes both 'usury' and 'interest'.

(*b*) Because *ribã* is generally translated as usury, and because in modern parlance 'usury' signifies only an 'exorbitant rate of interest', some people have fallen into the error that what the Holy Qur'ãn has really forbidden is an excessive rate of interest. In truth, it is only a misinterpretation of the term *ribã* and a perversion of the Qur'ãnic teaching. That the holy book does not distinguish between 'exorbitant' and 'reasonable' rates of interest is clear from the following:

يٰٓاَيُّهَا الَّذِيْنَ اٰمَنُوا اتَّقُوا اللّٰهَ وَذَرُوْا مَا بَقِيَ مِنَ الرِّبٰوٓا اِنْ كُنْتُمْ
مُّؤْمِنِيْنَ ۝ فَاِنْ لَّمْ تَفْعَلُوْا فَاْذَنُوْا بِحَرْبٍ مِّنَ اللّٰهِ وَرَسُوْلِهٖ ۚ وَاِنْ
تُبْتُمْ فَلَكُمْ رُءُوْسُ اَمْوَالِكُمْ ۚ لَا تَظْلِمُوْنَ وَلَا تُظْلَمُوْنَ ۝ وَاِنْ كَانَ ذُوْ
عُسْرَةٍ فَنَظِرَةٌ اِلٰى مَيْسَرَةٍ ۚ وَاَنْ تَصَدَّقُوْا خَيْرٌ لَّكُمْ اِنْ كُنْتُمْ
تَعْلَمُوْنَ ۝

---

21. *Mufradãt al-Qur'ãn* by Imãm Rãghib; *Tãj al-'Ãrus;* Lane's *Arabic-English Lexicon*.

"O ye who believe! Fear Allah, and give up what remains of your demand for *ribã*, if ye are indeed believers. If ye do it not, take notice of war from Allah and His Messenger: But if ye turn back (from charging interest), ye shall have your capital sums: deal not unjustly, and ye shall not be dealt with unjustly. If the debtor is in a difficulty, grant him time till it is easy for him to repay (the capital sum). But if ye remit it by way of charity, that is best for you if ye only know." (II:278-280).

Mark the words in verse 279. "ye shall have your capital sums". The Holy Qur'ãn does not say: "ye shall have your capital sums plus interest at a reasonable rate."

(vi) *Creation of monopolies in trade and industry prohibited:*

When the Holy Qur'ãn lays down the basic principle concerning wealth that "it may not (merely) make a circuit between the wealthy among you"[22] (LIX:7), it negates the legality of all those means and methods whereby wealth becomes concentrated in the hands of a few, making the rich richer. The aim of the creation of monopoly being nothing else than the concentration of wealth in the hands of the bigger business magnates and industrial barons, who either buy out the lesser fry or create mergers and trusts or enter into private agreements—all with a view to charging higher prices for their goods and thus exploiting and fleecing the consumers, its prohibition is directly contained in that verse.

Islam stands for the common man and not for the privileged few. It is thus that the Holy Prophet (Peace be on him) condemned the monopolist trader and forbade the hoarding of grain and its withholding from sale in times of scarcity[23]; and, in Islamic Law, the Hanafi jurists have explicitly ruled against monopoly in food-stuffs.[24]

(vii) *Speculative deals classed as gambling and prohibited:*

Speculative deals in trade are actually a form of gambling, and about gambling the Holy Qur'ãn says:

---

22. كَيْ لَا يَكُونَ دُولَةً بَيْنَ الْأَغْنِيَاءِ مِنْكُمْ ۚ

23. Muslim: *Sahîh*, vol. II., p. 31.

24. *Hedãya*, vol. IV, p. 47.

يٰٓاَيُّهَا الَّذِيْنَ اٰمَنُوْٓا اِنَّمَا الْخَمْرُ وَالْمَيْسِرُ . . . . . . رِجْسٌ
مِّنْ عَمَلِ الشَّيْطٰنِ فَاجْتَنِبُوْهُ لَعَلَّكُمْ تُفْلِحُوْنَ ○

"O ye who believe! Intoxicants and gambling....are an abomination,—of Satan's handiwork: eschew such (abomination), that ye may prosper." (V:93).

Expounding this detail of the Qur'ãnic teaching, the Holy Prophet (Peace be on him) has laid down positive injunctions. For instance:

"It is related by Ibn 'Umar that the Messenger of Allah (Peace be on him) prohibited the sale of commodity not in stock with another commodity also not in stock."[25]

"It is related on the authority of Hakim ibn Hizam, who said: 'The Messenger of Allah (Peace be on him) prohibited me bargaining about anything which I did not possess'. In another account, he (is reported to have) said, 'I said, O Messenger of Allah, a person comes to me and wishes me to bargain about a thing which I do not possess. May I purchase for him from the market?' The Prophet replied, 'Bargain not about that which is not with you'."[26]

"It is related on the authority of Anas (may Allah be pleased with him!) that the Prophet (Peace be on him) prohibited dealings in fruits, as long as they were not ripe. It was asked: 'How to know their ripeness?' He said, 'Until they grow red'. Then he said, 'Do you think that anyone of you would be able to take the property of his brother if Allah were to stop fruit from ripening?' In the account given by Ibn 'Umar, it is stated that the Prophet (Peace be on him) prohibited the purchase and sale of date trees until the dates ripened, and from dealings in ears of corn until they grew (ripe and) white, or they were safe from calamities. He prohibited both the seller and the purchaser from such transactions."[27]

The speculation market has unfortunately become a part and parcel of the present-day commerce. It is, however, nothing better than a gambling den. An economist says:

---

25. *Mishkãt al-Masãbih*, Vol. I., pp. 247, 248.

26. *Ibid.*, Vol. I., p. 248.

27. *Ibid.*, Vol. I., p. 247.

"In the speculation market, the person who gains most is the broker. His role is that of the managing committee of a racecourse or the keeper of a gambling den. The operator buy and sell through him and he goes on charging his brokerage on each purchase and sale, just as the punters or the card players gain or lose among themselves and the race-committee or the den-keeper go on deducting their commission at a finish of each event. Money that ought to have been invested in industry or commerce finds its way into the speculative market, where it is feeding disguised and parasitical works like brokers and shrewd operators. In a world clamouring for capital formation in, and capital diversion into, the under developed countries, a futures market is a regressive step."

(viii) *Betting in races prohibited:*

In the Qur'ãnic verse quoted above in respect of speculative deals, the word used for 'gambling' is *maisir*, which means 'getting something too easily': hence getting a profit without proper labour. In its wider acceptance, it means 'any game of hazard, or play or stakes, or wagers'.[28]

As 'game of hazard', it refers to speculative deals.

As 'play of stakes or wagers', it refers to froms of gambling like betting in races—an evil which is quite old but which has assumed devastating proportions in the present age in the form of the Derby horse-race in England and of the Preakness and the Kentucky Derby races in the United States.

(ix) *Lottery or Raffle, prohibited:*

Let us refer to verse V:93 again. Commenting on this verse Abdullah Yusuf Ali says:

"The form most familiar to the Arabs was gambling by casting lots by means of arrows, on the principle of a lottery: the arrows were marked, and served the same purpose as a modern lottery ticket. Something, e.g., the car case of a slaughtered animal, was divided into unequal parts. The marked arrows were drawn from a bag. Some were blank and those who drew them got nothing. Others indicated prizes, which were big or small. Whether you got a big share or a small share, or nothing depended on pure luck, unless there was fraud also on the part of

28. Lane's *Arabic-English Lexicon.*

some persons concerned. The principle on which the objection is based is: that, even if there is no fraud, you gain what you have not earned, or lose on a mere chance. Dice and wagering are rightly held to be within the definition of gambling...." (*op.cit.*, p. 86).

3. Duties Relating to Active Struggle for Ensuring and Promoting the Political Stability of the Muslim Society

(a) *Duties of Commission:*

(i) *Collective discipline enjoined:*

The Holy Qur'ãn says:

وَرَابِطُوا

"....and strengthen ye one another...." (III:200).

وَأَطِيعُوا اللَّهَ وَرَسُولَهُ وَلَا تَنَازَعُوا فَتَفْشَلُوا وَتَذْهَبَ رِيحُكُمْ وَ
اصْبِرُوا إِنَّ اللَّهَ مَعَ الصَّابِرِينَ ۝

"And obey Allah and His Messenger; and dispute not one with another, lest ye lose heart and your power depart; and be patient and persevering: for Allah is with those who patiently persevere."(VIII:46).

(ii) *Disciplined obedience to the Leader, in so far as he leads according to, and in the best interests of Islam, enjoined:*

فَاتَّقُوا اللَّهَ مَا اسْتَطَعْتُمْ وَاسْمَعُوا وَأَطِيعُوا وَأَنْفِقُوا خَيْرًا
لِأَنْفُسِكُمْ ۗ وَمَنْ يُوقَ شُحَّ نَفْسِهِ فَأُولَٰئِكَ هُمُ الْمُفْلِحُونَ ۝

"So keep your duty to Allah as best as ye can, and listen (obediently to the Divine Call that comes through the Leader), and spend (in the Way of Allah) for the benefit of your own souls. And those saved from the covetousness of their own souls (i.e., those who rise above personal interests)—they are the ones that attain felicity." (LXIV:16).

يَا أَيُّهَا الَّذِينَ آمَنُوا أَطِيعُوا اللَّهَ وَأَطِيعُوا الرَّسُولَ وَأُولِي الْأَمْرِ مِنْكُمْ ۖ فَإِنْ
تَنَازَعْتُمْ فِي شَيْءٍ فَرُدُّوهُ إِلَى اللَّهِ وَالرَّسُولِ إِنْ كُنْتُمْ تُؤْمِنُونَ
بِاللَّهِ وَالْيَوْمِ الْآخِرِ ۚ ذَٰلِكَ خَيْرٌ وَأَحْسَنُ تَأْوِيلًا ۝

"O ye who believe! obey Allah and obey the Messenger (Muhammad) and owners of authority from amongst you (as leaders and administrators or as leaders only)[29]; then if ye differ in aught, refer it to Allah and His Messenger, if ye do believe in Allah and the Last Day. That is best, and most suitable for final determination." (IV:59).

(iii) *Constant effort for the consolidation of Muslim Brotherhood, enjoined:*

وَاعْتَصِمُوا بِحَبْلِ اللّٰهِ جَمِيعًا

"And hold fast, all together, by the Rope which Allah (stretches out for you)....." (III:103).

(iv) Active, profound, ceaseless and balanced struggle for making the Muslim community immune from all internal and external evils in order to promote piety, progress and peace, enjoined:

مَنْ قَتَلَ نَفْسًا بِغَيْرِ نَفْسٍ اَوْ فَسَادٍ فِي الْاَرْضِ فَكَاَنَّمَا قَتَلَ النَّاسَ جَمِيعًا ؕ وَمَنْ اَحْيَاهَا فَكَاَنَّمَآ اَحْيَا النَّاسَ جَمِيعًا

".....If any one slew a person—unless it be for murder or for spreading mischief in the land—it would be as if he slew the whole people: and if any one saved a life, it would be as if he saved the life of the whole people....." (V:35).

وَجَاهِدُوا فِي اللّٰهِ حَقَّ جِهَادِهٖ ؕ هُوَ اجْتَبٰكُمْ وَمَا جَعَلَ عَلَيْكُمْ فِي الدِّيْنِ مِنْ حَرَجٍ ؕ مِلَّةَ اَبِيْكُمْ اِبْرٰهِيْمَ ؕ هُوَ سَمّٰىكُمُ الْمُسْلِمِيْنَ ۙ مِنْ قَبْلُ وَفِيْ هٰذَا لِيَكُوْنَ الرَّسُوْلُ شَهِيْدًا عَلَيْكُمْ وَتَكُوْنُوْا شُهَدَآءَ عَلَى النَّاسِ ۚ فَاَقِيْمُوا الصَّلٰوةَ وَاٰتُوا الزَّكٰوةَ وَاعْتَصِمُوْا بِاللّٰهِ ؕ هُوَ مَوْلٰىكُمْ ۚ فَنِعْمَ الْمَوْلٰى وَنِعْمَ النَّصِيْرُ ۝

"And strive in His cause as ye ought to strive (with sincerity and under discipline). He has chosen you, and has imposed no difficulties on

---

29. According to Lane's *Lexicon*:

"In general, those who are termed *Ulu al-Amr* of the Muslims, are those who superinted the affairs of such with respect of religion, and everything conducing to the right disposal of their affairs."

you in religion; it is the Faith of your father Abraham. It is He Who has named you Muslims, both before and in this (Revelation); that the Messenger may be a witness for you, and ye be witnesses for mankind! So establish regular Prayer, give regular charity, and hold fast to Allah! He is your Protector—the best to protect and the best to help!" (XXII:78).

يٰٓاَيُّهَا الَّذِيْنَ اٰمَنُوْا هَلْ اَدُلُّكُمْ عَلٰى تِجَارَةٍ تُنْجِيْكُمْ مِّنْ عَذَابٍ اَلِيْمٍ ○
تُؤْمِنُوْنَ بِاللّٰهِ وَرَسُوْلِهٖ وَتُجَاهِدُوْنَ فِيْ سَبِيْلِ اللّٰهِ بِاَمْوَالِكُمْ وَ
اَنْفُسِكُمْ ؕ ذٰلِكُمْ خَيْرٌ لَّكُمْ اِنْ كُنْتُمْ تَعْلَمُوْنَ ○ يَغْفِرْ لَكُمْ ذُنُوْبَكُمْ
وَيُدْخِلْكُمْ جَنّٰتٍ تَجْرِيْ مِنْ تَحْتِهَا الْاَنْهٰرُ وَمَسٰكِنَ طَيِّبَةً فِيْ
جَنّٰتِ عَدْنٍ ؕ ذٰلِكَ الْفَوْزُ الْعَظِيْمُ ○ وَاُخْرٰى تُحِبُّوْنَهَا ؕ
نَصْرٌ مِّنَ اللّٰهِ وَفَتْحٌ قَرِيْبٌ ؕ وَبَشِّرِ الْمُؤْمِنِيْنَ ○

"O ye who believe! shall I lead you to a bargain that will save you from a grievous penalty?—that ye believe in Allah and His Messenger, and that ye strive (your utmost) in the Cause of Allah with your property and your persons: that will be best for you, if ye but knew! He will forgive you your sins, and admit you to a Garden beneath which rivers flow, and to beautiful Mansions in Gardens of Eternity: that is indeed the supreme Achievement. And another (favour will He bestow), which ye do love,—help from Allah and a speedy victory. So give the Glad Tidings to the Believers". (LXI:10-13).

(v) *Fighting against the enemies of Islam in defence of truth, justice and righteousness and for making Islam and Muslims safe against all aggression, enjoined:*

وَقَاتِلُوْا فِيْ سَبِيْلِ اللّٰهِ الَّذِيْنَ يُقَاتِلُوْنَكُمْ وَلَا تَعْتَدُوْا ؕ اِنَّ اللّٰهَ لَا يُحِبُّ
الْمُعْتَدِيْنَ ○

"Fight in the Cause of Allah those who fight you, but do not transgress limits; for Allah loveth not transgressors." (II:190).

وَقٰتِلُوْهُمْ حَتّٰى لَا تَكُوْنَ فِتْنَةٌ وَّيَكُوْنَ الدِّيْنُ لِلّٰهِ ؕ فَاِنِ انْتَهَوْا فَلَا
عُدْوَانَ اِلَّا عَلَى الظّٰلِمِيْنَ ○

"And fight them on until there is no more tumult or oppression, and there prevail justice and faith in Allah; but if they cease, let there be no hostility except to those who practice oppression." (II:193).

أُذِنَ لِلَّذِينَ يُقَاتَلُونَ بِأَنَّهُمْ ظُلِمُوا ۚ وَإِنَّ اللَّهَ عَلَىٰ نَصْرِهِمْ
لَقَدِيرٌ ۝

"To those against whom war is made, permission is given (to fight), because they are wronged:—and verily Allah is Most Powerful for their aid:....." (XXII:39).

(vi) *Migrating from such places where Islam is persecuted and suppressed, thus saving one's own faith and strengthening the Cause of Islam and the Muslim community elsewhere, even though it involves losses from the material point of view, enjoined:*

إِنَّ الَّذِينَ تَوَفَّاهُمُ الْمَلَائِكَةُ ظَالِمِي أَنْفُسِهِمْ قَالُوا فِيمَ كُنْتُمْ ۖ
قَالُوا كُنَّا مُسْتَضْعَفِينَ فِي الْأَرْضِ ۚ قَالُوا أَلَمْ تَكُنْ أَرْضُ اللَّهِ وَاسِعَةً
فَتُهَاجِرُوا فِيهَا ۚ فَأُولَٰئِكَ مَأْوَاهُمْ جَهَنَّمُ ۖ وَسَاءَتْ مَصِيرًا ۝
إِلَّا الْمُسْتَضْعَفِينَ مِنَ الرِّجَالِ وَالنِّسَاءِ وَالْوِلْدَانِ لَا يَسْتَطِيعُونَ
حِيلَةً وَلَا يَهْتَدُونَ سَبِيلًا ۝ فَأُولَٰئِكَ عَسَى اللَّهُ أَنْ يَعْفُوَ عَنْهُمْ ۚ
وَكَانَ اللَّهُ عَفُوًّا غَفُورًا ۝ وَمَنْ يُهَاجِرْ فِي سَبِيلِ اللَّهِ يَجِدْ فِي
الْأَرْضِ مُرَاغَمًا كَثِيرًا وَسَعَةً ۚ وَمَنْ يَخْرُجْ مِنْ بَيْتِهِ مُهَاجِرًا
إِلَى اللَّهِ وَرَسُولِهِ ثُمَّ يُدْرِكْهُ الْمَوْتُ فَقَدْ وَقَعَ أَجْرُهُ عَلَى اللَّهِ ۗ
وَكَانَ اللَّهُ غَفُورًا رَحِيمًا ۝

"When angels take the souls of those who die in sin against their souls, they say: 'In what (fight) were ye?' They reply: 'Weak and oppressed were we in the earth.' They say: 'Was not the earth of Allah spacious enough for you to move yourselves away (from evil)?' Such men will find their abode in Hell,—what an evil refuge!—Except those who are (really) weak and oppressed— men, women, and children—who have no means in their power, nor a guide-post to direct their way. For these, there is hope that Allah will forgive: for Allah doth blot out (sins) and forgive again and again. He who forsakes his home in the Cause of Allah, finds in the earth many a refuge, wide and spacious: should he die as a refugee from home for Allah and His Messenger, his reward becomes due and sure with Allah: and Allah is Oft-Forgiving, Most Merciful." (IV:97-100).

(*b*) Duties of Omission:

(i) *Doing anything which might create disruption and disunity among the Muslim community, prohibited:*

وَلَا تَفَرَّقُوا ۚ وَاذْكُرُوا نِعْمَتَ اللَّهِ عَلَيْكُمْ إِذْ كُنْتُمْ أَعْدَاءً فَأَلَّفَ بَيْنَ
قُلُوبِكُمْ فَأَصْبَحْتُمْ بِنِعْمَتِهِ إِخْوَانًا ۚ وَكُنْتُمْ عَلَىٰ شَفَا حُفْرَةٍ مِنَ النَّارِ فَأَنْقَذَكُمْ
مِنْهَا ۗ كَذَٰلِكَ يُبَيِّنُ اللَّهُ لَكُمْ آيَاتِهِ لَعَلَّكُمْ تَهْتَدُونَ ۝

".....and be not divided among yourselves; and remember with gratitude Allah's favour on you; for ye were enemies and He joined your hearts in love, so that by His Grace by became brethren; and yet ye were on the brink of the Pit of Fire, and He saved you from it. Thus doth He make His Signs clear to you: that ye may be guided" (III:103).

وَلَا تَنَازَعُوا

".....and dispute not one with another...." (VIII:46).

(ii) *Creating religious sects and thus dividing the Muslim community into hostile sections, prohibited.*

وَلَا تَكُونُوا كَالَّذِينَ تَفَرَّقُوا وَاخْتَلَفُوا مِنْ بَعْدِ مَا جَاءَهُمُ الْبَيِّنَاتُ ۚ
وَأُولَٰئِكَ لَهُمْ عَذَابٌ عَظِيمٌ ۝

"Be not like those who are divided among themselves and fall into disputations after receiving Clear Sings: for them is a dreadful Penalty...." (III:105).

مُنِيبِينَ إِلَيْهِ وَاتَّقُوهُ وَأَقِيمُوا الصَّلَاةَ وَلَا تَكُونُوا مِنَ الْمُشْرِكِينَ ۝ مِنَ الَّذِينَ
فَرَّقُوا دِينَهُمْ وَكَانُوا شِيَعًا ۖ كُلُّ حِزْبٍ بِمَا لَدَيْهِمْ فَرِحُونَ ۝

"Turn ye back in repentance to Him, and fear Him; establish regular prayers, and be not ye among those who join gods with Allah,—those who split up their Religion, and become (mere) Sects,—each party rejoicing in that which is with itself!" (XXX:31, 32).

(iii) *Tyrannising over other Muslims prohibited:*

قُلْ إِنَّمَا حَرَّمَ رَبِّيَ الْفَوَاحِشَ مَا ظَهَرَ مِنْهَا وَمَا بَطَنَ وَالْإِثْمَ وَالْبَغْيَ
بِغَيْرِ الْحَقِّ وَأَنْ تُشْرِكُوا بِاللَّهِ مَا لَمْ يُنَزِّلْ بِهِ سُلْطَانًا وَأَنْ تَقُولُوا عَلَى اللَّهِ
مَا لَا تَعْلَمُونَ ○

"Say: 'My Lord forbiddeth only indecencies, such of them as are apparent and such as are within, and sin and *wrongful oppression*, and that ye associate with Allah that for which no warrant hath been revealed, and that ye tell concerning Allah that which ye know not." (VII:33).

(iv) *Creation of and participation in secret societies whose object is destruction of truth and justice, prohibited:*

يَا أَيُّهَا الَّذِينَ آمَنُوا إِذَا تَنَاجَيْتُمْ فَلَا تَتَنَاجَوْا بِالْإِثْمِ وَالْعُدْوَانِ وَمَعْصِيَتِ
الرَّسُولِ

"O ye who believe! When ye conspire together, conspire not together for crime and wrongdoing and disobedience toward the Messenger....." (LVIII:9).

Part II

DUTIES OF MUSLIM SOCIETY TOWARDS THE INDIVIDUAL

***END*:**

Collective effort by the Muslim society (*Millat*) for:

(*a*) Moral perfection of the individual;

(*b*) Happiness of the individual.

I.— Fundamental Principles governing the Muslim Society and the Islamic State.

II.— Duties:

(1) Duty of ensuring the spiritual welfare of the people.

(2) Duty of ensuring the moral welfare of the people.

(3) Duty relating to the intellectual development of the people.

(4) Duties relating to the political and social welfare of the people.

(5) Duties relating to the economic welfare of the people.

Chapter I

FUNDAMENTAL PRINCIPLES GOVERNING THE MUSLIM SOCIETY AND THE ISLAMIC STATE

I. Individual vis-a-vis Society

(*i*) As we have already seen in the foregoing,[1] the Holy Qur'ãn has emphasised the importance of social life and its demands. Here we may emphasise that simultaneously *it recognises the worth of the individual and the development of individual personality.* The holy book says:

مَنْ قَتَلَ نَفْسًا بِغَيْرِ نَفْسٍ أَوْ فَسَادٍ فِي الْأَرْضِ فَكَأَنَّمَا قَتَلَ النَّاسَ جَمِيعًا

"....whosoever killeth a human being for other than manslaughter or corruption in the earth, it shall be as if he had killed all mankind...." (V:35).

Again, it says:

وَأَمْرُهُمْ شُورَىٰ بَيْنَهُمْ

".....Their affairs are by mutual Consultation". (XLII:38).

Mark that in this verse the principle of consultation is founded on the concept of the importance of the individual.

(*ii*) *The Holy Qur'ãn makes it the obligation of the Millat to look after and promote the spiritual, moral and general welfare of the individual.* Collective effort for establishing what is right and eradicating what is wrong for the individual, and the creation of conditions wherein truth, perseverance in truth and mutual compassion and well-doing prevail for the benefit of the individual, has been directly affirmed and emphasised. The holy book says:

تَأْمُرُونَ بِالْمَعْرُوفِ وَتَنْهَوْنَ عَنِ الْمُنكَرِ

"....ye enjoin what is right and forbid what is wrong...." (III:110).

---

1. See pages 285-287.

وَتَوَاصَوْا بِالْمَرْحَمَةِ ۝

".....and exhort one another to compassion." (XC:17).

إِلَّا الَّذِينَ آمَنُوا وَعَمِلُوا الصَّالِحَاتِ وَتَوَاصَوْا بِالْحَقِّ وَتَوَاصَوْا بِالصَّبْرِ ۝

".....Save those who believe and do good works, and exhort one another to truth and exhort one another to endurance (in the cause of truth)....." (CIII:3).

(*iii*) Side by side with that, *the concept of collectivism is the very warp and woof of Islam*, and it has to be cultivated in Muslim society to the extent that even in his prescribed prayers a Muslim has to pray using the plural "we"[1]

2. Obligation of organising collective welfare of Muslims even where they are a Small Group only

This necessitates the establishment of the Islamic state. That does not mean, however, that Muslim minorities living in non-Muslim state have no obligation with respect to their collective life. Because *Islam insists on collective duties to such an extent as to make it imperative for the Muslims, even when they do not possess a state of their own, to organise themselves into a well-knit community which should function under one leader*. That leader should be elected by the Muslims on the basis of his piety, knowledge and other merits of leadership; and, united under him, they should employ every means and strive in every way to build up their lives, individually as well as collectively, in a manner whereby they may be able to imbibe and assimilate the spiritual, moral and social blessings of Islam in as wide a range and on as high a level as possible.

All this is borne out by the organisation of the Muslim community under the direction of, and according to the instructions given in, the Holy Qur'ãn, during the Makkan period of the Holy Prophet's career. In addition to that, the following among several verses, have a direct bearing on the above-mentioned obligation:

يَا أَيُّهَا الَّذِينَ آمَنُوا ادْخُلُوا فِي السِّلْمِ كَافَّةً

1. See *Sura al-Fãtihah* (Chapter I) and other prayers taught by the Holy Qur'ãn.

"O ye who believe! Enter into Islam (i.e., its comprehensive discipline) all ye together....." (II:208).

وَاعْتَصِمُوا بِحَبْلِ اللهِ جَمِيعًا وَّلَا تَفَرَّقُوا

"And hold fast, all together, by the Rope which Allah (stretches out for you) and be not divided among yourselves...." (III:103).

يٰٓاَيُّهَا الَّذِيْنَ اٰمَنُوْٓا اَطِيْعُوا اللهَ وَاَطِيْعُوا الرَّسُوْلَ وَاُولِي الْاَمْرِ مِنْكُمْ

"O ye who believe! obey Allah, and obey the Messenger, and those charged with authority among you....." (IV:59).

3. Obligation of Establishing the Islamic State

The collective effort of the *Millat* for the moral perfection and happiness of the individual cannot, however, gain its ends truly and comprehensively unless it transforms itself into a free theo-democratic state, whose function should be to enforce the Islamic Way of Life in its totality and to act as a condition for the natural flowering of the ideals of Islam. Hence *the establishment of the Islamic State, whenever and wherever possible, forms, according to the Holy Qur'ãn, the duty of the Millat, not only towards Islam but also towards the individual.*

That it is an unavoidable duty, in case of ability, is borne out by the fact that the Holy Prophet (Peace be on him) established the state at Madinah at the very first opportunity.

Further, this duty is contained and emphasised in the following verse:

هُوَ الَّذِيْٓ اَرْسَلَ رَسُوْلَهٗ بِالْهُدٰى وَدِيْنِ الْحَقِّ لِيُظْهِرَهٗ عَلَى الدِّيْنِ كُلِّهٖ
وَلَوْ كَرِهَ الْمُشْرِكُوْنَ ○

"He it is Who hath sent His Messenger with the Guidance and the Religion of Truth, that He may cause it to prevail over all religion, however much the idolaters may be averse." (IX:33).

It should be noted that the domination of Islam as a Way of Life is not possible without the establishment of the Islamic State. Hence it is the collective duty of the Muslims to strive for it with might and main.

Again, the Muslims have been commanded:

وَ اَعِدُّوْا لَهُمْ مَّا اسْتَطَعْتُمْ مِّنْ قُوَّةٍ

"Against them (i.e., your enemies) make ready your Power to the utmost...." (VIII:60).

This injunction makes it an obligation to establish the Islamic State, because without that it is impossible to carry it out truly and comprehensively.

4. The Constitution of the Islamic State

The Qur'ãnic Constitution of the State rests on the following principles:

(*i*) Sovereignty:

Sovereignty belongs to God:

اِنِ الْحُكْمُ اِلَّا لِلّٰهِ ؕ اَمَرَ اَلَّا تَعْبُدُوْۤا اِلَّاۤ اِيَّاهُ ؕ ذٰلِكَ الدِّيْنُ الْقَيِّمُ وَلٰكِنَّ اَكْثَرَ النَّاسِ لَا يَعْلَمُوْنَ ۝

"....Authority and control belong to Allah only.[2] He hath commanded that ye serve none save Him: that is the right religion, but most human beings understand not." (XII:40).

اَلَا لَهُ الْحُكْمُ وَهُوَ اَسْرَعُ الْحٰسِبِيْنَ ۝

"Is not His the Command? And He is the Swiftest in taking account." (VI:62).

لَهٗ مُلْكُ السَّمٰوٰتِ وَ الْاَرْضِ

"To Him belongeth the kingdom of the heavens and the earth." (XLIII:85).

وَلَا يُشْرِكُ فِيْ حُكْمِهٖۤ اَحَدًا ۝

"He does not share His Command with any person whatsoever." (XVIII:26).

2. Cf. VI:57. XII:67; etc.

Besides the above verses, the following Excellent Names also bear reference to Divine Sovereignty:

رَبِّ الْعٰلَمِيْنَ	:	Lord of the worlds	(I:2);
رَبُّ الْعَرْشِ الْعَظِيْمِ	:	Lord of the Throne (of Glory) Supreme	(IX:129);
مٰلِكَ الْمُلْكِ	:	(Lord of Power and Rule	(III:26);
اَحْكَمُ الْحٰكِمِيْنَ	:	Ruler of rulers, or, Greatest of rulers	(XI:45).
اَلْمَلِكُ	:	the Sovereign	(LIX:23);
مَلِكِ النَّاسِ	:	the King (i.e., Ruler and Legislator) of mankind	(CXIV:2).

(*ii*) <u>*The right to legislate*</u>:

(a) The right to legislate belongs basically to God:

In the Holy Qur'ãn we read:

اِنَّآ اَنْزَلْنَآ اِلَيْكَ الْكِتٰبَ بِالْحَقِّ لِتَحْكُمَ بَيْنَ النَّاسِ بِمَآ اَرٰىكَ اللّٰهُ ط

"Lo! We (God) have revealed unto thee (O Muhammad) the Scripture with truth, that thou mayest judge between mankind by that (Law) which Allah hath shown (i.e., hath revealed unto thee)." (IV:105).

لَقَدْ اَرْسَلْنَا رُسُلَنَا بِالْبَيِّنٰتِ وَاَنْزَلْنَا مَعَهُمُ الْكِتٰبَ
وَالْمِيْزَانَ لِيَقُوْمَ النَّاسُ بِالْقِسْطِ ج

"We (God) sent aforetime Our Messengers with clear Signs and sent down with them the Book and the Balance, that human beings may conduct themselves with equity" (LVII: 25).

These verses affirm direct Divine legislation.

(b) However, *the laws given by the Holy Prophet Muhammad (Peace be on him), in addition to the Qur'ãnic Laws, also fall under the category*

of what "Allah hath revealed" because:

وَمَا يَنْطِقُ عَنِ الْهَوٰى ○ إِنْ هُوَ إِلَّا وَحْيٌ يُّوْحٰى ○

"Nor does he (i.e., Muhammad) say (aught) of (his own) Desire. It is not less than inspiration sent down to him." (LIII:3, 4).

Hence: it has been commanded:

وَمَآ اٰتٰىكُمُ الرَّسُوْلُ فَخُذُوْهُ ۚ وَمَا نَهٰىكُمْ عَنْهُ فَانْتَهُوْا ۚ

"And whatever the Messenger (Muhammad) gives you, accept it, and from whatever he forbids you, keep back." (LIX:7).

(c) Having been given the Divine Law *it is not permitted to the Muslims to adopt, when they have their own State, any law which is repugnant to it.* The following verses emphasise this fact very vehemently:

وَمَنْ لَّمْ يَحْكُمْ بِمَآ اَنْزَلَ اللّٰهُ فَاُولٰٓئِكَ هُمُ الْكٰفِرُوْنَ ○

"If any do fail to judge and command by (the light of) what Allah hath revealed, they are Unbelievers." (V:47).

وَمَنْ لَّمْ يَحْكُمْ بِمَآ اَنْزَلَ اللّٰهُ فَاُولٰٓئِكَ هُمُ الظّٰلِمُوْنَ ○

"If any do fail to judge and command by (the light of) what Allah hath revealed, they are committers of severe wrong." (V:48).

وَمَنْ لَّمْ يَحْكُمْ بِمَآ اَنْزَلَ اللّٰهُ فَاُولٰٓئِكَ هُمُ الْفٰسِقُوْنَ ○

"If any do fail to judge and command by (the light of) what Allah hath revealed, they are the transgressors." (V:50).

(*d*) It should be noted that the Holy Qur'ãn prohibits only the violation of "what Allah hath revealed". But, it does not lay down, either in the verses just quoted or anywhere else, that Muslims are forbidden from following any laws which Allah has not revealed, thus leaving it open to frame new Laws for meeting the exigencies of new situations. Of course, all such laws should be in conformity with the Divine Guidance, as the holy book says:

أَفَحُكْمَ الْجَاهِلِيَّةِ يَبْغُونَ ۚ وَمَنْ أَحْسَنُ مِنَ اللَّهِ حُكْمًا لِّقَوْمٍ يُوقِنُونَ ○

"Seek they then the judgment of Paganism? And who is better in judgment than Allah unto a people whose faith is assured?" (V:53).

Thus, a *controlled and limited, but positive, freedom has been given to the Muslims in respect of legislation.*

(*iii*) *Status of Governmental Authority:*

Human beings are vicegerents of God: Hence, governmental authority can be held by them only as a delegated function and as a trust under the sovereignty of God:

The Holy Qur'ãn says:

وَإِذْ قَالَ رَبُّكَ لِلْمَلَٰٓئِكَةِ إِنِّي جَاعِلٌ فِي الْأَرْضِ خَلِيفَةً ۖ

"Behold, thy Lord said to the angels: 'Verily I am going to place a vicegerent on the earth." (II:30).

(*iv*) *Objectives of the Islamic State:*

The objectives of the Islamic State are:

(a) *To maintain internal order and ward off external aggression:*

In respect of maintenance of internal order, the Holy Qur'ãn says:

وَلَوْلَا دَفْعُ اللَّهِ النَّاسَ بَعْضَهُم بِبَعْضٍ لَّفَسَدَتِ الْأَرْضُ

".....And if Allah had not repelled some men by others, the earth would have been filled with mischief." (II:251).

Commenting on this verse, a learned commentator of the Holy Qur'ãn remarks: "This verse emphasises the importance of the State and establishes the fact that but for the existence of organised government, human society would have been destroyed. On truth is based the maxim that Religion and State are twins." (*Rûh al-Ma'ãnî*, vol. II, p. 173).

As regards warding off external aggression, we are told:

أُذِنَ لِلَّذِينَ يُقَاتَلُونَ بِأَنَّهُمْ ظُلِمُوا ۚ وَإِنَّ اللَّهَ عَلَىٰ نَصْرِهِمْ
لَقَدِيرٌ ۝

"To those against whom war is made, permission is given (to fight), because they are wronged;—and verily, Allah is Most Powerful for their aid." (XXII:39).

(b) *To establish absolute justice for all citizens:*

The Holy Qur'ãn says:

إِنَّ اللَّهَ يَأْمُرُكُمْ أَنْ تُؤَدُّوا الْأَمَانَاتِ إِلَىٰ أَهْلِهَا وَإِذَا حَكَمْتُمْ بَيْنَ النَّاسِ أَنْ
تَحْكُمُوا بِالْعَدْلِ ۚ إِنَّ اللَّهَ نِعِمَّا يَعِظُكُمْ بِهِ ۗ إِنَّ اللَّهَ كَانَ سَمِيعًا
بَصِيرًا ۝

"Allah doth command you to render back your Trusts to those to whom they are due; and when ye judge between man and man (whether Muslims or non-Muslims), that ye judge with justice: Lo! comely is the teaching which He giveth you! Lo! Allah is He Who heareth and seeth all things." (IV:58).

يَا أَيُّهَا الَّذِينَ آمَنُوا كُونُوا قَوَّامِينَ بِالْقِسْطِ شُهَدَاءَ لِلَّهِ وَلَوْ عَلَىٰ أَنْفُسِكُمْ
أَوِ الْوَالِدَيْنِ وَالْأَقْرَبِينَ ۚ إِنْ يَكُنْ غَنِيًّا أَوْ فَقِيرًا فَاللَّهُ أَوْلَىٰ بِهِمَا ۖ فَلَا
تَتَّبِعُوا الْهَوَىٰ أَنْ تَعْدِلُوا ۚ وَإِنْ تَلْوُوا أَوْ تُعْرِضُوا فَإِنَّ اللَّهَ كَانَ بِمَا
تَعْمَلُونَ خَبِيرًا ۝

"O ye who believe! stand out firmly for justice, as witnesses to Allah, even as against yourselves, or your parents, or your kin, and whether it be (against) rich or poor: For Allah can best protect both. Follow not the lusts of your hearts, lest ye swerve, and if ye distort (justice) or decline to do justice, verily Allah is well acquainted with all that ye do." (IV:135).

(c) *To do all that lies in its power and to employ all means and media, including tableegh,*[3] *for the establishment of "all that is right"* (al-ma'rûf) *and the elimination of "all that is wrong"* (al-munkar);

---

3. *i.e.*, dissemination and propagation of the teachings of Islam from the pulpit and the platform and through the press, the radio and the television, with a view to persuading and inspiring the people in respect of the Islamic Way of Life.

(d) *To organise institutions for spiritual and social welfare:*

In respect of (c) and (d) above, the Holy Qur'ãn says:

الَّذِينَ إِن مَّكَّنَّاهُمْ فِي الْأَرْضِ أَقَامُوا الصَّلَوٰةَ وَآتَوُا الزَّكَوٰةَ وَأَمَرُوا
بِالْمَعْرُوفِ وَنَهَوْا عَنِ الْمُنكَرِ ۗ وَلِلَّهِ عَاقِبَةُ الْأُمُورِ ○

"(Muslims are) those who, if we bestow on them (authority) in the land, establish regular prayer (—pursue spiritual welfare) and give regular charity (—pursue economic welfare), enjoin (all) that which is right and forbid (all) that which is wrong (—pursue moral and political welfare). And unto Allah is the end of (all) affairs." (XXII:41).

Again:

لَا خَيْرَ فِي كَثِيرٍ مِّن نَّجْوَاهُمْ إِلَّا مَنْ أَمَرَ بِصَدَقَةٍ أَوْ مَعْرُوفٍ أَوْ
إِصْلَاحٍ بَيْنَ النَّاسِ ۚ وَمَن يَفْعَلْ ذَٰلِكَ ابْتِغَاءَ مَرْضَاتِ اللَّهِ فَسَوْفَ نُؤْتِيهِ
أَجْرًا عَظِيمًا ○

"In most of their secret conferences there is no good: but if one commandeth a deed of economic well-doing or justice or *'islãh* (i.e., establishment of peace, happiness and order) among human beings: to him who does this, seeking the good pleasure of Allah, We shall soon give a reward of the highest value." (IV:114).

Moreover, from the social and economic point of view, the function of the Islamic State is to transform the Muslim community into a community of middle-roaders—or of the middle-class standard—with the elimination of the evils of poverty, on the one hand, and the evils of riches, on the other, as the Holy Qur'ãn proclaims:

وَكَذَٰلِكَ جَعَلْنَاكُمْ أُمَّةً وَسَطًا لِّتَكُونُوا شُهَدَاءَ عَلَى النَّاسِ وَيَكُونَ
الرَّسُولُ عَلَيْكُمْ شَهِيدًا ۗ

"Thus We have appointed you (O Muslims) a middle nation (or, a nation conforming to the just mean[4]), that ye may be witnesses against mankind, and that the Messenger (Muhammad) may be in regard to you a witness." (II:143).

4. Lane's *Lexicon*.

Islam steers the middle course between Capitalism and Communism and bears witness to the evil of their extremism—an evil from which they themselves are trying to recede gradually, thus proving the truth of Islam. The famous philosopher of history, Prof. Arnold Toynbee admits: "If Russia has moved to 'the right' her neighbours have moved to 'the left'.....the apparently irresistible encroachment of planning on the once unregimented economies of the democratic countries suggests that the social structure of all countries in the near future is likely to be both national and socialist. Not only do the Capitalist and Communist regimes seem likely to continue side by side; it may well be that Capitalism and Communism....are becoming different names for very much the same things."[5]

(e) *To actively endeavour for making Islam the supreme ideological force on the world-front:*

هُوَ الَّذِيْٓ اَرْسَلَ رَسُوْلَهٗ بِالْهُدٰى وَدِيْنِ الْحَقِّ لِيُظْهِرَهٗ عَلَى الدِّيْنِ كُلِّهٖ وَلَوْ كَرِهَ الْمُشْرِكُوْنَ ۝

"It is He Who has sent His Messenger with Guidance and the Religion of Truth, that he may proclaim it (as the supreme ideological force) over all religion (namely, over all systems of belief and action), even though the Pagans may detest (it)." (LXI:9).

Again:

وَاَعِدُّوْا لَهُمْ مَّا اسْتَطَعْتُمْ مِّنْ قُوَّةٍ

"Against them (i.e., your enemies) make ready your Power to the utmost...." (VIII:60).

(v) <u>*Democratic Rights of the People*</u>:

People are to be free and in possession of democratic rights:

People in the Islamic State are to be free subjection to any human being, because their government is the government of Law and they are subjects of God alone.

We have been told:

5. Arnold Toynbee: *A Study of History*. Abridgement of Volumes I—VI by D.C. Somervell, *ed.*, 1946, p. 400.

إِنِ الْحُكْمُ إِلَّا لِلَّهِ ۚ أَمَرَ أَلَّا تَعْبُدُوا إِلَّا إِيَّاهُ ۚ ذَٰلِكَ الدِّينُ الْقَيِّمُ وَلَٰكِنَّ أَكْثَرَ النَّاسِ لَا يَعْلَمُونَ ○

"The authority and control belong to Allah *only.* He hath commanded that ye serve none save Him. That is the right religion but most human beings understand not." (XII:40).

Then, the Holy Qur'ãn lays down the following principle in respect of the collective life of Muslims:

وَأَمْرُهُمْ شُورَىٰ بَيْنَهُمْ

".....Who (conduct) their affairs (or, government) by mutual consultation...." (XLII:38).

It is evident that the administration of the State on the basis of mutual consultation is impossible and unthinkable without the citizens enjoying freedom and full democratic rights.

Moreover, it is the essential condition and consequence of the establishment of absolute justice enjoined vehemently by the Holy Qur'ãn[6] that the people should be in possession of freedom and equality of opportunity—in other words, full democratic rights: and this actually has been realised in the Islamic State.

(vi) *Qualifications, status and functions of the Head of the Islamic State (Amîr al-Mo'minîn):*

1. *He must be a Muslim, endowed with a high standard of piety, knowledge, wisdom and physical qualities, including bravery:*

That he must be a Muslim is borne out by the words "from amongst you" in the following Qur'ãnic verse:

يَا أَيُّهَا الَّذِينَ آمَنُوا أَطِيعُوا اللَّهَ وَأَطِيعُوا الرَّسُولَ وَأُولِي الْأَمْرِ مِنكُمْ ۖ

"O ye who believe! obey Allah and obey the Messenger and those who wield authority from amongst you...." (IV:59).

Even from the purely rational point of view, the head of an ideological state can reasonably be only he who believes in and represents that ideology.

---

6. See (iv) (b), as also other reference on this topic.

As regards the high standard of piety, the Holy Qur'ãn lays down the law:

إِنَّ أَكْرَمَكُمْ عِنْدَ اللَّهِ أَتْقَاكُمْ

"....Verily, the most honoured of you with Allah is (he who is) the most pious of you....." (XLIX:13).

Knowledge, wisdom and physical merits have been affirmed in the following verses:

وَقَالَ لَهُمْ نَبِيُّهُمْ إِنَّ اللَّهَ قَدْ بَعَثَ لَكُمْ طَالُوتَ مَلِكًا ۚ قَالُوٓا أَنَّىٰ
يَكُونُ لَهُ الْمُلْكُ عَلَيْنَا وَنَحْنُ أَحَقُّ بِالْمُلْكِ مِنْهُ وَلَمْ يُؤْتَ سَعَةً مِّنَ
الْمَالِ ۚ قَالَ إِنَّ اللَّهَ اصْطَفَاهُ عَلَيْكُمْ وَزَادَهُ بَسْطَةً فِي الْعِلْمِ وَ
الْجِسْمِ ۚ وَاللَّهُ يُؤْتِي مُلْكَهُ مَنْ يَشَاءُ ۚ وَاللَّهُ وَاسِعٌ عَلِيمٌ ۝

"Their Prophet said to them, 'Allah hath appointed Talut as king over you'. They said: 'How can he exercise authority over us when we are better fitted than he to exercise authority, and he is not even gifted with wealth in abundance?' He said: 'Allah hath chosen him above you, and hath gifted him abundantly with knowledge and physique (i.e., physical merits): Allah bestoweth His power on whom He pleaseth. Allah careth for all, and He knoweth all things." (II:247).

وَقَتَلَ دَاوُدُ جَالُوتَ وَآتَاهُ اللَّهُ الْمُلْكَ وَالْحِكْمَةَ وَعَلَّمَهُ مِمَّا يَشَاءُ ۚ

"And David slew Goliath; and Allah gave him power and wisdom and taught him whatever (else) He willed." (II:251).

2. *His status is that of: (a) the Vicegerent of God; (b) the Successor to the Holy Prophet Muhammad (Peace be on him) (c) the Representative of the People who delegate their Authority to him:*

(a) He is the vicegerent of God: as it has been said about David (Peace be on him):

يَا دَاوُدُ إِنَّا جَعَلْنَاكَ خَلِيفَةً فِي الْأَرْضِ

"O David We did indeed make thee a vicegerent on earth...." (XXXVIII:26).

(This is his cosmic status, or status in relation to God).

(b) *He is the successor to the Holy Prophet Muhammad (Peace be on him):*

The Holy Prophet being the founder and the first head of the Islamic State, every other head of the Islamic State who comes after him is naturally his successor.

(This is his historical status, or status in relation to the Holy Prophet, Peace be on him).

(c) *He is the representative of the people, who, as vicegerents of God, delegate their authority, out of organisational and administrative necessity, to him.*

The administration of the Islamic State being based on "mutual consultation" , as seen in the foregoing[7], no one can impose himself as a despotic ruler on the Muslims. Rather, he is to be elected by them; and, as such, he is to be their representative.

(This is his political status, or status in relation to the people).

3. *His functions are:*

(a) As vicegerent of God, his natural function is *to live for God*, to carry out Divine commands and to surrender his ego completely to Divine Pleasure.

(b) As Successor to the Holy Prophet (Peace be on him), his natural function is *to imitate the Holy Prophet* as a Muslim and as head of the state, as best as he can.

(c) As representative of the people, his natural function is *to be the servant of the people* and not their master.

Hence *he should lead a life of austerity and self-negation.* It has been said about good Muslims that they sacrifice their own interests and comforts for the sake of other Muslims.[8] The head of the Islamic State is, therefore, duty-bound, more than any other Muslim, to base his life on self-sacrifice.

---

7. See p. 327.

8. LIX:9.

Thus, *his life must be exemplary for the people in respect of the Islamic Way of Life.*

4. *His relationship with his people:*

(a) *Parliament:*

He should rule the State in consultation with the people. Thus, there should be a *parliament.*

According to the Holy Qur'ãn, the Holy Prophet (Peace be on him) was commanded by God, in spite of his unique position as God's Messenger, to administer the State in consultation with the people, who were his followers. The command reads:

وَشَاوِرْهُمْ فِى الْأَمْرِ

".....And consult with them upon the conduct of affairs." (III:159).

Thus, as Successor to the Holy Prophet (Peace be on him), the head of the Islamic State cannot assume the position of an autocrat or a dictator and cannot disturb the democratic rights of the people.

(b) *People's Right to differ:*

The citizens of the Islamic State have the right to differ with the head of the State; and when such a situation arises, the dispute is to be referred to the Holy Qur'ãn and the Prophetic Guidance (*Sunnah*) for arbitration.

The right to differ is directly contained in the right to give opinion[9], while the principle for settlement of differences has been given in the following verse:

فَإِنْ تَنَازَعْتُمْ فِى شَىْءٍ فَرُدُّوهُ إِلَى اللّٰهِ وَالرَّسُولِ إِنْ كُنْتُمْ تُؤْمِنُونَ
بِاللّٰهِ وَالْيَوْمِ الْآخِرِ ذٰلِكَ خَيْرٌ وَّأَحْسَنُ تَأْوِيلًا ۝

"If ye differ in anything among yourselves, refer it to Allah and His Messenger, if ye do believe in Allah and the Last Day: That is best, and most suitable for final determination." (IV:59).

(c) *Supremacy of the Law:*

The above brings out that the head of the Islamic State is not above Law, his function being not to administer the State arbitrarily and

9. XLII:38, quoted on p. 327.

at will but positively on the basis of Truth and Justice as given in the Divine Law, as the following verse establishes:

فَاحْكُمْ بَيْنَ النَّاسِ بِالْحَقِّ وَلَا تَتَّبِعِ الْهَوٰى فَيُضِلَّكَ عَنْ سَبِيْلِ اللّٰهِ

".....So judge between mankind with truth, and follow not caprice and lust of the heart, lest it cause thee to err from the path of Allah (i.e., do not subordinate the welfare of the people to thy personal inclinations and interests, because that would lead thee away from absolute obedience to the Divine Law and upholding it as supreme)." (XXXVIII:26).

However, as long as he administers in conformity with the Guidance given by God and His Messenger Muhammad (Peace be on him), he should be implicitly obeyed by all, as it has been commanded:

يٰۤاَيُّهَا الَّذِيْنَ اٰمَنُوْۤا اَطِيْعُوا اللّٰهَ وَ اَطِيْعُوا الرَّسُوْلَ وَ اُولِي الْاَمْرِ مِنْكُمْ

"O ye who believe! Obey Allah, and obey the Messenger and those charged with authority among you." (IV:59).

(*vii*) Separation of the Executive and the Judiciary:

If as we have noted, the head of the Islamic State is subordinate to the Law given by God and His Messenger (Peace be on him), *the principle of the Supremacy of Law is established. Now, the only way to ensure the Supremacy of Law is the keeping of the judiciary independent of the executive and the total avoidance by the head of the State of tampering with the functioning of the judiciary.*

(*viii*) Qualifications of State's Functions:

Functionaries of the State are to be appointed on no other consideration but genuine merits like knowledge, practical wisdom, efficiency, honesty and integrity.

The Holy Qur'ãn says:

اِنَّ اللّٰهَ يَاْمُرُكُمْ اَنْ تُؤَدُّوا الْاَمٰنٰتِ اِلٰۤى اَهْلِهَا

"Verily Allah doth command you to make over Trusts to those to whom they are due (or to those who are worthy of them)". (IV:58).

We have already seen that those in authority hold the State and all that it stands for as a trust from God. All the offices of the State, from the highest to the lowest, are thus trusts; and one of the implications of above command, according to orthodox authoritative thought, is that which relates to the appointments to governmental services only of persons who are worthy of those jobs[10].

(*ix*) *Obedience in People's own interest:*

Obedience to the head of the state has been imposed as a duty upon the citizens for:

(*a*) the co-ordination of their democratic rights;

(*b*) the establishment and maintenance of collective discipline;

(*c*) the establishment and maintenance of a unitary policy for the State.

These three principles are contained in "enjoining what is right", which is one of the functions of the Islamic State, and, among other verses, in the following verse which lays down the command:

وَأَصْلِحُوا ذَاتَ بَيْنِكُمْ

"Establish happiness, peace and order among yourselves."

(VIII:1).

---

10. "The concept of 'trusts' covers the principle that offices should go only to the really deserving". (*Ruh al-Ma'ãnî*, vol. V, p. 64).

Chapter II

DUTIES

Preliminary

"Enjoining what is right and forbidding what is wrong"[1] assumes, as instrument of the state, the form of:

(*a*) the actual establishment of conditions and requirements which preserve and promote human good;

(*b*) the active obliteration of such conditions as destroy human good.

Now, *Good*, being a comprehensive term, includes all *goods*, namely, spiritual, moral, intellectual, political and economic.

In other words, the function of the Islamic State should be the spiritual, moral, intellectual, physical and social preservation and development of the individuals, with a view to the establishment of a righteous society, i.e., a society which is healthy in all respects.

In this connection, besides those duties which shall be shortly mentioned, *a basic duty of the Islamic State is the education and training of the experts of Islam[2] belonging to all the required levels of learning.* The following verses bear reference to this duty:

وَلْتَكُن مِّنكُمْ أُمَّةٌ يَدْعُونَ إِلَى الْخَيْرِ وَيَأْمُرُونَ بِالْمَعْرُوفِ وَيَنْهَوْنَ
عَنِ الْمُنكَرِ ۚ وَأُولَٰئِكَ هُمُ الْمُفْلِحُونَ ○

"Let there arise out of you a band of people inviting to all that is good, enjoining what is right, and forbidding what is wrong: They are the ones to attain felicity." (III:104).

فَلَوْلَا نَفَرَ مِن كُلِّ فِرْقَةٍ مِّنْهُمْ طَائِفَةٌ لِّيَتَفَقَّهُوا فِي الدِّينِ وَلِيُنذِرُوا
قَوْمَهُمْ إِذَا رَجَعُوا إِلَيْهِمْ لَعَلَّهُمْ يَحْذَرُونَ ○

---

1. III:110, XXII:41.

2. Basic education in Islam shall have to be provided to every Muslim citizen of the State, as we shall shortly see.

".....If a contingent from every expedition remained behind, they could devote themselves to studies in religion, and admonish the people when they return to them,—that thus they (may learn) to guard themselves (against evil)". (IX:122).

(1) Duty of Ensuring the Spiritual Welfare of the People

The Holy Qur'ãn proclaims "exhortation to Truth" as one of the essential conditions of human success (CIII:3). Hence, it is the duty of the Islamic State as the vicegerent of God, Successor to the Holy Prophet (God's blessings be on him), and representative of the people, to uphold, propagate and ensure the functioning of Truth, and consequently, the spiritual values—which form the basic content of Truth in the lives of the Muslims.

The Holy Qur'ãn says:

اَلَّذِيْنَ اِنْ مَّكَّنّٰهُمْ فِى الْاَرْضِ اَقَامُوا الصَّلٰوةَ وَاٰتَوُا الزَّكٰوةَ وَاَمَرُوْا
بِالْمَعْرُوْفِ وَنَهَوْا عَنِ الْمُنْكَرِ ۗ وَلِلّٰهِ عَاقِبَةُ الْاُمُوْرِ ○

"(Muslims are) those who, if We establish them (in authority and power) in the land, establish regular prayer and give regular charity, enjoin the right and forbid the wrong: With Allah rests the end (and decision) of (all) affairs". (XXII:41).

As a duty of the Islamic State, "establishment of regular prayer" and "enjoining what is right and forbidding what is wrong" in spiritual affairs, mean:—

(*a*) the construction and maintenance of mosques;

(*b*) appointment and maintenance of the requisite staff for the proper functioning of the mosques;

(*c*) organisation of spiritual education at the highest levels as well as at the level of the general masses, and making it compulsory for every Muslim citizen of the state to acquire that education;

(*d*) enforcement of laws whereby the above is ensured;

(*e*) curbing and eliminating all those forces, customs and institutions which are opposed to, or are capable of hindering, the proper functioning of the Islamic spiritual values.

(2) Duty of Ensuring the Moral Welfare of the People

Taking up the verse just quoted (i.e., XXII:41), it lays down "enjoining what is right and forbidding what is wrong" as one of the functions of the Islamic State. Viewing this function in the perspective of morals, the fact stands out as self-evident that *it is the duty of the Islamic State*:

(i) *to organise and institute the moral education of the people, and to do in that behalf all that is necessary*;

(ii) *to take all positive steps, including the enactment and enforcement of laws, for ensuring the proper practice of Islamic morals* with a view to preserve and promote moral welfare;

(iii) *to adopt all measures necessary, including the enactment and enforcement of laws, for combating all tendencies, acts and forces that are detrimental to the cause of moral welfare, and for punishing the actual offenders.*

In fact, the Holy Qur'ãn demands severe punishments for those who promote what is detrimental to the maintenance of the proper moral tone of society:

إِنَّ الَّذِينَ يُحِبُّونَ أَنْ تَشِيعَ الْفَاحِشَةُ فِي الَّذِينَ آمَنُوا لَهُمْ عَذَابٌ أَلِيمٌ فِي
الدُّنْيَا وَالْآخِرَةِ ۚ وَاللَّهُ يَعْلَمُ وَأَنْتُمْ لَا تَعْلَمُونَ ۝

"Verily those who love that immorality is propagated among the Believers, for them is a grievous penalty *in this life*[3] and in the Hereafter: and Allah knoweth (its far reaching evil effects) and ye know (or discern) not."[4] (XXIV:19).

3. Duty Relating to the Intellectual Development of the People

When we study the attitude of the Holy Qur'ãn regarding the intellectual development of human beings, we find that:

---

3. This refer to the punishment of the offenders by the Islamic State.

4. The punishments prescribed by the Holy Qur'ãn for different offences have been given in Part III.

(i) it classifies humanity distinctly into two groups: the possessors of knowledge and the ignorant, and emphasises clearly the superiority of the former over the latter:

هَلْ يَسْتَوِى الَّذِينَ يَعْلَمُونَ وَالَّذِينَ لَا يَعْلَمُونَ ۗ إِنَّمَا يَتَذَكَّرُ أُولُوا الْأَلْبَابِ ۝

"Are the possessors of knowledge equal with those who possess not knowledge? It is the possessors of understanding that are mindful." (XXXIX:9).

(ii) Nay, it goes beyond that. Because while emphasising most vehemently the importance of intellectual development in human life, it makes the quest of knowledge a duty of paramount importance for an individual. We have noticed that in detail already in Book I, chapter on "Duties to Self" (section: 'Duties as Rational Beings').

The problem with which we are concerned here is: Has the Islamic State any duty towards the citizens in respect of their intellectual development? The plain answer is: Yes, as the following observations bear out:

(*i*) According to the Holy Qur'ān, God educated Adam, the progenitor of the human race:

وَعَلَّمَ اٰدَمَ الْاَسْمَآءَ كُلَّهَا

"And He imparted to Adam the knowledge of the nature of all things[5]." (II:31).

Then, the Holy Qur'ān lays down the law that Divine Blessings are meant to be transmitted to others:

وَ اَحْسِنْ كَمَآ اَحْسَنَ اللّٰهُ اِلَيْكَ

5. The Arabic word is *asma'*, plural of *"ism"*. The commentators of the Holy Qur'ān explain this word to mean: "the attributes of things and their descriptions and their characteristics, the attributes of a thing being indicative of its nature." (See: Saiyid Qutb's Commentary named *Fī Zilāl-il-Qur'ān*, p. 126).

".....and do thou good (to others) as Allah has been good to thee...." (XXVIII:77).

Thus, the knowledge imparted by God to Adam was meant to be transmitted to mankind, generation after generation, and to be developed further by them.

Now: who can organise this difficult and great pursuit better than the possessor of the powers of collective vicegerency of God?

Thus, it is the duty of the Islamic State to organise universal education for the intellectual development of its citizens.

(ii) The Holy Qur'ãn has taught the prayer:

رَّبِّ زِدْنِي عِلْمًا ○

".....O my Lord! advance me in knowledge". (XX:114).

This shows that it is God who advances the human beings in knowledge. He does so, however, through human beings, of which the institution of prophethood is the proof.

All the prophets, from Adam to Muhammad (Allah bless them all) were the vicegerents of God par excellence and, as such, the teachers of mankind.

Every State is also the vicegerent of God, the Islamic State being supremely so, because besides its status as "state", it is also the inheritor of the blessings conferred on mankind by God through His Messengers.

This vicegerency makes it incumbent on the Islamic State to undertake the development of knowledge to higher and higher levels and to organise and enforce the education of all its citizens with a view to their intellectual advancement, with all the resources at its command.

(iii) The Holy Qur'ãn refers to the establishment of justice and balanced life among human beings as the objective of Divine Guidance and, consequently, as the objective of the Islamic State:

لَقَدْ أَرْسَلْنَا رُسُلَنَا بِالْبَيِّنٰتِ وَأَنْزَلْنَا مَعَهُمُ الْكِتٰبَ
وَالْمِيزَانَ لِيَقُومَ النَّاسُ بِالْقِسْطِ ۚ

"We sent aforetime Our Messengers with Clear Signs and sent down with them the Book and the Balance (of Right and Wrong), that men may stand forth in justice....." (LVII:25).

This objective cannot, however, be achieved without a universal dissemination among the people of the knowledge of Islamic Way of Life, as a compulsory measure.

The Islamic Way of Life is, in its turn, built upon Divine Guidance, which is the highest knowledge, and as such necessitates the acquisition of all knowledge for its proper understanding.

Thus free, compulsory and universal education, based on Divine Guidance, having the promotion of the Islamic Way of Life as its objective, and being widest in its scope, stands out as one of the foremost duties of the Islamic State.

(iv) The Holy Qur'ãn commands the Muslims to build up their *power* to the utmost and in all respects (VIII:60)[6]. That objective is only achievable, among other things[7], through:

(*a*) universal and basic religious and general[8] education of the people, and

(*b*) the highest theological, philosophical, scientific and technological education of those who possess the proper aptitude;

thereby building up a community of intellectuals which should endeavour ceaselessly to attain the highest level in every field of knowledge.

All that education should, of course, be inspired by the ideal of making Truth and Justice reign supreme in the world, whereby alone the mission of Islam is fulfilled.[9]

---

6. Already quoted on p. 351.

7. The eminent *Muhaddith* Daw'oodi has deduced the necessity of the development of agriculture from the verse under reference (*See: 'Ainî: Commentary* on Bukhãrî's *Sahîh*, vol. V, p. 712).

8. It may be emphasised here that Islam being the religion of Unity it does not recognise any distinction between the "religious" and the "secular". The distinction made here is purely nominal, and not functional.

9. It may be remarked here that the present day Islamic theological education is unbalanced, defective and narrow in conception; while the secular education

The crux of the above discussion is that:—

In respect of intellectual development, it is the duty of the Islamic State:

(*a*) *to organise, establish and enforce free compulsory basic universal education;*

(*b*) *to devise ways and means whereby all branches of knowledge are cultivated at the highest level; and*

(*c*) *to harness all intellectual endeavour in the cause of the advancement of Truth and Justice.*

(4) Duties Relating to the Political and Social Welfare of the People

(i) Establishment of happiness, peace and order for ensuring healthy existence and development of the individuals, enjoined:

The Holy Qur'ãn says:

فَاتَّقُوا اللّٰهَ وَأَصْلِحُوا ذَاتَ بَيْنِكُمْ

".....So fear Allah and pursue *islãh* (i.e., happiness, peace and order) between yourselves......" (VIII:1).

(ii) Administering justice without discrimination and without any extraneous consideration, for the preservation of life, honour and property of the individuals, enjoined:

The Holy Qur'ãn says:

يَاأَيُّهَا الَّذِينَ آمَنُوا كُونُوا قَوَّامِينَ بِالْقِسْطِ شُهَدَاءَ لِلّٰهِ وَلَوْ عَلَىٰ أَنْفُسِكُمْ
أَوِ الْوَالِدَيْنِ وَالْأَقْرَبِينَ ۚ إِنْ يَكُنْ غَنِيًّا أَوْ فَقِيرًا فَاللّٰهُ أَوْلَىٰ بِهِمَا ۖ فَلَا
تَتَّبِعُوا الْهَوَىٰ أَنْ تَعْدِلُوا ۚ وَإِنْ تَلْوُوا أَوْ تُعْرِضُوا فَإِنَّ اللّٰهَ كَانَ بِمَا
تَعْمَلُونَ خَبِيرًا ○

---

that is being imparted in the Muslim countries is breeding, because of its wrong orientation, aimlessness and even un-Islamic and anti-Islamic bias. (For a detailed discussion, see the author's: *The Present Crisis in Islam and Our Future Educational Programme*).

"O ye who believe! stand out firmly for justice, as witnesses to Allah, even as against yourselves or your parents, or your kin, and whether it be (against) rich or poor; for Allah can best protect both. Follow not the lusts of your hearts, lest ye swerve, and if ye desert (justice) or decline to do justice, verily Allah is well acquainted with all that ye do." (IV:135).

Again:

يَاأَيُّهَا الَّذِينَ آمَنُوا كُونُوا قَوَّامِينَ لِلَّهِ شُهَدَاءَ بِالْقِسْطِ وَلَا يَجْرِمَنَّكُمْ
شَنَآنُ قَوْمٍ عَلَىٰ أَلَّا تَعْدِلُوا اعْدِلُوا هُوَ أَقْرَبُ لِلتَّقْوَىٰ وَاتَّقُوا اللَّهَ إِنَّ
اللَّهَ خَبِيرٌ بِمَا تَعْمَلُونَ ○

"O ye who believe! be maintainers of your pact with Allah, as witnesses to fair dealing, and let not the hatred of others to you make you swerve to wrong and depart from justice. Be just: that is nearest to Piety: and fear Allah. For Allah is well acquainted with all that ye do." (V:9).

(iii) *Ensuring the democratic rights of the people, enjoined*:

إِنَّ اللَّهَ يَأْمُرُكُمْ أَنْ تُؤَدُّوا الْأَمَانَاتِ إِلَىٰ أَهْلِهَا

"Allah doth command you to render back your Trusts (i.e., all obligations towards God and fellow-beings)[10] to those to whom they are due....." (IV:58).

(iv) *Honouring all human beings as human beings: Hence no law, whereby the human dignity of any citizen is jeopardised unjustly, is to be adopted:*

The Holy Qur'ãn says:

وَلَقَدْ كَرَّمْنَا بَنِي آدَمَ

"We have honoured the children of Adam." (XVII:70).

(v) *Punishing the violators of law and those who endanger the security of the State made a function of the State: Hence State's duty:*

---

10. Ref: comments on this verse in *Ruh al-Ma'ãni*, vol. I. It should also be noted that every government which wields authority as a delegated privilege, is, in the very nature of the case, a trustee of the democratic rights of the people.

The Holy Qur'ãn says:

الَّذِينَ إِن مَّكَّنَّاهُمْ فِي الْأَرْضِ أَقَامُوا الصَّلَاةَ وَآتَوُا الزَّكَاةَ وَأَمَرُوا
بِالْمَعْرُوفِ وَنَهَوْا عَنِ الْمُنكَرِ ۗ وَلِلَّهِ عَاقِبَةُ الْأُمُورِ ۝

"(Muslims are) those who, if We establish them (in authority and power) in the land, establish regular prayer and give regular charity, enjoin the right and forbid what is wrong....." (XXII:41).

In this verse, "forbidding (or, restraining from) what is wrong" relates to the function of the Islamic State with regard to the punishment of offenders against Law.

Also: punishing the criminals[11] is a positive demand of justice; and the Holy Qur'ãn enjoins:

وَإِذَا حَكَمْتُم بَيْنَ النَّاسِ أَن تَحْكُمُوا بِالْعَدْلِ ۚ

".....And that when ye judge between human beings (whether Muslims or non-Muslims), ye judge with justice." (IV:58).

(vi) *Defence of Islam and Muslims against internal disruption:*

In this connection, it should be noted that:

(a) *Damaging Islam through the creation of mutually hostile religious groups has been condemned and prohibited by the Holy Qur'ãn*:

وَلَا تَكُونُوا مِنَ الْمُشْرِكِينَ ۝ مِنَ الَّذِينَ فَرَّقُوا دِينَهُمْ وَكَانُوا شِيَعًا ۖ كُلُّ حِزْبٍ
بِمَا لَدَيْهِمْ فَرِحُونَ ۝

"And be not ye among those who join gods with Allah,—those who split up their Religion, and become (mere) Sects, each party rejoicing in that which is with itself". (XXX:31, 32).

It is, therefore, the duty of the Islamic State as the defender of Islam, to foster religious unity among Muslims and to put down all attempts at religious disruption and disputes with an iron hand, leaving no place for religious adventurers.

---

11. Punishments shall be stated shortly. See pp. 352-364.

(b) *Damaging Muslim unity and solidarity socially and politically, through the formation of mutually hostile political, tribal, regional or racial*[12] *groups, has been condemned, and the duty of punishing those who are guilty of such offence, and enforcing unity with justice, has been enjoined by the Holy Qur'ãn:*

وَإِنْ طَآئِفَتَانِ مِنَ الْمُؤْمِنِينَ اقْتَتَلُوا فَأَصْلِحُوا بَيْنَهُمَا ۚ فَإِنْ
بَغَتْ إِحْدَاهُمَا عَلَى الْأُخْرَىٰ فَقَاتِلُوا الَّتِي تَبْغِي حَتَّىٰ تَفِيءَ
إِلَىٰ أَمْرِ اللَّهِ ۚ . . . . . إِنَّمَا الْمُؤْمِنُونَ إِخْوَةٌ فَأَصْلِحُوا بَيْنَ
أَخَوَيْكُمْ ۚ وَاتَّقُوا اللَّهَ لَعَلَّكُمْ تُرْحَمُونَ ○

"If two parties among the Believers fight (against one another), make ye peace between them: but if one of them transgresses beyond bounds against the other, then fight ye (all) against the one that transgresses until it complies with the command of Allah: but if it complies, then make peace between them with justice and be fair: for Allah loves those who are fair (and just). The Believers are but a single Brotherhood: so make peace and reconciliation between your two (contending) brothers; and fear Allah, that ye may receive Mercy". (XLIX:9-10).

It is, therefore, the duty of the Islamic State to combat and eliminate all such tendencies in the community on the basis of truth and justice.

(vii) *Defence of Islam and Muslims against external aggression, enjoined*:

أُذِنَ لِلَّذِينَ يُقَاتَلُونَ بِأَنَّهُمْ ظُلِمُوا ۚ

"To those against whom war is made, permission is given (to fight) because they are wronged....." (XXII:39).

Again:

وَأَعِدُّوا لَهُمْ مَا اسْتَطَعْتُمْ مِنْ قُوَّةٍ وَمِنْ رِبَاطِ الْخَيْلِ تُرْهِبُونَ بِهِ
عَدُوَّ اللَّهِ وَعَدُوَّكُمْ وَآخَرِينَ مِنْ دُونِهِمْ ۚ لَا تَعْلَمُونَهُمُ ۚ اللَّهُ

---

12. The Holy Qur'ãn recognises no tribal, racial, linguistic or regional distinctions as a basis for political divisions. (XLIX:13).

يَعْلَمُهُمْ ۚ وَمَا تُنفِقُوا مِن شَيْءٍ فِي سَبِيلِ اللَّهِ يُوَفَّ إِلَيْكُمْ وَأَنتُمْ
لَا تُظْلَمُونَ ۝

"Against them (i.e., your enemies) make ready your Power to the utmost of your capacity, including steeds of war, to strike terror into (the hearts of) the enemies of Allah and your enemies, and others besides, whom ye know not, but whom Allah doth know. Whatever ye shall spend in the Cause of Allah, shall be repaid unto you, and ye shall not be treated unjustly." (VIII:60).

(5) Duties Relating to the Economic Welfare of the People

I. *Harmonising different interests to end exploitation and the creation of a classless society, enjoined:*

In this respect:

(i) *The Holy Qur'ãn establishes the Brotherhood of Muslims:*

إِنَّمَا الْمُؤْمِنُونَ إِخْوَةٌ فَأَصْلِحُوا بَيْنَ أَخَوَيْكُمْ ۚ وَاتَّقُوا اللَّهَ لَعَلَّكُمْ
تُرْحَمُونَ ۝

"The Believers are but a single Brotherhood. Therefore, establish happiness, peace and order among two (contending) members of your Brotherhood, and observe your duty to Allah that haply ye may obtain mercy." (XLIX:10).

It should be noted that:

(a) the concept of the Brotherhood of Believers is outright the concept of a classless society;

(b) the establishment of happiness, peace and order in that Brotherhood refers to the preservation of the Brotherhood as a classless society through the requisite principles and laws: social, political and economic;

(c) the establishment of happiness, peace and order is truly possible only for the state which controls the life of the people comprehensively and with coercive authority. Hence, this verse relates primarily and essentially to the duties of the Islamic State.

(ii) The Holy Qur'ãn lays down the law for ending exploitation at all levels and in all respects:

لَا تَظْلِمُوْنَ وَ لَا تُظْلَمُوْنَ ○

"Ye shall neither wrong, nor be wronged". (II:279).

Again:

إِنَّمَا السَّبِيْلُ عَلَى الَّذِيْنَ يَظْلِمُوْنَ النَّاسَ وَ يَبْغُوْنَ فِي الْأَرْضِ بِغَيْرِ الْحَقِّ ؕ أُولٰٓئِكَ لَهُمْ عَذَابٌ أَلِيْمٌ ○

"The blame is only against those who oppress men with wrongdoing and insolently transgress beyond bounds through the land, denying right and justice: For such there will be a penalty grievous". (XLII:42).

(iii) The Holy Qur'ãn enjoins active steps, through coercive authority, for ending exploitation:

وَ إِنْ طَآئِفَتٰنِ مِنَ الْمُؤْمِنِيْنَ اقْتَتَلُوْا فَأَصْلِحُوْا بَيْنَهُمَا ۚ فَإِنْ بَغَتْ إِحْدٰىهُمَا عَلَى الْأُخْرٰى فَقَاتِلُوا الَّتِيْ تَبْغِيْ حَتّٰى تَفِيْٓءَ إِلٰٓى أَمْرِ اللّٰهِ ۚ

"If two parties among the Believers fall into a quarrel, make ye peace between them: but if one of them transgresses beyond bounds against the other then fight ye (all) against the one that transgresses until it complies with the command of Allah....." (XLIX:9).

The first implication of this verse is that which has been given in the previous section.

In its general bearing, it provides also the principle that if a group of Muslims tries to exploit another group, it is the duty of the Islamic State to restrain the exploiters by force.

Prohibition of usury and interest[13], whereby the rich exploit the poor, is a part of Qur'ãnic legislation in this regard.

---

13. See pp. 304-306..

II. Ensuring the economic characteristics of the Muslim society in terms of its being the "balanced community"[14] *by eliminating the evils of poverty as well as the evils of riches*[15] *enjoined:*

The means which the Holy Qur'ãn prescribes, for adoption by the Islamic State, are:

(i) *It propounds the principle that all human beings have equal right to the means of sustenance found on earth,*—and that, consequently, the citizens of the Islamic State have equal right to the means of sustenance found in the State:

هُوَ الَّذِي خَلَقَ لَكُم مَّا فِي الْأَرْضِ جَمِيعًا

"He (Allah) it is Who created for you (i.e., for the benefit of all of you, O mankind!) all that is on the earth." (II:29).

Mark that, according to this verse, no human being has originally any exclusive and absolute right to anything found on the earth.

Again:

وَجَعَلْنَا لَكُمْ فِيهَا مَعَايِشَ وَمَن لَّسْتُمْ لَهُ بِرَازِقِينَ ۝

"And We have provided therein (i.e., in the earth) means of subsistence,—for you and for those for whom ye provide not". (XV:20).

Still again:

وَقَدَّرَ فِيهَا أَقْوَاتَهَا فِي أَرْبَعَةِ أَيَّامٍ سَوَاءً لِّلسَّائِلِينَ ۝

---

14. II: 143, quoted on p. 325.

15. That this is a necessary condition for every social order for being healthy and strong has been referred to in the following verse which emphasises that deviation of the economic order of a community from the "just mean" leads to disaster as regards the very existence of that community. God says:

وَكَمْ أَهْلَكْنَا مِن قَرْيَةٍ بَطِرَتْ مَعِيشَتَهَا

"And how many populations We destroyed, whose way of life and livelihood became reckless (leading to corruption)........." (XXVIII:58).

".....and (Allah) ordained in due proportion therein (i.e., in the earth) the sustenance thereof (for the purpose of fulfilling the requirements of its inhabitants) in four Days: equal for those who seek (to fulfil their needs)". (XLI:10).

(ii) *It lays down the law that value lies in labour*:

أَن لَّيْسَ لِلْإِنسَانِ إِلَّا مَا سَعَىٰ ۝

"That man can have nothing but what he strives for (through labour)". (LIII:39).

(iii) It teaches that God rewards man's labour in full. Hence, *it is the duty of the Islamic State, as the vicegerent of God, to establish an economic order wherein the labour of every citizen is fully rewarded:*

وَأَنَّ سَعْيَهُ سَوْفَ يُرَىٰ ۝ ثُمَّ يُجْزَاهُ الْجَزَاءَ الْأَوْفَىٰ ۝

"And that his (man's) effort will be seen; then he will be repaid for it with fullest payment." (LIII:40, 41).

(iv) *It sets forth the principle that all human beings are equally honourable in respect of their humanity: It has been proclaimed:*

وَلَقَدْ كَرَّمْنَا بَنِي آدَمَ

"Verily We have honoured the children of Adam". (XVII:70).

Hence, it is the duty of the Islamic State, as God's vicegerent, to organise, ensure and promote honourable living and livelihood for all of its citizens.

(v) *It approves*[16] *the right to private property:*

لِّلرِّجَالِ نَصِيبٌ مِّمَّا تَرَكَ الْوَالِدَانِ وَالْأَقْرَبُونَ وَلِلنِّسَاءِ نَصِيبٌ مِّمَّا
تَرَكَ الْوَالِدَانِ وَالْأَقْرَبُونَ مِمَّا قَلَّ مِنْهُ أَوْ كَثُرَ ۚ نَصِيبًا مَّفْرُوضًا ۝

---

16. Let it be noted that the Holy Qur'ãn does not make ownership of private property an *obligation*.

"From what is left by parents and those nearest related there is a share for men (to own) and there is a share for women (to own), whether the property be small or large, a determinate share". (IV:7).

Again:

لِلرِّجَالِ نَصِيبٌ مِّمَّا اكْتَسَبُوا ۖ وَلِلنِّسَاءِ نَصِيبٌ مِّمَّا اكْتَسَبْنَ ۚ

".....To men the benefit of what they earn and to women the benefit of what they earn....." (IV:32).

(vi) *It protects the rights of the owner of private property against violations by others:*

وَلَا تَبْخَسُوا النَّاسَ أَشْيَاءَهُمْ

".....and wrong not mankind in their goods (i.e., possessions)[17]....." (VII:85).

(vii) *It does not, however, permit the institution of private property to promote the evil of concentration of wealth.* Rather, among other measures to which references have been made in the foregoing, it lays down the principle for the division of property among inheritors on a wide scale, by taking into consideration all the male and female categories of near relatives and permitting bequest of one-third property for the welfare of the non-inheritors, so that the Muslim community may remain essentially a community of middle-roaders from the economic point of view.

(See IV:11, 12, etc., where the share of the different beneficiaries in a Muslim's property have been given)[18].

The foregoing makes it evident that the Qur'ãnic point of view steers clear of both: free economy (capitalist) and controlled economy (communist), and prescribes a partially free and partially controlled economy.

---

17. Cf. Prescription of punishments for theft, robbery, etc. (pp. 358-360).

18. Speaking of the Qur'ãnic law of inheritance, Macknaughten observes in the 'Preliminary Remarks' to his *Principles and Presidents of Muhammadan Law";*.......indeed it is difficult to conceive any system containing rules more strictly just and equitable".

In that respect:—

(*a*) it sanctions the right of private ownership;

(*b*) its principle that value lies in labour envisages peasant-proprietorship of agricultural land and forms a condemnation of absentee landlordship;

(*c*) it advocates wages for the labourer commensurate with honourable living;

(*d*) its emphasis on the gifts of nature being meant for all human beings, the right to own mines, water, perennial forests, etc., should belong only to people as a whole, namely, to the State.

(*e*) its emphasis on the principle that wealth should not be permitted to become concentrated in a few hands makes it incumbent that the economic order should be such as to have no room for monopolists of wealth—the industrial barons and the business lords.

Besides these principles, however:

(viii) *It emphasises the Brotherhood of Muslims, as already noted.*

This makes the provision of social security a duty, because a Brotherhood without social security for its members is hardly worth the name.

Provision of social security will have no meaning, however, if the Islamic State does not, side by side with eliminating exploitation in all its forms[19], ensure:

(*a*) the right to work and employment;

(*b*) the right to free choice of profession;

(*c*) the right to decent wages for labour, and the consequent decent living.

These rights are directly traceable in the Holy Prophet's practice in respect of Qur'ãnic Guidance[20].

---

19. Reference has been made to this duty on p. 344.

20. See: Bukhãrî: *Sahîh*, Vol. I., p. 275; *Mishkãt al-Masãbîh*, Vol. I., pp. 242, 290.

(ix) *It:*

(*a*) *ensures economic assistance to those who, for any reason, are incapable of earning their livelihood, through the Welfare Taxes which we have discussed already*[21].

(b) *lays down the principle of spending profusely*[22] *for public good, thereby creating, in the case of the Islamic State, public works,—thus warding off unemployment.*

III. Provision of basic necessities of life to all the citizens, enjoined:

This problem has been covered indirectly and in different details in the foregoing. It is a problem of such vital importance, however, that the statement of its positive and direct affirmation by the Holy Qur'ãn is necessary.

In this connection, we have to consider:

(*a*) the Qur'ãnic concept of God;

(*b*) the Qur'ãnic description of the life of Adam and Eve—the parents of humanity—in the Heavenly Garden;

(*c*) the Qur'ãnic promise, given by God, after the Repentance by Adam and Eve, concerning the elimination of fear and sorrow from the lives of human beings, during their sojourn on earth, and the condition thereof.

As to (*a*), the Holy Qur'ãn says:

اَلْحَمْدُ لِلّٰهِ رَبِّ الْعٰلَمِيْنَ ۝

"Praise be to Allah, the Cherisher and Sustainer of the Worlds." (I:2).

Thus God is the Cherisher and Sustainer of all human beings.

Indeed, He has taken upon Himself the obligation of providing the livelihood, or, basic necessities of life, to all living beings:

وَمَا مِنْ دَآبَّةٍ فِي الْاَرْضِ اِلَّا عَلَى اللّٰهِ رِزْقُهَا

21. See: p. 314, *et foll.*

22. See: II:274.

"There is no moving creature on earth but upon Allah is the livelihood thereof." (XI:6).

As to (*b*), the Holy Qur'ãn refers to the basic necessities, provided by God to Adam and Eve in their heavenly Abode, as: food, clothing, health, shelter and education. The holy book says:

وَقُلْنَا يَآدَمُ اسْكُنْ أَنْتَ وَزَوْجُكَ الْجَنَّةَ وَكُلَا مِنْهَا رَغَدًا حَيْثُ شِئْتُمَا

"And We said: 'O Adam! dwell thou and thy wife in the Garden (in health and happiness); and eat of the bountiful things therein (in healthy enjoyment) as ye wish." (II:35).

Again:

فَقُلْنَا يَآدَمُ إِنَّ هٰذَا عَدُوٌّ لَّكَ وَلِزَوْجِكَ فَلَا يُخْرِجَنَّكُمَا مِنَ الْجَنَّةِ
فَتَشْقٰى ○ إِنَّ لَكَ أَلَّا تَجُوعَ فِيهَا وَلَا تَعْرٰى ○ وَأَنَّكَ لَا تَظْمَؤُا
فِيهَا وَلَا تَضْحٰى ○

"Then We said: 'O Adam! verily, this is an enemy to thee and thy wife: so let him not get you both out of the Garden, so that thou art landed in misery (in many ways, including the problem of suffering in respect of health). There is therein (enough provision) for thee not to go hungry (—food) nor to go naked (—clothing) nor to suffer from thirst (—food nor from the sun's heat (—shelter)." (XX: 117-119).

Still again:

وَعَلَّمَ آدَمَ الْأَسْمَاءَ كُلَّهَا

"And He imparted to Adam the knowledge of all things." (II:31).

As to (*c*), God says:

قُلْنَا اهْبِطُوا مِنْهَا جَمِيعًا ۚ فَإِمَّا يَأْتِيَنَّكُمْ مِّنِّي هُدًى فَمَنْ تَبِعَ هُدَايَ فَلَا خَوْفٌ
عَلَيْهِمْ وَلَا هُمْ يَحْزَنُونَ ○

"We said 'Get ye down all together; and if, as is sure, there comes to you Guidance from Me whosoever follows My Guidance, on them shall be no fear, nor shall they grieve!" (II:38).

This verse denotes that proper enforcement of Divine Guidance, which is possible only through State Authority, ensures, to the limit possible under the conditions obtaining on earth, freedom from all fears and sorrows, including the economic fear and sorrow.

This whole discussion brings out that:

The Islamic State, as functioning under the Sovereignty of God, and in the capacity of His vicegerent, and as governed by the Divine Law, is duty-bound to arrange and organise the economics of the state in such a way[23] *that every citizen obtains the basic necessities of life—those necessities being: food, clothing, health, shelter, and education, thereby obtaining all possible immunity from economic fear and sorrow.*

---

23. The provision of basic necessities to every citizen forms such an important part of the Qur'ãnic teaching that even the right of the individual to private ownership of wealth and of private enterprise can be curtailed by the State Authority in case there is no other way to meet that objective, as the eminent jurist Ibn Hazm affirms. (See: *al-Mohallã*, vol. 6, p. 156).

Part III

THE PENAL CODE

There are certain offences against the honour, property and life of the citizens, and against the security of the state, with respect to which the Holy Qur'ãn has ordained punishments[1] that are to be executed by the government of the Islamic State.

The punishments specifically mentioned in the Holy Qur'ãn are:

I. *Punishments pertaining to the interests of the Individuals:*

(i) *Punishments relating to Honour*—in respect of:

(*a*) Slandering of chaste women;

(*b*) Fornication and adultery;

(*c*) Homosexuality.

(ii) *Punishments relating to Property*—in respect of:

(*a*) Theft;

(*b*) Robbery.

(iii) *Punishments relating to Life*—in respect of:

(*a*) Murder:

(*b*) Mutilation.

II. *Punishments pertaining to the interests of the State:*

Treason.

---

1. Punishments for other offences, prescribed by the Islamic Code of Law, are traceable to the *Hadîth* or to the deductions of the Muslim jurists. (See: *al-Tãj al-Jãme'li al-Usûl*).

Part III

THE HUDOOD

[illegible] certain offences [illegible] the honour, property and [illegible] of the citizens, and [illegible] of the State, which [illegible] the Holy Qur'an [illegible] to be [illegible] the government of the Islamic State.

The [illegible] punishments [illegible] mentioned in the Holy Qur'an [illegible]

I. *Punishments pertaining to the [illegible] of the [illegible]*

(a) *Punishments relating to Honour and Chastity, in respect of*

(i) Slander [illegible]

(ii) [illegible] (adultery)

(c) Hirabah

(b) *Punishments relating to [illegible] in respect of*

(i) [illegible]

(ii) [illegible]

(c) *Punishments relating to life, in respect of*

(i) Murder

(ii) Mutilation

II. *Punishments pertaining to the interest of the State*

Treason

1. Punishments for other offences, prescribed by the Islamic Code of Law, are [illegible] to the *Hudud* or to the [illegible] of the Muslim jurists (See [illegible] *al-Din al-[illegible]*).

Chapter I

PUNISHMENTS PERTAINING TO THE INTERESTS OF THE INDIVIDUAL

1. Punishments Relating to Honour

(a) *In Respect of Slandering of Chaste Women*:

The Holy Qur'ãn says:

وَالَّذِينَ يَرْمُونَ الْمُحْصَنَٰتِ ثُمَّ لَمْ يَأْتُوا بِأَرْبَعَةِ شُهَدَآءَ فَاجْلِدُوهُمْ
ثَمَٰنِينَ جَلْدَةً وَلَا تَقْبَلُوا لَهُمْ شَهَٰدَةً أَبَدًا ۚ وَأُولَٰٓئِكَ هُمُ الْفَٰسِقُونَ ○ إِلَّا
الَّذِينَ تَابُوا مِنۢ بَعْدِ ذَٰلِكَ وَأَصْلَحُوا ۚ فَإِنَّ اللَّهَ غَفُورٌ رَّحِيمٌ ○

"And those who accuse chaste women (of unchastity), and produce not four witnesses (to support their allegations), flog them with eighty stripes; and reject their evidence ever after; for such men and wicked transgressors;—unless they repent thereafter and mend (their conduct); for Allah is Oft-Forgiving, Most Merciful." (XXIV:4, 5).

Thus, the punishment prescribed is that of:

(i) *flogging the offender with eighty stripes;*

(ii) *deprivation of the civic right of giving evidence—appearing as witness—in a court of law.*

As for the effects of repentance, "Abu Hanifa (the Imam of Hanafi school of Law) considers that neither the stripes nor the incompetence for giving further evidence is cancelled by repentance, but only the spiritual stigma of being 'wicked transgressor'. This of course is the more serious punishment, though it cannot be enforced in the Courts." (A. Yusuf Ali, *op.cit.*, p. 897).

In case the accusation of unchastity is brought by the husband against his wife, the Holy Qur'ãn lays down the following procedure to be observed in a court of law;

وَالَّذِينَ يَرْمُونَ أَزْوَٰجَهُمْ وَلَمْ يَكُن لَّهُمْ شُهَدَآءُ إِلَّآ أَنفُسُهُمْ فَشَهَٰدَةُ أَحَدِهِمْ
أَرْبَعُ شَهَٰدَٰتٍۭ بِاللَّهِ ۙ إِنَّهُ لَمِنَ الصَّٰدِقِينَ ○ وَالْخَٰمِسَةُ أَنَّ لَعْنَتَ اللَّهِ عَلَيْهِ إِن

كَانَ مِنَ الْكٰذِبِيْنَ ۝ وَيَدْرَؤُا عَنْهَا الْعَذَابَ اَنْ تَشْهَدَ اَرْبَعَ شَهٰدٰتٍۭ بِاللّٰهِ ۙ
اِنَّهٗ لَمِنَ الْكٰذِبِيْنَ ۝ وَالْخَامِسَةَ اَنَّ غَضَبَ اللّٰهِ عَلَيْهَآ اِنْ كَانَ مِنَ
الصّٰدِقِيْنَ ۝

"And for those who launch a charge (of unchastity) against their spouses, and have (in support) no evidence but their own, their solitary evidence (can be received) if they bear witness four times (with an oath) by Allah that they are solemnly telling the truth; and the fifth (oath) should be that they solemnly invoke the curse of Allah on themselves if they tell a lie. But it would avert the punishment from the wife, if she bears witness four times (with an oath) by Allah, that (her husband) is telling a lie; and the fifth (oath) should be that she solemnly invokes the wrath of Allah on herself if (her accuser) is telling the truth." (XXIV:6-9).

Commenting on this Qur'ãnic ordinance, A. Yusuf Ali says: "The case of married persons is different from that of outsiders. If one of them accuses the other of unchastity, the accusation partly reflects on the accuser as well. Moreover, the link which unites married people, even where differences supervene, is sure to act as a steadying influence against the concoction of false charges of unchastity, particularly where divorce is allowed (as in Islam) for reasons other than unchastity. Suppose a husband catches a wife in adultery. In the nature of thing four witnesses—or even one outside witness—would be impossible. Yet after such an experience it is against human nature that he can live a normal married life. The matter is then left to the honour of the two spouses. If the husband can solemnly swear four times to the fact, and in addition invoke a curse on himself if he lies, that is *prima facie* evidence of the wife's guilt. But if the wife swears similarly four times and similarly invokes a curse on herself, she is in law acquitted of the guilt. If she does not take this step, the charge is held proved and the punishment follows. In either case the marriage is dissolved, as it is against human nature that the parties can live together happily after such an incident". (*op.cit.*, p. 897).

(b) *In Respect of Adultery and Fornication:*

As for illicit sexual relations between man and woman, i.e., adultery and fornication, which are very widespread and devastating evils of the Western civilisation, the Holy Qur'ãn ordains:

الزَّانِيَةُ وَالزَّانِي فَاجْلِدُوا كُلَّ وَاحِدٍ مِّنْهُمَا مِائَةَ جَلْدَةٍ ۖ وَلَا تَأْخُذْكُم بِهِمَا
رَأْفَةٌ فِي دِينِ اللَّهِ إِن كُنتُمْ تُؤْمِنُونَ بِاللَّهِ وَالْيَوْمِ الْآخِرِ ۖ وَلْيَشْهَدْ عَذَابَهُمَا
طَائِفَةٌ مِّنَ الْمُؤْمِنِينَ ○ الزَّانِي لَا يَنكِحُ إِلَّا زَانِيَةً أَوْ مُشْرِكَةً وَالزَّانِيَةُ
لَا يَنكِحُهَا إِلَّا زَانٍ أَوْ مُشْرِكٌ ۚ وَحُرِّمَ ذَٰلِكَ عَلَى الْمُؤْمِنِينَ ○

"The woman and the man guilty of adultery or fornication, flog each of them with a hundred stripes: Let not compassion move you in their case, in a matter prescribed by Allah, if ye believe in Allah and the Last Day: and let a party of the Believers witness their punishment. Let no man guilty of adultery or fornication marry any but a woman similarly guilty, or an Unbeliever; nor let any but such a man or an Unbeliever marry such a woman; to the Believers such a thing is forbidden."

(XXIV:2, 3).[1]

Thus, the punishment prescribed for adultery and fornication is public flogging of the offenders with a hundred stripes.

Verse 3 speaks of further punishment of debarring those guilty of sexual immorality from establishing the marriage-tie in the circle of the chaste.

(c) In respect of Homosexuality[2]:

The Holy Qur'ãn says:

وَاللَّاتِي يَأْتِينَ الْفَاحِشَةَ مِن نِّسَائِكُمْ فَاسْتَشْهِدُوا عَلَيْهِنَّ أَرْبَعَةً مِّنكُمْ ۖ فَإِن
شَهِدُوا فَأَمْسِكُوهُنَّ فِي الْبُيُوتِ حَتَّىٰ يَتَوَفَّاهُنَّ الْمَوْتُ أَوْ يَجْعَلَ اللَّهُ
لَهُنَّ سَبِيلًا ○ وَاللَّذَانِ يَأْتِيَانِهَا مِنكُمْ فَآذُوهُمَا ۖ فَإِن تَابَا وَأَصْلَحَا
فَأَعْرِضُوا عَنْهُمَا ۗ إِنَّ اللَّهَ كَانَ تَوَّابًا رَّحِيمًا ○

"If any of your women are guilty of lewdness, take the evidence of four (reliable) witnesses from amongst you against them; and if they

1. The Holy Qur'ãn takes a very strong view of fornication and adultery, because they seriously damage the social health and because the Qur'ãnic Guidance has already provided such conditions of life as totally nullify the normal incentives to commit such crimes.

2. Mark the severe condemnation of sodomy in VII:81-84, XXIX: 28, etc.

testify, confine them to houses until death do claim them, or Allah ordains for them some (other) way. If two men among you are guilty of lewdness, punish them both. If they repent and amend, leave them alone; for Allah is Oft-Returning, Most Merciful." (IV:15, 16).

Commenting on verse 15, A. Yusuf Ali says: "Most commentators understand this to refer to adultery or fornication; in that case they consider that the punishment was altered to 100 stripes by the later verse XXIV:2. But I think it refers to unnatural crime between women, analogous to unnatural crime between men in verse 16 below; because (1) no punishment is specified here for the man, as would be the case where a man was involved in the crime; (2) the word *al-lãti*, is used for the parties to the crime; (3) the punishment is indefinite.....If we understand the crime to be unnatural crime, we might presume, in the absence of any definite order ("some other way") that the punishment would be similar to that for men in the next verse. That is itself indefinite, and perhaps intentionally so, as the crime is most shameful, and should be unknown in a well regulated society. The maximum punishment would of course be imprisonment for life." (*op.cit.*, pp. 183, 184).

2. Punishments Relating to Property

(a) In Respect of Theft:

The Holy Qur'ãn says:

وَالسَّارِقُ وَالسَّارِقَةُ فَاقْطَعُوٓا أَيْدِيَهُمَا جَزَآءً بِمَا كَسَبَا نَكَالًا مِّنَ
اللّٰهِ ؕ وَاللّٰهُ عَزِيزٌ حَكِيمٌ ○ فَمَنْ تَابَ مِنْۢ بَعْدِ ظُلْمِهٖ وَأَصْلَحَ فَإِنَّ اللّٰهَ
يَتُوبُ عَلَيْهِ ؕ إِنَّ اللّٰهَ غَفُورٌ رَّحِيمٌ ○

"As to the thief, male or female, cut off (O men of authority) his or her hands[3], a meed for that which they have earned,—an exemplary punishment from Allah; and Allah is Mighty, Wise. Then whosoever

3. "The Canon Law jurists are not unanimous as to the value of the property stolen, which would involve the penalty of the cutting off of the hand. The majority hold that petty thefts are exempt from this punishment. The general opinion is that only one hand should be cut off for the first theft, on the principle that 'if thy hand or thy foot offend thee, cut them off, and cast them from thee' (Matt. XVIII:8). Apparently in the age of Jesus thieves were crucified (Matt. XXVII:38)." (A. Yusuf Ali, *op.cit.*, p. 254).

According to Hanafi school of Islamic Law: a theif's hand shall not be cut off if the value of the thing stolen is less than one dinar, and if two male witnesses

repenteth after his wrongdoing (i.e., returns the stolen goods to, or is forgiven by the owner) and amendeth (his criminal attitude of stealing), verily Allah shall relent towards him. Verily Allah is Forgiving, Merciful."

(V:41, 42,).[4]

(b) <u>*In Respect of Robbery and Bloodshed*</u>:

The Holy Qur'ãn says:

إِنَّمَا جَزٰٓؤُا الَّذِيْنَ يُحَارِبُوْنَ اللّٰهَ وَ رَسُوْلَهٗ وَ يَسْعَوْنَ فِي الْاَرْضِ
فَسَادًا اَنْ يُّقَتَّلُوْٓا اَوْ يُصَلَّبُوْٓا اَوْ تُقَطَّعَ اَيْدِيْهِمْ وَ اَرْجُلُهُمْ مِّنْ خِلَافٍ
اَوْ يُنْفَوْا مِنَ الْاَرْضِ ؕ ذٰلِكَ لَهُمْ خِزْيٌ فِي الدُّنْيَا وَلَهُمْ فِي
الْاٰخِرَةِ عَذَابٌ عَظِيْمٌ ۝ اِلَّا الَّذِيْنَ تَابُوْا مِنْ قَبْلِ اَنْ تَقْدِرُوْا
عَلَيْهِمْ ۚ فَاعْلَمُوْٓا اَنَّ اللّٰهَ غَفُوْرٌ رَّحِيْمٌ ۝

"The punishment of those who wage war against Allah and His Messenger (by violating public security for the establishment of which the Divine law has come) and go about in the land causing corruption (in

---

of good character are not available for testimony. (*Hedaya al-awwalain*, p. 539). Also it "shall not be cut off for the theft of what cannot be guarded, or is not worth guarding, being found in the land in great quantity, such as dry wood, hay grass, reeds, game, fish, lime, etc ; also such articles of food as are quickly perishable, as milk, meat, fresh fruit, etc..... Finally, a thief's hand shall not be cut off if the thing stolen has no conventional value, even though it be otherwise regarded as of great worth." (Roberts: *Social Laws of the Qur'ãn*, p. 93).

4. We might compare this Qur'ãnic ordinance with the Biblical law. There we find that: "If a thief be found breaking up, and be smitten that he die, there shall no blood be shed for him." (*Ex.* 22:2). "If a man be found stealing any of his brethren of the children of Israel, and maketh merchandise of him, or selleth him; then that theif shall die." (*Dt.* 24:7).

In the Hammurabi, the Greek and the Roman codes, as also in the common law of England until recently, theft has been classed as a capital crime of grave nature. (See: *Encyclopaedia Britannica*, XIII, p. 721).

It should be noted that the deterrent effect of this mode of punishment has been very remarkable in all the Muslim lands where it has been enforced, *e.g.*, in Arabia.

It should also be noted that this severe punishment has been prescribed for the members of a society which ensures the provision of the basic human needs to every individual.

terms of robbery and bloodshed) is execution (in case they are guilty of murder), or crucifixion (in case they commit murder and robbery both), or the cutting off of hands and feet from opposite sides (if they commit robbery only), or exile from the land (if the murder or robbery has not yet been committed, but the persons concerned are arrested while on the point of doing so). That is their disgrace in this world, and a heavy punishment awaits them in the Hereafter; except for those who repent before they fall into your power (i.e., prior to their arrest); in that case, know that Allah is Oft-Forgiving, Most Merciful. (He will condone their guilt in respect of the punishment which is to be received in the Hereafter)". (V:36, 37).

Thus, the punishments are:

(*i*) Slaying the offenders, in case murder only has been committed and no robbery has taken place.

(*ii*) Cutting off of the opposite hand and foot of the offender, in case robbery alone has been committed.

(*iii*) Crucifying the offenders, in case both robbery and murder have been committed.

(*iv*) Exiling the offenders, in case they are arrested in the situation of crime before the actual commission.

3. Punishments Relating to Life

(a) <u>*In respect of Murder*</u>:

The Holy Qur'ān says:

يٰٓاَيُّهَا الَّذِيْنَ اٰمَنُوْا كُتِبَ عَلَيْكُمُ الْقِصَاصُ فِى الْقَتْلٰى ؕ اَلْحُرُّ بِالْحُرِّ
وَالْعَبْدُ بِالْعَبْدِ وَالْاُنْثٰى بِالْاُنْثٰى ؕ فَمَنْ عُفِىَ لَهٗ مِنْ اَخِيْهِ شَىْءٌ
فَاتِّبَاعٌ ۢ بِالْمَعْرُوْفِ وَاَدَآءٌ اِلَيْهِ بِاِحْسَانٍ ؕ ذٰلِكَ تَخْفِيْفٌ مِّنْ رَّبِّكُمْ وَ
رَحْمَةٌ ؕ فَمَنِ اعْتَدٰى بَعْدَ ذٰلِكَ فَلَهٗ عَذَابٌ اَلِيْمٌ ○ وَلَكُمْ فِى
الْقِصَاصِ حَيٰوةٌ يّٰٓاُولِى الْاَلْبَابِ لَعَلَّكُمْ تَتَّقُوْنَ ○

"O ye who believe! The Law of Equality is prescribed to you in case of murder: the free for the free, the slave for the slave, the woman for the woman[5]. But if any remission is

---

5. "Our law of equality only takes account of three conditions of civil society: free for free, slave for slave, woman for woman. Among free men or women,

made[6] by the brother (i.e., the heirs of the murdered person), then grant any reasonable demand, and compensate him (in the form of blood-money) with handsome gratitude. This is a concession[7] and a Mercy[8] from your Lord. After this, whoever exceeds the limits shall be in grave penalty. In the Law of Equality there is (saving of) Life to you (as it cuts the roots of endless blood-feuds) o ye men of understanding, that ye may restrain yourselves." (II:178, 179).

---

all are equal: you cannot ask that because a wealthy, or high-born, or influential man is killed, his life is equal to two or three lives among the poor or the lowly. Nor, in cases of murder, can you go into the value or abilities of a slave. A woman is mentioned separately because her position as a mother or an economic worker is different. She does not form a third class but a division of the other two classes. One life having been lost, do not waste many lives in retaliation: at most, let the Law take one life under strictly prescribed conditions, and shut the door to private vengeance or tribal realiation. But if the aggrieved party consents (and this condition of consent is laid down to prevent worse evils), forgiveness and brotherly love is better, and the door of Mercy is kept open." (Abdullah Yusuf Ali, *op.cit.*, p. 70, n. 182).

"According to the Hanafis", says Abdur Rahim, "the life of a slave stands on equal footing with that of a free-man, of woman with that of a man, of a non-Muslim subject with that of a Muslim." (*Muhammadan Jurisprudence*, p. 359).

6. "Islam while recognising retaliation as the basic principle of remedial right, favours compensation as being a principle which is most consistent with the peace and progress of society, and lays down rules for the purpose of confining retaliation within the narrowest possible limit." (Abdur Rahim, *op.cit.*, p. 359).

7. "Retaliation being the right of the person injured or of his heirs, they can compound with the offender for money, or, if they choose, pardon him. Wherever retaliation for murder or hurt is compounded, the money payable as consideration can be realised only from the offender himself. So also when compensation is ordered in cases where there is a doubt as to the wilful nature of the homicide. Similarly when the hurt caused has not resulted in death, the wrongdoer alone can be called upon to pay compensation. But when death has been caused by negligence or mistake, the offender's Akilas, that is his tribe or regiment, or the inhabitants of the town to which he belongs, are to pay the blood-money to the heirs of the deceased. The reason is that it is the duty of a persons' Akilas to watch over his conduct and the law presumes that the wrongdoer would not have acted in the way he did unless they neglected their duty." (Abdur Rahim, *op.cit.*, p. 359).

8. "The law, though it recognises retaliation in theory, discourages this form of remedy in every possible way. For example, if there be the least doubt as to the wilful character of the offence or the proof, retaliation will not be ordered." (Abdur Rahim, *op.cit.*, p. 359).

There are two points contained in these verses:

(*a*) Punishment for murder is the taking of the murderer's life.

(*b*) If, however, the heirs of the murdered person agree without any compulsion, the law of mercy can be allowed to operate on the basis of reasonable monetary compensation to the heirs,—that with a view to ward off worse evils;—and the government will allow it.

(b) <u>*In Respect of Mutilation*</u>:

The Holy Qur'ãn says:

وَكَتَبْنَا عَلَيْهِمْ فِيهَآ اَنَّ النَّفْسَ بِالنَّفْسِ وَالْعَيْنَ بِالْعَيْنِ وَالْاَنْفَ
بِالْاَنْفِ وَالْاُذُنَ بِالْاُذُنِ وَالسِّنَّ بِالسِّنِّ وَالْجُرُوْحَ قِصَاصٌ
فَمَنْ تَصَدَّقَ بِهٖ فَهُوَ كَفَّارَةٌ لَّهٗ وَمَنْ لَّمْ يَحْكُمْ بِمَآ اَنْزَلَ اللّٰهُ
فَاُولٰٓئِكَ هُمُ الظّٰلِمُوْنَ ○

"We ordained therein for them: 'Life for life, eye for eye, nose for nose, ear for ear, tooth for tooth, and wounds equal for equal. But if any one remits the retaliation by way of charity, it is an act of atonement for himself. And if any fail to judge by (the light of) what Allah hath revealed, they are (no better them) wrongdoers." (V: 48)[9]

This verse prescribes the Law of Equality in connection with murder as well as in respect to loss of, or damage to, the limbs of the human body caused by one person to another.

However, as in the case of murder, the permission of foregoing, in the interest of moral excellence, the right of demanding the enforcement of the Law of Equality has been given to the aggrieved party.

9. We may note with advantage the comments of A. Yusuf Ali on this verse. He says: "The retaliation is prescribed in three places in the *Pentateuch*, viz., *Exod*: XXI:23-25; *Leviticus* XXIV:8-21, and *Deut*. XIX:21. The wording in the three quotations is different. But in none of them is found the additional rider for mercy, as here. Note that in Matt. v: 38, Jesus quotes the Old Law 'eye for eye', etc., and modifies it in the direction of forgiveness, but the Qur'ãnic injunction is more practical. This appeal for Mercy is as between man and man in the spiritual world. Even where the injured one forgives the State or Ruler is competent to take such action as is necessary for the preservation of law and order in Society. For crime has a bearing that goes beyond the interests of the person injured: the Community is affected (See Q. V: 35)." (*op cit*., p. 25).